S0-AFN-698

With love and deep appreciation
to a valued friend
Margaret Stanton
from your friend
T. B. Yount III

Remembered for Love

Frontispiece. Lao Russell at the midpoint of her life.

Remembered for Love

LAO RUSSELL OF SWANNANOA

J. B. Yount III

BY J. B. YOUNT III

HOWELL PRESS, INC.
CHARLOTTESVILLE, VIRGINIA

P413
→ P442

To William Cranwell
and the Honorable Melford Okilo
and in loving memory of
Emelia Lombardi,
exemplars of the Message.

© 2004 University of Science and Philosophy

All rights reserved. This book, or any portions thereof, may not be reproduced or transmitted in any form or by any means, electronic or mechanical, including photocopying, recording, or by any information storage and retrieval system, without permission in writing from the publisher, except for brief quotations in critical reviews or articles.

Designed by Dara Powers Parker

Library of Congress Cataloging-in-Publication Data

Yount, J. B. (Joseph Byron) III
Remembered for love : Lao Russell of Swannanoa / by J.B. Yount III.
p. cm.
Includes bibliographical references and index.
ISBN 1-57427-153-9 (alk. paper)
1. Russell, Lao, 1904- I. Title.
BF1997.R85Y68 2004
192--dc22

Printed in the United States of America

ISBN 1-57427-153-9

13 12 11 10 09 08 07 06 05 04 10 9 8 7 6 5 4 3 2 1

Published by Howell Press, Inc.
1741 Allied Street
Charlottesville, VA 22903
(434) 977-4006
www.howellpress.com

The published works of Dr. Walter Russell and Lao Russell and other publications of the University of Science and Philosophy may be obtained from
University of Science and Philosophy
Post Office Drawer 520
Waynesboro, Virginia 22980
and via the following:
Telephone Fax Number: 1-330-650-0315
Telephone Number: 1-800-882-LOVE (5683)
Web sites: www.philosophy.org, www.twilightclub.org

CONTENTS

Interviewer "And for what would you most like to be remembered?"

Lao Russell "For Love."

—*P.M. Magazine* television
interview, January 1976

ILLUSTRATIONS

INTRODUCTION
BY EDDIE ALBERT

Author's Note: Of the many internationally known individuals who studied and befriended the Russells, Eddie Albert, the beloved and well-respected actor and humanitarian, was among those in the forefront. Albert and his remarkable wife, Margo, herself an acclaimed actress, came to know Lao Russell after reading her first book, *God Will Work with You but Not for You*. In the ensuing years, especially after his wife's untimely death in 1985, Albert found comfort and inspiration in the Russell philosophy and frequently conversed with Lao, who often spoke and wrote of him with admiration, citing him as one who had generously helped her extend the University's message of science and love. After Lao's sudden death in 1988, Albert filmed a personal message, which he permitted the University to use thenceforth as an introduction to the Russells. The words he used then are reprinted here in gratitude and appreciation.

Introducing you to the lives and work of Walter and Lao Russell is possibly one of the most satisfying things I could be asked to do. They were remarkable people, two extraordinary individuals. It seemed as if they were brought together in our time to offer mankind the knowledge necessary to replace the chaotic civilization we have today with a world of peace and balance.

They knew that the Science of Man held the key to all this, and they regretted the fact that the Science of Man was the least understood of all fields of learning. The Russells understood that discovering one's own special destiny and purpose is the greatest thing that can happen to any soul. They realized that this discovery came to an individual only when he learned to live his life in harmony with the universal law of Rhythmic Balanced Interchange.

Lives so balanced would create a truly civilized community that would ultimately embrace the entire world. But the ultimate began with the individual, and they used the following maxim as the byword of their teachings: "In vain we build the city if we do not first build the man."

The Russells tapped the secrets of the universe, and their lives exemplified this universal balance. Walter Russell was a master so diversified in an array of talents that he was called "the modern Leonardo," "the most versatile man in America." People who came to see the work of this painter, architect, and sculptor stayed to admire the talents of the musician, philosopher, and poet, or listened in awe to the scientist, physicist, and humanitarian.

Lao Russell's brilliant and beautiful life was parallel to his. She demonstrated her intuitive philosophy of cosmic harmony through her own paintings, sculptures, books, and lectures. Her crowning achievement was the establishment of the Walter Russell Foundation, which became the University of Science and Philosophy, providing students all over the world with insight and illumination through the development of the inner person and one's love of fellow man.

—Eddie Albert
Pacific Palisades, California

PREFACE

The opportunity to write a comprehensive biography of Lao Russell was an enormous challenge and a labor of love. From 1994, when the board of directors of her University of Science and Philosophy authorized me to undertake the project, until the manuscript was delivered to the publisher ten years later, I spent most of the time I could spare from my profession working on what I hoped would be the definitive life story of a remarkable woman.

She was a significant figure in my life from the day I met her when I was nine years old. Throughout my youth and early adulthood she was my father's friend and client and an inspiring counselor to my sister and me. After my father's death, I succeeded him as her personal attorney and by her nomination joined the University's board. I knew her first and foremost as a trusted friend on whom I could always depend for good advice, cheerful conversation, and the warm if puzzling admonition, "Some day you will play an important role in this work."

Born in an English country village where her family's position made her feel secure, Lao Russell was orphaned early and left in the care of a loving but overly protective older sister. Although unusually introspective, she was bright in school, beautiful and athletic, and prone to find joy in every experience. Her seniors and peers found her delightful company.

She developed a streak of independence, a determination to succeed, and a highly competitive spirit. Falling in love with a handsome young advertising executive, she was fascinated by the potential of mass media marketing and swiftly conceived a successful health and beauty business. After they married, he quit his job to join her in what became a highly profitable venture with a rapidly expanding sales volume.

Ahead of her lay happiness, heartbreak, and challenge, but her travel, reading, and spiritual insight enriched her in ways that far transcended the eventual loss of her business and much of her fortune. Her strong character was reflected beyond her physical beauty in the warmth of her smile, her animation of movement, and the obvious concern she felt for other people. She had an enchanting personality and an inspiring presence. She made legions of loyal friends on both sides of the Atlantic.

Lao insisted throughout her lifetime that the role of women be respected and encouraged equally with that of men. She believed that balance between the sexes was essential for world harmony and that hope for the future was futile indeed unless the modern world allowed women full and free range of opportunity and expression. She embraced this conviction in her early years and lived to realize that her unique perspective and living philosophy would dramatically impact both sexes for generations to come.

She spent years seeking answers to the ultimate questions of life and came to understand the unchanging power of the love that had motivated Jesus of Nazareth and other great illuminates of history. In mid-life she met a genius whose unique scientific perspective explained the dynamics of creation and life with stark but undeniable simplicity. His ideas were incredibly compatible with hers. They married and spent the rest of their lives sharing their message with the entire world. Their work lives today.

In the years following her death it seemed at times that her vital role in the inspiring partnership of Walter and Lao Russell had been somewhat subsumed in her husband's well-deserved reputation. This was ironic because Walter had always emphasized her pivotal role in their joint accomplishments. Without Lao, the Walter Russell Foundation and the University of Science and Philosophy would not have come into being. Without her, the art collection at Swannanoa would not have been an inspiration to thousands from around the world for a half-century. She was a woman whose advanced ideas often broke with tradition but were as timeless as the rhythms of the universe. She was Walter Russell's acknowledged equal and benefactor in many realms, not the least of them the remarkable manner in which she used her management skills to market their joint message to the world.

Many people gave me invaluable assistance in this work. To acknowledge them here is inadequate but necessary. Those recognized deserve credit for the book's qualities and no blame for its errors.

Several who volunteered countless hours to furthering this project include my friend Professor Peter Graham, award-winning author of books on Byron and distinguished educator at both Virginia Polytechnic Institute and State University and the Byron Research Center of Messsolonghi, Greece; Ms. Laara Lindo, poet, philosopher, and thirty-year friend of Lao Russell, an expert on Mrs. Russell's life and teachings, who also intuitively suggested the book's title; Waynesboro historian and former librarian Dorothy Anne Reinbold, dear friend and demanding critic; and New York artist, therapist, and author Dr. George Speck, whose Renaissance personality reflected that of Lao Russell and greatly appealed to her.

Andrea Terry was my skilled project secretary and manuscript manager through years of research. Kathleen Graves Cornell never complained when biographical tasks infringed upon her work in my private law office. Without them the task could never have been completed.

I owe much to the generously shared reminiscences of Lao's nephew, Peter Harold Summerfield of Derby, England, and his gracious wife, Betty, and to Mr. John William Ernest French of London. The extensive files maintained over the course of nearly forty years by Lao's faithful friend, the late Emelia Lombardi, were an essential source.

Mrs. Elizabeth Murray, the best researcher in London, took much time from famous and important clients to guide me through intricate sources, archives, and places in Great Britain and uncovered many facts that proved important to telling Lao's story. In America I was helped by Jennifer Hummel Rayburn and by T. Austin Graham, a talented writer, musician, and scholar, now pursuing his doctorate in English at the University of California at Los Angeles. Mr. Lloyd C. Hawkins of Jackson, Mississippi, provided access to the trove of professional photographs he created during the years he and his wife were board members at Swannanoa and valued friends of Lao Russell.

In addition to Laara Lindo, my own past and present colleagues on the board of the University of Science and Philosophy who helped and encouraged me in particular include Dr. Timothy A. Binder; William C. Cranwell; Richard A. Dulaney, Esquire; Connie A. Flaugher; Michael P. Hudak; Tyler M. Moore, Esquire; and His Excellency Senator Melford Okilo of Nigeria.

Others who deserve gratitude for providing significant help in this venture include P. M. H. Atwater (www.cinemind.com/atwater, atwater@cinemind.com), Angela Carr, Sarah Graham, Joey Korn (Joey@dowsers.com); Reverend Charles Lelly, Patricia Levoff, Cindy Lewis, John David Mann (johndmann@earthlink.net), Reverend Edward A. Plunkett, Shirley Calkins Smith, Samuel and Martha Spicher, Dr. James Radford Stone, and Lucinda Strickler.

Finally, I am extremely pleased that Ross Howell of Howell Press, Inc., deemed the book worthy of publication and am grateful to him and his editor, Dara Powers Parker, for bringing it to life with such skill and expertise.

—J. B. Yount III
Waynesboro, Virginia
April 2004

1. Lao Russell as a young woman.

CHAPTER ONE

Beginnings (1904-26)

Lao Russell's birthplace, Ivinghoe, lies in a beautiful part of England's green and pleasant countryside, near Buckinghamshire's common boundary with Bedfordshire and Hertfordshire. The town is thirty-six miles northeast of London, but in atmosphere it seems a world apart from that metropolis. This is rich agricultural land. Much of the soil in the Chiltern Hills is chalky, but the area near Ivinghoe consists of strong clay and rich loam.

Every local child learned that Sir Walter Scott had so admired the special "Englishness" of the town that he immortalized its name in his famous novel *Ivanhoe*. He appreciated the local folklore and enjoyed the ancient sayings that the older townspeople recited for him when he visited the area.

Lao Russell was born Daisy Grace Cook on November 6, 1904, the youngest of three daughters of Alfred William and Florence Lizzie Hills Cook. Not for forty-three years would she assume the name Lao, and another year would pass before she became Lao Russell, but much personal history preceded those two events.

Notable landmarks, some of them significant in medieval times, surround the village of her birth. A mile away looms Ivinghoe Beacon, 800 feet above sea level, one of the highest peaks of the Chiltern Hills. A thousand years ago great fires were lit upon the top of Ivinghoe Beacon to alert the countryside to invasions from the east.

Daisy knew the Beacon as a challenging site of joyful hikes, picnics with her father and friends, and frequent times of solitary childhood meditation with God. Today the Beacon hosts world-class glider competitions and other popular recreational activities.

2. Lao Russell (Daisy Cook) at the age of five.

Little more than a mile from Ivinghoe, along

the Dunstable Road, stands the Pittsdown Windmill, the oldest remaining post-mill in England, built in 1627 and easily seen from the village churchyard. This landmark, now owned by the National Trust, is closely identified with Ivinghoe, and Daisy often spoke of it.

Today's visitor to Ivinghoe finds a perfectly kept, gentrified village so restored to its supposed fifteenth-century appearance that it seems older by far than eyewitnesses described it in 1904, the year of Daisy's birth. Then it was a teeming, dusty, country crossroads with a dense but declining population. Like other nearby hamlets it was essentially little more than a satellite to the burgeoning industrial city of Luton, some twelve miles to the east.

In those early years of the twentieth century, most of Ivinghoe's inhabitants were farm laborers, brewery workers, or straw-plaiters. Straw plaiting had been the area's major cottage industry for over a hundred years, and without it, in the mid-nineteenth, century many people in Ivinghoe might well have starved. This was the great age of English manufacturing, and the region surrounding Luton comprised the straw-hat center of the world, but the plait schools were virtual sweatshops, crowded and unhealthy, in which young children worked long hours.

In the year of Daisy's birth, a plait school was still being conducted for children of the village laborers in the Ivinghoe market a block from her house. The status and relative wealth of Daisy's family spared her from this occupation.

St. Mary's Church stands in Ivinghoe's center, one block from the site of Holly Cobb Cottage, Daisy's birthplace. The 800-year-old church displays lavishly ornamented roofs, wooden angels holding shields, pew-ends quaintly carved with poppy heads, and other fanciful religious ornamentation. The seventeenth-century pulpit is the church's most recent architectural feature. On the wall surrounding the church an unusually large thatch hook remains from medieval days when it was used to pull off burning thatched roofs in order to save as much as possible of a house or structure that had caught fire.

Daisy knew St. Mary's well. She attended church services there as a child and witnessed the funerals of her paternal grandparents before she was five years old. She was always restless when she attended the formal Church of England services and much preferred her own personal communion with God, which developed when she was exceptionally young.

Her eldest sister, Florrie, remembered distinctly the infant Daisy clenching her fists at Vicar Treffry Hawly as he baptized her in the church on December 18, 1904. Doubtless the baby was expressing reflexive indignity at having water sprinkled on her head by the aged cleric. Florrie nonetheless always interpreted her infant sister's reaction to baptism as an eerily early demonstration of Daisy's innate disdain for religious ritual.

The name Daisy Cook is unknown to parishioners worshipping today in that picturesque village church. It would surprise them to know that an infant girl baptized there in 1904 later wrote books, under the name of Lao Russell, that have been translated and sold on six continents, and that she founded a home study university with tens of thousands of alumni and students around the world.

Daisy's sister Florrie revisited Ivinghoe in 1964 and noted the traffic racing through the town and the absence of many scenes and rural activities of their youth. She wrote to Daisy in America, "The village has altered and, like many more, has lost quite a bit of its character." Most apparent to Florrie at that time was the fact that her youngest sister's birthplace, Holly Cobb Cottage, the ivy-entranced home of their parents and grandparents, had been pulled down for road-widening, along with the adjacent six cottages that had comprised a substantial part of the family patrimony. Today the site of Daisy's birthplace is a vacant lot.

Daisy's earliest years centered on an Ivinghoe neighborhood where her parents were well-respected, her older sisters doted on her, and her grandfather George Cook seemed to her the Lord of the Manor. In reality this genial man was far from the top of the area's stratified class structure, but he was indeed a popular and substantial man of property. Besides some farmlands outside the village, his holdings had long consisted of Holly Cobb Cottage and the six two-story brick dwellings he had erected on the adjoining lots. In the last fifteen years of Cook's life, his son Alfred helped him erect an additional ten rental cottages on a back street several blocks away. This greatly augmented the family income.

George Cook was well read. Perhaps the oldest heirlooms Daisy possessed at the time of her death were two books, *A New and Easy Guide to the Use of the Globes*, by Joseph Moon, mathematician, published in London in 1792, and an apparently older *Rudiments of Geography*. George Cook's signature appears on the flyleaf of each book.

The earliest paternal ancestor of whom the family had record was Robert Cook, born in 1730, who married Ann Burrows and fathered John Cook, born in 1754. John married Ann Dover, and their eldest son, William, was a grocer in Ivinghoe who married Jane Simmons.

George Cook, the third son of William and Jane, was born in Ivinghoe in

3. Lao's parents, elder sisters, and paternal grandparents about 1900, Holly Cobb Cottage, Ivinghoe, England.

1828 and was Daisy's grandfather. He became a shoemaker and bookmaker. When he was only eighteen, he married Sarah Lester, two years his senior, a native of nearby Aylesbury. Their wedding took place in St. Ann's Church. George and Sarah worked hard and became successful in business. A talented dressmaker, Sarah was soon denoted a dress designer in local records. Her business thrived, and she trained a succession of apprentices.

George and Sarah had four sons and three daughters. Three of the children died young. Daughters Emily Anne Ayres and Sarah Jane Jamison married and reared their own families. Son Edwin George moved as a young man to America, where he established his family in St. Louis, Missouri. His brother, Alfred William, Daisy's father, preceded him to America about 1870. By 1900 Alfred had returned to Ivinghoe with his wife and two daughters, Florrie and Emily Anne. A three-generation photograph of grandparents, parents, and granddaughters taken about this time in front of Holly Cobb Cottage shows an obviously prosperous family. This was the loving circle into which Daisy was born in 1904.

By then George Cook had transferred Holly Cobb Cottage to his son Alfred and moved with his wife, Sarah, into one of his adjoining brick houses, next door to the house occupied by their daughter and son-in-law, Joseph and Emily Anne Ayres. Tenants occupied George's remaining cottages.

George Cook's kindness to his tenants, the deference with which he was recognized and acknowledged by his neighbors, and the self-earned dignity with which he carried himself and conducted his life left a deep impression on Daisy. When the Aylesbury Hunt, led by Lord Rothschild and his hounds, gathered nearby at St. Ann's Church, these aristocrats seemed no more impressive to Daisy than her loving, obviously well-liked grandfather.

In January 1904 George Cook executed his will, naming as his executors and trustees Vicar Hawly of St. Mary's Church and Walter Lester of nearby Dunstable, a nephew or younger brother of Sarah Cook. The entire estate was to be held in trust for Sarah during her lifetime. After her death, the personal property would be divided among all their children and the real estate among all except Alfred, who had already received Holly Cobb Cottage as his share of the real estate.

Sarah Cook died at eighty-one in January 1907. George Cook, the impressive old squire of his granddaughter's memory, lived on until the day after Christmas in 1909, nine days shy of his eighty-second birthday. Daisy was five years old when he died. She never forgot her grandfather's kindness and character, or the horror she felt at seeing him in his coffin.

Daisy sensed God's presence in her life almost from the very beginning. In 1946, the virtual midpoint of her life, she recalled, "Deep, deep within I have always known God. When I was a tiny child, He was closer to me than any human being."

At three years of age she first became dimly aware of her destiny. She would line up her dolls and tell them that when she grew up she would save the world. Her sister Florrie remembered that Daisy could read and write better at three than the normal child of eight or ten. At seven years of age she wrote fairy stories of exceptional quality and taught herself to paint watercolor landscapes and seascapes.

Daisy was precocious in other ways. From early childhood she excelled at the varied games that she played with her father and sisters. She recalled how her mother taught her to get her father's slippers and help him change his shoes when he came in tired in the evening. "This I was allowed to do as soon as I could toddle," she remembered, adding, "I was walking before I was a year old, thanks to our precious Scotch-Collie dog." This was probably the first dog she ever knew, and the animal's friendship left her with a love of canine companionship that lasted throughout her life.

Across the road from Holly Cobb Cottage the vast Ashridge meadows and woods where Daisy wandered as a child are still undeveloped, held in perpetual trust by the village as greenspace for public use. In this pastoral retreat of 116 acres she found her early spiritual awakening. She recalled this in later years: "I was born in the heart of the country in England, and I recall certain meadows where I used to go and sit with my dog, talking away to God and imagining all kinds of weird and wonderful pictures forming in the heavens."

Daisy felt she had derived much from solitude. "Circumstances forced me into a great aloneness in my youth," she recalled, "and these were my rich years, my formative years."

Except for memories of her paternal grandfather as the village squire,

Daisy took her major pride of ancestry from her maternal side. Horsham, the West Sussex community where her mother was born, is thirty-nine miles south of London and was a flourishing commercial and educational center. When Daisy visited her relatives there as a young girl, the town was home to the newly relocated Christ's Hospital School for Bluecoat Boys, moved from central London to a 1,200-acre hilltop campus with a glorious view of the Sussex downs.

The town of Horsham itself was built around a famous thirteenth-century church, whose silver-shingled spire rose 175 feet on a tower circled with grotesque corbels. The church stood at the end of a causeway in an oasis of tranquility, across a small bridge in a remembrance garden surrounded by ancient elms. The causeway itself equaled the church as a distinctive feature of the town. It was a tree-lined street passing old houses with no body of water nearby despite its name.

Daisy's grandparents had lived near the causeway at Number Five Richmond Terrace before their daughter Florence married Alfred Cook. As Daisy grew up, her aunt Alice Anne Hills was her closest relative still living in Horsham, but Florence Cook and her three daughters visited the area often during those years, and Daisy became familiar with stories of her mother's family.

She never knew her mother's parents. Daisy's maternal grandmother, Ellen Eliza Parker Hills, had died in 1877, twenty-six years before Daisy's birth. Ellen Eliza's husband, Thomas Hills, lived on in Horsham until 1892, when he died at sixty-eight. Thomas was an intelligent man who rose in employment from work as a draper to the position of bank teller, and later bank officer and accountant. He was an officer in the Freemasons Lodge at Horsham, and his portrait in Masonic regalia was treasured and displayed by Daisy throughout her life. Interestingly enough, her Horsham grandparents were Presbyterians, although Daisy's mother belonged to the Church of England. William Hills, Thomas's father and Daisy's great-grandfather, died at the age of ninety-eight, two days after Christmas in 1881 in Folkstone on the English Channel. He had been curator of the Chichester Museum. The family took its greatest pride in the ancestry of Thomas's wife, Ellen Eliza Parker.

Her father, Lieutenant Henry Lucas Parker, held a government post at the time of his death at forty-nine in 1842. He had served in the Royal Corps of Marines, going to sea first during the War of 1812 on HMS *Cressy*, in which he saw action in the West Indies, along the eastern coast of the United States, and in the defeat of the British Navy on Lake Champlain two years later. In 1824 he was serving on HMS *Ganges* in the Indian Ocean near Bombay, but a year later he was transferred to HMS *Wellesley* and sailed to South America.

His last assignment at sea was in the Mediterranean on HMS *Briton* in 1831. His descendants often alluded to his relation to the Parker family, which during Napoleonic times had given Britain two of its most distinguished admirals, Sir William Parker and Sir Peter Parker, but there seems to have been no close family connection.

Lieutenant Parker's wife, Frances Margaret Hennessy, who survived him by six years, was from a well-respected family. Daisy's grandmother Ellen Eliza Hills was the third of the Parkers' six children.

Thomas and Ellen Eliza Parker Hills were the subjects of large, well-framed pastel portrait drawings, which their granddaughter brought to America and proudly displayed during her years at Swannanoa Palace in Virginia.

Daisy was orphaned early, a fact she lamented in conversation with others until the day before she died. Despite their early deaths, her mother and particularly her father left a strong impression on her. Her father gave her a perspective quite different from that of the usual Ivinghoe native of the time. He was fifty-four when Daisy was born. She was his great favorite. He delighted her by recounting the adventures of his early life.

Particularly she loved to hear him tell of America. Alfred had married soon after his arrival in America about 1870. His bride was a young English lady who he had met and courted on the voyage to New York. Soon afterwards an illness or accident confined her to a wheelchair, and she remained disabled until her death, seventeen years after their marriage. They had no children. Alfred's second wife, who he met and married in the American Midwest, died after seven years of marriage while giving birth to their only child, a stillborn daughter.

These adverse circumstances caused Alfred to leave America and return to England in the early 1890s. There was much demand for his skill as a master brick mason in London, and he was working there when he met and fell in love with his third wife, Florence Lizzie Hills. They were married at St. Peter's Bayswater in London on February 24, 1895.

Florence's brother Richard Thomas Hennessy Hills witnessed the wedding. The couple lived in the western suburbs of the capital city until after the birth of their second daughter. Their eldest daughter, Florrie May, named for her mother, was born there on September 15, 1895, and registered at Woolwich near London. The second daughter, Emily Anne, was born on January 8, 1897, and registered at Paddington in Central London. Soon afterwards, Alfred's father invited him to bring his wife and daughters back to Ivinghoe and take possession of the family home, Holly Cobb Cottage, where

Alfred and Florence lived for several years before their third and youngest child, Daisy Grace, was born.

Her father always told Daisy that travel was the greatest education one could have. This stimulated her love of travel. When she was seventeen, she felt an uncontrollable urge to go to America. Such a journey was impossible, of course, but years later she realized that this was the exact time that her future husband Walter Russell was experiencing his great illumination in Connecticut. Florrie marveled at the coincidence, because she remembered well the difficulty with which she had dissuaded her young sister and ward from running away and sailing to America.

In 1909, after the death of George Cook, Alfred sold Holly Cobb Cottage, and he and Florence moved with their three daughters from Ivinghoe to Luton, a city of 45,000 people, twelve miles to the east. Here Alfred purchased a substantial two-story commercial building at 12 Mill Street, with a commodious apartment upstairs where the family made its home. Alfred was contemplating retirement, and the relatively new brick building in a growing part of Luton was an investment that provided them a comfortable home as well as rental income.

Downstairs was Fry's Chocolate Shop. Daisy often reminisced about this confectionary and the wide array of delicacies that were artistically displayed in its windows. The broad smile with which she was greeted by Mr. Fry seemed more important to her than thoughts of the chocolate treat he had always given her. She lived in the Mill Street home from her fifth to thirteenth year. A studio photograph of her, taken about 1910, supports descriptions of her as happy, inquisitive, fun loving, and precocious. Before she was ten, she was selling her watercolors, mostly seascapes, through Mr. Fry's chocolate shop and elsewhere in the neighborhood. Years later, seeing several of these early watercolors on display at Swannanoa, international artist and pioneer art therapist Dr. George Speck expressed amazement at the aesthetic ability and sensitivity Daisy showed at this early age, pronouncing her watercolors worthy of a trained artist of thirty rather than a mere child.

4. Fry's Chocolate Shop, Luton, England.

From her home above the chocolate shop, Daisy went to and from the local school, and also to the private tutorials in art and other cultural studies that were regularly provided her. Autograph books were popular in her youth, and she received a beautiful one on her thirteenth birthday. Soon it was filled with drawings, happy messages, and signatures from many of her young friends. Her French teacher entered a particularly solicitous message.

5. Watercolor painted by Lao at age ten.

The happy years over the chocolate shop ended all too soon. Suddenly, on May 21, 1917, Florence Cook died at the Mill Street home, five or ten minutes after suffering a heart attack or stroke in the middle of a fierce thunderstorm. She was alone with her husband, and they had quarreled. Daisy was at a friend's birthday party, and her two sisters were out with their friends. Alfred had discovered some household bills that his wife had neglected to pay. "My father was such an honest man, and he couldn't stand owing anybody a penny," Daisy recalled. "That's the English, you know."

6. Florence Lizzie Hills Cook, Lao's mother.

"If only she'd told me," he told his daughters. "She knew she could have anything that she wanted!" He was heartbroken and filled with grief and guilt.

Her mother's favorite flower was the pink carnation, and her daughters placed a bouquet of pink carnations in her hand as she lay in her coffin. As long as she lived, Daisy never saw pink carnations without remembering her mother.

Daisy was convinced that the shock and sorrow of her mother's death brought on her father's cancer, which was diagnosed several months after Florence's death. "In one month he lost twenty-eight pounds, and he soon died," Daisy recalled. Alfred survived his wife by fifteen months, succumbing on August 5, 1918, after a long hospitalization. It was less than three months before Daisy's fourteenth birthday. She had spent some of the intervening time at Viscob Camp, a school in the country, where Percy King, an actor who played the character Ruff in one of the dramas performed for the students there, autographed his photograph for her on January 12, 1918.

7. Alfred William Cook, Lao's father.

Her father provided in his will that all his estate be held in trust for Daisy's benefit until she was twenty-one, at which time it would be liquidated and divided among the three daughters. Florrie, the eldest, at twenty-three, served both as her father's executor and Daisy's guardian. Emily, the middle sister, moved soon afterwards to Derby, some hundred miles to the north near Nottingham, where she married Harold Summerfield on June 25, 1921, and began her own family.

Daisy spent the spring and summer school term in 1920 at Crescent House in Brighton, where many of her friends signed yet another autograph book. Some simply wished her health and happiness, but others were more expressive. One boy entered the following: "Man wants but little here below; he is not hard to please; but woman, bless her little heart, wants everything she sees!" Her friend Mabel Budd at Crescent House wrote the secret of happiness in the book: "Keep your face always toward the sunshine, and the shadows will always fall behind you."

Daisy also had a sketchbook in which many of her school friends illustrated an individual page for her. Most of these entries occurred in September 1919, but the place is not indicated. Erik Lambert seems to have been her special swain at the time. He drew for her on several pages. G. Patrin drew a beautiful ink portrait of Daisy.

All her life Daisy was deeply grateful to Florrie for caring for her when their parents died, and believed their rare and wonderful sharing was unusual for siblings so far apart in age. Even though their personalities were different, Daisy always held her sister in genuine esteem.

8. Lao about 1918.

Florrie was a slender, striking young lady, well dressed and professional in appearance, who wore round horn-rimmed glasses. Trained as a bookkeeper, she had developed a conservative, sound business sense. She took her responsibility as Daisy's guardian and surrogate mother very seriously.

Florrie was strict with her youngest sister, and Daisy often remarked on the rigid rules that she was forced to obey. As she grew older she came to understand the onerous responsibility her sister felt toward her. They were young and alone. There was no man in the household. On two occasions, when Daisy was in her early teens, strangers tried to abduct her. She was uncommonly beautiful and mature for her age, and there was bustling white slave traffic in cities like Luton and London. Florrie knew there was a real danger that her sister might be kidnapped and sold into a life of prostitution. For this reason she was constantly on guard and overly protective.

9. Lao with her sister and guardian, Florrie.

Almost immediately after their father's death, Florrie sold the building at 12 Mill Street and moved with Daisy into a genteel boarding house, where they lived while Daisy continued her schooling until she graduated at the age of sixteen. Throughout this time and afterwards she was tutored in classical music, art, dance, composition, and elocution. Her rural Buckingham country accent began to disappear as she was taught to improve and refine her voice, vocabulary, sense of fashion, and knowledge of literature. Daisy was a voracious reader, blessed with a natural sense of style, and she responded well to this tutelage.

10. Lao at sixteen on a motorbike.

In a 1944 resumé Daisy prepared and sent to prospective employers in New York, she seems to have exaggerated the extent of her formal education. She claimed to have attended Prospect House School in Tring, five miles from Ivinghoe, which in fact was a boy's school, demolished and relocated to Brookfield before Daisy was of school age. She may well have attended Miss Young's school in Luton, as she claimed, but it was not the young girls' college she described, but most likely a secretarial or business training school.

Without question she had a compelling quest for knowledge, strong self-discipline, and an intensity of purpose, and, during the years between her father's death and her first marriage, she also grounded her

11. Lao reading near Ivinghoe Beacon.

education in beauty care, health, philosophy, and physical culture. Florrie, her best friend as well as her guardian, took vicarious pleasure in witnessing the transformation of her stunning youngest sister from a beautiful country girl to a wholesome young lady of apparent aristocratic background.

Music and dancing were a part of Daisy's youth. She enjoyed "The Valeta" and the "Military Two-Step." She mastered the tango and waltz as well as other popular dances.

12. Lao about 1922.

During World War I, Florrie took a bookkeeping position with Gristwoods, a large firm of wholesale grocers on Wellington Street in Luton. She worked closely with the manager, William Henry French, who acquired the firm when Mr. Gristwood died about 1923. The company had been responsible for allocating all rationed food items throughout the Luton area during the war, and Harry French, as he was known, had shared handsomely in the profits. Part of his acquisition of the business included trading the French family home, located in the smartest part of Luton, for the Wellington Street business property, an elegant mansion that had been extended and modified to include residential and office quarters at the front and a large shipping department with some thirty clerks in the rear.

Harry French and his wife, Eva Rosaline, had a strained marriage and an intelligent young son, John William Ernest French, some six years younger than Daisy. Florrie soon demonstrated sufficient management skill to win promotion to the position of Harry's principal assistant. She worked alone in a bookkeeping office at the front of the building, next to his office, and served as general supervisor of all the shipping clerks. Harry trusted and relied on Florrie. Soon his respect for her intelligence and ability gave rise to pleasure in her company and a romantic attachment. In a very short time, Harry, estranged from his wife, grew devoted to Florrie. He provided a home for his wife and son at 217 Luton Road in nearby Dunstable and supported them appropriately, but spent most of his time with Florrie. By the mid-1920s, Florrie was his secretary,

13. Florrie May Cook.

14. *Harry French.*

accountant, best friend, and loving companion. She might well have become his wife, but under the strict laws of the time he could not obtain a divorce without Eva's cooperation, which was not forthcoming.

Harry and Florrie made an excellent team. Dedicated to the success of the business, they spared little time for travel or social pastimes. It was obvious to Harry that Daisy's well-being was a major priority for Florrie, and he showed extreme kindness to the younger sister. His son remembered that Daisy worked for the company at times, probably after school and always in her sister Florrie's front bookkeeping office, rather than in the larger order room at the rear. Decades later John French recalled with pleasure Daisy's cheerful greeting and happy smile as she came to the office or left for the day. On November 11, 1925, John, who would become a professional construction engineer, drew a moated castle with crenellated towers in a blank page of Daisy's 1919 sketchbook.

Harry and Florrie remained together for the rest of their lives. When he sold the business in 1946, he and Florrie purchased a house in Canford Cliffs near Poole, to which they retired, living together as Mr. and Mrs. French until his death in 1953. His wife, Eva, had legalized her separate maintenance arrangement in 1946. When Harry died he divided his estate among Eva, their son, John, and Florrie. After Harry's death, Florrie legally changed her name to Florrie French. She always remained close to Harry's son and daughter-in-law and corresponded with them regularly. When John French and his wife retired to England after his successful engineering career in Canada, they settled near Florrie and looked after her. She felt as close to them as she did to her successful and talented nephew, Peter Summerfield. Harry was buried at Poole, and Eva, who died six years later in 1959, was buried in Dunstable, but when Florrie died some twenty years afterwards, John French declined to allow her to be buried next to his father. She was buried instead in Luton with her parents.

Close by Daisy's home in Ivinghoe, yet a world away from her in style of life, lived members of what was then considered the richest family in the world. Evidence is convincing that Daisy's exposure to members of the Rothschild family of international bankers deeply influenced her determination to rise above her modest background and move with ease in wealthy, artistic, and intellectual circles.

At the time, Rothschilds sat in the British Parliament and held primary positions in London's corridors of power. No fewer than five spectacular estates had been restored or created by members of the family in the green hills of Buckinghamshire near Ivinghoe. Only one of these palatial residences, Waddeston Manor, remains unchanged today, but by 1900, the Rothschild enclaves had strongly altered the character of the region and stood as objects of awe to the local people, many of whom counted themselves fortunate indeed to staff the palaces of the near-princely family.

The Rothschild presence in the area had come into being when Mrs. Nathan Rothschild bought some green hunting country in the Vale of Aylesbury. Here Mayer, her youngest son, hired Joseph Paxton, architect of London's famed Crystal Palace, to build Mentmore Towers, an Anglo-Norman super villa, not far north of Ivinghoe. Mayer's brother, Anthony, developed the Aston Clinton estate just outside Aylesbury, and Lionel Rothschild settled just over the Hertfordshire line, adjacent to his kinsmen, on 3,500 acres surrounding Tring Manor, a seventeenth-century house designed by Sir Christopher Wren as King Charles II's gift to his mistress Nell Gwynn. At Tring, the Rothschilds developed the finest private zoological museum in the world. Leo Rothschild owned Ascott Wing, the family's most tasteful country manor, and the only one inhabited by the family to this day. Alfred Roths-child's vast Halton House clashed luridly with the nearby countryside.

After 1932 the Rothschilds sold the Tring collection of over a quarter million birds to the New York Museum of Natural History. The family donated Tring Park to the public. Aston Clinton, home to the greatest Rothschild huntsmen, whose hunt and hounds often converged in Ivinghoe itself, became a hotel. Halton House was transformed into a training center for the Royal Air Force. Waddeston Manor was given fully furnished to the National Trust and opened to visitors.

Daisy's memorabilia include photographs and souvenirs of Tring and Waddeston Manor. Years later she occasionally referred to her time with the Rothschilds. She had apparently been employed at Tring and through her employment there had occasion to visit other nearby Rothschild estates, including Waddeston Manor. She told Waynesboro, Virginia, historian George Hawke, as well as her Afton Mountain neighbors, William Edwards and his piano virtuoso wife, Virginia, of her experiences when she was in her early twenties working on a Rothschild staff as an office clerk, personal secretary, and companion.

15. Lao at the time she worked for the Rothschilds.

CHAPTER TWO

Business of Marriage (1927-33)

About 1927 Daisy conceived and started a business supplying physical culture and beauty treatment instructional courses by mail. She soon augmented this by selling beauty products made for her by an Italian chemist in Luton. Through skillful advertising, her business met early success.

At the advertising agency, a tall, handsome, and talented copywriter named Lionel Charles Stebbing worked closely with her in promoting her mail-order business. He lived at 167 High Street in Lowestoft on the North Sea, nearly 150 miles from Luton. He was six months younger than Daisy, having been born June 11, 1905, at Findon, Washington, some fifteen miles south of Horsham in Sussex. It is possible that he and Daisy had met when she was visiting her mother's relatives in the area. Lionel's father was Charles William Stebbing, a pastry cook and confectioner, and his mother's maiden name was Daisy Ellen Claypoole.

Daisy Grace Cook and Lionel Charles Stebbing were married on November 5, 1928, at Luton's Christ Church, by its curate, A. Baley, with Florrie and a friend, Jeanne Haver, as witnesses. At the time, Daisy was living with her sister Florrie at 30 Cardiff Road in Luton. In later years she often told friends that she had married Lionel primarily to escape from Florrie's over-protectiveness, but in fact it seems to have been a genuine love match.

16. Lionel Stebbing and Lao about the time of their marriage.

After their marriage, Daisy and Lionel gave their full attention to her mail-order business, which soon was sufficiently established to enable Lionel to leave his employment and join her in what quickly became the largest mail-order beauty and health business of its type in England.

At the height of her success as England's loveliest and best-known purveyor of

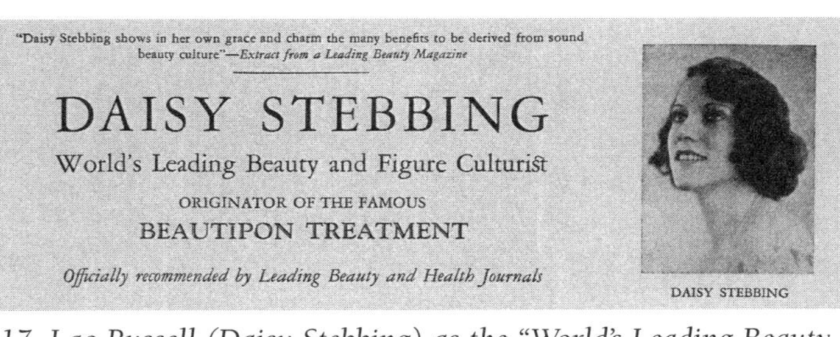

17. Lao Russell (Daisy Stebbing) as the "World's Leading Beauty and Figure Culturist."

beauty secrets and remedies, Daisy marketed many salves and elixirs prepared for her by British and Italian chemists. These products appealed to a large number of British consumers. She enthusiastically exaggerated the effectiveness of her cosmetics and remedies and did little, if any, testing of them. None of this violated British law in effect at the time. As a beauty specialist, Daisy enjoyed even greater success in marketing the courses and pamphlets she wrote to complement her products. She was expert at convincing her mail-order customers that they possessed within themselves the ability to achieve their health and beauty goals. She always stressed that the user's self-confidence was more important than any potion.

In many cases Daisy's beauty customers seem to have achieved remarkable results. The testimonials she published with her advertisements were legitimate. The individuals who were quoted had actually written to Daisy and authorized her to use their comments in her publicity. Her beauty business was only part of the Stebbings' enterprises and seemed at times overshadowed by Lionel's more extensive advertising of his men's strength, health, and body-building courses and products related to them. Nonetheless, Daisy invariably brought in half their income with her loyal legions of beauty customers.

Advertising principally in such popular magazines as *Women and Beauty*, *Health for All*, and *Health and Efficiency*, Daisy demonstrated great skill at reaching the masses of English women who felt they needed expert help to become more glamorous. She wrote booklets on beauty and slimming, which were sent "free" to purchasers of her products. Her courses and booklets on *Fascinating Loveliness* and her top products Slim Cream and Beautipon were bestsellers.

For five shillings she offered a slimming course that provided "a lovely Slim Figure in 30 days or your Money Back!" Her "remarkable New Beauty-Slimming Treatment

18. Composite of Lao used in her brochures.

positively cures bust-flabbiness, large hips, ugly ankles, double chin, thick wrists," she wrote, noting that it used no drugs, pills, hard exercises, appliances, dangerous diets, or baths. For those already too slim, she promised in the same advertisement that an "opposite treatment cures thinness, scraggy arms, unsightly hollows," quickly bringing "nicely, rounded figures." A further explanatory booklet was available "free and privately."

Her line included other Italian beauty creations with remarkable attributes, according to the ads. Slim Cream was purported to remove fat "anywhere" and was deemed "safe and certain." A vegetable reducing cream, it was marketed as "The Certain Way you can have a lovely, stylish, slim figure and end obesity safely and permanently." Rubbed in at night, she promised, it would produce amazing results.

Her Slenderettes were tablets that promised slimming with no dieting. One user wrote that Slim Cream and Slenderettes had reduced her weight by two stone (twenty-eight pounds) in twenty-eight days. Another, pictured with the ads in several magazines, wrote of similar success, and the ads offered to send further "wonderful testimonials" by mail. Beautipon was marketed as "the great flesh-former" to develop bust, arms, and legs. "Simply rub this harmless cream into the skin last thing at night, and in a few weeks you will have a glorious figure," Daisy pledged, noting that it "develops busts 3-6 inches."

Some advertisements pictured Miss G. Anderson, who was quoted as saying, "I have actually developed my bust four and a half inches and my breasts are now a lovely shape, high and firm. It is a joy to me to be told how young I look. I am so pleased with Beautipon Cream."

Miss V. Deciman, also pictured, likewise praised the product: "I measured my bust after fourteen days, and I had already reduced two inches. After thirty days my bust was reduced another two inches, a thrilling result. The double chin had quite disappeared, and I also use Slim Cream for my ankles, which are now as slender as ever. I reduced twenty-four pounds."

Not all of her testimonials were from unknown customers. Ella Logan, the famous star of stage, film, and radio, allowed her photograph to be used in Stebbing brochures and advertising in the better magazines, along with the

DAISY STEBBING BEAUTY PRODUCTS

Praised by Famous Radio and Stage Star

"I want you to know how thoroughly pleased I am with your wonderful beauty products—not alone for their final effect, so to speak, but also because I KNOW they are beneficial to my skin in comparison to all others I have ever used." —*Ella Logan.*

ELLA LOGAN

19. Famous actress Ella Logan praised the Stebbing Beauty Products.

following statement: "I want you to know how thoroughly pleased I am with your wonderful beauty products—not alone for their final effect, so to speak, but also because I know they are beneficial to my skin, in comparison to all others I have ever used."

The most successful advertisements pictured Daisy herself. Invariably her photograph in a magazine drew rapturous fan letters from young men as well as increased sales from women.

A PERFECT FIGURE

Radiant Health

You can have a lovely figure, radiant health, new beauty and magnetic charm. **I Guarantee** to reduce or develop your figure as desired. **I Guarantee** that you will be delighted with my famous Figure-Beauty and Health Course, or I will **return** the modest fee of **5/-** in full, without question. This wonderful Course is packed with priceless figure beauty secrets, now revealed for the first time. It will bring you glorious health and a superb physique of alluring loveliness. Enrol now and enter the "H. & S." £100 Physical Excellence Competition. Complete Course **5/-**, on Money Back terms.

MRS. LIONEL STEBBING
Dept. H.S., 28, Dean Road, London, N.W.2.

20. Lao promoting fitness and health.

Cream of Milan Cleansing Skin Food was sold to reduce wrinkles, lines, and enlarged pores. Rosine Lipstick promised a smart, new red shade that made lips silky soft and was claimed to be used by the film stars. Cream Marcheta was "the vanishing cream deluxe" to give one white hands and smooth skin.

Every month Daisy added auxiliary products. Soon she was also selling blackhead-acne remover, eyelash grower and darkener, Nordic sunshine blond hair wash, a "complete outfit" nail biting cure, and "my famous Beauty Chin Strap, as used by Society ladies" to reverse double chin.

At the same time, she worked strenuously on articles published under Lionel's name in an array of men's magazines, and on publicity focusing on several applied psychology courses they offered to "nervous and self-conscious readers." Recognizing the growing popularity of psychiatry, she wrote and sold booklets and courses on conquering inferiority complexes, mastering nerves, and winning success. "Success in business and social life comes easily to those who have learnt the amazing secrets of the mind and developed their mental powers to the full," she avowed, offering students the knowledge that could spell increased earning power by multiplying one's mental efficiency, energy, and general capabilities a hundred-fold.

The Secret of My Beauty Preparations lies in the years of experience I have had in solving the special problems presented by all kinds and descriptions of skins. Daisy Stebbing products are guaranteed to be absolutely pure and, of course, entirely harmless. So confident am I in the beauty benefits my products will bring to you that I offer to refund your money at any time, and for any reason, immediately upon your return of the unused portion of the product to me.

DAISY STEBBING BEAUTY PRODUCTS ARE SOLD DIRECT ONLY — *For your convenience use this circular as an order blank. Simply*

21. Lao advertising her products.

She augmented the material of the Menticault System of Applied Psychology, which the Stebbings had bought and which they advertised as the way to "release the hidden powers within you, transform your personality, and revitalize your whole being." In the women's magazines this bland old course was offered in a new guise under the headline "WHAT MEN SEEK." Touted as a famous psychologist's remarkable course filled with priceless secrets revealed at last to give the student "that rare feminine charm and vital inner nerve-power which men cannot resist," the curriculum was advertised to promise readers results that Daisy knew appealed to the would-be modern woman.

22. Lionel advertising their products.

Within two years of their marriage Lionel and Daisy were financially secure and began enjoying luxuries they had neither experienced in the past. They frequently vacationed at Scarborough on the Yorkshire coast, spending several weeks there during the summer of 1930 at the Hotel Montrosa on Avenue Victoria, Southcliff. Scarborough, one of the world's oldest seaside resorts, had attracted visitors for almost four centuries and was considered the queen city of the Yorkshire coast, with its two splendid bays separated by its mighty castle headland.

A handsome photograph album containing many snapshots chronicled this belated honeymoon trip, depicting the happy couple enjoying their leisure amid the beautiful sights of Scarborough. They strolled through the Italian gardens, climbed nearby Hayburn Wyke and saw its dramatic waterfalls, and rested and read at the top while enjoying the view. They strolled the Yorkshire beaches, played tennis, and gazed at the grandeur of nearby Oliver's Mount from their bedroom window.

Daisy's captions suggest the fun and relaxation that characterized the trip. They visited Filey with their friends the Camerons, watched the nearby British fleet from the harbor, enjoyed the spa and bathing pool, toured the castle, hiked through Primrose Valley, posed with horses in a stonewalled paddock, and made friends with the sun. Daisy captioned a snapshot of Lionel walking with her along the rocky coast as "'Stebbing' stones to success!" She also noted the marked difference between their Saturday afternoon and Sunday morning attire as shown on film.

Their photograph albums from this era show scenes of other holidays and vacation trips, views of Folkstone on the south coast near Dover, scenes of the

23. *"Banjo babies," the Lionel Stebbings at Scarborough, England.*

couple relaxing by the sea at Brighton, pictures of monkeys and polar bears at a zoo, a shot of an elephant parade, and one of an exuberant Daisy in her new white automobile. There are scenes of Haddon Hall and Chatsworth, two of England's greatest stately homes, even then open to the public. There is also a photograph of Lionel and a Scottish Terrier, doubtless Daisy's beloved Jimmie, the first of a long line of Scotties she would love and care for during her lifetime.

On another trip they visited Daisy's sister Emily at Derby, posed with Emily and her son, Peter, went on picnics in the country and long hikes, toured Dovedale and the beautiful Peak district, and enjoyed to the fullest the pastoral atmosphere and wildlife.

According to their accountant, their business had grossed £3,000 in the previous two months, a figure that probably did not include the considerable sums sent in cash by mail.

In 1930 they purchased several acres in Elstree, the British Hollywood, where filmmaking had begun in 1914, not long after the invention of cinema itself. Early British filmmakers considered Elstree an ideal location for film production, because it was close enough to London for easy access but far enough away to escape the city's smog.

24. *Lao and her nephew, Peter Summerfield.*

Here in an atmosphere of film directors, producers, and movie stars, on an elegant residential street called Deacon's Hill Road, Daisy designed and supervised construction of Sun Haven, the only home she ever owned. The site was a pleasant walk of five or six blocks from the quiet suburban train station that stood within view of the major film studios, where most of the great English films of that era were made. The acreage was a rough field when they bought the land for £650. Laying out the garden and tennis court cost five times as much.

Sun Haven was the house of Daisy's dreams. She loved it and always remembered it, although it was subsequently the scene of unhappiness for her. Years later she would promote Swannanoa Palace in Virginia as a shrine of beauty on a sacred mountain, but Sun Haven was the house she built for herself in the film capital of England, at a time when it seemed she would

25. Lao at Brighton, 1929.

achieve international fame as the exemplar of feminine beauty.

The house was Tudor in style with main floor reception rooms, including a large hall, lounge or living room, formal dining room, and large recreation room, bright and sunny, filled with exercise equipment and Daisy's ping-pong table. These were complemented by a powder room, cloakroom, plate and cutlery storeroom, garage, loggia, larder, kitchen, service cupboard, furnace room, closets, and servants' apartment. Upstairs were five bedrooms, a hall, baths, closets, and linen cupboards.

A driveway accessing the garage and linking two pairs of entrance gates intersected the front garden. "Sun Haven" appeared in gold letters on one of the north gates. A front hedge gave privacy to a small lawn bordered by herbaceous beds and rose beds. A large stone birdbath adorned the front lawn, and an iron boot scraper shaped like a Scottish Terrier was at the front doorstep. Daisy and Lionel spent a great deal of extra money in making the house elegant. The windows were all vita-glass. There was a water softening system. Daisy spent much of the summer in 1931 furnishing the house from fashionable London sales rooms.

Documents allow us the opportunity to tour Sun Haven as it appeared in 1936. The front hall extended from the front door to the rear loggia. A cocoa fiber mat in Greek key pattern lay just inside on the polished oak floor, which also supported a fawn- and blue-bordered floral Wilton carpet. Highlights of the hall included a bronze lady reclining on alabaster, a red lacquer dinner gong stand with striker, Indian brass accent pieces, a handsome oak and brass china press, and an oak table and side chairs.

All the electrical fixtures were silver, and all the rooms had brass doorknockers on the outside doors. Adding warmth to the formal dining room was a red brick fireplace on a raised brick hearth, flanked by oak bookshelves. A silver fire screen, scuttle, and fireplace tools were in their expected places.

26. Sun Haven, Elstree, England, 1930.

The rear lawn encompassed several acres, hedged and fenced, with a large tennis court and a pastoral view of farm fields beyond. Seventy years later it remained a handsome home, its acreage severely reduced, but its dignity and architectural distinction unmistakable. As the twenty-first century began, the house was known as Ambergyll and owned by Patrick and Margaret McNicholas.

The house provided Daisy and Lionel a respite from the challenges of operating a fast-growing business, and allowed them the opportunity to offer hospitality to family, friends, and many interesting people well known in the world of entertainment. Daisy did her writing for their business here. She honed the advertisements and drafted the courses that helped sell her beauty products, and polished and modified her husband's texts that championed a line of men's products, whih had grown as lucrative for them as hers for women. Here she read voraciously, delving deeply into the growing number of books on women's equality, and seeking in the writings of early and contemporary mystics explanations for her own intense psychic sensitivity.

Their neighbors in Elstree were principally engaged in filmmaking and the London stage. Walter Mycroft, their next-door neighbor, was director of production at the Elstree Studios and a giant in the British film industry. He was known for his Alexander-Pope-like wit, his compassion, and his exceptionally happy married life. His wife supplied the Stebbings with homegrown black currants and raspberries and kept them informed of the town gossip. She had been in some of the flying scenes in her husband's film *King's Cup*.

Through her the Stebbings met the American film actress Bebe Daniels and her husband, Ben Lyon, at their glorious hundred-acre estate at Windsor, lent them by the millionaire Dodge. Moving in these circles, Daisy and Lionel met such important opinion makers as Sydney Carroll and celebrated stars such as Constance Cummings. The members of this talented and sophisticated group often entertained one another.

Through these connections Daisy and Lionel were able to get copies of new or unreleased films and show them at home for their own private pleasure and that of their guests. Often they invited their live-in staff couple, Elsie and "Bennie" Benney, to join them. Movies, of course, were the talk of the town, and being able to screen new films at home was quite a luxury.

Lionel enjoyed making home movies. Most of his film-making was limited to the garden at Sun Haven: "Bennie weeding, hoeing, and digging; Elsie picking roses, hanging up washing; the car outside the house; Jimmie racing Bif up and down the path; David playing with both dogs; Mrs. Mycroft picking black currants in pajamas!"

When Daisy was away, Lionel filmed for her a garden party to which he had been invited in the neighborhood. Dorothy Dickson, Lawrence Olivier, Dodo Watts, and Jack Hulbert were among the guests who humored him on that occasion. Many of his letters indicate the type of activities they customarily enjoyed together at Elstree and the energizing nature of the film colony company they kept.

Elsie saw to it that the Stebbings kept a good table at Sun Haven. They and their guests could always rely on elegant but nutritious dinners of "lovely steamed fish, marvelous peas, and baked custard" or "chicken, bread sauce, strawberry flan, and cream." Elsie's husband, Bennie, drove them to their more important business engagements. The Stebbings often rewarded Elsie and Bennie with such special favors as tickets to the Royal Air Force display, a patriotic demonstration they appreciated and enjoyed.

Lionel managed their business office at 28 Dean Road, Cricklewood, in east London. The longtime secretaries recalled seeing Daisy on the premises only on rare occasions.

Lionel was there every day, hard at work, marketing new advertising strategies and working up copy for new products and courses, almost all of which he sent to Daisy for her special editing and final approval. He did most of the routine work and thrived on it. When imagination and ingenuity were required, he turned to her, as he had done since she first convinced him to leave his job with the advertising agency and help her pursue the business venture she had conceived.

Besides many banknotes, there was always something interesting in the mail. One reader wrote the Stebbing Institute worried about the size of his sexual organ and wondering if he would be effective in sexual intercourse. To their amazement he actually sent an outline of the organ in question. "He had drawn around 'it,'" Lionel reported, "on a piece of paper."

Lionel found the daily tasks generated by the mail-order business a godsend. He spent days revising and proofreading reprints of their existing literature and trying to decide on the best name for a new tanning product. "Mrs. Crabb (at the office) thought we might call it 'tanzu,' or 'Brol,' or 'San.' I thought 'Tanzu' was too much like 'Sez you!' and 'San' rather suggests sanitary towels. What do you think?" he asked Daisy. She chose "Sol."

Business was excellent. Their work was the subject of an editorial in *Health and Strength*, a popular physical culture magazine in which they regularly advertised. They also pushed their courses and products in brief filmstrips shown prior to feature films at the cinema. One such ad produced 106 inquiries in several days.

Lionel vigorously promoted a physical culture health camp they sponsored during the summer. Fitness instructors conducted it, using Lionel's curriculum under his absentee supervision. The camp was popular, and enrollment regularly filled up. "Booked about sixty pounds worth of space for the Camp yesterday—made lots of special deals on the phone," he wrote to Daisy when she was at Juan des Pins on the French Riviera. He told her that their profit margin was a full twenty percent.

Lionel regularly stressed how busy he was at home when Daisy was away on holiday. Even when he was preparing to join her on the Riviera, he sent

27. Lao (Mrs. Lionel Stebbing), cover of Health and Strength.

her a schedule of his activities to show that he was busier than ever preparing new copy, booking ads in advance at summer bargain prices in a number of newspapers and periodicals, and ensuring that the staff was handling all inquiries as swiftly as possible. He saved pounds and pounds on printing jobs, worked on the dummy booklet for the new *Guide To Beauty*, and ordered 20,000 copies with Daisy's picture on the cover as large as he could get it. That summer the heat in England was intense, but despite it, sales of the Stebbings' "four-in-one" package were booming. Lionel told Daisy how much he enjoyed his work and felt it a wonderful thing to have a congenial career.

In 1932, the Stebbings purchased J. R. Lindsay Limited (Rycol Co., Ltd.), a profitable business founded in 1880 that yielded some £12,000 sterling in annual profit. The Rycol treatment was originated by a medical man attached to the staff of the famous "iron man," Eugene Sandow, and had been accepted by the general public as a sound medical treatment for nasal catarrh, faulty nose breathing, and correcting mechanical injuries to the nose and nasal passages. The Stebbings deemed it entirely suitable for the United States, where such ailments were thought to be much more in evidence. Because it was not a patent medicine or secret remedy, it could be readily advertised without incurring the objection of American health authorities, who regulated mail-order medical treatments vigilantly and often barred them from the mail and prosecuted their proprietors. England had no such laws until the early 1950s. In the case of the Rycol treatment, the inspirators, in which antiseptic-impregnated tampons were used while the patient slept, constituted part of the treatment and were a registered design, but no internally taken medicine or tablets were necessary for the effectiveness of the treatment. Profits depended on the amount spent on advertising and the business ability of the owners. Rycol had been advertised in all the leading London dailies for years. The previous owner reported that he had received so many voluntary testimonials on Rycol from satisfied private individuals and physicians that he grew tired of keeping them and threw many away. Some weeks after selling it to the Stebbings, the seller was offered twice the sales price for the business.

For all the success they were enjoying in business and the pride they took in Sun Haven, strains began to show in the Stebbings' relationship. It is difficult to know which of the two was more to blame. Daisy's letters to Lionel do not survive, and his letters to her are the only available primary evidence. Many of the problems raised in their subsequent divorce proceedings seem to have existed by 1932, only four years after their marriage.

Daisy felt that Lionel tended to ignore her. She was insecure about their relationship and jealous of the time he wanted to spend with his friends, both male and female. She knew she was the more intelligent and ingenious of the two and that her vision had set Lionel on a successful business track. She was beautiful, sweet, and loving, but needed constant reassurance and insisted on managing their business and his life from behind the scenes.

Lionel was full of bravura, took credit for their financial success, and chafed under her constant demands that he reassure her of his love. On the other hand, he liked the company of other attractive young women and did not think it unreasonable to enjoy such company, whether or not Daisy was present.

The tension between them was real. Lionel felt that Daisy focused on him too much and let herself be hurt by inconsequential failings on his part. He insisted that he loved her as much as she loved him, but did not show it in the way she needed, stressing that his love did not depend on the number of times a day he kissed her or the number of hours a week he spent with her. They simply expressed their love differently, he assured her. What he wanted was a sense of freedom, the license to go to the cinema or buy records alone, join a club or two, or dine alone with his male or female friends without hurting her feelings or arousing her suspicions.

Lionel urged Daisy to expect less of him and to make necessary adjustments to their lifestyle in a sensible way, only because he did "want their lives to run smoothly and happily." He suggested moderation in all things between them, insisting that his love for her was unabated but that he needed more time to himself. Lionel believed that their problems arose from their spending too much time together; he doubted he could ever live up to her expectations and felt that his constant presence aggravated her. They would enjoy each other more than ever, he felt, if she understood that he loved her in his own special way.

Daisy's side of the argument may only be inferred. In the beginning she loved and needed him very much. She wanted him to be her mainstay, the focal point of her life. He had rescued her from the strict supervision of her elder sister. Daisy had given him a vivacious, beautiful, and intelligent woman for his bride. Yet for all her skill, guile, and strength, she found it difficult to accept the day-to-day routine by which they lived. Their newfound wealth was not enough to satisfy her. She had lost her parents in childhood, and she was determined to keep close watch on her handsome husband.

28. Lao at Lancing, 1931.

In August 1932, hoping the distance would help solve their problems, Daisy went alone to Lancing for a four-day holiday at their rented seaside villa near Brighton on England's southern coast. Left behind in Elstree, Lionel missed her greatly. He pictured himself as "the loneliest 'bachelor' alive, kicking himself for allowing the world's best wife to be seventy miles away" for what seemed to him to be three months instead of three days.

They both believed that time apart would ultimately bring them closer together, but Lionel wrote her the first day that "this seems the craziest of ideas now that we are actually carrying it out." While Daisy was away he seemed to have more freedom than he wanted.

She had fun meeting interesting people whenever she went out to dinner or the theater, but on the home front, Lionel's frustration was obvious. He found it hard to write her a love letter, noting that what he felt "just can't be put on paper," yet he implored her to write one to him. Although this brief first separation was additionally undertaken for the legitimate purpose of allowing Daisy some respite from a busy schedule of working with the business and planning the addition to Sun Haven, it was an ill omen of things to come.

Lionel seemed desperate to show her how much she was missed. "There are heaps of things to do at the office," he wrote. "The phone was ringing for me as I opened the door." He sent good news. The accountants had sent an encouraging report for the previous two weeks' income. Further, Daisy, who Lionel teasingly called "Little Miss Beautipon," was set to appear on September 10 in a beautiful photograph with the new advertisement for the magical creme in the ubiquitous *Daily Mail*.

Despite his frequent pleas for independence, the days with his wife away seemed far too long for Lionel. "Time drags even worse than I thought it would." Sun Haven seemed dead without her. He compared it to the line in a popular song, "Lord, you made the night too long!" He concluded his letter by asserting, "I love you ten times as much as you love me!"

She returned, relaxed and loving, and it seemed as though they were newlyweds again. They spoke often of having a baby, even discussed the possibility as certain when they noticed the odd coincidence that their major advertisement campaigns seemed to appear with more and more frequency in newspaper issues featuring lead articles about babies. Half jokingly, they considered these occurrences good omens. They were serious enough about it to rush to their friend Noel Jaquin, a well-known psychic, to confirm their experiences. No children were ever born to their marriage.

By mid-1933, their weekends apart grew more frequent. Daisy went to Lancing for a week in late May. Again, in daily letters Lionel lamented being home alone. Daisy's Scottie Jimmie had remained at Sun Haven. While Lionel and the staff walked and spoiled him regularly, Lionel wrote that there was a faraway look in the dog's soft brown eyes, and he often looked out of the bedroom window in the morning, appearing to think his mistress was somewhere in the garden.

"There's a funny, empty hollow quietness about Sun Haven without you, darling. You seem to breathe life into the house and make it home," he wrote. She wrote him a long, loving letter the first day she was gone, but he scolded her for spending too much time writing him. "I want you to spend every possible minute in the fresh air."

He replied that he was overburdened with work on the very day he had enjoyed a midday sunbath, a long walk in Hyde Park, and several late afternoon hours at the office.

She was meeting many interesting people. Daisy had always had an uncanny ability to attract the attention of worldly and sophisticated strangers who often became her lifelong friends.

"Trust you to meet people, you funny 'socky' darling with your highly developed gift of intimacy," Lionel wrote. "That's where we are different. People are nearly almost too much fag [boring] for me." He told her he much preferred being alone with her, and when that was not possible he would choose simply being alone.

In early June 1933, Daisy embarked on six weeks' vacation at Juan-les-Pins on the French Riviera, the elegant Mediterranean resort just outside Cap d'Antibes. Once a forest of pines surrounded by sandy beaches, Juan-les-Pins had been discovered by the Duke of Albany in 1880 and, during the 1920s, had become internationally famous as a playground for British and American film stars, European celebrities, and jazz aficionados.

Obtaining a visa at the last minute had caused her no little trouble. The authorities presumed from the attractive photograph that Daisy was an actress. French officials made obtaining a visa as difficult as possible for English artists, honoring passports only when they were accompanied by a signed agreement that the holder would not accept any kind of acting engagement on the Continent. Eight months earlier, an Englishwoman on bail had used a false passport and escaped to France, after which both countries had been doubly cautious in reviewing passport applications for single women planning travel to the Riviera.

Daisy's banker assured officials that Daisy was in advertising and not on the stage, and that she was "quite married and not going over in connection with white slave traffic." The issuing officer apologized, commenting that it was very rare that "such a beautiful photograph passed through his hands." Lionel teased his wife about the imbroglio. "Your trouble, darling," he wrote her, "is that you are far too lovely, as I have said many times."

Daisy loved the Riviera. She soon shook off the stuffy travel feeling in the exhilarating warmth of the ocean air. As she combed her hair in the morning, it gave her pleasure to look out on the Mediterranean.

She had booked a double room at Les Ambassadeurs, a luxurious hotel, but soon changed to a suite at the Grande, an equally attractive place, made more appealing to Daisy not so much by its more elegant clientele as by its greater spaciousness, its table tennis and other athletic amenities, and such luxuries as gracious picnic luncheons served on the beach. The Grande even provided her with a practice room for calisthenics once they were clear as to what it was she wished to practice. She had considered renting an apartment, but Lionel advised against it, and now she was happy she had taken his advice as she was making many friends living in the more public Grande.

For a few days she was alarmed at a downturn in her health. She grew tired and woke up chilled and coughing up blood. The local physician prescribed effective treatment, seemed to think it was not serious, and apparently suggested that her blood had become overheated. She began resting at midday and curtailed the late hours and dancing for several days. She attributed the spell to the change in weather, as well as her rigorous schedule of going in the water "for the first time in ages," riding horseback, and frolicking at all hours.

Daisy became well known at Juan-les-Pins for her beauty, vivacity, and charm. She knew her limits. She gambled in a small way, recognizing that she could afford to lose a little money but would really be winning if she met more of the right people.

She was regularly seen at the local night spot Maxim's, and no one yet had bested her tango. By now Daisy had a glorious tan, and she wrote she felt very much at home on the Riviera. She was photographed playing ping-pong rather successfully with well-known visiting champions at the sport. Her photograph was taken for a society article in *The Tatler Mail*. She was learning to ride horseback and doing it extremely well. "Now at last you are riding," Lionel wrote. "You never expected to ride first on the Riviera, did you, dear?"

She joined the Juan-les-Pins Riding Club and was pictured on horseback in the Thursday, July 13, 1933, *Daily Mail*, in a page-one photograph with fellow club members Anne and Genevieve Walker of New York, Count J. Biagini, and M. E. Decout, Manager of the Club. The caption identified her as

29. Juan-les-Pins, French Riviera, July 13, 1933.

"Mrs. Daisy Stebbing, the English film actress."

She and Lionel wrote each other daily, and although she constantly declared her love for him, she made it clear she was "having a topping time." Nonetheless, she assured him, "they all call me 'the faithful wife.'"

She had professional disappointments while at Juan-les-Pins. An earlier screen test at Elstree had proved discouraging, and the studio declined to offer her a contract. A self-proclaimed film director who she met on the Riviera assured her that he could make her a star, but she soon discovered his ultimate goal for her was simply a visit to his hotel room.

Lionel assured her. "I am sorry the film offer fell through and that you had such trouble, poor darling, but don't let it depress you. Very few people in this world wear wings. The thing is not to expect them to. Am glad you were so sensible about not going to his apartment. You know how to look after yourself. Terribly sorry it turned out that way, angel darling."

Before she left Elstree she had taken French lessons at Sun Haven from a gushing French woman they teasingly referred to as "Madame," who told Lionel how brilliant his wife was and what remarkable progress she had made in a wonderfully short time. Nevertheless, Daisy knew that the perfect way to acquire the language was to immerse herself in the country itself.

"When I come," Lionel wrote her, "you must ask me something in French that I can answer in German, so that we can feel quite cosmopolitan!"

Daisy met the English actor Sydney Howard at the pool, and they had a long conversation. She also met a number of well-known and well-connected Americans.

She surprised herself by being amazingly at ease in striking up conversations with fellow sun worshippers on the Lido. She pronounced herself cured of being too reserved and suspicious of strangers, a handicap she had recognized in herself from her protected youth.

Soon she met a Spanish dancer who taught her to improve her technique in dancing the tango. They won a dance contest together, which she dutifully reported to Lionel, who lamented playfully, "I will seem a very poor dancer now." The Spaniard tried to pursue Daisy and soon became insistent that she join him at another resort where they could continue to dance together publicly but non-professionally.

She wrote Lionel about the possibility, but he was extremely negative in response. "Do stay in Juan, dearest darling," he wrote. "Even though you like the Spaniard, you can't possibly alter your plans for him. It would look as though you were keen and would be a mistake." She let the Spaniard go on without her.

She wrote Lionel of other temptations and experiences, but he trusted her implicitly, more perhaps than he should have, responding that she was "too refined and lovely," "too fastidious and finely textured and reserved" to do "nasty cheap things."

He joined her at Juan-les-Pins in late July, and after a loving reunion of several weeks, they journeyed home, stopping in Paris for a week, where they visited a number of clubs and restaurants recommended to Lionel by a client in London during Daisy's absence.

Their reunion in France had been a happy time, but the return to Sun Haven seemed to revive Daisy's insecurities and Lionel's absorption in their business. By now separate vacations were hardly a novelty for them. Lionel would tell her that parting from her was "a terrible wrench" that gave him a lost feeling. Nonetheless, he always had "a mountain of stuff to go through" at the office and stressed to her he was "amazed at the accumulation." He sent her proofs to review, asked her for copy for upcoming advertisements, then apologized for not realizing she most likely "would rather forget business while away."

From all accounts Lionel was as yet refraining from the companionship with young unmarried women that would ultimately be the downfall of their marriage. When Daisy had been away from home, he claimed he had spent his free time attending films, working in the garden of Sun Haven, taking home movies, and enjoying onstage performances in London. His evening comrades were frequently his friend Ted or Mannell, a business associate well acquainted in the theatrical world.

Still Daisy worried that Lionel was spending too much time socializing alone with other women. "Darling," he wrote her, "You speak as if I am going to eighteen shows. That's just not what I am doing. I'm having a very quiet time indeed and working like hell. Of course I've been alone when Ted and Mannell have not been available," he wrote her, pleading with her to realize how much he loved her.

"I love being with you," he wrote, "but love doesn't depend upon how much time two people happen to be with each other. I love you more now than ever and we've been nearly a month apart."

His last letters before joining her in France focused on the difficulties they had apparently been having for some time. "You won't be unhappy about me any more will you?" he pled. "There is no need for upsets at all. They are killing, destructive, and futile. I love you. You know I love you. Don't spoil it by wanting me to do certain things, which you think prove my love....

"This month has given me a lot of time to think, and I am convinced that marriage is made lovelier and sweeter and life more interesting, varied, full, and higher if two people spend a proper amount of time apart as part of their normal life. You always look lovelier, and companionship is sweeter, when I haven't seen you for a while. Try hard not to attempt to dominate me, or manage me, but let me just be myself and love you in my own way."

In September 1933 Lionel reemphasized his desire to establish an American branch of their increasingly successful business. Daisy suggested that she be the one to undertake this venture.

Lionel had become increasingly moody, which distressed her, as she did not understand the reason. An ocean between them, she thought, might truly make him miss her and give them the opportunity to build a stronger relationship.

Perhaps more important to her was the opportunity she would have to realize at last her longtime dream of seeing America. To her it was the land of opportunity, the golden shore to which her father and uncle had emigrated as young men, and about which she had heard so many stories as a little girl in Ivinghoe at her father's knee.

With Lionel's full blessing she left in October for her first six months in America. With that separation things were never again to be the same between Daisy and Lionel.

CHAPTER THREE

America
(1933-34)

Daisy was admitted to New York on a six-month visa on October 27, 1933. After finding herself small but suitable accommodation in Gladstone Apartments in Forest Hills, she leased an office and employed a secretary, Kitty Weald, who was to remain her friend for decades. The office was located in nearby Flushing, and from this address Daisy began advertising and marketing the courses and products that were making the Stebbings wealthy in England.

Daisy knew that America regulated medical remedies and claims much more stringently than England. She realized that some of the Stebbings' preparations were close to the line legally. The American Medical Association and Better Business Bureau could also cause her trouble if she were not careful in her promotion. They were ruthless, powerful, and strictly to be avoided, she knew. As well, they were even more subjective than the postal authorities.

30. Lao in New York, 1934.

Under American law at the time the post office generally investigated a company only after receiving an individual complaint. The company was given the opportunity to explain itself and often to correct matters regarding claims in advertisements.

If the post office were satisfied, the business could continue. If not, a fraud order was issued, which meant that all mail coming in to a given company would be stamped, "A fraud, return to sender." This effectively stopped all inquiries and any money from being sent to the business address.

The post office's sole interest was to protect the public, and it usually allowed a company to speak for itself and change its ways before issuing an order against it. The post office had no institutional axe to grind and was generally satisfied with selling all the stamps it could.

One major loophole in the law was that a fraud order was always issued in the name of a given company or producer. Therefore, a fraud order against Stebbing Systems would not have any effect whatsoever against items marketed by Daisy Stebbing, Slim Cream, Beautipon, or Lionel Stebbing.

Accordingly, Daisy realized it would be safer and wiser to have Daisy Stebbing selling Slim Cream and a differently named organization marketing Beautipon. It would be wiser, she knew, not to make the precise claims and use the same advertising copy they had used in England. Modifying them for the American audience might even yield greater success while at the same time minimizing any threat from the authorities.

Daisy was beautiful and vivacious, and it was natural that she made many friends in the excitement of New York. She read and studied, worked and played, attended the theater, and found the different rhythm of life in New York thrilling. She frequented a restaurant called Chez Maurice at 49 West 47th Street, which advertised itself as "a corner of France in New York."

She had scarcely been in America a month before she attended a symposium on direct mail order techniques at the Waldorf-Astoria Hotel. The man she sat next to became one of the greatest friends she ever had. More than anyone else she knew, he encouraged her to break her ties with England and settle permanently in the United States. He was also, she would say in later years, a person she loved deeply, almost as much as she later came to love Walter Russell. Her new friend's name was also Walter. He was suave, dashing, well-spoken, and Harvard-educated. He fell in love with Daisy virtually at first sight.

Walter Powell worked for one of the important advertising agencies in New York, a company owned by his father, and the young man promptly offered the firm's professional services to the beautiful English lady. At the time Walter was unhappy in his own marriage, although concerned and caring for his two young sons. Inhibited by his cultured and traditional parents, he soon became so emotionally attached to Daisy that he avowed he was ready to sacrifice anything for the woman he called his "English wife." She was still very much in love with Lionel and made certain that Walter understood she was a happily married woman.

Soon, however, they were spending much time together, ostensibly promoting her business. During the first week that he helped her place the advertising, Fawcett Publications alone yielded thirty-eight Slim Cream sales. Walter considered this a very good start.

He went regularly to see her in Forest Hills, generally accompanying her

31. Fascinating Eyes, Lao (Daisy Stebbing), 1934.

home after dinner or the theater and returning to Manhattan on the ferry late at night. When they were apart, he wrote that he lived on the thought of having her sit next to him, smiling and ready to be kissed, as they looked out across the moonlit river.

Walter's mother was a talented musician who for years had been enraptured by the French Romantic authoress George Sand and her love affair with the composer Chopin. Walter told Daisy she reminded him of George Sand. Both, he felt, were brilliant and beautiful women who were drawn to men of genius. Walter felt that Daisy was capable through her own genius of inspiring any man she loved to deliver himself of his own genius.

As their friendship developed, they shared intellectual stimulation, enjoying literary talk. Daisy teased Walter with an epigram by H. L. Mencken, who had written, "Romance is the wine of love; marriage its bier."

At first Walter read more into Daisy's banter than she intended. He was clearly smitten with her. He took his beautiful English client to visit his parents' estate in New Jersey. They liked Daisy, too. On one occasion he jammed the movie projector, and the film unraveled over the floor. Daisy deftly rewound the film with great composure, making an excellent impression on all present. At times she could be touchy; one day, in the Forest Hills apartment, he dropped her toaster, and she snapped at him. Much was going on in their lives, and they were both often tired and nervous.

Daisy took a brief and restful vacation alone, staying for a week at the fashionable Sagamore Hotel at Lake George. She found the place exhilarating. "There were so many wonderful things to do, wonderful sights, wonderful people to meet," she wrote him.

Walter bombarded her with daily letters. She told him that she envied his gift of words, termed his letters "beautiful," and spoke of her own as "miserable scraps." They laughed about the dozens of love letters they sent each other. His white ones and her green and buff ones would make an interesting collection, they mused.

She wrote him that she wanted him to be happy. "You must be!" she exclaimed. "All the poetry of life will be yours. Always remember I shall never forget what you are doing for me."

Whenever she was away, he worked doubly hard on her business and often dined with Kitty, usually taking her to the Cosmos Club, Daisy's favorite place to dine. Daisy was always their main topic of conversation.

Walter found Daisy more in love with life than anyone he had ever known. Anyone, he felt, would find life with her more beautiful than without her. He loved her, he said, for her gift for happiness, for knowing that life and most of the things in it are beautiful. He was intrigued by Daisy's theory that a happy person always had the better ideas, and he made it clear he felt that this was a concept worth practicing. He enjoyed her naturalness, stylish as it often seemed. Daisy told him her sense of fashion kept her from wearing low-heeled shoes even though they were much better for cross-country walking.

Walter wrote her that he loved her for her personal attractiveness and the beauty of her face and eyes and smile, which he described as a "stimulating, articulate beauty that radiates a strong and happy nature." He found himself awed by her charm and the sweetness of her outspoken personality. Although she made it clear she loved her husband and would not submit to an adulterous affair, he longed for her companionship. Still he marveled at her "tender responsiveness to love, not passionate, not fawning, but simple and warmly sincere."

One day when they met for a quick luncheon at Schrafft's, Walter challenged Daisy lightly on the seeming inconsistency of a person of her sweetness and character being in the mail order business.

She smiled knowingly in a way that satisfied him perfectly, he wrote. They had often discussed her ultimate goal of bringing love to an unhappy world. Her present emphasis on physical health and beauty was but the first essential step to the more cosmic understanding she sought to embrace. Walter told her that he thought constantly of the fact that at the age of thirty-six, when he thought love was dead within him, he had met her and she had restored it all.

Walter had a professional graphologist review the analysis he himself had made of Daisy's handwriting, which revealed her to have traits of strength and fineness of character balanced with sympathy, sincerity, and affection. The analysis showed her to be straightforward and dependable, sincere and sympathetic, warm-natured but self-conscious, spiritual, and reticent. She could be secretive, shrewd, subtle, and diplomatic, sometimes logical and at others intuitive. She was modest and simple in her taste, but also proud, energetic, ambitious, and jealous. She was keenly attracted to literature and other cultural subjects. "Such a writer is nearly always an excellent business executive and a good judge of character," Walter told her. "Now how do you like yourself? Even your handwriting shows what a wonderfully nice person you are, but not quite how nice. In addition you are sweet, tender, kind, and loving but those words weren't in the graphology book!"

Daisy returned to England early in April 1934 and stayed with Lionel at Sun Haven for several weeks. Using Hotel Tudor stationery, Walter wrote her soon after she left New York: "You are now in Elstree, home for a week at least. You have seen Lionel and had many happy times with him renewing all that means so much between you. You have seen Jimmie and Bennie and Elsie and wandered down your paths and through the gardens and have seen old familiar things that have made your life happy in England." He seemed fearful she might forget him.

She was pleased to see their English business booming. In America business was likewise going briskly. Walter wrote her that he had felt confident enough to place advertising for her in the May magazines "with a vengeance," spending $990 for Slim Cream and $500 for Beautipon.

She sent him the Beautipon script from England, but he was afraid to use it because it emphasized herbal ingredients. He warned her that unless it were revised, the Federal Trade Commission would most likely come down hard on it. She cabled her agreement, and he saw to it that revised literature was printed up immediately with the changes and modifications he felt were necessary to placate the American authorities.

Much of the correspondence Daisy received from Walter during her sojourn in England was not so business-like. He wrote her on stationery he had taken from various hotels. "I swiped this to disguise another letter from me," he wrote. He was eager to avoid arousing Lionel's suspicions and likewise feared that Elsie and Bennie might comment if too many letters came to Sun Haven for Daisy from Walter's business address.

She wrote Walter that she looked forward to seeing him again. "We were always happy together," she reminded him. "What fun we have had doing just nothing!" Nonetheless, she warned her American friend that she still loved her husband and hoped to save her marriage. "I know that you would not leave me under the same conditions," she wrote Walter.

Daisy was surprised at how happily things went in her time with Lionel. The three-week visit home, besides satisfying her homesickness for England, also gave her the opportunity to visit Florrie in Luton and see many old friends in Elstree. Most of all, she felt it had strengthened her marriage.

Before leaving for New York in May, she sent Walter a set of parameters she proposed they should establish to govern their relationship when she returned.

> I have thought a lot about us, or perhaps I should say about your love for me. You know, my dear, your future happiness cannot lie with me. And I want you to be very happy.
>
> You know how much I love Lionel. I have always told you this. I would hate for you to be hurt later because you really love me too much and are

> dependent on me for your happiness.
>
> You are really so very unselfish, and I have deep feelings for you. I hope with all my heart that a really beautiful love will come to you. You deserve it so much and need it to wipe out the past.
>
> I had hoped that you would find happiness in your new plan of living, and I do not want you to talk of dead ends, darling. You have always been unselfish, and I know you do not want to make me unhappy. I feel from your letter that you are depressed, and I would never forgive myself if I were the cause of bringing you unhappiness.
>
> Please, dear, do not be hurt, and try to understand how much I want you to be happy, now and always.

Lionel was intensely curious as to what Daisy was accomplishing in New York. Reassuring him that her work in America on their behalf was yielding highly positive results, she was determined that when she returned to New York, she would be ready to work again with Walter but with confidence that her marriage to Lionel was on a solid foundation.

Daisy had formed a warm friendship with her London physician, Dr. Christopher Howard, and after her return to New York they maintained a regular correspondence. Learning that she had failed to consult him for a mild illness just before she left London, he chided her for not asking him for help. "What am I supposed to be for?" he inquired, reassuring her with the comment, "Honestly, I'm a good doctor, or at least I think so, which is half the battle." He told her he hoped his work had given "lasting good results" and urged her not to be hesitant in writing what she thought. They promised each other one letter a week.

The depth of their personal attachment is clear in his letters. "If you are ever lucky enough in this world to find someone you can understand and who understands you, the friendship can be valuable and perfect if you resolutely put aside self-consciousness," he assured her, "so write me whatever comes into your head and send me your poems. I will read them carefully and return them and tell you all about them."

She had explored Yoga. Christopher Howard told her to forget it, asserting that to westerners it was a burnt-out concept. Calling it "an advanced form of autosuggestion," he warned her that "to get any of the effects, physical or mental, requires years of doing nothing and concentrating. To study Yoga is to plead guilty to taking yourself and life too seriously. The secrets of the infinite are not for us to know—yet."

This advice was directly contrary to Daisy's growing intuitive need to practice and learn more about meditation. Christopher warned her that "every person falls into the trap of considering his thoughts unique ones" and somewhat patronized her by noting that "nothing really matters in life except happiness and health." Daisy replied, cultivating the good will of her handsome physician, but she ignored his efforts to dissuade her from meditation.

Christopher agreed that philosophers and adherents of spiritual religions were far more prone than medical specialists to consider the body merely the temple of the spirit and to believe that the highest vocation of the body was to provide a dwelling place for the spirit. He encouraged Daisy to read two books, *Mere Mortals* and *Post Mortem*, both by Charles Maclaurin, an Australian doctor. He argued that discovery of the active principles of the ductless glands had once and for all showed to the intelligent few the importance of the body itself.

Christopher enjoyed teasing Daisy when she spoke of the primacy of spirit over matter. "From another point of view," he wrote, "one must remember that we do not exist at all as entities but are only ourselves when given the complement of another personality. The you that your mother knows, the you that your husband knows, the you that you know, and the you that I know are all different. I suppose the answer is that in eternity it doesn't matter much anyway, so away with sterile reflections. On with the dance, and the devil take the hindmost!" he wrote her in July 1934.

Daisy listened to Christopher's comments but persevered on her spiritual quest, sending many of her favorite spiritual books to him through the years. By then Christopher had grown more conservative in his thoughts on religion and had decided that he drew more comfort from the Anglican *Book of Common Prayer* and the New Testament than from what he perceived to be the more esoteric teachings that Daisy favored.

On Saturday, May 19, 1934, Daisy was among the first-class passengers sailing from Southampton to New York via Cherbourg on the White Star Line's RMS *Majestic*, the largest steamer in the world. It docked in New York at seven in the morning on May 25. Walter met her an hour later, trying to be calm and restrained because Kitty had come with him. He drove Daisy directly to her apartment in Forest Hills, delivered her most correctly, and took his leave in a most proper way.

She remained in America until September, spending five busy months expanding her business and growing increasingly involved with Walter. As an advertising man, Walter was intrigued by the fact that mail order brought advertising as near as possible to a science. He had read the theories in book after book, but his work with Daisy had given him his first hands-on experience with it. He had never before truly approached the business of making money in what he felt was a proper way. This had to do with his father, his training, and his entire upbringing that had stressed the unimportance of money. Now he was keenly excited to see the impact of their mail order business as measured in net receipts, not least because he was helping Daisy.

America was a country of 120 million magazine reading, mail-order-buying people. Daisy had sales ability and a business future for which she was willing to fight. Walter wanted the money for her. Personally, he would be satisfied simply with the achievement as long as he was not broke.

He knew they both loved fine things, but she always made it clear that things of the heart and mind and soul took precedence with her. She told him that they would win, and win in everything for the sake of winning and for the sake of each other, and he agreed.

While Daisy was in England, Kitty had involved the American office in a problem that greatly concerned Walter. Kitty's brother and father concocted a pyorrhea remedy with the help of a local doctor. Kitty told Walter that Daisy had authorized a $500 check to be written to Kitty's father with wishes for success.

Kitty said she thought it was wonderful of Daisy to help her this way, noting that she had merely mentioned casually in a letter to Daisy that her father was thinking of the mail order proposition. Walter took Kitty at her word and went with her to meet her father and the doctor. After their briefing, Walter strongly advised Kitty against the venture, but the next thing he heard of the matter was ten days later when he learned that her father had decided to undertake it despite Walter's advice.

Since they had no American testimonials, at Kitty's request Walter wrote copy for the remedy, leaning on supposed reports of French dentists and thousands of cases of successful treatments in France. He advised Kitty's father to run the ad in *Grit* and the predate sections of *The New York News*, the cheapest thorough test. Soon he learned they had already booked advertising in the expensive *Pathfinder* magazine, as well as *Grit* and the *News*, through an advertising agency of which Walter had never heard.

Bills for $800 came in from the agency, but the advertisements yielded no results. Walter hit the ceiling. The doctor and Kitty's father hung their heads in shame. Instead of a $50 test, they had made an $800 test. The only thing left to do was to stop advertising at once and hope and pray that they would get enough business to break even over the coming months. This failed venture cost Daisy $500 at a time the American office could ill afford it, but she never wavered in her loyalty to Kitty, who had been so faithful in handling the day-to-day operations in New York.

Together Walter and Daisy organized a new company, a mail order concern named Beauty Specialists, and with enthusiasm they shared the first two dollars it earned. The Beauty Specialists letterhead showed 505 Fifth Avenue, New York, as the address and directed inquiries to a post office box, which, in fact, constituted the firm's entire Fifth Avenue premises.

The new company was designed to promote products and courses to which Daisy and Walter would have exclusive rights, shielded from Lionel's half-ownership in the Stebbings' businesses. In New York these custom-made cosmetics were produced by Tourneur Beauty Products, Inc., at 136 East 57th Street.

They proceeded to work on an asthma remedy. Realizing that they could not claim to have a cure, they decided on the heading, "ASTHMA—AT LAST!" advertising a course that appealed to the psychology if not the physiology of the millions of asthma sufferers who were so desperate to get rid of asthmatic symptoms.

Treatment for asthma was being effectively marketed by mail in England, but they soon found that in America money for an asthma cure could not be earned simply from an advertisement or even from literature without providing the customer with a sample.

In the meantime Walter worked secretly on his own surprise for Daisy, the Face Lifter. He ran a test market in the *Columbus Sunday Star*, noted as a fast-acting media, and prepared an advertisement with "before and after" illustrations, which he thought should give the Face Lifter a market boost. In his third advertisement he quoted a price of two dollars with a special introductory offer priced at a dollar.

The first order from the Face Lifter advertisements came from the small town of Centerburg, Ohio. By then the product had been advertised in *Grit* and *Screen Romances* and was beginning to pay off.

To their surprise, in the final analysis *Screen Romances* did much better than *Grit* in marketing the product, although initially *Screen Romances* brought in no mail whatsoever and had led them to conclude that the appeal was too old for the magazine's readership.

Walter had a great deal of fun with the Face Lifter, continuing to test copy appeals and different price offers in the Columbus newspaper. *Grit* had produced nothing but inquiries so far, but soon *Screen Romances* yielded encouraging sales. Daisy enjoyed Walter's enthusiasm and called him "so much the man!" They joked with each other about their respective experiments. Walter explored the possibility of finding a treatment for superfluous body hair, which he thought was a golden market opportunity for one who mastered the permanent removal angle.

He studied all angles of the depilatories business and thought there was the opportunity to make a great deal of money out of a legitimate and safe claim for removing hair permanently without electrolysis. Daisy teased him for being so immersed in the subject. He mentioned to her that he had been spending a lot of time on a depilatory proposition. She responded, "You naughty boy!"

Walter loved to shock her. At times they would laugh about the business they found themselves in and "all the talk of asthma, female pills, big tits and little tits, and money, money, money."

Daisy proposed a concoction called Love Drops with copy slanted at the idea that the drops had the power to awaken the desire of love. They both agreed the further the copy stayed from mentioning "perfume," the better it would be.

They wondered if the magazines would take it, and they soon found out. The editors knew that the product was simply perfume with a slant, and they knew that the slant was scarcely new. Obviously, the very basis for a woman's use of perfume was to appeal to a man through the power of scent. The beauty, charm, and voluptuousness of the scent transferred a man's fascination for the scent to a desire for the woman using it. The editors embraced the concept, and Love Drops proved a strong moneymaker.

They knew that their business had every potential for growth. Running an advertisement in six consecutive issues of *Grit* virtually told the public that the ad in question was getting responses. To find the same ad in *Pathfinder*, *Gentlewoman*, *Bickery and Hill*, and the like told the public, "Someone is making some money." Indeed their advertising was attracting significant response, and they were determined to beat their competitors at their own game.

Every day in her work with Walter, Daisy revealed her competitive trait, the determination to win that had so often annoyed her self-centered husband, Lionel. Walter laughed to notice Daisy's competitiveness in the first game of cards they played. "You are a little rascal when you get into competition," he wrote, "but I love you for it because it is a good trait."

Height advertisements in *Pathfinder* were producing numerous sales at a cost to them of thirty cents for the course, inquiry literature, and overhead and fifty cents for advertising. This yielded a profit of one dollar and fifty cents on each two dollars realized.

Daisy and Walter knew that given the time and financial resources, they surely had the ability to revise the courses time after time with every expectation that they would ultimately succeed, testing out and adding new lines to take the place of any they had to discontinue.

Daisy's major asset, they knew, was not the courses themselves or even the names or the money in the business. It was the knowledge that courses like Height and products like Slim Cream and Beautipon could turn money into more money.

Newsstand fiction groups *Real Detective* and *Sweetheart Stories* were the two main publications that Walter was focusing on, and this approach had greatly increased their business. They both sensed that Daisy had a marvelous opportunity to expand; Beautipon and Slim Cream seemed destined to be very successful in America with their accompanying packets of literature heavily edited from what had been successful in England.

The reprinted booklets removed statements that the formulae were the triumphant result of years of scientific experiment. No longer did they claim the potions contained certain valuable fat-destroying vegetables and herbal ingredients certain to have amazing effects.

Slim Cream had been dropped by *Screen Land* magazine, but once the ad was modified, it was again accepted as the only bust preparation in the magazine. The same was true of the Fawcett magazines and *Modern* magazine, both of which accepted the modified copy. Slim Cream yielded good returns in the first eight weeks the modified ad was run.

Bernarr Macfadden's successful books gave them a pattern to follow, but Walter knew that in official circles Macfadden was distinctly persona non grata. Macfadden had been a target of the postal authorities in his early days before he knew better. Although a genuinely serious physical culturist and on the whole a decent sort of citizen, Macfadden knew that the real trick of his great success came from the popularity of the pictures of unclothed females he showed in his enormously successful magazine, *Physical Culture*.

Macfadden had followed this success by publishing articles with a sex angle in *True Experiences*, which led to similar magazines such as *True Stories*, *True Romances*, and *True* this and *True* that until he became a millionaire.

Walter and Daisy met Macfadden. Walter was amazed that "the old fellow still sneaks behind the barn and does his daily dozen and puts his palms right smack down on the floor without bending his knees."

Johnnie Lee Macfadden, his beautiful, much-younger fourth wife, whom he married in 1948, was a frequent lecturer on health and exercise at Carnegie Hall prior to her marriage and would meet Daisy in later years at Swannanoa, after which they became lifelong friends.

Realizing that Bernarr Macfadden's use of beautiful models had contributed greatly to his success in business, Walter and Daisy soon discovered that using Daisy's so-called "Danish pictures" in connection with their own products brought in business much more rapidly, just as it had done in England. Her beauty transfixed Walter, so he was not surprised at this result.

The turnover of the American business matched a similar success in England, where sales reached a considerable figure in the year 1934 with the Stebbings doing business under the names of Lionel Stebbing, the Stebbing Institute, the Institute of Applied Psychology, the Grosvenor Institute, and Daisy Stebbing.

Daisy and Walter enjoyed a relationship that was spiritual and philosophical, however physical it may have grown. They had long talks about the serenity of the soul as an absolutely essential basis for happiness. Thrills, sensations, and kicks out of life were important, but not unless there was serenity to which to come back. Without serenity excitement was futile and fatal to happiness.

They had fun, too. One evening after they had drunk too much apple-jack, he took her home and wrote a love letter to her on the pink sheets of her bed before taking the ferry back to Manhattan.

Their relationship could be frisky. When he was depressed, he wrote her that if she were there, he would slap her on the can and muss her hair just to prove that behind his professional whiskers he was only a kiddish, bashful lover with slightly sadistic tendencies that he would like to indulge.

Walter talked about writing a book called *Lives of Men of Genius*. The opening slant would question why in all of time since civilization began there had been no woman among the geniuses of the world, among the DaVincis, Copernicuses, Shakespeares, Beethovens, Newtons, and Einsteins. The book would develop the ideas that had it not been for the love and inspiration of the unsung women, no one would have realized his genius. Daisy undermined a portion of his thesis by arguing aggressively that there had been a number of great women who had changed the world in their own right through their courage and genius.

Daisy had become absorbed in a remarkable novel titled *Salome, The Wandering Jewess: My First Two Thousand Years of Love*. Written by George S. Viereck and Paul Eldridge as a companion to their earlier bestseller, *The Wandering Jew*, this book proved even more successful. It fascinated Daisy, helping her clarify her long-held convictions that woman's equality was not only morally justified but also essential to the progress of civilization.

Termed by distinguished critics of the time as "one of America's most notable contributions to the study of love," the book was called "brilliant and daring," a fictionalized account beginning with the Biblical story of Salome, whose dance scandalized the lascivious court of King Herod, her father, but earned her the severed head of John the Baptist, the saint who had scorned her. Salome's eternal punishment was the miraculous gift of perpetual life, youth, and frustration. "She became the Wandering Jewess, forever seeking the fulfillment of her role as a woman, yet at the same time striving for victory over the physical bondage of her sex," the dust jacket describes the plot. In the novel she had many loves, but her principal effort was to influence the lives of many famous men and women over two millennia.

Tens of thousands of readers bought hardcover editions of the book that had come to Daisy's attention promptly after its publication. The caliber of the critics who praised it proved it to be far more than a sensational potboiler. Havelock Ellis pronounced it "done well with a large sweep." Dr. Franz Wittels called it "undoubtedly the most searching analysis of the eternal woman." The *Los Angeles Messenger* termed its vividness of imagination, poetry of expression, and vastness of concept unique in modern fiction and compared it favorably with Milton's *Paradise Lost*, Dante's *Inferno*, and Goethe's *Faust*. *The Boston Transcript* called it exciting and fascinating. *The Cambridge Review* and *New York Kadelpian Review* heralded its scope and pageantry, and the *Newcastle Chronicle* called it "the first book that shows woman facing life in its entirety and attempting to adjust herself to her destiny."

Daisy gave copies to Walter and many of her friends. She assimilated the book's thesis into her own philosophy. She agreed with its premise that woman's condition was tragic, bound by body and soul with the heavy shackles of man's domination. In this fictional account of Salome, she saw an alternative to woman's docile acceptance of her subordination. Although it continued to sell through the decades in paperback editions, the book was soon forgotten by scholars and critics and left no sociological impact on the western world. It had registered its message in Daisy's mind, however, and reinforced her determination to awaken the infinite possibilities that would come to a world of sexual equality. "The cruelty, the injustice, the bestiality which the rule of man has brought upon earth shall disappear," Viereck and Paul Eldridge predicted, and Daisy agreed. She would refine her knowledge and understanding through the years to come, but Man-Woman equality remained a major foundation of her living philosophy. Twenty and thirty years later it would echo through her books and teachings.

Walter pled with Daisy to accept his proposal and give him in spirit the full love and devotion of her heart. He assured her he was physically, mentally, and spiritually divorced and hoped that the same would someday soon be true of her. He readily acknowledged that Daisy was still in love with her husband. His only hope was that she would get over that in time. He tried to stress to Daisy that Lionel had grossly and deliberately thrown over his right to her love because of his selfishness. Daisy recognized that she was faced with the failure of a husband who did not love her enough. She felt besieged. Daisy warned Walter that they should guard their happiness.

Dell Publishing threatened to drop advertising for Height. Walter went down to see the manager in charge of advertising, and they had a cordial meeting. Walter told him that he had once spent an evening with a man who mentioned that his watch chain had become an inch longer in a number of years. His explanation was that each of the thirty-two links has worn away a thirty-second of an inch. Walter told the Dell executive that the same thing happened to the cartilaginous cushions of the human spine. He outlined the course convincingly enough to cause Dell to renew the advertising in a number of Dell publications, including *Sweethearts Stories* and *Film Fun*, which had already begun producing good results for Height.

Daisy and Walter worked together to make her Height business safer. They tried to limit the changes in what had been an effective business in

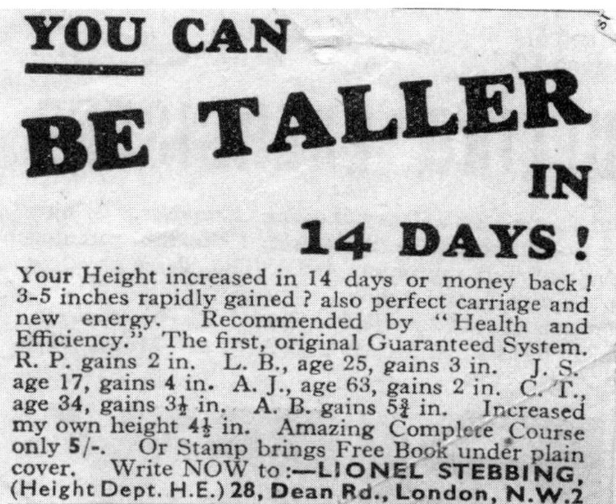

32. Advertisement for Height.

England to those that would not reduce its pulling power in the market. They reviewed the advertisements and the Height course content and eliminated or toned down a number of things they felt might antagonize the scientific mind

"Three to five inches rapidly gained" was edited to read "Amazing course $2.00 complete or send for book giving guarantee and testimonials of three to five inches gained." The heading "BE TALL" was changed to "BE TALLER." They both agreed the latter was more conceivable and more believable.

Walter tried to obtain before and after photographs of former students. He and Daisy both knew from statistics on the heights of male adults in the United States that any product promoting increase in height would find a great market. The trouble was that despite all his research, Walter could find nothing anywhere in the course, the literature, or the ads to prove that individual height had actually been increased by so much as a fraction of an inch. Only the testimonials made that claim.

Walter spent hours and days at the public library, searching for the faintest bit of scientific data on the matter of extending the human frame. The closest he came was some evidence from a physician of 1870 whose experiments tended to show that the ligaments in the spine might be expanded through mechanical stretching rather than exercise.

A previous owner of Height had fought for three years to gain the approval of the American authorities for the course but had ultimately lost. Still Daisy and Walter felt that Slim Cream, Beautipon, and Height could probably be saved. At the time, the fledgling American business had a good savings account built up. Under the cover of that cash and the weekly profits, they had every good chance of building and developing a solid mail-order business that would not be attacked or threatened in the future.

In May, Daisy had brought back from England photostats of the testimonial letters used in the Height literature there. They knew these would be important to have on hand if they were called upon to produce them.

CHAPTER FOUR

Multiple Disasters (1934-36)

All the while she was in America, Daisy and Lionel corresponded regularly, but in March, July, and August 1934 his letters emphasized his desire to be free to seek other women's company, even within the continuation of their marriage.

Despite these signs of alienation, they planned a European holiday together for September. Even though Daisy was growing ever closer to her brilliant new protector in New York, she looked forward to the opportunity to be with her husband and renew their love. She sailed from America, arriving home on September 6, and she and Lionel left for Italy nine days later. Crossing the English Channel, they debarked at Boulogne, crossed France by train, and reached the Italian frontier on September 16.

They stayed at Lake Como for two weeks. At first the holiday seemed to restore some of the romance that they had shared in the earlier years of their marriage, but Lionel continued to display his worst traits. He was extremely jealous of Daisy, which was apparent throughout their stay. It was close to Walter Powell's birthday, and Daisy had to plot and plan to find a time to send a letter to him in New York. Nevertheless, Daisy and Lionel generally relaxed and seem to have delighted in many pleasant Italian distractions. At Lake Como they danced, played tennis, and took deep breathing classes. She loved exercise and recreation. She also managed to make new friends despite Lionel's possessiveness. They stopped in Switzerland for a brief holiday on their return trip to England.

Soon after this Daisy wrote Walter a letter describing Lionel's shabby and shocking treatment of her in Italy, complaining that while the vacation on Lake Como had been planned at Lionel's insistence as "a lovely holiday with the only woman in the world that I love," he had cut their trip short and insisted they hurry back to London because of a supposed business meeting that turned out to be a rendezvous with another woman.

Lionel told Daisy he must have his evenings out and be free to lead his own life. This was enormously disappointing to her. She could not accept the fact that Lionel had been unfaithful. He claimed that he needed the intellectual companionship of his other women friends. This was equally insulting to Daisy, who considered her own intellect more than an adequate match for Lionel's.

On October 8, Lionel arose about eleven in the morning and left for London, returning between one and two o'clock the following morning. The next day he told Daisy he had been out with lady friends the previous evening for dinner and the theater. She thought he seemed very morose. The next Saturday, October 14, they went together to a cinema, and on their return to Sun Haven she asked him what was troubling him. He said he was sorry he kept hurting her but confessed he could not help it because he had changed and did not love her as he had in the past.

Daisy, ever sensitive, asked him what she had done to provoke the change, and he told her it was entirely his fault. He seemed unable to give her a clear explanation of what was happening to him. The next day, Sunday, Daisy stayed in bed, very upset over the events of the previous evening. Lionel was very kind and considerate, and said he was sorry he had hurt her so much. This raised her hopes that they might be able to live together happily again. That afternoon friends called to see them. Lionel entertained them, but Daisy stayed in bed.

The next morning when Daisy arose, Elsie told her that Lionel was sleeping late and would see her at lunch. Thinking he might be ill, Daisy went into his room to find out what was the matter. He told her he had had a bad night and started crying. She was upset to find him so unhappy and asked him if there was anything she could possibly do to make him feel better. In between crying spells he told her that he would consult Noel Jaquin, their fortuneteller friend, as to whether or not they should separate. Daisy was shocked at the very suggestion of going to such a person to discuss so important a personal matter. She told him that he must know in his own heart what he wanted to do and urged him not to confide in Jaquin. Lionel then told her that he would go away, as he must be free to lead his own life. He wanted to be with his own friends, who were all girls, and he said he needed a place where he could entertain them when he wished.

Daisy remembered a previous instance when he had suggested that she might go out alone while he had one of his girlfriends to Sun Haven for dinner. That suggestion had hurt her at the time, and Lionel had chastised her for being too old-fashioned for modern times. He now told Daisy he needed the freedom to go where and when he wished without telling anyone. She assured him she had always wanted him to feel free and would try not to object to his meeting various women friends.

He told her he had decided he would be happier if he went away. Hurt and frustrated, Daisy went back to her room to rest. Soon Lionel entered the room and told her he was leaving. He kissed her goodbye and left the house without any luggage. His shaving items remained in the bathroom as usual, and his clothes were lying about in his room as if he intended to return soon.

That afternoon he telephoned from Mayfair Chambers, Balderton Street, near Grosvenor Square, and asked the maid to send him some clothes and various tinned food and provisions from the Sun Haven pantry. Daisy called Florrie in Luton and asked her to come to Sun Haven to stay for several days. Florrie told her sister that it was ridiculous to send Lionel food. The maid was dispatched with his clothes. By the end of the week Lionel notified Daisy that he would be staying permanently in London at a flat on Abbey Road.

From that time on Lionel refused to let Daisy take an active part in the English business and insisted that she give up her half ownership in it. She vigorously challenged his claim that the business was entirely his. She asserted that if Lionel were not prepared to live with her and likewise wanted the entirety of the English business, he would have to make her an attractive settlement offer. By now Daisy feared that she had put herself in a weak position by hesitating. She was still Lionel's wife and as such was entitled to his support and companionship, but he wanted to give her neither. She knew that the law required Lionel to comport himself as a husband. While she had been in America and after her return, he had grown accustomed to enjoying his freedom without any restraint from her, which she had permitted him to do it at little or no cost. She now felt she needed to make it clear there would be a price for his enjoying the pleasantness of an independent life. She was dissatisfied with the present situation but did not want a separation. She had been happy in the marriage and considered their present estrangement to be entirely Lionel's fault. She felt he needed to understand what the law required of him as her husband whether their business continued or not, but Lionel turned down every proposition she made for a settlement. She grew frustrated. He was getting the best of her. It was not her nature to make a nuisance of herself or try to prove his misconduct by having a detective follow him, but she knew she would need a lawyer if she were to protect her interests. She hired H. B. Hughes as her solicitor to handle the negotiations with Lionel.

Daisy knew that the accounts Lionel kept did not reflect their business's full income or show many assets they had accumulated and sheltered. She knew that Lionel had underreported their income for Inland Revenue purposes and that cash payments sent them by mail had generally been stashed away and not reflected on the company's books.

She was filled with conflicting emotions. She had much at stake and felt that Lionel was being intentionally cruel to her. She suspected that he would delay giving her a divorce, simply because he knew that by being dilatory he would drive her to despair and induce her to accept a settlement favorable to him. She began to think if she could save the American business for herself, it might be well for her to relinquish her interest in the English operations if it brought her freedom from Lionel.

Daisy told H. B. Hughes she would give up all claims to the English venture in exchange for full ownership of the American business, as well as title to Sun Haven and its furnishings and an allowance of seventy pounds a month. It proved a fateful decision for her.

Hughes warned her there were risks in such a proposal. He reminded her that if Lionel should die or go bankrupt, she would most likely receive no further monthly payments and would have to live solely on the uncertain income from the American business and whatever capital she could realize from selling the house and furniture. Hughes pressed Lionel's solicitor for a more generous settlement, making it clear that Lionel had left Daisy without justification and had firmly announced his intention of not returning. This left her free to apply to the court for restitution and other relief, and she threatened to do so.

The solicitors continued their prolonged negotiations. Even though Lionel clearly wanted to keep the successful English business for himself, at first he opposed a geographical division of the business between America and England and offered Daisy one hundred percent of the beauty business wherever located in consideration of leaving the health and physical culture assets for him. Daisy knew that if either of them were to obtain any benefit from the American business, she would have to return to New York to develop it herself. She had confidence in her ability to build on what she had begun there and was willing to take her chances on its future. She knew Walter would help her and was certain they would be successful. She considered Beauty Specialists already hers and Walter's and knew that Lionel could not prove that she had been acting in America solely as his agent or as a representative of their own joint business. She had never signed a document that might lead to that conclusion.

She knew if she agreed to take less than a controlling interest and if she had no right to dictate policies and management of the English business, things could easily go awry and Lionel could take advantage of her. It would be far better for her to own the American business outright than to have a minority interest in a larger English venture that might be badly or crookedly managed. Nonetheless, as a negotiating ploy, she first asked for twenty-five percent of the English business in addition to the entire American business, plus £750 a year for her own support.

Daisy knew she would require a substantial allowance from the larger English receipts if she were to relinquish her ownership interest in the British companies. Recognizing that there would be no binding guarantee that an allowance would continue after Lionel's death, she insisted that Lionel take out a twenty-year endowment insurance policy and assign it to her in satisfaction of any claim for maintenance after his death. This would still leave her potentially vulnerable in case of Lionel's bankruptcy. Lionel whined that he should be able to reduce her monthly allowance if his business income were to drop in the future. She reminded him that the divorce court would only give him that option as part of a settlement that additionally provided a higher allowance for her if his income increased.

The peripheral issues were equally difficult to resolve. Paramount among these was the disposition of Sun Haven, to which Daisy was deeply attached. Lionel insisted that it be sold and the proceeds divided between them. Walter was very concerned about the possibility of Daisy losing Sun Haven. She had written him it would cost her £15,000 at a minimum if it were sold in such a deteriorating market. She was convinced that holding onto it would prove beneficial to her in the long term. When she eventually agreed that it should be rented and was forced to move out, it was agonizing for her. She decided to spare herself actual contact with the new tenant and was not present when he moved in.

Daisy demanded that in the future the name "Mrs. Lionel Stebbing" be used in any English advertising in place of the name "Daisy Stebbing" and wanted it clearly understood that whenever Lionel used her photograph in connection with the business, it would only be done in connection with text that Daisy had previously approved.

Through all her ordeal of haggling with Lionel, Walter regularly offered her sound advice and moral support from New York. He insisted that Lionel was getting off too easily in the proposed settlement. He told her Lionel was using her and urged her to be definite in her demands and reject any reduction in her claims.

Walter feared sending her a present for her birthday in 1934. He was afraid that even if he sent her a book, it might contain a single phrase that would upset her. He urged her to seek sympathy and help from Florrie, who was on the scene, suggesting, "Surely she could be able to give you some comfort," but when Daisy's negotiations with Lionel seemed stymied, Walter seriously considered traveling to England to help her, despite the fact that his doing so might only damage their cause.

Amidst the legal wrangling, Daisy found herself in an emotional upheaval quite apart from the practical side of her estrangement from Lionel and the possible consequences of their separation. She wrote Walter that she was afraid she was losing her sweetness and her faith in human nature. It was clear that Lionel's unfairness to her was having a deleterious effect on her natural optimism.

In New York, Walter experienced little success in obtaining evidence of marital misconduct on the part of his wife. He wrote Daisy a humorous and self-mocking account of one such effort when, after watching her apartment with binoculars from a nearby office building, he suspected she was alone there with a male friend when he saw the lights go off in the bedroom. He went to the apartment building, entered the side door, and walked up fourteen flights of stairs to elude the doorman and elevator operator, whom he thought might call to alert his wife that he was in the building. Entering the apartment, he eavesdropped on the conversation taking place in the bedroom, only to realize that his wife was sharing the bed with one of their young sons, who was reluctant to go to sleep and whom he heard her tell, "Come now, go to sleep or I'll give you a spanking, a real one the way Daddy does. Mother is tired and wants to go to sleep." Walter reported this misadventure in a letter to Daisy, concluding, "So the super sleuth crawls back down over the fourteen flights, informs his partners in crime, and off we go to battle over the NRA, the gold standard, and Roosevelt over a few beers at the Lexington Tap Room!"

Both Walter and Daisy feared that his wife might file an action for alienation of affection against Daisy, and for this reason Walter was extremely hesitant to institute his own divorce proceedings. He knew that Daisy would win such a suit but wanted to spare her the embarrassment of possibly having her American property attached. "Anyone can bring suit against anybody else for anything and the person suited will be treated like a defendant until the case is over," he wrote. Daisy rejected Walter's suggestion that she consider selling the Beauty Specialists business temporarily to Kitty for a dollar to ensure that it would be shielded from any claims his wife might file.

Daisy wrote Walter that in her mind she was depending more and more upon the potential of the American business. They both understood that its success was built on judgment and vision, and they mutually agreed that they had an ample supply of both qualities. Daisy felt that since she had established the business in New York, she had the moral right to own it and doubted if Lionel had a legal claim to anything more than the money they had originally put into it.

She seriously considered returning to New York before her negotiations with Lionel were concluded, but Walter advised her against abruptly leaving England. Her "American husband" wanted two things, he wrote: "You and security for you." Walter knew that her staying in England and countering Lionel's successive ploys kept them apart, but he realized Daisy's gamesmanship with Lionel on their home turf increased her chances for ultimate security in America.

Over a seventeen-week period from August through November 1934, Height, Slim Cream, Slim Cream Advanced, Beautipon, and Beautipon

Advanced had yielded $9,586, leaving a profit of $3,434. Walter emphasized there were dozens of avenues for expanding the American business. He asked her to envision its limitless horizons, urging her to negotiate a settlement giving her the American business before Lionel realized its potential.

Daisy knew that she and Lionel were engaged in a fight to the finish and recognized the importance of keeping from him the real success of the American business. The American business was already earning a net profit of $10,000 a year, and she was only beginning to explore the opportunities for developing new lines to expand it and increase the profits. Walter had checked with his patent and trademark attorney and determined that no one had any copyright claim in America on any of the courses, literature, names, signatures, or illustrations she and Lionel had been using in England. As a practical matter, they were all Daisy's.

She and Walter established an elaborate code for cabling as negotiations between her and Lionel grew more tense and a financial settlement with him seemed more difficult to obtain. In late November Lionel balked, apparently suspicious of the financial information Daisy had given them regarding the New York business. He now insisted that it was no longer possible to work out the settlement along geographical lines and demanded an absolute division with Daisy taking the beauty side of the business, "the part dealing with the female sex," and leaving the remainder dealing with the male sex for him.

At the time the beauty business yielded between forty and fifty percent of the net English sales. Lionel proposed that Daisy carry on the beauty business at a separate address, and each party would agree not to carry on business similar to that carried on by the other. This would leave no room for any clash of policy and no need for the parties to meet in connection with their activities. Lionel would give Daisy his share of Sun Haven and pay the mortgage as long as she lived there. If the house were sold, the mortgage would be satisfied out of the sale proceeds, and if it were rented, the rent would be applied to the payments.

Daisy would have the Vauxhall automobile, one-third of the investments Lionel had made, and £250 sterling a year for life whether the marriage was dissolved or not. Lionel argued that this plan had the merit of giving Daisy a valuable business, a house, a sum of capital, and a definite income which, when augmented with the proceeds of the beauty side of the business, would prove much more beneficial to her.

1934 ended with Daisy facing a dilemma. After a lonely Christmas and New Year, she knew that it would be better if she and Lionel made a final break. His distant, unusual attitude toward her had not changed, and he was enjoying the society of a number of other women. Hughes wrote her on December 30, telling her that she must decide which course of action to pursue. He continued to believe that the American business was a poor business proposition and advised her that it would be much safer to retain the beauty business in England, seek a separate location on Regent Street, try to persuade Lionel to give her the entire American business for a nominal sum, and seek to obtain an additional payment of £350 a year. On New Year's Eve he communicated this proposal to Lionel's solicitor, Crane. Through the lawyers the parties wished each other a happy and prosperous New Year.

There were fundamental differences to be resolved. Lionel feared future business calamities or periods of economic depression. He stressed that if he were to have the entire English business it must include the name Daisy Stebbing and the right to continue using Daisy's photographs in course literature but not for advertising. Lionel agreed to raise Daisy's annual allowance to £750 sterling, but only for two years.

While Daisy could keep all their wedding presents, there were further problems involving personal property. Lionel had removed Daisy's golf clubs and certain pictures from Sun Haven on the impression they were his. He agreed to return them. She had let two months go by without sending him all his personal belongings. He entered Sun Haven to search for the remainder. He alleged that on several occasions Daisy had been through his private desk at the office and asked her to send him her key to the desk.

The assets Lionel offered Daisy as part of the settlement included the American rights to Rycol, a patented cure for catarrh; the Grosvenor Institute of Psychology Course, all physical training courses and appliances; all beauty courses and cosmetics; the course in nerve treatment; and the course entitled Word Force and Social Magnetism.

Lionel's solicitor emphasized that in his opinion only the course in nerve treatment might prove objectionable to the Better Business Bureau or the postal authorities in America. Lionel was convinced that Daisy could build a very substantial business there on these courses. Giving her these rights plus Sun Haven, the car, and £750 sterling a year seemed to him a more than ample settlement.

Daisy tried to look dispassionately at her situation. With difficulty she sought to put emotion aside and judge things purely and simply as a business proposition. Some years before, she had started a mail order business in England and brought in Lionel as her partner. They had produced courses that sold well. Initially she had a limited amount of cash and virtually no business experience, but she soon came to understand what attracted customers and which magazines would draw business. By hard work and trial and error they had built a very successful business.

Now she was older, wiser, and more experienced. America was much richer in mail order possibilities because it was bigger and its people were more responsive and easier to reach through magazines with much larger circulation. She had over $10,000 in cash, which Walter felt was more than enough seed money. She had a history of "pulling power," which she knew was very valuable. There was no reason why she and Walter could not continue to expand the American business, using Height to pay her living expenses and the cost of experimenting and testing new lines.

Lionel's father seemed very solicitous of Daisy, telling her he hoped things would work out in her marriage and assuring her that neither he nor Lionel's mother could understand the change in their son. "We are always worrying about it," he wrote her. "Lionel is neither happy nor wealthy." Mr. Stebbing said he wanted Daisy to give him "blue-eyed Stebbing grandchildren." He understood that Daisy wanted to keep Sun Haven for a while until she decided definitely whether or not to pursue the New York business. She wanted to keep the Benneys employed at the house in Elstree until March, but Mr. Stebbing assured her he could secure cheaper caretakers and offered to help her himself in taking care of details in England. He told her that Lionel would surely be "proud of you when you've made the New York side as good if not better than London."

By February the delay in reaching a settlement appeared to be affecting the health of both parties. Soon they compromised on the remaining issues and on February 27 they signed a deed of separation. In exchange for an annuity of £750 a year free of tax, Daisy assigned her share in the English business to Lionel. She received title to Sun Haven, as well as all furniture and personal effects on the premises and the Vauxhall Saloon motorcar. Thenceforth she would be responsible for her own personal expenses.

The business (including Rycol) was divided geographically with Lionel having exclusive rights to the United Kingdom, Irish Free State, continent of Europe, and all the British Empire excluding Canada and the West Indies. Daisy's exclusive territory encompassed the United States, Mexico, Canada, Central and South America, and all New World islands. Daisy retained sole right to use her photographs and the trade name of Mrs. Lionel Stebbing but granted Lionel limited use of the name Daisy Stebbing and certain of her photographs in his area of operation. He was forbidden to send any circulars or literature relating to any of the correspondence courses to America.

They each assumed existing debts in their respective territories. Lionel was given the office furniture at Dean's Street and the entire stock of stationery, cosmetics, and printed matter located there. Strict provisions were made to ensure that he kept proper accounts, something they both knew had not been done in the past. Lionel assigned her a non-profit insurance policy on his life under which she would receive £2,000 payable on his death.

Their partnership was dissolved. As for their marriage, they were permanently separated and free to live apart but not divorced. Apart from infrequent letters regarding their settlement, she did not see or hear from Lionel again until June 1937.

Daisy decided to stay in England longer. Walter urged her to return to New York as soon as possible because the business was being investigated, but Daisy felt she could not leave England until she settled her domestic affairs. She had planned to return to America in March 1935 but delayed her trip a month or more. In June 1935 she visited her aunt and uncle, Emily and Thomas Ayres, in Centralia, Illinois. Emily had been virtually bedfast for over a year, but Daisy's visit pleased her greatly, according to a letter Thomas wrote Florrie after his wife died on August 5. One of Emily's last requests was that Daisy receive a handsomely framed picture of Alfred William Cook, Emily's brother and Daisy's father. Both Daisy and Florrie were surprised that their Aunt Sarah Jane had outlived all her brothers and sisters and had celebrated her eighty-first birthday on the day her sister died. As Florrie noted, "She was always supposed to be very delicate."

In New York Daisy saw less of Walter. She had met Hans Kolb, an Austrian businessman managing a Pittsburgh department store and Manhattan restaurant and representing a European manufacturer of innovative and profitable cold drink machines. He was a champion swimmer who had fallen madly in love with Daisy. They corresponded regularly after she returned to England in early July, leaving Walter to confront the government officials investigating her business.

It was an exceptionally hot summer in New York in 1935, but Hans went to the beach every day, mornings and evenings, and was soon to start training again for his championship swim meets. He missed Daisy terribly and wrote her he could sit for hours before her photograph "and remember the beautiful days we had together, days filled with love and beauty." He hated being so sentimental and feared he was boring her to death. He told her he sometimes bought the magazines with her picture in the advertisements just so he could look at her. He teased her: "I still read your testimonials sometimes and how you lost thirty pounds in one week." He told her he wished he could be in the envelope with his letter.

33. Lao and Hans Kolb, 1936.

On August 21 Hans finally heard from Daisy.

She had not decided whether to rent Sun Haven or sell it. The next week she sent him two letters. She had decided to lease Sun Haven with its furnishings. In that way she could reclaim it if she ever wanted to return to Elstree. He encouraged her to obtain her divorce from Lionel and come back to America and marry him. She sent him newspaper clippings from England warning of the dangers of Hitler's rise to power in Germany. He told her some of the British press accounts were true and some were false, but he did not think a war involving England and Germany would occur in the near future.

Hans's New York opportunities were improving, and he moved to a larger apartment on Central Park, planning it as a future home for them both. He finished second in his first swimming tournament of the summer and told Daisy he had won her a nice trophy. The next Sunday he finished first. She had been in England for seven weeks and was expected back in New York in eight more weeks. He told her there were only a few more outdoor swim meets before the season ended. He expected her to be back before the indoor season started in November, suggesting that "by then I will have no time for swimming or will you let me practice every day?" He was negotiating with Coca-Cola to use his machines in New York. He planned a trip to visit her in Elstree but decided his presence would further complicate an already difficult situation for her.

Daisy continued to maintain a high fashion profile. On September 16, 1935, as both her marriage and her American business were under siege, she replenished her wardrobe with stylish gowns and a cape from Adrian's ("Exquisite Expressions in Gowns") on Regent Street off London's famed Piccadilly.

Earlier that month Noel Jaquin, the fortuneteller, telephoned her and arranged for her to meet him and his secretary, Ella Milne, over dinner. They suggested that Daisy have Lionel watched by a private detective and showed her a letter Lionel had written Jaquin asking him to read the character of his Danish lady friend. Daisy instructed Cooper's Detective Service to send a representative to Copenhagen to see if it were possible to obtain sufficient evidence for her to obtain a divorce from Lionel. Mr. Cooper's report of October 2, 1935, was inconclusive, but late the next month a similar surveillance was conducted for several days at Lionel's residence at Bay Tree Cottage in Maida Vale. Still no evidence could be obtained of any other woman sleeping at Lionel's address.

Before Daisy returned to New York on the *Normandie* on September 24, 1935, Walter told her of his extreme concern about the Federal Trade Commission investigation. He found it virtually impossible to convey the seriousness of the matter to Daisy while she was an ocean away, but he stressed there was hope they could carry on the business even if some of it were closed down.

Daisy was tense as she returned to America after leasing Sun Haven and storing many of her possessions, but her frustration seemed due to her inability to cope with the unpleasantness that Lionel had left in her life. She described her nervousness to Walter in some of her last letters from England that year. He replied that he could not get out of his mind her tales of screaming in her sleep. He promised to help her and tried to reassure her that his wife was most unlikely to file an alienation of affection suit against Daisy unless he began divorce proceedings. Walter's wife still loved him, and she knew she was financially better off not separated. Nevertheless, Walter promised to protect Daisy.

Soon, unbeknownst to Walter, Daisy was spending much of her time with Hans Kolb. After a few weeks Hans was working mostly in Pittsburgh and Philadelphia, while she and Walter turned their attention to the forthcoming hearing in Washington.

The Federal Trade Commission had scheduled its hearing on Height for the previous March, but Daisy's New York attorney, Mr. Hooker of Goodale, Hanson, and Hooker at 50 Broadway, obtained a long adjournment which enabled Daisy to advertise in the April magazines. By now Walter was optimistic that Beautipon and Slim Cream would survive the hearing and maybe even by some miracle, Height. In any event he knew that they could make several thousand dollars in Height in the interim even if an order were issued against it. He knew publications would take advertisements for it in spite of the pending hearing. "That's the best thing I do," he said. "If Height alone is ruled against, we will simply use a mailbox and a New York City address and mail it out in bulk to insure that income will continue while we are digging in and building new lines. Nothing will prevent us from correcting things according to our judgment of what has been challenged and starting again under a different name." The fraud order would go against the old name, but the new name would have every right to do business. Even though the post office might launch another investigation in the future, it would be more difficult for authorities to prevail because the new business would be designed to be unassailable.

In case the businesses were closed, Walter placed them on the strictest possible advertising budget. This was difficult to do when the new hearing date had not been set. He knew the government would present a tough case against Height but was not certain that Slim Cream and Beautipon would be involved. Hooker succeeded in postponing the proceedings until Daisy could come back from England. Walter felt he could defend the business "to the last word in his vocabulary," noting that in the past on similar matters he had proven his aptitude for that sort of thing.

An order to show cause issued by the federal government was served against Daisy on October 16, 1935, returnable November 25, 1935, seeking to determine why a fraud order should not be issued against Daisy Stebbing, Lionel Stebbing, Stebbing System, and the Stebbing System of Height Increase, all of Forest Hills, Flushing, New York.

Daisy's attorneys did a great deal of work in preparing the defense, and an answer was filed with the government on November 18, 1935. The administrative trial in the case was adjourned until December 3, 1935, when it was held in Washington, D.C., with Daisy attending. Despite her lawyers' best efforts, a government fraud order was issued which had the effect of closing up the entire business in the United States. Mr. Hooker was pessimistic about the possibilities of reversing this ruling and advised Daisy in a letter of January 2, 1936: "We are convinced that the acts of the government would never be reversed through application to the courts. As far as we know, the government has been sustained by the courts in every case of a similar character. In our opinion, everything that could be done was done in your behalf to save this business and there is nothing further that could possibly be done which would alter the outcome."

She authorized Kitty to close down the Forest Hills office and sell the remaining products to wholesalers.

On New Year's Day, 1936, Noel Jaquin wrote to Daisy in America telling her, "I have never forgotten your last night in England. It was marvelous. When are you likely to return to England? Obviously you will have to do this if your business is closed down in America. Don't forget my advice on that matter. Lionel is no longer anxious for divorce. He does not know what he does want."

Soon afterwards Noel Jaquin and Miss Milne reported to her that Lionel was staying with another woman at the Orchard Hotel, but this charge proved impossible to substantiate. Daisy concluded that either Jaquin was intentionally misleading her as a favor to Lionel, or was trying to cause trouble for them both because Lionel's excursions to Denmark left Jaquin the full burden of conducting their own joint venture in a correspondence course entitled *Remold Your Life*. Daisy felt as if she had been victimized in every aspect of her existence.

CHAPTER FIVE

Losses and Gains

(1936-38)

After the debacle with the Federal Trade Commission, Daisy left her Long Island apartment in Richmond Hill and sailed for England on the SS *Champlain* at noon on January 4, 1936. On her arrival she cabled her New York friend Billy Sheridan that it had been a rough trip. William H. Sheridan operated a thriving Pontiac dealership in the General Motors Building at 1775 Broadway. He had sold Daisy a new Pontiac automobile in mid-1935 before she drove west to visit her American relatives. She left it with him to sell for her.

He tried to encourage her in a letter of January 22, but it was clear to him that her state of mind was nearly as depressed as it had been just after the hearing. He continued to try to reassure her and told her she owed it to herself to take better care of her health. Billy had stored the inventory of many of the creams and devices that Daisy had been selling, and Kitty had come from the Forest Hills office to pick them up. Walter had advised them to fill the outstanding orders as soon as possible, and Billy was attempting to find a source through which the remaining products could be marketed without using the mails. There was some concern that if the federal officials found that any of the banned products had been mailed, it might adversely affect Daisy's ability to return to the United States. As if her business problems were not depressing enough, no sooner had Daisy returned to England than the country was plunged into mourning by the death of King George V. Billy's letter was little short of a love letter, full of assurances of his devotion and signed "your best and real friend, Billy."

Hans Kolb also missed Daisy. He wrote her every day while she was crossing the Atlantic so she would have a sheaf of letters awaiting her. He sent her photographs of an outing they had enjoyed together with another couple and urged her to settle matters with Lionel so that she would be free to marry him. In February, a month after she had left New York, he wrote her that it seemed as if she had been gone ten years. She was staying in London at a hotel for the time being. It was a time of major labor unrest in England. He told her he was sorry for the Londoners during the strikes, forced to do without their steaks and chops, but principally he focused his concern on one major question: Would she be coming back to America again?

Her first letter to Hans after her return expressed concern that she might not be able to obtain a divorce from Lionel. He told her teasingly that even in those regrettable circumstances, they would still be happy together someday. "Maybe I could adopt you so you can have my name," he mused. "We could live here together and nobody would know the difference. The main thing is, darling, that we can be together. We love each other and that is enough." He planned to meet her in England during the summer of 1936. He knew how happy she was to be with her Scottie, Jimmie, again for a while. Some day, he assured her, she would have her precious dog living with them, and they would be "happier than anybody in the whole world."

Hans offered to help market her remaining stock of beauty creams and asked her to send him a sample of each of her tubes and jars along with an inventory of how many she had in stock. They spoke of taking a cruise together in the sunshine of some warm climate, but each of them faced business and personal challenges that kept them apart. His business was flourishing. He had made a large commission on a deal with the Woolworth department stores.

H. B. Hughes was making scant progress in obtaining a divorce for Daisy. He tried unsuccessfully to contact Lionel. Cooper's Investigation Service reported that Lionel had taken a flat at Baytree Cottage, Langford Place, Abbey Road, Maida Vale, and they also heard from Ms. Milne of Jaquin's office that Lionel was staying with a woman at the Orchard Hotel on Portman Street in London. Hughes had asked the detective to inquire further and have Lionel watched, but the investigation indicated that Lionel was sleeping alone at Baytree Cottage, and there was no trace of his having registered at the hotel either in his own name or that of his purported alias Boswell. Daisy ordered the detectives to curtail their work until she instructed them further. She and Hughes both believed that Lionel was purposely sending them false leads through Noel Jaquin and Ms. Milne in order to encourage Daisy to spend more money on detectives. It was becoming clear that Lionel would not do anything to facilitate Daisy's obtaining a divorce.

Daisy read more and more on the occult, particularly books on Ancient Egypt and the pyramids. She kept a list of the books she had read on the subjects, and it reflects her deepening spirituality and growing mysticism. Obviously at loose ends because of her frustrating business and personal problems, she decided to reclaim possession of Sun Haven and began legal proceedings to evict the occupant, but first she sought inner peace in Egypt, a journey that would leave a lasting impact on her life. She sailed to Calais on February 27, proceeded across France and the Mediterranean, and arrived at

34. *Lao on horseback in Egypt, 1936.*

Port Said on March 4.

She remained in Egypt until late June. She toured the upper reaches of the Nile, explored the inner Sahara regions of western Egypt, meditated at length at the great pyramids of Giza, and relaxed in the company of Cairo's intellectual and stimulating Anglo-Egyptian society. She seems to have traveled alone from England, but as always she soon made many new friends, including an attorney, G. Koutitonsky, and R. Strekalovsky, an artist who also taught on the faculty of science at Egyptian University.

In her book *Love* she described spending days at the foot of the pyramids but focused primarily on the rapport she experienced with the Egyptian people. "I found an eagerness for friendly sharing, and soon realized that people everywhere desired the same thing—Love," she wrote. "I found that all women like to be admired for their beauty and all men like to possess and be admired for their power of leadership. Man did the borrowing of camels, and the women did the work in the fields. In one camp that we visited in the desert a young sixteen-year-old sixth wife of an old toothless Bedouin Arab took me into her tent and, shyly taking down her veil, showed me how pretty she was. I could not speak Arabic but with my eyes and hands I made it clear to her how very lovely I thought she was. The language of the eyes and heart has no language barriers. I discovered that, geographically, it matters not where men and women are; all have the same basic desires and the greatest desire of all is to love and to be loved. I found that men and women for a period delude themselves into believing that power and possessions will satisfy their desires, but experiences usually teach them—sometimes too late—that it was that elusive 'something' man calls love that they truly required."

35. *Lao with Egyptian children, 1936.*

Years later Walter Russell alluded to the importance of Daisy's journey to Egypt in the biographical sketch he wrote as an introduction to her book *God Will Work With You But Not For You*: "She likewise journeyed in far lands in her search for that secret which would awaken the Light in man and thus release him from the chains of his dark. 'Neath the pyramids of Sahara's sands, and to tropics of the Indies, and in crowded cities of four continents, she searched—but she did not look outside of man for that which she sought. She looked only within him. She looked only into the Light of his illumined Soul. And it was there in his illumined Soul she found the Holy Grail of her long search. For behold! All that she found there was good—naught but good."

36. Lao near Cairo, 1936.

On June 30 she sailed up the Mediterranean through the straits of Gibraltar on the SS *Balmoral*, stopping at Funchal, Madeira, for a week, where her sister Florrie joined her. They returned to England on the same vessel some ten days later.

Soon afterwards she visited her sister Emily in Derby and was charmed by Emily's young son, Peter Summerfield, who recalled that she brought the family beautiful souvenirs from Cairo.

By now she had received horrifying news of Walter Powell's deteriorating health. Ill at his parents' home in New Jersey, he wrote that he scarcely understood what was happening to him. It had all started with what he thought was cold. At first he attributed it to the change in weather. He was depressed and bedridden and constantly ran a high temperature. Still blessed with his sense of humor, he suggested that if she were to come and jump in bed with him his temperature would probably rise to 110 degrees. Near the end he wrote her what he believed would probably be the last letter he might ever write. He stressed he wanted to tell her his deepest and truest thoughts about her. He loved her, he said, as he would an ideal woman, for she had all the fineness he could ever conceive of finding in any member of the opposite sex. Her qualities were perfect, he told her.

37. Florrie and Lao, Funchal, Madeira, 1936.

Soon his fever worsened. His hand was too shaky to write, and he admitted he was becoming an invalid. Finally, he wrote

38. Lao in Madeira, 1936.

her brief notes using a typewriter, telling her if he were to write by hand she would not be able to read it. He reported feeling more exhausted than ever. When he died later in 1936, the newspaper headline attributed his death to the "relatively rare disease leukemia." Until the end he was lovingly cared for at home by his parents, sister, wife, and sons. Daisy treasured his memory and his letters for the rest of her life. For years she felt that she would never know the perfect love and understanding she had shared with Walter Powell during the three short years since they had met.

Immediately after her return from Madeira, she interviewed for an executive sales position in Wembley Hill, Middlesex, and on July 21 she traded her 1934 five-passenger Vauxhall Saloon roadster for a 1937 four-passenger coupe.

However, in August 1936 she made another trip to the continent, accompanied by Hans Kolb, who had come to London from New York to join her. They drove her car together through France, vacationing in Germany's southern mountains near Hitler's aerie at Berchtesgaden, crossing into Switzerland at Martinsbruck, and finally arriving in Vienna where Hans's family warmly received them. He delighted in showing her the splendors of the old imperial city and the glorious sites of his homeland.

The night before she left England, a suitcase containing many of her valuable personal belongings, including her reentry permit for America, was stolen from the car of a friend, who was to store it for her during her trip abroad. She had thought it safer to leave these passport attachments in England than to risk their loss as she crossed the many frontiers on the way to Vienna. When she returned home, she went to London's Marylebone Station and informed the police of the theft, but it was not until December 1936 that she reported the matter to the American con-

39. In northern Austria with Hans Kolb and friends, 1936.

sulate, inquiring as to whether the documents might have been turned in to the consulate officials and also as to the procedure for renewing her reentry permit, which was to expire in early January 1937. The consulate advised her to delay applying for a renewal until she was more definite as to the date she would be returning to the United States and assured her she could easily obtain a new permit at that time.

The Weisserts, Hans's mother and stepfather in Vienna, had written her the day after she left their city. They sympathized with her struggles to regain possession of Sun Haven from the stubborn lessee and referred her to a London attorney well acquainted with many Austrians and an expert in English property law. They liked Daisy very much, hoped her future with Hans would be a happy one, and urged her to return soon to Vienna and definitely to visit them at Christmastime.

Hans had returned to New York on the French Line's SS *Paris*. He wrote Daisy daily from the ship, telling her how terrible it felt to leave her behind. He told her the food was wonderful, as it had been in Vienna, but his fellow passengers seemed comical and uninteresting, including an elderly French woman who sat at his table "dressed up like a ham and eggs" and an avuncular Frenchman whose only conversation was to ask for the salt. The SS *Paris* had been recently renovated and seemed fresh and new. Hans had a lovely outside cabin in the middle of the vessel. He wished that Daisy were sharing it with him. She had arranged for presents to be smuggled into his cabin, including a shawl and neckties that delighted him. On the voyage he amused himself playing ping-pong. "There are some very good players here who beat the shirt off me. I wish you were here to show them a few of your ping-pong tricks," he wrote her.

By now he had found his table companions more agreeable. The French woman had revealed herself to be a published travel author. Each night when Hans went upstairs for fresh air and exercise, he looked at the stars and told them how much he loved Daisy. Midway across the Atlantic the ship experienced a dangerous thirty-six-hour hurricane with winds of eighty miles an hour. This disturbed all aboard, but soon after the storm abated and the sun appeared, Hans was delighted to look up and see the great German airship Hindenburg passing 100 feet above. "It made nearly no noise at all and looked absolutely unreal," he wrote her. He met more and more interesting people and received invitations to visit eight countries around the world. He talked with Thomas Wolfe, the celebrated American author, as well as Gustav Machaty, the producer and director of the shocking film *Ecstasy*, which had been banned in America for its nude swimming scene featuring the future Hollywood star Hedy Lamarr. Machaty knew Daisy's next-door neighbors in Elstree, the Mycrofts, and other English film personalities Hans knew Daisy had entertained at Sun Haven. He thought Daisy would have been delighted to be there with him and meet so many interesting people. He landed in New York in a thick fog on September 26. A long letter and a telegram, both from Daisy, were waiting for him at the dock.

Hans and Daisy had enjoyed a wonderful holiday, sharing many exploits and delights. They had raced through France at the end of their vacation and had even run out of gas one night in the French countryside. He was melancholy remembering the good times they had shared but overjoyed that she had met his parents in Vienna. They had asked him when he planned to marry her, and he told them they would marry once the Depression was over. He was invigorated and refreshed to get back to work.

In England, Daisy was not so happy. She missed him terribly. Her automobile had served them well on the continent, but as soon as she reached home, it required expensive repairs. She had obviously shown some misgivings as to their suitability for marriage for he wrote her plaintively, "Darling, whatever you say, I love you, and always will!"

Billy Sheridan had reportedly left New York, and Hans lamented that it seemed Daisy had lost both her Pontiac and the money she had invested in it. He had apparently severed his ties with General Motors. "I think he made some other deals like yours, and Pontiac got wind of it and fired him," Hans opined. A few months later he reported, "My lawyer has found Sheridan. He is still working at Pontiac and through some monkey business he made the mail-clerk say he wasn't there anymore." They served him with a lawsuit in Daisy's name, charging him with conversion and misappropriation, alleging that he had failed to account for the proceeds from the sale of her Pontiac as well as for the receipts from the discount sales of the large inventory of beauty products she had left with him.

Sheridan replied in an unfriendly and defensive letter to Daisy that he had done his best to secure the best possible price for her in both instances. He reminded her that in December 1935 she had sent him written instructions to use part of the proceeds from selling the car to purchase 100 shares of stock in a certain invention. This he had done, he said, and he had placed the shares in escrow for her. He mentioned her telling him that Hans Kolb owed her $1,000. It greatly irritated Billy that Daisy had filed suit against him instead of contacting him directly. "Now I have to get a lawyer to prepare a proper and good defense to an alleged serious charge against me," he complained, threatening her that should she decide to go through with this action, "I would have to bring in as part of my defense our business transactions and submit all correspondence between us in evidence to prove my case." To have done so would apparently have alerted the authorities that Daisy had continued to fill back orders for Beauty Specialist products after the Federal Trade Commission had ordered the business closed. Billy resented the annoyance and inconvenience he claimed she was causing him and termed her "someone who seems to bring distress to every person alive." At the end of his tirade he suggested they settle out of court, inquired as to the status of her marriage, and recommended that they adjust their own dispute amicably, which they did. It was a very different letter from his earlier handwritten messages to her. He no longer romanticized that he and Daisy might have a future together.

By October 1936, Daisy was more depressed then ever, as her correspondence with Hans Kolb revealed. She felt imprisoned, she said, but at least she had her Scottie Jimmie for company. Hans sought to console her: "You seem so unhappy, dearest, it really must be the worst time of your life. It seems so strange to see you go through all those troubles, dear, one after another, you who really deserve more happiness than any other person I can think of. You always want the best for everybody, and you seem to get the worst. We have to have a great deal of patience in this life sometimes, but sooner or later it all comes out all right." Hans genuinely sympathized with her. He felt that she would be sitting alone at Sun Haven "like an old grandmother" when in actuality she lived to "go out and do things with people."

The American newspapers were filled with stories of King Edward's love affair with Mrs. Simpson. Rumors were rife that the king would marry her the next year. Hans and Daisy agreed that the whole matter was disgraceful, but agreed that they themselves had their own worries and paid little attention to the royal scandals.

Hans urged Daisy to go to Vienna to be with his family once she sold Sun Haven. He felt that there she could soon restore herself to health and vitality. "The life they are leading there is just what you need to get you back on your feet again," he wrote her. His parents invited her to spend Christmas and New Year with them. By late November she had come to feel that there would be no more happiness ahead for her. He tried to cheer her up, reminding her of the fun they had traveling through Europe, telling her how fortunate she was to have friends like Pat and Marie Cassin with whom she was living. He reminded her of the happy evenings they had spent together, a splendid dinner in Cologne, and walks through New York's Central Park. They had met almost by chance, and he remembered their first encounter well. "I can see you still," he wrote her, "walking by me for the first time with your gray coat and red handbag. God only knows why you smiled that time, but I fell in love with you then and never got over it."

Later in the year Hans wrote her that his father was opening up a luxurious new buffet restaurant in Vienna and had offered her a partnership in the venture. "You couldn't find anybody better than him in that respect and you could both make money," Hans assured her, adding, "In the meantime you could teach my father English so that he can tell you nice things!"

40. The Milestone, Kensington, Lao's London home while Sun Haven was leased.

In November her attorney finally worked out a settlement with James Moffett, the Sun Haven tenant, and by Christmas Daisy had moved back into her beloved home in Elstree. In the meantime she had been living in London, principally with her friends Pat and Marie Cassin at 3A Edwardes Terrace, a small Georgian period house with a walled and paved garden in fashionable Kensington; at other times she stayed at the nearby Milestone's Hotel, a first-class hotel in Kensington Court, ideal for ladies who shopped at nearby Harrods, Fortnum and Mason, and other fashionable stores then located in the area.

The same month she closed her accounts at Corn Exchange Bank Trust Company in Forest Hills, New York, and transferred the balance to London's Midland Bank. She had been ill since her return from Austria but was now recovering with the help of Dr. Christopher Howard's medical expertise and Marie Cassin's gracious hospitality.

She went to Europe again in January 1937, spending ten days in Germany and again visiting Hans Kolb's parents in Vienna. In January 1937 she astounded Hans by deciding to invest in the new buffeteria his family was building in Vienna and to move there as its manager. He wrote her, "If you ever did anything that's really good for you, I think that is it. It will give you a new interest in life. You will like living in Vienna very much."

In May 1937 she began advertising Sun Haven for sale in the British papers. To Hans's surprise it proved difficult to find a willing buyer. By then Daisy had changed her mind about investing in the Viennese buffeteria, thus narrowly avoiding a situation that would in all probability have found her trapped as a British citizen in Nazi-occupied central Europe during the five years of World War II.

Daisy invited her nephew Peter to come visit her at Sun Haven on an extended vacation and even offered to adopt him and rear him as her son. His mother declined the offer of adoption but agreed that he could pay his glamorous aunt an extended visit at her lovely home. To young Peter, living at Sun Haven was far different from the austere life he knew back home in Derby.

Immediately his aunt hired an elocution tutor to help the boy expunge his Derby accent. After that Daisy introduced him to her cosmopolitan group of friends in and around Elstree. He remembered well the cocktail parties at Sun Haven where couples danced the latest dances accompanied by a hired pianist. Daisy's Austrian maid taught Peter to sing the German lyrics to the popular song, "Vienna, City of My Dreams," which Richard Tauber had sung in 1935 in the popular film *Heart's Desire*. When Peter performed this song at his aunt's parties, he was an instant hit with her sophisticated friends. Sixty years later he well remembered the German refrain to this sentimental tribute to the old imperial capital, lyrics which translate into English as follows: "Call, call, Vienna mine, / Round me a garland of love you twine, / Make all my wonderful dreams come true, / My heart belongs to you."

Daisy led an active social life. In those days elegant English "roadhouses" provided entertainment equivalent to American country clubs for the bright young people of her status. The Spider's Web on the Watford bypass, twelve miles from London, was one of the most popular roadhouses near the city, and Daisy frequented this establishment during the time Peter lived with her. A social history of the era describes the Spider's Web as having "beautiful gardens blazing with roses and shaded by lofty elms, a tea terrace, swimming pool, deck-tennis courts, and golf." Its indoor attractions included a restaurant, ballroom, and grillroom. As an indication of its popularity, it had parking for 2,000 cars.

41. Jay Bamberger's mansion at Stanmore.

Daisy was well acquainted with Joseph Jay Bamberger, a widower and international businessman who played an influential role at the Elstree Studios, in which he was a major shareholder as early as 1918. His wife, Marguerite Hutchinson, had died August 31, 1935, apparently of an infection from a mosquito bite. Their commodious mansion, the Dower House at Stanmore, was situated beside a large ornamental lake, across which a previous owner had constructed a rustic bridge using stones from a ruined Roman watchtower. Jay Bamberger had restored the mansion itself, but architectural critics noted that "even with all the modern resources at his command in the studios of Elstree, he could not succeed in getting a good duplicate of the balancing original gable end." The estate was adjacent to the famous Stanmore Park home that was commandeered by the Royal Air Force and razed in 1937.

Jay Bamberger was rich, cosmopolitan, and very happy in Daisy's company. He opened important doors for her when she was considering a career in motion pictures during this era and later on the American west coast. A successful import-export tycoon in addition to his major role in film production, he admired Daisy's business acumen and often entertained her at his

Stanmore Dower House parties. Peter Summerfield recalled accompanying his aunt on a private visit there one afternoon. The house was filled with servants, and he was left to enjoy an hour of boating on the lake while the adults visited. The Bamberger house was razed during or after World War II, but before that conflict erupted, Jay Bamberger and his business partner Walter Forte had moved to Hollywood, California, the new movie Mecca.

Daisy had not seen or heard from Lionel for two years, but suddenly at midnight on June 24, 1937, he telephoned her and told her he could not sleep because his mind was not at rest. She told him that she was sorry and wished that she could help him but expressed great surprise at his calling her at so late an hour after such a long silence. He insisted that he had been trying to reach her all day, which she doubted. She was very upset to hear from Lionel and refused to discuss their personal or business matters over the telephone. Six days later he called her again, purporting to be someone else, and finally confessed his ruse and told her she could get evidence necessary to obtain a divorce as he intended to stay at the Winston Hotel with a woman from Copenhagen. Daisy alerted Cooper's Investigation Service at once, suspecting that the information might be false, but on July 8 Lionel sent her a letter enclosing the hotel accounts showing that a Mr. and Ms. Stebbing had stayed at the Winston Hotel, Jermyn Street, Piccadilly Circus, from July 2 through 5 and at Ford's Hotel, Manchester Street, on July 5 through 6. The letter also enclosed a receipt for the deposit paid to the Winston Hotel and a bedroom card. Daisy's detectives had followed Lionel to these hotels, but the management at both places declined to assist them in obtaining the necessary evidence for a divorce. Now Lionel had sent her the evidence she needed, and she proceeded to file the complaint.

42. Lao in France, 1937.

Lionel cooperated and even paid into court the necessary costs. In a matter of weeks she had obtained a final decree dissolving her marriage to Lionel. At the time, she was visiting her cousin Mrs. Ayres at Norland, North Church, in Berkhamstead.

Immediately after her divorce Daisy spent the first two weeks of October vacationing in France. In January 1938 she briefly revisited Germany. Hans had been skiing in Canada for several weeks and had met a lady who had known Daisy at Sun Haven. His happiness turned to shock when Hitler occupied Austria on March 12, 1938. He was forced to change his nationality from Austrian to German. "It was a damned shame but maybe it's better that way, who knows? Some day the whole works over in Europe

43. Dr. Giusepe Cipelletti in Naples, 1938.

will blow up, and it will be a very sad story," he wrote. It seems to be the last letter she ever received from him.

She returned to Sun Haven for the next few months and remained active. She read incessantly, attended the latest films, enjoyed weekends at the country homes of friends, and was a member of the Queens Ice Skating Club. Her interest in astrology deepened. She frequented the British Astrological Society at its London headquarters on Southampton Row.

She visited Paris again where she moved in significant circles. Her daybook mentions Baron Othon de Bogaerde, Liberian delegate to the League of Nations; the Comte du Val de Beaulieu of Brussels; and Prince Georges Djoumkovsky. As usual, many of her new-found acquaintances fell madly in love with her. "You were a spark, and my heart was gasoline," Parisian Charles Terrier wrote her on her return to England.

She spent June and most of July that year in Italy, cruising again through the Mediterranean and landing in Naples. Dr. Giusepe Cipelletti, a Milanese physician whom she had met at Lake Como on her vacation with Lionel four years earlier, came south to see her again.

On July 14 Lionel sent Daisy's attorney a small check for the previous six months' sales to Canada and the British West Indies. Hughes questioned the paltry amount, but wrote Daisy that he would "retain the particulars" until she returned home.

Back in England she saw a great deal of her friends M. R. and Joan Crickmore, aristocratic country folk she had met through neighbors in Elstree. The Crickmores' handsome country house, Ellerton Abbey, stood in ninety acres of garden and parkland on the south bank of the river Swale, three miles east of Reeth, near Richmond, North Yorkshire. The house was built in 1830 for the Erie-Drax family on the site of an ancient village with fish breeding ponds fed by a spring not far from the tower and ruins of the eleventh-century Ellerton Priory. Daisy had frequently visited the Crickmores

44. Ellerton Abbey, Yorkshire, home of the Crickmores.

there.

She accepted their invitation to accompany them to Jamaica for the winter. It gave her an ideal opportunity to seek the sunshine of the Caribbean at a time when the situation in England was highly precarious. In fact she had every intention of going from Jamaica to the United States and in any event did not plan to return to England until the international situation improved.

She leased Sun Haven once again, but this time she removed her favorite furnishings and personal effects. Some she placed at Norland, North Church, Berkhamstead, with her cousins, the Ayres, with whom she spent her last few weeks in England. She sold her Beckstein piano to Charles Stiles, a London dealer. A highly publicized auction cleared Sun Haven of the rest of its excellent furnishings.

"Sun Haven."

Deacons Hill Road, Elstree

About eight minutes' walk from Elstree and Boreham Wood Station.

Catalogue of Sale by Auction of the

FURNISHINGS

COMPRISING:

Walnut and Limed Oak Bedroom Suites, "Put-u-up" Bed Settee in Tapestry, Eiderdowns and Bedding.

RARE JAPANESE LACQUER BEDROOM SUITE

Rugs, Carpets, Velvet and Silk Curtains. Lloyd Loom Chairs and Settees, Drawing Room Suite in Velvet, Easy Chairs, Chest of Drawers.

WELL MADE LIMED OAK DINING ROOM SUITE

Japanese Lacquer Cabinet, Splat Back Chair, Bureau and 3-tier Occasional Table *en suite*, Phillips' Electric Wireless, Vacuum Cleaner,

GLASS, CHINA AND COOKING UTENSILS

Lawn Mowers, Hose and Reel, Motor Jack, Ping Pong Table, Games, Deck Chairs, etc.

MESSRS.

Harland & Son

(*John Harding Young, F.A.I.*)

Have been favoured with instructions to Sell the above upon the Premises (owner going abroad)

ON THURSDAY, JUNE 9th, 1938

At TWO p.m.

On View day previous to Sale, 10 a.m. to 4.30 p.m.

Catalogues and full particulars from the

AUCTIONEERS, 69, HIGH STREET, BARNET, HERTS.

Telephone: BARNET 0070/1.

45. *Sun Haven furnishings sales catalog.*

46. *Lao with Jimmie in Jamaica, 1939.*

Daisy visited Paris for the last time in November, returned to England with influenza, and postponed the date of her trip to the Caribbean for a week because she was not well enough to travel. By December 4, 1938, she was in Kingston, Jamaica, with her friends.

CHAPTER SIX

Roundabout

(1938-45)

In autumn 1938 before Daisy left England, Lionel had fallen behind on his monthly payments to her. Her solicitor contacted his attorney but received a reply directly from Lionel confirming Daisy's suspicions that her former husband was purposefully slowing down the business and hiding its true profits from her in order to minimize what he owed her.

Lionel traveled to Copenhagen, Denmark, in August 1939 and was still there when England and France declared war on Germany after Hitler's forces invaded Poland in early September. A month later Lionel's solicitor reported that his client was confined to his bed in Copenhagen under medical supervision and unable to arrange any further payments to Daisy owing to his illness and "the present situation."

Almost immediately, Daisy learned that Lionel had been put into bankruptcy in absentia by one of his creditors on the grounds that he had left England and suspended payment to them. The official receiver sold the business to Lionel's father for £1,000 and marshaled Lionel's relatively few other assets for pro rata distribution among all creditors once a court order was issued.

Lionel's father was prepared to annul the bankruptcy as it applied to the business by paying the business creditors in full. In Lionel's father's hands, however, the business would be under no liability to continue any payment to Daisy. She rejected the senior Mr. Stebbings's offer to her of a fifteen percent settlement, and her former father-in-law refused to send her any further payment, temporarily declining even to keep up the premiums on Lionel's mandated life insurance policy on which she was a beneficiary.

This greatly frustrated her. She was convinced that Lionel and his father had doctored the company books to disguise the profits and arranged the bankruptcy as a ruse to avoid further payments to her. Even imputing to the senior Mr. Stebbing the more honorable motive of merely trying to save his son's reputation and business, Daisy doubted that the company could prosper without Lionel or her present to run it. She knew that it would yield an excellent profit if properly managed, but Lionel seemed indefinitely ill in Copenhagen, and she was very reluctant to return to wartime Britain without sufficient capital to ensure that her interests were fully protected.

She felt forced to choose between personally appearing in a British court to prove the value of Lionel's covenant to pay her or alternatively treating the bankruptcy as a default entitling her to start a competing business in wartime England. Neither course of action was attractive to her. She had no desire to return to England until the international situation was clarified. Instead, she pursued the ineffective course of having her solicitor spend the next six or seven months reviewing various settlement proposals from Lionel's father and seeking to induce him to pay the back payments due her.

A TRAVEL-WISE YOUNG JOURNALIST

Mrs. Stebbings of London is resting in Jamaica this winter and enjoying long motor rides on our country roads which she declares are quite pleasant going.

47. Lao in a Jamaican newspaper, 1939.

Because of the threat of war in Europe, the Crickmores remained in the Caribbean until 1940 and insisted that Daisy stay with them. In Jamaica she made many new friends, including a dental surgeon who promptly fell in love with her and escorted her to fashionable social events and private dinners throughout the 1938-39 Christmas and New Year's holiday. On December 28, he wrote her that spending Christmas with her had been the most thrilling occurrence in his very eventful life. He felt that at the very moment of meeting their souls had embraced one another as life partners. He spoke of his wonder that they had found so much in common in such a very short time. He told her he wanted to live only for her and dreaded the fact that in a few short weeks or months she might be gone. They saw each other incessantly for one week. As they watched the New Year in together over the beautiful Jamaican sea, Daisy asked him to forbear calling on her anymore, agreeing to let him write her, but insisting that she did not feel the same way he did about their relationship and had no interest in marrying him or settling in Jamaica. When she suggested that it was best they terminate a relationship she felt had no future, he was devastated and bombarded her with letters. For years afterwards he wrote her at Christmastime, when she was far from the tropical island on which they had shared the year-end holidays of 1938 and New Year's 1939. He told her he knew her eyes would lighten other hearts but her memory would always bring him joy and happiness.

Through the Crickmores, Daisy met a Canadian couple, Mr. and Mrs. Herbert Parker, who invited her to accompany them back to their home in Canada rather than returning to England. They assured her it would be easier for her to arrange permanent residency in the United States from Canada. She agreed. Although she was strapped for cash and eager to settle her financial dispute with Lionel, she longed to find refuge in the United States and willingly accepted the generosity of these new friends.

By now neither Daisy nor her attorneys knew Lionel's whereabouts for certain. They remained skeptical of the meager income figures the elder Mr. Stebbing continued to supply, but Daisy's only means of refuting them was to exercise her right to require a full audit of the company's books. She seriously considered this approach but was dissuaded by what she feared would be excessive accountants' fees. Her irritation at her former husband knew no bounds. Nonetheless, her feeling that he had "been so absolutely unscrupulous in his dealings with me (that) I have no faith or trust in anything he may promise to do or even in any agreement he may sign" was tempered by her unfailing good nature. She wanted to be fair in spite of everything, she wrote her solicitor, noting, "Whatever the motives are of Lionel and his parents, they must be having plenty of heartache at the present moment, and in spite of everything I find myself feeling sorry for them."

It annoyed her that Lionel had put her entire life in disarray for his own selfish purposes. She felt it only just that his reward for his treachery had been less than nothing. By mid-March she made a reasonable settlement with Lionel's father on the past due payments and was assigned ownership of the insurance policy on Lionel's life. Now if the Stebbings failed to keep it current, she would have the option of maintaining the premium payments or surrendering the coverage. Lionel would remain liable to her as before to pay one-third of any future income from the business.

On April 9, 1940, however, the German army occupied Denmark. Lionel was caught there on his honeymoon with his new Danish wife. He was interned as an enemy alien for the duration of the five-year war. In May the British home office received word that he was being held in a camp at Copenhagen. With Lionel trapped in enemy territory, Daisy had little expectation of any further business income from Stebbing Institute. She realized that with no major source of income she might well have to seek employment. Her stocks were in England, still in the hands of her broker, but she had received no dividends for months. In June she wrote her solicitor that she was "badly in need of some money over here, but the rate of exchange is so terribly low at the moment (that) I am very doubtful as to what is the best thing for me to do."

Several months earlier, just after New Year's 1940, she had entered the

United States through Canada with Mr. and Mrs. Harold Brown, Canadian friends who were spending the summer in New England and had invited Daisy to accompany them. At summer's end, Daisy settled in Boston in temporary quarters on St. George Street, but she did not tarry long in Massachusetts. She spent most of the winter of 1940 with friends in Hollywood, Florida, staying there through April.

"I have wonderful friends all over the place who have offered me a home for as long as I like," she wrote her solicitor, "but of course I would rather make money for myself and be independent."

On May 11, back in Boston, she moved to an apartment of her own at 217 Beacon Street. This would be her home base until June 1941, but she spent the summer of 1940 in California, trying to arrange contacts in the film industry through her friend Jay Bamberger and others whom she had known back in Elstree.

She returned to Boston when she learned that her bank accounts had been blocked and no money would be forthcoming from England except for the purpose of enabling her to leave America and reenter the "sterling area." Stymied once again, she authorized her councilor to purchase British securities or war bonds in her name with the income she received in England on her stocks, bank accounts, and the rental of Sun Haven. She now knew she must economize and live on her relatively few American assets.

Her residency status in America was soon of greater concern to Daisy than her lack of funds. Her 1935 visa was soon to expire, and she learned from immigration officials in Boston that there was little likelihood it would be extended. Desperate to remain in the United States, she gave a sworn deposition to an immigration inspector in Boston and called on prominent friends to help her. Their number and influence reflected the lofty social circles to which she had gained entry.

In November, President Franklin D. Roosevelt's son, John Roosevelt, who seemed eager to assist her, wrote a resumé of her case to his mother's private secretary at the White House. Another Boston friend, John Walsh, nephew of United States Senator David I. Walsh, spent months battling the bureaucracy on her behalf. United States Attorney Brandon in Boston, another of her supporters, asked Henry Nichols, head of the Boston Naturalization and Immigration office, to expedite her case. All of these men forwarded letters supporting her to Washington, D.C.

On December 12 yet another friend wrote a dramatic letter on her behalf to Congressman Richard B. Wigglesworth and to the American Counsel in Montreal, Canada. The writer stated that he had met Daisy a year before through mutual friends, Mr. and Mrs. George E. Phillips of Chestnut Hill, Brookline, Massachusetts. Mr. Phillips's brother, Ambassador William C. Phillips, endorsed her petition as well.

All of these important people did their utmost to secure Daisy's right to stay permanently in the United States. She had made a favorable impression on them all. "She sincerely desires to enter this country and remain here permanently," one wrote. "She does not wish to enter any particular occupation, but wishes to carry on the journalistic work which she did in England. I might add that she is a woman of considerable refinement and talent, well educated, and has traveled extensively. Since I have known her in Boston, she has many times expressed the hope that she could make a home permanently in this city where she has become well-acquainted with many of our good citizens." With such support she had little trouble in having her visitor's visa extended to December 30, 1940.

Time was of the essence, and on December 10 she obtained another interview with the chief of the Immigration Office in East Boston. She showed him her bankbooks, supporting letters, and other documents. Her financial position, modest as it was in fact, was impressive on paper. She had savings in a Boston bank as well as larger sums in London's Midland and Barclay banks and regular income from England. It seems not to have mattered to the American official that wartime restrictions prevented her from receiving the benefit of most of these assets while she was in the United States.

Her London solicitor had written that because of her health she might be able to obtain funds from England "if and when she so wished." It had taken no little guile for Daisy to obtain such assurances. A month before meeting the immigration official, she had written each of her English bankers a letter, copied to the Exchange Control Bank of England, explaining that for medical reasons she had been advised not to reside in England, especially during the winter months, and it was therefore practically impossible for her to return to England. She even managed to obtain a medical certificate confirming this. Her attorney had warned her that if the English banking authorities suspected she planned to live permanently in the United States, the Exchange Control Bank would not allow money to be sent abroad to her, but her suggestion that it was medically necessary for her to delay her return seemed to satisfy the British authorities.

The American immigration official suggested Daisy apply for a six months' extension of her visa to allow time for her to send to England by airmail for the necessary copies of her birth certificate, divorce decree, more detailed financial statements, and police affidavits as to her good character. Scotland Yard had verified the fact that the originals of these documents had been stolen in England in 1936. Her application for extension was forwarded with a favorable endorsement to the immigration office at Rouse's Point, New York, where the final review would occur.

On February 17, 1941, Mr. B. E. Levy of Charles of the Ritz at New York's Ritz-Carlton Hotel, a director and past president of Coty International, wrote the immigration officials that he had known Daisy for more than five years in England and America. He advised the officials that she was "a person of high repute and splendid character who would be a most desirable person for permanent admission to the United States." He offered to sign an affidavit to this effect and post bond as security for her admission as a permanent American resident.

Her first cousin, Dr. James T. Cook, a prominent physician and surgeon in St. Louis, Missouri, echoed these sentiments in a letter referring to her as having "the highest moral character," adding that "her background is excellent" and affirming that she had been "reared in a home where the strictest discipline and highest principles were maintained."

She was advised that the best way to obtain favorable action on her request for permanent residency in the United States would be for her to leave New York for Canada and trigger a review of her entire file on her return. On March 25, 1941, she went to Lacolle, Quebec, purportedly for a ten-day holiday. Two days later the American Consul in Montreal issued her a visa to return to New York. On March 29 she met with the immigration officials at Rouse's Point, New York. John H. Curley, Jr., U.S. Immigration Inspector, reviewed her voluminous file and granted her long-sought request for permanent residency in the United States. She told him that the United States was a country she loved and admired and a place she desired to make her home forever.

Boston was to be Daisy's official residence, now that she was a permanent resident of America, but once again she immediately left for California, still eager to build a career as a motion pictures actress. She lived on the Pacific coast for nearly a year, first at 1250 North Hayworth Avenue in Hollywood and, after two months, in South Laguna Beach for the rest of the summer. In October she returned to Los Angeles, where she took lessons in film arts and acting from Marie Stoddard, who was by all accounts the best acting coach in Hollywood at the time. The daughter of the founder of the famous Pinkerton Detective Agency, Marie Stoddard had acted on Broadway with such actors as John Gielgud and John Barrymore and appeared in various films over three decades. Late in life she was to receive wide notice as Mrs. Sanford in Alfred Hitchcock's 1955 classic *To Catch A Thief*.

48. Marie Stoddard, Hollywood, 1942.

For the next six months Daisy lived with

other aspiring movie actors at Miss Stoddard's home at 1350 Hazelhurst Drive. During this period she met her lifelong friend, Patricia Buttons, later Patricia Levoff, who became well-known as a singer and actress and enjoyed a long career in Las Vegas and elsewhere.

The records are inconclusive, but it was doubtless during this period that Daisy made the first of several American screen tests she often described. The filmmakers viewing them invariably rendered the same opinion. Her own personality was so strong that it seemed impossible for her to immerse herself in the role of another character.

She became well known in the arts community, helping a friend establish the Laguna Arts Forum in Laguna Beach and working to build her own contacts through which she could market reproductions and Spanish-style pottery in New York and Boston. The Laguna business soon floundered. Orders could not be filled, and the daily wartime blackouts so chilled the local economy that many Laguna Beach shops were forced to close.

Her business partner reestablished his business in Riverside, a larger city near military bases and new steel plants. Together they considered opening a smart Western gear specialty shop in Tucson, Arizona, but questioned if the timing was right.

All the while Daisy continued her acting classes under Marie Stoddard, banked on Sunset Boulevard, shopped for clothes on Wiltshire Boulevard, registered her car in California, and gave every indication that she would permanently settle on the west coast. Her grocery receipts reflect the health regimen she was following. Her diet emphasized wholesome milk from nearby Arden Farms. Nonetheless, her records from this period indicate that she was regularly consulting Dr. Homer F. Bailey, a Hollywood physician and surgeon. She hid from her friends the health problems that would lead within a year to a serious and nearly fatal operation.

Her Boston friends, Mr. and Mrs. Thomas E. Fee, came west and persuaded her to return with them to Boston in April 1942. Soon she wrote her California friends that social activities were taking up much of her time. Some of this was canteen work befriending troops temporarily stationed in Boston. Friends worried that she would overtax her strength.

"Get all the fun you can out of life," her former business partner wrote her from California, "but don't pay too dearly in health for it. Do all you can for the Royal Air Force boys and the Aussies if you run across them. They are a fine lot of boys and the best is none too good for them. I'll bet your protégés will never forget you. How could anyone ever forget Daisy?"

Within a month Daisy moved from Boston to New York, where she lived from May to November 1942 at 38 East 68th Street. In 1942 she was enrolled in the Reginald Goode Studio of the Drama at 133 MacDougal Street, New York.

Here she applied for employment as manager of the advertising depart-

49. Lao in New York, 1942.

ment of the Asiatic Petroleum Company, 50 West 50th Street, in New York.

Thomas E. Fee, who headed Boston's Preferred Accident Insurance Company at 40 Broad Street, highly recommended her to Asiatic, writing the company that he "had known her since she came to this country three years ago. I have found her to be a person of splendid character and highest integrity."

Mr. Fee added that he had been instrumental in helping Daisy "obtain permanent admission to this country and thereby am familiar with all of her personal and business records and can assure you that she is a most desirable person." He advised Asiatic that he had "every confidence in recommending her as a valuable employee for your organization in a managerial position because of her keen judgment and tact in handling people."

Again her cousin, Dr. James T. Cook of St. Louis, wrote a character reference, this time noting, "In business she has been extremely successful and built up a very large organization in London through her efforts. She has organizing abilities as well as managerial and if given an opportunity her services could be invaluable."

She was employed by Asiatic Petroleum Corporation and worked in their New York office from August to October 1942. During this time, Daisy answered a blind newspaper advertisement for a better position, noting that the scope and extent of her experience in promotional and sales work prompted her to apply. Her letter gives an interesting perspective on her view as to her own business qualifications and personal interests:

> As partner for ten years in a mail order business, which became the largest of its type in England, I had complete charge of the correspondence, as well as writing advertisements, direct mail folders and sales letters. I also did much contact work, which included interviewing editors of papers and magazines.
>
> During this time I participated in all purchasing and cost accounting; this entailed the ordering of printing, artwork and posters etc.
>
> I am 37 years of age and my special talents are: Sales promotion through direct mail; original and creative ideas; business management and personnel; cost accounting and the ability to analyze results.
>
> My ambition is to do creative writing.
>
> Hobbies and interests are: riding and bicycling; tennis and golf; bridge, music and painting. Psychology and philosophy are of great interest to me and I have studied both.

> Since I did not work on a salary basis in my own business, I would prefer to leave this matter for future discussion.
>
> If the above qualifications meet with your requirements, I would greatly appreciate an interview.

Soon her health failed, and on November 20, 1942, she entered New York's Post Graduate Hospital, where she spent several weeks following serious surgery. As soon as she left the hospital, she moved to Palm Beach, Florida, where she spent Christmas with her new friend, Charles W. Biddle, and lived at 415 Australian Avenue until May 1943. Her Scottish terrier Jimmie, who had been her constant companion for nearly fourteen years, died near the end of her stay in Florida, and she was devastated. In February she had entered her fears in a private journal: "Jimmie is to die and leave me. I love him so. He is the last little bit of my old life, the last living testimony of a love that was perfect."

Charlie Biddle was rich, handsome, gallant, and descended from the great American banking family of Philadelphia. He had spent decades before World War II in the Japanese and Chinese branches of one of America's largest international banks and had progressed from sub-manager at Osaka, Japan, to manager at Darien, China, where he was interned by the Japanese for six months after the attack on Pearl Harbor. He was freed in a general exchange of non-combatants and had returned to New York on the exchange ship Gripsholm. He had been assigned to the bank's head office in Manhattan "until better days."

Their mutual love of dogs seems to have brought Charlie Biddle into Daisy's life, and he swiftly became her protector and one of her greatest friends. Daisy's Scottish terrier Jimmie had been her companion since her years with Lionel at Sun Haven, and Charlie seemed to have won her heart with his devotion to the dog. She soon became his closest friend and came to know his extended family. Later, when she fell in love with another man, she wrote Charlie a gentle letter, describing the value she placed on his friendship with her.

"There is a great deal I enjoy in you as you do in me," she wrote him in a goodbye letter several years later. "The remembrance of much sweetness in our friendship and particularly the deep love we shared in little Jimmie and your wonderful kindness to him will remain with me all of my life. I shall love you for that forever and I believe that it

50. Charles W. Biddle.

is that side of your character that will win for you a great love. It takes a great heart to have such love and understanding as you had for Jimmie and for my Thor when I lost him. Because there had been no one else I had just thought I had given that little dog all my love for fourteen years, and only you will ever know how deep it went and how much it meant to me. I shall be grateful all of my life for your care and tenderness for me during that time."

Although Charlie and Daisy were inseparable at times during the two years after they met and would remain friends for the rest of his life, it seemed that from the first that they avoided thoughts of marrying. This ultimately led them both to seek a romantic involvement with someone else, and Daisy told him at the time, "Human nature being what it is, platonic friendship is a rare experience. It is not fair to you. You will meet a girl with whom you could be gay and happy and share your life. I know you are not happy living alone and unmarried. It is only half living and someday real love will come to you, too. If it had been right that we should marry, we would have married long ago. People do not wait and keep putting it off when there are no obstacles and they are in love. It will make me very happy if I one day hear you have met and married some lovely girl. I am sure that you will make a wonderful husband."

Daisy spent most of the next two years helping various American friends. She had more invitations than she could possibly fill. Because she had spent most of the time living with friends and had a very extensive wardrobe, she lived inexpensively and still had some of the capital she had transferred from England years before.

She took care in choosing her clothes, studying the scientific aspects of various colors she wore. A 1943 note in her daybook recommended that she wear pink or rose for relaxation and happiness, diamonds as jewels, and red to show her capabilities. When she wanted to attract opportunities to herself she chose red, gold, or coral as her jewel.

She was in New York in May and June 1943, living in a hotel at 25 East 67th Street, but she spent July and most of August with Charlie Biddle's cousins at Kearsage Hall, North Conway, New Hampshire, in the middle of the beautiful White Mountains. From there she went to visit Priscilla Fortescue, a close friend and possibly a Biddle relative, at 82 Day Street, Auburndale, Massachusetts, returning to the Manhattan hotel for the months of September and October.

Every day she practiced her creative writing. In one notebook she listed possible titles for a column of spiritual advice she hoped someday to publish and syndicate. Her favorite choices were *Restful Moments* and *Reverie Moments*, but other potential names she listed included *Moment of Reflection*,

A Moment to Ponder, *Quietniche*, *Wisdom Corner*, *Quiet Second*, *Repose*, *Silent Solace*, *Comfort Corner*, and *Corner Stone*.

Daisy was back in California by October and once again pursued her film career, living again at Marie Stoddard's commodious home in Hollywood until April 1944. Charlie Biddle encouraged her and helped her financially. He wrote her frequently on stationery from New York's Downtown Athletic Club, sending her photographs of himself, herself, and his extended family along with messages of good cheer.

In late spring 1944 she returned to Boston. Coming home from church one Sunday in June, she bought the Sunday paper, wondering if by chance there might be a job advertised for her. Scanning the "Female Help Wanted" list, her eyes traveled to the end of the last column. "The one that hit me," she later wrote, "was 'Sales assistant to engineer. Good personality. Earn up to $100 per week. Apply Monday a.m. Insulation Company."

The advertisement left her suspicious but aroused her curiosity sufficiently to follow it up. "I had discovered selling was my forte, and from somewhere I had to earn sufficient to support myself. My assets read well on paper as far as capabilities went, but to get going with them in practice and really earn a living was another story."

She had begun reading motivational books and meditating again. "What I really wanted to do, namely, try and make the world happy by spreading spiritual harmony, was not profitable in a material sense, and somehow I had to pay my rent and subsist. I felt in this work there might be an opportunity to meet people and in some way help them."

She was nervous during the employment interview, but the personnel manager was duly impressed and arranged for her to begin work as assistant sales manager in several days. She kept a fascinating journal of daily incidents during her three months with Bonded Oil System, Inc., 108 Massachusetts Avenue, in Boston. "Truth is stranger than any fiction, and everything in this book is true," she wrote.

After a few days of technical training, Daisy began working with potential customers. The challenge was difficult for her. "I shall never forget the sinking feeling I had when approaching the first door bell I had to push. Anyone who has been faced with this dreadful situation knows with what trepidation I walked up to that first front door. I wanted to turn and run—harder and faster than ever before in my life."

Ultimately she found she thoroughly enjoyed the experience and felt that she had truly achieved her objective of being of service. Her journal reflects the ease with which she met all types of people.

In one entry she relates, "Today I called upon a homeowner in a wonderful old New England home. Walking up the road to it, I met two little girls. They were all dressed up in the flowing long clothes of women. Their ages must have been from seven to nine. Their faces had been made up too."

Daisy told of calling on a talkative elderly woman of Scottish descent. "You wonder whether or not she is looking at you, and she talks and talks incessantly. She was worried because in the hurricane a week ago she heard a noise in the wall, which she likened to the noise of wool being blown into walls, namely, insulation. It must have been the wind howling down the side of the chimney and perhaps blowing loose stones from the roof down the opening. She is a kindly soul and if one bears with her, she will help by suggesting various friends to call on for the work we have to sell. When we got up to leave, she pulled out first this photograph and then that, delaying us for as long as she could. There was the picture of a handsome young soldier nephew, six feet one inch of fine manhood. How proud she was of him! Together with the portrait was a snapshot of him marching ahead of a number of other soldiers. We duly exclaimed on this masculine wonder and bid our adieus amid dog barking and gusty farewells. There is something about the simplicity of these peoples' lives that gives one a nostalgia for things long forgotten."

It is obvious from reading this journal that Daisy was growing more and more immersed in her spiritual study. She writes of meeting "Mrs. Donahue, sad faced and distraught by the recent loss of her husband. [A friend] had called on him the week before and had joked and laughed with him after his operation. As [the friend] left the house, her husband had an embolism, and his wife went to the room to find him dead. Poor little soul is heart-broken and incoherent in her grief. We tried to comfort her. I told her there was only one consolation and that was in God.

"The thought struck me again how poor we humans are when it comes to really comforting our fellow beings. There is only one comfort and only one real love to console, and that is God's Love. It is that we are here to discover that God's love is the only Eternal happiness? This good sweet woman today recounted how her beau had died suddenly too, falling down twenty-two steps and being instantly killed. It is strange how the same type of tragedy so often hits me as though through it there is a certain lesson for our growth and understanding. How much I am learning from this job. From it and through it one views Life from the inside."

Daisy added, "In each and every home one finds stories—some happy, some sad, some futile, but all rich with color."

She left the company soon afterwards and turned her attention to regaining her assets in England. She knew that war conditions were impeding the orderly conduct of business in Great Britain but was greatly concerned at the lack of news regarding her property there.

In early September 1944 her ever loyal friend Charlie Biddle wrote Ernest Dixon, a London friend and fellow official with the National City Bank of

New York, recalling their time together in training some two decades earlier in London and asking his help in ascertaining the status of Daisy's accounts and the condition of Sun Haven.

Charlie described Daisy as "a countrywoman of yours, a very nice English girl who has been living here for several years and is a dear friend of mine," noting that "she is very anxious about the [status of her property] and seems unable to get any satisfactory explanation from people who are supposed to be looking out for her interests."

Ernest Dixon immediately contacted Daisy's lawyer, H. B. Hughes, at Lincoln Inn Fields, and her real estate agent, Thomas Hughes, in Elstree. The former had written Daisy that he had been unable to obtain any reports from the latter, despite repeated efforts. Thomas Hughes was irritated and resentful at Daisy's persistent personal and proxy inquiries. The day Mr. Dixon's agent visited him, he had received yet another letter from Daisy and had recently been contacted by H. B. Hughes, Florrie, and Daisy's English friend Pat Cassin as to the status of Daisy's property. Mr. Hughes had previously had a staff of eleven, but wartime conditions had reduced him to typing his own letters. He used his staff shortage and labor difficulties as an excuse for not keeping current in his reports to Daisy and promised he would send her a full report within the week.

Mr. Price, the last tenant, had occupied Sun Haven until September 1942, when it had been requisitioned by the War Department at annual rental of £160. A small amount had purposely been kept outstanding on the mortgage so that the mortgagor would remain responsible for the deeds. All in all, it was clear to Ernest Dixon that Thomas Hughes had managed Sun Haven prudently and that laxity in making reports to Daisy was his most serious offense.

Surprisingly, they discovered that the Stebbing family was keeping Daisy's life insurance policy on Lionel current, after forcing Daisy to pay the premiums for 1941 and 1942. Charlie Biddle wondered if perhaps the elder Stebbing thought he still owned the policy and would benefit from it in the event of Lionel's death. H. B. Hughes held Lionel's signed "statement of intention" to make the assignment, but it was unclear whether or not he had actually assigned it before his internment in Denmark.

Daisy was much alarmed to learn that her rights to the policy remained in question since she knew it had been taken out to satisfy Lionel's obligation to her under their original agreement. She gave firm instructions that the premiums were to be paid out of her funds if the elder Stebbing failed to pay them. All the while there had been no certainty that Lionel was still alive until his father received word in early 1944 that after two years of hospitalization, his son remained in an internment camp in Copenhagen and appeared to be reasonably well. In fact, Lionel and his new wife had two young sons. Again the news touched Daisy's heart. "If you ever get further news of Lionel, please let me know," she wrote Thomas Hughes. "If you should be in touch with his parents regarding the policy, please convey my sympathies and regards."

In 1944 Daisy read a book by Glenn Clark entitled *I Will Lift Up Mine Eyes*. It greatly inspired her, and she eagerly sought to live its message. She began reading other books by this well-known author, including his widely popular first book, *The Soul's Sincere Desire*, which showed him to be a man who had learned to pray as naturally as to breathe and whose every prayer seemed to be answered. Clark stressed that individuals who found the peace of God within could be the leaven of a Kingdom of God movement on earth.

Clark was an English professor, track and football coach, religious philosopher, and the founder of the Camp Farthest Out movement. He addressed the question of peace and peace-making in many books, repeatedly affirming, "We can only become peacemakers when we first find the inner peace of God, after which through corporate prayer we possess tremendous potential for world transformation." He lectured from time to time at the Boston Home of Truth when Daisy was in the audience.

51. Glenn Clark.

The Home of Truth movement was founded in San Francisco in 1891 by Annie Rix Militz, one of the great leaders of the New Thought awakening. She was a student of Emma Curtis Hopkins, the so-called teacher of teachers, who had been associated with Mary Baker Eddy and Christian Science but had started her own school and grew to be acclaimed as a founder of the New Thought movement. After Mrs. Hopkins's death in 1925, her work had been carried on by her sister, aided by a teacher, Eleanor Mel. Later Eleanor Mel headed the successful Home of Truth Center at 175 Commonwealth Avenue in Boston, Massachusetts, and there, in the early 1940s, she became a close friend of Daisy Stebbing.

Daisy began to pray on a regular basis more deeply than ever before. In her journals she recorded her daily progress. Her path now was centered on Christ, more Biblically based and ritualistic than the universal truths she would later commit her life to serving, but the daily exercises she recorded clearly led her step-by-step towards a deeper and more fulfilling understanding of God than she had known before.

The physical world itself took on a new aura for her. "Today there is the breath of autumn in the air," she wrote. "How beautiful it is. Every shade of green and greens tipped with ruddy gold. The murmuring of nature, so wondrous. O, the beautiful, beautiful God-given world. O, that man could but realize how much he has. All heaven is here, in the heart of nature and Life, away from the noise and smell of city streets. Why do men crowd to the cities? Earth gives up herself to sustain him, but he in his folly feeds from the flood pests of dirt and grime and deludes himself with false hopes and elementary pleasures until death picks him up and laughs at him and so another life is over and another beginning—perhaps never to know and feel the beauty of all the richness of man's true heritage."

Because she felt the need of living alone for a while, Daisy took a small apartment (number 8-D) at 100 Beacon Street and planned to stay in Boston until the summer of 1945. Friends urged her to return to California, but she told them that "a personal attachment" would keep her in Massachusetts. With her remaining available funds she knew she could manage for a while longer. "Perhaps by the time the money is gone," she wrote Thomas Hughes, "my life will be settled in a different way."

In August 1944 she had met Michael, whom she felt certain would be the long-sought "love of her life." There is no record of his surname among her papers. He was married and involved in a lengthy divorce, and appears to have been either an officer in the American military or otherwise involved in government espionage work that took him back and forth across the Atlantic during the war. Daisy's journal entries began to center on Michael. She aspired to show courage, loyalty, and love...to be ever helpful, to be faithful, successful in bringing love to all humanity. She yearned for the power to unite, to write good spiritual works, and to marry Michael in God's good time.

She viewed this new love in cosmic terms and closely followed Glenn Clark's pattern of prayer. "Two to three months ago I expressed above my soul's sincere desires," she wrote in October 1944. "I knew God would answer the prayers of my heart. He has given me Michael. Thank you, God, for this wonderful demonstration. Michael is a true child of God, and my soul's sincere desire is that with him I can help bring true love and happiness to all men. My life is in God's keeping and my soul's sincere desire is to do His Will only. Please, God, give me the power of expression and lead me to my life's work. I know it is in the written word and my soul's sincere desire is to be shown the form. God—please.

"My soul's sincere desire is that Michael can marry me very soon," she vowed. "My soul's sincere desire is that we can be married for Christmas, if it is God's will." Daisy thanked God for showing her this great love and promised every hour of every day to be worthy of such a great and beautiful gift. She asked God to bless Michael and watch over him forever, averring that she saw so much of God in her newfound love. She feared greatly for his safety but felt that God had given him to her forever and that they would be together even into eternity.

She was developing a strong mysticism. She felt that God had renewed for her an opportunity for happiness that would have been available all the time had she embraced it. She thought of her love for Walter Powell, so cruelly cut short by his death at thirty-six. She addressed Walter in her journal, promising with deep emotion, “I love you, Walter. You know that now. You shall not have died in vain, darling. Somehow, sometime, I shall try to redeem the wrong I did you by helping others. As my guilt touched many lives, so shall my redemption, for no man lives to himself alone.” She had always felt that her refusal to hasten her divorce from Lionel so she and Walter Powell could marry had hastened Walter's death.

Michael was often away from Boston and in great danger. He left Daisy three days before Christmas, holding her to his heart and murmuring, “God bless and keep you. Chin up!” She knew that she needed to be brave for both of them, but she felt that with his leaving he had taken the very light away with him. She frequently had nightmares in which he was lost to her. A voice told her, “When the body becomes as nothing, these things will cause no pain.” She awakened with the dream very real within her mind. She lay alone, writing, “All is dark and quiet but for a ticking of the clock.” She analyzed the depth of her feelings every day in her journal entries. “We come into the world to learn the meaning of love. I have learned that meaning, darling. I have learned that the mystery of life is very simple. All the prophets through the ages tried to make it clear to us. Jesus taught it in all His works. It is not really very mysterious. It is really very easy, too easy I suppose. The key to the whole universe is in the letters L O V E. There is no problem too great to be solved with those four letters. Jesus Christ died on the cross to prove it and men have gone on trying to prove it ever since. Men are dying for it all over the world today. Love is called by many other names.”

New Year's approached, and her loneliness almost overwhelmed her. “I cannot sleep tonight. I am so lonely for you: I wonder where you are! All day I have felt your loneliness too. Outside it is stormy and snowing. It is lashing against the windows, and I feel cut off from the rest of the world. I have worked hard all day, writing and doing household chores. I did not stop until midnight. I thought then I should sleep. I will not let self-pity get me, sweetheart. I will force myself to think of all the other waiting women.”

Yet she railed against “all and every thing that has brought this war,” noting how easily “a little personal suffering can strip us of our inside logic. Tomorrow, it will all be different. Hope will fill my being again, and I shall join the throng of other hearts who look forward to a day of returning and arms of love melting loneliness.”

Her life became a series of “sleepless nights reading or sewing with the radio playing for company, the sound of the elevator stopping on our floor and waiting, always waiting, with a hope, however unreasonable, it is you." Then there would be silence, only the sound of the clock ticking, the radio stations all signed off for the night.

The old year ended, and it was 1945. Again she had her horoscope cast, as she had so often done before. It offered her advice for the coming year: "After five years of hard work, you will be finishing up many things. You will have to make your own decisions and start on your own in a commercial way. It will be a year of some emotional upsets. You may have the opportunity to marry in the spring. Don't marry before October and better still, wait until 1946. There is some possibility of travel during the summer. The end of the year will see you repeating the first three months of the year on a higher spiral."

She sent Christmas cards to friends far and wide, enclosing a photograph of herself and her new Scottie, Jinnie. Her friend Marie Cassin wrote her a sad letter from London. The war was winding down, and Marie told her that in England everyone's vitality seemed at a low ebb.

Michael cabled Daisy on January 4 and at last returned to her in Boston just before Valentine's Day. In the meantime, she tried to assuage her loneliness for him by dining out with a friend. "It was foolish of me," she wrote him. "I tried it and once again it was a dismal failure. I came home missing you more than ever. And so every night this week I have cooked my dinner and dined in solitude."

Michael worried about her depressed state and poor diet. When they were together he took time to go shopping and stocked her apartment with wholesome food. They discussed books. She reread some of her favorites and suggested them to him. "There are so many books I want to share with you," she told him, "thoughts expressed by master minds that conjure up unbelievable beauty and unexplored evenings of life."

In her journal she began recording a voice that seemed to be channeling advice to her: "Keep up with your prayers for Michael. You both have a sacred trust and I know you will always keep it. The time before your marriage is shorter than you think now." The voice admonished her to keep every thought God's thought, adding that Michael would be guarded always. The voice grew even more specific: "You will see Florrie next year. She will come to the States. Now read your Bible and rest. I shall speak with you tomorrow. Remember Michael loves you always and is safe. Goodbye."

She wrote a personal soliloquy to love. She even envisioned that she was carrying Michael's love child. She transcribed the following extraordinary message: "This peace that you feel today is the peace of the love child within you. He is going to bring love to you and Michael and to thousands of people in your world. When he is born there will be many signs to show the miracle. There will be lights and shooting stars. This is why you met Michael. You will never again falter in your path of Godliness. God is all and the strength will sustain you forever and ever. The marriage is already being arranged. It will be sooner than you expect. We want the love child to have every protection and advantage. He is all love and will bring you all peace. Always remember this. You were born to spread love and you always will, and your child will be born knowing his work. Everyone will love him and everyone's life will grow in love after contact with him. Your spiritual attribute is Love. Michael's is Duty. He is loving you and thinking of you now. Soon he will be back and will have great news for you."

The next day the voice told her the preceding message was but "a demonstration of Eternity. When you have become accustomed to the wonder of it you will be able to think more constructively. This unity you have works like the law of gravitation. Since all is mental in reality in the Universe, no natural claim can keep you separated. The law of Oneness will keep you together. You will one day write the most beautiful love story that has ever been written. Keep on with your scribbling. It will come."

Their February meeting seems to have been one of their last. Daisy was careful not to ask him about his divorce. The voice had told her he was doing all he could, adding ominously, "Michael needs a rest now and we are going to free him to take it."

After he left she wrote of dreaming of him in the dark, "remembering all the wonderful and prophetic things you said and loving every precious moment." Her intuition told her to take one step at a time, trusting that by the summer all would be clear. Michael would always be with her. Let God take care of the future, she told herself, adding, "Only good can come from good thoughts. Remember thoughts are things. Your thoughts brought Michael's love into manifestation. Marriage will follow as sure as day follows night. Stop worrying and leave it all to God."

The guide urged her to continue with her writing. "You will be very successful. Use the name of Dana Lester. We shall help you always. You are being directed by the spirit of Walter (Powell). He loves you and Michael." Marie Stoddard invited her to come back to California and help her with her dramatic students, but her intuition told her to remain in Boston. She strongly believed that she and Michael had been together in previous incarnations. The voice told her to have patience and thank God for being one of His chosen people.

But Michael was not to return. He appears to have been killed in the war or in a wartime accident. Daisy was devastated. She wondered how the voice could have been so wrong.

By March Daisy wrote of her sadness. The deep, dark choking of doubt and uncertainty were strangling her. The loneliest of lonely despair filled every atom of her body. Daily she wondered when it would all be over, when life would completely leave her grief-racked body. Time, space, and action were all blotted out from her consciousness. Michael was dead. She had reached the line of demarcation all meet at such times. Now the battle raged between sense and soul. Which would win? Sooner or later, she felt, soul must overcome.

By September 1945 she was more philosophical about Michael's death. "I have been very busy the last few months and am better in health," she wrote Florrie. "I almost died losing Michael, but I do not want to express my self-pity. I have so very much to be grateful for. Perhaps sorrow fills us with a greater understanding than happiness." She had overcome her grief and doubts. "Great is the joy known of happiness," she wrote, "but greater is the joy born of sorrow, and everlasting is the joy born of overcoming." She felt that life was one long lesson in overcoming self and that the pleasures of Self were but illusions of everlasting happiness. She confided to her journal that she had learned the great lesson that most people found greater happiness in giving than receiving. "In giving we are being true to our real self, and that is why we see such uplifting happiness." It was a truth that would echo through the rest of her lifespan of eighty-three years.

She felt that the lesson of losing Michael had been given to her to induce her to spread the love she possessed. "You who know so much of love must not concentrate it on one person. One day you will marry, but it is wrong for you to sit and wait and waste God's precious time and love. You are ready and equipped to help many souls and you must do it to live happily. What use is your spiritual growth if you do not use its radiance? Each man must work for God."

She still felt the urge to write. Looking back over her notes, she found that she had been just beginning to make progress when she had met Michael. She knew that she needed to regulate her time. "When I do this, I shall be able to think constructively. I would not be lonely if I made myself work."

Daisy reflected on her last decade. "For ten years I had wandered the world in search of that illusive thing we call happiness. All the playgrounds of the world had been mine: Paris, Vienna, Cairo and the French and Italian Rivieras. All the manufactured gaiety of the world was mine—all but happiness.

"I thought, as perhaps all unattached and lonely mortals think, that here in one of these earthly paradises I should find what my whole heart and soul yearned for—love. But no, it eluded me. Oh, yes, there were admirers, many of them, but never one that satisfied me."

She now came to realize that the world was the manifestation of wrong and chaotic thought and actions that had accumulated over thousands of years. The war itself had been inevitable, she concluded. Unless man individually cleared his own mind of selfish thoughts and gave love to God, there would continue to be wars until there was no one left to demonstrate hate. "The fear of man thinking that someone else possesses what he should have would lead to our becoming another lost world, like Atlantis."

Once again she seemed to sense growth and change in ever-faithful Charlie Biddle. She thought that he expressed himself to her in a more positive manner and saw more clearly than ever his inner goodness. "He really loves me," she confided to her journal. "This is the safest kind of love. It has gradually grown and I believe it will grow and grow through the years and will be a wholly satisfying influence in our lives."

She knew that she must strive for balance in her life, otherwise her health would be ruined. She chided herself for being a bad self-starter. She knew there was nothing she could not accomplish if she put her mind to it, but she felt that she had become mentally lazy and vowed to make herself more productive.

Even before the war ended in Europe in April 1945, Daisy began working with her English friend Pat Cassin and others to establish an import-export business in Boston. Her efforts to interest the major toothpaste and shaving cream manufacturers in a specially patented automatically-closing collapsible toothpaste tube led her to several important meetings with Arthur B. Bellwood, an entrepreneur and promoter of new inventions. Although the cost of producing the tube Daisy was promoting was deemed prohibitive, she was not deterred from seeking further ventures.

She spent much of 1945 trying to find new American products that Pat could market in England. She urged him to consider coming to Boston to help get their joint venture established and regretted that they had waited so long to get such a business underway. "I am sorry I did not write you long ago about this," she told him. "By now we could have been started on something. I shall not rest until I find something."

She asked Pat to send her full details of his background, past business experiences, bank references, and other connections. She knew that in order to be selected as a manufacturer's import-export agent one needed an established organization and the highest references.

In late September she returned to New York to discuss the English export business prospects with a friend who had many business connections in Mexico. She was very encouraged. "If I can prove to these people that we have the outlets in England and also the entrée for purchasing good English merchandise, they are ready and willing to give us all the financial backing necessary," she wrote Pat.

For much of 1945 Daisy was employed as a consultant to Lyle Boulware, a famous architect who had taught for years at the Pratt Institute, subsequently had offices in New York and Boston, and would spend decades in the future as the leading architect in Philadelphia. Her title was business coordinator, and she used her considerable connections in New York and Boston to obtain commissions for him.

Daisy was certain she had the necessary American connections to make the venture prosper. "Because I have had such phenomenal success selling an architect's services in New England (which is said to be the hardest nut in the States to crack), they have confidence (in me) here in Boston," she assured Pat, adding, "Somehow the best people of the town have taken me 'right in,' and that, too, apparently, is something to be reckoned with in Boston, which, as they say, is 'ultra-ultra'."

DAISY STEBBING
Business Co-ordinator
LYLE BOULWARE
Architect
100 Beacon Street
Boston, Mass.
KENmore 3332
654 Madison Avenue
New York 21, New York
RHinelander 4-4752

52. Lao's professional card with Lyle Boulware.

Pat sent her samples of a new English product, a "fumiphone," which could be attached to the telephone and serve as a room deodorant. Daisy promptly contacted Mr. Bellwood, who presented the product to executives of American Telephone and Telegraph Company. Their response was not favorable. The company had made exhaustive tests to prove that telephones did not spread colds or other respiratory diseases, and using them to disperse pleasant fragrances might suggest otherwise. Likewise, the company had a firm policy against authorizing any attachment to their phones and feared establishing a precedent by approving any such device in view of the hundreds of similar proposals with which they were besieged each year. Daisy and Bellwood felt that there would be nothing to prevent a manufacturer from marketing the fumiphone directly to telephone users, and she continued to work with Pat in seeking a royalty agreement with the inventor. After some weeks she was optimistic that a deal could be brokered, and Pat sent the patents to her with a power of attorney allowing her to negotiate a proper licensing agreement.

In the meantime Pat had invented an impregnable door and sent Daisy the specifications. He also offered her a share of royalties on other products he had invented. "What a fertile mind you have," Daisy wrote him. She felt their business partnership had great potential and wrote him: "Through it I can help you and myself, and perhaps we can help many others. After all, that is the only thing worthwhile in life—just loving and helping each other."

As soon as the war ended, Daisy made plans to sell Sun Haven. She took it out of Thomas Hughes's hands due to his failure to communicate with her. The War Department had vacated the premises, and it was deteriorating inside and out. In September 1945 she entrusted the sale of Sun Haven to Pat Cassin and also wrote Florrie, briefing her sister on every aspect of the property and asking her to help Pat with the matter. She sent him her power of attorney to enable him to execute the sale and finally relieved H. B. Hughes, her attorney, from further responsibility for the property.

Pat faced numerous problems in consummating a sale for Daisy. The War Department still had the house keys. There was property tax to settle, insurance premiums and the miniscule final mortgage payment to pay, and much repair and restoration to undertake before a successful sale could be accomplished. Pat soon found that another obstacle might prevent a ready sale. The War Department had not fully relinquished the property but had transferred its rights to the Rural District Council, which proposed dividing the house into three flats for the resettlement of homeless, bombed-out families. At last this plan was thwarted, and the property was fully released to Daisy.

"Your lovely house does not appear to have a scratch on the outside or the roof," Pat wrote her, "but not having the keys, I could not go in. Your garden is overgrown so much, and the tennis court has thistles growing through, and what is more the soldiers have pinched all the little apples for the season."

Once Pat gained entry to the house, he found considerable dilapidation. All the heating radiators were ruined, and Daisy's valuable lighting fixtures and bathroom fittings were gone. Many of the expensive vita-glass windows were cracked, and the costly water softening system was beyond repair. Walls and woodwork needed painting, but the basic structure was sound.

Thomas Hughes continued to interfere in Pat's efforts, and Pat warned Daisy to advise her former realtor once and for all that he would no longer be needed on the Sun Haven sale. Pat's attorney had dealt with the Army and local authorities "in a diplomatic way," Pat told Daisy, "and I have wonderful prospects once it is free."

Daisy was firm but appreciative in relieving her longtime real estate agent. "I have been away from England for so long that I am sure you, as well as the [local authorities], will understand how difficult it is for me at this distance to make detailed representations. Even if I did desire to occupy the premises myself, it would take considerable time to repair and make good the damage that had already been done. It looked so beautiful when I left, and that is the picture of it I shall always carry in my heart, that and all the memories of my good friends in England."

To Pat she was considerably more frank regarding the property. "Sun Haven has always been a 'problem child' for me," she admitted. "From the day I bought the land, it has brought me sadness, worry, and trial. I put so many dreams into it and loved every flower in the garden, but evidently it was not for me!

"I am sure you will dress Sun Haven up a bit, and I hope whoever buys her will be happy there. I built the house with love and at least someone should find happiness under her roof."

CHAPTER SEVEN

Works in Progress (1945-47)

Daisy continued to study Glenn Clark's books and regularly practiced his suggested journaling exercises as set forth in *I Will Lift Up Mine Eyes*. She entitled these *Daily Ponderings*, and they clearly reveal her increasing spiritual development.

As attracted as Daisy was to Clark and his writings, she was unaware of the book on which he was currently working. Nor was she acquainted with its subject, Walter Russell, a man whose international reputation as a painter, sculptor, and scientist, as well as his success in architecture, figure skating, and horsemanship, had earned him a reputation as "the most versatile man in America," "the modern Leonardo," and "the man who has lived five lives."

Executives of the International Business Machines corporation had been so fascinated with the underlying principles through which Russell had incredibly multiplied his abilities that for years they employed him to train the company's thousands of employees in these techniques of self-multiplication and self-creativeness. Many of those involved credited this training with helping IBM founder, Thomas J. Watson, make the company the strongest organization of its kind in the world.

53. Walter Russell and Thomas J. Watson.

Clark believed that Walter Russell had discovered the universal law behind Christ's Sermon on the Mount and that he consciously used that law with awareness of its meaning and obedience to its principles. Walter had read Clark's biography of Dr. George Washington Carver, a figure with whom both men strongly identified. "I loved that book," he wrote Clark, "for [Dr. Carver] so frankly put words to 'I talked to God' as plainly as I have working with God in my studio. Many times have I opened the door to let the ego of me out and let God in. It was a ritual with me. I felt Him come in as a friend would come in."

Clark planned a trilogy. The Carver biography would exemplify man working through God the Father. A biography of Reverend Charles Sheldon, author of the bestselling *In His Steps*, would tell of man working through Jesus, the Son of God, and the third book would describe Walter Russell as the prototype of man working through the Holy Spirit.

Through a busy spring and summer of 1945 Clark worked on the manuscript of his Russell book, which he originally titled *The Man Who Tapped the Reservoirs of God*. He took fragments of his conversations with Walter and expanded them through a liberal use of Russell's lectures at IBM. He followed closely the format he had used in his Carver book, *The Man Who Talks with the Flowers*.

In September 1945 he sent Walter Russell a carbon copy of his still-incomplete draft, asking the subject to add or subtract from it and to insert from two to ten pages of how he had anticipated Einstein, as well as something of Walter's own scientific achievements. "I have left blank pages in the manuscript, crying to be filled," wrote Clark, asking Walter to insert somewhat briefly the story of his life, all of which Clark would edit and rewrite in his own words "to protect your sense of modesty."

Walter was thrilled with Clark's draft. The one thing that struck him unpleasantly was the title. He knew that people tended to shun such titles because they seemed incredible. Charlatans and hypocrites hid behind loudly spoken claims of unique ties to God and Jesus, and generally this repelled the intelligent public. Walter feared the proposed title would give people the impression that he was just another Messiah-complexed charlatan. Clark agreed and soon gave the book the name under which it achieved seeming immortality, *The Man Who Tapped the Secrets of the Universe*.

The paperback edition of the book was published in early December. Copies were mailed to all of America's senators and congressmen in the hope that it would influence favorable congressional action on commissioning Russell to develop his Four Freedoms sculpture as a national memorial to Franklin Delano Roosevelt. In early November Clark had augmented his mailing of 30,000 Macalaster Press catalogues with special letters to major business executives. Reading the book was declared an entrance requirement for all students at Clark's Camp Farthest Out sessions. Every effort was made to give it a favorable reception.

Daisy's horoscope for the New Year was revealing: "January 1, 1946, starts a new cycle for you. You will undoubtedly do something new even if it means only moving to a new residence, and you'll be very active this year." About the same time a friend gave her a copy of John Burroughs's poem, "Waiting." It became her touchstone, her favorite assurance. She particularly loved the lines, "Serene, I fold my hands and wait, / Nor care for wind nor tide nor sea; / I rave no more 'gainst time or fate, / For lo! My own shall come to me." Thirty-six years later she wrote a friend, "Each and every day I repeated the poem to myself, and it brought me the great inner peace of knowing that my true love would soon be by my side."

Daisy experienced enormous change in 1946. The first dramatic event occurred in January in her small, exquisite apartment on the eighth floor of 100 Beacon Street in Boston.

From January 17 to 19 she had an out-of-body experience. She described it as a severance from body sensing, a time when she knew herself to be as one with the rhythmic 1-2-3-4 pulsing of God's electric universe. She felt wholly centered and received clear instructions in an attitude she perceived as "wordless knowing." As she returned to body-consciousness, she found herself spiritually on a mountaintop looking down into a beautiful valley. She often spoke of the experience: "The glorious figure of Christ was behind me. His hands were on my shoulders and the final words, which were indented into my Consciousness, were, 'Thou Shalt Know Space But Never Emptiness.'"

For years she compared the suddenness and clarity of the occasion with the illumination that had come during the previous century to the Canadian psychiatrist Richard M. Bucke, as described in his book *Cosmic Consciousness*.

Daisy was sympathetic with her English friends and understood the privations they continued to endure. She regularly sent packages of tinned meats and other delicacies that were heavily rationed in England. She remembered all her favorite people, including Dr. Christopher Howard, Pat and Marie Cassin, her sisters and other relatives, and even the two Hughes families, despite her feeling that both H. B. and Thomas Hughes had failed to represent her interests adequately during the war. In February Florrie wrote her that Sarah Ayres, the midwife who attended their mother when Daisy was born, had died near Ivinghoe.

Pat and Marie Cassin had been Daisy's friends from the darkest days of her separation from Lionel. Pat's willingness to give his prompt attention to the sale of Sun Haven was but the latest example of how he had always stood by Daisy when she needed love and friendship. They had met on shipboard crossing the Atlantic. Now once again Pat was demonstrating love and friendship. "I only hope I can add materially to your happiness," she wrote him. "You and Marie have done so much for me."

In March 1946 the Duke de Nemours had appointed Pat sole British agent for his popular Armagnac brandy. This important appointment brought some

£12,000 sterling in immediate capital to Pat and Marie, and they were willing to use it as start-up funding for a new import-export business with Daisy.

By February 1946 the sale of Sun Haven had been concluded. Daisy realized over £25,000 on the property. Getting it out of England to Daisy in America was another matter. By early April Pat advised her that the Bank of England had authorized an $8,000 transfer to her Boston account, but after six more weeks had passed the Exchange Control had still not finalized the transaction and Daisy's funds were languishing in one of Pat's business accounts.

Charlie Biddle had spoken with several of his English banking colleagues who advised that her funds should be kept in England in a so-called "American account," but Pat seemed preoccupied with his brandy business and delayed answering her letters. To add to her worries H. B. Hughes wrote that her English income taxes were overdue and needed settling at once.

Exasperated, she decided that a roundtrip visit to England was the only way to protect her interests, and she wrote a blistering letter to Pat, chastising him for placing her funds in his business account and demanding that he settle with her immediately. She had consulted a Boston attorney who called Pat's action unethical and warned Daisy that her position would be most untenable if Pat were to die. She knew from experience that men who handled women's money were often prone to be careless and had to be watched. "It hurts me indescribably to write you this way," she told Pat, "but in view of your actions how can you expect me from doubting your honesty?" These funds were extremely important to her. The Sun Haven proceeds and a lesser amount of stock, bonds, and bank savings in England represented her entire capital. This surprised those she told, but it was a major factor in preventing her from making further progress in the business ventures she and Pat were hoping to launch in America.

She still feared that leaving America might render her residency status precarious and prevent her returning to Boston. Nonetheless, she was determined to visit England before the end of 1946 at the latest.

54. R. Wheeler Bennett.

From January to May Daisy did promotional work for the Boston Symphony Youth Council Youth Concert Association, committing many volunteer hours in support of this charitable effort to introduce young elementary and high school students to the joys of classical music.

She worked closely with the association's board of trustees, which comprised some of Boston's most prominent patrons of the musical arts, and with the conductor, R. Wheeler Bennett, whose home was in Englewood, New Jersey, but who spent much time in Boston. The board included Edward A. Taft, Edwin S. Webster, and Charles F. Hovey, all well-to-do capitalists from the Boston elite.

In early March 1946 Daisy described her daily struggles in a letter to Pat. She knew she was far better off in Boston than her friends were in postwar Britain, but still she had troubles: "My throat is not good again, and I am trying to work on a temporary job [with the Youth Concert Association]. I work, shop, clean, and cook, and do everything myself, and it is not easy when one is not too strong. There are no deliveries, and I have to carry things quite a way, and eating out is far too expensive for me. I get invited out quite a lot, but a social life does not go with a working life here. Distances are too great and time too short, and I have to get my sleep. Things are difficult in this country, too, unless you have money."

Unknown to Daisy, Glenn Clark's biography of Walter Russell had begun to gain considerable public attention, but problems had arisen since the book's publication. Walter's obvious pride in the book was accompanied by glee at the opportunity he anticipated it would give him to "throw a well-vaselined, harmless atom bomb into the very citadel of science." He had nearly completed the manuscript of *The Secret of Light*, his first full-length book since the 1920s. He made no secret of his claim that he had been cosmically prepared to deliver the definitive message for the New Age during seven transitional years from 1946 to 1953.

"My work for the next seven years is to give new scientific and spiritual knowledge to the world, knowledge which is not yet in the world, knowledge which will make wars unthinkable and impossible, knowledge which will scientifically tie the human race together as ONE, which will make nationalism impossible in our thinking and unify religious and racial thinking," he wrote.

Walter Russell testified to the spiritual illumination of light, which science also embraced. Traditionally science focused on the physical, but the profound scientific discoveries and advancements of the modern era confirmed that the material universe is a construction and function of light.

The first criticism of *The Man Who Tapped the Secrets of the Universe* came in February 1946 when one of Glenn Clark's strongest supporters demanded to know "what Mr. Russell is doing with his great power to uplift and benefit mankind," suggesting that the book dealt primarily "with his great power to work out his own plans to his own satisfaction, his unfailing success in managing his own affairs." Glenn Clark replied that Walter Russell's special contribution to others had been the bringing of beauty to their eyes and illumination to their minds. He forwarded the letters to Walter.

The criticism saddened Walter, who had made and lost several fortunes in his lifetime and knew that he had given far more to the world than he had received from it. He recounted his work in educating musicians, helping artists, working for years for absolutely nothing to advance cultural life, lecturing hundreds and hundreds of times without charge, being paid modestly and then only by a few major business concerns, and nearly impoverishing himself for over a quarter-century by seeking to follow the command he had received from the Universal One in 1921 to give this Message to the world.

He objected strongly to any suggestion that he had lived a playboy existence. On the contrary, at seventy-five he often worked seventeen hours a day to fulfill his professional and spiritual obligations, including summer weekends when he might well have been with his family in the country. His estate in Connecticut was the only thing he had set apart for his family, he noted, and he had given both the houses and lands to his children so that he might feel free to give the rest of his life to the world without feeling he was depriving them of an inheritance.

Despite his selflessness, Walter Russell lectured with a self-importance that often brought him enemies. Glenn Clark had staked his own reputation on *The Man Who Tapped the Secrets of the Universe*, and even though the book was selling by the thousands, it caused them both great concern to receive comments such as these: "While Russell is a super-egotist, I don't have the slightest ill-will against him personally, and his philosophy is harmless, though he hungers to banish Christ and take His place in the New Age."

It took four months for *The Man Who Tapped the Secrets of the Universe* to come to the attention of Daisy Stebbing in Boston. It intrigued her. Just as Walter Russell felt that he had been looking into a mirror when he had first read Glenn Clark's book, so did Daisy Stebbing identify with the wisdom and philosophy of Walter Russell when she found them expressed within its pages. She described how she came to discover the book: "A friend brought me a book that had been written about Walter's work. She said, 'You should read this, Daisy. Here's someone who thinks like you.' Well, I read it in three days and at the end of the period called Walter Russell in New York. We spoke for three hours, and agreed to meet."

55. The Man Who Tapped the Secrets of the Universe.

In later years Daisy would say that April 9, 1946, was the most important day of her life. On that day she took the initiative and telephoned Walter Russell at his Carnegie Hall studio in New York. As she often recalled, she introduced herself with the explanation, "I don't make a practice of telephoning men who are strangers to me, but I have read Glenn Clark's book about you, and I find that every word is as if I had expressed it myself."

Walter replied enthusiastically, saying that he recognized her voice as one he had often heard before in his meditations and telling her that he had long waited for her to come into his life. He expressed an eagerness to meet her.

That night she wrote to thank him for understanding her call, reiterating that she had felt a deep desire to know him since reading *The Man Who Tapped the Secrets of the Universe*. She knew that he was deluged with similar requests, she said, but on that night the desire to contact him had overcome all else. When he came to Boston, she promised to attend his lecture and invited him to have a quiet cup of tea with her. If his schedule proved too crowded, she offered to come to New York if he could find the time to receive her. "Everything about you and your words and your art work fills me with the realization of a great soul's awareness," she concluded, "and I feel a deep humility and longing to know you."

Walter wrote her the next day, confirming his plans to lecture at the Boston Home of Truth on April 17 and 18. She replied, expressing happiness that they would soon meet, and made him reservations at the Bellevue Hotel atop Beacon Hill at 21 Beacon Street so he could be near his beloved Boston Common. Daisy freed her schedule for those two days and urged him to take the afternoon plane from New York so they could meet and visit on the night of his arrival. They had discussed his early years in Boston. Daisy identified with his nostalgia and anticipated with pleasure "poking around remembered and loved haunts of your childhood."

Both were prudently chaperoned. Mrs. Maddox, a student who had been serving as his secretary at Carnegie Hall, accompanied him on the trip. Daisy brought with her Mrs. Cummings, the friend who had introduced her to *The Man Who Tapped the Secrets of the Universe*.

Their initial meeting was a spectacular success. It was clear to each of them that they were kindred spirits. She treasured the *Salutation to the Day* he had sent her and asked him to read aloud his *Invocation for the Night*. Daisy felt that he could provide the final answer to her life-long quest. "Because you express so truly much that I feel and cannot express," she told him, "I feel through your expression a completion of my own entity." In Walter she felt she had at last found the answer to her search for God-realization. "My seeking has been my sole quest, since I felt all loss gain if I could but find the true realization of God," she wrote him. From the time he went back to New York they kept in regular contact by telephone and letter.

Glenn Clark also lectured with Walter Russell in Boston during those two April days in 1946, and on that occasion he met Daisy Stebbing. He wrote her that she had greatly impressed him with her sincerity and spirituality.

They discussed Walter Russell, and Clark told Daisy that she could be invaluable in helping him to organize and disseminate his Message. Years later they agreed that if she had joined Walter in his work that April instead of thirteen months later, "many months of 'wrong roads' might have been avoided."

Daisy began promoting *The Man Who Tapped the Secrets of the Universe* among her friends as soon as she and Walter met. Meanwhile she was busily working for the Youth Concerts. She met with Mrs. Richard Saltonstall of Charles Cote Farm, Sherwin, Massachusetts, who expressed interest in both projects and promised both to read the Glenn Clark book and to support the music series through concert sponsorship and recommending it to wealthy friends.

This greatly encouraged Wheeler Bennett, who wrote her of his certainty that the music project would ultimately win widespread public backing. "Our cause must appeal to some," he wrote Daisy. "It is one of those things which lie close to the apex of the pyramid. Up there are the few rare spirits who are responsive to things spiritual. The arts have lost out lately with the masses because of the cult of the ugly and the dissonant. We forget that this is but temporary and that beauty is eternal and will return again in music and painting. The fact that we play only beautiful music is in our favor, we keep the channels open!"

She had sent copies of Glenn Clark's book about Walter to Jane and Wheeler Bennett. They were personally fond of Daisy and deeply interested in her interaction with Walter Russell. Daisy suggested that *The Man Who Tapped the Secrets of the Universe* could prove a natural means of attracting like-minded people to support the Youth Concerts. "I await news of your meeting with Walter Russell and Mrs. Saltonstall with eager anticipation," Mr. Bennett had written her, noting that 15,000 promotional booklets on the Youth Concert Association's work were being printed that day.

Daisy's usual charm and personality had worked its magic on Mrs. Saltonstall. She offered to add a personal handwritten appeal to her friends to the mailing that was being prepared. "I think that sometimes the personal touch can be effective," she graciously wrote Daisy.

Two days before Walter Russell met Daisy, Wheeler Bennett wrote to tell her that he and Jane had read *The Man Who Tapped the Secrets of the Universe* and found it "true and inspiring." He noted the many things Walter Russell had mentioned as fundamental were things that Daisy and the Wheeler Bennetts had believed intuitively for years but had failed to make use of in the practical manner Walter Russell exemplified. "Thanks awfully for sending the book," he wrote Daisy. "I shall reread it many times. It is just packed with important things. Good as it is, I am reminded that it is second hand—Walter Russell as seen through the eyes of another person. How much finer it would be to meet him personally and talk. I envy you your opportunity and await the impressions you will send with impatience. After reading the book, I forgot all about the Youth Concerts."

Mrs. Thomas D. Cabot of Westin, Massachusetts, was typical of the influential supporters of New England arts whom Daisy delighted by introducing her to *The Man Who Tapped the Secrets of the Universe* and inspiring her to support the Youth Concerts. There were many others who happily contributed to the concerts' financial drive after they had been visited by the vivacious Mrs. Stebbing and given a copy of Glenn Clark's book.

On May 31 Daisy renewed her British passport at the consulate in Boston. The document described her as "a writer, living in Boston, 5'6", blue eyes, brown hair." The passport was valid only for the United Kingdom and the United States, inasmuch as Daisy had declared her intention of becoming an American citizen.

She was plagued by business hassles from England. While Pat Cassin sought to interest her in an import-export venture, sending her a long list of French and Spanish wines and cognacs of all kind, which he now was successfully importing to Britain, she was preoccupied with her own financial plight and was distressed when her accountants sent a summary of her wartime investment earnings showing a closing income balance of only 615 pounds, two shillings, and five pence.

She demanded that Pat transfer all her funds to her London bank immediately and give her a full accounting. "What are friendships," she asked Pat, "if they cannot be implicitly relied on?" Pat was in Bordeaux on the duke's business when Daisy's letter reached London, and Marie opened it, noting it was marked urgent. Pat cabled Daisy on June 19: "Just arrived back from Bordeaux. Horrified by the tone of your letter. Attending to your affairs at once." Still suspicious, Daisy used the next three weeks to get her affairs in order before flying home to England to settle her business personally.

In early July she wrote Florrie, whom she had named as her sole heir and executor, giving details of her American holdings. She listed two Boston bank accounts, as well as personal effects in storage in New York and at 100 Beacon Street in Boston. She took out an additional $10,000 aviation accident insurance policy payable to Florrie, and advised her to consult with Mr. Thomas E. Fee, "a dear and old friend [who] would advise you and help you in all matters connected with the settlement of my affairs in this country." She sent copies to Thomas Fee, along with details of her English accounts, which Florrie already knew.

On July 9, 1946, she flew to England. Charlie Biddle, now happily married, took her to the New York airport for the transatlantic flight. He and his wife returned to Manhattan for dinner and sent a cable to her at Mount Royal Hotel at Marble Arch in London: "Pierre's Restaurant, 52 East 53rd Street.

Dear Daisy: Mary and I are dining here after seeing you disappear in the sky. Who was that robust character who held your arm going up the gang-plank? Come back soon. Love, Charlie and Mary."

While she was away, she allowed her friend and landlord, Maurice Saval, to open her Boston apartment for occupancy by one of his important out-of-town clients and wife. This spared Daisy liability for her Boston rent while she was visiting relatives and friends and handling business in England.

Except for the impossibility of removing most of her capital from Great Britain due to currency restrictions, she found things generally in order when she reached London. Pat had given her an extra £300 to cover the interest she had lost by his delay in investing the Sun Haven proceeds. She sold and invested her English communications stock.

To her surprise, Lionel's lawyers advised her that they had not heard from Lionel since 1940 and had not heard from his father for almost as long. Nonetheless, the General Life Insurance Company confirmed that the policy on Lionel's life was still in force and the current premium had been paid. She flew back to America within the month.

At Walter's invitation Daisy flew to Grand Rapids, Michigan, in October 1946 to hear him lecture. This autumn tour, arranged by Glenn Clark and his regional students and sponsors, included lectures in Michigan, Colorado, Texas, and California. Walter's wife, Helen, accompanied him. Daisy returned to Boston after the Colorado lectures before the Russells reached Texas and California, but she had proven to be indispensable in helping Walter arrange the minutest detail of his schedule. She made it clear that she would do anything she could to help him. Her radiant personality and wholesome helpfulness endeared her to the Michigan sponsors and hosts, and she made many personal friends among those who came to hear Walter lecture.

There had been dissension at some of the meetings. As popular as *The Man Who Tapped the Secrets of the Universe* seemed to be among a growing number of readers, the so-called modern Leonardo offended many of Glenn Clark's friends on the lecture circuit. In Grand Rapids, Michigan, Russell was accused of exalting himself and belittling Jesus. He was also roundly criticized for charging admission to some of his lectures, as well as for pricing his small booklet, *Your Day and Night*, at a dollar a copy, more than Macalester Press had initially charged for *The Man Who Tapped the Secrets of the Universe*. Some students objected to the fee of ten dollars an hour that Walter often charged for individual consultation. He acquitted himself of the charges that he was too mercenary by citing his own precarious financial position. He had not received the $15,000 due him from Congress for his 1939 World's Fair bust and could barely pay for the 300 copies of *The Man Who Tapped the Secrets of the Universe* he had personally ordered to distribute to friends. He had risked his financial position and reputation to bring new knowledge to the world, not to seek personal glory from it. Even Clark recognized Russell's "sweet humility in seeking to adapt the central truth the world needs to weaker minds."

The initial animosity among a few Grand Rapids listeners threatened to spread throughout the audience. "They all seemed ready to flee and side with the opposition, especially the ones who had appeared to be all for you," Daisy later recalled in a letter to Walter. She stood beside him and argued for him, and this made a deep impression on him. She also studied his style of delivery, noted peoples' reaction, and pondered ways in which he could better impart his Message.

In Colorado Russell reportedly said that when his forthcoming *Divine Iliad* was published, the Bible could be discarded, and no other book would be needed for the New Age. A student complained to Clark that Russell was a pernicious egomaniac and a madman. In California the wife of the great Christian minister Starr Daily took umbrage when Russell seemed to claim he was the only man with God-power and the greatest messenger since Christ.

This caused Clark no little concern. A major Michigan minister warned him that all the great work Clark was doing to promote prayer could be undermined if he continued to support Russell's work. Russell, the Michigan minister reported, implied he himself was the only omniscient individual since Jesus, who he admitted had gone a little further because he could heal. Physicians in the Michigan audience saw these claims as signs of egomania and initial stages of paranoia.

Nonetheless, many favorable reports on Walter also came to Clark's attention. Vida Reed Stone, well known as the author of *Come Now Into Your Freedom*, was a philosopher who greatly admired Walter Russell. She attended all of Russell's lectures in Los Angeles, recognized the inspiration they had brought to hundreds of people, and wrote Clark that she found Walter Russell to be a person of deep integrity, kindness, personal humility, and wisdom. "He is certainly not claiming to be the only enlightened one," Stone reassured him. "He made no statements while here that differed in any way from my own teaching and writing during the last few years. I know the truth of his statements by my own inner revealments."

A prominent clergyman heard Walter Russell speak at the Divine Science School in Dallas and telephoned Clark to express his support. "He loves you greatly, has great respect for you, and feels you have a great Message," Clark wrote Russell.

Walter Russell and Glenn Clark both felt that despite his years of lecturing, Walter needed to master the art of public speaking, balancing the ideal speaker's three indispensable qualities of sincerity, geniality, and momentum.

"Remember above all that the reason people flock to hear you is not to see you put on airs and...claim to be the only person in modern times who can tap the secrets of the universe. They come to learn how they can tap the secrets of the universe themselves," Clark cautioned him. Daisy had already advised him on means of improving his delivery.

Clark sternly warned Russell that he would disavow his work unless he showed more humility. He threatened to modify language in the next edition of *The Man Who Tapped the Secrets of the Universe* to identify Russell as one of many, rather than the supreme exemplar, as he was named in the original printing. Russell replied that such an alteration in text would call into question the credibility of both author and subject. Clark countered that Russell himself called humility the first law of life. "Unless you change your method, I shall have to send a circular letter ahead of you disclaiming anything to do with you. If you are the greatest messenger of modern times, you must prove it by your humility, your wisdom, and your love."

Without question, traditional evangelical Christians often found themselves challenged by Walter's Message. Students of such teachings as Unity and Divine Science, on the other hand, proved much more open to him. They were not disturbed by hearing people affirm faith in the God-like, God-inspired quality of oneself, for they believed that all people had an inner, real, Divine Self that represented the God-consciousness functioning on earth. They knew as well that each individual had an external, visible, little self that was often confused with the Divine Self. When Russell described his own illumination with exuberance, it was clear to his more enlightened students that he was extolling his Divine Self. To others it sounded like egomania.

For Thanksgiving, Clifford Clinton, a friend of Glenn Clark, offered Dr. and Mrs. Russell the privacy of his cabin in the redwoods near Santa Cruz, California. Here they rested and reflected on the hectic, controversial lecture tour, while Walter completed his manuscript of *The Secret of Light*. During World War II Clinton had developed the Meals-for-Millions program with the help of Dr. Henry Borsook at the California Institute of Technology.

Meanwhile Daisy learned that she had made a lasting impression on many of the people she had met on the lecture tour. Mrs. Olah Buist, with whom she had stayed in Grand Rapids, Michigan, corresponded with her on their mutual reading of L. Adams Beck's spiritual romance set in the Himalayas, *The House of Fulfillment*. "My dear blue-eyed Daisy," she wrote, "It has been a long time since I read of the splendor of Asia, but books like that leave so deep an impression one never forgets them. I wish I might get a clear picture of our past friendships. The impression is so great that I may have been with you in many lives. Thank you, dear, for the encouragement you give. The need is great, but those who can understand are so few."

She urged Daisy to place herself "where the winds do not blow," and added a prayer for the fulfillment of her mission. "I do not know your deepest plans, my dear, but my prayers will be that you may succeed." They both knew that Walter Russell was ahead of his time. "Few will understand, and many will crucify," she noted, reassuring Daisy, however, that "Karma will later compel their obedience to the laws. Life has a way of compelling our attention through the law of cause and effect."

The British Exchange Control had at last allowed Daisy to transfer a substantial sum to America over a four-year period. This made things very much easier for her on her return to Boston. At Christmastime she lavished gifts on her friends in England, choosing items she knew they could not get at home due to the rationing and restrictions. Her banker wrote to thank her for the "parcel of delicious luxuries" and stressed that "the vitamin tablets have done me a great deal of good, and I have religiously taken one each day."

Conditions she had witnessed in England earlier in the year had been a shock to her. She strongly felt that most people were not getting a fair deal in her homeland and deserved a better life after having gone through the war with such sacrifices. Things were better for some of her English friends. Pat and Marie Cassin were prospering, and her friend Joan, who had taken her to Jamaica in 1938, wrote from Ellerton Abbey that she and her husband hoped to winter again in Jamaica for the first time since that year.

Joan wrote her that country life in Yorkshire still had its charm: "Hunted today, quite enjoyed it. It really is a wonderful sport and so exhilarating." At the same time she told Daisy, "I certainly think you have done the right thing in getting out of England. It is more and more depressing."

On January 1, 1947, Daisy read her fortune: "This is a year to cultivate friendships, become interested in new studies or new people, and be economical. Be sure to save for the end of the year when you may need it."

For several months she worked again as a consultant to Lyle Boulware, the well-known architect she had earlier promoted so successfully. This time she spent very little time on the project and appears to have used the position chiefly to demonstrate to the naturalization officials that she was gainfully employed.

56. Dr. Carl Heath Kopf.

Her friend and mentor, Dr. Carl Heath Kopf, pastor of the Mt. Vernon Congregational Church and the most popular young minister in Boston, encouraged her to set aside her work with the youth concerts and the architectural firm and begin devoting her full-time efforts to Walter Russell. Daisy had read Dr. Kopf's books, *Windows on Life*, published in 1941, and *Personal Crisis*, which was just off the press, and was strongly influenced by his spirituality, manliness, and tolerant outlook on life.

He packed his church at every service and, as Daisy wrote, "They all love him because he has moved away from the old time type of sermon and is never afraid to say what he thinks." His weekly radio program over the Columbia network, called *From a Window on Beacon Street*, had been broadcast for over nine years. His down-to-earth messages endeared him to listeners of many faiths, and he spoke eloquently for racial tolerance and a less rigid dogma. Dr. Kopf enjoyed Daisy's visits and told her that talking with her was like having an electric treatment because she was so enthusiastic about life. She described Walter's forthcoming book, and he promised to read it when it appeared on the market.

Dr. Kopf met with her again just before Easter. Just as he was leaving, he questioned, "When are you going to start doing the work you should be doing?" She asked him what he meant, and he said, "Lecturing on philosophy and religion." Daisy told him that perhaps one day she would follow that course, but that up to that time she had never felt she could possibly become affiliated with any one doctrine, and for that reason she wanted to learn more of Walter's work and teaching, which she found more logical and true than anything she had ever studied.

Daisy showed few such reservations in her daily communication with Walter. By now she and he were discussing their deepest thoughts and sharing their impressions of other authors whose thoughts were similar to theirs. After months of knowing him personally, she began to share with him the knowledge she had gained through the years. To know there was a human being who could share and understand this quest for God knowledge gave her great fulfillment. Her deepest desire now became to help others reach this fulfillment.

Her friend from Grand Rapids, Olah Buist, had sent her a copy of *The Invisible Fulcrum*, by J. John Gilbert, which Daisy and Walter greatly enjoyed. Daisy was still a voracious reader and agreed with Olah: "Sometimes we read many books to find only one thought that is new to us, but that one thought is worth all the rest!" She applauded the book's direct and simple manner, noting that while Gilbert lacked Walter's advanced thought and scientific knowledge, much of the book seemed a voicing of Walter's own thought.

Walter expressed great interest in the book and clearly relished the carefully selected quotations from it that Daisy emphasized. She had been particularly drawn to one statement when she opened the book: "All are only divine phantoms rising from the changeless center of all things, and learning the eternal peace of earth."

Walter had just completed work on his own important book, *The Secret of*

Light, and his next project was to bring his long-envisioned masterpiece, *The Message of the Divine Iliad*, into print. Daisy stressed that she was in the front rank of those eagerly awaiting both books, telling him, "I hope that I shall soon be able to read and study them!" In February she wrote to him: "Tonight I am invited to a birthday party and shall drink a toast to the day your book is published with desire for its eternal good." In late March, Walter sent Daisy a printer's dummy of *The Secret of Light*. It was much more impressive even than she had expected. "The direct simplicity of it moves me deeply," she wrote him. "Truly God has spoken through you, and I cannot fail to recognize your interpretation as an exquisite and tremendous masterpiece."

She added, "I know that your book and your teachings can enlighten the mind of man so that life for all mankind can be harmonious and beautiful, full of all things to bring him joy. However, I know too, that since the majority of people have not sought deeply to unravel life's mysteries and find the answer to the overcoming of strife in their own lives and that of the world, there will be many unwilling to accept your great Message. There will be those ready to condemn at the slightest hint of public opinion in the opposite direction. We evidenced this in Grand Rapids. They all seemed ready to flee and side with the opposition, especially the ones who had appeared to be all for you. That lesson has remained with me and always will. Only time can test true friendship. There will always be flocks of supporters when the sailing is fair, but the test comes in storms."

She reassured him: "I want you to know, Walter, that come what may, I shall stand beside you and for you, as I did last October. I know how far-reaching and tremendous is the Message in the book, and I know, too, of the years of working and personal sacrifice you must have put in to make it possible."

Her discussions with Walter led her to an impassioned study of the *Tao Te Ching* (*The Way and Its Power*), by the great Chinese philosopher Lao Tzu, which Daisy had read years before. One Sunday in March she attended a discussion on the great Taoist, probably at the Boston Vedanta Centre. Lao Tzu, whose very name meant "Old Sage," was said to have been the archivist of the imperial Chinese court during the sixth century before Christ. When he was eighty years old, according to legend, he grew disillusioned at man's failure to strive for goodness and sought to leave the court to die in the wilderness towards Tibet. Asked by a border guard to record his teachings before he left, he composed the 5,000 characters of the *Tao Te Ching*. Daisy felt that the sayings of Lao Tzu held such good counsel that they would endure until the end of time.

Some weeks later Daisy returned from a long Easter holiday weekend spent with friends in Wollaston to find waiting for her a copy of Walter's book, *The Secret of Light*, published at last. She was overwhelmed with its appearance and wrote to thank him immediately. "I shall treasure it always," she wrote, "and I can never tell you how much your teaching has meant to me."

Noting that there were many weary ones throughout the world and that the zest for life itself had already left many hearts, she hoped that the few thousands who realized their Oneness would multiply rapidly due to Walter's book, "so that joy can take the place of sorrow, and love overcome all hate."

Daisy felt that Walter's chapter "The Life Principle" brought to life Lao Tzu's words: "Yet one who is anciently aware of existence is master of every moment, feels no break since time beyond time in the way life flows."

She reread this chapter a number of times. "I have never read anything so inspirational and so satisfying, and it leaves one with an amazing awareness of the timelessness of life," she wrote him. "This question of Life and Death is always the one asked by ninety percent of the people, and I feel that there has never been such a lucid answer given as you have given. You are truly a great Teacher."

She liked the title of his upcoming book, *The Message of the Divine Iliad*, believing it should have a very wide appeal.

Daisy promoted Walter's teachings among her broad array of influential friends, including Captain Caleb Laning, United States Navy, assigned to the Office of the Chief of Naval Operations in Washington, who visited her and expressed "more than interest." He was in a position to use Walter's great knowledge with very far-reaching effects. He had been responsible for the favorable turn in submarine warfare in the Pacific; his destroyer had been the first ship to enter the Philippines, as well as the first to use radar. He was chairman of the radar committee for the Army and Navy, a modest and fine man, and it was a source of great pleasure to Daisy that he valued her opinions on matters he believed could lead toward a better way of life for all mankind. Daisy had worked with him on a psychological plan almost two years before, and it had been accepted for use at the conferences leading to the establishment of the United Nations. Daisy correctly believed that Walter's book could be of tremendous value to such a person as Captain Laning, and she spent much time with him discussing Walter's work.

She also convinced other intelligent friends to order Walter's book. Manuel Pinto, a Harvard-educated man and a language professor at the prestigious Phillips Academy in Andover, ordered a copy for himself and an extra one to donate to the school library.

Mrs. Waterman, who had a huge and beautiful apartment in the same building as Daisy at 100 Beacon Street, shared a copy with her husband, an important engineer who constantly traveled the world. They were deep students of Yoga and often discussed such esoteric subjects with Daisy.

Muriel French, secretary of the Harvard Musical Association and past chairman of the Boston Symphony Youth Concerts, was a fine woman who had bravely endured a medical affliction her doctor had likened to a short circuit in electricity. Daisy could not help but feel there was hope for her recovery in Walter Russell's Message and procured a copy for her.

All the while Daisy kept in close communication with her sisters and friends in England. The winter of 1947, coming on top of postwar hardships and economic depression, seemed unbearable in Europe. Conditions in her homeland seemed to worsen daily.

"I receive the most pathetic letters from all parts of England," she wrote Walter. "The bad weather has been the final test for their stoicism. I trust and pray that the spring will bring sunshine, and a surcease of the terrible hardship that has surrounded them on all sides for so long."

She supported the Meals-for-Millions Foundation, which was sending tons of pre-packaged food through the American Friends Service Committee to famine sufferers in Europe and elsewhere. When she had lived in New York she had worked as a volunteer in their office at 109 East 19th Street.

She regularly remembered her English friends with frequent special gift packages of items they found it difficult to get. E. S. Alexander, the longtime London banker who had befriended her so many times in years past, described the generosity she regularly showered on him and his staff: "I think it is extremely nice of you to send us another parcel, and we all feel that you are being very generous to us, but we wish that there was some way in which we could recompense you for all the trouble and expense which you have incurred. Perhaps some way will open up in the future and will enable us to show you how grateful we really are. We are relieved to know that you no longer collect and pack the food yourself, as we have understood what this must really mean to you. You have very kindly suggested that we should let you know which of the parcels listed by Overseas Associates Inc. would be most welcome, and we have unanimously decided on the Sandringham parcel."

Her nephew Peter Summerfield, who was serving in the British Navy, wrote her regularly. She kept in close touch with her sister Emily and exchanged weekly letters with her beloved eldest sister, Florrie.

She received a happy letter from her longtime friend Dorothy in England, who was publishing popular fiction under three names: Dorothy Beck, Paul Beck, and Dorrington A. Beckett. As with many of Daisy's old friends, their ties of affection remained strong for years, and they mutually avowed that were they to see one another again, it would be as if they had not been apart. Dorothy was writing literature of the more serious type, and Daisy regularly sent her American magazines that she might contact for possible publication of her work.

Another excellent example of her continuing bonds across the Atlantic was the friendship she shared with her London physician, Dr. Christopher Howard. The year after they had seen each other in England in 1946, she wrote to invite him to bring his wife and daughter to visit her in America. "I dare not move from England as long as I am not hundred percent sure to be able to return without any difficulty," he replied. "If you really wish to dance again with me, well, do come. I also would love to dance again with you, and you will certainly see me smiling."

Her correspondence with Pat and Marie Cassin was now warm and regular. Marie's description of postwar life in Britain made Daisy ever more happy that she was living permanently in the United States. "You cannot imagine what we have been through," Marie wrote. "No coal, no light, blizzards such as I can never remember in my lifetime, and now floods! It seems too awful that we should have to live like this and I, for one, am so tired of it all. I often feel it is no use going on. No one outside this country can imagine what we are going through, but I expect Florrie writes and tells you the same. Believe me, Daisy, you are well out of this country. Even though I would like you to be here to see you and be with you I wouldn't wish anyone to live this sort of existence. I was thoroughly exhausted after the war, but now I feel so tired that I really cannot take any interest in anything."

Actually, Florrie seldom complained in her letters to her sister. Later in 1947 she wrote from England, "You would be surprised how busy we are, but very happy in spite of shortages. All my love and tons of good wishes, Florrie."

Daisy was eager to become an American citizen. "I cannot help but love Americans," she wrote. "They are so warm and expressive. I thank God every day for my being here. Of course I love my England and all my very dear old friends there, but America is so vital and here when people like you, they are not too shy to show it, and I guess we all like to be loved."

Letters like Marie Cassin's and what Daisy had seen for herself on her 1946 journey to England chilled any interest she might have had in permanently returning there. More so, the work she was doing with Walter and his persistent encouragement led her to begin the procedure to become a naturalized American citizen. On April 25, 1947, she filed her petition for naturalization as a United States citizen in the federal district court in Boston. The next month the government issued subpoenas for Pat and Sydney Buttons and Marie Stoddard to testify on her behalf in California. In June, Marie Stoddard testified as to Daisy's suitability for citizenship before an immigration officer there. Patricia Buttons did the same two weeks later, stating that she had met Daisy through Marie, and that she and her husband, Sydney Buttons, found Daisy "charming, intelligent, and desirous as an American citizen" and knew "of nothing detrimental regarding her morals, political affiliations or personal acquaintances."

Daisy's daily attention focused more and more on Walter. Publication of *The Secret of Light*, the anticipated completion of *The Message of the Divine Iliad*, and plans for another successful series in Grand Rapids filled Daisy with excitement. "All is ours now, and the key to personal as well as world problems is unity and faith, both in ourselves and in the world. But who am I to say this to you?" she asked Walter, adding, "You know I am merely expressing myself, don't you?" She constantly offered her help. "I do hope that you are well and that The Plan is fulfilling itself with as little personal strain as possible for you. I know how terribly much you must have to do and please remember that I will, and want to, help you in any way I possibly can."

In her letters from Boston she stressed that she was hungry to learn from Walter, so that she could continue in some small way to help others to greater understanding, and therefore to greater happiness and peace in this life. She felt that people were badly mixed up emotionally and mentally because of their lack of basic knowledge, resulting in deep insecurity. She reassured Walter that she hoped to attend all of his lectures.

When she had first read *The Man Who Tapped the Secrets of the Universe* in March 1946, she wrote Walter, "It reached me as the most practical as well as the most inspirational Word I had ever read. And as you know, my seeking has been deep and varied. For the first time I felt myself in alignment with a philosophy I felt was workable in this Age. I may never write you or express to you, in the flowery language of some of your admirers, what I feel for your work, but believe me, Walter, I have a sincere and deep admiration for your work, and I want to live and work to see it accepted universally. If you are The Messenger that I feel you to be, and God has work for me to do with you I know that His Plan will unfold. My only desire is for fulfillment of God's Will. I know that you know this and I shall not mention it again."

Knowing how deluged with mail Walter was, Daisy offered to answer queries for him without troubling him. "I could do much of this work for you. Do not fail to use me all you can on this trip. Because I really love all people, I know that I can listen to many long stories from your public, as I did here [in Boston] and in Grand Rapids and thus save you much time. I would do anything to be of real help and make the way a little easier for you, if it is possible at all. I can always arrange to come down."

It seemed to Walter that she was always giving her time to help others. She confirmed this by her actions. "One of my girl friends has just had an operation and is now home to recuperate, and I am head cook and bottle washer for her again," she told him. "I just love to help people though. It is the breath of life to me. I have lots of friends and I love them all, and life gives me a rich return for the love I try to give to them."

Daisy knew how terribly busy Walter must be attending to the dispatching of the books, so she offered to come to New York to help him with this work. "If you could use me in this respect be sure to let me know," she pledged. "You know that I will come down and do anything that I can to help. If there are any public relation jobs, or anything else you want me to do, be sure to let me know."

A number of copies of *The Secret of Light* were misaddressed and failed to reach the purchaser. Daisy felt that some of this was due to fatigue and overwork on Walter's part. She wished she could help him and continued to offer to do so. Walter was receiving some help from other sources. A businessman in New York, Mr. World, retired on March 15 to devote himself full time to spreading Walter's philosophy. Nonetheless, the seventy-six-year-old scientist and philosopher was growing to rely on Daisy more and more.

Before the 1947 lecture tour, Daisy and Walter discussed in detail their plans for establishing what Walter called the Institute of Man. They both agreed that such a university of man could be the best possible means of spreading the New Age philosophy. It would be their center of operation, emphasizing education, which would lay the foundations for a concept of life that must be accepted if civilization were to have a bloodless rebirth. It would avoid attracting the sensation seekers who were always seeking some new form of psychic phenomena. Daisy had watched many good movements from the outside and had observed that the "self-love" of their leaders had often destroyed their effectiveness in promoting true brotherhood and sharing. In all her life, she told him, she had never met anyone less interested in self than Walter. "I feel that this proposed Institution, with you as its head, could accomplish miraculous things. The cry for brotherly love through understanding may be a voice in the wilderness, but it is God's voice, and it shall and will be heard. It is the skeptics who have to be reached. The believers try to live the Golden Rule. Admittedly some make a poor showing, but the desire to do better is there. But the man who thinks he has no beliefs (and that when he is dead, he is dead for all time) is the one that must be reached, if all are to know a measure of happiness. How wonderful it would be if your work could bring Light to these poor lost souls!"

Daisy deeply prayed that scientists would listen to Walter. "There are so few with the vision and courage to get away from the beaten path," she told him, "but such an Institute as you propose would draw them with your leadership."

By now she was deeply involved in the planning for Walter's lecture tour. As early as March she had received several letters from friends in Michigan regarding his new book and the lectures scheduled there for 1947. His reputation was growing in Grand Rapids, and he was to be sponsored by the city's major business and professional club. Students Daisy had met the previous year in Grand Rapids urged her to come with him, and one offered Daisy accommodations in her home and the use of her car should Walter need to be driven anywhere at any time.

Daisy agreed to meet Walter and his wife, Helen, in Detroit in May. Helen Russell, who lived in Connecticut and had been cordially estranged from her husband for many years, had accompanied her husband on the prior tour and was planning to do so again. Daisy was particularly solicitous of Walter's wife on the few occasions they met, and she always included Helen in holiday greetings she sent to Walter.

The Michigan tour focused on a major series of lectures in Detroit, underwritten by twelve major businessmen. From Michigan the itinerary would take them to Colorado Springs and on to California. Daisy was grateful for the opportunity to see the West Coast once again. The hotels Walter had booked were beautiful places and typical of the lovely, sunny California Daisy so well remembered. She brought her driver's license and knew she would likely be needed to drive the Russells around the various cities on their route.

The folder advertising Walter's Detroit lectures greatly appealed to Daisy, who thought it artistically done and sensed it should attract the kind of people most receptive to the Message. She was convinced that the logic of Walter's teaching would meet with acclaim in his lectures in Detroit. She knew that if business leaders in such a highly commercial city broadly embraced Universal Law in action, it could prove the quickest and surest first step on the road to peace and prosperity for all.

In the days before he left New York, she wrote Walter regularly from Boston, stressing her commitment to him: "You must be very busy preparing your lectures now. Am more than anxious to hear them. You have taught me so much and I want

57. 1947 Detroit lectures brochure.

to go on absorbing your knowledge, so that I in turn may give to others. I feel that this is my destiny, and I but live to fulfill it."

They shared favorite poetry. Both of them admired the work of Kahlil Gibran, the poet, philosopher, and painter from Lebanon, whose book *The Prophet* was one of the bestsellers of the first half of the twentieth century. Gibran's writings had meant much to Daisy from her childhood. She often told people she learned at an early age to understand what he meant when he said, "The deeper that sorrow carves into your heart, the more joy you can contain."

Daisy flew to Detroit on May 8. Henry Maday, co-owner of Cross Index Directory Company, one of the prominent Detroit businessmen who sponsored the 1947 lecture tour, met Walter at the airport. The Russells seem to have been guests at the home of Mr. and Mrs. Hyde, strong supporters of his work. The Hydes had invited them all to come as soon as possible and stay as long as they chose. Daisy drove them from place to place in Mrs. Hyde's car. There were social activities planned throughout their stay, including a birthday party for Walter at which the ladies wore formal dresses. Christine Hyde, who had met Daisy the previous year, had sent Daisy many photographs of Detroit.

Fulton Oursler was preparing an article on Walter Russell that *Reader's Digest* intended to publish, but Daisy found Oursler's metaphysical writing far less inspirational than Walter's or Glenn Clark's. She was certain that Dr. Oursler would feel his inadequacy when he read Walter's book, *The Secret of Light*. Nonetheless, she felt strongly that Oursler's *Human Destiny* and Glenn Clark's *I Will Lift Up Mine Eyes* were wonderful forerunners for Walter's book, which, she assured him, "would give readers what Lecomte du Nuoy repeatedly asserts is missing in scientific and metaphysical writing."

She also knew that an article by Oursler on Walter Russell read all over the world in many different languages would have an enormous impact on their work, and Daisy continued to press Walter as to how soon the Oursler article would be published. The advertising for the Grand Rapids lectures was to begin any day, and the Michigan promoters wanted to include mention of the *Reader's Digest* article. Daisy told them she thought the article was to appear in either June or July and should likewise enhance interest in the subsequent lecture Walter would give in Detroit.

It was finally determined that the Fulton Oursler article had not been scheduled as yet. Walter and Daisy took comfort in the knowledge that the magazine was made up months in advance and had faith that the article would appear when the time was most propitious for the work. Daisy had a deep inner feeling that it would be next year before they saw the real fruits of Walter's past labors.

On Easter Day 1947, Dr. Francis Trevelyan Miller, Historian General of New York's Historical Foundation and one of America's most admired historians, had written an important letter of congratulations to his friend on reading *The Secret of Light*:

> My dear Walter Russell:
>
> I hasten, as the first historian, to congratulate you on your epoch-making achievement in giving the world *The Secret of Light*, in which you set forth with mathematical precision principles that command universal attention.
>
> In this little volume, with its tremendous magnitude of thought, you have given Science and human knowledge a rebirth—transmigration from its physical plane to its potential grandeur on the cosmic plane.
>
> You have opened the door into the infinite—Science must enter. It may hesitate; it may engage in controversy, but it cannot afford to ignore the principles you have established which eventually will revolutionize man's concept of himself, his world, his universe, and his human problems.
>
> As an historian, I have long been searching for the law of cause and effect behind all progress (as individuals and as nations). Your astounding revelations, with their trigonometrical charts and mathematical syntaxes, give me new fields for exploration.
>
> You have done for us in this Twentieth Century what Ptolemy, Euclid, Copernicus, Galileo, Kepler did for their earlier centuries. But you have further penetrated all physical barriers and extended your discoveries into definitive forms of the infinite law that created our universe and keeps it in operation with mathematical precision through the millions of years.
>
> Hitherto, Science while delving into these infinite sources has not attempted to define them. It has left the terminology to the ecclesiastics and theological dialectics. You have the courage and vision to start where they leave off—to explore the creative or spiritual law that motivates everything that exists, principles of far greater import than Einstein's relativity.
>
> I hail you as the forerunner of our New Age of Science.
>
> Cordially yours,
> Dr. Francis Trevelyan Miller
> Historical Foundation

This endorsement greatly stimulated interest in the book. Walter saw to it that his friends in Detroit and elsewhere received copies of the Miller letter, and he immediately sent a copy to Daisy. She replied by Western Union: "Deepest congratulations on Miller letter. It is wonderful and only the beginning." Two days later she elaborated on her feelings in a letter: "I was so overjoyed to read the letter from Dr. Miller I just could not refrain from sending you congratulations at once. He covered so much in his appreciation and praise, and I hope that for you it was a little compensation for the long years you have put in on the tremendous work behind the scenes."

They both felt that Dr. Miller's letter would vindicate Walter once and for all in Glenn Clark's eyes. His criticism of the previous year still hurt. "I cannot help but recall some of his remarks along the way," Daisy noted. "Words of praise for others, as well as ourselves, give us such a wonderful lift. When the praise is worthy praise, it seems to strike a note deep within one's being, which brings forth tears of humility, that purest of humility that perhaps is the greatest thing in man, being God himself."

Two weeks before Daisy flew to meet him in Detroit she wrote Walter a letter in which she expressed her own philosophy in her own words: "God unfolds for us little by little our depths which were unknown to us, and in the unfolding we are hurt time and time again by the loss of those whom we love, or the things that we love, in too personal a sense. All of these losses and disappointments are to turn us ever more and more to God alone, and when we at long last lose all sense of personal attachment, we are free and happy—happy in its truest sense. As long as we still know loneliness, jealousy, or attachment to the personal, we do not know Oneness in its completion. I believe the more that God wants to purify us, the more he tries us within. I know that this is not your form of expression, but the sum total is the same."

Daisy sought to reassure Walter that she was not seeking a personal love any longer: "God gave me my first lesson in the loss of attachment very young when he took my mother and father from me. Later I lost again those I most loved and cherished, and now, at long last, I believe I can truly say, that I do not want to become attached to a personal love again. I want to share all life with all people. I know irrevocably that this is to be my way of life as long as I live. I want nothing that is not in the Divine Plan for me and I long to share with others the joy that I have known since I gave up the sense of personal attachment."

She told him it had been a long hard road for her, and that only in January 1946 had she finally experienced cosmic consciousness and the full realization of inner peace and wisdom that had never left her. She had not told him of her past experiences as frankly before. "I may know a few moments of disappointment in human failings, in myself and others, but I have never had any doubt that God would unfold my work for him when the time was right. Wherever I am to go or whatever I am to do, I am ready to do all with joy. I do not ask for a personal life anymore. I have found my greatest happiness in the Universal Love of all mankind."

She would soon have both.

Walter arranged for Vida Reed Stone to share hotel accommodations with Daisy because of the difficulty in obtaining bookings in Detroit and Grand Rapids. Daisy hoped Vida would not mind sharing the room with her, as Daisy was so in harmony with Vida's writings that she felt she could not fail to be in harmony with her personally.

Daisy knew that it had taken little less than a miracle to get her hotel accommodations in those days and appreciated all of Walter's efforts in procuring places for them to stay. She knew that this would be a momentous trip for her and that what they would learn would be invaluable to her in future work. Daisy knew too that in unity of purpose lay their greatest strength. One day, perhaps millions of years from now, she knew they would live in the Light of Universal Love. That day would surely come, she felt, and they would all be part of it.

Vida had expressed concern, fearing she would not sleep because of causing a sleeping partner discomfort! When Daisy met Vida she promised she would try to put her fears to rest and ensure that she slept comfortably and soundly, especially after their busy days. Vida herself was about to publish a book with a letter by Walter as its foreword.

Daisy later wrote Walter that despite Vida's cosmic consciousness, Daisy sensed a deep loneliness about her and in turn felt a deep desire to love her. "All those who seek to know and live the glory of God, pass through this loneliness until they can feel and hold their Oneness in God," wrote Daisy. "All the great saints and seekers, like Lao Tzu, Confucius, and our own Kahlil Gibran, knew this inner 'aloneness.' Such is the 'price' for knowing the glory that is God. It is a beautiful and inspired letter that you have written for her book. It must be a glorious book, and I shall look forward to reading it."

Not all of Walter and Daisy's friends approved of his endorsement of Vida's new book. Some months later Forrest Griffith, head of Westward Health Products in Studio City, California, an important person who had publicly endorsed Walter's *The Secret of Light*, wrote them of encountering Vida in a restaurant where the Griffiths were dining. "She came to our table with much enthusiasm, having just received a copy of the statements of persons who had endorsed Walter's writings, of which mine was one. She did not know that I had been back to New York. Her book, *Behold My Song*, had just come from the press, so she gave Mrs. Griffith one, we think mainly because of Walter's introduction. From reading this introduction and after reading the book, one cannot help but feel that Walter's other arm is being twisted." Griffith hesitated to appear unkind, he said, but, referring to the photograph on Reed's book, he opined, "The book should be entitled, *Behold My Bosom*!!!" He told them that he had heard others who had read Vida Stone's books make the same remark and wonder how Walter could endorse them so highly. Walter doubtless remembered how strongly Vida had defended him to Glenn Clark in the maelstrom of criticism that surrounded Walter's 1946 lecture tour. To him that was reason enough to endorse her book.

58. *Detroit Masonic Temple, site of Lao's first speech.*

In May 1947 Daisy delivered her maiden speech in Detroit's new Masonic Temple, a luxurious structure facing Cass Park. Daisy had been intrigued by the fact that during one of his soul-stirring lectures in Detroit, Walter had briefly begun to lose his audience by dwelling on technicalities. She immediately concentrated on his need to return to a more audience-embracing approach. Remarkably, it seems as if he picked up on her thoughts at once, abruptly changing the pace and content of his speech until once again he was having a profound impact on his hearers. Their friends were fascinated with this interplay of thoughts between the two. One wrote her that it was "interesting that [Walter] picked up your thoughts. In fact, you and he are most interesting to me in your relationship. It is like stories I've read about but have never seen before. I'm glad to have been privileged to see and know that."

In California Walter was determined to avoid the criticism Mrs. Starr Daily had leveled against him the previous year. He paid a stenographer to transcribe every public word he uttered in California, including the question-and-answer sessions that followed his lectures. This, he felt certain, would reassure Clark that the reports of egotism and self-aggrandizement were erroneous at best and malicious at worst. He and Daisy complained when the court reporter billed him excessively, but felt they had taken a prudent defensive measure.

They also realized that *The Secret of Light* might upset the medical profession just as the teaching of nutrition riled the purveyors of dead, unhealthy food. Generally, however, Walter was well received this year, and his critics treated him far more kindly than they had done the year before.

While they were away from New York, Daisy kept closely in touch with their friend Frances, who was handling Walter's correspondence at the Carnegie Hall studio during their absence. The previous secretary did not like to take responsibility, found it difficult to make decisions, and preferred to leave things for Walter's decision. With Frances each day's work was done as it came in. "I feel that things are going quite well here in the office," she wrote Daisy. "I hope Mr. Russell will feel the same way when he gets back tomorrow. I have copied all of the manuscript that was ready (only wish there had been more of it); I have done a great deal of carding and filing that was left to be done; at odd times I have tried to take care of those things which had been left as 'unfinished business'. Some of it I have been able to handle, some of it must await W.R.'s return; but at least I shall try to be intelligent about it. I think Mr. Russell is going to have to take at least a day to go over things with me and clear the decks of everything. Well, I must get back to work. I do want everything 'ship-shape' when the boss gets back. It will be good to see him, but honestly I haven't had a bit of the feeling of loneliness. I believe you would see a change in me if you were to see me now. I know more clearly than ever that my coming here is the 'rightest' thing I ever did."

Walter returned to New York on July 11. Daisy flew directly back to Boston, but she had every intention of coming back to help Walter in New York as soon as she could finish her few remaining projects for Lyle Boulware and Wheeler Bennett.

Their Colorado friend, Gladys Cauley, urged her to use her time in Boston to relax. It was obvious to everyone who had seen them on the tour that Daisy had become an important part of Walter's life, but her friends feared that she had been working too strenuously. "You look wonderful, and I appreciate your light and the great amount of life you have," her friend advised, "but you must not let anyone nor anything impose on that body of yours." At the same time, Gladys wrote Walter in New York, noting that she had told many people "that I thought you were training Mrs. Stebbing to help you carry on your work. I have not heard any one say anything against the idea and have felt no resistance from anyone. She would be wonderful for she understands so well." Nevertheless, she admonished Walter not to take advantage of Daisy's indefatigability: "I hope that Daisy is getting her rest now since you have finished your book. She must take good care of that body for she is a very valuable instrument these days. See that she does it. She is such a loyal soul and loves truth so much that she could get out of balance as far as her body is concerned. I am sure you understand what I mean for you understand so well. Sometimes we are so close to a person or thing that we do not get the right perspective and that is why I am writing you this." Walter would find that it was impossible to temper Daisy's enthusiasm for him and his work.

Daisy had long instructed her friends on the nuances of numerology. She urged them to buy Florence Campbell's book, *Your Days Are Numbered*, and work out their charts, advising them on finding their key numbers and utilizing the more subtle factors of the art. Her friend Gladys found the results comforting and amazingly accurate and longed for more time to study the subject. It became an absorbing interest for Daisy, one she never tired of applying to friends and acquaintances even more diligently than considering their astrological aspects. She knew that numerology was like astrology in that it "impelled but never compelled" the subject to action, but she felt that both practices gave sobering admonitions as to decisions that one might wisely avoid or alter.

By May 1947 prospective readers were daily sending five dollars to Dr. Russell for the author's autographed edition of *The Message of the Divine Iliad* that he had announced would be ready for delivery during the coming summer. This was a schedule they were late in meeting. Throughout the summer in Boston Daisy helped Walter correct proofs of the book. She was very detailed. She went with him to the printers in New York. She insisted that capitalization, punctuation, and organization be uniform.

Daisy was determined that the new book would be free of mistakes and typographical errors. She thought there had been far too many errors in *The Secret of Light*. "It looks very bad in such a high-priced book," she wrote. "I know it is going to be a winner. Darling, you are so clever, and I am so proud of you even if I do get steamed up when you make little mistakes. We must have perfection if we are going to teach perfection."

She wrote Walter that she had not stopped working on the proofs since they came at 8:15 A.M. She had not stopped to dress or eat, but started working on them right away, canceling an appointment she had about her insurance. Late in the afternoon she stopped long enough to make herself a cup of tea. She missed Walter; doing all this work without him near was not nearly as much fun for her as when they were working together at Carnegie Hall, but she had given it her undivided attention. She realized how united their Mind was when they worked apart and seemed to reach the exact conclusions on matters in question.

Walter wrote a friend in California, "You have no idea how much fun we have working together correcting galleys, et cetera. I do not see how I ever could have given this Message without her." It was difficult for Walter to maintain a regular writing schedule when he was alone in New York. Mary, the housekeeper, helped him keep the studio clean but never stopped talking and greatly disrupted his routine. Daisy suggested he explain to her that he could wait until Daisy returned from Boston to handle the routine work. In the meantime Walter could spend his time on creative work.

"You know I think you are the cleverest man in the world, don't you?" she wrote him, "and what is more important, I think you are the sweetest."

CHAPTER EIGHT

Name and Aspirations (1947-48)

Walter Russell seems to have chosen the name "Lao" for Daisy during or just after the summer 1947 lecture tour. Many sources suggest that he had long felt that "Daisy" was not appropriate for her. It was old-fashioned, and to the average American of the time it brought forth thoughts of the country girl Daisy Mae in Al Capp's popular comic strip, *Li'l Abner*. Most significant to Walter, he felt strongly that Daisy's wisdom and spirituality suggested that she herself was the great Lao Tzu reincarnated.

Her name had always seemed inappropriate. Fourteen years before, her London physician and friend, Christopher Howard, irritated at the way Lionel was treating her, had refused to address her as "Mrs. Stebbing" but insisted, "Daisy doesn't suit you."

In late July 1947 Daisy purchased a dozen or more copies of Lao Tzu's *Tao Te Ching* at a Boston bookshop and sent them to friends with letters announcing that Walter had re-christened her "Lao Stebbing." Some of the reaction was interesting, but in virtually every case the new name was accepted with good will. Estlieu, a longtime Russell student, wrote Lao: "I received the little Lao Tzu book and I have feasted, soared, and rested in it. Isn't it wonderful! Thank you for sending it, and again for what you wrote in it. It all means more to me than I can tell."

Christine, another Detroit friend, sent her a copy of Charles Stocking's novel, *Thou Israel*, in return, addressed her as "Dearest Daisy, 'Lao,'" and asked her, "What matters it, the heroine's name, be it Daisy, Lao, or Marion? It is the daring, faithful, loving truths of her living that resounds as a clarion." Marion was the main character in *Thou Israel*, and Christine told her, "I know that you'll enjoy reading this glorious novel and for the greater part of it I feel quite certain that you'll see yourself in Marion as others see you."

Kay Linky, with whose group they were exploring the possibility of establishing their Institute of Man as a Walter Russell Temple of Light in Colorado Springs, was warm and grateful, writing, "My dear, your lovely little book that formed a new name for you has arrived, and we are delving into it. What a lot of wisdom it holds and what a lovely inscription it has."

Her Boston friend Priscilla Fortescue was one of several old friends who hesitated to adopt the new name. "Dearest Daisy," she wrote, "don't mind too much if I continue to call you by the name I've always used. It represents to me the years we've known each other, in which we've shared so many thoughts and words with great understanding. You're still Daisy to me, darling!"

In the middle of their effort to re-christen Daisy as Lao, a very supportive student who felt that Daisy and Walter were living "the constant realization of God and all that it means," wrote a letter addressed to her as "Daisy Steppingstone." This gave all of them a good laugh, although the embarrassed student, Mary A. Robinson, when corrected, countered that she hadn't "the slightest idea where I got the 'stone' part. Perhaps I simply thought of you as a stepping stone along my path to the realization of my inner desires so I took the liberty to name you to suit myself." Daisy had deeply impressed her. "The genuine light in your eyes plus the gentle warmth which you radiated both in speech and in person has lingered in my consciousness," Mary wrote.

It took some months to persuade most of her friends and acquaintances to adopt the new name, and some of them simply declined to make the change. By the year's end, however, she was seldom referred to as "Daisy" or "Daisy Grace," and in her regular letters even Florrie cheerfully addressed her youngest sister and former ward as "Lao."

Within a year or so she was receiving letters like the following from a new student in California: "I love your first name. It falls from the tongue just like a soft mantra, and when I first read it, I felt enfolded in your love and knew that I knew you."

Lao's gift for organization and promotion had been obvious to all she had met on the 1947 lecture tour. Many took note of her business skill. In Detroit, Ray Morton Hardy followed her suggestion and incorporated The Freedom Foundation he had established. In Minneapolis, another new friend, Frances, wrote Lao eagerly "to hear from you how things are progressing. I hope you were able to get the rest of the manuscript [of *The Divine Iliad*] to the printer all right. I am knowing that the Canadian deal comes through perfectly, and also the matter with the Macalester Publishing Co. You have a big job on your hands, Daisy, but I know you are the one to pull it through—the only one who can!"

Henry Maday, one of Walter's preeminent sponsors in Detroit, was smitten with Lao and suggested that she might well want to come to work for his company. He promised to sponsor a radio program featuring her. "How are you doing these days, little girl? I miss you so much, but if you are finding what you need, and everything is fitting together, you remain right where you are, and see yourself through this situation. The fact that I hope you can return in a few weeks is secondary at the moment; you must sprout the feelers that will make this stage of your development an achievement in itself, and I want you back now only if it would allow you that opportunity in better manner than where you are now staying. Rest assured that if you came, however, we would work on something specifically, for I have not yet outlined the radio program which I know can be sold right here in Detroit, in between the talks you could give."

Daisy had charmed Henry Maday as she had captivated the entire audience with her speech at the Masonic Temple. "You have a mother's tenderness and a sage's understanding," he told her, "and if you assembled your thoughts into a sequential framework, I could help the way to open majestically so that your own work is begun.

"Your eyes are perfectly beautiful, and you are God's simple little child," he told her with bravado, but his letter made it clear that the relationship he was seeking would be spiritual. "Life is indeed wonderful, and its magical ointment makes crescendos of every moment if we are caught up into its magnificent rhythm! On this high plane of nobility I meet you, for ours is a work that must be done. Don't let anything interfere with your high concept of Self, Daisy, and let us rest assured that God will bring something so miraculous into our lives that we one day will be glad that we drank the cup all of the way.

"I know I can say these things to you without your feeling that I encumber you with a narrow personalness. On the contrary, this is Universal consciousness which I am representing, and in this way I can do so much more for you and for myself than if I repressed the same thought. Let this suffice for all time. I am your friend and far more—I pray daily for your own unfoldment and mine, knowing for a certainty that no one or nothing can keep your good away from you, and that you will always be what you ever are."

At the same time, Henry Maday and Walter Russell were corresponding about the impact of the 1947 lecture tour, and each of them incorporated high praise for Lao in their letters.

In mid-September Walter wrote apologetically of his delay in replying to a letter from Henry, noting, "Each day Lao (that is Daisy's new name, which is short for Lao Tzu) would say—'Now we must write to Henry!'—but not a chance showed up. We worked on the book itself, editing, eliminating, condensing, improving, sentence-by-sentence and word-by-word, often till midnight. Now we are correcting galleys the same way, but Lao just had to jump on a plane for Boston last night for a few days to attend to important things she has been neglecting, and the last thing she said at the plane was, 'Be sure and write Henry, and give him my best and tell him why I could not write.' So I am obeying instructions."

In this letter to his old friend who needed no reassurance as to Lao's abilities, Walter described in great detail the indispensable role she had come to play in his life at Carnegie Hall and in the final preparation and editing of his forthcoming book:

> Under separate cover I mailed you a letter about *The Message of The Divine Iliad* which is self-explanatory. She wrote that letter herself—mostly—She does most everything—She has redone me and the furniture—not with the same cleansers but with the same spirit. She must have everything right—and the studio was not right—it was a junk heap. She converted it into a beautiful and restful place by the process of elimination of nonessentials and unrhythmic, unbalanced jitteriness.
>
> She did the same thing to me—or is doing it—but that is a job—for I sure was worse than even you would be because I had lived a bachelor existence so much longer and took on all the faults of being too much alone and without the helpfulness of the feminine mind—for I have been in the city most all the time while the family is in the country.
>
> Really, Henry, she is wonderful in every respect. More and more I admire her mentality. She has a career ahead of her and is as ready for it as a loaded gun is ready to fire. She has a destiny which will not be interfered with by anything on earth, and she was born for it, and she knows it.
>
> Also she has a wonderful nature. Everybody loves her, from prince to pauper. I couldn't even get our maintenance workman (Larry) to come to clean unless he was sure she was there, and the brat just plainly said so, just like that. And all during the trip she was being invited to dinners, theatres, [was] proposed to twice (to my knowledge—how many more I don't know of is conjectural) and has made as many friends among the women as among the men.
>
> Also the children. In San Francisco one morning at the Mark Hopkins, a beautiful little boy just kept looking at her across the breakfast tables, and she looked Lao-like at him (which means a lot) until the youngster just flew across the room and threw his arms around her and buried his face in her dress. It was beautiful to see.

Letters like this provide the evidence of Lao's increasing significance to Walter and the beginning of the love affair of their lifetimes. Henry seems not to have recognized the signs sufficiently. A month later he wrote a detailed letter to Lao on marketing Walter's newest book. Thanking her for the copy she had sent of Lao Tzu's book and still addressing her as "Daisy Grace," Henry added the following coy proposal: "I do believe I could convince you, however, without dire implications, of the fresh zeal that would come in our holding hands together. Wouldn't that be really joyful, Daisy Grace? Walter Russell's "adopted" daughter my lady of an evening—what a thrilling thought both for her and for me. Since she is "Everywoman" (not just "Lao") it might give her a balance that is most desirable—with some unfinished business to complete in the bargain!"

Lao overlooked his importuning, and as events transpired, it soon became clear to Henry that her relationship with Walter was destined to be different from that of father and daughter. The three of them continued to enjoy a mutual admiration, friendship, and support that lasted the rest of their lives.

At noon on September 30, 1947, Lao received her final citizenship papers in Boston. Walter was euphoric. Her English and American friends alike shared her joy on her becoming an American citizen. From Willesden Green her English banker, E. S. Alexander, wrote: "We were very glad to hear from you and will even forgive you for becoming an American citizen!" Gladys in Detroit rejoiced that she had gained her citizenship, adding, "I am sure that you feel a burden lifted, and I don't believe that America as a whole will disappoint you. You will be much freer here in many ways."

Walter had long urged her to relinquish her Boston apartment and move to New York, but she hesitated to do so, writing him, "Dearest, the days are going, and I still have much to do. Do not think I will give the apartment up this time. When things are definitely settled would be a better time. I like that inner feeling of a tiny 'home' to come to. I know my only home is with you—it always will be—and it will come because we know it will. I realize all the time how fortunate we are to have this wonderful companionship. If all people could have understanding, they could all have such a relationship. My heart aches for the unhappiness people experience in their unbalanced relationships. Our life belongs to God. We could never be happy with any other way of life."

Once she obtained her American citizenship, she was ready to come permanently to New York. She came by plane the next morning, sending eleven pieces of luggage by a friend's car with her trunks following by express.

She had advised her Boston building management that she was giving up 8D at 100 Beacon Street. She loved Boston and hated to leave it, but, as she wrote her friends there, "Although I have been so happy in the little apartment and have loved everyone there so much, it is really a lot for me to swing if I am not going to use it at all. I have been away from Boston now for at least six months, and as you know I was in England for weeks last year." Her work with Walter would keep her in New York indefinitely, she added.

She had worked helping Walter on the forthcoming book and his other correspondence day and night every day since they had returned from the lecture tour without even taking off a Sunday. On her moving to New York she found Walter happy but struggling with a miserable cold. She knew it was due to overwork. She wrote a friend that she no longer had a minute to take care of her wardrobe. "All my own personal things have been neglected. I am just head cook and bottle washer, secretary, co-worker and what-not...and I love it." Lao was living at the Hotel Wellington "just next door," Walter reported, "but she is there mighty little for we have much work to do here, correcting galley proofs, et cetera, and she answers all my letters now except from friends."

Lao wrote a friend: "I hope that when we eventually get the book out we can both rest up a bit. It has been a pretty tough job getting everything done and the heat all the summer did not help us any. Walter is a wonderful thinker and we produce an awful lot working together.... Somehow I never get to my own correspondence. Owing to internal labor troubles the printers will be unable to deliver to us now until late November. We have had some job getting proofs and all the things going in connection with the actual printing of the book."

She bewailed the state of labor unrest in America, fearing that the nation-wide telephone strike would cripple business and lead to inflationary prices if it were not settled soon. "No good purpose is ever served [by strikes]," she concluded. "It is like war. Error creates more error."

Events were moving fast in Colorado Springs where Kay Linky had generated great interest among civic leaders in providing a home for Walter and Lao and their Institute of Man. On October 10, Kay wrote Walter that the time had come for them to talk to the local officials and personally choose the site they desired. She was working regularly with the mayor and head of the local chamber of commerce, and they all felt that without question they could provide a suitable site in a very short time. Only they could make the final selection, she realized, but she suggested a wide range of tantalizing options.

"The city might have much better things to offer you and might take a large park and rename it the Walter Russell Memorial Park. Can you fly in for two days at least?" She assured them that the city leaders were most enthusiastic about what they considered a "magnificent thing" and would demonstrate to them that they had many elegant stretches of land available. She was certain the project would come to fruition and that they would be happy in Colorado Springs. "Do try to come as soon as possible. All cooperation here is assured. Stay with us. The city budget is now being made. Weather is perfect. Come soon if possible while you can depend on the weather in selecting your spot. I don't think things could be any better than they are," she told them.

She was happy that Lao was living full time in New York, she wrote, "as I know Walter relies on you a lot and you must have wonderful joy together.

[But] I just know you will be even happier here where you will be in your Beauty Shrine together and you can imagine my joy at the prospects of our being friends together here. We must be destined in your numbers."

Lao responded two days later, telling her how excited they were at the prospects her letter raised. "It must be God's great Plan for us, Kay, because that is how things unfold when we live and work toward our desires. Walter is so happy about it all. I cannot express to you how happy. It has been his life dream to see all of his beautiful works 'under one roof' and now this very morning you send him news that perhaps this is IT!

"Our idea is to have a non-profit organization and put all of our work into it—all the books and sculpture, paintings, etc. We would draw a life-salary and leave all to posterity after we have gone. In doing it this way the whole of Walter's life work would remain forever and belong to the State and therefore to the world. We think a Foundation should be formed so that donations could be made by the public to help pay the costs for erecting the monuments and the upkeep of the place."

Lao felt that a short trip to Colorado Springs would be just what she and Walter needed to energize them both. They still had much work to do on the book. "In coming we shall have to leave the book proofs, and it will delay the books coming out that much longer," she told Kay Linky, "but we know how important it is to come now while you have everything so beautifully prepared, and we shall not spare ourselves. You know that."

They made plane reservations for early November, planning to fly to Denver and drive from there to Colorado Springs. They urged Kay not to mention the Colorado Springs possibilities to any of the Russell students in Denver or anyone else until matters materialized further.

Lao wrote Kay that she and Walter could scarcely contain their enthusiasm at the prospects. They would bring as many photographs, letters, and clippings as they could assemble and wished that many things they wanted to show were not too heavy to bring. Lao described many of these. As she wrote, she was looking at the beautiful model of the Mark Twain monument that she knew would make a wonderful museum piece.

In addition, Walter had just had his bust of Franklin D. Roosevelt brought from the foundry. A colossal bust nearly forty inches high, Walter envisioned it erected on a pedestal twelve feet high with one of the Four Freedoms on each of the four sides.

They wanted to do much in the scientific field in 1948 in order to give the world the things that were prophesied in *The Message of the Divine Iliad*. "The time has now come," Lao wrote Kay, "and these must be given." Lao added that it had always been one of her dreams "to mess about in the laboratory." Now she had a deep feeling that particular dream might come true.

In September, Raymond and Kay Linky wrote Walter and Lao that they had toured the prospective sites for the "Temple of Beauty" on the rolling foothills across from the Linky house in Colorado Springs. This beautiful part of western America had been named in 1859 when two surveyors were laying out the city site and one remarked to the other that the glorious sandstone formations made the area a place fit for the gods to assemble. It had ever after been called the Garden of the Gods.

Walter and Lao remembered one beautiful spot with high pines all around. There they could visualize Walter's various marble monuments set in natural places among the pines and oaks. They reported views that were breathtaking with the mountains in the background and lovely views of the plains and the famous Broadmoor Hotel with its adjacent well-kept golf course in rolling green. By late September the proposal was under consideration by the property owners. Kay sent Walter a photograph of the local Baha'i Temple "supposed to be one of the most beautiful in the world."

Walter was quick to respond more specifically as to what he had in mind for Colorado Springs:

> I do not like that Baha'i Temple you sent. The Greeks would have had a fit if they saw it. That belongs to Baghdad, not to America. It is oriental, not occidental. My idea is assuming shape. I'll enclose a rough sketch. The cube and the sphere are Nature's two perfect forms. Each is a mate of the other. (See *The Secret of Light*—Part III.) I think of doing the cubes and spheres like domes surmounting the cubes, and connect the three sections by wonderful galleries where sculpture could fill the arched niches outside and inside for landscapes and color drawings on the one side and portraits and pencil and charcoal drawing on the other.
>
> The central section will be for big pieces, full figures, larger paintings, etc., and pedestals for heads and small figures can line the connecting sections.
>
> What we do outside depends upon the amount of land given. Sculpture must not be crowded. For the Mark Twain it needs a vista and approach, while planting must go in the rear for a background. The more land, the more out-of-door sculpture. Let us build the most beautiful thing in the world so that people will be uplifted by it and come from long distances to see it.
>
> When the land is allotted I will begin the designs, and make clay models of the buildings which I will cast in plaster. There will be three buildings—the little house, the laboratory, storage and garage section, and the Temple. We are anxious to build the little house next spring. I could design that in ten minutes for I know exactly what we want. We could go there and get it started with the hope it could be done by fall. The storehouse should also be built at the same time so we could ship everything out there. It would take several big vans, very big ones, and cost plenty.

> We want to build a little place for a studio with three bedrooms, three baths and kitchen, just to live and work in, for we would never live in the big place. I think that would be too pretentious and too much like a museum to live in. It may cost half a million or more. I am giving all I have to it plus all my income from books to support it after Lao and I have gone.

Walter's lease at Carnegie Hall was to end in October 1948, and he was tired of being cooped up there without sunshine or air, he wrote Robert E. Law, the President of the Colorado Chamber of Commerce with whom he had met to discuss the proposed project in Colorado Springs.

He sent photographs of *The Might of Ages*, which he described as "my most noted masterpiece," and other of his artwork on display at his Carnegie Hall studio or stored in his vaults in New York. The photographs gave the planners in Colorado a comparative size of the pictures he wanted to display in the proposed Temple of Beauty. The Carnegie Hall studio was seventy by twenty feet in area and fifteen feet high. The proposed central area of the three studios in the temple would be sixty-five by forty-five feet in area and thirty feet high with the two auxiliary studio areas thirty by forty-five feet and twenty feet high. He sent a small print of his colossal bust of Ossip Gabrilowitsch, son-in-law of Mark Twain and a renowned Russian-American pianist who had conducted the Detroit Symphony Orchestra for many years. Walter noted that this was "Mrs. Stebbing's favorite of all my works" and added, "It will indeed by a happy day for us when we can dedicate this and the entire collection to the glory of art in your city."

He reported that interest in *The Secret of Light* was growing in circulation daily and told them of his great desire to get established in Colorado Springs in 1948 so he might start the scientific research necessary to "give the world new cheap fuel which will render the coal mines useless, therefore simplifying industrial and transportation difficulties. From these discoveries a new civilization could arise."

59. Walter Russell and Lao with friends, Raymond Linky home, Colorado Springs, 1947.

After their few days in Colorado Springs, they returned to New York with every intention of following through on these plans. Lao wrote their friends in Colorado that they had been "busier than busy since our return. All kinds of important folk have crossed the threshold. You would appreciate these progressive and interesting people. The few we have told about Colorado Springs are very enthusiastic and want to see Mr. Russell's work in just such a setting. The support we need will come to us when we need it—that is certain!" They had learned that their friend Roger W. Babson, the investment banker and business analyst, was establishing an important center in Colorado Springs. One of their Colorado boosters had asked her about Walter Russell's social standing, and she forwarded a copy of his biography from *Who's Who*.

The Right Honorable William Lyon Mackenzie King, Prime Minster of Canada, visited them at Carnegie Hall in early November. They had been corresponding with him since September regarding his interest in the Roosevelt bust. Lao wrote Kay that she had spent three whole days drafting their first letter to the Canadian leader. They hoped that this commission from Canada would include much more than the bust. Walter had completed a beautiful painting he hoped to interest the prime minister in purchasing. They knew that if such an important commission came through, it would enable them to build their house in Colorado Springs early the next year as well as a laboratory and a store place for all the sculpture until it could be erected in the new museum.

The prime minister was delighted with both of the Roosevelt heads and agreed to purchase one for Canada where he hoped to have it placed as a companion piece with one of Winston Churchill in the Parliament House in Ottawa. He wanted to see both of Walter's busts of Roosevelt before deciding which one to take. He told them he tremendously liked the one he had seen at Springwood, the Roosevelt home at Hyde Park. Leaving for Princess Elizabeth's wedding in London, he promised to call on them again on his return from England.

Walter described the occasion. "Mrs. Stebbing and I had a very nice visit with him. He is very interested in our New Age Philosophy and asked if he could have a copy of *The Secret of Light* to read on the boat. He had already had a copy of *The Man Who Tapped The Secrets of the Universe* and told us he was more than interested in such things."

They had grown close to Reverend and Mrs. Ross H. Flanaghan of Vernon, New Jersey, whom they had met in late August. He was well-known as minister of the Church of the Good Shepherd, St. Thomas's Church, in Vernon and had written Walter after their first meeting: "I was interested in your 'exodus' into New Thought. If your teachings are New Thought, they are of a higher order than most of those I am acquainted with. It seems to me that most of the New Thought teaching I used to read revolved around the idea of material prosperity for the thinker. Your teaching is much more spiritual. I should say it is of the highest spiritual order, yet intensely practical.

That is what all true teaching should be—both spiritual and practical: from the realm of Spirit into the realm of Matter."

The Flanaghans came to New York and shared Thanksgiving dinner with Walter and Lao and others, during which they all reflected on how they might contribute to the millions in Europe and Asia who were hungry. They committed themselves to do more to share with others. Walter and Lao began a long correspondence with the Flanaghans, who compared Lao's letters to "a cool breeze on a summer evening" and Walter's to "the incense fragrance of deep prayer." Lao shared Lao Tzu's *The Way of Life* with them, and they marveled at the fact that in Lao Tzu's day God had raised up several great teachers—Lao Tzu, Isaiah, and later Confucius—for various parts of the inhabited world.

Lao quickly endeared herself to Walter's longtime students. Gertrude de Kock wrote her affectionately from Capetown, South Africa, after they had met in New York and enjoyed a happy evening together at the St. Regis Hotel.

Gertrude also wrote Walter, "It is lovely to think of you and Lao working together harmoniously and in love, to fulfill the purpose of revealing Truth to mankind. I am with you in spirit always. Whenever anyone sees your photographs, they ask who the lovely girl is, and I reply, 'the lady whom Walter Russell loves.'"

Her letters to Lao were equally warm: "Dear little sister, I feel quite sure that I shall see you again. We were meant to meet, and you are as near to me now as you always have been and will always be. How happily I shall follow the coming events of your life and how part of it all I am. I can just picture the studio now, clean and tidy and everything shining, bright with these loving and lovely people sitting down to a little breakfast or lunch and a rest-well deserved after much labor." Gertrude was well aware of the love Lao and Walter were developing for each other. Gertrude told them of corresponding with the African-American evangelist Father Divine, whom she admired because he refused donations and took no collections because he was "free to mankind." She commended to Lao the loveliness of acting from "the permanent consciousness of being One with all that Is." Lao knew that they would do much on faith alone, but that the practicalities of meeting daily expenses often tempered their altruism.

Mrs. Roy Curby was highly complimentary of Lao in a February letter to Walter, stressing, "I know, too, what Lao has meant to you and to this work for I know her great strength and sincerity. To be sincere is the greatest quality anyone can have, and her spiritual strength added to that sincerity makes a 'something' that can't be matched. This I know of her. Give her my deepest love."

Some of her oldest friends found it difficult to share her enthusiasm for

Walter's science and philosophy. Dr. Christopher Howard wrote to congratulate her on her maiden speech for Walter. "I am delighted to divine from your letter that working with him has brought you so much happiness and spiritual satisfaction," he told her. Dr. Howard, with whom she loved to dance, had warned her against eastern mysticism and yoga fourteen years before in England and had grown ever more conservative in his views. "I have read Walter Russell's book," he told her, "and it is far too intelligent for my understanding. The older I grow the more I find that faith replaces reason, and as I have told you before both in talking and writing, I am more and more content with the New Testament and the English Prayer book. I shall, however, keep Walter Russell's book and reread it as I know that you value his work and his writings so highly. My best love to you, Chris." She never lost touch with him. Soon afterwards she sent gift parcels to him and his family that brought them shrieks of delight. "We have not seen rice here for years," he replied, "and everything else in the parcel was equally a pleasure."

Henry Maday, ever the good businessman, did his best to advise Lao as how to help Walter in marketing *The Message of the Divine Iliad* effectively. In October 1947 he wrote her, obviously remembering what Walter had written him about her role in preparing the book for publication:

> I am glad you finally completed the work on Walter Russell's second book. No doubt no small share of its arrangement and editing will be due to your careful analysis and inspired synthesis, which will make the book ring true if it is genuinely brought out with the purpose of diffusing Truth. If it is consecrated in the proper way, Walter need not worry about the financial return. *The Secret of Light* was partially spoiled because of the outcry, which naturally followed the increase of price that should have been prevented beforehand.
>
> Please do not mind my stating this, but Walter certainly has needed steering, and I have no doubt that you are an able companion and associate to him. His last letter to me was full of praise about you and apparently in his older age he is finding what he lacked and needed years ago. It must make you very happy, for things have apparently worked out for you better than you had hoped regarding Walter.

Henry gave Lao explicit advice from his long experience in sales and marketing, suggesting that there was nothing wrong with making a charge, but urging her not to fall into the pattern of many new age teachers who were dictatorial in the very opposite way Jesus was democratic. He clearly felt that Lao was genuine, and he warned her to always "keep up the real work" and never to miscast herself, even with altruistic intention. "Certain types of women in this work become dangerous to themselves because of the inordinate pressure that is required," he reminded her. "You won't make that mistake. You are too universal, cosmopolitan, inspired and worthy to overemphasize a partial note by calling a major symphony the whole theme of music. Don't imitate anyone but be your own original inspiration. The world needs you, God needs you, and Truth Must be You."

He reassured her that he was not presuming to tell her that anything she had done was unwise. He urged that she always remember that the "end of the road" is but another way of saying that "here starts a new beginning." Lao respected his opinion, appreciated his advice, and sent him Lao Tzu's book as a friendship gift in remembrance of their days together.

Henry had recently met and spoken about Walter with Glenn Clark, who had been in Michigan for a two-day conference. He found Clark to be utterly true, simple in speech, but profound in insight. He believed Clark was doing magnificent missionary work among the churches and that his techniques of prayer were monuments of actual demonstration. Henry had questioned Clark's motives after Clark had seemed to challenge Walter's sincerity following the 1946 lecture tour, but he now made it clear to Lao that he wished to withdraw any unkind thought concerning the author of *The Man Who Tapped the Secrets of the Universe*.

Lao was in perfect agreement with Walter in all-out protection against his teachings becoming a "cult." She felt there was always a great danger in this when the groups listening were mostly made up of women. That is why she was so happy that the Detroit lectures had been sponsored by top business leaders there. She felt that if Walter could reach the right men, the tremendous import of the Message would have far-reaching effect in less time. She realized that his book was for the advanced thinker and relished the fact that men like Dr. Miller really appreciated its stupendous import. Recognition and help from other men of this caliber would come, she knew, and it would be then that the greatness of Walter's work would be appreciated. Should it ever be 'typed' as yet another cult, they both knew that such people would lose interest without investigation.

Lao was exuberant now that she was wholly committed to working with Walter. "You seem to have been very busy since your arrival in New York and you certainly appear to have become a permanent part of the work of Dr. Russell. It is nice to know you are so happy," wrote E. S. Alexander. She had also won the trust of Walter's New York attorney, Clark L. Jordan, who would play a vital role in their work in Manhattan and Virginia for many years to come.

One of her best friends in Boston, Georgia Eliza Reid, was a force to be reckoned with in New England in advertising, publicity, merchandising, and sales promotion. She was highly complimentary of Lao's ability to write:

"Your last letter was wonderful, darling. I know that if you write as well with your thoughts flowing as logically and purely in what you have done on the book with Walter, it will be truly worthwhile."

Georgia encouraged her to keep planning every day for the center they now hoped to establish in Colorado Springs. She knew they must wait until *The Message of the Divine Iliad* was published before they really began work on the center but assured them "I am cognizant of the fact that it is something so big that neither of you can discard it from your mind."

Henry Maday had finally succeeded in introducing Walter to Joseph Sadony, the enigmatic German-born sage of the Valley of the Pines, White River Township, Muskegon, Michigan, whom Henry considered to be one of earth's real noblemen with a divinely inspired gift of prophecy. Thirty years before, Sadony had written Gandhi that India would be freed by the British in 1947. He had correctly prognosticated thousands of events, was practically born with this gift, yet claimed no credence for himself. He made no claim to be a fortune-teller or seer, but felt himself merely a simple shepherd endeavoring to help his fellow man.

Sadony, who amazingly balanced his gift with a masterful scientific application in his sanctified Valley of the Pines laboratory, reminded Henry Maday of Walter and had written the latter a wonderful letter after learning of his Detroit's lectures. Sadony warned Walter's friend, Ossip Gabrilowitsch, Mark Twain's son-in-law, to maintain strong spirituality as a defense against a lingering illness Sadony foresaw. Henry wrote Walter: "Had Ossip listened to Joseph and kept the spiritual tie intact that Joseph suggested, the wonderful soul whom you once sculptured would no doubt have lived longer than he did. Ossip did so for two months, but then lost the continuity and before passing on, told Mrs. Gabrilowitsch [Clara Clemens] that he should have listened to Joseph." Henry correctly predicted that a genuine interweaving of interests with universal implications would develop between Joseph Sadony and Walter Russell. Joseph Sadony's experiences were later related in his autobiographical masterpiece, *Gates of the Mind*, published by New York's Exposition Press in 1964.

By December 1947 an expanded Committee for Walter Russell Lectures was actively promoting Walter from offices at 648 South Broadway in Los Angeles.

Lao's reading for January 1, 1948, was succinct and accurate: "This is your inspirational year, make the most of it!"

She received many letters of thanks from friends and relatives in England whom she had once again showered with gift boxes for the holidays. "Good old Daisy, so nice of her," one cousin told his wife.

Florrie and Harry had sold their business in Luton and were enjoying retirement near the shore. When their gardener took ill with cancer, Harry worked the flower and vegetable gardens himself, and Florrie wrote that he had never felt more fit.

The friends who had taken her to Jamaica in 1938 were delighted to hear of her exploits.""Your description of your travels and occupation has greatly fired Joan's imagination," her husband, M. R. Crickmore, wrote.

In late January, Walter and Lao wrote Jack Crandall in Colorado Springs that they would be unable to follow through with plans for relocation there, given the fact that they had been offered only a relatively small plot of ground adjacent to the Fine Arts Center. They were grateful and polite in declining the proposed Institute of Man site, but both of them had felt discouraged when it had been shown to them, although at the time neither recognized the reason for their feelings. The plot was so beautiful and well-landscaped that they had both momentarily forgotten that the main issue and reason for their wanting to move to Colorado Springs was to gain a needed isolation from people, city influences, automobile horns, and "the eternal flow of unannounced visitors which makes life here so difficult."

"When we think of the ceaseless flow of cars around that circle and the ease with which all people could walk in on us to make work impossible, we feel that taking such a place would be like stepping out of the frying pan into the fire," Walter explained. "When we looked across the valley from the Linky residence, we saw just what our ideals were desiring, a wilderness at the foot of great, protecting mountains, but on the edge of a beautiful city, [a site] which was sufficiently accessible for us and for visitors but still remote enough [for us] to hear the whisperings of nature instead of the raucous noises of crowded civilization."

Kay Linky had explored their dream site but found it to be inaccessible by road. Walter told them: "We would rather make the road if necessary, or we would rather buy the property ourselves if necessary and make it the way we want it than to spend a fortune in building something from which we would eventually want to escape. We feel that Colorado Springs wanted to give us its best and you offered what one would think was the best, but it does not live up to our dreams of building a Temple of Beauty in the beautiful outdoors of Nature. We deeply appreciate your great personal interest in our dream, and the hospitality of the city itself in offering us its best, and I am sure you will understand our reasons for thus deciding."

"I can readily see your point of view," Jack wistfully replied, "but I sincerely hope that this change will not affect your decision to come to this region with your proposed plans."

Lao returned briefly to Boston for business and to see friends, reassuring Walter that she missed her little dinners and games of gin rummy with him.

The celebrated author and mystic Paul Brunton had tried to arrange a meeting with Walter for over a year and suggested that they might get together during two weeks in May when Brunton would be in New York en route from the Southwestern United States to Europe. Lao replied, explaining, "Dr. Russell has had intense illumination this year. It started in April and has continued through until now. Knowing your own cosmic consciousness through reading your books, I know that you understand and appreciate Dr. Russell's silence. All of his personal correspondence has been answered by me, and I found your letter today in one of his personal files when trying to find something for him." She asked Brunton's forgiveness for this seeming discourtesy and urged him to contact Walter on returning from Europe "in order that he may have the pleasure which he has so long anticipated of meeting you and sharing some moments of Oneness with you." She signed this letter, as she did all of Walter's correspondence during those months, "Yours sincerely, Mrs. Lao Stebbing, Associate and co-worker with Dr. Russell." It would be 1957 before Paul Brunton met the Russells when he visited them at Swannanoa.

The books were attracting widespread attention. In May 1948 an important Czechoslovakian physician wrote of his deep interest in *The Secret of Light*, which had been forwarded to him by one of the Russell students in Indiana.

The first volume of Walter's *Message of the Divine Iliad* included "The Book of Desire" and "The Book of Rest," describing the sources of power and fundamental principles through which the physical universe of motion springs from the spiritual universe. Desire and rest were revealed as the sources of all power manifested by humanity by actions. The book concluded with ten lectures, supplemented by questions and answers, through which Walter sought to simplify the entire process of Universal Law and its applicability to personal power and balance in human relations.

The Message of the Divine Iliad drew praise from Gayatri Devi, head of the Boston Vedanta Centre and a longtime friend of Lao, who had sent her an autographed copy with an inscription in which Walter referred to Lao and her connection with the Centre. Gayatri Devi replied, "I have often thought of you and felt eagerness to know where you are and what you are doing. I do hope the association with Mr. Russell and his work has brought you security and happiness. When you come to Boston, please let us know, as we would like to see you very much." Lao had spent many hours during the 1940s at the Centre, whose roots in New England went back to Swami Vivekananda's visit to Boston in 1893, prior to his becoming a world renowned figure at the World Parliament of Religions held later that year in Chicago. The Boston Centre had been moved to a new location at 58 Deerfield Street in 1941.

CHAPTER NINE

Cosmic Romance

(1948)

By early 1948 Walter and Lao had decided they must marry. They knew that such action would be controversial, but it seemed essential if they were to dedicate the rest of their lives to delivering the Message to the world.

Walter left New York for Reno on May 20, 1948, to wait for his divorce. He traveled by bus so he could more easily meet with students along the way. He stopped to visit privately with his friends George and Dorothy Gibson in Columbus, Ohio. There he met Dr. Roy Burkhart, pastor of the 3,800-member Community Church. "Dr. Burkhart arrived at 4 o'clock," Dorothy wrote Lao, "and the meeting between these two was really something to observe. They think alike, and Walter's return visit here in July should produce wonderful results. Arrangements were discussed about meetings to be held at that time, so I am sure something worthwhile will result from the next visit. Dr. Burkhart asked permission to have several of his young members call here at our home in the evening to meet Walter, since the minister had distributed so many copies of *The Man Who Tapped the Secrets of the Universe* among his congregation. Permission was granted, so the meeting was arranged for 7:30 P.M."

Walter told the Gibsons about his and Lao's plans to marry. "We are extremely happy for both of you," Dorothy added in her letter. "We love you both dearly, and our good wishes shall be with you always."

Lao was certain that her Scottish terrier Jimmie had returned to her in a new dog, Jinnie, of the same breed. "O, but she is lovely," she wrote. "She looks exactly like him and acts like him and even has the same physical tendencies such as trouble with her ears." Jinnie accompanied Lao everywhere and would go with her to Nevada for the wedding and then join them on their honeymoon.

Lao had written Walter the same day. "Dearest Dear One: I cannot believe you have gone from me for so long. You have only just left and it is like a million years and little Jinnie waits by the door. Am so hoping the bus will prove restful and that you will arrive at Mrs. Gibson's a little rested. Am so glad you will have those few hours there and then you can finish your journey more relaxed for the longer distance. You looked so darling when you left. You are my whole world and no one will ever replace you."

Lao was confident that Walter would accomplish much important work in his weeks of waiting in Nevada for the divorce. She also knew that event and their subsequent marriage would lessen the tension in their lives and give them freedom to dedicate their energy to their future work. "You are God's own son and you will always be taken care of by Him," she assured her future husband. "Our lives belong only to God, and He will guide us but we must heed His Voice always. In quietness we shall hear and not go wrong."

Both Walter and Helen Russell had Connecticut attorneys representing their interests, and each had affiliated himself with a lawyer in Reno to ensure that the Nevada divorce went smoothly. Walter had filed the suit initially, but his wife's attorney advised Walter's lawyer that Helen preferred to obtain the divorce herself on a cross-claim in absentia.

There was much correspondence between the parties' legal representatives regarding Walter's personal property at the Washington, Connecticut, home. Helen was eager to see that all these items were removed as quickly as possible, but with Walter in Nevada and he and Lao planning a prolonged honeymoon before his return to New York, it was difficult to comply with Helen's wishes. Walter was leaving her all furnishings and fixtures at the Connecticut home and only wanted items pertaining to his sculpture and painting, as well as all of his artwork. She was eager to oblige. This was important because he had sent many of his works to the Connecticut residence for storage when he had taken a smaller studio at Carnegie Hall. She advised him through her attorney that she would send him all the casts and molds in the Connecticut studio as soon as he returned to New York. His casts of Mark Twain, Franklin D. Roosevelt, Thomas Lipton, and Cass Gilbert were all located in Connecticut, and she was not definite as to what else she might find, but made it clear to Walter that she would be "glad to have these casts and molds removed and to have the matter closed."

In letters to students Lao apologized for Walter not answering their inquiries personally. She advised them that he had left for seclusion and "had spent all of May and June intensely in the Light."

It was important to both Walter and Lao that they tell Glenn Clark of their plans, but he had been busy attending Camp Farthest Out meetings across the country. He arranged to see Lao in New York during a two-day stay in late July prior to flying to Paris, but a delay in the mail prevented her from receiving his invitation to meet, and Lao was forced to advise him of their plans by letter.

She stressed that she had wished to tell him in person of their future plans because she knew with Clark's "great spiritual inner knowing" he "would be glad that at last all obstacles were being removed for the greater unfolding of God's Plan." She reminded him that more than anyone else, he understood "that it was [her] destiny to bring the balance necessary for Walter to deliver the Message God gave him for mankind at this time. Walter had to empty the vacuum in order that it may be filled with only pure motives. The Message of Rhythmic Balanced Interchange could not be given when his own life was not such and now that his entire life is being lived on this principle. All is unfolding."

Lao told Glenn that she and Walter understood that there would be those who would condemn them, but she was confident that "those who understand and recognize God's unfolding will stand by and demonstrate their understanding that all that Walter and I live for is to give His Message of Scientific Laws, a message of science that will one day relieve the whole world." She assured Glenn that she and Walter had forgotten their little selves "in the unfolding of the Self—which is all men. We shall go on working and if any illusion of unpleasantness faces us, we know that that too will be voided because God has given us peace in His assurance.

"If we are right with God and wrong with the world we know that God will materially demonstrate this one day to all men. However all those near and dear to us know what is happening is God's unfolding of His Plan."

She told Glenn that to protect Walter's work certain human steps had to be taken, explaining that God had sent them abundant supply that was purely the result of Walter's work with his own hands. "When the soil is prepared good seeds bring forth wonderful flowers, and so it shall be," she added, noting further that "if Walter had had a divorce forty-six years ago, he would most likely have married another who would not have shared this work, but God's Plan was otherwise, and Walter knew great aloneness [in which] he created beauty in color and stone. God would not thus bring such a one into the Light that was not worthy in every way. I shall stand by Walter forever—I know how truly worthy he is—I have witnessed the depth of his humility and it is a humility that inspires humility."

She told Glenn that cosmic love was the breath of life to her. "Personal love plays no part in this greater love which holds my whole being," she assured him.

Glenn Clark replied that his intuition had told him they were contemplating marriage. "It is certainly a step that should be bathed in prayer," he advised. When their letters crossed, and their meeting in New York was precluded, she wrote him in Paris, "How I would have treasured a few moments' prayer with you, but please remember us in your heart always."

During all of May and June, Walter felt strongly in "the Light" again. His intense illumination of 1921 was repeated—only this time it seemed to him to be accompanied with God's Cosmic Orchestra. Walter said the music he heard was more beautiful than any he had ever experienced on earth. He found it difficult to get back into his body and both he and Lao were glad he was away on the Palomino Ranch in the mountains near Reno where he had little contact with the outside world.

In late June Walter wrote to Lao from the ranch, stressing the beauty of the Nevada environment and its beneficial effect on his health: "I have rested all the morning out in the air and fell asleep out there, for the sun is behind great clouds most of the time and the air was so fine, and I felt so tired and lazy and I just took the morning off and thought of you and Jinnie and our trip. It is the first time I have loafed like that since I got here. It never gets really hot here. There is always a cool breeze, and at night one must sleep under two blankets. In the morning a sport coat is needed, but I wear my blue smock and beret. Again about five a sport coat is again needed for one's bare arms feel the coolness of the evening everywhere. The air feels good on my feet—and the sandals are wonderful. I cannot get over the joy of the effect of the sun on my knees. If we both had plenty of sun and air for a few months, we would both be better."

He was clearly looking forward to their honeymoon trip. "The people who rent the cars say that they will try to arrange it so that I can deliver the car in New York so that we can go all the way home with our baggage, pictures, et cetera, and Jinnie. We should go through Yellowstone…and paint…. I will make two boxes to carry six wet panels each so that we can let them dry in their boxes without touching each other….We will stop somewhere each day and paint one picture each day just as I did on the way to Texas. In our thirty-day trip you will emerge as quite a painter. I will short-cut you to masterliness in no time—for you know—and it will be easy." For the first time he mentioned a marble palace called Swannanoa, located in the Blue Ridge Mountains of Virginia. Walter had tried to interest his friends in purchasing it with him for use as an art center in the late 1930s, but the effort had been unsuccessful. Now he wondered if the mountaintop retreat was meant instead for Lao and him.

Walter had completed eight pictures for a small exhibition in Nevada, and already he was getting phone calls about them. The local radio station announced the exhibition, and the local newspaper ran a feature accompanied by a photograph of Walter carving the Franklin D. Roosevelt bust.

Lao was delighted at the pace with which the Message was spreading. The week of July 4 visitors came to the Carnegie Hall studio from Sweden and Scotland. She wrote that "we sat and talked for a long time and when they left they took several of each of the books with them. They are both anxious to impart this great Message to their fellow countrymen."

She introduced herself and Walter's books to the owners of New York's important metaphysical bookshops and libraries. There was increasing demand for his works. Many readers of *The Secret of Light* promptly wrote for *The Message of the Divine Iliad* and vice versa, and a large number of these inquirers expressed a desire to own *The Universal One*, the magnum opus Walter had written after his 1921 illumination and published five years later in a limited edition. This book was mentioned in *The Man Who Tapped the Secrets of the Universe* but had long been out of print.

Lao soon worked herself to exhaustion, forcing herself to put in twenty-hour days in an effort to complete all of their necessary business correspondence before the time came for her to travel to Reno. She soon took ill. Their friend, Hildegarde Burmeister, a New York art dealer who had long attended Walter's lectures and lately become a close friend of Lao, looked in on her the first Sunday in June and thought she was critically sick. The seriousness of Lao's condition was obvious to Walter when he talked to Lao by telephone. She reassured him that she would rest and urged him to do the same. "God has work for me to do, and I shall not fail Him or you (or our Jinnie)," she wrote playfully, mentioning as always her beloved Scottish terrier who guarded their Carnegie Hall studio so earnestly. She did caution Walter not to talk about their plans too exuberantly or reveal their financial situation.

Walter had written his close friend Sherman Kiser, an important civilian employee with the Army, that he was having a grand time in Nevada and found it a great relief to be away from the telephone and the constant stream of callers, as well as to be located so that anywhere he looked, God in nature was staring him in the face. Sherman replied on September 9, agreeing, "The beautiful distant mountains always sing in harmony with the entire universe. You are experiencing a great freedom. I wish I could be with you. While you are painting, I would like to be near you writing." Sherman had called Lao the day before to see if she had followed advice and taken some time to enjoy the sunshine in the park, but she reported that she had only been out ten minutes during the day. He reprimanded her but to no avail; she continued to work incessantly, answering the inspiring letters they received. He stressed that Lao needed a skilled secretary to help her with her work, telling Walter, "It is too much for one person." Sherman planned to retire on September 30, and he and his wife Margaret told Walter they would await word from him before making a final decision as to where they would spend the next winter.

He reassured Walter. "It might be that all of our dreams so far have been just a beginning of the real events that will crystallize as God gives us more light. It seems to me somehow that we must start our laboratory work this fall or winter. The successful completion of that first venture would prove, to a doubting Thomas world, that what you have is Cosmic-Perfect. If we can give them something that their sensing can fathom, they will all fight to get your books, and no one will be able to block the spread of your God's ideas until they reach millions and millions of people in all countries. Something will turn up soon to make this possible, I am sure. The world is ready now to accept what you have to give, but only if they have some proof that they can understand. If we develop any gadget or any machine or any principle or process, it must bear your name. This must be understood and put in writing, and your lawyer must see that it is ironclad before we start. Only in this way can we get the maximum spread of what God has given you. As soon as possible, you and Lao must be freed of financial worries because they sap your energies and mesmerize you, putting a fog at times between you and the light. We will find a way soon I believe, hopefully by the time of your return." Sherman continued to look in on Lao regularly during Walter's absence and tried to be of assistance to her.

Walter pled with Anne from Glenn Clark's Camp Stadie to come to New York to keep the correspondence answered and look after the Carnegie Hall studio while Lao was in Nevada and they were on their honeymoon. "Naturally," Anne responded, "I want to do all I can to further the Message and will indeed go to New York to relieve Lao of responsibilities." She arrived in Manhattan the first week of July and spent several weeks working with Lao before assuming the clerical duties alone.

Anne was thrilled at the news of Walter and Lao's impending marriage: "Praise God from Whom all Blessings flow for Lao! She is a dear, and you are too," she told Walter. "I am so happy for you for I know what it means to you. I do know that you are triumphantly happy!"

Marie Stoddard wrote Lao from Hollywood when she heard of their wedding plans: "Dearest One, I have greased my face, cut my toenails, and now I am ready for anything!" The great acting teacher had many happy memories of Lao's months with her as an aspiring movie actress. "I think of you always, Daisy. The silver bells hang in the ceiling where you put them. The pretty things you sent Jean and me for the birthdays are on display. We often think, 'I'd like to hear Daisy laugh,' and Topsy still pricks her ears when I say, 'Where is Daisy?' and we all still love you and wish your happiness always, whatever it may be."

Charles Earley wrote in July that *The Message of the Divine Iliad* had restored his mental serenity. He had read and reread the book while sunning on the Lake Michigan beach and had gone to the library to retrieve the *Essay on Love* that Walter had recommended. He expressed happiness that the Russell books were receiving the recognition due them. "Often thinkers of his caliber must suffer aloneness and crucifixion for being ahead of their time," Earley told Lao. He and Walter had discussed their views of the graft and commercial aspect of most medical programs. Earley believed, as did the Russells, that following the few simple laws of nature was the only road to true health and happiness, but he faced the same dogmatic views in the healing profession as the Russells sometimes experienced in the spiritual and scientific realms. Earley was deeply engrossed in the study of herbs and the chemical types of people. He felt that each type of person needed specific minerals for his or her special constitution. They discussed the scientific foundation of the theory as it had been practiced in Germany forty or fifty years before. Like phrenology, he felt, "it is bound to have a revival, as it is based on truth." Earley had over fifty books on phrenology and had just found a valuable treatise on the subject by a Dr. Hollander of England. "All his facts were found on observation of nature," Earley wrote, "and to disprove it, one would have to prove that his observations were incorrect and his data not scientifically recorded, and that would be quite a feat for some of these microscopic-minded scientists of today." He had given the Russells a copy of Winsor's *Phrenology*.

California chiropractors specializing in white light radionics ordered *The Secret of Light*. Lao advised them, "A gentleman from Scotland this week called and told me he thought it was the most valuable book in the world today. He said he gains more and more knowledge from it with each reading."

Mixed marriage couples wrote that they found the teachings very helpful. "My husband is Jewish and I am Protestant, and none of the so-called churches really fill our needs. You have given us great comfort....I started my two youngsters in a Unity Sunday school, as I felt they must have spiritual teaching and I wanted them to have that secure inward feeling and reverence, I've known. My husband and I shall follow your more mature teachings and have already found great satisfaction in reading *The Man Who Tapped the Secrets of the Universe*."

Students often sent the books to their professors. Faculty members at the post-graduate Osteopathic Institute of Andrew Taylor Still's Research and Practice in Davenport, Iowa, regularly ordered copies of both of Walter's latest books.

Dr. William G. Sutherland, father of Osteopathy in the Cranial Field, who viewed the human body as a sophisticated "machine" and believed that dysfunction or impairment in one area was bound to compromise the entire structure, pioneered concepts about the constant rhythmic motions of the human body, "living anatomy," as he called it. Dr. Sutherland and his brilliant student, Dr. Robert Fulford, urged their fellow cranial osteopaths to study Walter Russell's work. Sutherland, working with Russell, first photographed "the Light" emanating at the time of a person's death. Mrs. Sutherland and Lao corresponded frequently in later years.

From Detroit Mr. Leland, who had headed the Cadillac Motor Company, endorsed their work. He had visited them at Carnegie Hall just prior to being involved in major labor negotiations with General Motors. Lao wrote him, "I shall never forget your face. I recognized the God Love in it before I was introduced to you." She stressed the need for people like him to support Walter in his work. "Walter and I must be free for the creative side. There is much to be released in these next five years, and we shall not fail if we do not compromise. All is unfolding harmoniously."

Word of Walter's impending divorce had reached Los Angeles and Sacramento. It resulted in unpleasant publicity and some criticism among their students, but once the news of their impending wedding became common knowledge, they received many congratulatory letters and cards from across America and abroad.

Sherman corresponded regularly with Walter in the weeks before the wedding. He wrote him three days before the divorce was to be final: "Then you will sign up again, but this time the partnership will be on the highest plane that man on this earth will ever reach. I feel as sure of it as I know you do." He had kept watch over Lao and dined with her several times and was totally convinced that Walter was making the right decision. "She is so completely devoted to your work and to you that every moment of her time is taken up. What a glorious mission both you and she are on. I feel it more deeply every day and sincerely hope that I can have a small part in your great mission as long as I live. It is the only thing that counts."

Walter wrote Sherman that he had sold the Mark Twain bust to a Virginia City newspaper and that he and Lao were already planning to attend the dedication there on Mark Twain's birthday, November 30. His friend replied on July 14: "Congratulations on your business as well as your artistic accomplishments. You are right. God always supplies our needs. This little windfall should give you and Lao a beautiful trip and much needed relaxation and change. Lao was really very ill for that one week and a change will do wonders for her. She has not returned to normal yet. Of course, a part of that is not having you to cheer her up. As you so beautifully state, 'It is joy and ecstasy that bring back the energy.' You are lucky, very lucky that you have her to assist you in your great mission. She will never let you or your great work suffer from lack of energy or loyalty. As time goes on your little flock will multiply and we will have such fun and thrills working together." Sherman had lost all zest for his military job and was forcing himself to keep his spirit high until his retirement. He and Lao felt that 1948 was a planning year, 1949 would see the seeds planted, and 1950 would yield the early blossom of their work.

In fact the sale of the Mark Twain bust was not definite. Walter had offered it at the token cost of $2,500 to those interested in restoring the historic Comstock Lode town, the biggest of the mining boom towns of the old West, where Mark Twain began writing his fiction while working for the old *Territorial Enterprise* newspaper. Reno's Latimer Club, comprising its leading

60. Walter Russell and Mark Twain's granddaughter.

citizens, pledged to raise the funds and had begun laying plans for a dedication that would feature an unveiling by Nevada's governor. A banner headline in the July 1, 1948, *Reno Reporter* proclaimed: "Virginia City To Fete Twain; Author's Bust Done By Famous Sculptor Is To Be Acquired." Another local newspaper featured a photograph of the Mark Twain bust with Walter and Mark Twain's granddaughter, Nina Gabrilowitsch, standing beside it.

News of Walter's major reason for being in Reno had not yet reached the press. The *Reporter* story noted that he "has been visiting in Reno as part of a sketching tour of the west" and noted that he "is internationally famous as an artist and sculptor and has gained national recognition as a physicist, philosopher, and musician." The article reported that he had completed eleven oil paintings since arriving in Reno in May. The oils were being exhibited locally. Interestingly, the reporter noted, "The doctor, also a proficient horseman and ice skater, is the father of several children, grandchildren, and has two great grandchildren."

Gilmour Young, a marketing expert and Russell devotee, was pressing Walter with details of the northwestern study center he hoped to open in Seattle for the Russell students. Sherman told Walter that Young sounded like a natural for the task.

Ten days before she left New York, Lao wrote Walter a letter full of love and filled with details of their busy lives. She was making arrangements for the Mark Twain head that the *Sacramento Bee* had commissioned to be cast in New York by the Modern Art Foundry, although it appeared unlikely that it could be cast before November l unless Walter delivered it to them before September 15. She handled the details. "I presume they want it in bronze," she inquired.

Walter's rental account with Carnegie Hall was in arrears, but Lao had spoken with management and felt confident they would have a home to return to after their honeymoon if they made a substantial part payment on the arrearage. She regretted not buying a car in New York and driving to Reno. She was certain it would have been cheaper than coming west by train.

"It is costing a fortune," she told him. "I will not tell you how much at this point, but it is too much." He had written her about a Plymouth he planned to rent for several months for them to use on their honeymoon. She urged him to pursue purchasing it if it could be had for a bargain and was clean inside. "A Plymouth is easily resold, being in the lower bracket. We could buy our own car for what it is going to cost us to hire this for so many months." She urged Walter to use his best discretion. "Perhaps it would be better just to hire it and then buy a good station wagon in a few months," she concluded, adding that Sherman had just bought a practically new Chevrolet for $1,500.

Lao loved the photographs he had sent her of the paintings he had done, particularly one with the mountains and tall trees. He sold several of his paintings there, but he reserved most of them constituting, a wedding present for her.

They faced a potential legal hassle. Walter had signed a contract several years before giving a friend, Mary deZevallas, exclusive rights to write his illustrated biography. "Why, o why, did you sign everything away in this manner?" Lao asked. Clark Jordan, their attorney, suggested the best course of action was to forget about the prior agreement and wait quietly to see if Mary actually pressed her claim. Only then would they need to consider offering her a settlement, which Lao feared would only induce her to ask for more. "In any case nothing would be done without you here, and it is better to go into it all carefully when we get back," she assured Walter. "There is no immediate rush. The proposition is too big. It is a much bigger thing than you realize at this point. Keep quiet about it all and let it unfold as it is doing. I do not believe that God would let Mary deZevallas get away with ill-gotten gain in that way. If you tried to buy her off for $2,500, she would ask for $25,000 or more because she would think something was happening. We must wait and let things take their course. When you come back, we will go over the whole thing with Clark."

Walter encouraged Lao to be ready to paint with him on their honeymoon, and this greatly excited her. She well remembered the watercolors she had done as a little girl and sold so readily back in Luton. "It is years and years since I even held a brush, but I will paint, and I shall love it," she told him.

She received many compliments on the letters she had written for Walter. Some of the recipients replied, asking if they could quote some of her statements. This convinced Lao that she should keep a file of her letters and reuse specific paragraphs as the need occurred. Beatrice Pelletier, a Russell student, described Lao's letters as "so wonderful that I know you will not mind my giving my friends the benefit of their freedom-giving effect. Such truths should not be hidden under a bushel."

The statements by Lao that Beatrice particularly liked included these:

"When we face life with compassion, we face it with courage"; "The climb is not hard when we do not compromise, but all unfolds harmoniously"; and "When we cease to compromise with life, Life ceases to compromise with us."

Helen Russell, Walter's wife, had not returned the papers consenting to the divorce. Clark Jordan advised Walter and Lao that if Helen did not return them immediately, Walter should file for the divorce himself. They suspected that Helen felt that she could delay Walter's remarriage by failing to send her consent. Clark and Lao both agreed that it was unfair of Helen to make Walter wait any longer. They felt they had given her ample time. More important, Clark thought that it would be best for Walter and Lao if the divorce were a *fait accompli* at least for several days before Lao arrived in Reno. Lao agreed with this and was happy she had not come west to join him earlier. She definitely wanted to delay her arrival until after Walter's divorce was settled.

Walter's original bill of complaint asked for a divorce on the grounds of extreme mental cruelty. On July 8 Helen's attorney filed a cross-complaint asking that she be granted a divorce on the same grounds. Six days before she was to leave for Nevada, Lao learned that the court had granted Helen a divorce on July 20.

The Associated Press carried the story on its wire, and many newspapers carried it. The release did not reflect well on Walter, quoting him as saying, after Judge A. J. Maestretti granted the divorce, "After fifty-five years, a man is entitled to some happiness." He and Helen had married January 10, 1893.

Walter and Lao had anticipated broad criticism from a public that would naturally sympathize with Helen Russell and criticize the seventy-seven-year-old Walter for deserting his wife of fifty-five years for a beautiful new bride of forty-four. What they did not expect was the castigation they received from many of their friends and colleagues.

Eleanor Mel, Lao's close confidante from the Boston Home of Truth, was attending a Religious Science conference in Sacramento in mid-July when the news of Walter's impending divorce and remarriage first surfaced among many of those who had supported him on his national lecture tours in 1946 and 1947. Devoted as she was to Lao, Eleanor hastened to write her on July 16: "I want to send you observations as gathered here and let you know that there is much deep feeling about this affair. It is very much of a shock to all who have known Walter and Helen to think that he should take such a step. I feel it will decidedly hurt the sale of the book and bring unnecessary disfavor to so many who have taken you all into their hearts." It was apparent to Eleanor that Helen Russell had endeared herself to the hearts of all who had met her on the lecture tours. Walter had appeared so solicitous of his wife's welfare at the time, and she had seemed so interested in his work, telling their friends how she and their children had done everything possible to help him bring out his first book in 1926.

Lao appreciated Eleanor's friendship and loyalty and sought to allay her concerns at once. "I am glad you sent the letter you did this morning," Lao replied, "and I took your words into the Light." She told her friend that all she lived for was to help Walter with his work and emphasized, "All we wanted is to do it in His way, and the way we are doing it seemed right and honorable."

Friends who had known Walter for forty years had told Lao that Helen's professed support of his work contradicted what they had witnessed over that time. Walter himself had assured Lao that he and Helen had never had a real marriage in the sense of a union of heart and soul, and that for forty-six years there had been no union whatsoever.

Lao was reluctant to discuss such matters, even with so close a friend, but she wrote Eleanor, "I believe in the years to come all those who are talking adversely will know and understand that this had to be. My guidance has been complete, and Walter has been in the Light of God since May. Could one be so close to God in complete knowing and be doing something that was not God's Will? I would rather be right with God than appear right to all men and wrong to God." She emphasized that she valued Eleanor's concerns and would never intentionally hurt another person. "But I must follow God's guidance and not listen to men's words which I know to be an illusion," she continued.

Lao told Eleanor she was forwarding her letter to Reno. "If Walter feels our marriage wrong after reading your report, I certainly would not marry him." Walter responded to Eleanor in a convincing manner. She replied immediately: "I have been approached by many, and my answer has always been, 'I believe in my heart of hearts that there is no one in the world better fitted to be Walter Russell's helpmate than Mrs. Stebbing.' I have always said, 'She is a gentlewoman, educated, refined, and is everything Walter Russell needs, especially in her understanding of the Light as it has come through Walter Russell.' Further, I have said that you had no cooperation from your family. This has always settled matters."

Eleanor related that when she reached Sacramento she had heard so many unpleasant reactions to Walter and Lao's plans to marry that she felt she must alert them. They were both dear friends to her, and she felt particularly that she had a hand in bringing them together since she had invited Walter to come to Boston in 1946 when he first met Lao. They had shared happy times. She had joined them for supper one evening at Carnegie Hall, she recalled, and even then she could see their love for each other and felt it to be a God-appointed combination. Both Walter and Lao had now reassured her "in every way," she said, and given her everything she needed to meet the reactions of the ignorant world. "You can count on me to be a good shock absorber and backstop for you both. It is right and it is good. God will richly bless your union and will use you richly to bless the world with the Light."

On July 24, a Saturday night, Lao wrote Walter at 8:00 P.M. to announce with pride that all of their old back letters had been answered. Accomplishing this had been her main priority. "I have all my own back personal letters to answer," she mused, "but they must wait until I am away or come back. Perhaps I have already lost all my good friends but I cannot help it." She had paid most of their current New York bills and withdrawn $2,000 of her own money for the journey west.

She was overjoyed at the favorable letters they had been receiving about Walter's books and was convinced that the forthcoming second volume of *The Message of the Divine Iliad* would be even more inspiring than the first. Walter's intense illumination that year was as strong as it had been in 1921 and continued unabated, accompanied by ethereal music that he felt came from Lao because "she was the song in his heart!"

Lao was convinced that the music was God's way of telling them that what they were doing was right. She felt that Walter was more "at One" than ever before and believed he would be able to step back and forth from the Light at will from then on.

She had written Gertrude de Kock in South Africa to tell her that Walter was finally free. "There are those who will condemn, but when we know we are Right with God, what does it matter what the world says? God told Walter in his illumination that Truth lies beyond the crucifixion. There are those who are crucifying, but there are also those who are deeply rejoicing, and we have more with us today than we did a year ago. Walter is unfolding God's Plan more surely, and the supply is coming as it never did before."

Lao's last letter to Walter before she left New York made clear the depth of her commitment to him: "I love you because you know God, and we can share Him. I could not share God with anyone as I share Him with you, and that is why I suppose we love each other more than anyone else in the Universe. I know God will guide us. We must never compromise in any one thing. Then all must come right. I feel you so close to me. You are the sweetest love in the whole world, and I want so much to share the music with you. I wonder if I ever shall. I feel that I will."

Lao left for Nevada by train on July 26. Minutes before she left Carnegie Hall she had written their scientist friend, Andrew Wilson, in Scotland, telling him of her plans with Walter and sending him a copy of Lao Tzu's *Tao* as a little gift in remembrance of their meeting.

Earlier she had written Walter: "I shall be mighty glad to lose the name Stebbing. Perhaps all will open up beautifully when that is gone."

CHAPTER TEN

The Sacred Mountain (1948-50)

News of Walter's filing for divorce and his impending remarriage drew sensational headlines in *The New York Daily News* ("Sculptor Russell, Divorced at 77, Will Marry Another"). The story was carried by the Associated Press and headlined in newspapers across the country (e.g., "Sculptor Asks Divorce From Wife of 54 Years"). In telephone interviews to the major New York dailies Walter was frank in expressing his delight at receiving his divorce but coyly declined to reveal the name of his intended bride.

The day before his divorce was granted, he wrote an intensely personal letter to Bessie Fourton, a vivacious young woman who had long been his friend and surrogate daughter: "Lao has rescued both me and the Message." Bessie knew about the pressures and complications that had so frustrated Walter in the mid-1940s and had encouraged him to eliminate the nonessentials from his life and to focus on his cosmic priorities. Walter related that Lao had come into his life, "reorganized everything, and reversed the downtrend, for I vitally needed her great genius." He told Bessie, "I know you will love her," adding that so many other friends from coast to coast "already love her."

61. Bessie Fourton at Walter Russell's Carnegie Hall studio.

The next day, July 19, 1948, Walter rebutted various women's groups that had reportedly criticized his seeking divorce after so many years of marriage. He asked *The New York Daily News*, "They would not want a man sentenced to prison for fifty-five years to stay in for life, would they?" In the same article he declined to name his new heart interest, but said that she lived in New York City. "We may marry in a few days, three weeks, or decide to wait a year," he told the reporter.

62. Marriage of Walter and Lao Russell, Geiger's Outlook, Nevada, 1948.

Actually Walter was well aware of the date he and Lao had set for their wedding and was keenly excited about their forthcoming honeymoon. He wrote Bessie Fourton: "Send your blessings to us over the silences of God's heaven at eight o'clock, Thursday, July 29, which is five o'clock here, for Lao and I are to be married up on top of one of the High Sierras at that time—and then our work will go on. Lao and I will go on a six weeks' sketching trip in Banff, Yosemite, Yellowstone, and Glacier National Parks—something we both need for recuperation and something I have always wanted to do. I have not painted out-of-doors in fifteen years, and it is heaven."

Some thirty friends were present at Lao's and Walter's marriage. Numerous reporters joined them at the subsequent reception to report the May-December marriage of the "internationally known painter and sculptor" and the young English lady, and their photograph and story were transmitted on the Associated Press wire to newspapers in New York, Los Angeles, and across the country.

On July 30 and 31 scores of newspapers highlighted the romantic news of Walter and Lao's marriage. *The New York Herald Tribune* reported in a special July 30 report from Reno: "Walter Russell, artist, sculptor, and physicist, and Mrs. Lao Cook Stebbing of New York were married last night on Geiger Lookout, a high point between Reno and Virginia City. The ceremony was performed by the Reverend Richard Caswell, pastor of the Reno Unity Center. The couple left on an automobile tour of the Pacific northwest."

63. Walter and Lao cut their wedding cake.

Newspapers from coast to coast echoed *The New York Daily News* in highlighting the age difference between Walter and Lao (e.g., "Walter Russell, 77, Painter, Sculptor, Weds Mrs. Stebbing—Bride, 43, of N.Y., British Born; Their Marriage Takes Place Near Reno"). *The New York Daily News* featured a two-column photograph with the caption, "The newlyweds cut the cake." The story reiterated the earlier report that Walter's divorce complaint had charged his first wife, Helen, with extreme mental cruelty and reported that he stated again after his marriage to Lao, "After fifty-five years, a man is entitled to some happiness." A national women's magazine repeated the statement in a romanticized two-page article, which once again drew sympathy for Helen Russell from the average reader.

64. The bride and groom survey the horizon.

Oblivious to the press criticism, Walter and Lao embarked on their long-anticipated wedding trip. After touring Yosemite National Park and various sites in the northwestern United States for ten days, they stopped to visit their friend Gilmour Young in Seattle, Washington. They found waiting for them a letter from Helen Russell's Connecticut lawyer acknowledging receipt of Walter's first alimony payment and conveying his ex-wife's instructions for him to remove all of his remaining personal property from her Washington, Connecticut, home as soon as Walter and Lao returned to New York in mid-September. At Seattle they also received a congratulatory letter from the manager of Carnegie Hall, wishing them happiness and apologizing for interrupting their honeymoon with an inquiry as to whether they desired a two-year renewal of the lease on the studio at a sixteen percent increase in rent. They accepted the offer and left for several weeks of seclusion at Cannon Beach, Oregon, in what Walter described in a letter as "a lovely little cottage high up on a cliff above the sea, the world of singing waters over broad sands, pounding against rocky pyramids standing right out of the sea like a marine Garden of the Gods. The world seems all our own here, for a great pine forest screens the land approach and the ocean protects us from contact with everything this side of Asia." Here they rested and painted and enjoyed their honeymoon.

65. Lao Russell on her honeymoon, Cannon Beach, Oregon.

They had intended to return to Fresno and

Virginia City and be back at the Palomino Ranch in Reno at the end of August, but the service clubs in Virginia City were unsuccessful in raising sufficient funding to erect Walter's colossal bust of Mark Twain as a memorial to the author's literary birthplace, so there was no need for them to return to California. Instead, they focused their attention on making a final decision as to where they would locate the Foundation.

They had visited a number of sites in the west, but Walter continued to describe Swannanoa in the Blue Ridge Mountains of Virginia as a possible site for their shrine of beauty. Walter had realized the potential of this stunning edifice when it had first become vacant in the late 1930s. Now Lao intuitively felt that they should discontinue further searching in the west until they had seen firsthand the present condition of the marble palace and gardens Walter described to her. They left Oregon for Virginia on August 23. On their journey they stopped by Banff, Canada, and Muskegon, Michigan, where they enjoyed a visit with Joseph Sadony at his Educational Research Laboratories in Valley of the Pines. In Ohio they stopped again with the Burkhardts. Meanwhile they contacted the owners of Swannanoa and arranged to see the amazing structure that would become their future home.

Located some twenty miles west of Charlottesville, Virginia, Swannanoa is a fifty-two-room palace that reportedly cost Major James Dooley three million dollars to build between 1908 and 1912. In 1948 its replacement value was estimated at ten times that amount. It boasted an exterior of white Georgian marble with Italian Carrara and sienna marble interior refinements. Above the grand marble staircase that centered the great hall was a magnificent stained glass window of a Roman matron, reportedly depicting Major Dooley's wife, Sallie May Dooley, in an Italian garden. The window was the work of the great Louis Comfort Tiffany and had itself reportedly cost Dooley $100,000. The palace was named to commemorate Mrs. Dooley's predilection for swans. Much of the massive furniture installed after construction was complete bore a "swan" motif. These pieces had been removed from Swannanoa after the Dooleys

66. Swannanoa Palace, Afton Mountain, Waynesboro, Virginia.

died, but certain of them, including a remarkable bedstead carved with swans, remained in Maymont, their Richmond, Virginia, home, which they bequeathed to that city as a park. Lao came to appreciate the additional symbolism of the name Swannanoa. In West Indian it meant "land of beauty" and in East Indian it meant "the absolute, or mother of heaven."

Lao often told of her first view of the palace. They had arrived in Charlottesville after a leisurely trip across the continent and arranged with the owners of the mountaintop property to be driven there by a local realtor. On September 4 the party of three drove to Rockfish Gap, where the Jefferson Highway crossed the mountain overlooking the Shenandoah Valley city of Waynesboro to the west and the magnificent Rockfish Valley to the east. At the gap, a mile below the palace site, was the highway's intersection with the Skyline Drive and the Blue Ridge Parkway, two scenic roads constructed by the federal government, the former heading north some ninety miles through the fabled Shenandoah National Park, the latter meandering south through national forests and scenic easements over a route that would eventually take it to the vicinity of Asheville, North Carolina. These byways were rapidly becoming major tourist attractions in postwar America.

At the time, the entrance gates to the desolate Swannanoa estate stood grandly within view of the crossroads at Rockfish Gap. Development of the adjacent area was a year or more away, and it would be even longer before a second motel rose over the intersection facing east, its own access road necessitating the grading and filling that would obliterate the original entrance to the palace grounds and require its relocation a mile or more away along the eastern ridge of the mountain off a secondary state road.

The Russells and their escort made their way through the gates onto the legendary estate. The road was rocky and unpaved. Although it provided access through the 500 acres of the palace grounds, it passed unkempt plantings surrounded by forest. Dense overgrowth had closed in on the Dooleys' lawns and gardens in the years since the palace had been abandoned. The caretaker, a lady who lived in one of the adjacent cottages, was to meet them at the great house, which was seldom if ever called the palace in those days but referred to among area residents formally as "Swannanoa," or in their vernacular as "Dooley's Mansion."

As the car made the final turn bringing the vast white marble edifice into view, Walter and the realtor had been describing it glowingly to Lao, warning her not to be dismayed by its abandoned condition and alerting her to the fact that she was about to see one of the most unlikely, remarkable sights in the eastern United States. The palace came into view. It was a scene that would have left a lasting impact on anyone, even a lady who was familiar with the grand houses of Britain, the proud sights of Europe, and the pyramids of Egypt.

Yet, as the car stopped in front of the palace and its occupants alighted to be met by the caretaker and escorted through the empty house, Lao paid scant attention to the architectural marvel that stood before her.

Immediately and instinctively she hurried past the palace a few hundred feet to look down the mountain at the glorious panoramic view to the east. She stood transfixed. It seemed to be the exact scene she had viewed in her January experience two years before in her Boston apartment when she stood facing an identical valley with Jesus himself standing behind her and telling her that this was the place to which her destiny would lead her.

From the beginning, Lao had felt that God was directing them toward the Blue Ridge Mountains of the South, but in their search they had traveled some 8,000 miles through the western United States before turning southward. They had visited Mt. Rainier, Mt. Hood, Mt. Shasta, and Pike's Peak. They had seriously considered various sites in the Garden of the Gods at Colorado Springs, but none of these potential locations seemed to give them what they wanted.

According to Walter's account, he had been led to abandon his studio in Carnegie Hall entirely as a result of a Lao's vision. She had seen a majestic statue of Christ standing on a "sacred mountain" in an attitude of compassion for suffering mankind. She felt that they had been called to find the site and to establish there a "world cultural center," dominated by an imposing statue of the Savior. Russell, always a man of action, had confidence enough in his wife's vision to leave the security of his position in New York and at the age of seventy-seven to undertake its fulfillment.

Lao never ceased to tell the story of the remarkable feeling she experienced when she first found herself physically standing on the mountaintop she had been to in her illumination. She knew it was no mere coincidence, and the occurrence told her at once that Swannanoa was the place where she and Walter would settle. She joined Walter and the others for the obligatory tour of the palace rooms, desolate and derelict as they appeared. Practical as ever, she tried to focus on the building's suitability for their purposes and its potential for being returned to landmark appearance within the limited budget she knew she and Walter would have. Bringing Swannanoa to the public as a shrine of beauty would be a momentous challenge for them, yet to her it was an unavoidable, inescapable destiny. This was

67. View of Rockfish Valley from Swannanoa.

the sacred mountain of her vision. This would be the place where their work would thrive.

On September 14, after ten days of negotiations, John R. Morris, president of Skyline-Swannanoa, Inc., the group of investors who owned the property, wrote the Russells offering them a thirty-day option to purchase the 629-acre Swannanoa tract at a price of $160,000, $5,000 of which was to be paid on execution and delivery of the contract; $15,000 on or before December 15, 1948, with $120,000 deferred purchase money to be secured by ten successive annual $12,000 bonds at four percent interest and a first deed of trust; and the remaining $20,000 secured by a second deed of trust to be paid July 1, 1949, at five percent interest.

The Russells would receive possession of the garage, stable building, and palace on receipt of the down payment and full possession of the property when the transaction was closed. The owners reserved 100 acres fronting on highways 250 and 609 where they planned to build motels and commercial structures, but the Russells would be entitled to use the existing entranceway crossing the reserved acreage until the sellers found it necessary to relocate the palace access road, which they did some years later to the serious detriment of the palace tourist traffic.

As eager as they were to obtain the property, it was clear to Walter and Lao that the proposed contract was well beyond their means. On their return to New York they had diligently pursued funding sources they thought were readily available, but their efforts were unsuccessful. It soon became clear to them that it would be at least a year before they could commit themselves to the proposed option. Their attorney Clark Jordan advised them that the only fair approach was to let the owners know immediately that an immediate exercise of the option was impossible. He thought perhaps they had been premature and impulsive in rushing down to Charlottesville in early September and sensed that the owners would be severely disappointed when they learned that a sale to the Russells was not imminent.

Jordan stressed that the Russells truly believed that Swannanoa was ideal for their purposes but were reluctant to embark on any course of action they were not certain could be carried through to a successful conclusion. He recommended that instead of an outright purchase, a lease agreement might be to the mutual advantage of all parties and suggested that the limited volume of tourists who regularly came to see the unfurnished palace would be greatly multiplied if the Russell collection were installed there. As an alternative he suggested that the thirty-day option term be extended to one year. He delicately acknowledged the difficulty of discussing these matters by mail and offered to accompany the Russells on a return visit to Charlottesville if the owners deemed it advisable. Jordan thought that this might encourage the owners to welcome further negotiations.

The thought of displaying Walter's vast collection of sculptures, paintings, and works of art in the palace, where they could be shown publicly for the betterment of mankind by a self-perpetuating non-profit organization, clearly appealed to the owners. Jordan stressed that Walter's income from his writings was sufficient to provide for the couple during his and Lao's lifetimes. In early October the owners proposed extending the option on the same terms until April l, 1949, but fears that they could not meet the obligation induced the Russells to decline the offer.

They had relied on their friend Donald K. Vanneman of Chamblee, Georgia, to secure the bulk of the funding, assisted by a wealthy couple, Mr. and Mrs. Frew. Vanneman visited Swannanoa in mid-September, conferring on site and in nearby Charlottesville with Mr. Morris and one of Skyline-Swannanoa's major stockholders, Mr. Alvin T. Dulaney, Sr., a wealthy oil distributor and civic leader. After returning to Georgia, Vanneman wrote Dulaney to express sincere appreciation for the manner in which Dulaney and Morris were handling the Swannanoa transaction and to advise them that he had met with the Russells and some of their associates in Columbus, Ohio, following his trip to Virginia.

Vanneman seemed particularly flattered that Dulaney had offered to sponsor the Russells and Vanneman for non-resident membership in Charlottesville's prestigious Farmington Country Club, where they might entertain important visitors in the historic clubhouse partly designed by Thomas Jefferson. He reported that Mr. and Mrs. Frew had tentatively agreed to lend every aid and assistance in bringing the project to fruition, including providing estimates for the equipment necessary to heat the palace rooms that the Russells would be using. While Vanneman was at Swannanoa he had reassured the caretaker, who was concerned that any change in ownership might adversely affect her. Vanneman planned to meet the Russells in Charlottesville about October 25 to continue negotiations with the owners.

On October 14, however, Walter wrote Vanneman that it would be impossible for the Russells to continue working with him on the project because of irreconcilable differences in their ideas, plans, and motives. Vanneman had planned to sell his Georgia business and come to Virginia to manage Swannanoa, but his high-handed attitude at their meeting in Columbus had destroyed any hope that their working together at the palace would be harmonious. The Russells said they could not live with what they felt was his insistence on running things his way instead of theirs and told him he had made the entire Ohio meeting "one of combat and inharmony." This was in sharp contrast to their relationship with their longtime associates Clark Jordan, Gilmour Young, and George Gibson, who were present at the meeting and never mentioned titles, voting power, or comparative salaries in discussing the proposed organization.

Lao and Walter had intended that the Foundation be guided by a board of trustees, of which Vanneman was to be one, but their ten days with him in Ohio convinced them that by bringing him into management they would lose their own freedom to follow instructions given them by God in *The Message of the Divine Iliad*. Compromising with combative minds like Vanneman's in order to keep peace, they felt, would surely introduce material motives that would undermine the organization from the start. Walter reminded him, "Each day we were confronted with blueprints and formulas on pages of your yellow sheets on which you said you had worked late into the night. Hours of argument were spent upon these matters—hours which should have been spent in constructive planning. No matter how forcefully we refused to consider your self-aggrandizing plan which graded everyone in accordance with your concept of where they should fit in and what salaries they should draw, you would always bring out new sheets next morning to start the argument all over again." Vanneman had always listed himself as business manager and placed Hilda, his wife, as administrator. This had proven upsetting to the Gibsons, who were their hosts in Ohio and who were themselves likely candidates for the administrative roles at Swannanoa.

Vanneman had even questioned where the Russells should live and suggested that allocating one of the small houses as their residence would leave the entire palace available for exhibition purposes. The Russells knew that at Swannanoa they would in all probability be visited by dignitaries who could hardly be entertained in a cottage. They were also irritated that Vanneman had discounted offhand Gilmour Young's excellent suggestions. Their greatest shock came when Vanneman proposed that $10,000 be deposited in a regularly replenished discretionary fund to be kept in a bank in another city subject to checks of Vanneman, Hilda, Lao, and Walter with no accountability to the rest of the board. The Russells felt that for the four of them to be able to draw at will upon such a fund and replenish it from the Foundation without accounting to the others would be both dishonest and criminal. Vanneman's direct dealings with the palace owners and with the Frews likewise displeased the Russells. All of these circumstances led them to abort their prospective business association with the Georgian although they hoped that what they deemed a necessary business decision would not disturb "a highly treasured personal relationship."

With Vanneman relieved of responsibility, the Russells returned to Charlottesville with Clark Jordan, and at last an agreement was reached which allowed them to make a good faith payment of $5,000 and to occupy the palace in early November. They returned to Carnegie Hall with less than two months to arrange their move. It was a massive undertaking.

On November 1, 1948, they left New York and drove to Swannanoa. Lao described the condition of the palace in her *Love* book. It was a ruin when they arrived, and required more hard work than they had anticipated to restore it to livable condition and prepare the main floor for public admission. "Electrical connections had to be installed, pipe repairs made to have water and heat, windows restored, doorknobs replaced, and walls plastered. The grounds were a jungle." It had obviously been left to the elements for fifteen or more years. For thirteen weeks Lao worked eighteen to twenty hours a day to complete the minimum preparation while Walter restored sculptures that had long been in storage and completed numerous paintings. In addition, they worked together on several books in the brief six-month period prior to the dedication and opening.

In an interview several years later the Russells described their arrival to Edward A. Plunkett, a minister friend from the area:

> A heavy fog covered Virginia's Blue Ridge Mountains on November 2, 1948. Three large moving vans from New York City moved into the fog at the foot of Afton Mountain and began to grope toward its summit. At the intersection of U.S. Highway 250 and the Skyline Drive they left the highway and rolled onto the narrow, broken pavement of a long-neglected mountain road.
>
> Laborers, hastily recruited in the towns below, slashed away at a thick growth of trees and vines to clear the way. A man with a flashlight walked ahead of the vans to guide them through the weird mid-afternoon twilight.
>
> Only the remnants of a hard-surface road beneath the wheels of their vehicles gave any hint to the drivers that civilization had once been there. Had the fog been less dense they might have seen a summer cottage here and there, now boarded up for the winter. But the fog closed in relentlessly and they could see only a nightmare of tangled vines and low-hanging tree limbs.
>
> Suddenly the road leveled off and the strange caravan halted. As they looked out of their cabs, some of the drivers wondered if they had been bewitched. They had brought thirty-six tons of sculpture and other works of art from New York to a mountain in Virginia. Rising above the jungle-like wilderness was the ghostly outline of an immense marble palace.
>
> For three days, during which the fog seldom lifted, the men of the moving crew worked to move heavy cases of sculpture, paintings, and furniture into the dank, cold rooms of the palace.

On December 3 Alvin T. Dulaney, Sr., wrote Walter that Skyline-Swannanoa was arranging financing to cover the cost of the hotel it was preparing to construct near the palace gateway and needed definite information as to whether Walter would pay the required $35,000 payment on January 1, 1949. Walter had indicated that he might be able to do this in a visit that Dulaney, Morris, and their wives had paid the Russells at the palace just before Thanksgiving. This would have enabled the Russells to obtain an encumbered deed to the premises, but the title would rest in the name of the Walter Russell Foundation.

Dulaney also noted that there had been an article in the Waynesboro paper on December 2, 1948. The *News Virginian* article, written by award-winning staff writer Woodrow Stone, caused quite a sensation in the area. It filled the top two-thirds of page three of the popular newspaper with three large photographs and a banner headline, "Russells Turning Swannanoa Estate Into Art Lover's Paradise." Sub-headings in nearly as large type proclaimed: "Exhibition Is Planned April 2, 3"; "Widely Known Artist, Wife, Hold Option on Dooley Property."

While the article dealt principally with Walter's artistic achievements and seeming "quirks of destiny" that had brought them to Swannanoa and seemed to be "appearing as the days roll on," the initial paragraph stated clearly that the Russells had "secured an option purchase agreement on Swannanoa," and the concluding paragraph confirmed, "The Russells' one desire is to build what Mrs. Russell has named a 'Shrine of Beauty' where the whole world can come for inspiration. To this end they have dedicated their lives and possessions in building The Walter Russell Foundation which they are willing to posterity forever."

In the meantime their friend, Sherman Kiser, who was now enjoying his retirement, had feted his daughter at an expensive wedding, purchased a new car, and spent a winter vacation in Florida with his family. Yet he had failed to offer the Russells either physical or financial help in the monumental undertaking of their moving to Virginia. He still expected to be their general manager at Swannanoa, but in February Walter wrote to advise him that they had decided he should not be a working part of their operation. Chiding him for failing to provide any constructive help so far, they compared Sherman's inaction with the sacrifices their friends Gilmour Young and Clark Jordan had made to help them. "Knowing that Gilmour and Clark would do a hundred times as much if they could, we have gone through this whole great change alone ourselves," Walter told Sherman.

He related how he and Lao had done all the backbreaking work of writing hundreds of letters, writing the books, packing tons of sculpture and all of the studio things, moving to Virginia, unpacking, cooking, cleaning, and all other required activities themselves. "You could have helped very materially during that hard week of packing at the shop and the other ten days of packing at the studio, but you were playing tennis," he reminded his old friend.

The Russells had originally thought Sherman ideally qualified to direct day-to-day efforts to build their organization, but when they told him of their first problem, the immediate need of $1,500, he suggested they find a fundraiser and opined that God was testing them. They were hurt that Sherman had not even offered to pay the $100 difference between bus and train fare to save them the long cross-country bus trip from Oregon to Virginia when their time was so precious. Subsequently, before they finally left New York, he had discouraged them at every turn, suggesting that they should not assume the burden of Swannanoa without $100,000 in hand. All this made it obvious to Walter that the Message was a low priority with Sherman. He would always have a place in their hearts and a welcome in their home, but they were convinced he was not suitable to manage their business.

Walter felt that God was testing people as to their fitness for the work. They had come to Virginia with less than $1,000 and had managed very well. Lao had written hundreds of letters in a campaign that yielded several thousand dollars in book sales and numerous donations. Walter described her as "the perfect example of what it means by 'the Message coming first'," adding, "From the moment of her coming into it, her own desires and needs were secondary. Time and money—all she had—went to the Message. Money came from England for her living. She gave it to the Message with no surety whatsoever that it would not be lost. Again more of her money came, just as we needed it for the printer. Again another $5,000 of her money went to secure the lease and option on Swannanoa." Walter explained that he had personally met the same test over and over again. He had gradually let a very lucrative profession slip by during twenty-five years of grueling preparation for worthiness to deliver the Message to the world. He stressed that no one would ever know the self-effacement he had had to practice through the years to give the Message first claim on everything he possessed.

Walter and Lao had hoped to have George and Dorothy Gibson move to Swannanoa from Columbus, Ohio, to help manage the operation, but their budget could not bear the expense. They would not be able to obtain a release from Skyline-Swannanoa allowing them the use of any of the nearby cottages for at least two years, and they had no money to repair them in any case. The palace itself had been organized to accommodate their classes, offices, and bedroom. There were two extra unfurnished bedrooms that they felt obliged to hold in reserve in case they were forced to furnish and rent them.

It had cost an additional $3,500 to bring the last of the artwork from their New York warehouses. The first month at Swannanoa had swallowed an additional $3,000 in unexpected costs, including the purchase of twenty tons of coal and the clearing of the jungle from the very door. Walter described "the blood and sweat of it, the crying in the night from the agony of insecurity," the threat of losing the palace and all the sculpture and paintings, and having nowhere to go. Even in the first weeks they were obliged to entertain the curious but powerful local elite. They rented a used automobile, hoping to be able to purchase it in a few months.

On November 19 they met with Clark Jordan in the Charlottesville law office of Michie and Fishburne and signed the papers necessary to incorporate the Walter Russell Foundation as a Virginia non-profit organization. Walter was listed as president, Lao as corporate secretary, and Clark as the third of the corporation's three directors. The board held its first meeting at the same place on January 10, 1949, at which time Lao was named to the additional offices of vice president and treasurer and far-reaching documents were signed delineating an agreement by which the Russells committed themselves to transfer all right and title to Walter's artwork, archives, and books to the Foundation as soon as it acquired title to the Swannanoa estate. In the meantime the Foundation would assume stewardship of the collection and arrange for it to be shown to the public at the palace.

By late winter the progress they had made at Swannanoa was obvious. They had hired labor on a daily basis. They had cut down nineteen superfluous trees, and the jungle of undergrowth that surrounded the palace was fast disappearing. In late February Walter was proud to proclaim, "A ruin is becoming a well-groomed place, alive instead of dead, and important people are now entertained by our well-ordered fireside."

They had hoped to hold four monthly sessions of classes in 1949, beginning in April, with daily lectures and three-hour afternoon question-and-answer periods that would focus on giving students a constructive scientific foundation for the transition from sensing to knowing cosmically the source of all things. Walter would personally conduct the classes as the sole instructor. They announced their anticipated schedule in their first newsletter from the mountain, dated Valentine's Day 1949.

Their work at Swannanoa attracted publicity and aroused great interest throughout Virginia, but soon it was obvious to them that the house and grounds would not be ready for dedication until May. There was no alternative but to continue the struggle and postpone the celebrations. There would only be one month-long class at Swannanoa in 1949, and that was delayed until August. A brief seminar was conducted for a smaller group in October.

In later years the palace's furnishings included antiques that came from an era of wealth in Italy, in addition to an elaborate pearl-inlaid chest and several smaller pieces from Sun Haven. The high renaissance and Gothic revival were reflected in numerous impressive items carved by Walter, including his desk from Carnegie Hall, several matching pieces, and numerous

Gothic chairs. Highlighting every room were drawings, paintings, and sculpture reflecting Walter's versatile endeavors.

Future visitors to Swannanoa would see the Mark Hanna banquet table at the top of the double marble staircase. One of two elegant mid-European armchairs on the landing had come from Schoenbrun palace in Vienna and bore the petit point arms of the imperial Hapsburgs. Lao had purchased several additional rare pieces at the 1951 auction at nearby Mirador when Lady Nancy Astor's niece, Mrs. Ronald Tree, sold the contents of the famous Langhorne family mansion, where Lady Astor, Mrs. Charles Dana Gibson, and their sisters had been acclaimed at the turn of the twentieth century as Virginia's fairest belles.

Despite its appearance of great wealth, the Swannanoa Palace interior during the Russell era actually contained much comfortable but unspectacular furniture that Lao had obtained at less exalted auctions and antique shops around Nelson County and Charlottesville.

In April 1949, while the Russells were finalizing the plans for their dedication, Alvin T. Dulaney, Sr., died unexpectedly on the mountain. His automobile was seen near the palace entrance late one night, and upon investigation he was found dead in a nearby lake. He was an insulin-dependent diabetic who had slipped into a coma and fallen into the water while fishing. His son, James F. Dulaney, Sr., was the principal heir and the landlord with whom the Russells would deal through the next twenty-one years. Their relationship was often far from pleasant.

Virginia's popular former governor, Dr. Colgate W. Darden, Jr., president of the University of Virginia, dedicated the Walter Russell Foundation at Swannanoa in a festive ceremony and reception on May 2, 1949, calling it "a world cultural center for the unification of mankind through greater knowledge of God's Message." The Reverend Kenneth Anthony, rector of Waynesboro's St. John's Episcopal Church, gave the invocation.

68. Former Governor Colgate W. Darden, Jr., at the Swannanoa dedication.

By circumstance, just prior to the dedication ceremony, Walter received the news that his daughter, Louise Russell, had died in Connecticut.

The opening of a "one-man museum," set in a beautiful marble palace and classic Italian gardens, and the Russells' stated intention of some day erecting a 300-foot high statue of Jesus surmounting an equally high pedestal temple on the top of the mountain was national news carried in newspapers across the country. The sculptured five-foot model of the Christ statue and Walter's painting of the finished temple surmounted by the massive statue fascinated the 1,500 guests who assembled for the dedication. The Christ statue was intended to be higher than the Washington Monument when finished and erected.

The day before the dedication, on Sunday, May 1, 1949, *The New York Times* featured a three-column article with a two-column photograph of the palace under the headline, "Sculptor's Estate to Become 'Shrine'—Swannanoa, Mountain Home of Dr. Walter Russell, Will Be Dedicated Tomorrow—World Cultural Center in Virginia."

Announcing the fact that President Darden would dedicate the site as a "shrine of beauty" on Monday before an "invitation audience" of more than a thousand persons, the reporter stated that the Russell Foundation would immediately begin functioning officially as a "force for unifying mankind."

The article described the artworks on display in the palace and gardens, noting that the Russells' plans for the two-million-dollar estate include a 300-foot illumined statue of Christ as "The Light of the World," which, Walter stated, "expresses the central theme of our work here, as an example of the marriage of science with religion—shown by using light with Christ—[which] we hope will become a symbol to unify man for peace and happiness as against war and oppression."

Noting that many of those who had read Walter's books had expressed a desire to know more about their philosophy, Lao told the reporter that the Russell Foundation planned formal educational courses at Swannanoa and cautioned him, "We do not want Swannanoa to become just a museum. We want it to be a place of inspiration for all men, who will see that one man, working with God in one lifetime, can accomplish so much."

69. The Russells' receiving line, May 2, 1949.

Few of those receiving invitations declined to attend. Most were eager to see firsthand the work that the Russells were undertaking at the mountain palace.

In Waynesboro Lao had met the irrepressible Lucille Haney, who owned and operated Haney's Pharmacy with her husband and shone as the town's most extravagant hostess at her frequent cocktail parties and receptions at the local country club or the General Wayne Hotel. Lao had ventured into Haney's in search of neat's-foot oil and had quickly engaged in conversation with Lucille, whom she told she was now living in "the Little White Cottage on the Mountain." They were fast friends after that, and when Lao inadvertently omitted the Haneys from the special invitation list to the formal dedication, Lucille did not hesitate to write and remind her, "I do so want to come to the formal exercises on May second, but you have forgotten all about me, and now I find myself so audacious as to ask you for an invitation for me and my husband on that day. Please do not think me too rude. Believe me, I am quite embarrassed letting my desire tempt me to ask you. It would truly serve me right if you were not to send me an invitation." Of course, the Haneys received their invitation and for years counted themselves among Lao's close confidants in the town.

Lucille Haney was not the only person to ask for an invitation for that day. William Dilworth of Richmond wrote that he was one of the old servants of Major and Mrs. Dooley and had had the honor of serving them as butler for many years until Major Dooley died in 1923 and Mrs. Dooley died in 1925. "They thought very much of me, and I loved them both dearly, and Swannanoa always will be dear to my heart even though I may never see it again as it has haunted me nightly and has been in my daily thoughts even since I left there. After reading in the paper that it had sunk into disrepair from those who purchased it soon after Major's death, I could not help from weeping over the downfall of such a glorious place as Swannanoa. I have never gone back since I left in 1925. I don't think I could stand seeing it in the bad condition it was said to have been in, but after reading in the paper last Sunday that it had been purchased by you and the Madam and was going to be restored back to what it was and even beyond that, it filled me with so much joy and happiness I just had to write and tell you how glad I was to read such good news. I would really appreciate to be allowed to come up and see the dear place once more." Walter and Lao happily invited him, vouched for as he was by Mrs. Dooley's nieces in nearby Staunton.

There were always critics. Ten days before the dedication, a lady from nearby Fort Defiance wrote them after reading of their intentions in the Sunday *Richmond Times-Dispatch*. She complimented them on their philanthropy but urged them to substitute a quiet chapel with a small statue of Jesus for their projected gigantic Christ of the Blue Ridge. "A statue 300 feet high of clay, marble, or stone at close view would be grotesque," she complained. She reminded them of the Biblical story that Christ's disciples had failed to heal the child at the base of the Mount of Transfiguration because of lack of prayer and faith. "In place of the statue why not have a shrine as a memorial," she continued, "a small statue of Christ in a small chapel where travelers who wished to stop for a brief worship would find sanctuary on a

70. Walter and Lao relax at Swannanoa.

hallowed mountaintop."

Reaction like this came often through the years and constantly reminded Walter and Lao that they were in an area of conservative Christians, many of whom felt little inclination to listen to the Russells' scientific explanation of God's Universe and Jesus' ministry.

That Monday at Swannanoa left a deep impression on the large audience. A visitor from Maryland expressed her "appreciation and gratitude for the simplicity and beauty of the ceremony, the things you both said, the inspiring surroundings, an occasion we would never forget. We all felt that we had been spiritually as well as physically on the mountaintop, and it seemed difficult to bring ourselves back to the ordinary plane of existence. You have done a priceless thing in making this shrine possible for those of us who have done nothing to deserve it!" A student cabled them from the West Coast just prior to the dedication: "The chord of beauty you are sounding at Swannanoa will reach its crescendo as a great paean of light uniting the world."

71. Lao's blue brochure was used for half a century.

Virginia's poet laureate, Ruby Altizer Roberts, who had known Walter Russell since 1934 and written a dedicatory sonnet for the first edition of *The Man Who Tapped the Secrets of the Universe*, was present with many of her distinguished colleagues in art and society.

The widespread publicity the dedication received also reached the ears of Walter's remaining creditors in New York. William Jay Schieffelin wrote to remind him of the money he had advanced Walter in March 1944, adding, "The newspapers report your lavish philanthropies at Swannanoa. Your books present Spiritual ideals! Please send me a cheque."

Within months of the dedication they had

published the blue brochure titled *Romance of Swannanoa*. It described in Lao's glowing prose their personal story of how God had directed them to the mountaintop palace for the purpose of creating there a spiritual home from which the Message of Love could spread to all mankind.

"This is the story we have waited to tell you for a long time," she wrote. A professional photographer had taken aerial photographs of Swannanoa that they used in the brochure and to produce popular postcards.

Lao's magnetic personality worked its way with visitors to Swannanoa as it had in her dealings with others throughout her life. Two months after May 2 a lady from Philadelphia wrote her: "I am wondering if you will remember me. My visit to Swannanoa on the 4th of July has left a very deep impression—the clasp of your hand and the compulsion in your voice as we left when you said, 'You will be back!'"

Her letters proved very effective marketing tools. Charles Earley continued to praise them vociferously and suggested they be published. "What you say is better expressed than most of the literature on which these philosophies all rest. What you say is true, surely from faith, trust, and a personal relationship to God."

Many people who met them thirsted for more. Many who could spare the time volunteered to come to Virginia to help with the work. A young man from Ann Arbor, Michigan, wrote them three days after the dedication: "I am still too closely bound and deceived by this electrically conditioned and sensed world of ours, and so, if in any way I could give you my services at Swannanoa this summer and have some opportunity of learning from you, I should be overjoyed. As long as it is vitally imperative for me to work during the summer, I would rather do it at Swannanoa."

Lao had written Elsie and Bennie, the loyal couple who had comprised her resident staff at Sun Haven in Elstree, asking them to consider coming to America to work for Walter and her at Swannanoa. Benny's answer of June 2, 1949, gives an intriguing picture of the impression this faithful English couple had gleaned from Lao's letters and the photographs she sent of the palace.

"We were very interested in your new home. It is a most delightful place, and after reading all about it, and Dr. Russell, I think that you have a wonderful, kind and generous gentleman for a husband. I think that he is wonderful for the beautiful things he has created, and generous and kind because of the messages he has sent; and the interest he is taking in the welfare of what would be regarded by most men in his position as those silly little people in far away England. And you know, Madam, I feel quite a bit scared that I may not come up to his expectations. He may ask me to do something that I am not capable of doing, and he may think me a fool. But for all that I would risk it and come tomorrow if it were just me, but Elsie feels that she would like Anna to be just a wee bit older before we come. Would the offer still be open in say six months time? Could we bring enough money to furnish a little place? Would I be a personal servant, butler, chauffeur, or general handy man? Is there an army of other servants? The place looks so big and grand that we feel that there must be."

By early June the second volume of *The Message of the Divine Iliad* was still months from publication. Walter had received hundreds of subscriptions for the volume and was forced to issue a general letter explaining that the printer's proofs had only reached them when they were in the middle of "elaborate preparations for our opening and dedication. This important event in our history so fully consumed our time and energies that the proof reading could hardly be started until the great day took place."

Actually, as Walter later explained, when he and Lao finally felt they could give their concerted efforts to the proofreading, they became convinced that radical changes needed to be made in the book. The major change was the addition of a most important chapter entitled "The New World Thought," which he had intended to include in a third volume. He now believed that world conditions demanded its immediate release.

The second volume of *The Message of the Divine Iliad*, complete within itself, included "The Book of Love," "The Book of Beauty," and "The Book of Healing," three books describing God's nature and His means of manifesting that nature to man. Appended lectures treated many related subjects and outlined the need for a global transition to new world thought in human relations. After many delays, it was printed by Jarman Printing Company in nearby Charlottesville and was ready for mailing on February 1, 1950.

The Scientific Answer to Sex Promiscuity, reprinted from the second volume of *The Message of the Divine Iliad* and in some respects a precursor to Lao's *Love* book, lauded sex as the holiest of all God's laws and explained that every transaction in Nature is based upon the sex-principle. It was published separately at the request of physicians who wanted inexpensive reprints to give to patients whose nervous disorders and frustrations were based on lack of knowledge or unbalanced sex practices.

Lao replied to serious and important inquiries about their work with a concise explanation of the purpose of the Foundation and their present activities at Swannanoa, along with a packet containing one of the blue brochures, a copy of Dr. Francis Trevelyn Miller's letter praising *The Secret of Light*, and a copy of Glenn Clark's biography of Walter, which, she noted, "has been read by thousands of people all over the world." She stated that through *The Man Who Tapped the Secrets of the Universe* many world leaders had sought to familiarize themselves with the scientific knowledge that Walter was releasing yearly to the world through his books. "Dr. Russell," she wrote, "has had to prove through his life and works the power man has when he lives knowing his unity with God and His universe. He is the only man in the world today (or perhaps ever) who has proven himself master in all the five fine arts, and one day the world will be more aware of his great contributions in the world of science."

She generally included a sheet of excerpts from and brief reviews of Walter's books. She described *The Secret of Light* as "Dr. Russell's basic book which scientifically explains the nature of God and His electric wave universe of Light by means of which He manifests His all-knowing and all-power in forms of matter in motion. God's processes of Creation, which are ours also, are well-illustrated in diagrams which fully explain these processes in as simple words as possible." She stressed that *The Message of the Divine Iliad* had been "released for the purpose of helping mankind make the transition from his past ages of sensing all things materially to knowing all things cosmically," adding that the book contained knowledge given to Walter in his 1921 illumination in which he was directed to prepare a message whereby man could comprehend the underlying principle of all creation. This knowledge of people's relationships one to another and to God was described as the sole means by which the unification of mankind could be achieved and a climate of world peace maintained.

Walter seldom read other people's books. Since his first illumination at the age of seven, he had felt that he could differentiate truth from falsehood. When he opened a book to a paragraph that the cosmic in him told him was untrue, he closed the book. He felt that so many books that people read consisted of information oriented into symmetrical patterns to please the eye, ignoring the truth that good design begins with unbalance extended in repetitions until an unbalanced line assumed the beautiful symmetry of a crystal.

On the other hand, he had learned early that a masterpiece could not be written quickly. During his entire life he wrote and destroyed much of his work, only to rewrite it after the next annual illumination. After the extensive illumination he received in 1921, he wrote *The Universal One*, an effort that took him until 1926. He had printed a limited edition of 1,000 copies and distributed many of them to the leading scientists and philosophers in Europe and America. When the edition was exhausted, he refused to republish it, instead working twenty years to rewrite it into the simpler *The Secret of Light*, which he proclaimed "one fifth as long but a thousand times better." He was quick to tell those who asked that giving form to an immortal concept was a time-consuming effort requiring skill, technique, design, composition, and mathematical expertise.

He continued: "God illumines one in a timeless flash. I thought I could tell the whole story of Creation in three minutes after my illumination. I actually wanted to get the scientists of the world together to tell them that their very foundations were not in conformity with Nature. What a foolhardy thing that would have been. The simplest story is the hardest to tell."

He recognized that Lao had followed much the same path. "My beloved Lao wrote profound thinking all of her life and tore her writings up because she thought they should be better. She intuitively knew that the Source of her writings was cosmic, but God would not let her publish a word of them until she ripened her thinking with the sunlight of knowing. Not until then was she able to cast off the influences which caused her to fit her writings into her traditional training instead of freeing her from them. Now, at the age of forty-four, she is arriving at the masterpiece stage, and her two books should be out next year."

72. The first summer class at Swannanoa, 1949.

The first class at Swannanoa was held in August 1949 and consisted of students from thirteen states and South West Africa. Lao was pleased with the initial enrollment and felt that the August classes "went off perfectly." Three students could only stay for one week, and one remained for two weeks, but twenty-four of them participated in the entire month-long program. "We have a very fine group of students," Lao wrote Bessie Fourton, "and we know that they will go out into the world and spread the Message most effectively."

So successful was this intimate seminar that classes were scheduled the following year for June, July, and August. Dr. Russell was seventy-eight, but he seemed indefatigable, encouraged as he was by Lao, who always saw to his comfort and that of the students.

The 1949 class set the pattern for future years and consisted of four weeks with daily lectures followed by question-and-answer periods. Afternoons and weekends were left free for reviewing lessons and working individually on the "transition from sensing to the New Age of knowing all things cosmically." The gardens and palace were open to students all day and evening, and recorded organ music filled the air from the palace towers.

Lao took great care in arranging facilities that would be suitable to students of all means and all ages. Special arrangements were made at nearby hotels and tourist homes from which daily transportation to the Palace was provided. Tuition itself was only $100 for the entire month. Bessie Fourton and Florence Spaulding spent most of June and July at Swannanoa helping Lao with preparations. Bessie's exuberance was contagious. "You are the champion bookseller," Lao wrote her later. "I always smile when I picture you taking the students aside and telling your story."

Some of the students were succinct in their assessment of what they learned. "I came up to see a marble palace and found the answer of my lifetime," wrote one.

Another, from Des Moines, Iowa, gave a detailed account of her 1949 experience in the Russell classes. "The class was conducted very much as any good physics instructor would conduct a class in Chicago University. We studied God, Light, Electricity, and the laws governing them. There was not a single experience during the entire four weeks disappointing, or that we had any desire to be changed."

Lao knew that personal contact with Walter Russell added greatly to the student's grasp of his writings. "I grieved as a child that I did not have an opportunity to see Jesus," one student wrote, "and I always regretted that I did not take the opportunity to see Mary Baker Eddy. Anyone who is really interested in Dr. Russell's message should not miss an opportunity to see him or be in his class. The next best thing would be to study his writings earnestly and take work under one of his students."

The impact of that first class at Swannanoa was profound. A Florida doctor called it "the opportunity of a lifetime." A Texas physician marveled that "it was some time before all the mass of knowledge I got there began to systematize within myself so I could talk about it."

"The mountain top of my awakening" was fondly remembered by an Oklahoma student, while clergymen from Kentucky and Washington, D.C., respectively termed the experience as "out of this world" and the beginning of "a new era in my life."

To the question as to whether the students were "peculiar" or what type of work Dr. Russell offered, the student from Des Moines was reassuring in her description: "There were no mental, physical, or spiritual calisthenics and absolutely no suggestion of any oriental occult practice." Interestingly enough, another student praised the course for allowing her to expand her horizon and enabling her to read intelligently and knowingly for the first time the religious teachings of the Orient.

Their first year on the mountain had seen the completion of the second *Iliad* volume and the preparation for publication of Walter's popular meditations, *The Book of Early Whisperings*. Some of the *Early Whisperings* manuscripts had been lost and forgotten for years and were found by Lao packed away with Walter's papers. She felt that they belonged to the world and insisted on their publication in early 1950. *The Book of Early Whisperings* immediately struck a responsive chord with hundreds of readers. Lao had anticipated that it would evoke memories of the readers' own early treasured communions with God.

When Bessie Fourton wrote Walter in March 1950 to thank him for sending her an inscribed copy of *The Book of Early Whisperings*, he promptly replied: "Your letter of appreciation has been here several days. You thanked me for sending it by addressing the letter to me, but I do not deserve the thanks. It was Lao who thought of it—for she is ever thoughtful, and I am not. It was she who wrote you and did up the package with her loving hands. Therefore it was Lao to whom you should have written, not me, except as an accessory. In fact, the book would never have been published except for Lao, for she collected the manuscripts and had it done. She attends to our worldwide correspondence and manages everything wonderfully. I am just not much good at that—hence I am the very luckiest 'dog' in the whole world, for without her skillful management and good judgment in relation to policy I would be at sea and make so many mistakes that we would never recover from them."

In the meantime the Russells received many fully paid enrollments for their long-anticipated *Home Study Course*. This yearlong curriculum of forty-eight lessons was still in preparation. It would replace the projected next three volumes of the *Iliad* and attract thousands of students over the coming years.

While the volume of tourism at the palace over the first year of their residence had been severely disappointing, there were encouraging signs. Many students journeyed thousands of miles to visit the Russells at Swannanoa. Over 200 people toured the palace on the last Sunday in July. Lao noted it was their "biggest day yet" and was pleased to report, "Book sales were good, too." Labor Day weekend in 1949 drew even larger crowds to the palace, largely the result of an article published in late August in *The American Weekly*, the result of material Lao had sent the editor months before in response to a telephone call. Letters and book orders came from all over the world in ever increasing numbers.

For many local people in Waynesboro the inspiration of that dedication day soon passed, and it began to dawn on the traditional folks of the Shenandoah Valley that the palace on the mountain was now the home of two people most unlike the conservative, less cosmically oriented folks who populated the area near Swannanoa in the late 1940s.

There were striking scenes the locals recalled of Walter stopping in the record shop to pick up an album of '78s, going into the sound booth to hear several others, and absorbing himself in music, oblivious to the fact that Lao was driving around the block waiting for him to return.

The Russells soon became the talk of the town. Waynesboro was not accustomed to seeing a beautiful woman in flowing silks alight from a large sedan and enter the post office or a local bank. Sales clerks were dazzled when Lao entered their stores and even more fascinated when she proved to be knowledgeable as to quality and not at all indifferent to a bargain. Folks looked across their blue-plate specials when the Russells dined at the Southern Restaurant, in those days the city's only establishment listed in the better travel books.

There was much exaggeration in the town gossip. The Russells were reputed to be multimillionaires who entertained famous movie stars and the Duke and Duchess of Windsor atop the mountain. Lao herself was reputedly a cousin of the English royal family. She and Walter were said to spend their mornings meditating in the opposite towers of the palace.

For a season or so in Waynesboro it was quite the current thing to pass around copies of *The Man Who Tapped the Secrets of the Universe*. Lao's own first book, *God Will Work with You But Not for You*, was a bestseller in the local downtown gift shops after it achieved national success in 1955. Soon these books passed from local vogue, and the awe of the locals grew jaded.

No adult group was ever formed in Waynesboro to study the Russells' works, and even if some forward-thinking chemists and scientists passed photostatic copies of Walter's long out-of-print masterpiece, *The Universal One*, among the Wilmington-Camden-Waynesboro DuPont laboratory circuit, the fact remained that the Russell books were locally little read and not altogether respected, despite the fact that in later years most area brides received at least one copy of Lao Russell's *Love* book as a wedding present. It was the classic case of prophets being without honor in their own country.

73. Lao dressed for the 1950 Waynesboro Cotillion.

Perhaps the most striking and pitiful example of the mixed hospitality the Russells received in Waynesboro occurred early their first year at Swannanoa, when they were invited by the local Cotillion Club to a formal dance at the new country club. Lao arrived in a Parisian-cut red evening dress that dazzled the men and provoked the ladies, and she and Walter were warmly greeted. But they had not come alone. A young, dashing, European gentleman, whose elegant manners and movie-star looks evoked thoughts of the decadent aristocrat or even the gigolo, accompanied them. At a break in the dancing, Walter came forward and clapped his hands, announcing to the crowd,

"Now if the orchestra will play the tango, my lovely Lao and our guest will perform the dance for which she won the prize on the Riviera," and soon the startled folks of Waynesboro society were treated to a tango that might have come right out of Hollywood.

For years the people at that cotillion—or many of them—dined out on the story of poor, elderly Walter Russell, oblivious to the fact that his beautiful young wife and her male friend were carrying on an affair right under his eyes. It became a staple part of local gossip that grew more seasoned with the telling, and many an exaggeration made the ever-widening rounds of regional conversation. Those who knew better were too few to counter the rumors and could only defend the Russells with charity and kindness whenever the matter came up. The truth of that cotillion night and much-discussed tango was entirely innocent.

As busy as they were, the Russells had been happy to be asked to the cotillion, but at noon on that very day a friend of Walter's, a professional dancer from Europe whom Lao had never met, telephoned to say that he was in Washington and wanted to drive down to Swannanoa for a visit. The Russells brought him with them to the dance. Walter knew that Lao had danced the tango years before at Juan les Pins to the acclaim of all who saw her, so he stopped the music and asked them to play a tango for his wife and their guest. Lao recalled, "We did our best, although it was the first and only time we ever danced together. He left the next day, and I never saw him again, although I often wondered what the local folks thought about the tango."

The main factor that caused a cordial chasm to develop between the Russells and the town was the need the Russells felt to spend every waking hour with matters of more importance than mixing in local society.

Their impact on people who encountered them briefly at Swannanoa could be life-moving, and they used the same approach in meeting the natives. They respected merit in people, not wealth, prominence, or so-called aristocracy. They reached out to people in pure and simple kindness. Lao particularly would encounter the shyest person in the group, bring him or her to the forefront, and draw out the radiance of a long-sheltered soul.

Often it was the deliveryman, hairdresser, woodcutter, or the sales clerk in the downtown store who came in contact with the Russells in the ordinary course of everyday work and saw then and there the real beauty of their presence. These modest, hard-working people often retained a fierce loyalty to the dynamic couple.

One seldom heard criticism from local residents who knew the Russells. The critics were people who had only heard about them.

CHAPTER ELEVEN

Courses of Action (1950-53)

Arthur Winslow McGrath of the Sun Center, West Falls, New York, considered Jesus to be the connecting link between the unknowable and the knowable. His physical description of the man from Galilee was well authenticated by reports on Jesus sent to the Roman Senate by the Roman Legion. After reading *The Message of the Divine Iliad*, McGrath urged Walter to create at least one more great work of art. McGrath felt that Walter was the one artist skilled and enlightened enough to bring forth the true image of Jesus Christ either as a painting or statue. He wondered why Walter had not already done it.

In fact, for nearly a year, beginning in mid-1949, Walter and Lao had been working together in the main hall of the palace on the full-scale clay model of their great figure of Jesus. Their conception of Christ was different from most. They knew he was a carpenter and that in those days the profession took muscle. Walter felt that the moneychangers in the temple would have thrown Jesus out instead of being forced by him to leave the hallowed precinct if he had not been muscular and strong.

74. The Russells in the palace hall with the clay model of their Christ statue.

Dr. Christopher Howard, Lao's physician friend in England, wrote of his delight at the great success they were achieving at Swannanoa. The fact that they were sculpting the Christ statue together convinced Dr. Howard that he had indeed been correct in predicting that Walter and Lao would come to realize that Jesus was the only power in the spiritual world. "You used to laugh at me and say there was nothing to choose between all the other prophets because they all reflected in their differ-

75. Friends gather as the plaster casting of the Christ is placed in the gardens.

ent ways the Glory of God," he reminded her, adding, "I don't believe that you still believe that." Lao knew that this friend of her early years would never fully embrace the Russells' Message.

A thirty-foot casting of their Christ of the Blue Ridge was erected in the center of the palace gardens and dedicated on July 29, 1950. Before a distinguished audience, Lao consecrated it "to the principle of Love and the Unity of Man, which Jesus gave to mankind as a Truth by which all men could live together forever in the peace and happiness of world brotherhood."

Major General E. Walton Opie, editor and publisher of the *Staunton News-Leader*, extolled the occasion in a widely reprinted editorial, "A Statue of Christ on the Mountain," in the August 1, 1950, issue of the newspaper: "With the first throes of World War III upon us, it seems a fruitless time to be erecting a statue of Christ on Blue Ridge Mountain in an effort to emphasize His adjuration, 'Love ye one another.' That's what Dr. and Mrs. Walter Russell are doing at Swanna-noa, however, with abiding faith that another war will be but an interlude in man's slow rise to the heights of the Sermon on the Mount."

General Opie described the previous Saturday's dedication ceremony with eloquent praise, noting the "deep sincerity [that] marked the expressions of the noted sculptor and his wife as they told how God had brought them to "the sacred mountain" to erect the statue of the Redeemer as the Light of the World." He added, "There was a note of cheer in Dr. Russell's dignified statement at the very well-attended dedicatory exercises. Contrasting man's progress since the coming of Christ with his thousands of years of barbarous living, he said that great progress has been made toward attainment of the Christian

76. Walter and Lao at the dedication of the Christ statue, July 29, 1950.

precepts. He confessed confidence that in spite of periodic wars and persistence in selfishness, in spite of failure to live by the Sermon on the Mount, mankind will move on toward brotherhood and love." The editor described Lao's consecration of the statue "forever in the name of love" and her stated hope that "it always be a symbol of peace."

Walter told the audience that Lao had inspired him when he was seventy-nine to undertake a sculpture that would present Christ not in His traditionally effeminate appearance in sculpture and painting, but as a man strong in physique and character. "In this he has strikingly succeeded," General Opie reported. "His Christ has a noble, uplifted head, a countenance of love, and a body which bespeaks power."

"The lovely statue in the gardens is now being called 'The Christ of the Blue Ridge,' and people are planning holidays here from all parts of the country," Lao wrote Mr. McGrath.

A few months later columnist Howard Sizemore described his own experience in the Swannanoa gardens in his popular column, "Country Folks," written for the *South Boston Record-Advertiser*, a widely-circulated Southside Virginia newspaper: "I worshipped God Sunday, not in a church, but on a mountain top. And it was one of the deepest, most inspiring periods of worship I have ever experienced. I spent an hour at Swannanoa, the Shrine of Beauty on the Sacred Mountain, four miles this side of Waynesboro, Virginia.

"As gorgeous and wonderful as Swannanoa palace is, the greatest thing about the place now is the soul-stirring statue of Christ which has been created there by Dr. Walter Russell. The 30-foot praying statue of Christ now stands in the beautiful garden back of the palace. It was there in this garden, all alone, that I worshiped, as I looked into the love-filled face of the Christ statue, and as I listened to the beautiful music of the great old hymns coming from the loudspeaker in the palace tower. I marveled at how Dr. Russell had brought such an expression—such a countenance of love and compassion into the face of the Christ statue. It seemed almost unbelievable that something so human-looking, and at the same time, so Divine-looking, could have been created by man."

77. The Christ of the Blue Ridge.

Most of those who admired the newly dedicated Christ statue felt its greatest manifestation was yet to come. They embraced the Russells' vision of a bronze replica of the statue, 300 feet tall, to be erected atop an

78. *Aerial view of palace and gardens, 1951.*

equally tall "Temple of Light" on the highest point of the mountain. It would symbolize Christ's message of love, day and night, for thousands who passed by Rockfish Gap and for others throughout the region.

There was no let-up in the pressure on the Russells, but Lao was determined to see that Walter husbanded his strength. When Bessie Fourton arranged an invitation for him to give a free lecture at Virginia's prestigious Hollins College, an outstanding school for women, Lao insisted that he decline, reminding Bessie, "We must concentrate our entire efforts on producing funds now, and long-range good will is something for future consideration." Bessie was willing to uproot her family and move to Swannanoa to join the Russells' staff full-time, but Walter explained the realities of their situation to her: "Our own plans are uncertain, for things are pending which may alter them materially. We have not taken title yet and must raise a lot of money to do so. Until we own this place, we must not have anyone pull up their grass roots for us. It may be five years before we feel stability enough [for that]."

In summer 1949 Peter Parker and his sister Emelia came to visit the Russells at Swannanoa from New Jersey. Peter, a successful commercial artist, had purchased a copy of *The Man Who Tapped the Secrets of the Universe* for a quarter from a used bookshop in Manhattan. He and his sister, who was a professional court reporter, were awed by the book and at first sought out Walter Russell at Carnegie Hall. When they learned that the Russells had moved to a palace in the Blue Ridge Mountains of Virginia, they drove south to meet them. From the very first the four of them became close friends. Soon after returning home, Emelia wrote to tell Lao how much they were enjoying *The Book of Early Whisperings* and to volunteer her limited spare time to help with clerical and editorial work. Soon both Peter and Emelia had enrolled in the *Home Study Course.*

Emelia Lombardi became Lao's closest friend over the decades the Russells spent at Swannanoa. She was also devoted to Walter. In 1950 Emelia had the joy of helping Lao furnish portions of the palace from Richmond and Charlottesville auction houses and antique shops. She later helped the Russells edit the *Home Study Course* revisions and their many subsequent books.

79. Arthur and Val Thompson.

Among Walter's early students who remained close to him and Lao during the years at Swannanoa was a remarkable couple, the Arthur VanRensselear Thompsons, who had been reared in great wealth. They were devoted to the Russell work. In 1937 the doctors had given up Valborg Thompson as incurable and soon to die. Five years later, her husband reported, "she is a well woman. We owe her recovery to right eating and right thinking."

Desiring to pass this knowledge on to others, in 1941 they had remodeled their barn at Boxwood Farms, Mendham, New Jersey, made it their modest but comfortable residence, and turned the mansion and estate into an unusual health farm that they operated on a non-profit basis. They still had sufficient income to live on, but on cool nights they delighted in gathering fellow Russell students to discuss the many phases of what the Thompsons called "right thinking." They believed the solution for the world's inequities could be found in Edward Bellamy's *Looking Backward*, which they felt depicted a society based on Walter Russell's philosophy. "It is obvious that a great change has to come," Mrs. Thompson said. "We've seen what money does to our class." She felt that her fellow rich people had become intolerable by 1929, snobbish and selfish. "In 1932 they were making frenzied last dashes to the banks which were closing," she recalled, adding, "Now that most of us have lost everything material, we are beginning to be pretty decent." The Thompsons became close friends of Emelia and her brother, and years later, when the widowed Val Thompson died, she left a unique archive of early Walter Russell items to Emelia, who subsequently bequeathed them to the University of Science and Philosophy at Swannanoa.

Lao's Scottish terrier Jinnie, whom she had brought to the palace from New York, died in the fall of 1949. Students wrote to sympathize with Lao. They knew the dog had been a loving friend and that she was grieving her loss, but Lao kept closely in touch with important New Jersey and Virginia breeders of Scottish terriers, and at Swannanoa she would never be long without a beloved Scottie. By springtime the next year, Wendy was the terrier in residence at the palace.

Lao's health was deteriorating, and she consulted their friend Dr. J. F. Vannerson, who prescribed hormone therapy but was concerned when she failed to react satisfactorily to the estrogen tablets he prescribed for her. Convinced that she had no malignancy, he altered the treatments and temporarily succeeded in bringing her system into chemical balance. He believed that the frustration and disappointment Lao had experienced in the past contributed to this imbalance. Her intense mother love for Jinnie and the grieving that followed the dog's death caused a change in her system, the doctor told her. He treated her with varying doses of both the male and female hormones and natural B-complex vitamins.

The Russells learned from Gilmour Young that his so-called "Northwest Headquarters" of the Walter Russell Foundation in Seattle, Washington, was in serious danger of collapse. His key associate, Mrs. Nugent, had left the headquarters after allegedly antagonizing many students. She had grown incensed when Walter and Lao had written that they could not come to Seattle in November as planned. "This information made [Mrs. Nugent] boiling mad, for she had been planning to turn your stay at her home into a gala social event of afternoon teas and receptions with lots of publicity (her name in the papers, etc.), all of which would have worn out both of you," Gilmour reported. Her dream of reflected glory shattered, she profanely demanded that the key study group members be called together for the purpose of closing the headquarters, but the seven-member executive committee unanimously rejected the proposal. Although shaken financially, the Seattle group continued its work, attracting additional students and selling the books and course. "Because of the loyalty of the majority of our Study Group to the Message and to you both," Gilmour continued, "the tempest did eventually fit snugly in a teapot."

The first announcement of *Universal Law, Natural Science and Philosophy: A Home Study Course* was issued in October 1950 with the promise that it would provide students with the master key to the attainment of great heights of power and happiness by giving them awareness of their unity with God and their oneness with His creative processes. Walter was positive that the knowledge revealed in this intimate course would teach students to govern their own way of life and improve their home, profession, and business lives, as well as their personal relationships.

Although the course as published attributed authorship solely to Walter, this omission was rectified in the second edition and thereafter when Lao was listed as coauthor. In any event Walter made it clear on many occasions that they had written the *Home Study Course* together. In 1950 he was the clear focal point of their work, an acclaimed genius in the eyes of the public. Lao was not well known and had yet to produce her own bestselling first book. It is understandable why they chose to launch the course under Walter's name alone, although from the very first Walter seems to have regretted this omission and desired to recognize Lao's significant co-authorship.

They intended to issue the one-year course in monthly mailings of four lessons each, but the Russells launched their charter enrollees on the vigorous curriculum when no more than two-thirds of the twelve units had been completed and published. The initial students received their first unit in December 1950, but the twelfth unit was not ready for mailing until June 1952. Thereafter, however, the course was given on the more regular twelve-month basis. Enrollment was open at any time, and the four-lesson units were mailed once a month for an entire year.

Unit 1 dealt with meditation in all its ramifications, offering the student a definition and scientific explanation of what the Russells termed the key to "working knowingly with God" and seeking to stimulate the reader to awaken his or her own genius through the power of idea and the glory of the unseen and unheard. Meditation technique was carefully delineated, as was the individual's ability to use the process to create. In these first sixty-six pages of the course, the fundamentals of the light-wave universe were broached, and the student was introduced to concepts of God and Man as Light, the love nature of God, and the truth that all nature manifests love. In short, the unit brought the neophyte face to face with the world of imagining in all its limitless power. Their preferred form of meditation was decentration, a practice Lao described by analogy by telling their students that when one decentrated, one became, in direct proportion to the degree of decentration, less aware of the body and more aware of the all-inclusive Light.

Lao's longtime mentor from Boston, Eleanor Mel, director of the Boston Home of Truth Divine Science Center, was ecstatic when she received the first unit. She termed it "a masterpiece, crystal clear, enlightening, and illuminating," and doubted that anyone reading it could fail to understand the power, joy, results, and absolute necessity of meditation. She promoted the course among her students and proclaimed it as "evidence of [the Russells'] perfect awareness of God." She predicted that the course would naturally appeal to the scientific mind because of its inclusiveness and explicit truth. "I understand perfectly that you have brought it forth because of your ability to keep so aware of God that He works through you and with you as you work with Him," she wrote them, uncannily suggesting the future title of Lao's first great book.

As the *Home Study Course* was released, Glenn Clark wrote to tell them that he was reveling in it and felt that they were truly spreading light from heaven. Jay Katz, a chemist and Russell student, established the Foundation's scholarship fund in 1952 to pay tuition for students who could not afford to take the course. Many subsequent donors joined in to enlarge this fund and make possible free or reduced tuition for low-salaried people, ministers, and students from countries from which money could not be sent because of government regulations.

Unit 2 focused on prayer, its relationship to meditation, common misconceptions regarding its purpose, appropriate techniques, and its usefulness in striving for cosmic consciousness. The unit included a dramatic account of Walter's 1921 illumination. Unit 3 taught the student the first principles of cosmic thinking, deeper meditation, the reality of the sexed electric Universe, the role of opposites in a two-way radial cosmos, and the means of achieving an understanding of the Universal heartbeat. Unit 4 treated God's Law of Balance in a divided Universe and explained the source of all energy. At each juncture the Russells provided postulates, axioms, and answers to anticipated questions in order to facilitate the student's understanding. Unit 5 explained the fulcrum and the lever, the power of stillness, and illusion in the making. Now the student took the first steps toward understanding what the Russells termed "the supreme mystery of life and death." By this point, the persevering enrollee had completed twenty lessons in 350 pages and encountered a new approach to traditional concepts of the individual, God, and the Universe as they include, affect, and encompass each other.

In December 1950, the Russells' work was carefully described in *The Ushers Bulletin*, a widely distributed weekly publication of New York City's Riverside Church, whose famous minister, Dr. Harry Emerson Fosdick, often quoted Walter Russell from the pulpit and had visited them at Swannanoa. They attracted attention from unexpected quarters. Archconservative evangelist Gerald L. K. Smith of St. Louis congratulated them on exercising their spiritual gifts in the most constructive manner.

The Message was spreading around the world. New Thought leaders in Helsinki, Finland, circulated *The Secret of Life* and both volumes of *The Message of the Divine Iliad* in governmental and scientific circles there. They urged the Russells to arrange for their books to be translated into other languages for those unable to read English. In Helsinki a state geologist, an engineering publisher, and a local physician were all absorbed in Walter's work and eager to enroll in the *Home Study Course*. Lao sent photographs for one of the Finnish students to use with an article on the Russell work at Swannanoa published in a popular Helsinki journal.

The Russells spent Christmas 1950 at Swannanoa hard at work on completing the *Home Study Course*. They had made the acquaintance of a family in St. Louis that would play an important role in expanding the Message. Arthur J. Jones was an executive with the May Department Stores. He and his wife had shared a deep interest in the Russells' work for several years, and Walter and Lao had entertained them at Swannanoa. Dr. Bowan Jones,

Arthur's son, was a talented massage therapist and naturopathic physician who for seventeen years had helped many patients through the House of Health, his professional center in St. Louis. He wrote Lao that he had never been as uplifted or inspired by anything as by the course. He showed Walter's first personal letter to him to his father, and Arthur's comment was that the "letter is worth the cost of the whole course." Walter Russell called Bowan the most enlightened student he had ever taught.

80. Swannanoa summer cottage, the Russells' retreat.

Arthur Jones made a substantial down payment on the summer cottage behind the palace gardens. The Foundation acquired this inviting retreat from the heirs of the late owners, a Mr. and Mrs. Miller. Lao furnished it comfortably, and it became a treasured retreat on Lao's daily walks. She hoped that Emelia and Peter and their mother would some day be happily ensconced there.

By early 1951, Emelia began sending generous monthly contributions to the Foundation. The first such donation paid for printing the invitations and programs for the first Easter Sunrise Service. It was held at 6:00 A.M. on Easter morning, March 29, 1951, in the shadow of "The Christ of the Blue Ridge" in the palace garden. The local ministerial association conducted the service, assisted by local choirs and churches. More than 2,000 people attended on what was a bitterly cold morning. Lao realized that in the next few years Easter would come on a later date when the temperature at sunrise would likely be warmer, and she immediately decided to make the Easter service an annual event. "Jesus looked glorious as the sun shone on His face, and it was a beautiful sunny morning although terribly cold. I know we shall have some beautiful Easter Sunrise Services here in the years to come, and we are hoping that next year you and Peter will be here," she wrote Emelia. Later in the year Emelia sent another sizable donation, which Lao used to purchase a carload of coal, two tons of which she sent to the summer cottage. "Whatever else we lack this winter," she wrote her generous friend, "we shall have heat!"

By Unit 6 the *Home Study Course* students were ready for deeper thoughts of life and death as motion and to understand the type of knowledge that made one the master and not the servant of matter. Energy was demonstrated to be in mind and not in matter. Cosmic illusion was dispelled by an explanation of the one reality, and the student was taught the power of self-control. Unit 7 sought to simplify the concepts already taught and bring the student to a full appreciation of what the Russells called "the universal balance wheel." The immutable law of cause and effect was brought to bear on common misconceptions regarding the efficacy of prayer and faith, but the true value of faith and belief was stressed. Unit 8 stressed the spiritual significance of electric polarity, the unity and oneness of all creation, the illusion of disappearance and reappearance, and the concept of reincarnation, which the Russells termed "the supreme mystery of the ages."

Occasionally the Russells ventured off the mountain for public appearances. Their friend and insurance broker, J. R. Goodwin, Jr., induced them to speak jointly to the Salem Kiwanis Club on April 5, 1951. He owned a large burial park in Salem, Virginia, and later commissioned sculpture from Walter for the park. The Goodwins saw that the Russells were splendidly accommodated at the gracious Hotel Roanoke nearby and introduced them to many prominent civic and business leaders in southwestern Virginia. Among these was Norman R. McVeigh, president of the Mick-or-Mack grocery chain, who contributed financially to their work, read their books, and vowed that they had taught him an increased sense of love for his fellow man and respect for the potential of every individual, including himself.

They worked closely with a large and successful group of Alcoholics Anonymous members in nearby Charlottesville, who found that the Russell lessons buttressed their twelve-step program and saved many of their members months of torment. "God is seeing that His Message is received by many who can do much good in our poor old world," she told their students.

The next month they were invited to Portsmouth, Virginia, by Frank Lawrence, a leading banker and founder of the Virginia Athletic Hall of Fame, who had asked Walter to deliver a major address at the Portsmouth Civic Center on Armed Forces Day, May 19, 1951, Walter's eightieth birthday. An audience of 10,000 was present. This was the Russells' introduction to the heavily populated Tidewater area, and their hosts saw to it that they met the leading citizens of Portsmouth, Norfolk, and Virginia Beach. Walter's speech was carried on radio throughout eastern Virginia. Many who heard it had anticipated a speech that would excuse America from any blame in the Korean conflict, but Walter addressed the causes and dangers of war and the sane alternatives. As one listener wrote, "to hear such forthright honesty was indeed reassuring."

Walter's address that evening followed a day Lao described as "one we shall always remember, for so many unusual happenings took place to stamp it on our memories." Earlier in the day they attended a luncheon given in their honor at the Officers' Mess at the nearby Norfolk Naval Shipyard, with

Rear Admiral David H. Clark, USN, as their host. Walter was not aware that he was scheduled as the main speaker at the luncheon, but his impromptu remarks recounting his own experiences as an honorary Lieutenant Commander in the Navy as artist to the fleet during the Spanish-American War proved so entertaining and full of his natural wit that it left the luncheon guests convulsed in laughter. He emphasized the differences he saw between America's white squadrons of 1898 with its largest guns eight inches in diameter and the giant gray American fleets of 1951 that had so recently won a world war on two oceans.

Walter's speech that evening was titled *The Dawn of a New Day in Human Relations: Why Men Wage War on Each Other and How to Prevent It*. The speech synthesized the themes that would prove so popular as Unit 9 of the *Home Study Course*. The day afterwards the telephone lines at Mr. Lawrence's American National Bank in Portsmouth were tied up by people asking for copies of the speech. A committee of leading citizens was formed to see to the speech's publication, and in the interim the bank officials decided to dedicate the bank's advertising space in the area's daily newspapers to print the entire address in eleven sections over eleven days. Thousands of copies of the booklet were distributed on request by Frank Lawrence, who received complimentary letters on Walter's remarks from some of the leading businessmen in America.

Lao took ill shortly after their return to Swannanoa. Earlier she had consulted gynecologists in Staunton who advised her to enter the hospital for surgery, but she had delayed seeking treatment until after the Portsmouth trip. She endured a successful uterine operation on May 23, followed by ten days of recovery in the hospital and weeks of recuperation at home.

Dr. Bowan Jones offered to come to Swannanoa when he heard that Lao had been hospitalized. He wrote her regularly during her convalescence and reassured her that her busy schedule would not impede her recovery. He told her that she knew better than he did that the body gives vitality only in proportion to what is demanded of it.

Lao's sister Florrie, now enjoying a happy seaside retirement with Harry French on England's southern coast, wrote to cheer her, promise her a certain recovery, and tell her to "keep smiling through." The approach of the busy summer season at Swannanoa cut her convalescence rudely short. Walter had finished the rough draft of four

81. Arthur and Adele Jones with their son, Dr. Bowan Jones.

more home study lessons, and it was essential for Lao to review and edit them. They had given the students an intermission of three months for the summer season while Lao recovered from her operation. Students were due to arrive for the summer sessions. "My Knowing will have to keep me going," she told Emelia.

Members of the Swannanoa summer classes generally kept in touch with one another through the rest of the year by means of round robin letters and proved the nuclei of many study groups across the country. Miss Brick and Miss Boyer, two ladies from Des Moines, attended the Swannanoa summer sessions every year and helped establish several study groups in Iowa, advertising their exuberance at the Russell Message with the exclamation, "Nothing known to man compares with the freedom, health, and joy one may find in this new life!"

Lao's old friend Marie Cassin, now widowed and eager to leave postwar England for America, sailed for New York on the *Queen Elizabeth*. Emelia met her at the dock on July 26, gave her a warm welcome to the New World, and drove her to Swannanoa. Emelia stayed on for the summer classes and helped immeasurably as usual. Lao felt that with Marie as her fulltime assistant she would finally have someone suitable to help with operating the office and managing the palace staff.

Labor Day was hectic, following the end of the second year of August classes, but Lao at once went back to her writing, telling Emelia that she planned to write a book about Dr. Russell that would appeal to the businessman as much as *The Man Who Tapped The Secrets of the Universe* had appealed to the metaphysician. "Doctor's name will appear in the title since it matters not about my name not being known," wrote Lao. Throughout the years at Swannanoa, Lao and the staff referred to Walter affectionately as "Doctor."

After their initial *Home Study Course* students had completed eight units encompassing thirty-two lessons and totaling nearly 600 pages, the Russells interrupted the course's progressive explanation of the Cosmos to provide their students with a special human relations unit. They deemed this 100-page digression of vital importance given the world situation at the time. It was a remarkable guide designed to help mankind set right global, national, local, and individual wrongs.

Lao had grown enthusiastic at the prospect of bringing their new ideas and teachings into industry. Unit 9 explained how this could be accomplished. The methodology, based on Walter's heralded work with Thomas Watson and the employees of the International Business Machines Corporation during the 1930s, lay in bringing higher ethics into human relations. Lao thought that every city and town should form a center of people from all walks of life to focus on the task. Soon, she envisioned, the national organizational effort would be so demanding that it would provide Peter Parker a suitable position with the Foundation, providing him an opportunity that would challenge him, suit his sensibilities, and take him all over America. In late October 1951 they sent advance copies of Unit 9 to Emelia and Peter and eagerly awaited their response. It was highly favorable and greatly boosted Lao's spirits.

Somewhat apocalyptic in tone, the unit stressed that "knowledge alone can save the human race from another dark age." Recognizing that the world had never known peace and that mankind seemed on the verge of destruction, the Russells posited unity in the home, industry, religion, and personal relationships as the basic root of a balanced civilization. The catastrophes of the first half of the twentieth century were used to demonstrate the accelerating degeneracy of civilization. Aggressive cooperation must replace cutthroat competition, the Russells asserted, citing effective measures by which labor could be taken into partnership with management, public service could translate the brotherhood of mankind into reality from the local to the international level, and higher ethics could infiltrate public, private, and individual transactions. Warning their readers that nature never bargains but always balances, the Russells told them that the world was at the eleventh hour and that civilization's disintegration could in the long run only be averted by universal, definitive use of the golden thread of sharing.

Unit 9 was issued in early November 1950 to a limited audience but soon engendered overwhelmingly favorable reaction. Within two weeks of the mailing the Russells began receiving wonderful letters about it. In a matter of months, study groups were formed in many states, and extra copies of the individual unit were much in demand. Walter and Lao urged their students to circulate it, telling them, "We have no time to lose. You are one seed. Every seed lost from inaction means a lowering of the world harvest." The entire Arthur Jones family had enrolled in the *Home Study Course*. Arthur Jones believed that the power and overwhelming logic of Unit 9 made it the most potent message available and sought earnestly to interest his fellow businessmen in what he deemed its enormous potential.

Writing Unit 9 had brought both Walter and Lao to the point of exhaustion, but they had been so fired with its urgency that they persevered until it was finished. Once it was printed and mailed, Lao faced mountains of back mail to answer and no time to get a newsletter out before Christmas. Physically they were both at the end of their strength. They were too busy to take their daily walk together, and when they did, Walter grew so faint he could hardly get back to the palace. Increasingly he experienced dizziness. Lao had never fully recovered from her operation and suffered continual colds, sore throats, and ear infections.

The tenth home study unit was nearly completed. Lao had sent Dr. Russell's Armed Forces Day address to *Reader's Digest* and *Saturday Evening Post*, but neither reprinted it. She was eager to get his name before the public in big letters again.

Emelia spent much time at her New Jersey home transcribing tapes of Walter's lectures and preparing mailing labels for use in mailing out monthly lessons and articles for possible use as radio scripts touting the Russells.

82. Dr. Howard Walter Lavender.

Dr. H. Walter Lavender, a prominent chiropractor from Fulton, New York, enrolled in the *Home Study Course* and wrote to express his enthusiasm for their work. He told them he had considered gravity as the omnipotent power, as he had been taught that everything in the universe, unless restrained, flows inexorably from an area of higher potential to an area of lower. Walter Russell's suggestion that had Sir Isaac Newton waited long enough, the apple that fell from the tree would have ascended again as other atoms, made common sense to Dr. Lavender, who reported he had gained much in his quest of more light from Walter's *Book of Early Whisperings* and *The Message of the Divine Iliad.*

Dr. Lavender soon visited the Russells in Virginia and became an important supporter both financially and personally. He served on the board of directors for twelve years, and he led other healers to the work.

In 1951 a nationally known clinical hypnotist came to Swannanoa and drew inspiration from the Russells' idea of applying Universal Law to Christ's Sermon on the Mount. He agreed with them that modern educators had been lax in devising methods for widening the range and acuity of human perceptions by relying solely on verbal educational techniques.

The palace staff, as usual, gave Lao problems. Marie seemed satisfied, as was the elderly housekeeper, but the latter's husband, Lao reported, was as lazy as ever and full of complaints. Lao felt sorry for his wife, but noted "there is little one can do to help her for she spoils him and allows him to hurt her far too often." Lao believed he had only married her to have someone to care for him when he lost his traveling job. Their friend Mr. Goodwin had located a maintenance man for them in Salem, a man strong enough to fire the furnace, a job no one else at the palace could perform. Lao hoped that seeing the housekeeper's husband sitting around idle would not spoil the new man. She also worried about the accelerating expense of a growing staff.

In November the Russells again felt a desperate need for additional staff.

The housekeeper had gone, and Dorothy Vannerson, a student from Arizona who had spent five weeks at Swannanoa the previous summer, agreed to return. She was easy to be with, would cook, clean, and do anything to help, and was devoted to The Message. Lao offered her the same salary she was paying Marie, although Dorothy generally declined payment for her work. Marie looked better than when she had arrived from England, but she had recurring stomach pains and was still having trouble adjusting to her new situation. Still Lao hoped for the best. She knew that the cheerful and versatile Dorothy would soon have the palace housekeeping well in hand. The new man from Salem would do the heavy cleaning, and the others could open the mail, fill book orders, and handle new course enrollments whenever the Russells were away from the palace. If they took a brief vacation, Lao would send all the courses out before they left and do it again on their return.

Walter and Lao issued Unit 10 and wrote their students that the next two units would be delayed for several months. They promised that Unit 11 and Unit 12 would follow as early as possible in 1952. "So heavy is our work at this time that it may not be possible to send further personal greetings on Christmas Day," Lao added, "so we are enclosing with Unit 10 a copy of The *Sea Children Waltz*, composed by Dr. Russell when he was fifteen years old."

Unit 10 focused on the unending cycle life and death, the illusion of the senses, and misconceptions of intelligence. It emphasized spiritual strengthening and the relationship of man and woman. The student was taught thought mechanics and shown how the individual may multiply himself into a transcendent being through cosmic knowledge.

They also issued *The Scientific Answer to Human Relations, A Blueprint for Harmony in Industry*. Essentially a reprint of Unit 9 of the *Home Study Course*, it argued for friendly, fair dealing among nations and businesses, describing the benefits all mankind would reap when balanced interchange replaced avarice in government and industry.

Lao's relationship with students taking the course was deeply personal. She worked late into the night virtually every night corresponding with each and every student, helping them adapt the Message to their own immediate needs. "Only ones with great souls and love for humanity would spend so much painstaking effort to give knowledge to others," wrote a Texan. "From the very first lessons I have felt your loving friendship for me, as well as for all humanity."

Enthusiastic students who completed the course found themselves reluctant to break off their connection with the University. The handsome graduation certificate was a poor substitute for continued communication with the illuminates at Swannanoa, and they generally implored Lao to keep them on her mailing lists and advise them of future classes and publications. Frequently they wrote to ask further questions as they read and reread the books and lessons.

When a new student perceived that the course was too complicated for the average person to understand, Lao always took time to encourage the student to persevere. An Ohio enrollee expressed "dismay at the contents of the lessons," noting that "since about the fourth or fifth manual when the complex explanations began, I have not been able to understand it." Lao promptly replied, telling the dismayed student that another letter she received in the same mail had reflected a very different reaction to the course. Lao shared the more positive response with the unhappy correspondent. The other student had written: "I freely confess that I shall need to study these lessons over and over again for I am not an enlightened one, but I hope at least I am one who is climbing the ladder of understanding. Sometime, even though it is not in this life, I shall find the enlightenment I seek."

On July 8, 1953, Lao wrote a letter headed "A Response to a Needlessly Discouraged Woman." It read in part:

> In our teachings, all through our *Home Study Course*, we say that each one makes his own destiny. He can be what he chooses. You made your own destiny; you are what you chose to be, and if you are unhappy with your choice, you can turn your rudder around and steer toward another goal. That you can only do for yourself. We cannot do it for you. All we can do is what we have done for our thousands of discouraged students whom we have helped to become utterly transformed by giving them the knowledge that awakens their own genius powers within them. If you had that knowledge you would not ask encouragement from us or any other person. You would know how to meet it and replan your destiny along newly desired lines.
>
> The spiritual development of man comes through his ever-increasing culture or descends if his culture descends. Man's culture comes from world geniuses and mystics whose inspirations are direct from God through the interpretations of nature's rhythm. Inspired geniuses do not get their music, art, literature, and poetry from séance rooms. Their inspired works do not come through ascended masters or other unnatural creatures. The great mystics such as Jesus, Buddha, Lao Tzu, and Confucius, or Plato, Socrates, or Shakespeare are directly inspired by the Creator, the One God. We speak to you thus frankly. We have no desire to sell our books to those who expect to be helped abnormally. We look forward to the day when mankind will recognize the divine spark of his own inheritance and awaken to the realization of his own divinity and the source from which his spiritual unfolding stems.

Lao urged the discouraged student not to despair at being unable to understand "all that you read in your first year's study of the lessons. Many students have said ours is a lifetime's course of study, and they always say that each time they re-study it, they understand a little more that proves invaluable to them." She always emphasized that whatever comes easily seldom produces much gain. She told students that no one should expect to sit and play Rachmaninoff after a first piano lesson.

83. Lao relaxing on a Florida beach.

By now Walter and Lao desperately needed the peace and tranquility of a vacation. They had followed through on one huge project after another for five years straight without rest. Just before Thanksgiving 1951, they drove to Fort Myers Beach, Florida, and spent the month of December there on the oceanfront at Hotel Rancho del Mar. They kept busy, and the days slipped by. Lao cooked all their food. To eat out was expensive, and restaurant food was not as wholesome as they desired. They avoided going out for even an occasional meal.

At first they were homesick. The weather was not too warm and they wished they had stayed at Swannanoa for Christmas, but when they remembered how badly they needed the change and how necessary it was for them to escape the tension of daily routine, they soon extended their stay until January 17. When they arrived in Florida, arthritis was crippling Walter's knee, and Lao suffered from an infected ear. After several weeks of rest and lying in the sun, enjoying daily massages that invigorated them both, Lao had recovered, and Walter seemed much healthier. This pleased Lao greatly for she knew they needed to fortify themselves for all the work that lay ahead.

They were delighted when one of the Thomas Edison family's friends in Fort Myers told them that Walter had captured the likeness and feeling of Edison in his sculpture and painting to an extent far above anything else he had seen. He arranged for one of Walter's busts of the great inventor to be shown at the Edison house in Fort Myers where thousands of visitors could enjoy it annually.

They kept in close contact with the three staff members left behind at Swannanoa. These loyal employees had faced an unusual problem. Wild dogs had killed several deer within sight of the palace. The game warden offered them a gun to use in shooting the dogs if they came near again, but neither Dorothy nor Marie would use it, and John announced that he could never kill a dog. "We're not a very killing lot," Dorothy wrote Lao.

On the Russells' return to Virginia in late January 1952, they found a full agenda awaiting them. The last two units of the *Home Study Course* and a newsletter needed final editing, after which they hoped to go to New York to meet with their old auditor on accounting matters and to inquire about the cost and feasibility of having their foundry manufacture small replicas of Walter's sculptures.

Lao found that their time away had had a disastrous effect on business. The volume of mail had been reduced to virtually none. Emelia had anticipated this and had sent a loving letter and substantial contribution to await them on their return. Lao wasted no time in returning to her busy work schedule, but the change in climate was physically hard on Walter, who went outside without scarf or gloves on their second day home and soon contracted a lingering chest cold. His coughing disturbed their sleep for weeks. Lao worried, but he had no fever, and she felt that with proper care he would soon be well.

Students in Boulder, Colorado, were among many who asked them their opinion of L. Ron Hubbard's new book, *Dianetics*. Their friend Dr. Raymond L. Nimmo, a Fort Worth chiropractor who had attended summer sessions at Swannanoa for two years, was also investigating this book to see if the Scientology techniques it contained could effectively restore memory loss. None of the inquirers seemed to think that *Dianetics* conflicted with the Russell cosmogony, and although they had many Scientologists among their students in the years to come, the Russells never embraced Hubbard's teaching as an adjunct to their Message.

Dr. Nimmo recommended the Russells' work to the editor of *Scientific American* magazine, calling it "the answer for a vast number of people." He chided colleagues who considered the Russell lessons too difficult and turned instead to "something easy, like Shakespeare," suggesting that they meditate on a sentence from *The Secret of Light* for six hours or a week as he had done. Dr. Nimmo recalled that Dr. Albert Einstein had always emphasized that the generalizations of philosophy should have a scientific basis. "Dr. Russell has given philosophy such a basis." Nimmo told the editor. "He has made a philosophy of science and a scientific philosophy one thing. I wonder why this man is overlooked by science. I wonder if the reason could be that he is not 'academic' or that he is an outsider."

A Detroit osteopath thanked them for clarifying prayer for her as no one else had ever done. Students likewise expressed eagerness to learn how to increase their intuition, which the Russells described as "mind awareness concerning the destiny of one's idea" with no physical or emotional disturbance, sound or visible presence, merely knowing without question. A Christian pastor in Arizona told them every minister in the world should be a student of their course of lessons. "I am constantly finding in it marvelous inspiration for sermons," he wrote. In six months he had doubled the membership of his own congregation.

A Unity Center leader from New Jersey found that Walter's admonition, "Never ask of anyone before asking God," seemed to offer people a fresh start. Twenty-year Rosicrucian students from Colorado wrote that the Russells' *Home Study Course* provided them with "flash after flash" of inspiration and led to a definite improvement in their health, nerves, and work.

The same was true of longtime Christian Scientists across the country who found the course helpful with their healings. The fact that the Russells proclaimed church founder Mary Baker Eddy to have been a super-genius did not escape her church members' attention, and many enrolled in the Russell course, although the Christian Scientist Church only sponsored lessons and materials officially issued by its mother church in Boston. Walter and Lao understood their position, recognizing that the denomination was dedicated to the sole purpose of bringing Christian Science to those who were receptive to it and could not be expected to partner formally with the Walter Russell Foundation. Lao applauded the success of Christian Science schools and realized the reason for their effectiveness, although she admitted she had not studied their curriculum carefully.

Members of a small prayer and meditation group in Kingsport, Tennessee, wrote that for the first time in their lives, after studying the course, God became something more than a far-off, unreachable being. A California teacher told them that if every schoolteacher in the world would live by the logical statements contained in their course, "we should soon have a world peopled with those who live to love instead of to grab." Students also suggested that the Russells prepare a beginner's level course for businessmen who never pray or think about their spiritual nature. They agreed that truth must be introduced at the individual's level of understanding.

Lao received a large shipment of furniture and personal items from England, mostly furniture and objects d'art she had stored with a cousin near Ivinghoe after selling Sun Haven. Ruth Colbert in Portsmouth, Virginia, found beautiful silver platters and a set of flatware for Lao to purchase to replace items that had been sold in 1938 or stolen from Sun Haven or storage during the war years. Emelia and Lao continued to explore the antique galleries of Richmond and Charlottesville and brought bargain-priced rarities back to Swannanoa. The palace was regaining some of the glory it had boasted in the years when James and Sallie May Dooley had occupied it.

The Russells paid more and more attention to their diet and found a new food supplement called Nutrilite to be a virtual brain food, improving their vision, energy, and strength. Nutrilite consisted of the best of alfalfa, water-cress, and parsley, grown on specially treated organic soil. Students urged them not to undertake more than their strength would permit. Lao seemed indefatigable even with her midlife health problems, and Walter's vitality and heavy schedule of activity astounded those who noted it.

Their friend, the Reverend Ross H. Flanagan, was one of the earliest traditional ministers to agree with the Russells' disavowal of faith healing and "useless affirmations in the hope and belief that God would work magic at request," stressing that he shared their feeling that many loyal orthodox Christians misread Jesus' admonition to "Ask, and ye shall receive" by not recognizing that the phrase was coupled with the admonition to "Seek, and ye shall find" and "Knock, and it shall be opened unto you." They all believed that Jesus meant for the three words, "ask, seek, and knock" to be taken together, and that wishful thinking alone was no substitute for personal action when it came to handling problems.

They frequently met and corresponded with students of the late Edgar Cayce, the famous clairvoyant who had died at Virginia Beach in 1946. The Russells found that their own philosophy appealed to many Cayce students, and they were well-acquainted with the Association for Research and Enlightenment, the Cayce organization at Virginia Beach, as well as with its leaders and authors, including Cayce's son, Hugh Lynn Cayce, who cheerfully gave Cayce students the Russells' address and suggested that those interested write directly to Swannanoa to purchase their books.

Through his Metaphysical Forum in Lacey, Washington, Elmer W. Shaw was conducting a class on the *Home Study Course* with an enrollment of twenty-two students. Their motto, "We serve those who seek with us the truth that sings within," complemented the Russells' own purpose statement, and their members regularly ordered virtually all of the Russell publications. "Paradoxically, although I am the youngest one of the whole group," Shaw wrote them, "I will need many years of preparation yet to attain the high goals I have set for myself." Walter had written a foreword for Shaw's own privately published book.

Easter was April 13, and Lao again in 1952 scheduled a special Sunrise Service at Swannanoa, sponsored by the Waynesboro Chamber of Commerce and ministerial association. It was well attended. By then it was obvious that their planned New York trip would have to be delayed. They were working hard to complete the *Home Study Course*, but the final unit proved a greater challenge than expected. Lao was still behind in answering her mail in spite of writing stacks of letters every day.

Mrs. Bailey, a wealthy widow whom Emelia had sent to Swannanoa to see Walter's sculpture, complained on returning to New Jersey that she liked the teachings but found the Russells cold. Lao told Emelia that Mrs. Bailey had given the impression that she wanted everyone to make a great fuss over her and was disappointed when no one did. Her husband had left $5,000 for a colossal monument to be erected at their grave. Such a sum would at best pay for a simple casting. Mrs. Bailey was quite uninformed as to what it would cost to have such a large finished sculpture made.

Merrian Jones had arrived at Swannanoa in early May. A sweet, quiet girl with beautiful red hair, she was the daughter of Arthur and Adele Jones, the Russells' major friends and supporters from St. Louis. Lao felt that Merrian had led a frustrated life to date and thought surely romance would come to her at Swannanoa. She and her sister-in-law Geri planned to run the gift shop in the tower cottage and live in the summer cottage adjacent to the palace gardens. Geri was a virtuoso pianist although she had not had ready access to a piano for eleven years. Merrian remained at Swannanoa through the fall and then left for Fort Lauderdale where she planned to work with elderly folk.

Emelia and her brother Peter came to Swannanoa to help celebrate Walter's eighty-first birthday on May 19, 1952. It was Emelia's birthday month, too, and the Swannanoa group feted both of them. Ever the matchmaker, Lao felt that Merrian Jones was the perfect girl for Peter Parker. Neither of them agreed.

By mid-June the final units of the course had been completed, printed, and mailed to students. Walter and Lao shared the hope that the time was ripe for the scientific world to recognize their new cosmogony, but despite the fact that new enrollments were received in every mail, such recognition was slow in coming.

Unit 11 focused on the inviolate law of rhythmic balanced interchange, the fundamental axiom of all creation. Advanced knowledge of pressures, energy, and motion was presented along with simplifying explanations and examples. The Russells described the "cosmic cinema," explored the four-dimensional universe of time and curved motion, and led the student to an appreciation of the cube-sphere wave field. Far from theoretical, the practical importance of the unit was demonstrated in examples as vital as the meaning of interchange in breathing.

Unit 12, the final unit, brought the course's scientific and philosophical premises to focus on "the greatest of all lessons, the supreme question and mystery of creation." The expanding-contracting, two-way balanced universe was explained in its complex ramifications and awe-inspiring simplicity. Earlier lessons were reinforced. The mystery of curvature, the making of matter, the significance of radii or so-called magnetic lines of force, the nine octave cycle, elements and isotopes, inert gases, universal mathematics, and atomic physics all were brought into cosmic symmetry as the student reached the ultimate realization that knowledge is the one universal power. The course concluded with a summary of new concepts for cosmic man. Those who had traveled with the Russells through the entire forty-eight lessons had enjoyed a remarkable journey.

Emelia sent special donations to help defray Lao's personal expenses, but Lao knew the secret of looking stylish without spending much money on clothes. "I shall wear my old sweaters again this winter," she wrote her friend, noting, "Doctor loves me whatever I wear. I never feel I should spend anything on us personally." Nonetheless, she took Emelia's advice and bought two white suits. Adele Jones had sent her a fine dress from St. Louis for the delayed trip to New York. Their journey was quick and their mission successful, although their schedule there left little time for socializing. On their last night they joined a number of old and new students and friends for a final evening on the town at an elegant Manhattan restaurant. By July 9 they were safely home.

The Russells were still paying off the rental account that remained due on their old Carnegie Hall studio. Clark L. Jordan helped negotiate the settlement of other debts Walter had left behind in New York.

It exasperated Walter to be quizzed by his readers on the extent of his formal education. In asking Lao to respond to such a letter from a Mr. Berry on August 13, 1951, he said, "Tell him I never went to a university nor even finished grammar school. Tell him also that university degrees given to pupils who can answer examination questions correctly are numerous, but degrees given for work performed are few. Edison and hundreds of others who have proven their worth to mankind could not get an earned degree from a university. For that reason the Academy of Sciences was formed to give such honors to those who had earned them." That academy, which Lao noted had as full authority from the State of New York as any university, had granted Walter his doctorate of science on November 21, 1941, for his work in hydrogen that led to the discovery of heavy water, among other things, and for his chemical charts and new Periodic Table of the Elements, which had also led to other important discoveries.

She related that previously for seven years over a period of twenty years Walter had been president of a similar organization, the Society of Arts and Science, which awarded degrees to Edison and others whom the universities would have excluded. That Society had also given earned medals to Robert Millikan, A. E. Michelson, Harlow Shapley, and many others. "I personally set no value upon unearned degrees," Walter wrote. "I have eleven such honors in all and have earned every one of them."

Emelia planned to attend the August classes, and Lao hoped her friend would meet the love of her life among the surprisingly large number of men who had signed up to attend the sessions. She asked Emelia to bring Hildegarde Burmeister to Virginia for the classes. Hildegarde had attended Walter Russell's lectures and read his books since 1946. She had met Lao in New York before the Russells were married and had often helped Lao at Carnegie Hall in those busy days. Lao, who never forgot true acts of friendship, considered her selfless and kind. Hildegarde had come for the 1949 dedication of Swannanoa, after which both she and Lao had been too busy to correspond regularly with each other. Hildegarde's own hard work and considerable talent had made her decorative arts gift shop in Jackson Heights, New York, a resounding success. Lao was eager for Emelia to meet her. The two drove down together, arriving in time for the opening dance at Swannanoa on August 6. Doctors and nurses from the local hospitals had been invited to join the students for the occasion.

Lao had worked for weeks to prepare for the students' arrival and was busy with preparations until the last minute, but the week before classes began she and Walter felt obliged to attend a party hosted by Lucille Haney, one of their first Waynesboro friends and the city's premiere hostess. There were some occasions on the local social calendar that even the Russells did not choose to miss.

In late August Lao's pet canary Dickie died, much to her sorrow. Walter made a cast marble casket for him and carved a little bird on it. The incident reminded Lao of Walter's advancing age and mortality, and she asked Emelia to promise her that if Walter should die first, Emelia would come to help her carry on the work. By now Emelia had met and was dating John Anthony Lombardi, a successful young New Jersey attorney, and Lao already envisioned their being married at Swannanoa with Emelia walking down the great marble staircase on Walter's arm. She told Emelia that they would give them a reception at the palace to introduce them to the townspeople and that John could open a law practice in Waynesboro. The bridal couple could live in the summer cottage and enjoy a grand life of simple tastes with the mountain providing all the fruit, vegetables, chickens, and basic necessities needed in palace or cottage. Emelia brought her fiancé for his first visit to Swannanoa prior to Lao's birthday in November. He greatly impressed the Russells. John and Emelia returned again at New Year's to join their friends in welcoming 1953. Afterwards

84. John and Emelia Lombardi.

John wrote Lao a joyful letter, crediting her with giving them the best beginning to a new year that he had ever experienced. Emelia and John married and paid many visits to Swannanoa, but their wedding took place in New Jersey and they never moved to Virginia.

After their marriage, John and Emelia generally committed every available holiday weekend and vacation to the Russell work. They were early officers and directors of the Foundation. After a few years Emelia's dedication to the Russells grew too intense for John, who wanted to start a family, and they agreed upon an amiable divorce. Emelia continued to serve as a Foundation director and was secretary of the successor University until some ten years before Lao's death. She and Lao spoke virtually every week by telephone, and she visited Lao frequently at Swannanoa through the years. At great effort Emelia worked to maintain her beautiful home in Far Hills, New Jersey, often suggesting to Lao that it would be available as a new headquarters for the University in the event that Lao should ever be forced to leave Swannanoa. She served as executor of Lao's estate, editor of their unpublished work, and promoted the Message until she died, some eleven years after Lao, leaving nearly a million dollars to the University.

In September 1952 Andrew Wilson, the Scotsman who had visited Lao at Carnegie Hall just before she left for Nevada, came to Swannanoa and spent all day taking tape recordings about Walter's scientific contributions. There was continuing trouble on the staff. Marie refused to get up early and grumbled about everything. She berated Dorothy for not being downstairs to help greet visitors, even when the tourist flow was slow and Dorothy was busy scrubbing and dusting. Another staff member was a wonderful cook when she was not drinking but tended to go off on four-day binges. Marie quit on September 22 and took a job at Martha Lawrence, Waynesboro's couture dress shop. From then on she caused trouble for the Russells. She wrote their mutual friends in England that Lao was mentally ill and had

85. The Russells host a buffet on the Mark Hanna banquet table.

buried her dog Jimmie in the Christ of the Blue Ridge statue. She also told them that when the canary died, Lao had gone into hysterics for three days. None of this was true, and it provided a sour ending to their long friendship.

On November 7, 1952, Lao received the Mark Hanna banquet table from a student in the Midwest. It thrilled her. "It proved the most beautiful old table I have seen on this side of the ocean, and it just fits on the balcony facing the stained glass window. Opened it is about eighteen feet long." Given by a Hanna descendant, the table came with the admonition that just as Mark Hanna had gathered around it with the leaders of America in the interests of the country at the turn of the century, so, too, should the Russells strive to bring the leaders of the world around it to work for the cause of peace.

The Swannanoa Christmas greeting for 1952 was a photograph of Walter and Lao and a copy of the sheet music for Lao's song, "Swannanoa." Both were well received. For months students wrote Lao, complimenting her on the song and reporting their delight in displaying both pictures of Lao in their homes. The photograph of Lao on the sheet music cover had been taken on her forty-eighth birthday.

Harry French died the day after Christmas 1952 at Bournemouth, Hampshire, in the south of England. He left their home at Bournemouth to his beloved Florrie, whom he described in his will as his late secretary and friend. The house in Dunstable was left to his long-estranged wife Eva for her life, and the balance of his estate went in trust to Florrie and Eva for their respective lives and afterwards to his son John French.

In early 1953 the Russells' mail was encouraging. A California student had forwarded *The Dawn of a New Day in Human Relations* to a Texas philosopher, who ordered fifty copies for distribution among his friends. Winter that year was relatively mild, although a January storm prevented the Russells from accepting an invitation to a gala affair in Portsmouth hosted by their friends the Frank Lawrences.

Their 1953 newsletter reported publication of a special edition of *The Russell Cosmogony*, a small volume Walter had published prior to completing *The Secret of Light*. The new edition had been printed for scientists in general and as a thirteenth unit for students who had completed the twelve units of the course. Soon *The Russell Cosmogony* was being confirmed in many places. A New York student wrote that one of the chief scientists at Bell Telephone Company in New York had concluded that no matter existed in the entire universe, only electric potential, all of which convinced Walter that his science was becoming more accepted in the mainstream of advanced research.

The Russell Cosmogony was being read across America, and an Indianapolis student had sent it to her son in Saudi Arabia, who shared it with local scientists and leaders there. The Guttersons in San Francisco became ardent students of the Russell Cosmogony as soon as it came to their attention. They promoted the course successfully and urged the Russells to have the forty-eight *Home Study Course* lessons recorded in Walter Russell's own voice on the newly popular long-playing phonograph records or wire and tape recordings. Walter never found time or stamina to accomplish this major project.

Questions came in virtually every mail, some none too pertinent to their teachings. One student inquired, "Sometime I would like to ask you or Dr. Russell if it is possible for a person to work on another planet while asleep?" Another student had in mind that since the sun makes a circuit once in 25,000 years, taking in each sign in the zodiac through which it takes the sun about 2,000 years to pass, it could be accurately calculated that an individual experiences a new beginning on a regular schedule. She wanted a precise answer to the question, "Do we come back at stated intervals and is the interval 25,000 years or 2,000 years?"

Walter's books prompted unexpected reactions from some readers. A leader in the group of scholars who believed Sir Francis Bacon had actually written the plays of William Shakespeare was so impressed with the Russells' assertion that any student could claim all knowledge for his own simply for the asking that he inquired, "I recall vividly the sentence Francis Bacon wrote as a young man: 'I have taken all knowledge for my province.' Are you he in a later reappearance? My other question is to ask if you have the knowing of whether Francis Bacon is the author of Shakespeare's plays or not?"

Their efforts to reach high government officials yielded some results. A student distributed a dozen copies of *The Man Who Tapped the Secrets of the Universe* to the director of the United States Treasury and members of its international finance division. Lao was cheered by a letter from a student highly placed in the outgoing Truman administration who told of the broad circulation the book had been given among top cabinet members and high functionaries.

Lao was much taken with President Eisenhower's Inaugural Address on January 20, 1953, particularly when the war hero President stated, "In the swift rush of great events, we find ourselves groping to know the full sense and meaning of the times in which we live. In our quest of understanding, we beseech God's guidance. We summon all our knowledge of the past and we scan all signs of the future. We bring all our wit and will to meet the question: How far have we come in man's long pilgrimage from darkness towards light? Are we nearing the light—a day of freedom and of peace for all mankind? Or are the shadows of another night closing in upon us?"

Salvatore Gibilaro of Bridgeport, Connecticut, saw to it that Dr. Edward L. R. Elson, the new president's personal minister, presented copies of the Russells' Message personally to the great world leader. Lao believed that President Eisenhower would find that the answer to his earnest inaugural plea had already been given in Walter's *The Secret of Light*.

CHAPTER TWELVE

From the Castle Threshold (1953)

As February 1953 drew near, Walter and Lao were preparing an important letter that they intended to send to world scientists, political leaders, and major theologians. Only a few of their inner circle were aware of its ramifications. "As the time grows closer for the transmittal of your letter," John Lombardi wrote, "my thoughts and prayers for your every success are increasingly with you."

Soon after the *Open Letter to the World of Science* was issued, the Chairman of the Department of Physics at Harvard University, an admirer of *The Russell Cosmogony*, began corresponding with Walter. Their letters ranged beyond the subject of physics. They discussed prayer, and Walter noted that they agreed that "true repentance is a sort of regiving. It is a giving of genuine sorrow for the wrong done either to others or to Self. It involves restoration or restitution and a genuine change of thought from things lower to things higher."

The *Open Letter* was circulated extensively among the world's important scientists but received far less response than the Russells had anticipated. A well-known chemist sent them this advice: "Do not be concerned over the apparent silence of the skeptics. You and your beloved sent that message out with love. The results in love will come. It requires much deep reading. It is so simple to you two who are cosmically conscious. You forget that most of the letters were sent to sense-conscious men concerned about their jobs, new textbooks, stockholder rebuffs, et cetera. We have found in our work that this atomic age has its loyal devotees [who are] reluctant to give one inch outside of the few so-called rules they go by."

Walter and Lao were frustrated. Walter had sought to keep his explanation simple and to follow the advice he had been given years earlier by William Maxwell, one of Thomas Edison's early vice presidents, who always said, "You must talk to a man in his language."

An official from the French Embassy in Washington visited them in July and wrote afterwards: "Right from the castle's threshold I felt the mystical invocation and its soothing uplift. I left it with an inner, deeper, and broader appreciation of our human life." A visitor called them "two happy people living in Nirvana on top of the world in beauty and divine government." Walter believed, "When you know your mind is the source of your power, you will command your body to strength and health."

"It is almost unbelievable all you have done at Swannanoa," wrote another supporter. "It could not have been accomplished had it not been part of the fulfillment of the greater plan. Lao, you have rare executive and staying powers. You and Walter make the perfect whole, and we are so glad to watch your rich fulfillment come to pass." An executive of the American Broadcasting Company visited them and called Swannanoa the most exquisite paradise on earth.

The Russells remained in close contact with Dr. Francis Trevelyan Miller and his wife, Ann, who had moved to the Morgan estate in New York. The Millers brought important guests to Swannanoa and sent the Russells frequent encouragement. They introduced Walter and Lao to the Stauffer sisters, cousins of President Eisenhower, and these delightful ladies came to Swannanoa with the Millers for what was described as "an old-time family gathering" and later related the experience to their cousin in the White House. Jennings C. Wise, author of many scholarly books and a friend of Dr. Miller from Lexington, Virginia, wrote from Florida that he would soon be coming to Swannanoa. His *Philosophic History of Civilization* was ready for publication. He had written a pro forma introduction but wanted Dr. Russell and Dr. Miller to write a final preface. Mr. Wise corresponded with the Russells for many years and frequently visited them.

A day's mail brought a variety of missives to the Russells. The world situation presented new challenges. People wrote to express their concern over Stalin's death, wondering what the result would be in the Soviet Union. In the same mail one of Lao's Boston friends might write to tell of her unhappy marriage and ask Lao for a numerology reading. The same day a supply of vitamins might arrive from Bowan Jones. They never knew what to expect as a new day dawned on the mountain.

Lao's friend Georgia Eliza Reid, the Boston advertising executive, was amazed at what they had accomplished in Virginia. "You must both be very happy there in your work and your surroundings. As I read what you have sent, I am appalled at the amount of work you have done and wonder how on earth you ever managed to do it. It is stupendous. How could you and Walter turn out so much? Do you have help there working with you? It is miraculous and I am so happy and proud for you both."

Students who came for the weekend to meditate and study often found themselves struggling on Saturday night to learn the card game canasta from the Russells and, in any event, came away from Swannanoa fully realizing that meditation must be an around-the-clock, everyday pastime encompassing rest, work, and play.

The Esoteric School of Cosmic Sciences in Indiana distributed copies of *The Secret of Light* among its members. Its founder, Dr. Audra Younkin, a homeopathic physician and Egyptologist of note, had organized a group to study the Russell writings. Dr. Martin G. Manch of nearby Staunton's Institute of Musical Art visited Swannanoa, concluding, "It is most satisfying to learn firsthand of your fine works and thoughts in many matters of great importance." Their friend Dr. Raymond L. Nimmo corresponded extensively with them on health. He stressed the importance of biochemistry in nutrition and always kept his first edition of Walter's book, *The Universal One*, close by in his bookcase. A Presbyterian minister in Georgia signed up for the course and called the Message "so revolutionary it sometimes frightens me, yet I believe it is the fulfillment of our Christian gospel."

From Bridgeport, Connecticut, a prospective student who had long studied under Paul Brunton, had recently found a used copy of *The Secret of Light* inscribed to Benjamin E. Levy by Daisy Stebbing. Lao grew nostalgic when the incident reminded her of the great friend whom she had first met in England and who had later proved so helpful to her when she sought permanent residency in America.

A Texas state government official noted that the special *Human Relations Unit* was so forcefully written he could not put it down. He wrote them, "As a government employee for many years, I have been distressed over the power of politics, the terrific waste of time and money, the rapid growth of bureaucracy, and the deterioration of morale and morals among younger workers, to say nothing of the corruption in government on the higher levels." The writer thanked the Russells for clarifying that the Golden Rule provided the answer to all of these problems.

A Kansas City attorney told them she found the Law of Balance as explained in their course to be applicable to every lawsuit she handled and infinitely more important than all the legal precedents in the code and statute books. In 1953 C. L. Wheeler, editor of *Mind* magazine in San Francisco, wrote several articles on the work at Swannanoa.

In 1953 the Russells bought additional lots adjoining the palace grounds from the heirs of Mary F. Andrews and also made the final payment on the summer cottage. John and Emelia came again in the spring. He told them it was wonderful to be even briefly in the atmosphere of Swannanoa and offered them his help "whenever you feel my legal training can be of any assistance. My desire is to work at law, and if it ever happens that Swannanoa needs my work, I shall be more than willing to give it for I do feel a need for Swannanoa." In June he joined the prestigious firm of Hughes and Hartlaub in Summit, New Jersey. Emelia was happy to help Lao at Swannanoa for a week whenever time permitted and gladly continued editing and typing for the Russells at her home in New Jersey.

Their spring (1953) announcement stated positively that the coming summer would be the last time Walter Russell would personally teach his August classes at Swannanoa. They were burdened by ever increasing "behind the scenes work" as they sought to keep in contact with thousands of students all over the world. In addition, Walter was deeply immersed in writing lectures and was preparing to undertake additional laboratory work, a daunting task for a man of eighty-two. The summer courses were popular, the Russells knew, but they both agreed that at Walter's age "he must do those things which can mean the most to the many."

The curriculum for the August lectures that year was carefully concentrated on teaching students the techniques needed for personal guidance and mastery over everything one desires to do in life. The subject was *The Great Secret of Creation Which Lies in the Wave*.

Walter intended to focus on this topic for the entire month to the exclusion of everything else. Other study was unnecessary, he believed, if one understood this principle. He was convinced, "We are creatures of guesswork and experiment because of our lack of knowledge of the wave. We have failures, bankruptcies, loss of friendships, unhappiness, misery, agony, divorces, ill health and other ills because we do not know the fundamentals of universal law that lie in nature's waves.

"The greater the knowledge of balance and the orderliness of octave wave rhythms which anyone acquires, the greater his mastery over his achievements, his command over matter, and his power over other men."

Their premise was explicit. Years could be wasted in university study without learning one percent of the valuable truths that Walter Russell would teach in one month's study of the Universal Wave.

New students came by the scores, and many old students returned for what Lao promised would one day be among their most treasured memories. They shared informal evenings at the palace and quietly meditated in the gardens. Students from previous classes brought slides and colored movies of previous sessions to entertain their fellow alumni and newcomers as well. The schedule was arranged so as to give students an opportunity to ask Walter personal questions and have the inspiration of personal contact with the Russells while absorbing the loveliness of Swannanoa.

Four hundred students attended the 1953 classes, including engineers, doctors, three clergymen of differing denominations, four Jewish students, one student from Japan and one from China, a Muslim, many Christian Scientists, Unity members, an investment counselor from Detroit, a number of professional men and women, and representatives of many other disciplines. Lao called the varied group "an example of the unity which comes to those who speak the same language, for we have but one language here, growing out of our mutual understanding of God's ways and processes."

86. Walter Russell with his students in the palace gardens.

Kitty Boaz, Lao's friend from her early days in New York, spent three and a half weeks that August at Swannanoa, which she found to be "not only a shrine of beauty but a shrine of peace and inspiration which is a blessing in and of itself even without your valuable teachings." She told them, "There I found the fifth freedom, freedom from the din and clutter of civilization, the blaring of the radio, the telephone, the idle chatter of those who wallow in materialism. Last but not least, I found freedom from the eternal 'getting and spending' with which we lay waste our powers."

Many who stayed a week told Lao they wished they had stayed for the month. Mrs. Clarence Day wrote, "My two weeks with you were about the most precious in my life, and daily I find myself referring to some incident or inspiration received there."

The self-styled Brick and Boyers, two ladies from Des Moines who always attended the sessions and regularly filmed the summer's highlights to share with their study groups in Iowa, pronounced the summer of 1953 "the most enjoyable session at Swannanoa they had ever experienced. As we carry on our work regardless of what it is, we feel more and more the thrill of the teachings we received on the mountain. These were precious hours."

The Iowa ladies operated a large and progressive farm and at Walter's suggestion had stopped in Harrisburg, Pennsylvania, to discuss biological farming and related techniques with B. A. Rockwell, director of research for the

Pennsylvania Farm Bureau. "How many times as he talked we could feel his idea being worked out in some of the sketches placed on the board during Dr. Russell's lectures," they wrote the Russells after their return to Iowa. "Lots of times Mr. Rockwell would say, 'Now I know you will think I am crazy!' Didn't we hear that many times at Swannanoa? We told them of our experiences at Swannanoa. Our visit will never be forgotten. The way Lao talked at and to the mountain itself gave us much encouragement and understanding."

Charlotte Stevens, an enrollee from Florida, wrote Lao to say how much she appreciated the profound simplicity of the message of the wave, as well as "your warm eyes and vibrant voices, the close affinity of the other students, the beauty and grace of Swannanoa, the peace of the mountaintop."

J. M. Leickheim, another student, wrote Ralph Bellamy, editor of the Cleveland, Ohio, *Plain Dealer* and his mother, the widow of the author of *Looking Backward*: "What I heard and saw last week at Swannanoa I believe is your father's vision coming into manifestation between now and the year 2000. It will occur on account of the scientific discoveries made by Dr. Walter Russell and not by any political system." Walter had discussed *Looking Backward* in one of his classes.

The Stauffer sisters had returned for the class as they had promised. Two popular Russell students were married at the foot of the Christ statue the weekend following the 1953 classes. More than forty of their fellow students hosted a celebratory dinner for the couple.

During the summer Walter began sketches for a series of busts of American leaders he hoped to execute during the coming winter. The first was a bust of George Washington on whom he had done extensive research to ensure its accuracy. The curator of the Winchester-Frederick County Historical Society suggested that their 1798 drawing of Washington by St. Memin provided the best basis for discerning Washington's actual appearance, and Walter promised to lend a plaster cast of the completed work to the museum for exhibition. Artists and sculptors often asked Walter to give them private instruction in painting and sculpture. He declined all such requests because of the demands on his time.

David Kramer, Helen Russell's attorney, wrote them that Walter's former wife had died at Washington, Connecticut, on July 24, 1953. "The payments specified in the agreement are thereby terminated." July 29 was the Russells' fifth anniversary, a time of keen reflection for Lao.

On September 1, 1953, Dr. Francis Trevelyan Miller wrote them: "You are doing a magnificent work at Swannanoa and becoming world-famous. We have recommended your courses highly to folks here in Greenwich and they seem deeply interested. I am tremendously interested in your great work and often wish I were engaged in it with you in making Swannanoa a world shrine. There is a classic to be written about Lao and Walter in the marble palace on the mountaintop." They were always encouraged by his words of support, and Lao often expressed regret that the great historian had never written Walter's biography.

Dr. Emmet Fox, whom they both had known from his lectures at Carnegie Hall and elsewhere, had recently died, and his posthumous book *The Ten Commandments* was vying for popularity with the Walter's *New Cosmogony* on college campuses among serious science and philosophy students, according to a leading faculty member at the University of Michigan.

Their Pontiac sedan was seriously damaged in an auto accident on October 27 in Waynesboro, but neither of them was hurt, and a week later they celebrated Lao's birthday at a large dinner party hosted by friends.

As a special surprise, Lao's sister Florrie arrived from England on her first visit to Swannanoa. A friend wrote Lao, "I think I know who has been the happiest lady on the Appalachian range since last Saturday. Being somewhat of a globetrotter myself, I think I can fully appreciate what the occasion meant to you to have your sister arrive here and join you at Swannanoa."

An anonymous benefactor in California provided executives of Pan American World Airways with copies of the Russells' *Science of Human Relations*. Dr. Edna K. Williams, an African-American osteopath in Philadelphia, enrolled in the course and promoted it through her practice. Charles H. Story and his wife took the classes and soon afterwards began a successful study group in Tulsa, Oklahoma. Arthur and Adele Jones had attended the entire summer session in 1953. They were now living in the summer cottage they had helped procure for the Russells.

The Russells' 1953 Christmas card was a reproduction of Walter's pencil study of the Christ child accompanied by a special message from Lao. Several thousand were mailed, and by December 20 they were receiving many grateful replies. "I'm going to frame mine and keep it forever" was a typical response. They shared a joyful Christmas at Swannanoa with the Jones family. Just in time for the holiday their Portsmouth friend Frank Lawrence shipped them a large commercial box of fresh seafood from the Chesapeake Bay.

The Russells received much publicity. In addition to many of the Virginia dailies, *The Nashville Tennessean Magazine* featured the palace in a story, as did *The Indianapolis Star and News*. Both articles had been suggested by Russell students in the respective areas. Walter and Lao soon discovered that such regional notices were their most effective method of free advertisement next to the word-of-mouth endorsement of their readers and students.

Other small newspapers in various parts of the country promoted the work. The editor of the *Lake Ellsinore Valley Sun* in California expressed the unique way in which she had seen the Russells' science in action in her pressroom: "One of the greatest thrills came when I discovered the massive fulcrum on my big newspaper press one busy and monotonous night and stood by for long hours while operating it, watching the levers with their simultaneous action-reaction operating from the fulcrum. Life has infinitely more meaning since studying your wonderful works."

Walter's 1951 Armed Forces Day speech had been reprinted in out-of-state newspapers, among them the *Salisbury Post* in North Carolina. This brought the speech to the attention of Dr. Enid S. Smith of nearby Pfeiffer College, who found it "the best, most complete and understandable explanation of all life and history of mankind that I have ever heard, simple, concise, and dynamic." A prominent sociologist, she thereafter used the Russell work in her classes and on her regular radio programs. She had studied in India, spent seven years in Hawaii, and had many important contacts throughout the United States and abroad. Her support drew additional students to the work. When she visited Lao and Walter at Swannanoa, she was delighted to find that they all loved the *Bhagavad-Gita* and shared her vision of world unification and peace. At the time the *Bhagavad-Gita* and Bucke's *Cosmic Consciousness* ranked with Alexis Carrel's *Man the Unknown* and Glenn Clark's book on Walter Russell as the four books on their supplementary reading list.

The Russells were reluctant to launch any serious plea for financial backing in these early years. A student from Texas sent Lao the *Autobiography of a Yogi* by Paramhansa Yogananda and suggested they emulate the great yogi's practice and ask each of their students to donate $500 to the work. They declined, but unsolicited donations continued to arrive.

One of their strong local supporters was Louis Spilman, owner and editor of the *Waynesboro News-Virginian*. He turned their 1953 open letter news release and booklet over to his managing editor, Edward P. Berlin, Jr., with the suggestion that the award-winning journalist develop a feature story. It was difficult to encompass the scope and depth of the Russell message in a small town daily paper. "You are making such a marvelous contribution to life that I am deeply humiliated over my own inability to exhibit more specifically the admiration that is in my heart for you," Mr. Spilman wrote them.

At times the Russells declined to be interviewed by newspaper reporters. Walter was often adamant on this and explained the reason for his reluctance: "All interviews I have ever given resulted in superficially told stories which lacked the meaning of our lives. Nobody could faithfully depict either of us by the kind of clothes we wear and other such immaterial descriptive matter. Mrs. Russell's and my books and study course together are girdling the world. Yet writers ask for interviews with a view to entertaining their audiences with an account of a kind of queer person or specimen which is new to them instead of reading what has made us into such a queer specimen. And so it is that writers describe the palace and gardens where we live, the sculpture and paintings that demonstrate our versatility, but never a word do they relate of that in our writings which transforms man. It is like giving one a copy of songs and hearing them described as a beautiful morocco-bound gilded book which will neatly fit into one's pocket or adorn a library table with not a word of their music."

A skilled journalist interviewed Walter at the palace, wrote a colorful article, and submitted it to *Coronet* magazine, a popular periodical of the early 1950s. Walter was sent an advance copy of the article and deemed it so shallow he wrote the editor of the magazine to insist that it not be published. The article contained scant information as to the content of their books, course, or teachings. Instead it stressed their restoration of the palace itself. Walter reminded the writer that a true work of art eliminates nonessentials in order to accent the essentials. He recalled that he had interviewed many great men for news and scientific purposes and had likewise been interviewed by such writers as Richard Harding Davis and Elbert Hubbard, "both of whom dug deep into the essentials of a story to get the Soul of it." *Coronet* dropped the article.

In 1953 the University's insurance broker in Salem placed an article on their work at Swannanoa in *Mutuality*, the magazine of the North Western Mutual Fire Association in 1953. A funeral director and his wife who visited the palace were so impressed that they sent information to the *American Cemetery Association Bulletin*, which featured the Russells in an article about Swannanoa in the May issue that year. These trade publications were limited in their circulation, but they and others like them drew book sales and course enrollments, and more and more the teachings seemed to be spreading.

Virgila Tiffany Stevens wrote Lao that she had written a story on Swannanoa that would be published Sunday, October 25, 1953, in the *Washington Times-Herald*. "You may be disappointed in some of the omissions in my article, but I did it over three times in an effort to include the high points most likely to interest the most people," she noted.

Lao's abiding interest in astrology, shared to an extent by Walter, drew additional students to them, although astrology was not emphasized in their works. A stellar science practitioner in Dallas called it "an added pleasure to know that you understand astrology" and asked Lao for help in ushering in the Aquarian age. In 1953 Mary Jane Brusseau, a well-known astrologer, analyzed Lao's chart and advised her to "lock the door on the past, enjoy the present, and anticipate the future under Saturn and Jupiter," noting that the period from October 1953 to March 1956 would mark a significant epoch in her life pattern with a "crowning glory" by 1956. By then Lao had published her widely acclaimed first book.

Years later Walter was featured in an article entitled "Faith and Genius," written by Rita del Mar, published in *Astrology* magazine in 1981. She considered Walter Russell to be one of the forerunners of the Aquarian Age who worked to lift consciousness beyond selfishness and transform greed into a realization of the power and accomplishment one can attain by learning and obeying natural and cosmic law. She told the extensive readership, "One of the important principles that Walter Russell exemplified is that there is no limit to what man can accomplish if he makes use of the inherent possibilities within himself." This outstanding article gave much biographical information on Walter Russell not published elsewhere at the time.

A well-known New York astrologer sent them brief interpretative notes comparing the Russells' astrological charts. He was intrigued to find the planet Mars, representing dynamic energy and action, in the same zodiacal position by sign and degree in both of their charts. Jupiter in Lao's chart was on Walter's Neptune, both indicating religious and philosophical strength. Lao's Mercury was opposite Walter's Pluto. Lao's Jupiter was found in the same "occult" house as Walter's Saturn. The astrologer stated that the line of personality thus found a perfect completeness in this combined position in the eighth house, which signified release from personal limitations, the realm of birth and rebirth, regeneration through spiritual and mental enlargement of viewpoint, and involuntary subjugation of the personal self.

Stanley Jones, a noted New York economist and stock market analyst, contacted them in 1951 to say that since 1942 he had been calculating the future of securities with certainty by using the precise formula Walter espoused, namely, that "all motion begins at zero to run its course to the end and begin again at another point of zero." Frederic Snyder, rated as one of the ten leading platform speakers in the United States, noted the publicity surrounding the dedication of Swannanoa and later read the Russells' Unit 9. "You can realize how amazed I was when the powerful directive from Dr. Russell arrived," he wrote to Beverly Hills, California, attorney Chauncey Snow. "It comes as a direct answer to prayer. Right now I am booked to speak to some important industrial groups, hence my electric interest in what you sent." Snow himself adopted the Russell plan for his law office on January 1, 1953, and within ten days he told them all of his colleagues and employees had come to recognize and appreciate the power and balance inherent in Unit 9.

There were disappointments. Companies such as Western Union, where they had personal contacts with top management, decided against adopting the Russell instructions on human relations for their employees, doubting its practicality. "I do not intend any disparagement of the universal force which *The Russell Cosmogony* reveals, but I feel it would be too huge an undertaking to sell and apply in that it would not be worthwhile financially," a top company official wrote them.

Arthur Gohmsted, an engineer at a large chemical plant in Ohio, who was responsible for the purchase of twenty-five million dollars worth of engineered equipment and construction contracts over six years, wrote them: "During this time there has not been one instance of difficulty in adjusting all errors and misunderstanding without recourse to our legal department. I feel that the Russell teachings played a major part in this good record." J. Gordon Roberts, owner of Roberts Dairy Company in Omaha, wrote them that he had followed their suggestion in applying the Golden Rule to free enterprise with marked success.

It thrilled them that, as they intended, the course appealed to people of all races. An exuberant new student from Brisbane sent them her photograph, cheerfully explaining, "I'm as brown as a chocolate drop. I look like a tree in the fall of the year, that nice mahogany brown, or a huckleberry in a pan of milk." Another Australian wrote them, "I shall be guided in all matters by God's guidance through Mr. Russell."

Subscribers from Auckland, New Zealand, sought to promote the giving, regiving principle in their city. One wrote Lao, "Just lately I have come to realize how much I have to do to make restitution to others, and I have need to make concessions to many people. At this time of crisis I have been reading, as though for the first time, Glenn Clark's book about Dr. Russell, and I will daily meditate on the great truths that Dr. Russell gives in Glenn Clark's book. This will take me a long way and indeed the whole way because it is the mind of God which alone can supply my need." By December there was an active study group in Auckland.

Students from Bavaria contacted the Russells through Macalester Park and signed up for the course. From Bombay one of their active students wrote them, "As advised by you, I have started to love my work, however exacting it may be. Little by little the strain of it is reducing. I hope to master the situation very soon." In answer to repeated suggestions they explored the possibility of having the lessons translated into French and Spanish, but they were unable to budget the expense of such an undertaking.

By 1953 a South African publisher, Alex Pizarro, urged them to open a branch there and publish South African editions of *The Secret of Light* and the two volumes of *The Message of the Divine Iliad*. He had found it difficult to reconcile the churches' attitude to God with his own, nor did he believe, as Eastern mystics seemed to suggest, that God wanted him to spend his life in meditation without helping his fellow man. The Russell books had resolved his problem at first reading. Pizarro was one of many persons around the world who felt that the Message "could do more than anything else to bridge the wide gap of hatred and fear in this country between European and non-European, between English and Afrikaners, and between natives and Indians." He believed there were thousands in South Africa who were thirsting for the Russells' message of Universal Law. They arranged to send bulk shipments of books to him at a substantial discount.

Many of Lao's friends in England were thrilled with information she sent them on her work with Walter. R. T. Knight wrote her from Hampstead, "Your letter this morning was a great surprise and pleasure to me like light from an oasis in the desert of the present prostitution of all harmony and beauty. I have the picture of the Four Freedoms on the mantelpiece of my study and constantly under my eye and say 'Lao Deo' for it, often and often." In London the editor of England's popular periodical *The Book Exchange* reviewed *The Message of the Divine Iliad.* The Russells arranged with a London firm to secure copyright protection for their books in all countries signatory to the Berne Convention.

On April 28, 1953, Andrew Wilson wrote that in London the previous week he had met Dame Caroline Haslet. "Your books are known to her through her close friendship with the late Sir Stafford Cripps and Lady Cripps," he added.

Inquiries came from London's Truth Forum, founded by Dr. Joseph Murphy, a large and progressive metaphysical study group that met fortnightly in Caxton Hall, Westminster, where they engaged leading and eminent international metaphysical teachers and leaders. "Our members are in the position to preshape the very highest and best teachings as all the prominent leaders visit London as a center some time or another during their career, and I am in touch with them all when they arrive," Dr. Murphy wrote them. "Our people would very greatly appreciate personal contact with Dr. Walter Russell if and when that could be arranged."

Donald Sturgeon, one of their earliest English students, regularly stocked their books with major British book dealers and distributed the *Home Study Course* and Swannanoa newsletter among progressive thinkers in his country. He felt a special rapport with Lao because of her English roots. By now Lao had reestablished her account at Barclay's Bank in London and frequently English students sent their payments to that account. A donation of fifty pounds sterling was deposited there on May 2.

Two months later the Russells hosted a luncheon at Swannanoa for Mr. and Mrs. Michael George Touma of Beirut, Lebanon, a very influential Middle East opinion-maker who served both as Chairman of the Arab Section of the International Union of Official Travel Organizations and Commissioner General of Tourism in Lebanon.

Adele and Arthur Jones sent word that they had formally submitted a nomination to Stockholm proposing Walter for a Nobel Prize.

Students from Malaya enrolled in the course. The owner of a large financing, architecture, and construction corporation in São Paulo, Brazil, wrote Lao a detailed discussion of how the Russells' work had helped him and his employees prosper in their multi-faceted business.

Two Ontario physicians and surgeons wrote in 1953 that they had been studying the *Home Study Course* as faithfully as time would permit and had conducted group study on the Message for over eighteen months. A second group was due to hold its first meeting there the next month. They had described the Russells' work before Rotary and other service clubs, stressing its vital significance. They wrote of their frequent amazement at reading in the general press and scientific journals accounts of outstanding scientists who were gradually coming around to Walter's point of view and presenting to the world as apparent new theories many of the concepts that Walter had already presented in his lectures.

"I believe I now practice much better medicine and have more to give," wrote one of the Canadian surgeons, Dr. Sydney R. Bennett, who had taken the summer class at Swannanoa. The Canadian physicians introduced a number of fellow medical doctors to the *Home Study Course* and regularly corresponded with Lao on aspects of the science. One told her, "If I could decentrate as well as I am able to concentrate, I would have had cosmic consciousness long ago."

In 1953 a New Mexico student bewailed his inability to interest people in his hometown in the Russell cosmogony. "It is their loss if they do not accept it," he wrote her. "I have tried to get people here started on reading your books to open the way a bit. Like the town of Waynesboro, Virginia, my town is not ripe, I guess." Yet for every discouraging letter she received, numerous jubilant ones arrived. A Pennsylvania nurse, sixty years old, wrote Lao on Valentine's Day 1953: "Since I have been studying with you, I have found my work less tiring, and last night a friend who has not seen me for almost two years said that I looked years younger."

A family in France volunteered to come to America and spend a year helping the Russells at the palace in return for the opportunity to learn the science and philosophy firsthand. An oil company executive stationed in Kuwait had begun a small study group based on the Russell books. The work had indeed extended beyond Swannanoa.

Dr. B. R. Shenoy of India had visited them on a June Sunday in 1953. He sent them an English rendering of the *Bhagavad-Gita* by W. Hugh Judge and told them how impressed he was to see how closely the Russell principles were to the ancient Hindu teachings. He stressed, "I may note in particular the comments I read on reincarnation, the divinity in man, the ceaseless law of cause and effect which we call karma, the immutable law governing the universe in the working of which there is no room for accident, the identity of religion, how every man has within him the supreme custodian of all wisdom, and the fact that philosophy is not a matter of intellectual gymnastics but a way of life."

Minister James E. Suehiro of the Los Angeles Holiness Church (Oriental

Missionary Society) enrolled in the course in 1953, writing them, "Although I am a minister of an orthodox church, I have been a lover of Walt Whitman since my high school days and Bucke's *Cosmic Consciousness* has inspired me as much, but no one has ever shown me the way to cosmic consciousness until I read Dr. Russell's books. We have been studying similar concepts from several sources of information such as Scientology as developed by L. Ron Hubbard and Ron Howes; the works of Dr. Emmet Fox; *Science and Health* by Mary Baker Eddy; and the teachings of Christ from the Bible. I might add that since the Russell Message has been opened up to us, the Bible has taken on an entirely different meaning, and I am sure that the study course will help us continue this spiritual growth. We have found that the same basic truths run through all these sciences and that they differ only in their methods in obtaining the higher states of being. Each has been another stepping stone for us, and we hope to reach the final step in your science and philosophy."

Throughout his study, Minister Suehiro was pleased with what he was learning. "I am receiving much inspiration and knowledge that I could not get anywhere else," he told them, adding, "the last three units were so wonderful that I can hardly wait for the next one." By the time he completed the *Home Study Course*, he wrote them enthusiastically that it had proven a turning point in his life.

A well-known investment broker from Detroit, Leonard M. Eckland, told them he had more than 100 students in two adult classes and added, "I believe I am doing a good job because of your inspiration and teachings."

Reverend and Mrs. Willard I. Plough visited in September 1953 and purchased *The Scientific Answer to Human Relations*. As pastor of the Church of the Christian Brotherhood Hour, "a United Church for a Divided World," in Rivenna, Ohio, he told them that he quoted much from the Russells, "I think I agree thoroughly with the principles set forth. As a minister, I would say that Jesus personified these principles and there was a nucleus in the early church that demonstrated these principles and thus there has always probably been that nucleus. My thought is that the nominal Christian world as a whole does not practice these principles in their everyday relationships. It would seem that the work you are doing makes it much easier for us ministers to make an impact on the world in the work we are trying to do. Thanks! On the other hand, I hope we are making it easier and more effective the work you are endeavoring to do."

CHAPTER THIRTEEN

A Way of Life (1953-57)

The Russells' own illuminations remained a constant source of awe to their students. Students wondered if Lao had been forced to work hard for her illumination or if it came suddenly as it had with Walter.

Statements like these amused Lao, whose illumination had come only after years of reading, inquiry, thinking, prayer, and hard work. Hers was an active meditation at best, a knowing while doing, a progression to the Light through many sorrows and profound losses. She had never known the luxury of standing idly by and waiting for the knowledge she sought to be unfolded to her. On the contrary, her life had been so full of challenges that she often wondered how indeed the Light had ever come to her. She worked as she meditated, strove as she aspired, and was quite surprised when, in the midst of her twelve- and fourteen-hour daily routine, students asked if her illumination had been a tranquil experience. Lao knew that rest was essential for the enlightened spirit, and she always strove to find the time to rest her weary mind and body, but hers was a pinnacle achieved in the thrust of activity.

Lao knew that it was vitally important for those who desired to experience illumination to see the qualities of life and not simply its quantities. "The qualities," she wrote, "create one's character, and one's character is one's identity. The spiritual self of man is the true reality, and the physical self but an illusion."

Walter readily acknowledged that his work was far more valuable when enriched with Lao's contribution. He explained his feelings in a letter to a close friend: "Proof of that fact lies in *The Secret of Light*, which I wrote alone, just before Lao came. *The Home Study Course* (which we wrote together) is *The Secret of Light* multiplied a thousand-fold for it has in it the Light of all knowledge and the wisdom of its use commanding one's destiny.

"A way of life is what Lao espouses so earnestly. The Message would only be embraced by the multitudes if they felt it deeply within their hearts. It would only extend throughout the world if it struck mankind and womankind with the simplicity of its truth. 'Love ye one another,' Christ admonished his hearers, and in this clear and unmistakable direction He has touched the Universal Soul and

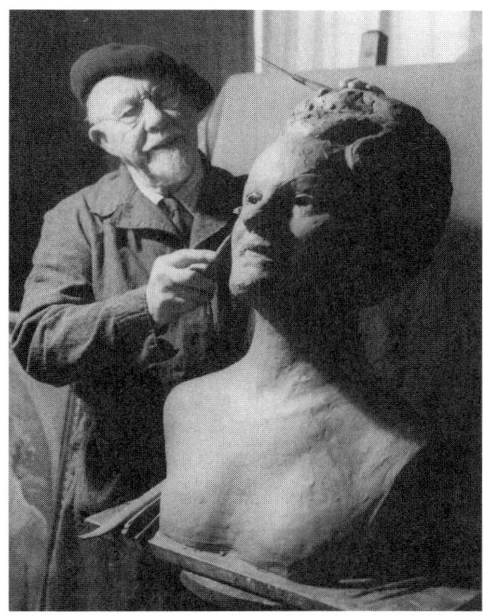

87. Walter sculpting his bust of Lao.

demonstrated the ultimate way of life."

Juxtaposed with the genius of Walter's science, Lao's consummate belief that their philosophy must be actively lived every day gave enormous power to their joint work. Walter again acknowledged this in his essay *The Purpose of the Message*: "A scientific interpretation of the Message alone is not enough," he wrote. "To give it full value it must also have the philosophical interpretation in order that it may become a way of life!"

Walter truly believed that Lao's life experience had paralleled his. "Ever since the age of three she has not only known her destiny, but has freely told it to her parents and sisters who put it down as childish imaginings." Lao was cosmic, Walter knew. "She not only recognized the rhythms of the universal heartbeat at an early age but has intuition and extra sensory perception far beyond mine."

In 1951 Walter told A. Warren Way, a scientist from Philadelphia, that Lao was the only cosmic woman he has ever known, and probably the only one on earth. He suggested that God had sent her to him because at his advanced age he was "getting in deep—over his head—and needed a super-intellectual mate in order to carry on."

Lao's *Code of Ethics*, first published under Walter's name as part of the introduction to Unit 1 of the course, was made available as a handsome broadside distributed to students and strangers by the thousands, providing a succinct one-page blueprint of Lao's living philosophy. It was much more readily accessible to the general public in this format than submerged in the copious thousand-page *Home Study Course*, even though Lao wrote of the latter as "the Kingdom of God on paper."

Many students agreed that Lao's *Code of Ethics* was indeed the "basic foundation for a living philosophy," as she often described it. It was a practical elucidation of the Golden Rule, "Do unto others as you would have them do unto you." From the *Code's* first line, "To bring blessings upon yourself bless your neighbor," to its dynamic conclusion, "Love is like unto the ascent of a mountain. It comes ever nearer to you as you go ever nearer to it," the *Code* set forth in less than a page profound guidelines for a joyous life.

Lao was much more practical than Walter about the need for keen business judgment in marketing the Message. When a student ordered books to sell at a Texas health food center and noted in passing that a Russell student in town was lending her *Home Study Course* lessons to six interested fellow students, allowing each one to borrow a lesson for three days before they met to discuss it, Lao gently suggested that truly supportive students would refrain from lending or copying their lessons and would instead seek to demonstrate regiving by encouraging each interested party to enroll individually. Soon a note to that effect accompanied all introductory course packets. She was likewise firm with those who dared to reproduce unauthorized copies of Walter's early works.

Lao Russell's

Code of Ethics

for a living philosophy

To bring blessings upon yourself bless your neighbor.

To enrich yourself enrich your neighbor.

Honor your neighbor and your neighbor will honor you.

To sorely hurt yourself hurt your neighbor.

He who seeks love will find it by giving it.

The measure of a man's wealth is the measure of wealth he has given.

To enrich yourself with many friends enrich your friends with yourself.

That which you take away from any man the world will take away from you.

When you take the first step to give yourself to that which you want, it will also take the first step to give itself to you.

Peace and happiness do not come to you from your horizon. They spread from you out to infinity beyond your horizon.

The whole universe is a mirror which reflects back to you that which you reflect into it.

Love is like unto the ascent of a high mountain peak. It comes ever nearer to you as you go ever nearer to it.

88. *Lao Russell's* Code of Ethics.

Lao had a warm and thoughtful disposition. People found her extremely kind. She was appalled by medical experiments on animals and through the years actively supported the antivivisection movement. It horrified her to see animals tortured for purposes of product testing and research. She considered such activity inhumane and barbaric, and it brought her a sense of nausea and revolt. "My one prayer is that in these next months I shall be given the means to play a greater role in the antivivisection movement," she wrote a student.

As a child she had worked diligently as a volunteer for the National Society for the Prevention of Cruelty to Animals and its companion organization that worked to reduce cruelty to children. In those days both animals and children generally suffered because of lack of care by their owners and parents. In later years she would constantly speak out against these evils.

Lao believed that animals and all life forms had souls. It disturbed her that orthodox religious people so often seemed ignorant of this. As her understanding of the universe developed and she came to recognize that "everything in God's universe is a conscious thought of God," she was ever more convinced that cruelty to animals was one of the worst crimes perpetrated by man. For most of her life she was a vegetarian because, as she stated, "The thought of eating a little animal that has been killed so inhumanely sickens me. Can I say more?"

It was important to the Russells that people realized that their teachings were purely scientific and had no religious connotation whatsoever. Walter asserted that the greatest age of character and righteousness the world ever knew existed before religion came into mankind's consciousness. During that time, he believed, the world's greatest literature and teachings had been written, including the Psalms, the Proverbs, the Golden Rule (in its root form), and most of the inspired literature in the Bible. Both he and Lao recommended that their students read *The Dawn of Conscience* by Henry Breasted, which they now included on their supplementary book list and offered for sale whenever it was available.

Lao often cited one of Walter's clearest explanations as to why their Message should not be considered religious whenever students sought to cobble such a connotation onto it. He had stressed, "In our illuminations we were especially commanded to awaken the Light in others by teaching them God's ways and processes (and the understanding of the kingdom within) through action, rather than through faith and belief or through doctrines and creeds. Right action or righteousness is ethical, not doctrinal. The Golden Rule is strictly ethical. You must practice it in order to be righteous. It refers to what you do to your neighbor, not what you believe about a hereafter. We cannot conscientiously teach man a way to righteousness through doctrines when we were commanded to teach him by right action."

Those who suspected there were aspects of the occult in their work were promptly corrected by Lao: "You are under a grave misapprehension regarding the value of any of our knowledge to groups who are interested in psychic research and allied thought. There is nothing whatsoever in any and all of our works and teachings which even remotely bears upon psychic phenomena, séance rooms, or anything pertaining to the unnatural, supernatural, or any other phase of distortion or abnormality."

Nonetheless, it was no less a spiritual teacher and mystic than Sarah Weld Blake who introduced the Russells' work to nationally known radio commentator Fulton Lewis, Jr., in 1951. He discussed their human relations program on his syndicated Mutual Broadcasting System program.

By 1953 there were no more copies of *The Secret of Light* available for sale and seemingly no used copies to be purchased "as no one will part with their copies," but Lao advised students, "We will reprint it in due time, but the interest in new scientific knowledge which it stirred up all over the world compelled us to expand it into the year's *Home Study Course*, which we both wrote together. For the present that serves the purpose."

Teachers of other disciplines seemed intrigued with the *Home Study Course*, and many used it as part of their own curricula. In 1951, Rose Van Mater of Summit, New Jersey, wrote to tell the Russells that she planned to integrate their principles into the curriculum she used for students studying the *Kabbalah*, a subject she had taught since 1932. Years later Joey Korn of Augusta, Georgia, who brought his wife, Jill, to Swannanoa for personal meetings with Lao on several occasions, followed the same approach. From Detroit a teacher of Joel S. Goldsmith's *The Infinite Way* noted a marked congruency between Goldsmith's and the Russells' paths to cosmic truth.

A chiropractor from Missouri was happy to find Bahá´u´lláh mentioned in Lao's first book and emphasized the similarity between the Russells' beliefs and *The Book of Certitude* of the Baha'i faith. Bahá´u´lláh had said that science and religion must agree. The writer felt that the Russells' scientific approach to God and the Baha'i concept of spirituality were consistent and comprised the ultimate of knowledge. From Riverside, California, Dr. W. J. Gallean, an early practitioner of Scientology, wrote "to express deep appreciation for the wonderful knowledge you are giving to the world through the *Home Study Course*. We have come to realize that this is not simply a twelve-unit course that one finishes in a period of one year, but rather a lifetime program of ever increasing illumination."

From the years of Walter Russell's earliest lectures in New York, students of Religious Science Church founder Dr. Ernest Holmes from California to Florida were inspired to study them and, later, when the *Home Study Course* was issued, to enroll in the course and study the other Russell books. In 1956 Dr. Holmes wrote Lao, "How wonderful it is to think we are doing our little bit in what we hope is the building of a greater realization of life and health on earth!"

Dr. Clifford Chaffee, a leading Religious Science minister and scholar in California, noted the remarkable similarities between Lao's book, *God Will Work with You but Not for You*, and Holmes's seminal work *The Science of Mind*, as well as Chaffee's own popular treatise *A Stairway to Freedom*. Dr. Victor Willey, another Religious Science minister active in the International New Thought Alliance in St. Petersburg, Florida, praised the Russells' inclusiveness. "Surely the love and inner-knowing now being awakened in unfolding man will be able to reverse the evil of race-thinking before it is too late," he wrote, adding his conviction that the Russells' true and wonderful work would lead to lasting peace. The Religious Science minister in nearby Orlando enrolled in the course and told his congregation, "Thank God for the Russells! I wouldn't take a billion dollars in exchange for this material. It is beyond price."

Walter and Lao believed that it was not their purpose to teach what others had taught except as worthy examples of God's Message. For this reason, at times, they felt it appropriate to question what they perceived as shortcomings in other illuminates and made no apology for not promoting those who held beliefs contrary to theirs. Emanuel Swedenborg was one such mystic whose conclusions often troubled them, and when his devotees challenged the Russells for not embracing his cosmogony, they replied that many of Swedenborg's teachings suggested to them that he had not fully understood the Cosmos. He believed in creation by nebular hypothesis, in evil and the devil, and in conversing with angels. The Russells, on the other hand, asserted that evil is created by man and could not have been created by an omnipotent and omnipresent God of Love. At times they were accused of paying insufficient respect to Paramhansa Yogananda and the Self-Realization Fellowship.

From their first years at Swannanoa, Lao and Walter were active in the local Chambers of Commerce and the Shenandoah Valley and Virginia Travel Associations. Their very livelihood depended on tourism. The Virginia Travel Council in Richmond distributed 25,000 of the Swannanoa brochures throughout the state every quarter. When the number of visitors to the palace inexplicably decreased during the summer of 1951 despite twenty-five percent increases for other Virginia attractions, members of the council staff met with them and suggested ways to boost their numbers. That year the Council asked Dr. Russell to share the spotlight at its annual conference in Virginia Beach with W. W. Hubbard, a Washington economist who edited *The American Motorist*. Although the Russells generally followed a policy of not accepting invitations off the mountain, Lao told them he would make yet another exception, feeling that the appearance would bring Swannanoa good publicity and possibly lead to a syndicated newspaper column for Dr. Russell. At the last minute they were forced to cancel his speech because of Walter's failing health.

Throughout the summer that year they engaged in a pitched battle with bureaucrats from the Virginia Department of Highways who demanded that they remove their advertising signs from any place within 500 feet of the Blue Ridge Parkway. The Russells argued that their signs were only temporary and would soon be replaced by "a beautiful structure architecturally and sculpturally." They pled that for the present they vitally needed the signs to help people find the palace. To remove them now would surely be the death warrant of all they were trying to achieve at Swannanoa, they asserted, noting that without tourist revenue, their private income and earnings from books and courses would be insufficient to allow them to continue their growth. The noted Virginia architect Stanhope Johnson endorsed their plan for beautifying the Parkway where it joined the Swannanoa property at the junction of Route 250. John S. Graves, president of Skyline Swannanoa, Inc., which owned the palace, told them that he had studied the law carefully and concluded that no state official could grant them an exception. The Russells persisted, and after granting them an extension of time, the officials in Richmond suddenly concluded that the entrance signs at Swannanoa were exempt from the ban because of their distance from the palace itself. The victory was welcome, but the wrangle had caused the Russells undue alarm at a difficult time.

In 1952 Peter Parker designed a new sign for the main entrance, which by then had been greatly improved with attractive landscaping and two marble pillars supporting figures from Walter's monumental Four Freedoms. The palace gardens were radiant. The tulips were out, the grass was green and beautiful, and next month the roses would bloom in all their glory, but May brought relatively few visitors and expenses mounted. They built a small information booth at the entrance gates in an effort to increase attendance.

Lao remained active in Shenandoah Valley, Inc., throughout their first decade at the palace and served on its board. Waynesboro and the area were beginning to recognize the importance of the tourist dollar, and Lao worked with enthusiasm to bring the Valley organization into league with the National Association of Travel Organizations, the United States Chamber of Commerce, and the American Automobile Association. She developed a good rapport with national travel agents who specialized in tours to Virginia's historic shrines. Statistics supported her claim that "tourists who come primarily to Virginia to see Swannanoa alone spend at a minimum half a million dollars in the state during a five-month season. This money is spent in Virginia hotels, motels, restaurants, gift shops, fruit stands, entertainment businesses, other tourist attractions, and sundry services." She often attended legislative hearings in Richmond to promote tourism in the state. In March 1953 the Russells entertained the Virginia Travel Council with a buffet dance at the palace to honor thirty-one Trailways Travel Bureau directors from across the country.

Locally, Lao encouraged the Waynesboro Chamber of Commerce in its efforts to attract visitors to its local tourist attractions. These regional promotional groups often met at Ingleside Resort near Staunton. Through the years this was one of the Russells' favorite area restaurants. Its talented and philosophical chef became their close personal friend and student and frequently came to Swannanoa with prominent members of the area's African-American community.

The Southern Restaurant, accredited by well-known American gourmet and travel expert Duncan Hines, was the focal point of downtown social life in Waynesboro. Its genial and talented owners, George and Aristea Gianokos, welcomed overflow crowds to excellent meals. They became close friends of the Russells in 1949 and always showed them warm hospitality when they brought out-of-town guests to dinner or came down from the mountain to dine alone. In the 1950s, when the restaurant's interior was destroyed by fire, the Russells provided five-by-six-foot, sepia-toned photographic murals of the palace, Christ statute, and gardens, which for years adorned the walls of the inviting restaurant.

By spring 1954 many acres of the mountaintop between the stables and greenhouse had been cleared of the former wilderness. Many dwarf fruit trees had been planted to form the nucleus of a great formal garden. This was the special vision of the Russells' faithful friends Adele and Arthur Jones and their daughter Wendy, who intended to dedicate the rest of their lives to the work at Swannanoa and were living in the summer cottage near the swan pond.

Another Easter Sunrise Service was held at the foot of the Christ of the Blue Ridge. "It was a very awesome and inspiring sight," Lao wrote, "to see the first red light of the sun illuminate the face of the Christ and then creep slowly down the figure as the vast throng of worshippers lifted their eyes on that glorious sight, uplifted by the voices of Waynesboro's many choirs."

The Russells had instituted an experimental seven-week radio series in Lynchburg, Virginia, as a step towards what they hoped would ultimately be a national radio and television hook-up for dissemination of the *Divine Iliad* Message. The enormous volume of correspondence they received reflected the tremendous growth of the Foundation in the short five years since it had been established at Swannanoa. Hundreds of letters now arrived at the palace every month. By now they had active students on every inhabited continent.

Their new housekeeping couple, the McConnells, worked hard to keep the palace going, but it was obvious they were too old to meet the challenge. The cook continued to drink and lose weeks at a time, and the need for a more professional staff was ever more evident. As usual, Lao regarded willing workers with tenderness. They purchased Mr. McConnell a hearing aid so he could effectively man the gatehouse. "He will be wonderful for the gate," Lao knew. "People like him because he is nice, and I am awfully fond of him." Later in the spring, the Tome Williams family joined the palace staff. They understood the teachings well and worked in harmony with the Russells and the other employees. The one exception was the cook, who reportedly had threatened to stab any of her friends in Waynesboro who dared think of applying for the job when she went on her drinking binges. By early summer jealousy had broken out among the staff, and Lao was required to take on the managership burden herself. "At least," she sighed, "the Williamses were keeping the house beautifully clean."

From England, former Prime Minister Sir Winston Churchill wrote to congratulate them on their work, "I have your bust of President Roosevelt at my country home, Chartwell. It is a striking work of art as well as a memorial of my great friend."

Lao urged Emelia to try to spend the spring and summer at Swannanoa, realizing that Emelia could take charge of the office and leave the Russells free to spend more time with palace visitors, hopefully selling more courses. Lao had refitted the office, which then occupied the southeast upstairs room and was generally filled with sunshine from its southwestern exposure.

Emelia spent two weeks at the palace in early April helping Lao catch up on her work. Lao's schedule was more and more demanding. With Emelia's help she found time to work on a newsletter and catch up on correspondence. For a week she got by on two or three hours sleep a night in an effort to send out the newsletter. In two days she had written 800 personal letters and had 200 more to write. Out-of-town visitors took up more and more of her time, and she felt strongly obliged to spend much time with old students who often came thousands of miles just to see them. "We must get a number of students this year and sell more courses," she noted, "for that is our bread and butter money."

They hoped for greater access to the nation's leaders. Marjorie Stauffer, President Eisenhower's cousin, had carried through on her promise to keep the popular president alerted to the Russells' expanding work.

Dr. Russell seemed hale and happy. The mountain air was like wine to him. Lao presented herself glamorously, paying careful attention to her wardrobe, even though most of her clothes were gifts of friends. She built outfits around a navy blue hat John Lombardi sent her, but focused more attention on red and pale blue.

89. Walter and Lao Russell, 1955.

Summer arrived and with it the hectic pace of preparing for the 1954 August classes they had reluctantly decided to hold. A hundred students were expected the first week, but attendance dropped to a disappointing seventy-five. Walter was tired but enthusiastic, and after the first week he moved his lectures to the summer cottage. This provided a more relaxed atmosphere, free from interruption by the steady flow of tourists at the palace.

Progress seemed slow overall, but Lao was optimistic, earnestly feeling that "The Message is finding its place in the world and one day will be recognized by all mankind for what it truly is—God's Message for this age."

The Joneses prepared a special intimate birthday dinner for Lao that November, which she enjoyed as much as the usual large party. She herself would have had to work out the arrangements for a bigger event, and this year she was simply too tired. "I still work every hour of the day and night, but I find that I tire more easily these days, and I know that I shall have to learn to take it much more easy—a hard thing to do around here!" She was making progress on her new book, writing much of it in the quiet hours after midnight.

In December 1954 John Lombardi was sworn in as assistant county prosecutor, an important and demanding post for which there was much competition. His extensive criminal practice garnered him this position. He and Emelia celebrated his success by spending several days at Swannanoa during Christmas.

Lao guarded their work, firmly refusing to allow excerpts from *The Russell Cosmogony* to be printed in Alphia Hart's magazine, *The ABERREE*, even though Mrs. Hart had sent copies of the *Cosmogony* to Mayor Robert Wagner and sixteen other leaders in New York City.

When famed theologian Paul Tillich publicly expressed his opinion that Protestant Christianity needed to be more relevant, adding, "Unless one's religious views can be found to have a foundation in the individual's daily world and are pertinent to his daily living, they would appear to have little value," Lao was even more convinced that the Russells' time had come. She sent Tillich information on their work and corresponded briefly with him.

New students enrolling in the course reflected a variety of backgrounds. The president of the United States Army Air Defense Board wrote for copies of their books. A child psychiatrist, already an advanced initiate in Kriya Yoga through the Self-Realization Fellowship, made several visits to the palace and used the Russell books in his practice. "The message of God is always the same yet it is very refreshing to see it expressed in different styles and tongues," he told Lao. "Your personal approach and that of Dr. Russell is very striking. It could be the most up-to-date message offered to the western world!"

A leader of the New Thought movement in England, the well-loved Brother Mandus, leader of the World Healing Crusade centered in Blackpool, read and reread the news from Swannanoa with absorbing interest and advised the Russells that he intuitively accepted as true their main conclusions. He featured Walter in the leading article of the February 1957 issue of his *Crusader* magazine, which was widely read in the United States and other English-speaking countries. He believed that the work the Russells were doing would "take their allotted part in stirring public opinion, and quicken progression towards the only possible solution to the world problem."

Walter was quick to state that the entirety of his and Lao's teachings could never be expressed in one book, asserting that it takes many phases of expression to depict a way of life, knowledge of the Cosmos, and also knowledge of God. He always urged those who praised one of their books to read the others and take the *Home Study Course*.

When it was published in 1955, Lao's first book, *God Will Work with You but Not for You*, which many consider her masterpiece, was widely advertised as neither religious nor metaphysical but as science and philosophy based on natural law.

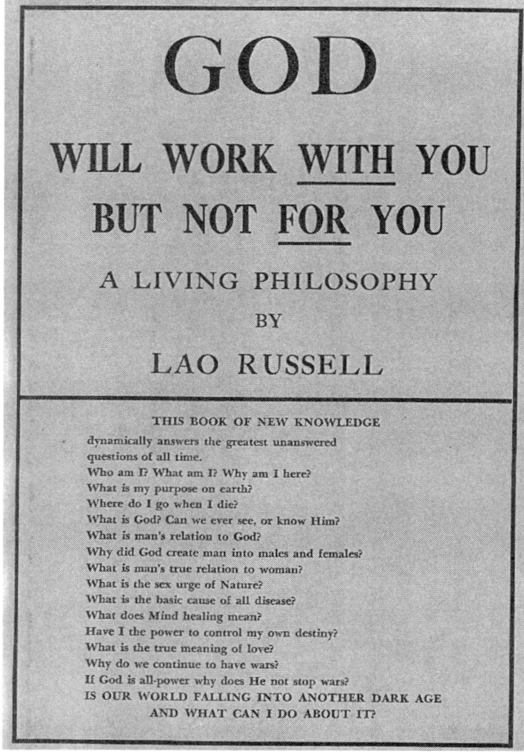

90. God Will Work with You but Not for You.

Promoted as new knowledge that the author had acquired cosmically, the book emphasized that the human body is an electrical illusion no more solid than the air one breathes. She wrote *God Will Work with You but Not for You* to convey a purposeful, living philosophy especially to those seeking to fathom the mysteries and realities leading to spiritual unfolding. Prefaced by Oscar Wilde's lament, "I must say to myself that I ruined myself and that nobody great or small can be ruined save by his own hand," the first section explained the individual nature of man and explored mind, cosmic, and Christ consciousness. The second part dealt with the truth of universal oneness, man-woman equality, and the consequences of ignoring God's law of balance. Its theme was drawn from Edwin Markham's avowal, "In vain we build the city if we do not first build the Man." The final section of the book was centered on a factual and scientific interpretation of the Golden Rule, exploring essential aspects of character and means of creating one's own destiny. The book, although written for an all-inclusive audience, concluded with a special message for women.

In this living philosophy Lao sought to clarify for mankind what she considered the three largely uncomprehended statements of Jesus, namely, "Seek ye the kingdom of heaven within yourself"; "What I do ye can also do"; and

91. Walter Russell's portrait of Lao, 1955.

"I and my Father are One." These were not mere abstract phrases, she avowed logically and with obvious comprehension, but conclusive truths explaining the power of thought when one thinks with one's mind instead of one's senses. Both Walter and Lao considered the book the fulfillment of Herbert Spencer's vision and the essential textbook for any study of the Science of Man.

Immediately after publication of the book had been announced in *The New York Times*, *New York Herald Tribune*, and other newspapers, thousands of letters began arriving at Swannanoa expressing the appreciation of the book's readers for the new understanding it had given them. Libraries across America were obliged to purchase copies by extensive requests from their patrons. The New York Public Library initially ordered twelve copies to fill its immediate demand and subsequently ordered more.

The 1956 University newsletter reported numerous orders from foreign countries, "even from so far as Finland, New Zealand, South Africa, and South America," as well as requests for separate printings for the English sterling countries and translation into Spanish and other languages. Three months after the book's initial announcement *The New York Herald Tribune* pronounced it one of the six greatest books of the year. Ten thousand copies were sold in four months.

Typical of the widespread praise Lao received was this letter: "It is the finest book I've ever read. It is the answer to the real religion that I'm sure the Master talked about when he was here." Booksellers from as far away as New Zealand and Holland ordered supplies of the book. Scores of interested parties wrote to complain that the Russell books were difficult to obtain in local bookstores. Many ministers, including a leading Episcopalian bishop and the Catholic bishop of Pittsburgh, read *God Will Work with You but Not for You* and subsequently enrolled in the *Home Study Course*.

The Russells continued to receive reports of important work done previously and more recently in the field of parapsychology. Just before Lao's first book was published in 1955, she engaged in correspondence regarding the work of Lotte von Strahl, who had been an important figure in the field in

Europe. Lao advised her correspondent: "It pleased us to know how greatly these indications of spiritual unfoldings in people are increasing. We are very much interested in knowing about every evidence of either Cosmic Consciousness or extrasensory perception in people; in fact, we journeyed over to Edgar Cayce's house to know more [from his son] about his powers in that direction, for we teach the basic principles which underlie both, but we do not in any way operate a clinic for either of them, or for Mind Healing, which has not the same basis. I have devoted a full chapter in my new book to Mind Healing which takes away quite a little of the mystery of it and puts it upon a scientific basis."

In May 1956 the widely known actress Tallulah Bankhead wrote Lao to praise her book and plan a visit to Swannanoa. Walter had been well acquainted with Miss Bankhead's father, long the Speaker of the United States House of Representatives, and Lao recalled seeing her on the English stage in *Her Cardboard Lover* during the 1930s. Both the Russells were fans of Miss Bankhead's enormously popular Sunday evening radio program, "The Big Show."

During 1956 Dr. Charles Lelly, a pharmacist from Delray Beach, Florida, who had earlier read *The Man Who Tapped the Secrets of the Universe*, visited the Russells at Swannanoa and enrolled in the *Home Study Course*. Unexpectedly, he was told by the tour guide that Walter wished to see him in his laboratory. He was warmly welcomed, and they shared a deeply insightful conversation that profoundly affected Dr. Lelly. As he drove away, Lao, whom he had not met, waved goodbye to him from the palace balcony. Eight years later, after he had completed the course and reviewed it no less than twice, he sold his pharmacy and entered Unity ministerial training at Lee's Summit, Missouri. Again he stopped at Swannanoa. To his amazement, Lao recognized him immediately, introduced him to others in the room, and embraced him with all the warmth of her personality. He explained to her how the Russell teachings had revealed hidden dimensions within him over the years, and they solidified a lasting friendship. Soon afterwards he sent her a personally inscribed copy of his first book, *The Beautiful Way of Life*, published by the Unity School.

The first week of April 1956 saw the *Home Study Course* enrollment of Laara Lindo, a young teacher from Powell River, British Columbia, who would become a faithful supporter of the Russells and maintain a regular correspondence with Lao for the next thirty-two years, even though their long-anticipated personal meeting would not occur until the first week in May of 1988. By 1954 Laara had chosen to move from teaching in urban schools to working in a rural district, and her obvious success in this profession was stimulated, she wrote Lao, by her use of Russell principles in encouraging the young students in her rural school to develop their individual talents and creativity. Lao was delighted, and wrote Laara, "I cannot help but reflect on the influence our teachings will have on these young minds. They will start life feeling an inner security few humans ever experience. I am sure God has put you right where you are for a great purpose. Those children growing up in Nature and having you to teach them will not be so influenced as children in a big city, and it will be interesting to follow their lives into manhood."

By now Lao had introduced Laara to other Russell students in British Columbia, and the young teacher was not only sharing her personal copies of the Russell books with others but likewise donating entire sets of these volumes to libraries in the area. When Laara married a kind, intelligent widower in 1960 and settled in the Vancouver Island area, Lao sent her a small model of the Christ statue as a wedding present. Laara continued to teach and regularly shared her earnings with the University. She wrote Lao heartfelt letters of support and consolation during the long months of Walter's final illness. Lao wrote her, "You have learned so early in life that the only happiness man ever holds is the happiness he first gives." Lao considered this the most important and the hardest lesson a person could learn.

By March 1958 a large textbook manufacturer wrote Lao that many of its traveling salesmen were recommending *God Will Work with You but Not for You* as a likely textbook to public school superintendents and teachers across the country. Businessmen liked the book. A steel company executive called it "the greatest book I have ever read in my life, and I am a severe and searching critic." A popular television dance show host came to Swannanoa from Columbus, Ohio, and filmed a palace tour in color for use on his broadcast. "If tomorrow civilization should enter a dark age and I were allowed to take just one item with me," he told Lao, "it would be *God Will Work with You but Not for You*."

From Alberta, Canada, a reader praised Lao's description of every human being as "a divine, immortal, invisible soul" as opposed to the hopeless creature described in many a pulpit as "made from dust and returning to dust." A college student from the Marshall Islands told her "*God Will Work with You but Not for You* is the most priceless book in all of my collection with the exception of the Holy Bible." He added that it had opened to him a new door into the future, teaching him how badly the world needs love and what a cruel and evil part mankind has played throughout history. "Since reading your book," he told her, "my entire attitude toward woman has been completely changed because I have come to see and realize their value in this one-world family of man."

Robert B. Stone, founder and president of the Associated Plan Service, a popular third-party insurance company specializing in customized self-funded option employee benefit and insurance plans, called *God Will Work with You but Not for You* "an epic," but when he wrote the Russells lamenting that "nowhere is there a nationally recognized school receiving and emanating wisdom about the universe and the infinite intelligence that permeates it," Lao was quick to respond that he was incorrect; the school they had established at Swannanoa for the study of the science of man fulfilled that very purpose.

A West Virginia Congresswoman found Lao's book inspiring and advised Lao, "the Library of Congress is able to lend it out for only a short period of time since there is a long waiting list for it," and ordered copies for her personal use and as gifts for friends. At Michigan State University, a professor who had authored *A Guide to Effective Speaking* wrote Lao that he no longer taught his students in communications skills to remember and repeat, but regularly followed her recommended method of unfolding their imaginative faculties by teaching them to think and know. "The students under me find it a pretty stiff dose," he reported, "but those who can take it are better for it."

Warner Aull from Hollywood, California, wrote, "I enjoyed your wonderful book *God Will Work with You but Not for You* and would welcome more of your ideas. I remember very well my first visit with Dr. Russell at Carnegie Hall an afternoon in March 1947. It was inspiring and illuminating."

Lao's earlier Hollywood connections had not been lost. She kept in touch with all-star agents in films and television. Professional writers contacted her with proposals for films, coffee-table books, and biographies about the Russells. An important writer of children's books proposed that a juvenile book be written about Lao, Walter, and Swannanoa. The book's message would naturally be delivered in simplified form, and the author was certain it would prove of inestimable value to children and the world. Later an Illinois businessman suggested that Lao design a line of children's toys that would reflect the Russell teachings. Lao thought this would be wonderful not only for the children, but likewise for the parents who bought them. She urged the manufacturer to act on his vision and design the toys himself.

By 1957 Lao could identify Russell students all over the world who had the "higher level" knowledge, knew what God is and where to find Him, and understood the relation of the invisible Mind to their visible body not metaphysically but scientifically. Lao admitted that the world of tradition seemed to pass the Russells by and gave its grants in millions of dollars to the old science that saw reality in substance, motion, and matter. "Fortunately," Lao said, somewhat wistfully, "we do not need grants and have never asked for them. The seekers are many and we support our University here, together with the palace and gardens, by supplying those seekers for knowledge with what they desire for inner unfolding."

Lao knew that the percentage of people who would understand their Message was small, but she was proud that the number of their supporters throughout the world was steadily growing and hoped that institutions of learning would someday transcend empirical knowledge gained by the senses and recognize the value of basic knowledge from inspired spiritual sources.

The leader of a study group in Missouri wrote her on May 1, 1957: "Studying the lessons, I am reminded of how as a child I was always held spellbound by the sky at night. I would stand for long periods looking up and whispering to myself, 'Why can't I know how all of this came into being? Why is all of this and what does it mean?' I never thought then that I would someday receive the answers to all of those questions and to all of the deeper questionings as well which came later into my life and kept me searching and probing for so many years without solution and fulfillment. This entire message you are giving to the world from the Light is such a stupendous thing. The more I unfold and understand, the more I comprehend through reading, study, and concentration, just so much more do I see far ahead, the immensity of your message which I feel I am only beginning to glimpse. In a world of turmoil, conflict and confusion where people seek answers to their questions and find no answers, we students are being given the Truth and I wonder if we are truly grateful enough for that which we have received. I hope that we all deeply realize that your message from the Light is the most profound ever given to Man."

The same day, Lao wrote advice to a student: "Study alone for this is as important as to create alone. Just as you would not write a symphony with others, so you should not be influenced by the thoughts of others while forming your own, especially when new awareness is awakening." She cautioned a new student that his "conception of Light is not in accord with the natural law and science contained in our teachings. I am sure you will find many of your inner questions answered for there has never been a course of this nature and with this knowledge and your ability to write I feel sure your contribution to the world will someday be a great one."

Successful professional men at the end of their careers wrote to say that they had been helped immeasurably by the course. From Indiana came word, "I must say that your course has changed my life to an amazing degree. I didn't understand my urges and desires, and the future looked apprehensive and insecure to me, but your guidance has changed all that. It has given me self-confidence as it has revealed vital and wonderful powers of man that I wasn't aware of before. I didn't understand the significance and meaning of many statements in the New Testament but now they just glow with divine beauty, wisdom, and practicality. I just can't explain in words how pleased I am with your marvelous teachings."

By August 1957 Walter and Lao's revised edition of the course was in print, listing Lao as co-author with Walter for the first time and including a section on her own illumination.

CHAPTER FOURTEEN

The Growing University (1956-58)

Classes were held on the mountain during the summer of 1956. It was a time of poetically fascinating moonlight concerts in the gardens, broadcast over the grounds through loudspeakers. Dances were held in the palace and on the terraces in the light of an August full moon. The students enjoyed picnic parties in the adjacent forests and long walks on the mountain trails.

One long-remembered event from that session followed students' requests to see Walter at work in his studio. In one hour he sculpted in rough form a lifelike bust of George Washington. In the next hour he completed sketches from memory for a painting of the Villa Balbianelli on Lake Como. Those who witnessed this remarkable exhibition of power said they would never forget the eighty-five year old genius's demonstration of his mastery of these media, an exercise meant to serve as an illustration of how rapidly one can work knowingly with God. Those who returned to the palace the next season saw the completed bust and painting.

As early as January 1956 the directors of the Walter Russell Foundation addressed the long-delayed plan to rename the foundation and rewrite its corporate purposes to bring them more in keeping with the organization's actual activities. Russell University was proposed as a suitable name, but Walter and Lao preferred the more descriptive "University of Science and Philosophy." On April 4, 1957, the corporate charter was legally amended to adopt the new name and clarify the essential purposes, which were "to maintain and establish a university to teach the science of man, philosophy and art, and to engage exclusively in said educational activities in furtherance of the public welfare and to promote the well-being and well-doing of mankind in general."

Numerous students had offered to invest in the University, but their offers were politely declined. The corporation was non-stock, tax-exempt, and charitable in nature. Clark L. Jordan, their New York attorney, considered the organization of the new University of Science and Philosophy a landmark accomplishment and used the occasion to announce his retirement from the board, emphasizing that he was now confident the framework had been established for the permanent fulfillment of their mission and assuring his longtime colleagues that he would be proud and eager to be associated with the University in a pro bono advisory capacity as long as he lived.

The first meeting of the University's board was held at Swannanoa on May 17, 1957. Arthur Jones, Dr. Lavender, Charles L. Banister, and the Lombardis joined the Russells on the newly constituted board. Banister had cited the Russells in an article published in Newark, New Jersey, entitled "Is the Golden Rule Necessary in our Human Relations?" One of their most faithful students since 1951, he was a consultant for the federal government and was charged with the task of planning and programming methods of disposing millions of dollars worth of surplus personal property.

Lao was elected president and treasurer, Walter vice-president and secretary, and Emelia Lombardi recording secretary. The Russells were given unrestricted authority for the University's administration and management. Lao described the corporate reorganization as follows: "We started as a simple foundation for we could not acquire university status until we had a completed curriculum and many enrolled students. Our early students were grateful for what they received from us and spread their joy among their friends, which not only brought us more enrollments, but led to the establishment of our scholarship fund to provide financial assistance for people who could not afford to subscribe. That great cooperation by our students made it possible for us to become strong. Without it we would have had to close our doors long ago, and no one could have benefited from our teachings." After the meeting, Walter and Lao left for several weeks at The Cloister on Sea Island, Georgia, one of their favorite retreats.

In Rome, Italy, the University's chartering elicited a warm response from a longtime friend of Lao, Guiliana Bosio of Milan, who was staying at the famous Excelsior Hotel in Rome at the time she received the news. "Congratulations on the recognition of the University," she wrote. "I would like to have been with you that day to enjoy with you the marvelous news. I'm sorry I cannot express in English my feelings, but all I can say to you is that I am ever so happy." Guiliana had publicized the University in various Italian journals in articles that included photographs she had taken at Swannanoa.

The Russells were receiving many book orders from Italy. This was particularly true once *Atomic Suicide?* was published in 1957. A student in Milan asked permission to prepare and publish an Italian translation of the book, and they authorized him to proceed. Apparently the edition was small and quickly sold out and the translated work was never reprinted there.

By then over a thousand students had completed the *Home Study Course*.

A far greater number had read the Russells' books and visited or corresponded with them. Lao was proud of the diversity of their student body. A year after the Foundation was rechartered, she was happy to write, "Our students come from every walk of life among the more intellectual and from such groups as Christian Science and Unity. We have no religious connotation whatsoever in our teachings. The giving of knowledge does not require it. Yes, we believe in Jesus and Lao Tzu and Benjamin Franklin. They gave much to the world, Jesus more than any other man, but we do not believe the things about Jesus that the church claims it is heresy not to believe. In that sense you and we are alike in our thinking."

In 1957 Dr. Russell stopped carrying on his general correspondence because at the age of eighty-five he wanted to devote his full time to more important creative work. He wrote cheerfully to Bessie Fourton: "This may be the last letter I will ever write you. That sounds tragic, but it does not mean what it sounds. It only means that I am to be gradually freed from letter writing or even letter reading, except those from our inner circle. Won't that be grand? Lao freed me from the handling of money long ago, and that is even more grand, so I am now looking forward to a wonderful life of poverty and ease with nothing to do but work—which is the grandest kind of a life!"

At times he made an exception. Together in 1958 he and Lao outlined the basis of the course in a letter to a Texas student: "We both preferred waiting to see if the lessons themselves would not answer your questions. The law of love is expressed in the course by balanced interchange in equal givings and regivings. No civilization or individual who does not practice it can prosper. That is the very essence of the Golden Rule ethics upon which our teaching of human relations depends. Let us put it another way. Mrs. Russell and I have worked very hard for many years to make this course possible. I cannot tell you the hardships we experienced and the hard work of it, plus giving of all we possessed, [working] without salary for ten years, in order that you and others might transform your lives through having the kind of knowledge that transformed ours."

Lao was deeply appreciative of Dr. B. J. Palmer, the innovative college president whose work for humanity she felt to be of monumental importance. Until his death in 1961, Dr. Palmer, the most significant figure in twentieth-century chiropractic, regularly distributed hundreds of copies of Glenn Clark's *The Man Who Tapped the Secrets of the Universe* to his graduates and referred many brilliant scholars and healers to the Russells' books and course. He pronounced *The Message of the Divine Iliad* one of the best books he had ever read and gave copies to the staff and faculty at his Davenport, Iowa, college of chiropractic medicine. "The ones who took advantage of this opportunity and read the book have benefited," he reported to the Russells. Dr.

Palmer sent them an autographed copy of his own volume, *The Bigness of the Fellow Within*, which, he noted, emphasized the concept of innate intelligence in a manner that greatly reflected the Russells' own teaching.

Other leading chiropractors who promoted the Russell course and teachings during the last decade of Walter's life included R. C. Bolen of Greenwood, South Carolina, who conducted home study groups on the Russell work, sold hundreds of their books from his Chiropractic Institute, and regularly brought his classes for visits to Swannanoa.

Soon after this, Lao wrote that nearly 100 chiropractors were engaged in active correspondence with her or enrolled in the course. She believed that chiropractors were often more committed than medical doctors to reaching the body through the mind. At times they came in groups of fifteen or twenty, often prior to or following a state or regional conference.

In Fulton, New York, Dr. Lavender also urged his fellow chiropractors to enroll in the course. He had encouraged the Russells to produce small castings of Walter's sculptures of the hands and head of Christ, as well as of the Christ statue itself, and had correctly predicted that these reproductions would be popular with his professional colleagues and find their way into many of their office reception rooms.

Groups of chiropractors implemented the Russell teachings in their business policies. In 1958 a Conway, New Hampshire, practitioner advised Lao that twenty-nine of his colleagues in that New England state were working closely to implement the universal law of giving in their profession. "Our services are rendered on a cooperative basis with patients so that they might be able to receive health more abundantly from the Source, the Giver of life. We have completely done away with the fee system. All patients pay within their means. This is something new in the healing arts, as far as a group goes, and we mention it as a matter of interest to you."

Lao and Walter stressed that the "new knowledge" they offered their students could not be gained casually. When letters reached them filled with deep scientific questions, Lao would promptly reply that the answers could be found in their one-year *Home Study Course*. She often added that answering questions individually might well take as much space as the "twelve hundred pages and eighty diagrams of the course itself. You might just as well ask a musician to tell you all about music in a letter," she often noted. "We have the answers for you, but they cannot become yours by magic or wishful thinking. You must do what all others do to acquire knowledge and power. You must work and study! There is no other easy way." She regularly told her readers that she and Walter did not like to give explicit advice on individual problems because they knew that through an understanding of the Science of Man, individuals could learn to answer their own questions and solve their own problems.

Meditation was the starting point for the inquiring mind, she always said, and normal spiritual unfolding was a perfectly natural experience in which the student became more and more aware of God's presence within himself. This was important to Lao, who advised her students that no one could attain cosmic awareness by following a formula or performing a set of exercises. She told them it had to be earned like everything else in life, and "when true cosmic awareness comes to a person, the individual knows without any doubt that he has been born in the light of God and is left with no doubt as to the authenticity of the experience."

Lao also knew that even illumined people could go astray if they overvalued their own experience. This category included persons who claimed to be reincarnations of Jesus, Paul, or John the Baptist. Thus, while she urged students to think inwardly "because the cosmic mind within represented the true kingdom of heaven," she also warned them that true illumination took time to achieve. Recounting the Russells' own life journeys, she wrote, "My husband had forty-two such experiences before his great one in 1921 described by Glenn Clark. Even then he kept silent for years. I, likewise, had many years of knowing within me before I was ready to tell others. No one can help you but other illuminates, so guard yourself against religious and metaphysical cults and above all else guard your speech and keep your sanity. Keep yourself in what people call normal condition. They would not understand you, and those who do not understand will often persecute."

Walter and Lao sought earnestly to avoid the metaphysical phrases of the orthodox preachers, as well as the creeds and doctrines of the hundreds of disunited beliefs they felt had divided the unified whole of Christianity into an unrecognizable mass. They emphasized the worship of one universal God of Love, teaching that healing and inspiration comes from God and that worshipping individuals like Jesus, Lao Tzu, Krishna, Buddha, Beethoven, or Emerson often led to pure idolatry. They agreed with those who said that Christ lives in everyone, but they thought it equally correct to say that all the immortals whose teachings make us what we are live within us. They were quick to honor a student's right to believe as he or she chose, but they claimed the right to keep idolatry out of their own lexicon.

The Russells received bizarre requests. The following letter from Roanoke Rapids, North Carolina, arrived on July 25, 1957. "Dear sir: I've heard a report that astronomers from Waynesboro have seen in the heavens a great, golden city coming down from heaven as John the Revelator saw in the vision from the Isle of Patmos. [Revelations 1: 9-11, Revelations 21: 1, 2, 10, 18.] Now I would be glad to obtain the information if you have such or know where it can be obtained. Please inform me by return mail. Also I've been told scientists have used the very delicate radar device that magnifies sound so greatly and have heard prayers and pleas for air and water from another world that they have not directly located as yet. You being a great scientist as you are, I feel you are in authority to know this if these statements are fact. Please send me information at once on this."

Lao wrote a response, which Walter signed: "We have received your valued letter asking about some strange happenings in the heavens above Waynesboro. We have not heard of any such things and would have paid no attention to it for we do not believe that man ever defined heaven in any better way than the way Jesus taught when he commanded man to seek the Kingdom of Heaven within. We are sorry that we can send you no further information because we have heard nothing ourselves."

Another writer wrote complaining that the Russell teachings seemed to call into question much he had been taught concerning Christianity and religion, including the fact that Jesus Christ was mankind's Lord and Savior. "How can we select that part of the Holy Bible which we like? All Bible teachings indicate that the world will be destroyed in fire so that it can be purified of all evil by fire in preparation for receiving the new Jerusalem. God's universe is running right on time, and if it is His plan for it to burn up, than it most surely will burn up. The atomic bomb is the best way to accomplish this prophecy. I'd like your comments on the devil, hell, and the lake of fire. The Devil is very real and tempts every human, even trying to tempt Jesus Himself." This request required a longer response, but the Russells' conclusion was the same: "Everything is of God. Evil is man's imagination. The kingdom of heaven is found within." Their advanced students generally understood the purpose of their course.

A Kansas City student wrote, "As you may know, I live in what is known throughout the United States as the Bible belt. There is a crying need for a transitional type of book that will transform the minds of those who think only in terms of the metaphysical into the new knowing of the cosmic consciousness. I feel that your books are to be used for that transition."

The Russells knew that the world economy was based on the production of munitions and machinery, the sole ultimate purpose of which was to help people kill other people. They recognized that this made it difficult for their teachings to gain credibility among the world's industrialists and power brokers. Nevertheless, they had been working ceaselessly for over a year on a book they believed would awaken the whole world to the dangers of the proliferating use of atomic energy. On June 11, 1957, they wrote their friends and students that work on this forthcoming book made it impossible for them to issue their usual yearly newsletter or hold a summer class. Successful summer classes had been held at the palace in 1955 and 1956, although they were limited in length and attendance. Supporters understood that complet-

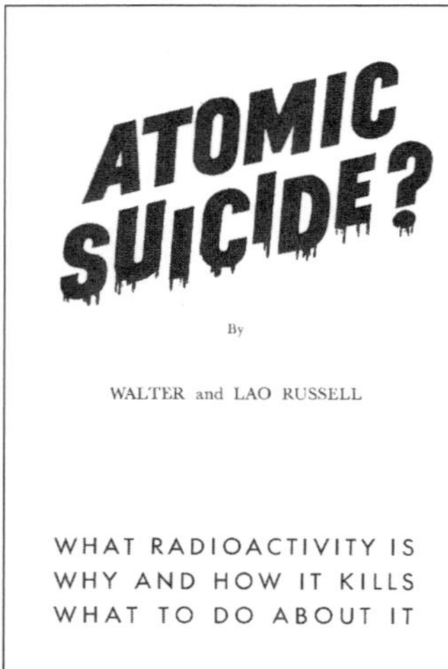

92. Atomic Suicide?

ing the book precluded holding on-site classes in 1957 but expressed hope that at the very least there would be a reunion of alumni at the palace in 1958.

Atomic Suicide? was announced in the book review section of the Sunday *New York Times* on June 23, advertised on all three national television networks, and reviewed in the *New York Herald-Tribune*. Russell students had already learned from Walter and Lao the nature of radioactive activity and how it kills, but the Russells' new book was the direct result of the authors' urgent desire to alert the entire world to this danger and save humanity from self-suicide. Students anticipating the Russell book urged them to rush it into print before the Atomic Energy Commission began a new round of dangerous experiments.

Publication of the volume could hardly have been timelier. Two months earlier, Dr. Albert Schweitzer had issued a dramatic warning against atomic bomb testing, saying his aim was to awaken public opinion before it was too late, and warning that the human race was heading for catastrophe if atomic bomb explosions were allowed to continue. At the same time, Norway had reported a recent radioactive rain over Scandinavia caused by Soviet nuclear testing. Dr. Russell had written Dr. Schweitzer of his own similar concerns and on request sent an advance copy of *Atomic Suicide?* to the great Nobel Prize-winner. Lao wrote a personal note to him, saying he was "the one man in the world today who comprehends its contents and import and can do something about it." Half of the first printing of 10,000 copies was soon sold out.

Atomic Suicide? warned the world against the dangers of using radioactive fission for either war or peace. The authors' authority to make such a claim stemmed from Walter's discovery of the existence of the trans-uranium elements decades before and his unique recognition of their dangers. Even further, the book sought to reveal secrets of Nature, including the means by which matter is constructed, how life is sustained, and why death inevitably comes from ignorance of universal processes.

In Tulsa, Oklahoma, Charles H. Story, prominent in nuclear control efforts, wrote telling the Russells that he prayed that the reaction to *Atomic Suicide?* would help restore sanity to the world, noting sadly, "Even though there has been a universal appeal to the President [Eisenhower] among scientific, educational, and religious leaders for an agreement to end nuclear testing of weapons, it seems to fall on deaf ears." Proponents of testing argued that within four or five years they could produce an absolutely clean hydrogen bomb. The very concept horrified the Russells, who wondered how any destructive bomb could ever be made "clean."

Popular morning television star Dave Garroway of National Broadcasting Company's *Today* show mentioned the book on the air and corresponded with the Russells. K. Z. Morgan, Director of the Oak Ridge National Laboratory in Tennessee, sent them word of his deep interest in talking personally with them about the book. Headquarters of America's Military Air Transport Service at Andrews Air Force Base ordered copies of *Atomic Suicide?* as did top staff officers in the United States Navy. On September 7, 1957, a member of the Atomic Energy Commission visited the Russells at Swannanoa and explained that the United States government was not ignoring their warning but felt helpless to stop nuclear testing until the Soviet Union agreed to do the same.

Over thirty years after *Atomic Suicide?* was published, John David Mann wrote an incisive article in his *Solstice* magazine outlining the remarkable accuracy of many of the predictions made by the Russells in their book and chronicling how three decades had favorably altered public and scientific perception of the Russells' fundamental warning. Recalling that the Russells' concern over radiation's effect on the atmosphere came twenty years before Sherwood Rowland's ozone prognosis, Mann described the attitude of nuclear carelessness that both sides in the Cold War demonstrated in the 1950s. The Soviet Union was conducting atmospheric bomb testing in Siberia, and the United States, embracing the promise of President Eisenhower's "Atoms for Peace" program, was doing the same on the Bikini atoll. The Russells had issued their initial warning in 1954 in their open letter to science, asserting that oxygen and radioactive materials could not coexist and warning the world that atmospheric nuclear testing was a recipe for disaster. In 1957, the basic premise of their book *Atomic Suicide?* was that continued development of nuclear arms and industry would eventually destroy earth's oxygen.

93. Solstice *magazine featuring the Russells.*

Mann found it more than coincidental that the Russells' "uncannily accurate forecast" in their book "that the oxygen-destroying effects of radiation would not be noticed 'until the late seventies'" seemed to correspond precisely with scientists' discovery of ozone depletion over the Antarctic in 1982 and the subsequent conclusion that this depletion had first appeared in 1979. Earlier, John W. Gofman in his 1971 book, *Poisoned Power*, included documentary statistics that confirm the Russells to have been correct.

In June 1957 alone over 500 students ordered books and courses and most wrote long personal letters to the Russells. Lao told Emelia that the best comment that month came from a couple who wrote, "The benefits we have received from the study of your course are too numerous to tell, but our living has acquired a great calmness, that our purposes are being more and more focused in one direction. Each day comes with great awareness and a realization that there is no life without the life of God. Know that your efforts on our behalf are deeply appreciated."

Professors at Lincoln College of Chiropractic in Nebraska wrote that they frequently referred to *Atomic Suicide?* in their classes. A number of Lincoln College graduates purchased copies of the book and enrolled in the *Home Study Course*. In August 1957 twenty of them came to Swannanoa to engage in prolonged discussion with Walter and Lao on the nuclear threat.

In October 1957 the editors of *American Fabrics* published an article on nuclear energy, quoting effusively from *Atomic Suicide?* The next month the book was favorably reviewed by the *International Review of Chiropractic*. From Melbourne, Florida, Dr. Charles Hanes, a great friend of Dr. Alexis Carrel, wrote the Russells and enthusiastically endorsed the book. Roger W. Babson, the notable American economic forecaster, whom they had known from the 1940s in New York, was extremely interested in the Russells' negative reaction to the development of atomic energy and shared their concern with his colleagues in investment banking and the international business community.

As much as Lao and Walter drew encouragement from the book's acceptance by an intelligent few, they were very disappointed when *Atomic Suicide?* failed to gain universal acceptance. In Minneapolis James D. Scarsdale had presented a review of the book to his business and professional colleagues, each of whom was given the privilege of making comments and asking questions for five minutes. The result, he reported to Lao, was "stunning silence." He sought to review the book in the major Minneapolis daily newspaper, but the editor rejected the article on the same day the newspaper featured an article on the discovery of atomic particles in the atmosphere by scientists at the Univesity of Minnesota.

By now Lao was demonstrating obvious skill at addressing detailed scientific matters in her own letters. She answered a student's question by explaining that nothing could counteract radioactivity once it lodged in a human body. She warned against a person having too many x-ray tests, noting that in the body radioactivity is accumulative, especially in the bone. As to the dangers from nuclear hardware, she advised the questioner that a two-ton shield on a locomotive reactor had become sufficiently radioactive in two years to suggest that it would become dangerously radioactive in a decade. Scientists proved this by their own mathematical calculations and tests from which the Russells quoted, Lao explained, noting, "God does not give us text book information but principle only. This answers your question as to how Dr. Russell knew that plutonium loses only half its radioactivity in twenty-three thousand years. You must always remember that information regarding effects is not the same as knowledge of cause."

She knew that important scientists like Dr. William F. Quillian of nearby Randolph-Macon Woman's College were aware of *Atomic Suicide?* but doubted that he or his colleagues would participate in a public discussion on the subject with Walter, who, she asserted, would welcome such a challenge even at the age of eighty-six. It was significant to Lao that no mainstream scientist had ever denied Walter's claim to have been the first to assert the existence of the two radioactive elements. He had claimed this priority many times, and it appeared again on the jacket of *Atomic Suicide?*.

To Lao the real unfairness lay in the fact that her husband had never received adequate public recognition for his discoveries, despite the fact that many traditional scientists had assured her that Walter was indeed recognized privately among his peers in the scientific world, especially in Europe, where, she was told, his new science would soon be taught in some major universities.

The New York Times Book Review vacation reading issue in 1958 contained a large advertisement for their books. Brother Mandus, the illustrious spiritual healer of Great Britain, brought *Atomic Suicide?* to the attention of Dr. George Arnsby Jones, author and founder of Unified World Communion, a non-organizational group of world servers founded in 1933. It was concerned with the imminence of nuclear self-destruction and the necessity of propounding a synthesis of science, art, philosophy, and religion, in order to reorient the thoughts and emotions of humanity. Dr. Jones reviewed *Atomic Suicide?* in the 1958 New Year's issue of his *New Horizons* magazine. Jones's own paper, *Synthesis of Science and Spiritual Religion*, had been published in several magazines and also issued by the International Institute of Scientific Research Societies. Jones fully endorsed the Russell teachings and brought them to the notice of scientists around the world. He envisioned a role for the Russells in his proposed Academy for Greater Living, which was to have as its goal the complete education of Man as a consummate spiritual being. Jones, who was also the world's leading proponent of the universal language called Globago, had worked on the blueprint for such an Academy for years and had tentatively been elected its Rector.

In the midst of all the correspondence on the future of the planet came several pleas from students whose matrimonial plans had not received sufficient attention from Lao. "Lao, dearest, please write me right away. Why are you afraid for me? Am I doing a right thing by marrying the man whom I brought you to meet? Why were you afraid for me and from what did you want to warn me? Write, darling, and be with me always." Advice to the lovelorn seemed to be always expected of Lao.

For Lao, 1957, numerologically a twenty-two year for her, was a time to give, give, and give. Students were amazed at her indefatigability and Walter's energy, which seemed to be boundless for a man of eighty-six. Visitors to Swannanoa found it amazing that Walter still enjoyed playing the organ at his advanced age. The truth about the man who tapped the secrets of the universe seemed to lie in Walter's knowledge that activity is the key to successful life on all levels. If one wants to stay young and able, he believed, one must be creatively active without ceasing. He projected his vigor well. A Connecticut student spoke to them both on the telephone and wrote Lao a week later, "It was one of the happiest moments to hear your lovely melodious voice and Doctor's young and vibrant one that night last week." John David Mann considered Walter Russell's strict adherence to natural law "a quintessentially macrobiotic ideal." Noting Walter's "legendary ability to work long hours with ceaseless good humor and without fatigue," Mann credited it to Walter's meticulous habits, prodigious work schedule, and the manner by which "he carefully rotated projects so that his focus changed to a different problem or medium every two hours—a rhythm known in macrobiotic circles as corresponding to the energy cycle of acupuncture meridians."

94. Walter playing the organ for Lao.

Lao was always quick to emphasize that age was no barrier to success, either economically or socially. "When my husband and I were married he was seventy-seven, and we have accomplished more since we were married in our God-given work than he did in all the years before. When you have a balanced mate, you will accomplish anything you set out to do."

Nevertheless, Lao, then only fifty-three, frequently urged close friends to visit them at the palace. "Let's see each other soon for we all are getting older," she would say. The few friends who remembered understood how she had felt back in Carnegie Hall when Walter seemed on the verge of a nervous breakdown. The Russells had one thing that the average man did not have. They knew where to turn when the going seemed too hard. They looked within to the One. Often Lao said she could not imagine how people endured without that security.

Eleanor Mel, their friend who headed the Boston Home of Truth Divine Science Center, wrote that its location at 175 Commonwealth Avenue was only two blocks from the new $100 million Prudential Life Center, a complex that would be larger than New York's Rockefeller Center. This seemed to be bringing new stimulation to Boston, she wrote, fondly recalling the days when Lao had frequented the Home of Truth and had first heard Walter lecture there in 1946. "A lot has gone under the bridge since then in your lives, in my life, the life of my work, and the life of the world," she wrote Lao. This treasured friend remained close to the Russells through the years until her death on July 18, 1964.

The Russells had begun a productive association with Kingsport Press in Kingsport, Tennessee, a complete book manufacturer, which did most of their publishing over the next years. Amish Hamilton, Ltd., which handled the British copyright for Alexis Carrel's *Man the Unknown*, offered to do the same for the Russell books. Swiss and Polish readers of their books wrote urging them to authorize translations into French, German, and Polish. The University of Virginia's Alderman Library wrote that their books had been extremely popular and ordered additional copies.

From Fulton, New York, Dr. Lavender, a faithful member of the board of directors since 1957, continued to support the Russells in their work. He visited Swannanoa in the summer and thought both of them looked far more rested than they had in the previous spring when they were under the tremendous pressure of finishing their new book.

The well-known mystic and writer Paul Brunton came to visit Walter and Lao at Swannanoa. They were familiar with each other's books and had sought to meet at Carnegie Hall in 1948, but their schedules had conflicted at that time. Creative Institute founder Allen Orizon Goodwin of Houston, Texas, a sponsor of Russell study groups there, came to the palace.

The Russells contracted with a Norristown, Pennsylvania, professional photographer named Grantland Rice to work with them on scientific laboratory experiments, but it soon became obvious that Rice's work was not suitable and his price excessive. They discharged him, but he threatened a lawsuit and withheld indispensable drawings and other University property they had allowed him to take to his studio. Through John Lombardi's negotiating skill a settlement was reached, but to recover their materials the Russells were forced to agree to a compromise payment of over $2,000.

In August 1957 Lao wrote one of her rare letters regarding physiology and medical treatment. A student had asked, "Is mind the visible ring or is it the invisible black center?" She used text and drawings from the course to show that the mind universe was invisible and the motion universe visible. The second question regarded the advisability of shock treatment, which doctors at the Mayo Clinic had prescribed for the student's wife's severe depression. Lao replied, "You must use your own judgment for we are not allowed to give medical advice, but we believe that shock treatments are injurious and would not allow it for ourselves under any circumstances."

The same month they went briefly to New England to visit old friends and students. They spent several nights with the Lombardis in New Jersey and with old friends in New York.

Students crossed the country to obtain the Russells' books by the case from the University, volunteered weeks of their time at the palace before returning to California, and distributed the books all across the country along the way. One Californian reported to the palace and offered to help the gardener take care of the grounds, or wash dishes, or do anything there was to do. She had been with the Rosicrucian fellowship since 1944 and had worked in the print shop, dining room, and on the grounds at their headquarters in San Jose. Another volunteer told Lao he could do plumbing, painting, carpentry work, sell books, or anything that was needed. All he asked was a place to eat and sleep.

Lao received many invitations to speak but declined them all because Walter needed her at Swannanoa. The Chapel of Truth in Philadelphia invited her to be its May speaker, adding, "We have been making out very well, but a great many people have asked me, 'When do we hear Lao Russell?'" A Russell study group met in Philadelphia the first Monday of each month.

Every day Lao could expect to receive at least two ten-page letters from various students with problems in their marriage or other serious personal family problems. Many of these people were already taking the course. They often asked for medical or psychiatric advice. Lao lovingly answered each request, making certain to focus on the Message.

From Mount Vernon, New York, the Director of Ideas for the Success, Unlimited, organization wrote them. A disciple of truth, who had reeducated herself along scientific lines and promoted the theory "You only need one idea to make a fortune," she signed up for the *Home Study Course*, ordered *The Man Who Tapped the Secrets of the Universe*, and suggested the Russells establish an endowment to provide scholarships for those who could not afford the course.

Word of the Russells' work reached Jill Jackson, author of the great hymn "Let There Be Peace On Earth and Let it Begin With Me." Calling them an inspiration, Jill related how in her own life the theme song of a small teenage workshop in human relations had in three months become so popular that 125,000 copies had been requested by schools, churches, service organizations, youth groups, and other organizations all over the world. Thereafter, Lao often encouraged young people to sing the song.

Sales were up on Walter's booklet *Your Day and Night*, which one Florida student called 'the most tremendous and beautiful, Soul-inspiring, divine little masterpiece I have seen after searching for many years." The mayor of Morganfield, Union County, Kentucky, enrolled in the course and found it of great value in helping him carry out his public duties.

By now there were 50,000 students all over the world, including those who had taken the course, bought their books, or corresponded with them about their teachings. Peter Parker found this fact "particularly impressive because it had been accomplished in such a short time under adverse circumstances and without any high-powered advertising."

Her sister Florrie wrote Lao a long description of changes in their old home city of Luton, enclosing photographs of its condition in the 1950s. "Luton is still growing. It is getting really important now and is always in the news. The people who bought our business sold the premises a couple of years ago and are now in a more convenient location. If you remember, when we went to Luton in 1909, it had a population of 45,000. Now it is 160,000. You would not believe it! Even after only twelve years away, I don't!"

In January 1958 Lao wrote their students that she and Walter were writing yet another book to awaken people to the one and only road to peace and security of life for all mankind. She expected this book to be published by April.

The same month a student had personally delivered a copy of *The Russell Cosmogony* to United States Secretary of Defense Neil McElroy. This brought a surge of joy to Lao, who wrote, "Many people call and want to send books to distinguished people whom they personally know, and often I feel impelled to tell them that the book will probably not even be opened, for such people are flooded with all kinds of useless material. Somehow I did not get this reaction when you mentioned Mr. McElroy. We have long felt him to be a man of destiny and have noted his courage in advocating the principles he considers right." Lao feared Mr. McElroy's schedule would be so heavy that he would pass it on to the Atomic Energy Commission, as President Eisenhower had done when Walter had offered his great scientific knowledge to the government in 1955. Lao related, "At that time Walter had received a curt three line letter of rejection through the Atomic Energy Commission, to whom the letter had been referred. Great minds all down through history have experienced this same treatment. We can only hope that Mr. McElroy is the one to recognize the basic knowledge contained in *Atomic Suicide?*"

When *The Russell Cosmogony* had been released in 1953, the Russells sent it to more than 800 of the greatest scientists in the world. Universities in Europe gave Walter due credit. Cambridge University went so far as to send two scientists from the Cavendish Laboratories to study with him for two weeks. Before they returned to England they had made photostatic copies of every one of Walter's out-of-print works, including the 250 pages of *The Universal One*, Walter's 1926 book that scientists and intellectuals in America had largely ignored.

Lao related the Russells' deep worry that the Soviet advance over America in science was due to the comprehension by Soviet scientists of the clues to greater power sources that Walter had given in all of his scientific writings. She concluded, "Our great hope now is that the Soviets have not yet solved the problem of power projection, which would make present cables and transmission lines obsolete, as well as the anti-missiles."

In February 1958 the Russells were put in contact with industrialist Cyrus Eaton through the spiritual efforts of his wife. He expressed interest but failed to follow through in any tangible way of support.

Lao's mail was piled high and Walter helped her with replies to some of the more curious letters: "Your letter is next, but it is one of those which gives me deep pain to answer," they wrote one writer who questioned their failure to acknowledge the presence of extraterrestrial beings masquerading as Earthlings, "for so many like it have come to us for years—and all have to be answered truthfully, whether we save people from their own love of the miraculous, unnatural and impossible or lose them by our frankness. I wonder why people ask such questions and make such statements as you have about space people walking our streets. Where and how did these people from Venus and Mars learn to speak English? Where did they get clothes like ours? You ask us why we do not include these 'space people' in our teachings. Our answer is that there are no such beings walking our streets and coming in space ships. Our knowledge of God and His ways insulates us from being taken in by the greatest hoax of this century, which criminal charlatans have invented to make money from credulous people who like to believe in unnatural phenomena. Why do you call them 'messengers from God'? What has any of them said or written that would justify any such wild statement? Yes, I know that these charlatans who are so profitably fooling the world are claiming that they receive the messages. So, also, do spiritualistic mediums make the same claim. That is their stock in trade."

Peter Parker lobbied the editors of *American Mercury* magazine to publish an article on the Russells. After a condensation of the Russells' newest book, *The World Crisis: Its Explanation and Solution*, appeared in the magazine's October 1958 issue, nationally known writer and publisher David Lawrence asked for and received an autographed copy of the book.

The World Crisis: Its Explanation and Solution argued that civilization's ills were not caused by faulty economics but rather by lack of unity among mankind. It convincingly portrayed the white race as destroying itself by preying on the other races and failing to recognize the oneness of humanity. "Every person in this world has a deep purpose," Lao often stated. "Happiness consists of finding one's own purpose and working to fulfill it." She was convinced that by so doing, everyone would contribute to the one-world purpose of unity and harmony, which would result when men and women of character, power, imagination, and vision acted on valid scientific knowledge of their purpose on earth.

Earl Nightingale, Chairman of the Board of Nightingale-Conant Corporation in Chicago, and his wife both read *The World Crisis* and found it an "outstanding, brilliant, and penetrating analysis of the world today" with which they were in full agreement. Mr. Nightingale told Walter he had long been familiar "with your outstanding career and many times discussed you on my radio and television programs in the mid-west." They explored having Nightingale record some of their works for sale to the general public.

From Hollywood, California, the parents of an Olympic swimmer wrote to recount the impact the Russells' work had made on them and their son. "Glenn Clark's little book on your wonderful life and ability to tap the great powers has just fallen into my hands. I know that any works you have written will be of vital help and inspiration. We are in this country to help choose a college for our son, Murray Rose, the world swimming champion, who at the age of seventeen years won three gold medals at the Melbourne Olympic Games, the first time in the history of the games for one so young. He has been brought up on a vegetarian diet and in food reform lines and with metaphysical beliefs. Sometimes we have felt a little of the force you have known so well. Now we must leave him to his own resources and are seeking guidance and help in making wise decisions for him and ourselves. Please send a list of your books." This letter led to a long

95. Murray Rose, the Australian-born Olympic swimming champion.

correspondence and friendship with the Rose family.

Walter and Lao spent April 1958 at Sea Island, Georgia, where they had previously vacationed, and planned to take the same cottage at the same time in 1959. Dr. Bowan Jones in Fort Lauderdale, Florida, kept them supplied with health food supplements. The Russells both used royal jelly and supplemented their chiefly vegetarian diet with many minerals and vitamins. They had never smoked cigarettes or drunk coffee.

While their explicit views on diet appeared to vary somewhat from time to time, they summarized their fundamental conception of nutrition and health in *Atomic Suicide?* where they maintained that "the blood is of first importance of all the elements which compose the body. The nervous system could be entirely paralyzed and the body would still function, but the blood has deep instinctive awareness of its existence, and the body which does not have a happy, rhythmic blood condition cannot possibly retain its normalcy."

In the same book they emphasized, "Even the food one eats should be 'happy.' It should be cooked with love and eaten joyfully, and there should be a joyful realization of love in one's deep breathing and exaltation during the process of taking food into one's body. The food you eat becomes blood and flesh of your body, and the manner in which you eat it, and your mental attitude while eating it, decides your blood count, the balance between acidity and alkalinity of your digestive machinery, and your entire metabolism. Your Mind is You and your body is the record of your thoughts and actions. Your body is what your Mind electrically extends to it for recording."

It still annoyed Walter when people minimized Lao's contribution to their work. He stressed this in a letter of August 23, 1958, to his friend Harris:

> They are our teachings, Lao's equally with mine. I wish you would make it a habit to say "Walter and Lao" when you speak of our work, or "Walter and Lao Russells' teachings" or "the Russells' teachings," and drill it into the minds of your men never to say "Dr. Russell" alone when speaking of this university or our work. This is not a one-man affair. Lao created the whole body of the organization, then created its curriculum equally with me.
>
> When we started, Lao wanted to build me up, but she did as much on the course as I did, and for a while I put my name to it alone. After a while I was so ashamed of taking that credit for what Lao was doing equally that I refused to let her suppress her great Self to exalt me, so we put both names on it. In thus working together we learned the great lesson of the greater power of a man and woman who work together, and the discovery of it in practice became a part of our teachings.
>
> Lao is a greater person than the students who come here ever give her credit of being. Why is this? They see me doing all the glory work of painting, sculpting, and such things, and they see Lao writing letters in the

> office, doing the inconspicuous work of building the very foundation of this institution. They do not see her in the midnight hours working with me to produce the entire curriculum that we now have, which is a practical living philosophy. They do not see her creating her own great book, *God Will Work with You but Not for You*, which is as well known in Switzerland and South Africa as it is in the United States. They do not see her role because she insists on placing me in front, as she did in the introduction to *Atomic Suicide?* I know that I would be six feet underground long ago if she had not come along.

Walter was in no danger of being forgotten. In Pasadena, California, Jo Regan included him among the hundred "best Americans in all fields" to offer advice to teenagers in her proposed book, *The Best in Advice to Young Americans*. Walter wrote seven paragraphs reflective of the advice he generally gave "seriously ambitious young people." Noting that the "great geniuses of the world are hard workers who love their work" and "give long hours into making themselves into the kind of men they wish to be," he cautioned that "the richest father in the world cannot create a genius son. The son alone can do that. Genius is self-bestowed and mediocrity is self-inflicted." He concluded by telling the young people that the first and most important discovery in life "is the discovery of yourself as a deep well from which everything you desire can flow into whatever goal you may seek and make it become the image of your concept of yourself."

On December 9, 1958, the Internal Revenue Service issued a ruling granting exemption from taxation to the University of Science and Philosophy under Section 501(c)(3) of the Internal Revenue Code. The United State Tax Court subsequently made the exemption retroactive to 1948 and extended it so as to cover the predecessor organization, the Walter Russell Foundation. This vindicated Arthur Jones's treating as tax-deductible his mid-1950s gift to the Foundation of most of the purchase price of the summer cottage behind the Swannanoa garden.

Despite the fact that the ruling cleared the way for a major fund-raising effort, the Russells continued to adhere to what Lao described as "our strict policy of never in any way, directly or indirectly, asking for the donations and 'love offerings' which are customary in most human relations organizations. Our instructions in *The Message of the Divine Iliad* read as follows: 'Pass not thou the alms bowl. All thy life then hast been prepared as a rock against which thou, thyself, mayst lean, and it shall not fail.' We have both practiced it all of our lives, and it has never failed. We still adhere to that policy in order that no one who ever needs us will be turned away."

She knew that the University's benefit to mankind was limited by its income. "During all these years we have been its main source," she explained to those who inquired. "We have given all our personal fortunes, our fifty-three copyrights, and our valuable art collection, but we have been limited in our ability to give scholarships to those who could not afford our tuition and our ability to expand our laboratory and staff as needed for our scientific work. Walter Russell gave atomic energy to the world, as you know, and the world made bad use of it. We are now working to replace nuclear power with a better and safer power which will remove the war incentive."

After visiting Swannanoa, Harry Edward Neal of Washington published an article about the Christ of the Blue Ridge for *Sunday Digest*. He apologized to the Russells for the limited scope of the piece: "As I explained to you, the emphasis in this story is on the statue and the garden, and I could not dwell upon your interesting philosophies and work, but I do hope I have managed to present them fairly yet briefly." They replied favorably, but Lao told Emelia, "Such seems to be always the case. It is always the artwork and the palace that they emphasize."

The Russells had predicted major changes for 1960. A student wrote to tell them that April 17, 1960, Easter Day, had been revealed as a future day of great importance by Dr. Brown Landon, as a result of his study of the telos of the Great Pyramids.

Dr. Reba Kelly of Portland, Oregon, reported that a Claire Voyer there had reported that the Russells had helped her establish a center in Arizona for the purpose of preparing to receive space people. Participants had all been required to make substantial cash payments, and Lao purportedly had required each one to paint his or her house a certain color. Lao had never heard of the person. She replied, "Not only would we not be connected with such a movement as its backer, but we believe this space people phenomenon to be the greatest foible of the age. It has made millions for people who know nothing about the properties of space. One author claims to have held conversations with a man from Venus. The man looked like Earth people and had the same kind of flesh, yet the temperature on Venus is over 200 degrees, nearly the boiling point of water. You need not keep this confidential. The more you do to expose this woman, the better. We shall turn the matter over to our attorney."

Grace Desmond, a special Russell student, wrote, "Never had any human being in the world up until now, even Jesus, spoken with such authority in giving cosmic knowledge and such detailed explanation for all who will hear and receive as Dr. and Lao Russell. Jesus had the knowledge, of course, and some others too have given something of truth in their writings, but always it is in veiled style."

Lao commented on a student's theory that one might learn as much from the Bible as from their *Home Study Course*: "It is good to hear that you are a student of the Bible and that you write for such distinguished periodicals, but the Bible will not teach you to be a good painter, poet, or musician. That is not its purpose, not its intent. The scientist could not build an electrical generator from study of the Bible, and you should not expect that Book to go beyond its intent and purpose. Nowhere in it does it answer your question to us regarding the electrical nature of the thinking process, nor its rhythms, yet it is the most poetically rhythmic book ever written. The Psalms especially, express that 1-2-3-4-4-3-2-1 octave measure in poetry in as masterful a manner as Beethoven expresses it in his symphonies. That basic thing which you say you do not understand is known by every genius ever born without having been taught.

"I have written you at this length because you say you were awakened to new thinking by my book. You even say that my ideas are unique. They are not unique. They are basic, but the world is only just beginning to become aware of basic knowledge and thinks it is new. It is not new. It is as old as time. It is the awakening to their realization by man that is new, like visiting another country which was always there, but new to the first-time visitor only."

Lao wrote an explanation of inner sensory perception as it related to a case of supposed healing: "We were interested in your comment about your own malady and your experience with the woman who 'took on' your illness. There is nothing beyond Nature, so miracles are not involved as far as cause is concerned. Quite a few people have had inner sensory perception developed to the telepathic level. Edgar Cayce was a noted example of this. Various people have reached certain heights and powers which others have not reached. This woman may be one of these. We have no way of knowing. Neither have you, but no one can justly condemn that which is beyond his understanding, even though there are many who fraudulently claim such powers. What puzzles us is why she took your ailments on herself. Jesus did not do this. Cayce did not, and we have never heard of any who did. The fundamental of Mind healing is to extend your normalcy to another and not to take on his abnormalcy."

She was quick to explain that the University was a purely educational institution. "For us to render diagnoses or treatments of any kind, mental or physical, would endanger our charter. As an educational institution we can teach, however, and that means that we can give principle, examples, and reasons. If you carefully read the chapter in *God Will Work with You but Not for You* on the healing principles you will fully understand the relation of your Mind to God's Mind and to your own body. Most people are handicapped in that respect by believing that their body is their identity. It is but a machine that can get out of repair, but it can also be made to function abnormally by Mind-attitudes and emotions which cause abnormal strains and tensions on the body. Do the troubles come when your nerves have been on edge? Ask yourself that. If so guard against it. Happy people are almost always normal. A state of inner joyousness is better than a thousand doctors, but a cynic or grouch sours his own stomach as well as he repels his friends. We knew a man who was totally paralyzed for forty years; you would be amazed if you could hear him talk. He was also blind, yet he earned his own living and paid for his two or three personal attendants. By sheer will he made the muscles of his fingers work well enough to press a button, and that is all, yet he told us that he would rather have his Mind and his body that any athlete's body and an average Mind."

At times Lao gave detailed diagnoses as to the cause of illness, although stressing that she was not qualified to cure disease. Explaining their principles in a September 1958 letter to a San Mateo, California, student, she explored various ways through which a person could suffer injury. "Nicotine has its own ways, and yellow fever has its ways. We call them symptoms. Their patterns and effects are unlike. Many injuries to the body we call diseases, but a blow upon the body with a hammer injures it also, and you do not call that a disease, nor do you associate the idea of germs with it. I am quite sure that if you give thought to the many ways in which you can injure your body knowingly or unknowingly, you will readily understand that their different causes must produce different effects."

Major John B. Garnett, a scholarly English professor at nearby Fishburne Military School, was a frequent guest of the Russells at Swannanoa, as was local portraitist and artist Mrs. Thomas Jefferson Randolph IV. These cultured and sociable individuals passed the Russell works among their various intellectual and artistic circles and at last began to bring the University much favorable attention locally. Lao particularly appreciated the work Major Garnett and others were doing in educating young men at Fishburne, and she and Walter entertained groups of cadets, as well as students from the local girls school, Fairfax Hall, on springtime occasions when the palace gardens were beautiful and the young people could best enjoy the splendor of the mountain site. Among the Fishburne cadets who thus became acquainted with the Russells' teaching were future Virginia Governor Gerald L. Baliles and, years later, Otio Okilo, son of Lao's great friend, Melford Okilo, the Nigeria statesman.

John Miles had joined the staff in 1958 and for years was charged with keeping the gardens beautiful as well as handling maintenance problems on the estate. Even in years of drought, he seemed to work magic on the marble terraces behind the palace. In her 1964 Christmas message, Lao described how he had "lovingly fed the ground with natural fertilizer" and noted that "visitors were amazed at the size of his marigolds and zinnias. Our terraces were a mass of blues, reds, golds, and yellows. It was indeed a sight to behold. [He] also made lovely gardens at our entrance."

Harry Hone, who was to experience a remarkable revival from death about which he wrote in 1976 in his book, *The Light at the End of the Tunnel*, had been well acquainted with the Russells since 1958, when he followed a compelling desire to meet them and ventured to Swannanoa in a blinding snowstorm. Not surprisingly, he was deeply moved by his initial meeting with Walter and Lao, a pleasant encounter over afternoon tea, which nonetheless awakened him to the concept of working knowingly with God, a path he followed thereafter and found exemplified in his near-death experience eighteen years later. He developed a solid friendship with the Russells and advised them on estate and business planning techniques through which the University's students might help endow the future of the Message and the shrine of beauty the Russells had established at Swannanoa. Hone met with John Lombardi and agreed to contribute his services and experiences to the project even if an insurance company other than his were chosen to carry out the commitments of the contracts. Hone often described his initial meeting with Walter and Lao at Swannanoa and the circumstances surrounding it that seemed to Hone far more than coincidental.

Throughout the 1950s the Russells worked with Major Tudor Poole of London's worldwide Big Ben Silent Minute Observance in promoting an international moment during which individuals around the globe would be encouraged to pause for a single minute to realize silently their mutual dependence upon God and to pray for world peace.

Richard St. Barbe Baker, founder of the Men of the Trees organization, wrote them from Southampton, England, in August 1958. Glenn Clark had given Baker a copy of *The Man Who Tapped the Secrets of the Universe*, and after reading it, he was eager to meet Walter. Baker, who was famous for his successful nine-year struggle to save the California redwoods, had extended his work to New Zealand and the Sahara Desert. A native of Saskatchewan, Canada, he promoted environmental conservation in Kenya as early as 1920 and eventually worked on every continent except Antarctica to preserve and maintain the world's forests and halt the spread of its deserts. Christened "the Man of the Trees" by famous commentator Lowell Thomas, he began the first international conservation movement, the Men of the Trees. He also reportedly had first suggested the idea of the Civilian Conservation Corps that provided work for six million unemployed Americans during the great depression. Baker authored many books on trees and forestry.

The Russells invited St. Barbe Baker to Swannanoa that fall, telling him, "We have no redwoods, but we have miles of quite primitive forests and many quiet walks in our hills and ravines. You will love the palace itself—our home on the mountaintop. We anticipate some wondrous talks about things which we know in advance will be of deep mutual interest." Although St. Barbe Baker was unable to come to Virginia until several years later, when they did meet, he and the Russells proved to be kindred souls. Baker thereafter promoted their works on four continents and visited them again not long before Walter's death, after which he remained a close confidante of Lao for the rest of his life, visiting her frequently at Swannanoa and personally introducing her to his London publishers in 1963.

An osteopath from Salem, Oregon, wrote them for advice as to how to stimulate his business. Their response detailed their formula for success: "Many of our students have suffered from the same lack as you describe, but after taking our course and getting into the habit of more powerful inner thinking and gaining more knowledge of God's ways and processes, they have overcome their lack, not by overcoming it by conscientiously fighting it, but by unconsciously eliminating it by substituting better right thinking for it."

Walter told of another osteopath who had studied the course and then moved his practice from Arizona to Florida, where he had built a flourishing practice within three years without even putting out his sign. "Incidentally, I have never asked for work in my life, for the same reason," Walter recounted. "I make people see in me and in my work that to which their needs respond. People see that quality in our students' eyes and ask 'Why?'"

He had advised one struggling professional, also an osteopath, as follows:

> I cannot analyze your faults in detail, for it would take too much time and you would not comprehend them from an analysis. You would have to recognize them by replacing them with new thinking which our one-year course would give you. Briefly though, your human relations ideas are not focused. They are scattered. You are in a world where you have to manifest constantly the love idea in your every action, especially to your patients. Your thinking evidences that it is easier to interest you in flying saucers or unnatural phenomena than it is to interest you in illumining the world with the Light of your Self, so that all men will come to you as a light in the wilderness. You speak of "mystic philosophy" which you have studied. What you mean is mystic phenomena. You speak of "mystica" instead of natural laws. You speak of being punished by karma. Your Mind has been misled into unnatural paths instead of natural ones. You send people away from you instead of attracting them to you. People instinctively move out of the orbits of those who manifest unnatural beliefs and with equal instinctive eagerness move into the orbits of those who manifest God's ways and processes, whether that naturalness of the love idea is expressed by an illiterate farmer or a statesman.
>
> You got off on the wrong track early in life by studying the so called "occult and mystic" instead of talking with God in the quiet of the forests, or

> by meditation in your own seclusion. The kingdom of heaven is within, but you have looked for it in the miraculous. If ever a person needed what this university teaches, which is the philosophy of two who have built their lives to high points through knowing and working with God, you are that person.
>
> I have been frank with you, because you asked it. We are not a clinic. We do not diagnose and charge consultation fees. We are purely an educational institution which endeavors to give God-awareness to people who wish to make use of His omnipotence to multiply their own powers. You told us to consider your $5 as a donation or apply it to a fee. We will accept it with our sincere thanks as a donation, but not as a fee.

Walter advised him to make a clean break and to give earnest study and thought to the basic things of life. The osteopath and his wife soon enrolled in the *Home Study Course*, and in later years they thanked Lao for the opportunity the University had given them to live their lives abundantly, gloriously, and together.

A student from British Columbia asked them whether or not the mind is controlled by suggestion. Lao promptly responded, "The Mind is never controlled by anything because it is the controlling force of all things and all matter obeys its will. The senses receive their orders from the Mind and it is through the desire of Mind that the universe is constructed and operates. Such a suggestion as that the Mind is controlled by suggestion is so foreign to our teachings that you must have read it elsewhere."

Alexis Carrel's *Reflections on Life* had been translated from the French by Antonia White, and Lao arranged with Hawthorn Press, its American publisher, to stock the book for sale at the palace and list it on the University's supplementary reading list.

Lao showed special love for musicians and other creative artists who were attracted to the *Home Study Course*. She heartily endorsed the famous classical singer Marjory Taylor for her stimulating support for a newly organized symphony orchestra on the West coast and praised the costume designs that had gained a young Cuban expatriate major commissions in Hollywood. Both of them felt their creativity had been expanded by the course.

Of the thousands of letters they received, Lao noted, only the occasional one would come from an individual truly ready for cosmic knowledge. "The rewarding thing," Lao wrote Marjory Taylor, "is that they do come."

There was no summer reunion at Swannanoa in 1959, and Lao doubted that there would ever be any more organized summer classes. "When there are so many people here at one time," she noted, "there is little opportunity to see the students alone for more than five minutes." She thought it much more satisfactory when special students came individually or in small groups so that the Russells might meet with them individually for a longer time. Well-known Hollywood names often appeared in their mail. The Beverly Hills celebrity Lance Reventlow, son of Woolworth heiress Barbara Hutton, received and read their books.

A lifelong friendship with the noted actor Eddie Albert and his celebrated wife, Margo, developed from a letter Mr. Albert wrote the Russells on September 19, 1956, beginning, "A generous friend has given me Glenn Clark's pamphlet on you and your thinking, and in the two days that have passed since reading it, my behavior has taken on a joy and coherence, my thinking an ecstasy and purpose that have heretofore eluded me—and I am eager for more." He asked to enroll in the *Home Study Course* and requested some books of the Russells' choice, and both of the Alberts soon found themselves delighted with Lao's *God Will Work with You but Not for You*.

The same month Catherine Reynolds, personal secretary to the famous actress Gloria Swanson, wrote to tell the Russells of the film star's desire to come to Swannanoa and meet them. Lao sent her a copy of the same book, asking that Miss Swanson read it before they came to Virginia. Lao felt intuitively that Gloria Swanson might well be the great leader who could head the proposed global Man-Woman Equalization League envisioned in the book.

Miss Swanson insisted that she and her secretary come to Swannanoa in October 1958. She felt as if a great light had come into her vision, a dream come true, and she was determined to pursue it. The visit proved to be the beginning of a lifelong friendship between Lao Russell and Gloria Swanson. It would bring them together in New York and at Swannanoa on a number of occasions in the years to come and kept them in close touch with one another until the great actress died in 1983.

96. Gloria Swanson with the Russells at Swannanoa.

Almost immediately after her first visit to Swannanoa, Miss Swanson wrote Edward R. Murrow, urging him to focus a television program on the Russells. She also promoted the idea of a film based on Walter's composition, *The Sea Children's Waltz*.

CHAPTER FIFTEEN

Proving the Truths (1951-62)

Through the first fourteen years at Swannanoa, the Russells worked valiantly to find the time and funding to allow them to establish a laboratory at the palace, where Lao might help Walter replicate and expand the experiments he had completed years before, in order to prove the scientific truths set forth in their books and course. They found encouragement from many sources, but it proved almost impossible to focus attention on this demanding work while their worldwide correspondence proliferated and their books drew thousands of visitors to the mountain, many of whom they were obliged to meet personally.

A. Warren Way, the Philadelphia scientist, began a rich and extensive correspondence with them in 1951. They told him that they read his letters with the interest they gave to the special one in a hundred or thousand. He shared their fears that, without new knowledge, the world was on its inevitable way to another dark age. The Russells knew that such special students as Mr. Way understood the handicap faced by those eager to give a spiritual message in a materialistic world. They told Mr. Way that during World War II, Walter had authored a plan to build a series of towers around England fifty miles apart, through which no plane could pass with an explosive. He had offered to demonstrate how such a "detonator" could be constructed, but those in authority showed no interest.

In March 1953, the Walter Russell Foundation gave Andrew Wilson sole and exclusive right to form a research group to produce free hydrogen by transmutation from the atmosphere under the guidance of Walter Russell at Swannanoa.

Dr. Robert M. Page, a government expert on radar, came from Washington with his wife, Esther, and spent twenty-two hours with the Russells in January 1961. His purpose was to discuss Walter's new cosmogony and ascertain its potential for improving radar. The Russells studied up on current radar terms in their Encyclopedia Britannica, but found, as usual, "when one knows the basic principles of Creation and applies them to anything in Nature, the true answers come." Dr. Page left Swannanoa feeling he had known them all his life, and frequently corresponded with them through the following years.

Winifred Duncan, an Alabama theosophist, obtained Walter's permission to include several of his drawings and information on his theories in her extensive compendium *The Shape of Things*, published by New York's Ronald Press. She told them that Walter's clear analysis of the devolution of cubic space into spheres was by far the most precise she had found, and stood in sharp contrast with what Duncan termed the "hazy meanderings of Rudolf Steiner." Walter was complimented to be compared so favorably with the well-known founder of Anthroposophy, and he and Lao sent Mrs. Duncan the material she requested, reviewing her comments on their work before they were published in several remarkable letters that reveal Lao's immersion in Walter's scientific work.

A letter Lao wrote to Winifred on February 6, 1951, suggested that the Alabama author might best understand Walter's theory by producing a whole octave cycle "while you wait" and examining it: "Empty your lungs as far as you can. Then breathe in to fill them. That is a wave—an octave wave—a cyclic octave wave. In it are the four positive and negative efforts that the spectrum would record in color, substance would record as elements, and music would record as tones. You reincarnate the whole octave, not part of it."

Lao was proving herself as adept as Walter in addressing questions on the scientific principles of their teachings. In January 1951, she replied to a specific question about Walter's claim that he could summarize the secret of creation in one sentence. She quoted the sentence, "The electric wave divides the one Father-Mother of Creation into pairs of father-mother bodies, which unite as one to divide again into pairs of father-mother bodies." She told the inquirer, "I will make you a diagram showing this principle. As you have undoubtedly long ago learned, God's ways are simple, but men have made them complex, and in doing so have lost the key to God's great creative principles."

During the summer of 1953, the world's top physicists met in session in Kyoto, Japan. Each of them received a copy of *The Russell Cosmogony* and Walter's chart of the elements. Some of them responded directly to the Russells, but the real response came in their public statements, which were remarkably congruent with Walter's work.

Several months later, Walter noted with interest the announcement that Professor Halary of Indiana University had simplified Einstein's formula on gravity with implications that gravity and electromagnetism were related. This also reflected the work Walter had done decades before.

Phillip K. H. Yee, a manager of the Honolulu, Hawaii, municipal water system, learned of Walter Russell, and promptly read *The Man Who Tapped the Secrets of the Universe* and all four of Walter's available books, following which he began a productive correspondence and long friendship with the Russells, punctuated by several visits to Swannanoa and tireless efforts to publicize the Message through Honolulu newspapers and the local government there. It was a tremendous revelation to Mr. Yee to meet someone who knew the common ground between science and religion. A hydraulics engineer, he had studied chemistry, physics, electricity, magnetism, and calculus, and found in the Russell books answers to all the questions that had plagued him through the years. He shared this knowledge with many important friends in Hawaii, and dedicated himself to helping the necessary transformation of man. Regularly he sent colleagues attending the annual American Water Works Conferences on side pilgrimages to Swannanoa.

A psychology professor at Morningside College in Sioux City, Iowa, corresponded with the Russells on the nature of electrons and protons, questioning whether the substances were fission products, and whether creation begins by division followed by more complex integration into larger, more complex, and more unstable structures. They discussed the tensions of opposites, possible causes of the expanding universe, and Herbert Spencer's famous formula of differentiation and integration. Walter's replies never deviated from the basic cosmogony he had expressed in *The Secret of Light*. Scientists expressed interest in the fact that during Lao's three-day-and-night illumination in 1946, God had made known to her that scientists should not refer to electricity as negative and positive, but as a positive change using only the plus sign instead of plus and minus.

The connection between Walter Russell's scientific theory and that of Nikola Tesla continued to intrigue researchers who were working to evolve practical applications of both. Tesla's efforts to develop an apparatus capable of collecting atmospheric electric force was one such project. The full particulars of his experiments had never been divulged, and individuals frequently wrote Lao for information on related laboratory work by Walter.

From their first years at Swannanoa, the Russells had hoped to build a small laboratory in a large concrete room in the palace's chateau-like, abandoned stables. In August 1953, they told their friend Dr. J. F. Vannerson that the laboratory would be located temporarily upstairs in the palace until it could later be moved to the stables.

Dr. and Mrs. Everett Johnston wrote from Detroit of their success in locating a used spectroscope and other x-ray apparatus that Walter needed for further laboratory experiments at Swannanoa. The local hospital in Detroit had sold its old equipment to a Japanese physicist just before receiving Dr. Johnston's inquiry, but soon afterwards, the Johnstons located a self-rectifying hospital x-ray apparatus satisfactory for Walter's work and sent it on to Swannanoa, Martha Johnston advising him that "being a service to you is our pleasure."

In September, Grace L. Drummond sent two boxes of scientific equipment from California, including an excellent microscope. The new laboratory was in operation at the palace by November 1.

Work soon began in the laboratory to prove the Russell's contention that radioactive fission would destroy the earth's atmosphere and its water, and to prepare for the anticipated global water problem. As always, budgetary constraints inhibited their progress, but they were immensely aided by a 1953 student, Dr. Shag Okubo of the University of Hawaii, a brilliant physicist who grasped the urgency of the Russells' warning, took leave of his teaching position, and came to work in the hastily improvised laboratory at Swannanoa. At last Walter had a physicist to work with him at the palace, something he urgently needed. Starting with their limited and somewhat antiquated equipment, the team pursued their work, acquiring the necessary apparatus piece by piece as they could afford it and through additional donations from deeply interested students. Dr. Okubo's Chinese wife, Fung Kai, and their three talented children added to the happiness of the growing Swannanoa family. They occupied the cottage near the water tower. Lisa Okubo, one of the daughters, delighted the Russells with her piano virtuosity.

The Russells had felt compelled to continue their August course on the mountain through 1956, despite the toll it took on their progress in the laboratory. After attending the August 1953 classes, Mr. and Mrs. Jay Katz spent several months at the palace working with the Russells and Dr. Okubo. Mr. Katz had created the scholarship fund for those unable to pay their *Home Study Course* tuition.

Phillip Yee performed further related scientific work in Hawaii, carefully coordinating his experiments with Walter. Yee's work led to the Federal Government stepping up its search for a low-cost method of converting salt and brackish water into fresh water for human consumption, irrigation, and industrial uses. Eleven new exploratory research contracts were approved by the Department of the Interior under a two-million-dollar, five-year program of research on salt and brackish water conversion.

Dr. Russell was frank in admitting that he had first discovered the two atomic elements, but stressed that he would never have developed the atom bomb if science had consulted him, for he had intuited a more powerful weapon of defense, which would have saved lives rather than destroyed them.

He and Lao believed that it was their Message's scientific basis that distinguished it from others. They said, "We are not metaphysicians but rather metascientists. The difference is great."

In 1957, the manager of the Bell Aircraft Corporation research division obtained the Russell books and wrote them, "Our physicists feel that there is still much left unexplained by the presently accepted theory of physics. We feel that Dr. Russell's works may give us direction toward a better understanding of the forces of the universe. We also understand the Russell Foundation offers a series of lessons or a course on universal law, natural science and philosophy and would very much appreciate receiving any available information on this." The Bell scientists ordered *The Russell Cosmogony* and *The Universal One*. The latter had long been out of print, but Walter's *The Secret of Light*, essentially an updated version of *The Universal One*, was substituted.

Lao promptly replied to the Bell inquiry, "Your letter was unfortunately delayed in answering because of our absence for important conferences in relation to our recently published book *Atomic Suicide?* which has aroused so tremendous an interest in certain scientific circles that its reverberations have already reached into two European countries. We were very happy to know that your research group is awakened to the fact of the fundamental unsoundness of modern scientific concepts and are even eager to listen to the great truths about the nature of this electric wave universe that my husband has been releasing for thirty years. Science can advance 1,000 years in a year if men with vision such as your letter indicates that you have would make it possible to substitute the 'why' which we have to give in place of the 'how' of present day research practice.

"Our greatest desire is to remove the costly and wasteful element of experiment from all research and relocate it to the drawing board. That is possible only by knowing the why which lies in cause for all effect must inevitably image its cause and is therefore predictable in advance. When the why is known all electrical projects which in our focus upon resultant anodes will be focused upon their controlling cathodes. Likewise, all chemical and metallurgical effects, which are now focused upon the elements of matter, will be focused upon the inert gases, which control the processes of the unfolding of all matter. When that day of simplification comes, the cumbersome, space-consuming laboratories of today will disappear into miniatures of their present selves."

She also wrote, "You will find that our books are not easily read by the traditionally-trained scientist, for new knowledge demands new words and forms. When these become familiar to you, however, you will see the universe with other eyes and a more comprehensive understanding, for cosmic law is simple and the Russell cosmogony is consistent. We commend it to you with the hope that you will read it with an open mind and not sift it through full concepts that have been arrived at through evidence of man's senses."

In February 1958, Walter, then eighty-seven, was directing laboratory experiments on the coil dynamo he had diagrammed in his writings. The Lombardis encouraged him and provided financial support. By November the coil was functional. Walter was certain that the extent of its value would manifest itself in time. In addition to the coil proving itself, it was the basis for demonstrating the fact that the Russell science could be practically applied to industry. Walter sought first to address the growing water shortage. He then would prove his theory of the irreversibility of radioactivity.

Russell Maguire, the owner of American Mercury, assembled a group of potential investors to meet the Russells and discuss procedures for financing their continuing research. John Lombardi insisted that any understanding among the parties be reduced to a written agreement, and that Maguire be required to prepare and submit the first draft of such writing. This would give the Russells an idea as to their ultimate goals and intentions, and would disclose whether or not they intended to be fair in their dealings.

Within months all discussions between the Russells at Swannanoa and Russell Maguire and his companies had been terminated. The Maguire interests were not prepared to proceed to the University's satisfaction, and the University was not properly equipped to proceed on its own. A major sticking point was the Russells' unwillingness to make a full and complete public disclosure of the Russell coil and Russell dynamo project details.

The Russells had extra expense in having the model constructed, but were certain it would be a means of demonstrating their scientific principles in a dramatic and irrefutable way.

In a February 1958 letter to Marjory Taylor, Lao demonstrated her agility at explaining Walter's complicated scientific theories. Her letter states that she had discussed Marjory's questions with Walter but that the reply is her own, and she delineates in great detail how a wave turns spirally upon a shaft, just as wheels turn on shafts. "If you throw a stone into water, a series of rings is formed," she wrote. "Those rings are waves. As each wave is added, the shaft extends into it." She defined imagined infinity, noted that all waves were harmonic repetitions of their source, and explained that all matter comes to rest when its compression is maximum. "Any plane in either matter or space," she noted, "is a reflecting mirror." She explained the screen of space and described how rings are compressed into spheres. "Answers to such questions cannot be dictated," she told Margory, "and I have to answer them myself."

The Russells then began working with C. Guy Suits, director of General Electric's research laboratory at Schenectady, New York, offering his company first refusal on patent rights to the Russell coil dynamo, asserting that it would not only double to quadruple the power of General Electric's present dynamos, but also provide the company the key to power projection without cables.

The core of Walter's science suggested a fundamental application that could revolutionize every industry on earth. Lao described Walter's geometry of space as "the foundation for the science of tomorrow," calling the new coil "the key to the mechanics for transforming static space into dynamic motion and to its complete control while being transformed." In a letter to Dr. Suits dated June 13, 1958, she reiterated their certainty that "the Supreme Secret of Nature is her practice of multiplying vast areas of the zero nothingness of static space into huge gravity-centered, magnetic field generators like our suns." Soon afterwards, Suits made a journey to Swannanoa to see what the Russells had accomplished. Suits found their concepts fascinating but advised them that, without laboratory proof of their theories, which General Electric was unwilling to finance up front, the world's largest builder of dynamos was not willing to make a commitment to enter a partnership with them.

Soon there were further indications that the Russell science was beginning to unfold. In September 1961, they were visited by Euell Rubert, a contracting engineer who had just been to Oak Ridge, Tennessee, and was well acquainted with many top scientists in the laboratory there. He had asked a leading scientist in the Oak Ridge laboratory if he knew who had really discovered the transuranium elements, and the scientist replied, "Yes, I do. It was Walter Russell." This visitor told Lao that at Oak Ridge and throughout the Standard Oil Company scientists were circulating copies of *Atomic Suicide?* and that growing numbers of people in the world of science knew the truth as to Walter's epochal contribution.

By October, Lao wrote Emelia of their frustration with the project because of delays in obtaining materials, and also delays through their electrician assistant. His coming was delayed, and on his arrival, he hooked the apparatus up incorrectly. As a result, several days' progress was lost. Soon they had the services of the two men who had made the parts, and who had the technical experience necessary to handling the electric current. Dr. Russell reported that C. C. Keyser and Harvey Glass were engaged on a part-time basis to assist in the development of the Russells' gravity reactor project. They had signed a nondisclosure agreement. The preliminary experiments moved along as anticipated, but the project seemed to develop very slowly. Both of the Russells were increasingly impatient.

In late October, they tested a small model of the gravity reactor. The big model was not ready to use. Problems arose. Lao walked around the mountain for inspiration, and God told her what to do to correct them. Competing scientists visited them, one from NORAD, another from Raytheon. This convinced Lao more than ever that perfecting the work on hand was of utmost importance. It was critical that they make the correct decisions as to whom to trust. Lao was confident. “My intuition has never been wrong, and I believe we shall be guided step by step.” She and Walter never lost faith that God was working with them, and that all would unfold according to the Divine Plan at the right time.

In mid-November, the Air Force major who had accompanied the seven-man team from NORAD returned to warn them against becoming too involved with Henry C. Mulberger and other scientists from Raytheon, who had been doing their best to entice the Russells to release their laboratory notes and records of experiments to the New England technological giant. Lao had felt uneasy about working with Mulberger for some time. On November 15, they conducted the big test. Although promising, it was inconclusive.

Along with everything else at Swannanoa, laboratory work had been greatly impeded by lack of capital. If provided enough capital to equip and staff an adequate laboratory for a period of eighteen months, Walter was convinced that he and Lao could activate the principle that would yield water from the atmosphere or by desalting the ocean, give abundant fuel from space at negligible expense, and provide an unlimited supply of needed metals from silicon sand or granite. To make progress, the Russells needed enough money to keep two qualified technicians working full time. Without such staff it took weeks to do what should have been done in three days.

Their dedicated Florida student Pat duPont proposed a solution to this dilemma. Her idea was to form a corporation and sell stock. Familiar as she was with stock market procedures, she knew that it was far easier to attract investors than donors. The Russells’ Space Power Corporation would issue up to $300,000 in stock, reserving fifty-one percent to the Russells. Income of the corporation would be derived from licensing corporations all over the world, either directly or through a management company, to substitute the Russells’ knowledge of the power of gravity for current industrial dependency on water, fuel, oil, and metals. The returns would be inconceivably great.

Lao outlined the proposal in an enthusiastic draft prospectus sent to John Lombardi, whose advice and legal assistance she would need in bringing it to fruition. Overnight, however, she decided not to pursue the project. God had talked to her in the language of light and warned her against forming the corporation. Such a commercial approach violated the principle that all must be given in love with no thought of return. The investment approach carried with it the risk that the whole amount could be lost if it proved insufficient to complete the project. “Then there would be anxiety,” Lao came to realize, adding, “There must be no anxiety—only complete knowing is right.”

Pat duPont readily understood Lao’s reluctance and, as an alternative, promptly gave the Russells a donation of $10,000. Lao knew this would pay for reprinting the Swannanoa folders and publishing *The Scientific Answer To*

Human Relations on her return to Virginia.

Henry C. Mulberger, the Raytheon scientist, continued to inquire as to how they were progressing with the generator experiments. He described his company's recent progress with lasers, and the potential they saw for developing a means of generating coherent light beams powerful enough to destroy ballistic missiles at great distances in space. America's success in space seemed to be expanding the world's horizons and understanding of God's universe, he noted. The Russells' contacts at NORAD and Raytheon were keenly interested in any breakthroughs that might have occurred at Swannanoa. By late 1962, Walter's poor health forced them to suspend work in the Swannanoa laboratory.

Years later, John David Mann, editor of *Solstice* magazine, described Lao's role in the Russells' science work in a penetrating article published after her death. Recounting a visit with her at Swannanoa, he found her "thoroughly versed in her husband's cosmology and scientific perspective," but found it remarkable that Lao "held that technical solutions alone, no matter how cosmologically conceived, would not bring about the changes so urgently needed. That change, she taught, would come about only through the transformation of human beings, that we might realize the Law of Balance, and the Divine potential in ourselves and in each other."

Mann, one of the major macrobiotic scholars and practitioners of his generation, was intrigued by Lao's demeanor as she discussed such threats to humanity as nuclear proliferation and ozone depletion. "Oddly, despite the dire nature of her subject, there was nothing dark or gloomy in her words nor in her demeanor," he wrote. "Her measured statements emerged in a melodious flow that was at once precise and comfortable; they seemed uplifted by a quiet, unshakable faith. We sensed a conviction that all events fall into their natural time and place, with ultimate benefit for the whole.

97. John David Mann.

"Later that day, she addressed the assembled group: 'There is one central answer to all these terrible environmental problems, and that is a change in the nature of human relationships.' It was impossible not to understand what she meant, and agree."

CHAPTER SIXTEEN

Intimations of Mortality (1957-62)

From the time the University of Science and Philosophy was organized in 1957 as successor to the Walter Russell Foundation, its directors had convened for their annual meeting on New Year's Day at Swannanoa. This practice continued through the early sixties, and brought John and Emelia Lombardi from New Jersey to celebrate the obligatory holiday eve with the Russells.

The four of them often discussed the thought that they had been together in previous lifetimes, and had much work to do for God in their present ones. Lao in particular was struggling to achieve what God purposed for her, because she hoped not to have to return to earth again. "I feel like a stranger in a strange land," she wrote. "The ways of the world are not for me."

Generally the other three directors, Dr. Lavender, Charles L. Banister, and Arthur Jones, joined them for the meetings until Dr. Lavender's health made it difficult for him to travel from New York, Mr. Jones and his wife moved from the summer cottage to retirement in Florida, and Mr. Banister resigned due to other commitments.

The New Year's celebration was always festive and hearkened back to the large Christmas homecomings the Russells had held for students in their early years at the palace. An example of the later, smaller house parties occurred in 1962. An elderly student named Mabel joined Dr. Lavender, the Lombardis, and Emelia's artist-brother, Peter Parker, at the New Year's celebration that year. Lao hoped that Mabel would take more than a casual interest in Dr. Lavender, but Mabel demurred. She had expected to find John and Emelia much older than they were. Peter particularly enjoyed getting to know Dr. Lavender. He was impressed by the doctor's influence with his old friend Walter Russell. It amazed Peter to see Walter walking so much more uprightly the morning after Dr. Lavender had arrived.

Mabel's account provides an excellent description of the Russells' idea of gracious hospitality. "I feel as though I had the most wonderful, refreshing trip out of this world! I am so aware of the love given by each of you to make our visit just perfect," she wrote. "The palace was beautiful, my little room was completely comfortable, and I noticed all the thoughtful things that had been added. My gifts from you and Doctor were perfect, and the companionship of such wonderful people was an experience I shall never forget. I don't know how to thank you enough for making all this possible for me. Other things bring pleasure, but not the inner joy of association with such unfolded souls." The Swannanoa staff worked to ensure that guests enjoyed their stay at the palace. Pauline and Max, who had recently been employed by the Russells, drew praise from all who enjoyed her savory cooking and appreciated his readiness to provide transportation around the area at a moment's notice.

Next to Walter, Emelia was clearly Lao's closest friend. Lao was deeply grateful for her support. "Your love has sustained me through many a day for so many years, and there has never been a moment in all these years that I have not known my Oneness in God with you," she wrote her. Lao was convinced that God had put them all on Earth to save mankind, and that someday, the Lombardis would join the Russells full time at Swannanoa to extend the Message. Early in 1960, one of the palace staff was arrested drunk in Waynesboro and, after they forgave him, repeated the offense, this time stealing their camera and selling it to buy liquor. No sooner had he been discharged than a new student applied for work, and greatly impressed Lao with an apparent ability to write letters from a psychological angle. Lao desperately needed professional clerical help.

Despite being a prolific letter writer, Lao found it difficult to answer the onslaught of mail they received daily. She could write a full-page letter by hand in two or three minutes, but she realized that her time could be better used. As her correspondence increased in volume, she suffered more and more from lack of skilled secretarial help. Filling this need, she said, would be the greatest New Year's gift she could receive. "I need a dozen good secretaries, and at the moment I do not have one." During the years of writing the books and course with Walter, her hours had been so erratic that it had been impossible for her to find the sustained time to train a good secretary. She regularly worked all night when she was inspired, and knew that the demands she would make on a secretary would be quite different from a regular office routine.

In particular, she grew anxious over the time required for her to answer the multitude of questions posed by new students who were too impatient to await the answers in subsequent lessons. She stressed that it was to answer these inner questionings that they had written their books and *Home Study Course*. She reassured inquirers that they would understand the whole concept by the time they had completed the course. "To answer each individual question adequately would take many books," she wrote. "You should recognize that all of your questions are questions that every human being asks himself when he has reached the advanced stage of thinking and no longer lives completely in a sensed world. You are close to the secret of all life, and as you understand God's laws of the universe, you will understand Yourself."

By late 1959, Walter was in ever-failing health and needed constant attention to keep his body from deteriorating further. Daily he seemed to require more special care, and there was no one but Lao to administer it. Giving him natural treatments took four to five hours a day but became her top priority. Lao was terrified of calling a physician who might treat him with shots she felt certain would be fatal.

In January 1960, they had planned to attend an important three-day convention of the Virginia Travel Council, but at the last minute, Walter's legs began to swell, and they canceled the trip. Lao administered a salve to which she felt God had guided her, a combination of vitamins A, D, and E, and lanolin acid. This fed his skin and caused the swelling to subside. She put him on a regimen of oatmeal and soda baths, and massaged his legs day and night until they finally began to improve. "Some day when we are rich," she wrote Emelia, "we will have a resident masseuse to keep his circulation going. This is a necessity in one of his age." At the same time, Walter suffered from a painful skin rash, which Lao cured by eliminating their use of laundry detergents.

She also exercised constant supervision over his diet. They were both closely following the organic diet that Gloria Swanson had recommended. For much of the winter they were snowbound in the palace. The snowplow damaged their road so badly that they were reluctant to use it. Mr. Slusser in the stone house just below the palace took his jeep to pick up their mail when the roads were passable, but they hesitated to put too many demands on him. The bad weather reduced the palace gate receipts. As usual, Emelia sent the Russells regular donations. By spring Walter felt better, and at last, Lao believed they had found the proper curatives for both his external and internal ailments. She had seldom in her lifetime experienced as demanding a time, but her attitude and disposition remained strong and focused. She constantly sought to encourage troubled students and lead them to balanced thinking.

A Florida medical doctor, who had lost his own savings and his wife's inheritance, wrote that the course's first lessons left his mind stirring with questions. She replied that such a reaction was a good start, because "it means you are beginning to think again instead of drowning in a whirlpool of doubts about past mistakes." She told him that despite his financial reverses, the fact that he and his wife still loved each other gave each of them the balance of true matehood, the greatest asset on earth.

Lao was quick to reassure new students who considered themselves failures because of their limited finances or lack of success in business. "Remember always," she wrote, "you are far from being failures. To reach your present stage of God-awareness is to know the greatest wealth. It is not what one possesses materially which makes him a true success. All material things are transitory, but the wealth of soul-qualities is yours forever. I would rather die knowing God than die leaving the greatest fortune on earth. To know God is to know eternal life and love, whereas material riches create fear of loss and enemies."

She emphasized that it is always well to remember that all things are ultimately for good, because somewhere along the line they teach someone a valuable lesson. Suffering yields benefits because it induces one to go deeper within to know God and oneself. One's sole purpose on earth is to learn to know God, one's relationship to God, and one's relationship to mankind. When this is learned and lived universally, she said, "We shall then know heaven on earth."

She stood firm in her convictions. "Although to do good one must sometimes be silent, I do not believe in compromise. In fact, I believe when we compromise, we delay the good both universally and to ourselves. There is no compromise with what is right, and I am sure that if more people had the courage to be themselves the world would not now be in the impasse in which it finds itself."

She understood the difference between mankind and animals in their concept of killing. The lion killing the little gazelle made her heart ache, but then she would remember that the lion killed only to satisfy his hunger. In turn, the gazelle killed other forms of animal life in order to live. It was all an interchange. Man, on the other hand, killed by the millions, not to keep alive but out of sensual depravity.

Their friend and student Alberta M. O'Connell had sent them the manuscript of her book *Strange Prologue*, which included wholly unauthorized pages about the Russells and Swannanoa. Lao wrote Emelia that *Strange Prologue* was "unliterary tripe at best, a cheap exposé of a very personal life and a demonstration of personal ego beyond the pale." She used a more diplomatic approach in convincing O'Connell to remove the more flagrant references to the Russells.

Lao felt that parents could give their young children no better gift than the experience of growing up with the Russell philosophy. "It will be wonderful for your children to have the influence of the Message that God bestowed upon us. I remember a student calling me some years ago to tell me that her little five-year-old daughter had fallen twenty feet onto a concrete walk. Naturally, the mother was horrified and ran quickly to the child, but her little daughter stood up untouched and unhurt in any way. She said to her mother, 'Why are you so distressed, Mommy? You know that God fell with me. You have always told me that God does everything with me, so when I was falling, I said to God, I know you are with me.' So naturally, she was unharmed and not even frightened."

Parents who sought to teach the Russells' principles to their children often found it a challenging process. The parents of nine-year-old twins, a son and a daughter, and an eight-year-old son told of their experiences in applying the lessons found in *God Will Work with You but Not for You* and the *Home Study Course*. "We have taught our three children many of the principles as we go along, and they are using Dr. Russell's prayer, 'God, stand by, I need thee.' This seems to be needed most in school where the law of the jungle seems to be most dominant. We have been strict in their training and teaching them their responsibility to God and themselves, and, as you know, it is at variance with what they run into in the world. It is confusing to them at times, especially when they are so outnumbered that they must stand alone with what they believe to be right." Lao assured them that as the children saw the effect of their right thinking and action, they would gradually find their environment more peaceful and compatible.

Peter Parker, ever gallant and in many ways as dedicated to the Russells personally as his sister, Emelia, always marveled at how "stunningly chic and lovely" Lao looked after carrying such an enormous burden of work for so many years.

As photogenic as she had always been, Lao nonetheless always asserted that photographs taken of her seldom resembled her. "This has happened all my life. People who have seen my photographs are always surprised when they meet me because of this." She told many people that the portrait Walter had made of her for the frontispiece of *God Will Work with You but Not for You* was "still the best likeness I have ever had."

In any event, thousands of women as well as men found her "lovely, gracious, beautiful, and dedicated to her work," and sensed intuitively her integrity and honesty.

Visitors coming to Swannanoa often left feeling as if touring the palace and shaking hands with Lao had changed their lives. People frequently told her they felt better just by being at Swannanoa. She longed for time to talk with them and learn their specific problems so that she might be better able to help them, but keeping current with University enrollments and her correspondence took all the time she could spare from helping nurse her failing husband.

"How I wish I could do more and put the teachings of Natural Law into motion in peoples' homes, their businesses, and their social lives," she wrote Emelia. "I have such big dreams for mankind and I feel I can give so little at this point." Lao noticed a pronounced pessimism in the firsttime visitors to Swannanoa, a condition she saw speedily disappear in those who enrolled as students.

There were remarkable instances of her impact being felt from afar. Friends from Scotland wrote to describe how they were using *Atomic Suicide?* to restore physical, mental, and spiritual health to ailing friends: "Miss Woodall asked to see your book. The change was immediate. Within two days she was up and again busy in mind and physique." The Scottish group wished the Russells had given *Atomic Suicide?* another name, or at least a subtitle such as "The Entrance To Life," because of its profound impact as a healing instrument on the individual.

Their home study groups often developed rapidly. Guy Lloyd in Wilmington, Delaware, outlined the progress of his group over its first seven months. They had designed their monthly meetings to attract everyone. At times they had personally approached especially "alert individuals capable of understanding." Their group included a minister who was often invited to speak at churches and civic organizations, where he succeeded in awakening others.

One member of the group, a reformed alcoholic who had once attempted suicide, had progressed from being a patient in a local convalescent home into serving as a volunteer there, producing so-called miraculous cures with the patients, and making it possible for the group to provide a study course once a week for all the patients and staff. The administration had come to consider the group a part of its staff.

"All over town," Lloyd reported, "individuals are being shaken awake into full-time living, practicing spiritual balance. Doctors, lawyers, nurses, business people, housewives, et cetera, are suddenly very conspicuous and outspoken along these lines."

A member of the group had been named head of a local school for deaf and retarded children. The local ministerial alliance was persuaded by the group to take over responsibility for alcoholic rehabilitation for the entire community.

Lloyd noted that healing seemed to be an unexpected byproduct of the group's intervention. He told of paralyzed stroke victims who began talking and moving about. A patient with peritonitis from a ruptured appendix, given up as terminal by his doctors, recovered and went home on Thanksgiving Day. The group had worked with each of these individuals.

Organization of a second study group in Delaware was nearly complete. Not only did this enable the students to understand the Russell Message better, it also provided every participant with the opportunity to express character in their social friendships and business relations. "From small beginnings can come great events," Lao said, "and the world desperately needs a character building movement with basic knowledge of God's ways and processes at its root."

In May 1960, the directors held a special meeting to consider proposals from New York architect August F. Schmiedigen to develop the Swannanoa property as a retreat for senior citizens. Lao felt that publicity could be prepared promoting the project as an adjunct to the work of the University. Dr. Lavender and Mr. Banister agreed that there was an urgent need for such a development, where elderly residents could live in the manner manifested by the Russell principles. Walter and Lao were authorized to prepare and distribute a booklet to attract interested senior citizens to such a development on the Swannanoa property. At the same time, Mr. Schmiedigen would develop architectural plans, sketches, and drawings to be used in connection with such a program, and otherwise assist the Russells in bringing the project to fruition. Mr. Schmiedigen was affiliated with the forthcoming New York World's Fair, and recommended that the Swannanoa project might likewise be conceived to reflect the stated purpose of the fair, which had been declared to be "Peace through Understanding." Economic conditions prevented the project from being realized at Swannanoa.

The Russells' book *The One-World Purpose: A Plan to Dissolve War by a Power More Mighty than War* was published and distributed in early November 1960 in an initial edition of 10,000 copies, half of which were sold within the first few months. This excellent response was almost entirely due to orders from the University's students and from others on the mailing list who had been sent the announcement brochure. Virtually no response had been received from those on an expensive, commercial, general public mailing list the University had purchased and used for the first time. The book was written to explain woman's role as the indispensable force for everlasting peace and to promote the need for global man-woman equalization. John Lombardi prepared a draft of recommended procedures for students to follow in forming local chapters of the Man-Woman Equality League that the Russells had heralded in the new book.

At New Year's 1961, Walter's health seemed better, but only because Lao was now spending six hours every day helping him with naturopathic and other treatments.

That January, they eagerly awaited another visit from Dr. Page. Lao expressed anxiety to Emelia. "Somehow we must get through the coming 'big day' with flying colors, and when that is over, whatever the outcome, we are going to Florida, and I trust that Doctor's legs will be healed and that the change will help me." Lao knew that she would get little rest even on a vacation in the sun, because she would be preparing their meals and caring for Walter, but she felt certain the change without tensions would do her much good.

They were encouraged by Dr. Page's visit, and left immediately afterwards for several months in the Florida Keys. Florence Rabon interviewed Walter there for a feature story that appeared in the *Miami Herald* on Sunday, February 26. He recalled his experiences in the Florida Keys more than sixty-two years before, just prior to the Spanish-American War, when at the age of twenty-eight, he arrived there as artist for the U.S. fleet representing *Collier's Weekly* and *Century* magazines. Frederick Remington and Richard Harding Davis were among his companions then. Rabon noted that the Jefferson Hotel where they had stayed had been destroyed by fire, and "the men who made newspaper and literary history are memories, but today Dr. Russell, hale, hardy and keen-witted at 90, is paying a return visit to the island city." He described "his store of memories of the first visit and how news was relayed to the rest of the world" in that bygone era, and told of his treasured first meeting with Theodore Roosevelt, which subsequently led to his being named official artist to the Roosevelt family during the great Rough Rider's presidency.

98. The Russells in Key West, 1962.

Walter took pleasure in recalling his architectural work in Miami Beach, Coral Gables, and Coconut Grove, Florida, during the 1920s, when he had been a professional and business associate of Carl Fisher, August Heckscher, and other great Florida "gold coast" developers of the era. Walter described his role in designing many notable buildings in the area that still stood, and numerous other developments planned but never executed because of the world depression.

They were back at Swannanoa by early April. On May 19, Walter celebrated his long-anticipated ninetieth birthday. John and Emelia arrived to join in a small but festive celebration at Swannanoa, and presented him with a symbolic gift of ninety silver dollars.

Lao spent much time at the summer cottage revising the *Home Study Course* unit by unit. She and Walter carefully worked out changes before she drafted them, and once she was finished, she sent them to Emelia, who carefully edited them and worked directly with a printer in New Jersey in publishing them. This was very helpful to the Russells at a time when they had borne the heavy expense of preparing the model and purchasing equipment for laboratory work. At their own expense, the Lombardis shipped all the reprinted units to Swannanoa by Railway Express.

Summer was busy. Lao found it difficult to maintain the palace, see that tours were available, and keep up the correspondence with only John Miles, Pauline, and Max to help her.

By July, Lao was inundated with work. "Many days I get not a bite from breakfast to night, and it is awfully hot," she wrote Emelia. She was plagued with a recurring humming in her ear as she struggled to deal with the increasing stress of her daily life. 1961 was an unusually bad year for home study enrollments. There was no summer course on the mountain, and book sales were down. Inquiries were up, however, and Lao's office tables were piled high with correspondence to answer. She ruefully told friends that she had but one pair of hands to do what many should be doing. More than ever, she relied on donations from friends like the Lombardis to pay the bills.

By autumn Walter was feeling better. He thrived on Lao's loving care, which included the daily massage on his legs to keep the swelling down and his skin in order. The fact that there was no sign of swelling in the mornings seemed to Lao a good sign that his condition was no longer deteriorating. Tension and excitement over their continuing scientific work kept him alert, but left him susceptible to stress-induced respiratory infections. Now they were on a totally vegetarian diet, enjoying vegetable-based soups, vegetarian nutburgers, and a vegetable enzyme-calcium powder they used in apricot juice.

On November 6, Lao's birthday, their housekeeper Mrs. Teets was married at the palace to a local farmer. She had worked faithfully for the Russells, and Lao hoped the marriage would cure the loneliness she had suffered since Mr. Teets's death. The elderly bride was queen for the day at Swannanoa, but Florrie and the Lombardis saw to it that Lao was not forgotten. Florrie sent her sister an English egg cooker, and the Lombardis ordered her an antique silver dish, also from England.

Encouraged by his son and daughter-in-law, who had met the Russells in Florida, the internationally acclaimed Dr. Norman Vincent Peale, author of *The Power of Positive Thinking* and one of America's best-loved ministers, visited them at the palace in October 1961. Dr. Peale expressed great interest in all that they were doing and told them that wherever he went, he heard high praise for their work. The famous broadcaster Lowell Thomas, whose farm in upstate New York was near Dr. Peale's, had sent the Russells a highly complimentary letter after reading *The One-World Purpose,* and was among those who had recommended their work to his neighbor. On returning to New

York, Dr. Peale wrote to thank them for his heartwarming visit, reiterating his belief that the Russells were a great inspiration. He promised he would meet Lao again at Swannanoa to discuss the Christ of the Blue Ridge project.

"You two are doing so much good in the world," Dr. Peale added. "You are so important to mankind that I pray most earnestly that the Lord will continue to strengthen and guide you in the days that lie ahead."

Lao long remembered Dr. Peale's last words on this visit. After telling her to remember that he was their friend and hoped to keep in touch with them, he told Walter that Lao's *God Will Work with You but Not for You* was the greatest book of the century.

In late March 1963, Dr. Peale dedicated five minutes of his Sunday morning national radio hookup to the Russells and Swannanoa. "Have We Forgotten How to Live?" was his text for the program. He noted that even though Walter was past ninety, he never got tired and was constantly excited about life. He reported that as long as God permitted the Russells to live, they believed they were here for a continuing purpose and would act in that belief.

In March 1962, Dr. C. H. Yeang of Malaya distributed 240,000 copies of his booklist featuring *Atomic Suicide?* The list was printed in French, English, German, Spanish, and Indonesian, and a lady in Holland translated it into Russian and mailed out additional thousands. This produced a large number of inquiries at Swannanoa.

The same month, C. D. Livingston wrote Lao that the Friends of the Cottage Loom in Perthshire, Scotland, had issued 10,000 copies of a leaflet advertising the same Russell book. For the past five years, the group had distributed these leaflets each summer throughout Scotland. The 1962 edition also included a quotation from *Atomic Suicide?*

Charles L. Banister resigned from the board in September 1962. That month, Lao wrote Emelia that rewriting Unit 10 of the *Home Study Course* had been the greatest challenge of all. "I just cannot voice the agony of it all, and there are still Unit 11 and Unit 12 to do," she said.

In October Emelia wrote Lao reflecting her own frustration over the revised course units, particularly the last section of Unit 11 concerning transmutation and solar energy. "I have incorporated what Doctor had dictated to me when I was with you where I thought it should go," Emelia noted, adding, "However, it might not be the place where you want it to go."

Senator Stuart Symington was the most influential Missourian in Washington. Lao was enthusiastic over his advanced idea of providing specific training in Americanism for young people who would be allowed to enter foreign service regardless of college qualifications. She corresponded with him in early 1963, seeking his help in obtaining funding necessary to build a full-size replica of Walter's Mark Twain Memorial in St. Louis in time for the city's 1964 centennial. She reiterated the history of the memorial, and the zeal with which Missourians had promoted it until the attack on Pearl Harbor diverted national attention to the war effort. "This was the sole reason for its abandonment at that time," she told him, "and we have not made any attempt since then to have the monument erected, as our other work for mankind has demanded all of our thought and attention." Senator Symington worked with her to alert the people in Missouri who were leading the recognition of Mark Twain, but due to Walter's rapidly declining health, the project was once again delayed.

Congressman Jim Wright of Texas, later speaker of the House of Representatives, lamented that his busy schedule left him little time to engage in reflective thinking, but told her that people he respected in Washington had described the Russells enthusiastically, and "that is recommendation enough for me."

Their books continued to attract both traditional and innovative educators. Marie H. Carroll, Lao's friend at Virginia State College in Petersburg, told her that many of her neighbors and friends in the college community found the Russell books very inspiring. Dr. Robert P. Daniel, president of Virginia State, frequently referred to *God Will Work with You but Not for You* in his speeches, and the dean of the college and his wife, Dr. and Mrs. John H. Hunter, called the book "a most valuable possession," and termed the Russells' twelve-item basic foundation for a living philosophy "worthy of being copied and kept in sight on one's desk as a daily reminder." From Pennsylvania, President Edward L. Holman of the renowned Carson Long Military Institute at New Bloomfield visited Swannanoa with his wife almost every summer, and regularly corresponded with them on their philosophy.

There were always humorous moments. One visitor to the palace, author of a book called *Greeting and Hallucinations*, told Lao that when he saw her coming down the palace steps, he thought for a moment that she was the mythical Queen Tanna, who often appeared in his delirium tremens in a similar dress.

Lao had discovered Marie Corelli's 1911 book, *The Life Everlasting*, and felt it reflected her own earliest spiritual leanings. "I could have written it when I was fifteen," she told Emelia. Lao disagreed with Corelli's comments on visions, but she and Walter found strong vindication of their own beliefs in the book's thesis on age, love, and God.

From Denver's Natural Living Foundation, David Lane praised "what you have given to the world" as "by far the most enlightened [work] that has been presented to mankind in the past two thousand years. We highly recommend it to everyone."

Lao's old friend Charlie Biddle wrote to the Russells from Spain, where he lived in retirement. He had retired from banking in 1950; divorced his wife,

Mary; and spent several years in the Far East as financial advisor to the governments of Vietnam, Cambodia, and Laos. From there he returned to Spain with a new wife, Yetta, who he had courted in Singapore; brought to Virginia to visit the Russells at Swannanoa; and divorced in Holland several years later. Now sixty-seven and suffering from acute heart fibrillation, he lived in Barcelona and enjoyed the pleasant companionship of a well-educated Spanish lady, a general's daughter educated in England, with whom he had traveled widely until his heart trouble made travel unwise.

He had received Walter and Lao's Christmas card with their photograph, and was amazed to see Walter at ninety looking as jaunty and dapper and young as ever. As for Lao, Charlie found her unchanged from the time they had first met in 1942. "Yours is an indestructible kind of beauty," he wrote her, "so long as you keep your eyes! These I cannot quite see in the picture, but I can conjure them to mind very easily!" He was happy that their work and teachings were so successful, and marveled at the life they led. "You have done well to keep active with an absorbing and useful occupation. That is why you both look so young!"

Lao was delighted to hear from Charlie and at once invited him to Swannanoa. He replied on Valentine's Day, apologizing to Walter for asking her to be his Valentine. He was greatly cheered by her "wonderful letter, so deeply thoughtful and full of love—the letter of a person who is victorious in life, with a large share left over for other people! It was such a warm and glowing letter, Lao. I do thank you for it." He never returned to Swannanoa, and died in July 1971 in Barcelona.

The Lombardis came for the Christmas holidays, spent a long weekend at the palace, and joined the Russells for the board meeting. The third edition of the *Home Study Course* was expected to be completed by the end of the coming year. John and Emelia left Swannanoa for New Jersey on New Year's morning 1962, and a few hours afterwards, the mountain was blanketed in snow.

CHAPTER SEVENTEEN

Time of Transition (1962-63)

Winters on the mountain had grown increasingly impossible for Walter, and in mid-February, their staff members Pauline and Max drove the Russells to Florida. Soon Lao and Walter were comfortably settled in a temporary home at Fort Lauderdale, relaxing by bathing in the ocean and sunning themselves on the beach. For the first time in months they felt rested. Within a week, however, Lao was back to work, editing several more course unit revisions, which she sent to Emelia for printing.

John Miles wrote them that eight inches of snow at Swannanoa forced him to walk up and down the mountain with the mail. At the palace, there were few visitors and little revenue. In Florida, Pauline took ill, and for several days until she recovered, all the work of cooking, housekeeping, and Walter's care fell on Lao. Dr. Bowan Jones gave Walter and Lao regular therapeutic treatments, and his wife and daughters showered them with Florida hospitality. His parents, Arthur and Adelle, and sister, Wendy, came from Winter Haven to visit them. Arthur Jones, who was now seventy-six, had tendered his resignation from the board to John Lombardi, but he assured them all that his action in no way affected his deep devotion to the Russells or his feeling of responsibility toward the University. He simply felt that a younger, more active person should take his place, but he termed the years he had spent helping to establish the University the most pleasant of his life.

The brightest side of their 1962 vacation came when Walter and Lao finally met their enthusiastic new students Pat duPont and Elaine Wold, both beautiful, worldly women in their mid-thirties, who seemed to shine with the new knowledge they had gleaned from the *Home Study Course*. Elaine told Lao that her self-assurance and inner joy were now so wonderful that she considered her life and marriage perfect. Pat's life with her alcohol-prone, invalid husband had been unbearable before she discovered the Russell teachings. Both of these women told Lao and Walter that, more than anything else in the world, they wanted to further the Message.

According to Bowan Jones, Pat duPont was not wealthy in her own right, and Elaine Wold had as yet inherited but little of her reputed family millions, but he assured Lao that each of them were well able to make contacts that would incalculably further the Russell work. Only a few weeks before, the duPonts had entertained a son of King Saud of Arabia. The prince had given Pat's daughter a lovely watch, and to reciprocate, Pat had commissioned an artist to translate Lao's *Code of Ethics* into Arabic, and had framed the beautifully illuminated manuscript as a present for him. She planned to go to Egypt and Arabia later in the year, and was eager to interest the prince further in the work of the Russells.

Pat duPont proved herself to be "the most generous and wonderful girl one could ever hope to meet," Lao wrote. Pat insisted on taking Lao shopping and bought her three expensive dresses. Virtually every day she took Lao to luncheon at a different place. When Lao chipped a tooth while eating an olive, Pat arranged several visits to her excellent dentist for both Lao and Walter. The greatest treat for them was Pat's offer of three days of restful cruising on her yacht. The Russells went alone with the crew of three and were able to relax to a greater extent than they had done in years.

Walter returned from the boat trip in the pink of health, but while Lao tended to the mail after giving him an Epsom salts bath, Pauline administered a cream massage to his legs and left him exposed to the open windows. With his pores thus opened, he developed a serious cold that settled in his throat and left him with a high temperature and deathlike pallor. Lao prescribed bed rest for him and spirits of nitric, an old English remedy for high temperature (a teaspoon of spirits of nitric in two tablespoons of sweetened water every two hours until the fever breaks). She had been recovering from months of intense fatigue, but Walter's condition now kept her up day and night for a week. Soon she developed a bad cold that she attributed to the changeable weather, Max's incessant smoking, and the difference in her diet. Oddly enough, the juice regimen to which they were accustomed at the palace was difficult to obtain in Florida.

While the Russells were in Fort Lauderdale, Emelia and John Lombardi flew to Orlando in order that he could take depositions in a pending lawsuit. Afterwards, they came south to enjoy a sunny reunion with Walter and Lao and to meet Pat duPont and Elaine Wold.

The Russells flew from Miami to Washington, D.C., on April 10 for an interview with Senator George Smathers and Congressman Durward Hall the next day. Congress had turned down a proposal to use Walter's statue of the Four Freedoms as the centerpiece of the Franklin D. Roosevelt national memorial, and the Russells felt that Senator Smathers might be helpful in forcing a reconsideration of the rejection, or at the very least in authorizing erection of Walter's monumental work at another national park or site. The senator had earlier strongly praised *The Man Who Tapped the Secrets of the Universe* and *The One-World Purpose*.

Harry C. Morris and C. E. Palmer of Erie, Pennsylvania, had visited the palace in October 1961, and were intrigued by *Atomic Suicide?* and Walter's plans to renew his scientific experiments. Equipped with a machine shop and fine tooling equipment, they offered to help Walter by making any needed parts to his specification. Their obvious interest and desire to help led Lao to ask Mr. Palmer to come to Swannanoa and direct palace operations while she and Walter went to Florida in 1962. He agreed to come at his own expense as a volunteer and asked Harry Morris to accompany and assist him on the same basis. On their arrival, they realized that a skilled typist would be necessary to carry on the large volume of correspondence required by the University, as well as to see to Palmer's own business.

On his own initiative and at his sole expense, Palmer had employed Ruth Crane, a woman who he had met when she came to tour the palace, to work in the office and help with typing. She was a licensed minister, clairvoyant, and advanced Cayce student. This worried Lao. "It gave us such a shock that he would have a stranger come in that way. We trust all is right but you can imagine our feelings when he told us over the phone what he had done," she wrote Emelia. Further unsettled by Crane's claim to have had prolonged states of illumination congruent with the *Divine Iliad*, as well as letters in which she claimed to be a time traveler who had found various inconsistencies in the Russells' teaching, Lao suggested that Crane not be given access to the University's office and files and urged that she be discharged. The press of business was so great and the palace staff so small that Palmer retained her.

Other irritants arose in the Russells' long-distance relationship with Palmer, among them his giving students their Florida address and opening Lao's personal letters from England, and when Walter's illness required them to prolong their stay in Fort Lauderdale beyond April 15, Palmer was forced on several occasions to undertake a contracted research assignment in New York, and left the palace responsibility to Ruth Crane and Harry Morris for a week or more at a time. While Palmer provided an extra car for palace errands, and assured Lao that there was nothing irregular in the way Crane was answering University inquiries, all parties seem to have been exasperated with one another by the time the Russells returned to the palace in late April. However, even at the end of May, Harry Morris was still helping Lao in the office, and in December, they exchanged mutually complimentary letters.

An anonymous reader criticized the Russells for failing to include Moses among the names of great mystics in the *Home Study Course*, making the argument that Moses had introduced the concept of justice, supposedly a concept more in synchronicity with universal balance than Jesus' suggestion that an aggrieved person "turn the other cheek." Lao had asserted on several occasions that their list of initiates was not intended to be all-inclusive, and avoided the challenge of comparing the merits of Jesus and Moses.

Harry Morris wrote a succinct response to such critics during his months at Swannanoa in early 1962: "Please remember that Truth is Truth and that there is only one source and that each Illuminate interprets the light and clothes it in his own words, but basically it is one. The Russells' *Home Study Course* is by far the greatest because it is written by a united pair of God's Illuminated Messengers. All of their writings more clearly reveal the Truth, with both a Scientific and Philosophical technique, than all other teachers have ever done."

Even this eloquent defense was challenged by those who cited such other examples of joint cosmic work by husbands and wives, as the team efforts of Rudolf and Marie Steiner working together in developing Anthroposophy (especially the art of movement, Eurhythmy); Charles and Myrtle Fillmore in jointly setting up the Unity School of Christianity; and Flower and Lawrence Newhouse of Questhaven, California, who worked selflessly together to establish their Christward Ministry.

Meanwhile, Walter and Lao worked to complete the final *Home Study Course* unit revisions. With all of her other work backed up Lao felt as if she would never get on schedule. She also knew she must constantly look after Walter.

Nevertheless she took comfort in the fact that he remained mentally facile. "I know he is not as strong as he should be but thank God his great Mind is as alert as ever," she wrote Emelia. "At ninety-one, one's body does not function like it does at forty-one, and I cannot help but wish something truly wonderful would occur so that he could see some fruit for all his years of great work." It was obvious to Lao that Walter might not live much longer. "Last night I was up for two hours in the middle of the night changing the bed. The water stays in his body despite all the careful diet, and this is what worries me."

In July 1962, the Russells bought a new, six-passenger Ford country sedan, which was essential for conducting University business and ferrying special guests to and from the mountain.

Lao gave interviews to Lilith Lorraine, founder of Avalon and editor of *Flame*, its magazine, and to Mohammad Sarfraz, chief editor of *The Pakistan Times* in Lahore. She was featured in the English natural health quarterly *Grace*. The editor of *Guidepost* wrote for further biographical information on the Russells.

Despite the fact that they lived in a palace and gave the appearance of being wealthy, Lao was quick to reassure those who inquired that she had given the world her whole inheritance when she and Walter first came to Swannanoa. "I do not own one cent today, and I have never taken one cent royalty on any of our writings. Neither have we received one penny in salary. We have a most modest living. Our ways are extremely simple, since we do not smoke, drink, or eat rich foods. My husband is now in his ninety-second year, so a social life is not possible even if we desired it, which we do not."

By October, Walter was using a wheelchair and keeping his hemoglobin up by taking several tablespoons of crude blackstrap molasses and honey in hot water as a warm beverage at bedtime. He and Lao often drank the mineral and iron-rich water in which apricots had been cooked. It seemed to have the same effect.

Peter Parker reminded Walter that years before, when the Russell spirit was still new to Swannanoa, Walter had told a class that Jesus had performed his healings by passing his own strength and perfection on to those who were sick in order to make them strong again. He sought to cheer his ailing friend by recalling their happy times together, writing Lao just before he visited them, "I haven't played Canasta since my last visit to Swannanoa, but I hear that the Doctor has been practicing steadily. It would appear that I shall be badly beaten."

Lao was extremely uneasy as to Jim Dulaney's immediate intentions for the palace, and fraught with panic as to what he might do if Walter were to die. She confided her fears in Louis Spilman, her stalwart friend and the publisher of Waynesboro's daily newspaper, who urged her to ask Dulaney directly what he had on file as to the Russells' leasehold of Swannanoa. Lao distinctly remembered that they were to have a six-months right of first refusal to purchase the palace in the case Dulaney decided to sell it, but she could not find the documents confirming this fact. "I wish I could find those letters but Doctor had them, and I have no idea where they can be," she told Emelia. Kitty Heald and Florrie both reflected these concerns in their letters to her early in 1963.

Early that year, many new books on cosmic experiences seemed to vindicate the Russells. These included Paul Brunton's *Overself*, Glenn Clark's *Collaborating with Eternity*, and Norman Paulson's *Cosmic Consciousness*. Lao felt that this indicated a new awareness of truth, but believed that their own books were unique in emphasizing woman's equality with man, a concept that was then only beginning to gather the strength that by the century's end would make it a major wave of the future in most of the world.

With publication of the latest research on the Dead Sea Scrolls and the even more valuable Essene library, some felt the Russell teachings had been validated. Many believed that these recent discoveries had so threatened the

Roman Catholic Church as to force the pope to call the latest ecumenical council. These findings also strongly buttressed the Russells' view that many falsified statements had been attributed to Christ over the centuries by Paulist, Catholic, and Protestant scholars.

On January 1, 1963, Lao reported to the board that she had appointed Pat duPont to fill the unexpired term of Charles L. Banister. Walter's illness had made it necessary to abandon the Russells' gravity reactor project. Eleven units of the *Home Study Course* had been revised and printed, and the twelfth and final unit was in process and was expected to be ready for the printer within the next month or two. The price of the course had been increased to $100 to cover the added printing and handling costs.

The first Sunday of the year brought cheer to the University's West Coast students when they were surprised to hear Dr. Gene Emmet Clark devote his entire radio message to Walter Russell. Many students wrote the Russells to say they had heard this broadcast by the celebrated minister of the Beverly Hills Church of Religious Science, whose heavily attended Sunday service was held in the Fox Wilshire Theatre, and always offered a table filled with copies of *The Man Who Tapped the Secrets of the Universe* for sale. As spring approached, various regional television stations gave excellent coverage to Swannanoa, far more than in previous years.

The Canadian peak performance master Neil C. Davis, of Toronto's Success Training organization, shared ideas with Lao, who felt that such programs as his filled a great need in promoting creative thinking. Without such thinking, she was certain, mankind would eventually lose his freedom.

Samuel L. Lewis, who as Sufi Ahmed Murad was recruiting faculty and arranging reciprocal cultural relations for the newly established University of Islamabad in Pakistan, had devoted his long career to linking traditional wisdom with modern science, and first met Walter Russell in New York in 1945. Eighteen years later, he wrote Lao to express his view that despite its primary concern with physics and cosmogony, *Atomic Suicide?* included enough physiological material to support a sound doctrine for both the new psi-sciences and mental telepathy. Lao's own contribution to the book, he told her, was enough to form the basis of a healing system, combining material, metaphysical, spiritual, and Christ methods. This greatly encouraged the Muslim educator who had previously experienced great difficulty in penetrating the "Western" mind with concepts of "Eastern" mysticism.

President Virgil McCain of Athens College in Athens, Alabama, visited Swannanoa in late January, and wrote to Lao a week later, "The more I think about it, the more I realize that this was an important day in my life." A distinguished scholar, well read in the intellectual and religious frontiers of learning, he had long felt that there was a need to assemble leaders in such thinking for a seminar where they might share knowledge and experiences with each other. He returned to his campus and discussed the project with the college dean and faculty, suggesting that the first such symposium take place at Swannanoa. Lao declined the honor, given the critical state of Walter's health, but she kept in contact with the college president and dean, and subsequently visited their campus and spoke before the student body and townspeople. Meanwhile, several people from the Athens College community enrolled in the *Home Study Course* after hearing the dean refer to the Russells in lectures.

Life magazine ran a series on ancient Greece, in which author de Santillana described the ancient Athenian schools of philosophy as "palaces of pure thought," a reference that led a Canadian study group to write the managing editor suggesting that the Russells had created a modern "palace of pure thought" at Swannanoa. While the editor declined to feature a story on the Russells, the correspondence led to an exchange of letters between Lao and the famous photographer and writer Gordon Parks, who had photographed the series. Parks was attracted to Walter Russell, because he, like Walter, had been self-taught and felt he had learned to express the God-light from within.

In February 1963, Walter was filled with new ideas for the electronic reactor, which he believed would replace the dangerous and costly atomic reactor.

By March, Lao was exhausted and fearful. Her desk was stacked with unanswered correspondence. "I would love to go somewhere away from the world and bask in the sun and let the wind blow through my hair and lie and talk to God. Doctor worries me. But I cannot talk about that. My heart is too heavy."

By April, Lao wrote Euell and Joyce Rubert in Springfield, Missouri, that Walter was making slow progress, but they were grieved to hear that he was so weak that he had not been taking food. "The only important thing now is for him to get well again," they wrote. "The world sorely needs the application of this great mind to the many problems it faces. We know, too, how much you need him."

In the meantime, the Ruberts were working to try to bring some recognition to Walter for his tremendous contribution to the world of science. Pursuant to this, Euell met with a Dr. Pollard, who had recently resigned as chief director of the government's Oak Ridge Laboratory to become an Episcopal Priest. Euell had also promised Lao to help underwrite the University's proposed magazine, *Balance*. He returned to Swannanoa in late April, accompanied by Congressman Durward G. Hall of Missouri, who told them that the things they did were so challenging, and their actions and accomplishments spoke so loudly, he could scarcely hear what others said.

In April, Lao wrote their environmentalist friend St. Barbe Baker, "I have had a most heartbreaking year, and Doctor's life is hanging on by the merest thread. This is just a brief note because I want you to know that it would make me very happy to have you here this summer and I know your summer school would find this setting ideal in every way." Lao had been corresponding with him in an effort to help launch his forthcoming Sahara Reclamation Program, and to assure him that Swannanoa could serve as the site of his summer school for 1963. Walter's death made that impossible.

On May 1, 1963, Phyllis McConnell, a graduate student in education at Iowa State University, wrote Walter and Lao that she had received her *Home Study Course* lessons only a week before, but already felt an overwhelming desire to understand and comprehend them. Her letter reflected her enthusiasm:

> The first time I read the first booklet of your course I sailed through a good share of the ideas as though I were walking through a beautiful building filled with gold-framed closed doors. Of course I couldn't see the treasure of meaning in each room (idea) because I went by too fast but I sensed the indescribable knowledge behind each door.
>
> The thought came to me that these golden doors do not open unless you stand at the door patiently, reverently, and with a great desire to visit the treasures (inner understandings) of the room.
>
> The further thought occurred to me that one might enter the room and see the treasures but still not have deep understanding of them. Only as one stayed quietly and reverently long enough with the idea would it give up its deepest secrets to be absorbed into one's being.
>
> It is as though the ideas have to be thoroughly convinced that one really desires them before they give up their greatest secrets.
>
> I do not know whether I can convince these ideas that I sincerely desire them or not but I shall surely try. I feel very unworthy of such knowledge and feel indescribably grateful to you for allowing me to walk through the beautiful treasure of your ideas. Thank you kindly again.

Phyllis McConnell would soon come to join the palace staff as Angela Carr.

By the last week of April, it was clear that Walter's condition was critical. His edema had seriously worsened, and he was not taking nourishment. Dr. Thomas L. Gorsuch, then midway in the Waynesboro medical practice that gained him national repute as a heart specialist, arranged for his patient to be given intravenous feeding at the palace, and there was some hope that this might temporarily restore Walter's strength. Lao had come to realize that Walter was dying. She wrote the Lombardis, "Only God can save Doctor now. He is so terribly, terribly weak. He does not say a word or open his eyes. Surely God will let him live to see some fruit from his hard labors. I wish he could see you both once more. He expressed the desire so many times before he became so ill. Any moment I know could be the last one."

Lao was struggling to deal with the pressure. She was filled with anxieties, uncertainties, indecisiveness, frustration, and the feeling that her efforts to help Walter were useless. She also despaired that Walter might die without truly realizing the potential impact of his work. Later she would recognize that the last weeks of his life were the worst time of all for her. She was having difficulty with her new reading glasses. Her optometrist had prescribed significantly stronger lenses, and they were causing her major headaches. Her knees were in daily pain. Only after his death did she realize that the dreadful negatives were ended, her serenity had returned, and life had given her a renewed mission.

Euell and Joyce Rubert spent several days with Lao in April and did their best to encourage her. It was obvious to them that the strain had Lao almost at the breaking point. By early May, it was clear to everyone that the end was a mere matter of days away.

Emelia and John came to Swannanoa several days before Walter's ninety-second birthday. He was critically ill but recognized them. Besides their faithful friends and staff members Johnny Miles and Pat Hall, Evelyn Jones, a devoted friend, was there to lend her soothing and comforting presence. A day or so before his birthday, Walter told Evelyn, "Always remember, I am like a spring, but my Lao is like a deep well from which the fountains will ever flow." On May 19, 1963, his birthday, Emelia was holding his hand when he died. Lao had just stepped into the next room after consoling him in her arms for hours.

On Thursday, May 23, Walter was buried in the quiet garden of the summer cottage behind the palace gardens and pergola. Bordered on two sides by the mountain woodlands where he loved to walk and meditate with Lao, his grave would be adorned simply with a five-foot replica of the Christ figure. A bronze plaque imbedded in the base supporting the statue read in centered text, "WALTER RUSSELL—God's Son of Light—Came From God—May 19, 1871—Returned to God—May 19, 1963—He gave man the way to eternal life for he gave to man the Secret of Light."

99. Lao standing at Walter Russell's grave at Swannanoa.

Arthur and Bowan Jones, Euell J. Rubert, Peter Parker, and

100. Dr. Daniel Poling.

Charles L. Banister joined James Dulaney as pallbearers. Immediately preceding the interment, a memorial service had been held in the great hall of the palace at two o'clock that afternoon. The service was simple, punctuated with scripture, hymns, and organ music.

The highlight of the occasion was the eulogy delivered by Dr. Daniel A. Poling of New York, editor of the *Christian Herald* and one of America's best-known ministers. He focused on two texts from the New Testament: the words of Jesus, "The Father and I are one. He that hath seen me hath seen the Father," and John's words about Jesus, "This is the message that we have heard, that God is Light and in Him is no darkness at all."

Dr. Poling described Walter's achievements in science and the arts, calling special attention to the unique manner in which in his sculpture Walter had made the eye "a living reflector of the very light of the world." He stressed that for him two words comprehended "Dr. Russell's life and achievements. The word of five letters is 'Faith.' The word of four letters is 'Love.'"

"Up to now," he said, "the complete story of Dr. Russell has not been written and it may never be fully written, but in its physical and labor activities alone when measured by any known standard of success, his life is, I think, the Horatio Alger story of the century. Here was a man who became the highly regarded friend and confidant of Presidents and Kings, of philosophers and saints, and scientists, indeed, of the supreme figures of his time in practically every area of worthy human endeavor, but who remained always a commoner, 'loyal to the royal in himself.'"

Dr. Poling called Walter "a man who in his career and in all his activities, physical as well as mystical, was a personality without parallel in his century." He admired Walter's belief that every man had consummate genius within himself. He also stressed that to Walter Russell "time and space are but a breath, a whisper. He knew that physical existence is but the childhood of our immortality and that we finish here only to begin. How he will be missed," he asserted, "but though gone, he is never away." Dr. Poling concluded by recognizing that Lao, Walter's "beloved one," now had their destiny in her eyes. "Always and in all things they were complete in each other."

Walter's death was widely reported. The New York and Washington dailies published extensive obituaries, and friends sent Lao similar clippings from Chicago, Philadelphia, Los Angeles, and many other newspapers.

In England, Florrie felt grief beyond expression. She wrote her sister after telephoning her, "Darling, Peter's telegram has just arrived. The news is such a shock that I am not yet able to collect myself. There is so much I want to say to you but the right words will not come. Your loss, I know, is so very great, and my heart aches for you in your sorrow and bereavement. Walter was such a darling, and I know how much you loved him and what a great void his passing will leave for you."

Pat duPont came for the final service. Her presence was a great comfort to Lao. Estelle H. Ries wrote from New York, "Somehow I always believed that doctor's rare gifts included physical immortality." She decided on another way to express her sympathy. She later telephoned Lao, told her she was with her in spirit, and said that instead of coming to the service, she had decided to send Lao the probable cost of such a visit for her more practical use.

Gwen and Sid Grimmond, students and friends from Vancouver, British Columbia, who kept Lao supplied with choice English teas throughout the years, expressed great sympathy for her, as did Dr. George Chromiak of Los Angeles, who mourned the passing of a great soul. Louis J. Mitchell wrote her a particularly poignant letter, recalling their discussing the Russells' future plans together during his visit to the palace, and remembering especially how the ailing Walter had paid loving attention to the Mitchell children who were waiting patiently for the conference to conclude. Hundreds of letters and cards came from individuals who recalled similar personal encounters. Anna Rosa Fiorelli wrote Lao that a musical evening she and her sisters had spent with the Russells in August 1961 remained one of the most treasured memories of her life.

Those who had known the Russells well tried to express their appreciation of Lao's importance to the achievements of the previous seventeen years. A close friend wrote, "You have done all it was possible for anyone to do and far more than most others in similar circumstances would have done. The important work that you jointly undertook could never have been accomplished without you! Doctor was truly a very great and extraordinary man, and your understanding of him and beautiful devotion were comeasured with his great capacities. I fear he would have met a withering fate in the latter years of his life if it had not been for your great courage and clear vision of the urgency of your joint message and work!"

Charles Earley praised Lao's attitude at this time of grief as "a living symbol to all and living proof of the Truth." He told her he knew that Walter had been proud of her and that much work remained to be done, but he cautioned, "I realize the urgency, but you must take time to rest."

St. Barbe Baker's first impulse had been to step on the next plane in New Zealand and land at her side. With thousands of others, he had come to regard Walter as an eternal institution. He reminded Lao of Abdul Baha'i's prayer, "O my God, Thy trust has been returned unto Thee!" He assured her that his strong arms were around her in heart-to-heart loving sympathy.

Recent visitors to Swannanoa expressed joy that they had been able to get there to see Walter before he died. Among these was Brother Mandus of the World Healing Crusade in Blackpool, who wrote that he would always cherish the memory of his visit with them the previous year.

A number of students told Lao that they believed the Russells were the fulfillment of Jesus' promise to come again to fulfill the law. One student recalled that her first impression of Walter Russell was so strong she thought he was the embodiment of Jesus, Buddha, and Da Vinci, just as one mystic had remarked while looking at Lao's photograph, "I see God in that face."

A Hindu scholar working in Virginia told her his family had urged him to return home "and follow the footsteps of Swami Vivekananda," but he told Lao he could do nothing better than to follow her and Walter's steps. Friends realized that Walter's death was an enormous personal loss to Lao, but reassured her that he could be "of great assistance and inspiration to you from his realm of greater illumination." Another wrote her, "We have lost the Greatest Spirit in thousands of years, but you have lost so much more."

101. Dr. R. C. Bolen and his Concept Therapy Club.

From Greenwood, South Carolina, their great friend Dr. R. C. Bolen, who sent many of his chiropractic patients to Swannanoa for spiritual renewal, told her the world would ever be indebted to her, not only for her cosmic mind but also for being Walter's partner and inspiration so that the Message might come at this time. "It was your sheer projection of power and light that sustained him all these years," he said. A Unity minister in Northern Virginia wrote her, "I am sure he has opened avenues of progress of which we do not yet dream, and you, his partner, are part of all this and will carry on."

A month after Walter's death, she wrote a friend whose daughter had died suddenly. She poured out her compassion in this letter, consoling the grieving mother with confidence of their immortality. She also confided her own frequent yearnings to have children of her own. "How often I think how wonderful it would be now if I had a son or daughter," she wrote. "Then I remember that all the children of the world are my children. Never a day passes that I do not have beautiful letters from children who are living more glorious lives through our teachings. Nothing is in vain, and you who have given so much to life will go marching bravely on, and some distant day we shall fulfill our progress on earth and refold into our immortal selves. This is our reward for living."

There were those who questioned Lao's ability to carry on the work alone. Three days before Walter's death, Myrtle Moore, a versatile and highly successful natural healer from Miami Beach, offered her services to the University staff. A month later, she wrote Lao to recommend Dr. Sadhu Grewal of Detroit as Walter's successor at Swannanoa, assuring Lao that the University could still be a great philosophical center, and that Dr. Grewal was "better qualified to continue the work at Swannanoa than any one else I know."

Others volunteered their services and offered to take over the University, as if Lao were not capable of such a mission. A California architect and engineer asked her to let him know if he could help, adding, "it is possible that I would be able and interested enough to carry on the work."

It shocked Lao that anyone familiar with their work was under such a misapprehension as to how she and Walter had envisioned its continuity. Firmly, but with kindness, she advised the writer, "It was I who started this University and have made it a world-wide institution through my work. The last thing I want at this point is a manager. The one who has the concept must unfold that concept. What I need are good routine workers and top-notch stenographers capable of handling big mailings. The Message, which God gave to us, was a balanced male-female message, and this basic principle underlies all of our teachings, both philosophically and scientifically."

Most students were thrilled with Lao's determination to carry on with the work and felt her maturity of thought and spirit was greatly needed to bring sanity and direction to human relationships in the world at large. From California, Ann Elliott told her that Walter's passing reminded her of Junipero Serra's. The great Spanish missionary had planned the end of his earthly life in the same careful manner with which he had lived his life, believing he could accomplish even greater things for enlightening the world from another realm. This certainly seemed to be the case with Walter.

Lao replied warmly, "God gave me full instructions for my work on earth, and I live but to fulfill my purpose worthily. There has been great impetus in our work these past weeks, and after a holiday in England, I shall keep some important appointments and then fill lecture engagements early in the New Year." Obviously she was ready to continue the task.

CHAPTER EIGHTEEN

Meeting the Test (1963-66)

In late June, Lao began to prepare for what would be her last trip to England. It depressed her to go through her personal files to find her birth record, citizenship papers, and marriage license, but she knew she would need these to obtain her first American passport.

On July 21, 1963, just before she left for England, Lao wrote a very troubled letter to Jim Dulaney, telling him that she had wanted to talk to him for many months, but that Walter's illness and death had prevented her from doing so, and that subsequently, Dulaney had so persistently avoided meeting or talking with her, she felt she had no other choice but to write him. She reminded him how important the work at Swannanoa had become and cited the thousands of letters she received each year. She told him he had hurt Walter Russell deeply when he told them, at the time their book *The One-World Purpose* was released, that the Russells did not own anything at Swannanoa. That worried Walter until he died, she said. Both she and Walter had believed that the palace owners would honor what they considered a gentleman's agreement, that whenever the Russells could make the first large payment, they would be able to take title to the palace. During the years since they had first occupied Swannanoa in 1948, the owners had received fifty percent of the gate receipts, while the Russells had spent thousands of dollars to keep the premises in repair. They had even installed new sashes and windows in the barn not long after they had come to Swannanoa, but vandals had destroyed many of them over time.

Lao told Dulaney that both she and he had the power and ability to make millions of dollars in business; however, she understood that one doing God's work does not work to make money, but to obtain an eternal inner wealth beyond all earthly fortune. Dulaney had told her that money and politics were the important things today. Lao replied that such was indeed the case at present, but warned him that unless a great change occurred in mankind's way of life, some day there would not be any tomorrow. She reminded him of the support his father had expressed for the Russells' work back in 1948 and of his mother's continued support. She told him that if they could only work together, they would both benefit greatly.

Since coming to Swannanoa, Lao told him, the Russells had been greatly handicapped by the changes that the owners had made in the entrance to Swannanoa. The original gates to the palace grounds had been taken down and installed by Jim Dulaney at his house on Rugby Road in Charlottesville. Many visitors complained about their difficulty in finding the palace due to the poor entrance. Lao told Dulaney that prospective visitors, who had come thousands of miles, often passed fifty miles or more beyond Swannanoa before realizing their error and stopping to telephone for directions. He suggested cutting down trees so that the palace could be seen from the main highway, but Lao thought that was a poor solution to the problem.

She outlined her plans to lecture across America beginning in 1964, and advised him she was now leaving for England, but assured him that Swannanoa would be well taken care of during her absence. She asked Dulaney not to discuss her business affairs with anyone, even if Euell Rubert should return while she was gone, because she did not want anything done without her presence or approval. It shocked her that Jim Dulaney had recently talked with Johnny Miles of the palace staff about the shabby appearance of the palace, a conversation that had occurred in front of Dulaney's manager. She felt that these things should have been discussed directly with her. She would return to Swannanoa in September, she told him.

On July 22, Lao went to Washington, stopped at the State Department to procure her passport, and checked into the Willard Hotel on Pennsylvania Avenue. The trip had been timed to allow her to be present when Dr. Poling was honored as Clergyman of the Year by the Foundation for Religious Heritage of America. Many of Washington's elite were present at the gala reception and dinner. She sat next to the honorary president of the Mothers of America, and had a wonderful opportunity to become better acquainted with Mrs. Poling.

Lao found Dr. Poling by far the finest man present at the banquet, but she was happy to meet other people in leadership roles across the country. She had sent Mrs. Poling an orchid corsage, which greatly pleased the honoree's wife. The significant tributes Dr. Poling received made it obvious how hard he had worked through his ministry to help mankind.

Lao was radiant in her gold lamé dress, and many individuals at the head table stopped to meet her. She wrote Emelia that the dress was seventeen years old. "It is so useful for a dinner such as last night. I shall use it, I guess, as long as I live. I had it cleaned and held my breath in case it fell apart. I think it will last me another seventeen years if I live that long!"

It impressed Lao to see many Jews and African-Americans in key positions, a change she saw as a positive reversal of past prejudice. Justice Arthur Goldberg of the United States Supreme Court offered the major address of the evening. His theme was the need to build unity by ending racial discrimination. His speech left a strong and favorable impact on Lao.

Dr. Poling had declined any fee or expenses for coming to Swannanoa to preach Walter Russell's funeral, but Lao discerned that he and his wife would be delighted to receive a medium-scale replica of the Christ of the Blue Ridge as a focal point for the New Hampshire garden he had established in memory of his son, who was one of the famed four chaplains who yielded up their lifeboats to drowning sailors during one of World War II's many disasters at sea. Lao immediately ordered two five-foot replicas of the Christ statue, one as a gift for Dr. Poling and one for Walter's grave. She was able to have the statue delivered to the Polings in time for the planned dedication in New England.

In mid-July, John and Emelia had moved to their new home, a beautiful nine-acre estate on Spring Hollow Road in elegant Far Hills, New Jersey. Emelia treasured the house and often thought of it as a potential home for Lao and the University in case the lease on Swannanoa were ever lost. Emelia spent the rest of her life there and willed the property to the University on her death.

Before Lao left for England, John Lombardi prepared a new will for her. She left her English assets to Florrie, naming her niece and nephew, Olive and Peter, as contingent beneficiaries. All her American assets were left to Emelia to leave on display in the museum at Swannanoa if possible. This included Walter's personal effects. "I do not have the heart at this time to go through his things," she wrote to Emelia. "They all remain where they were when he was here." Subsequently she revised her will, naming the University as sole heir to her assets in the United States.

102. *Lao aboard the* Queen Elizabeth II.

Lao sailed for England aboard the *Queen Elizabeth* on July 31, after spending two days in New York with Pat duPont. As always, she traveled first class. Former President and Mrs. Eisenhower were in a nearby cabin, and Lao became acquainted with them early on the trip. Mrs. Eisenhower wrote Lao to thank her for her kindness and express her delight in "chatting with you." On the last day of the voyage, Lao was given a smallpox vaccination onboard to facilitate her return to America. She had never been vaccinated before and immediately developed a high reactive fever. Florrie met her ship, and the two sisters stayed in London for a week or more to allow Lao to see St. Barbe Baker and contact his and other English publishers. It rained and turned cold, and her stay in London was ruined because she was at first too ill and then too weak for much activity.

The first letter she received from Swannanoa told of expensive mechanical repairs needed at the palace. Once Pat Hall, Lao's assistant since 1962, learned how ill Lao was, she wrote again to reassure her that book sales and attendance figures were high and would cover the added expense. Pat had stopped two men in the palace garden, politely asking them to buy their tickets before they toured, only to realize that one of the men was Jim Dulaney. He enjoyed her mistake.

Two distinguished students, Colonel C. E. Boyer and his wife, Eugenia, joined Pat and her daughter Deanna at the palace to help carry on business, banking, and correspondence while Lao was away. Mrs. Boyer was one of Europe's most noted violinists.

103. Guy Chipman.

Guy Chipman was helping the staff on weekends, and had rearranged his own business appointments to allow him to spend more time at the palace. He would be there to help for the busy Labor Day holiday. He was a well-known human relations lecturer, who years before had become a popular inspirational speaker for industry by combining his hobbies of drawing clever cartoons and caricatures and performing fancy rope tricks with intuitive dialogue and heartfelt wisdom. His direct and simple manner, combined with his understanding of sales problems, allowed him to "hold a mirror to the individual's habits, emotions, and inner drives," and proved effective at employee performance clinics and sales motivational meetings. A successful radio personality, he authored a weekly syndicated newspaper feature, *How to Influence Yourself*. Tall and handsome, he would become a major support in Lao's life and an indispensable colleague, advisor, and manager on the national lecture tours she would undertake in the years to come.

The day after Lao left Swannanoa, another letter had arrived from Phyllis McConnell of Washington, Iowa, the schoolteacher with a master's degree in education who had become a serious student of the work. Phyllis would spend decades as a devoted member of the palace staff, where she was known and beloved by the name Angela Carr, given her by Lao, who she reminded of an angel.

Phyllis described the peonies blooming in her mother's garden with flowers in various stages of development, a few fully open, some tightly closed, and others partly opened. She thought the development of individual people paralleled that of the flowers. The Russells reminded her of beautiful, inspiring, fully opened flowers. Many others she knew were in various stages of development, but by far the greatest number of people were like the tightly closed blossoms, straining to awake or unfold but not quite ready. Phyllis loved music and was often asked to sing in Iowa churches. She told Lao her favorite song was one that reflected her overwhelming desire, "If with All Your Heart Ye Truly Seek Me, Ye Shall Ever Surely Find Me" from Mendelssohn's *Elijah*. She added, "In many ways I consider you and Dr. Russell to be my real Mother and Father even more than my physical parents. I say this not in lessening my respect for my physical parents but only in an ever deepening regard and love for you both." She was distributing copies of the Russells' books to friends and acquaintances in Iowa.

While Lao was in England, Henry C. Mulberger of Raytheon Company wrote to tell her that Congressman Durward Hall had contacted him, expressing a sincere interest in Walter's work on the optical generator. Inasmuch as Mulberger lacked the adequate facilities to assess the project's feasibility, he had referred Walter's letters and drawings to Dr. Silberg, a young scientist in one of Raytheon's advanced-project laboratories, who had worked extensively in the field of plasmoids and lightning balls, and who set out at once to obtain the necessary funds to attempt to prove the principles of the optical generator on a small scale in his laboratory. Mulberger promised to let Lao know the results of Dr. Silberg's experiments as soon as they were conclusive, but the project was soon stymied in oppressive corporate bureaucracy.

Florrie was happy to see Lao and seemed to look younger and better every day. She had experienced a very difficult time caring for their sister, Emily Summerfield, who had died on December 26, 1962, and being with Lao delighted her. At sixty-eight, Florrie was slowing down but still felt the need to stay busy and travel. As much as Lao longed for her sister to come permanently to Swannanoa, she knew that they would be ill suited to live together. Lao loved Florrie but recognized they were different in their thoughts. "I cannot share my thoughts on life and God with her at all. It would not do for us to live together—for either of us!" Lao wrote Emelia.

Lao longed for the quiet of her mountain. "The beautiful little English villages have become infected with thousands of cars that race around their little curved roads at a tremendous speed," she observed. "Domestic help is just about nil."

Florrie had no car or television, and there was little excitement at her home. Although Lao was ill for most of her time in England, she managed to visit Elsie Benney and her daughter Anna.

Lao missed Walter terribly, but she was eager to look to the future. "It seems as though I have no contact with life anymore. It is all so depressing, and I need love so much just now," she confided in a letter to Emelia. She spent much of her visit resting at Florrie's cottage, and soon it was time to return to America.

Lao left England for the last time on September 5, 1963, sailing on the *Queen Elizabeth*, arriving in New York five days later, suffering with bronchial pneumonia. Emelia had invited her to rest a few days in Far Hills, but Lao was far too ill. Guy Chipman met her ship, driving his comfortable Oldsmobile, and bundled her up in pillows and blankets before he drove her slowly back to Swannanoa. Guy was thankful to get her home alive, but once they arrived at Swannanoa, she seemed to grow stronger with each passing hour. She was clearly delighted to be home. "I feel I never want to leave the mountain again," she wrote Emelia.

On her return, she found that Jim Dulaney was clearing the fairways of the old Swannanoa golf course and had strung barbed wire right up to the water tower and alongside the roads leading to the palace. This distressed Lao, but she knew there was little purpose in discussing a more permanent lease purchase arrangement on the palace until she had more capital.

In October, the pain in her side was so great that she asked Dr. Clarabelle Hopkins, Waynesboro's legendary chiropractor, to come to the palace to treat her. Dr. Hopkins found several misalignments and one particularly bad spot in Lao's spleen, all of which the physician attributed to exhaustion and the smallpox vaccination. Dr. Hopkins told her that all Lao's Waynesboro friends had been terribly worried when Lao was nursing Walter so tirelessly, and feared that she would so weaken herself that she too would die.

"So I am striving to get back to normal," Lao told Emelia. She promptly went on a carrot juice diet to clear her system of toxins from the vaccination and the antibiotics she had subsequently been given for bronchial pneumonia on her arrival in New York. Soon her pain began to subside.

For the first time in many years, Lao spent her birthday alone. The Lombardis were unable to come to Swannanoa, and Lao recalled "all the years [when] we have made much of our birthdays and the air was filled with laughing and happy things. Now all is quiet, and my beloved tells my soul of our eternal love. Someday we shall be together again in new, young bodies. I cannot help but long to have you both near me."

She was invited to a party hosted by Senator Barry Goldwater in Washington on November 10. Numerous senators and congressmen were planning to attend, but she declined, convinced that her lungs could not take a smoke-laden atmosphere, and that such parties were not conducive to what she wished to convey. "God will bring to His mountaintop those who can help us," she wrote. Senator Goldwater had written her three years before, reassuring her in these words: "Certainly we are as one in that we both know it to be true that man is indeed a spiritual creature whose needs and desires can never be fully served by a material approach."

Emelia's mother died in December. Lao sought to console her friend. "There are no words that can assuage that awful dead feeling within you today. Last night I could not sleep. I was thinking of your mother and Doctor, and I thought how deep is the sorrow of the space they left their warmth, their love, their concern for us and their joy of just being with us. I felt such aloneness. And then I thought how in a few brief years we too shall go, and we shall leave 'aloneness' for someone else.

"Life is such a brief breath, and when we know joy we also know sorrow, for that which is joy one day is the very thing that will [some day] bring us sorrow." Still she felt that departed loved ones know our love, even after they were merged into the Light with God who had created everyone with a conscious thought.

Lao had always urged others never to waste a moment they had with those they loved. "Each moment is precious," she cautioned. Now she regretted the times she had been forced to work in the office during Walter's last days. "Doctor was dying, but to earn our daily bread I had to leave him. Each moment was agony away from him for I knew I soon would not have him there. When I left the room, the one left with him said he requested over and over again, 'Lao, my Lao, my Lao.' I would tell him when I came back I was sorry I had to go into the office, and he would smile his dear, sweet smile and say, 'Now the light has come on again.'"

Lao received mail from many exceptional new contacts who did not realize that Walter had died. Reverend Eugenia Bedford, of the Chapel in the Pines in Idyllwild, California, wrote to describe her own years of searching for validation of her convictions as to life and the creator of this universe. She recounted her intensive research with the pendulum concerning vibration and color. "Then came the wonderful day when a dear friend who knew how interested I was in Light gave me a copy of the *The Secret of Light*," she wrote. "As soon as I saw the painting of the light-wave I said, 'That's it, that's it, that is all there is!'" Letters like this opened new doors for Lao, but burdened her with the work of yet additional correspondence.

Attorney Louis J. Nizer, whose new book *My Life in Court* had brought him fame that season, had been interviewed earlier in the year on television's *Tonight Show* and asserted that in the future education would need to be of a different quality so as to teach that learning comes from within. Lao corresponded with this celebrated lawyer, who believed that "character and justice were one" and the success of any man greatly depended on his character.

Her old friend Frank D. Lawrence, founder of the Virginia Hall of Fame in Portsmouth, Virginia, asked her for a duplicate of the portrait she had sent him of Walter and her. He had one copy for his office at home, he told her, but wanted the second one for the Hall of Fame.

In December, St. Barbe Baker did his best to convince Lao to join him in Morocco for the Sahara International Conference, to be attended by representatives of the twenty-five countries surrounding the great African desert. "You are much in my thoughts and I am telling people here about your wonderful work," he told her, as he ordered another supply of University literature and books. Some of the books he personally presented to the sister of the King of Morocco.

Lao shared her concern over America's deepening racial crisis with her friend Ruby Dunn, a nutritionist from Tulsa. They both agreed that the white race in the United States had brought its current problems on itself by centuries of upsetting the balance in their dealings with African-Americans.

In early 1964, Lao was disturbed to read a newspaper article describing the proposed expansion of the Swannanoa Golf Club. She feared that this presaged trouble for her with the palace owners, and talked at length with the Lombardis as to the subtlest and most appropriate manner of clarifying matters with Jim Dulaney. At last she decided on writing a passionate letter to him and was pleased when she heard no more of the matter. She soon learned that the publicized project involved the other part of the original Swannanoa property, which had become a public golf course some years before.

That spring, the University board met at Swannanoa with Pat duPont; her new husband, James Stephanis; and John Lombardi joining Lao. Emelia was involved with settling her mother's estate and remained in New Jersey. The board formally agreed to sponsor Lao's forthcoming lecture tours and bear all incidental expenses. Arthur Jones and Dr. Lavender were both too frail to attend.

Pat duPont arranged for Lao to visit Florida the following month. Guy Chipman drove her down, accompanied by Johnny Miles, who she felt needed some restful sea air and who helped Lao care for her Scottie Wendy on the vacation.

In Florida, at a fundraising reception, Lao introduced the main speaker, Mayor Haydon Burns of Jacksonville, a candidate for governor who Pat duPont and Jim Stephanis were vigorously supporting. Mayor Burns told Lao that her introduction was the greatest he had ever received and had given him the cue and ground-

104. Lao in Florida.

105. *Patricia duPont and Jim Stephanis with Lao.*

work for the non-political, extemporaneous speech he had been asked to deliver. Through Pat and Jim, Lao made many important contacts in Miami and received broad publicity in newspapers throughout Florida.

Guy Chipman was proving more and more helpful to Lao. On their way back from Florida he drove her to Charlotte, North Carolina, where she gave a lecture on April 22, 1964, at the Esso building. Her topic was "Why You Must Now Awaken To Your Deep Purpose on Earth." Her sponsors in Charlotte were the Sydney Alversons, the Harold Steadmans, Mrs. Harold Dwelle, and the Dayrell Kortheurs.

Earlier in the day, Joann Coker interviewed her for the *Charlotte Observer*, concluding that Lao "spans the philosophical thought of two continents," and describing how her pink slouch hat "tilts up to reveal crystal-ball eyes and a cupid's bow mouth that pronounces words with a faint Buckinghamshire accent." This greatly amused Lao's sister Florrie when she read it. "I didn't realize you had any particular accent," she wrote her. "How did they get on to it?"

Coker painted the subject of her feature article in vivid prose. "She crosses her trim ankles and tugs at the skirt of her pale pink spring suit, making her salt and pepper ringlets peep from beneath the hat. You imagine Mrs. Russell thumbing through fashion magazines, not books of abstract thought, but she has been concentrating on changing the thinking of the world since the age of three. Living with a human dynamo, whose interests ranged from science to music, was only an extension of her own life for Mrs. Russell." Lao told the reporter that she and Walter "thought so much alike that we could share almost everything."

Even Guy Chipman was mentioned in the story. As Miss Coker continued, "A newspaper man turned novelist, who traveled with Mrs. Russell and is writing the couple's love story as a book, said their marriage was a May-December one, although the widow will not reveal her age."

"We're as old as our thoughts and attitudes. Chronological age has nothing to do with it," Lao told her interviewer, who stated that Lao's philosophy was based on "golden rule reincarnation, not the Hindu belief in steadily ascending or descending lives according to merit."

106. Charlotte Observer *interview, 1964.*

When asked her opinion of orthodox Christians who strongly questioned her belief in reincarnation by reminding her that the Bible said, "It is appointed to man once to die, and then the judgment," Lao countered, "You see reincarnation all around you. Look at the tiny rose you see in the winter and think it will never leaf, but spring comes and it is revived. The body is severed from consciousness in death, but life is eternal."

Her one-world philosophy held that if mankind recognized its true relationship one with another, the world would come into harmony. "If you recognized your oneness with me, you couldn't hurt me," Lao told the reporter.

Lao answered other questions posed to her in the interview. "Do the stars command one's destiny?" Miss Coker asked her. "Yes," Lao replied, "but all God's laws influence your destiny, and if you live by those laws then you command your own destiny."

Questioned as to her opinion of the then-current Bridey Murphy reincarnation case, she shook her head negatively and replied, "I don't know what to think about the Murphy case, but I do believe that the knowledge in the soul-seed is handed down from one life to another."

Lao had been away from the palace for nearly six weeks. On her return, she was concerned at the state of the gardens and hoped that Johnny and a new assistant gardener could soon bring it back to presentability. "It has never looked such a ruin," she told Emelia. Ann Kennedy, a student and retired bookkeeper, had assisted with the palace work while she was gone.

Supporters of Senator Margaret Chase Smith, who was thought likely to be the first women nominated by a major American political party as its presidential candidate, contacted Lao for encouragement and support.

Christopher Hills, who was to become her close friend, first wrote Lao in July 1964 after he had read *The Russell Cosmogony* and realized that it confirmed his own 300-page course in radiational physics. Amazed to find that there was anyone "ahead of us in this world," he told Lao he wished he had seen their work earlier, because he had given seven years of his life to reach self-realization, a quest he found "a thousand times easier" after reading the Russells' books.

Hills, a friend of Nehru, Andrew Wilson, and St. Barbe Baker, who with his colleague John Damonte popularized macrobiotics in England and promoted esotheurgia, a word drawn from two Greek words and defined as "in search of the miraculous within," often corresponded and visited with Lao. He presented her with a Tibetan stone, which he told her possessed spiritual energy. She was impressed with Hills's work, including his book *Rejuvenating the Body through Fasting with Spirulina Plankton*.

Although he could only trace his ancestry back six generations, he felt it most likely that he was related to Lao through her mother. Hills was not a common surname in England. His grandfather was one of the chief stewards of Freemasonry in England. Lao's Grandfather Hills had been an officer in his Masonic lodge. In any event, Christopher Hills and Lao felt related in spirit if not by blood.

The actor Cary Grant wrote Lao and extolled *God Will Work with You but Not for You*. St. Barbe Baker wrote her that he had given a copy of *The One-World Purpose* to a film producer, who wanted to come and make a news film and an educational film at Swannanoa. St. Barbe had urged Lowell Thomas to visit Swannanoa, and promised Lao to work extensively to promote the University when his Morocco Conference was concluded.

In 1964, Lao and Emelia had a spirited exchange over several references Lao desired to expunge from some of the Russells' previous writings, because they were being misunderstood. St. Barbe Baker had told her he would gladly have given copies of several Russell books to Khrushchev, but was reluctant to do so because of their castigating references to communism. St. Barbe told Lao, "If you knew what the U.S.A., England, and France were doing today in such places as Africa and Vietnam, you would not say Russia had done worse."

Lao was also upset because African students took exception to statements in their human relations booklet regarding the mongrelization of the races. The Russells felt their readers would recognize that race was an inconsequential concept in a light-wave universe, and that all races should be reluctant to see their respective civilizing achievements and heritages diluted by any process, while gladly sharing their wisdom with the rest of mankind. Neither Lao nor Walter intended any implication of white superiority.

"This Human Relations booklet is so important, and I would like to think we could send it to any country. Not a country can say they are right today. There is so much that is wrong everywhere," she wrote Emelia. "Sooner or later man must live God's Laws or we shall not have a planet left on which to live."

Emelia delayed responding for several weeks, and finally replied taking strenuous exception to any change in the Russells' original text. "It is a powerful unit. You have proof of it by the way it sold, first as part of the *Home Study Course* and then as a separate book. God inspired it. You said you woke up one morning and sat down and wrote it, and that is how it reads," Emelia told her, warning her not to listen to advice from others or to compromise her writing.

Lao left many of the references to communism intact, but altered the text in an effort to clarify her belief that all humanity was one, and that racial distinctions were purely matters of culture and environment and did not reflect any spiritual difference or individual separation from the "Universal Oneness."

The tax accountants had required Lao to repay the University for the expenses of Walter's funeral. It amazed her that this was necessary, inasmuch as she and Walter had given all they had to the University. Thereafter, Lao was paid a small salary and her expenses as a matter of course. It bothered her to accept this. She wrote Emelia, "I need so little for my personal needs and need not take so much salary unless I find a need for this when I start out on the road traveling. I may need more clothes then but as I live now, and with clothes I am sent for gifts, I need so little. I do not do anything that costs money, and I live but for the work."

In 1964, there were more interesting visitors, many of them deeply committed to the scientific work, including an English scientist who came in the fall, studied the science, and returned again the next spring. By July, Lao was feeling more like her old self. She wrote Florrie about the happy group she now had around her at the palace.

Florrie spent three weeks that summer in Derby and Luton. Her hosts took her on a grand tour of the countryside, where she and Lao had spent their youth. "We went along Dunstable Downs through Whipsnad, Ivinghoe, Chiddington, Kentmore, Leighton Buzzard, Woburn Park, Apsley, Guisi, et cetera," Florrie wrote. "I believe I told you before that Holly Cobb Cottage and all the cottages near had been pulled down for road widening. The village [of Ivinghoe] has altered and like many more has lost quite a bit of its character."

Florrie had visited Elsie Dillon, who had helped their family at Holly Cobb Cottage. "She wanted to know how you were and all about you and sent her love to you. She is still a very nice and simple soul," Florrie added. She sent Lao newspaper clippings of scenes they had shared in earlier years. One pictured the Pittstone Windmill in the middle of the field near Ivinghoe along the Dunstable Road.

Representatives of the John Phillip Sousa Society visited the palace and acclaimed Walter's music, particularly his *Sea Children's Waltz* that Paderewski had orchestrated. They arranged for the Marine Band to play and record this for Lao. They were greatly impressed with Walter's bust of Sousa, America's "March King."

The Roosevelt family was scheduled to meet on July 23 to discuss the F.D.R. memorial. Lao was eager for the University to obtain the commission for a monumental casting of Walter's Four Freedoms to be erected in Washington in memory of the great wartime president. Pat duPont told her that all of the Roosevelt family had been impressed with the Four Freedoms sculpture, and that the matter was now in the hands of the memorial commission itself.

Wendy Jones, the daughter of Arthur and Adele Jones, who had lived at the summer cottage with her parents and helped the Russells during the early years at Swannanoa, died in Florida on October 15, 1964, after a long illness. Lao had sent her roses two days before and had kept in touch with her throughout her struggle. "Poor, sweet Wendy," Lao wrote. "She was frustrated and yet so very brave and wonderful." The Jones family had been mainstays of the Russell work at Swannanoa. Their son, Bowan, used the Russell principles in his extensive healing practice and sent many students to Swannanoa.

Lao had argued with Guy Chipman. He was a close friend but very temperamental, she found. Florrie felt that he suffered from an acute inferiority complex, and knew that it put a nervous strain on Lao when the people around her continually seemed at variance. After this, Lao seems to have spent her sixtieth birthday in a melancholy state, writing Emelia and John a few days afterwards, "Life is all so uncertain today, and the only real joy is being with those we love. That is why I selfishly want to be with you both." By Thanksgiving she was in better spirits, planning her lecture tour, and urging Florrie to come to America and accompany her, but Florrie felt unable to manage the trip that year.

Lao gave serious thought to visiting her students in Australia and New Zealand, where the teachings seemed to be flourishing, but she decided the potential of such an extended tour did not justify the expense, and also feared the consequences of her being so far away from the Swannanoa for so long a time.

Her cousin Ellen Grant from St. Louis had visited the palace with her family earlier in the year, and enjoyed a happy reunion with Lao. Ellen wrote Florrie that she knew Lao felt very alone now that Walter was gone. "But is he really?" Ellen continued. "He was so full of life and love. His Soul lives on and on along with the wonderful memories of him. I thank God that Mother and Uncle Jim could visit with Lao and Walter before they passed on." Uncle Jim was Lao's first cousin, the St. Louis surgeon who had often written letters of reference for Lao in the early 1940s, when she was Daisy Stebbing desperately seeking permanent residency in the United States and better employment in New York.

Lao's Christmas message for 1964 was inspirational and prompted a large number of students to gather at Swannanoa for the holiday. This first Christmas message after Walter's death received such a favorable reception that Lao decided to keep it in print and call it "The Eternal Christmas Message" as a memorial to her husband. In it she described how she and Walter had written the song "Swannanoa, Shrine of Love" at three o'clock in the morning, while they were writing the first edition of the course. They had put the tea kettle on the stove, and Walter began improvising on the piano. The words came instantly to Lao, and she hurried to write them down.

The Christmas gathering in 1964 was an important occasion. It demonstrated that a new era had begun in the life of the University with Lao bearing full responsibility for the successful propagation of the Russell teachings. Her key staff helped her in dispensing the hospitality for which the palace had become known. Patricia Hall, charged with receiving visitors throughout the year, radiated the fulfillment she had personally found in the Russell teachings. Her daughter, Deanna, was in charge of the information center at the palace gates during her summer vacation from college.

Angela Carr, who Lao described as "our beautiful blonde little angel" and "a powerful being behind her delicate, Dresden china-like exterior," had become Lao's right-hand assistant in the office and storeroom, and spent many of her leisure hours hard at work beautifying the gardens.

Lao and Guy Chipman had reconciled their differences, and in early February 1965, they left Swannanoa for a major lecture tour. Lao knew that a woman alone on the road was no longer safe. "I did once drive alone from Boston to Los Angeles," she wrote Laara Lindo, "but I would not care to do so today. Traveling is not as easy as of yore or as safe." She was happy to have Guy Chipman drive for her and help with the onerous arrangements that seemed to multiply on every speaking tour.

They traveled first to Unity headquarters in Lee's Summit, Missouri, where Lao had been asked to give a series of lectures. Her reception there was even warmer than she had expected, and all of her sessions were well attended. They visited with Euell Rubert in Missouri and again in New Mexico where he was constructing a large Holiday Inn. Once again he promised Lao his financial support in helping her publish the proposed magazine *Balance* when she felt the time was right.

By early March, she was in Phoenix with lectures scheduled for Tucson on March 10, before a long series of engagements in Southern and Northern California. She was a success everywhere she spoke. By April 3, she was en route to San Francisco for four lectures and demand was so strong for her to speak that she retraced her route to give seven additional lectures in the Los Angeles area.

In Palo Alto she made the acquaintance of Billy Prior Bates, an attorney who considered her legal training merely a preparation for more cosmic work, and had fought for years for equal rights for women, becoming, she felt, destructively competitive, striving to excel over her husband. Meeting and listening to Lao convinced her that balance was the key to building a constructive home and life. She and her husband embraced the *Home Study Course*, and she soon wrote the first of many letters to explain to Lao how important the Message had become in their lives: "Having your philosophy to cling to was like being able to grab onto a redwood tree when one is about to slide off the path and down a steep slope. We caught ourselves before we made it necessary to climb all the way back up the incline, and are walking on the firm path hand in hand once again—in balance."

In the years to come, Billy Bates worked hard to help Lao spread her philosophy. For a while she worked on a book outlining her experiences with Lao and the University. Billy arranged many of Lao's lectures, promoted the books and course, and extolled the effectiveness of the Message in her own marriage. Her husband, she told Lao, was 100 percent behind her.

107. Guy Chipman, Lao Russell, Rev. and Mrs. Clifford Carpenter.

Lao attracted an unexpectedly large attendance at many of her lectures. Reverend Clifford Carpenter told members of his large Unity Temple in Glendale, "Besides being a woman of great charm and beauty, Mrs. Russell exudes a spiritual consciousness that bears witness to her close walk with God and her ability to translate that consciousness into practical daily living. She has the beautiful faculty of being able to convey this awareness to her listeners in such a manner that they are greatly edified and inspired to greater Christ-like thought and action." Dr. Martha Frank, Director of the Mothers' and Children's Educational Foundation, Inc., Child Guidance Center in Pacific Palisades, California, wrote Lao after her lecture there: "You have given us new vistas of understanding; in your presentation there were no walls separating science, philosophy, religion, and the arts. An answer was there for all, a call to sublimity, expressed by you in magnificent simplicity, clarity and strength. And above all of deepest significance is your gift to radiate that pure universal love so dynamically that we all felt deeply uplifted, inspired and transformed. The imprint and glow that you leave with each listener is beyond words."

Six years after she had successfully completed her study of the *Home Study Course*, Laara Lindo had written Lao that she continuously found the course helpful in her life and work. Lao recognized that Laara's "understanding is now coming into full flower," and advised the young teacher she knew "the joy which is yours because of this." They planned to meet in British Columbia in 1965, but Lao's unexpectedly heavy commitments in California prevented her from visiting the Vancouver area when she and Guy Chipman drove east through part of Canada.

Lao enjoyed hearing news of the young teacher's life in the classroom and at home. "I loved to hear that you will be putting fruits and vegetables into the freezer, and I trust that you will have time for some music and painting. It is wonderful to be able to express yourself in these mediums. It matters not whether you are amateur or professional in this expression, for the deep satisfaction that comes from any form of beauty expression is food for the Soul. Beauty is God, and you are truly one of his most blessed children."

Lao and Guy followed their Canadian route to Far Hills, New Jersey, where Lao had arranged to hold the board meeting on May 22, 1965, at the Lombardis' home. She had given twenty-one lectures and made numerous other special appearances over a period of three months. The Unity School of Christianity wanted her to return to Lee's Summit to speak again, and Unity congregations across the country were writing to invite her to their areas. In addition, she and Guy Chipman had made a special trip to the Mark Twain Birthplace Memorial Shrine at Florida, Missouri, where they met the curator and directors, and also discussed Walter's Mark Twain Memorial in a personal visit with former President Harry Truman.

Lao returned to an exceptionally hot summer at Swannanoa, but after such an extensive tour, she found it a joy to be home. She was confident, however, that her successful tour would be the first of many.

Guy Chipman was more enthusiastic than ever in his newly assumed role as the University's public relations director, and Lao was happy to have his help. He had proven indispensable to her on the long tour. He contacted Congressman Eugene J. Keogh, who was promoting the Franklin Delano Roosevelt Memorial, and gave the congressman considerable detail on the story of Walter and Lao's romance and their accomplishments. He advised the congressman of Elliott Roosevelt's conversations with Lao regarding the Roosevelt family's interest in Walter's Four Freedoms. He reminded the congressman that an appropriation for a colossal statue of the Four Freedoms was in the process of going through Congress at the time of President Roosevelt's death in 1945, but had remained in abeyance since that time. In addition, Guy was determined to see the cosmic story of Walter and Lao become a commercially successful film.

Peter Parker had helped Lao design a dark blue photograph of the Christ of the Blue Ridge to be sold by the box as individual note cards. This item proved extremely popular with tourists.

Lao regularly spoke to mentally ill veterans from the Army hospitals in

Salem and Richmond. In August alone she met with three such groups. "They say I reach the poor souls as no one else has," she told Emelia.

Jim Dulaney's awkwardness continued to bother her. Florrie tried to console her, suggesting that the tour would lead more visitors to Swannanoa, and that perhaps this would please Dulaney and render him more cooperative.

There were more and more signs that the Mark Twain Memorial might be realized in full scale in Missouri as originally envisioned. Lao confided to Florrie that this could help extend the Message to other countries that shared America's fondness for Mark Twain.

Melford Okilo of Nigeria visited Lao in 1965 when he was pursuing his education in New York City. Financially strapped, but firmly determined to take advantage of the opportunities available to him during his time in the United States, he had read *The Man Who Tapped the Secrets of the Universe*, which greatly inspired him. Lao never forgot his first visit to Swannanoa. It never occurred to her that some day this quiet but impressive scholar from a noble African family would prove the University's greatest supporter. She was sincerely impressed with his wisdom and humility. From the first, he found the teachings of the University of Science and Philosophy different from those of conventional universities. "These teachings pattern a way of life and include a full comprehension of nature's scientific ways and processes and the teachings of balanced matehood, which is as fundamental a law of Nature as the law of science which says that action and reaction are equal and opposite," he wrote. "These teachings help every man to awaken the Inner Light of the omnipotent power which centers the consciousness of every man."

108. Melford Okilo and Lao Russell.

Over the next few months he corresponded regularly with Lao. Despite the turmoil his beloved Nigeria had endured, he was optimistic for its future. "Perhaps my greatest heritage from your teachings is the new spirit of confidence I now have within myself," he wrote. "I no longer panic about life or any apparent disappointment. I now meet life calmly. I have grown and developed a heart and mind large enough to accommodate any problem cheerfully. While I mourn for the slain, my cheerfulness increases every day at the divine work of construction now taking place in my country. I hear and see the ideals for which I stood in parliament for the last five years being gradually implemented by the military government now in power, and I look to the day when it will please God that I return to continue the struggle for a better living for my people."

By October Lao was hard at work on her Christmas message. She was also working overtime on her *Love* book, struggling to make it simple but fill it with basic truth. "The world must listen and act now," she wrote. "I heard a news commentator say a couple of days ago that if crime increased at its present rate, in five years time it will not be safe to walk on the streets anywhere after dark. What a prospect—and what a world!" She was very optimistic at the prospects for her new book, for which she had evolved the working title of *Teen Sex*. Autumn was always a time of heavy tourism in the Blue Ridge. On one Sunday, Lao had spoken extemporaneously to an unexpected audience of over 200 tourists, all of whom expressed keen interest in owning her forthcoming book. "If this is a trend," Guy Chipman wrote the Lombar-dis, "it should go!"

On December 8 Lao took the manuscript to Kingsport Press in Tennessee. No one, least of all Lao, was satisfied with the proposed title, which was now *Teen-Age Sex*. Lao considered as an alternative *Youth—Awaken To the Power of Love*. Emelia preferred *A Scientific and Living Philosophy of Love and Sex*, and Lao adapted this as the subtitle. She finally decided that there could be no better title for the book than simply *Love*.

Love: A Scientific and Living Philosophy of Love and Sex was written by Lao, primarily to bring awakening teenagers an intimate blueprint of love and life, but to her pleasant surprise, it proved popular with all ages and became the best selling of all her books. Recognizing that many sex practices caused frustrations, because they failed to provide the inner satisfaction that all souls crave, Lao scientifically explained how love is cause and sex is merely an effect of love. Realizing that modern youth was rebellious because of widespread confusion about the nature of true love, she offered her readers dynamic solutions to many of their self-inflicted agonies. Her thesis was simple: man's eternal quest for true love

109. Christmas at the palace.

is never satisfied through sex alone.

Christmas was busy but highly successful. A number of friends came to cheer her during the holiday season, including her so-called "Texas family," Bill and Betty Horton and their eight children. On Christmas Eve, the baronial hall was decorated with Christmas trees and a huge fire crackled in the fireplace. Two sweethearts, Mary Garner and Jesse Van Hollman, who had met at Swannanoa the Christmas before, were united as man and wife before the grand staircase. Lao served as Mary's matron of honor, and Guy Chipman was best man. On Christmas Day, and for three days thereafter, the festivities continued. Music punctuated every waking hour. Orry Nottingham, a professional organist, and Hildegarde Nelson, an accomplished vocalist, led the group in carols and provided solo recitals. The V. Francis Reynolds family came from Waynesboro. Susan Reynolds, daughter of Lao's friend Louis Spilman, owner of *The News Virginian*, joined her husband and children in singing hymns and songs, as she did at several successive Christmas celebrations at the palace. "Her glorious voice was enchanting," Lao recalled. The United States Marine Corps band had specially recorded Walter's *Sea Children's Waltz*, and its assistant director, Captain Dale Harpham, sent the recordings to Lao as a special Christmas gift. Lao wrote her sister that everything went with a "real swing."

110. The V. Francis Reynolds family of Waynesboro, Christmas at Swannanoa.

Lao's old friend Isobel, Lady Cripps, wrote to obtain Lao's suggestions on the education of her two Ghanian grandchildren, who lived with her in England. The ladies reminisced over their first meeting, when Lady Cripps had stayed three extra days in New York to see Walter and Lao when they returned from their first visit to Swannanoa in 1948. Lady Cripps remembered that meeting, treasured her friendship with the Russells, and always promoted their work among her broad coterie of friends in British government circles. Lao was distressed to hear that the large country house of her Scottish friend Andrew Wilson had burned to the ground.

A Dutch scientist had attended one of her California lectures and later visited her at Swannanoa, telling her that, in scientific circles in the Netherlands, Walter Russell's face was better known than the portraits of most of America's past presidents. Similar praise from students in Yugoslavia and Germany suggested that there was an equally strong appreciation of Walter's scientific genius in those countries.

Lao received many invitations to lecture. Her calendar for 1966 was rapidly filling up. *The Scientific Answer To Human Relations* had been reprinted because of the growing demand.

111. Lao with Rowena, Lloyd, Jr., Julie, Janice, and Lloyd Hawkins.

Lloyd and Rowena Hawkins, early students from Jackson, Mississippi, owned a professional photography studio specializing in the finest quality of color work. Lloyd served on the University board from 1969 to 1982, when he was succeeded by the Univer-sity's longtime independent accountant, Leo Waterman. Rowena Hawkins served on the board for eight years during the 1970s. The Hawkinses frequently came to Swannanoa with their best camera equipment and took magnificent photographs, suitable for reproduction in any book or major magazine. After their visit in 1966, Lao wrote Emelia, "Their beautiful art work will enable us to publicize the Message in a highly effective manner."

The February blizzards of 1966 were so severe they were reported in the English news. Florrie inquired with anxiety as to conditions on the Virginia mountaintop. By March, Lao, recovering from a severe cough, was with Guy Chipman in Florida at Key West and then Fort Lauderdale. She gave a major lecture before 500 people in Miami on March 31. That morning she received a letter from Florrie, whose doctors had told her she could die at any time in one of the frequent blackouts caused by her heart trouble. "It was a shock, but I had to give the lecture," Lao said.

112. Miami book signing.

Pat and Jim Stephanis were present, and the Russell books sold by the dozens. Guy was kept busy making the sales. Lao had arranged for cases of the *Love* book to be shipped air express to her directly from the press for the Miami lecture.

They joined Pat and Jim afterwards at an Italian restaurant. Lao thought Pat looked wonderful. In a few weeks, she and Jim were to move into a new Spanish home, designed by Jim and furnished with antiques and objets d'art they had bought in Spain on their honeymoon.

The night before, they had attended a Derby Ball for Governor Haydon Burns, who was running for reelection. Burns and his wife gave Lao a loving

113. Lao speaking in Orlando, Florida.

welcome, and told her that Mrs. Burns wore the Cosmic Clock pin, based on Walter Russell's design, whenever she wanted good luck. Pat had commissioned her jeweler to fabricate them when Lao had introduced Burns at the Yacht Club luncheon the year before. The governor still recalled the "terrific introduction" Lao had given him then.

In early April, she addressed an audience of 850 at the Unity Church in Orlando, and on April 12, she spoke to 1,200 people in St. Petersburg. On their way north, she addressed a Unity congregation in Jacksonville on April 18, the last lecture before she and Guy returned home.

At Winter Haven they had visited Arthur and Adele Jones, who were still inconsolable over their daughter Wendy's illness and death. Their old friends Arthur and Val Thompson came to Lao's lecture in Miami. Lao told Emelia that they looked far younger than their age. On the way home, Guy and Lao stopped for several weeks at The Cloister, Sea Island, Georgia, where she was well remembered by the staff from her vacations there with Walter.

L. L. Dunnington wrote from Mercer Island, Georgia, sending her a copy of his latest book, which was in its eleventh large printing. The author of *Handles of Power*, *The Inner Splendor*, and *Power to Become* wrote her that it was clear they shared the same philosophy: "No problem is too great, no task too difficult, that it cannot be squarely faced and resolved with the help of God." He complimented her *Love* book, which he told her "comes straight to the point and concentrates on the love and light of the Spirit of God without dealing with the man-made theology that so often confuses and blinds men to the light." He told her he would be telling "the story of Walter Russell as given in Glenn Clark's beautiful little book" on March 7, the first Sunday in Lent.

In August 1966, Dunnington wrote Lao that he had distributed fifty additional copies of *The Man Who Tapped the Secrets of the Universe* among the members of a new church in Mercer Island, Washington. He told her that he always urged "the fortunate people who read of Dr. Walter Russell's unbelievable contributions to life to go on to read your great book, *God Will Work with You but Not for You*, which answers the most basic and haunting questions of life. Then I hope that people who go this far will be inspired to get one of the most remarkable books of this century, the one you and Dr. Russell wrote together in eight months and called *Atomic Suicide?* This book may yet save mankind from destruction. Above all, I hope they will first read your own introduction to the book with your own account of Dr. Russell's cosmic consciousness experience and of the amazing way you dear people met each other. Your own experience of cosmic consciousness had fitted you for the amazing cooperation that has resulted in a gift to our needy world whose blessed consequences are only now unfolding."

Melford Okilo, her Nigerian friend, wrote her from New York in late April. He thanked God for "my wonderful and historical meeting with you while you are here with us. It is impossible for me to attempt to express my deep appreciation for the unexpected reception and time you gave me." She knew him to be a man of destiny, and had happily received him at Swannanoa a second time. They maintained a regular correspondence. The civil war in Nigeria had prevented his return to his country. He told Lao that the events there had confirmed many aspects of her teachings and made them more tragically meaningful to him every passing day. He added that his study of her work gave him greater confidence and helped allay his alarm.

The board met at the Lombardis' home in Far Hills, New Jersey, on June 11, 1966. Only Dr. Lavender was there to join Lao and the Lombardis. Most of the discussion concerned the excellent reception the *Love* book had received on Lao's Florida lecture tour.

Florrie regularly sent Lao news of John French, Harry's son, now a successful engineer living in Islington, Ontario, Canada, where he had recently been promoted to the vice presidency of his large firm. John and his wife, Winnie, visited Lao at Swannanoa on several occasions, usually en route to or from a Florida vacation. They always received a warm reception from Lao. On one occasion, the Frenches arrived at the palace simultaneously with the prominent Frank Lawrences of Portsmouth, Virginia. The couples enjoyed each other's company, and John and Winnie accepted an invitation to return with the Lawrences to their home for a week of visiting in Tidewater Virginia. John French was very fond of Lao, remembering well when they were youngsters together, and she had brought joy and light to his otherwise drab existence in Luton.

Lao and Guy left Swannanoa for Denver, Colorado, on August 13, 1966, and planned to be in Fort Worth, Texas, by early September. Even the heat waves that blistered the southwestern United States that summer did not dim their enthusiasm. She was extremely well received everywhere they went. Lao was invited a year in advance to speak at the Hotel Blackhawk in Davenport, Iowa, on August 20, 1967, at the annual auxiliary luncheon of the International Chiropractors Association. The letter of invitation was highly flattering and included these words: "Your dynamic ability as a public speaker has been brought to our attention from various sources, and we are eager to have you serve in this capacity." Nearly 500 had attended the 1966 luncheon, including as many guests as doctors. Lao happily accepted.

The *Home Study Course* still had a remarkable impact on new students. In September 1966, one student wrote Lao after receiving the twelfth and final lesson, "My views on theology were of a 'Doubting-Thomas' agnostic nature before I started your course, but the course has indeed given me a concrete and perfect basis on which to establish belief and continue my life in an infinitely more satisfying manner. For my part I shall endeavor to spread your message, or rather spread 'the truth' to as many people as possible."

That fall, large groups of undergraduates from the University of Virginia came to the palace. One of the professors had given several of his large introductory classes the assignment of writing a paper on their impression of Swannanoa.

Lao made a brief third lecture tour in late October, speaking at Baltimore's Sheraton-Belvedere Hotel at a Unity service conducted by the Reverend Carmen Brannon, and two days later at two Unity services in Philadelphia as the guest speaker for Reverend Paul C. Barrett's congregation. She often gave her prescription for physical and mental health: "The greatest help in mental healing is to retain an inner sense of joyousness for this is God's greatest medicine. If one keeps mentally happy and adheres to Natural Law in the growing and eating of organic foods, one will keep well physically."

Two weeks later, on her birthday, she spoke in Northern Virginia at the Reverend Mildred Park's Unity of Fairfax congregation. The Fairfax lecture was an enormous success. They filled the church auditorium and put loudspeakers in the basement to accommodate the large overflow crowd. A recording of her remarks that day for years proved one of the University's best-selling items. At the Fairfax lecture she met a top personnel officer from the Pentagon, who told her he would do everything he could to circulate her books in the Pentagon.

Lao's return to Swannanoa found her facing a pile of unanswered mail and the need to prepare a Christmas message. It was mailed to three continents in late November, and had reached recipients in England by December 12. Lao's 1966 Christmas message was one of her best. She sent out 16,000 of them, most with brief individualized handwritten messages.

For a third consecutive year, a large group of friends and students gathered around Lao and her staff at Swannanoa to celebrate Christmas and the days following with all the joy and warmth they could summon.

CHAPTER NINETEEN

Purpose and Aim (1966-70)

A cousin from Missouri wrote Florrie at Christmas, "I must say that I admire Lao. She really is incredible. At least she enjoys life. She has a purpose and an aim. So many folks just drift along."

Dr. H. William Baum wrote Lao from New York to praise what he termed "your most beautiful and inspiring book entitled *Love*." He told her that every passage was a gem and strongly recommended it to the patients of his extensive health service. In the same week's mail, Paul Jimenly wrote her from Hollywood, California, "The philosophy and basic concepts as expressed in it should undergird and permeate all one's schooling from kindergarten through college. Next to being placed in the hands of influential industrialists, it should be put on the desks of all the influential educators."

The new book was selling well, despite the fact that some readers criticized its supposed overemphasis on love as merely a sexual response to life, as well as for its biased "woman's viewpoint and attitude." One reader noted that many illuminates considered sex as somewhat of a drawback to perfection, adding, "Jesus the Christ and some of his apostles eschewed sex entirely." Lao explained that she had written the book at a time when sexual promiscuity was rampant, and millions of young people were saying that God was dead. "My one desire and thought was to help not only young people—but all people—to know the sacredness of the Creative Principle of Life itself. Sex is God's holiest Law of Creation without which there would be no Creation in either human, animal or plant life."

She and Florrie wrote often now. Their letters to each other were warm and affectionate. Typically Florrie ended one, "I am now going to put the kettle on for a cup of tea. Would you like one?"

They often spoke of old-time music. Florrie sent her sister recordings of old Scottish airs by Kenneth McKellor. They both loved those old songs, particularly "The Song of the Clyde," which they had sung as girls. They likewise enjoyed Mozart's Horn Concerto played by Dennis Braine, who before his tragic death had been considered the finest horn player in the world.

Florrie wrote that their cousin Ada had died on February 8, 1967, in a London hospital. This was a severe shock to both of them. Florrie also sent news of Luton, where they had spent much of their youth together, and where their parents had died: "Luton is altered beyond recognition. The whole of Stuart Street on the left hand side coming from Chapel Street through the Dunstable Road including our old premises was empty and looked derelict. They are all to be demolished for road widening. Also all the center of the town is being rebuilt. Luton is really an enormous place now. It has just grown and grown, but not in beauty." Florrie had also visited Horsham, where their mother's family had lived. Unlike Ivinghoe and Luton, she found their beloved causeway neighborhood in Horsham relatively undamaged.

Lao wished Florrie would come to America and spend her last years with her at Swannanoa, but her sister guarded her own privacy and enjoyed her retirement cottage in southern England. Florrie thanked Lao, but confided to the younger sister she had so lovingly reared after their parents died, "You see, I spend many hours alone and often in the winter I often don't speak to a soul on the weekends for forty-eight hours, but please don't think I am lonely, as I quietly go on with my work and have a little rest in between."

With more and more people attending her lectures and coming to Swannanoa to meet her in person, Lao sensed that her life was growing more hectic, but she told Emelia, "It is wonderful to know that at long last the Message is going over."

114. Complimentary pass to Lao's 1967 Miami lecture.

After a brief winter vacation alone in Florida, which included several lectures, she returned to Swannanoa and prepared to leave with Guy Chipman for a major tour through California. Before launching her hectic West Coast speaking schedule, they stopped in Abilene, Texas, to meet informally with prospective students, as guests of the ten-member William Horton family. The Hortons had visited her at Swannanoa and saw to it that her visit in Abilene received excellent news coverage.

Beginning on April 20, 1967, at San Diego's Christ Church, as the guest of the Reverend Robert L. Steven, Lao spoke successively at the Psynetics Founda-tion in Orange, Clifford Carpenter's Unity Temple in Glendale, and at three Science of Mind congregations, Henry Gerhard's in Laguna Beach, Don Bertheau's in Long Beach, and Guy Lorraine's in La Crescenta. On May 13, she spoke at San Francisco's Metaphysical Town-Hall Book Shop, and a week later in Menlo Park's Masonic Temple, under the sponsorship of the Unity minister, Irene Wetzel. She spoke on the popular Owen Spann television

115. Lao Russell with Mrs. Bill Horton in Abilene, Texas.

show in San Francisco. She ended the month at Lillian Hopper's First Church of Religious Science in Oakland with a well-received lecture.

Every venue proved a successful one for Lao. Her hosts were open-minded theologians thrilled with her presentation, and every one of them asked her to return on her next tour. They sold thousands of dollars worth of books, using a new idea for book distribution that Guy Chipman had originated and found extremely successful.

Lao's excitement was hard for her to contain. Her letters to Emelia give enticing hints as to her optimistic state of mind, during what was a lecture tour free of disappointment. She wrote, "I long to share each exciting incident with you but each day is so full. The days fly by, and I am asleep as soon as I get into my room! We thought we would be able to take advantage of the lovely beaches here to walk but so far we have not been able to do so. Extra lectures are coming, and I guess they will continue to come right along."

On their return to Swannanoa, Lao was faced with unexpected expenses to eliminate termite infestation in the palace attic. Almost immediately they drove to the board meeting in Far Hills, where they met Dr. Lavender and the Lombardis. Present world conditions had stimulated a renewed interest and demand for *The World Crisis* and *Atomic Suicide?* The board authorized Lao to reprint both books, and approved an advanced marketing plan for *Love*, using interested students as agents through a personal approach method. There was much jubilation at the success of Lao's Florida and California tours, and she was encouraged to seek further radio and television exposure. The Lombardis entertained the board at an elegant party at their club, but the weather was unbearably hot in New Jersey, and Lao was happy to reach the relative coolness of her mountain in Virginia.

The head of the Anti-Pollution League of New York had read *Atomic Suicide?* and distributed copies among New York political leaders, successfully persuading Governor Rockefeller to block construction of major additional nuclear reactors in the state. The successful crusader lived in Annandale, New Jersey, and met Lao and the board members following their meeting. He told Lao that he welcomed the opportunity to meet the co-author of such a powerful book.

She returned to Swannanoa in time for a very special wedding. On June

15, 1967, Sam Spicher and Martha Smith were married in the palace gardens. Sam had been a faithful friend of Lao's since making her acquaintance in 1963. He had served as her special "Ambassador of Love" in Western Europe during 1966. Through the years he and his family grew particularly close to Lao. She often expressed her gratitude to Sam and Martha for their help, stressing that they had "never failed God's Message or me."

116. Sam Spicher with his bride, Martha Smith, and Guy Chipman, Lynn Spicher, and Lao Russell, June 15, 1967.

In August 1967, Lao left Virginia for Davenport, Iowa, where she spoke at the long-planned chiropractic luncheon before an audience of 375, and gave a special lecture several days later at Davenport College, whose president introduced her. She met Iowa Treasurer Paul Franzenburg and began a long correspondence with him. After a successful lecture in Akron, Ohio, and a detour to Birmingham, Michigan, where Lao spoke at several venues and appeared on television, Lao and her driver, Lowena, went to California, where they visited Jo Repan and several home study groups, and Lao made local television and radio appearances. She found it easier traveling with Lowena than it had been with Guy Chipman. She wrote Emelia, "She drives perfectly and takes care of things for me lovingly and efficiently. It is wonderful to have the harmony. Guy was always jealous of someone. Now I can go out for dinner if I wish or talk to interested people without interruption."

At year's end, Lao told Florrie she was again seriously contemplating a lecture tour to Australia and New Zealand. Although the pressure of obligations in America ultimately precluded it, Lao was clearly filled with more optimism than ever before. Her enthusiasm was contagious. Besides the large and appreciative audiences she always seemed to find on her lecture tours, her mail and visitors at Swannanoa remained sources of continued encouragement to her.

In the first week of 1968, a Harvard dropout, who had become addicted to drugs as an expatriate in Mexico, wrote of his experience after wandering into a used bookstore and picking up *The Man Who Tapped the Secrets of the Universe*. Reading the book led him to enroll in the *Home Study Course*, and he was now completing the eighth unit. He wrote her, "I thought it high time I write you and express my deepest love and appreciation for your life and work together with Doctor Russell. I cannot express the glory of the light that has visited me. Your course has been a great stabilizer in my life. I feel my feet firmly on the path into the New Age. Hopefully I will emerge into cosmic Consciousness, and be able to serve the world in the truest sense." Lao felt that uninterested and irresponsible parents were a major cause of increasing substance abuse in the younger generation. She always told college-age students that the proliferation of drug abuse must be stopped.

117. Rodger Hostettler.

A letter in mid-January introduced her to a handsome young man from Glenwood Springs, Colorado, who would for years be one of her favorite students. Rodger D. Hostettler was a physician's son who had nearly completed college and served two years in the United States military. Brilliant and talented, especially as a musician, he described a series of emotional upheavals and disillusionments that he felt had become a way of life for him. He told Lao, "From out of chaos I seek order. I seek but to love and to live in truth." She readily responded. He soon became a deep student of the *Home Study Course*, came to Swannanoa for an extended period, and remained close to Lao as he matured and enjoyed success.

Lao had refurnished and redecorated her bedroom in the room adjacent to the one she had shared with Walter. The new room was bright with its eastern exposure from the palace balcony. Filled with Walter's paintings, including her favorite, his own self-portrait, the room was as comfortable as it was luxurious. A student had given her a beautifully dressed doll of the Infant of Prague, and this elegant artifact had a place of honor on her bed.

The English rock group the Beatles had taken young American audiences by storm and, through the musical group's unexpected interest in Maharishi Mahesh Yogi, the founder of Transcendental Meditation and the worldwide Spiritual Regeneration Movement, had focused world attention on the guru and his teachings. Emelia wished that the rock group had been attracted to Swannanoa instead, writing Lao, "How we wish you could get an audience before the college generation. They need what you have to give them so badly. They are ripe for it now. This Maharishi somehow made contact with the Beatles in England, but the Russells' teachings could give them so much more!"

From Durban, South Africa, Rodney Manser offered to start a non-profit educational foundation to help spread the Russell teachings through his country. The proposed Science-Of-Man Foundation would buy large quantities of the books at discounts and market them aggressively in South Africa. Lao replied promptly: "It is hard to put into words just what your inspiring letter and your proposal for distribution of our teachings in South Africa mean to me. The need is so great and urgent, and it would seem that God has inspired you to formulate this plan at this most crucial time in world history." She sent him materials and books at once and crafted a careful proposal as to how she would wish him to proceed. She sent him a tape of her lecture at the Unity Church in Fairfax, a speech she considered even more comprehensive than her address to the International Chiropractic Association.

By February, Lao was desperately in need of sunshine as Swannanoa endured the worst weather ever, with solid deep ice, snow, and heavy fogs covering the mountain for far longer than normal. Lao wrote Emelia, "It has been a very cold, hard winter but I am keeping well because for weeks I have known the ecstasy within." John and Emelia had gone to San Francisco and Las Vegas, and Lao was happy for them, but likewise longed to embark on a southern journey as soon as she could.

As Lao left Swannanoa on April 15, 1968, to fill lecture commitments in Northern and Southern California she had made the year before, she received a disturbing letter from Dr. Lavender suggesting that his health and age made it advisable for him to resign as a director. This concerned her greatly because she valued her long association with the wise and supportive New York chiropractor, who had actively served with them virtually since the beginning of their work in Virginia. She asked John Lombardi to help persuade Dr. Lavender not to resign, and John suggested that the next board meeting be held in Dr. Lavender's hometown of Fulton, New York, in order to make it easier for him to attend.

"We all look forward to our annual get-togethers which, unfortunately, have become the only occasions when we see each other. I personally feel that it is a source of considerable strength for us to remain as a unit as long as possible and would prefer to see others added than any of the original Directors dropping out. I'm sure Dr. Russell would have wanted it that way," John wrote Dr. Lavender, who soon allayed their concerns by agreeing to stay on the board. He had received a long letter from Lao en route to California urging him to reconsider his resignation.

Lao received extensive local publicity throughout California, both in advance of and after her respective lectures. Her first speech was on April 28 at the Gunn Senior High School in Palo Alto, where she coordinated her efforts with a major Youth Crusade that had been inspired by her book *Love*. Once more she spoke to appreciative audiences at Unity and Science of Mind churches in La Crescenta, Glendale, Laguna Beach, and Long Beach. On May 12, she appeared on a television interview program called *The World of Books*, which prompted a good response to her lectures in San Francisco. Guy Chipman personally financed the appearance for her on what proved to be a very effective advertising medium. Her various radio interviews in California also led to increased lecture attendance and numerous book orders. She had another successful television interview in Sacramento, where she concluded her tour in late May with three lectures in three days, two of them arranged at the last minute.

The response she had received in California had been most encouraging. At the Youth Forum, her sponsors told her they were working to obtain financial backing for her to speak at the Hollywood Bowl within the next year. She recounted many stories from her Palo Alto visit that seemed to demonstrate the favorable impact her work there had had on the participating young people.

She was overjoyed at the diversity in her audiences and student body and told a South African friend, "We have wonderful students of every race, color and creed, and they are in every age bracket. The youth particularly are crying out for this new knowledge, and I feel that the hope of the world lies in its youth, and I trust we can reach them in time with this new knowledge." Her reputation as a speaker led to her election to membership in the International Platform Association, and her inclusion in the Royal Blue Book.

She sensed that in California conditions beneath the surface were deteriorating. People were afraid to go out at night. She wrote Emelia, "There were snipers on the Freeway last week and they had to close it off. People are fearful and unhappy, and yet the sunshine and the flowers are beautiful except in Los Angeles where the air pollution is so awful. The climax must come soon, for things could not possibly continue as they are."

The trip had been tiring for her, because the frequent relocations required much packing and unpacking. She was overwhelmed with the proliferation of traffic on California's busy freeways, but again Guy Chipman drove her from place to place, and saw to it she was kept as comfortable as possible.

She knew that she could not have made the trip without Guy and was grateful to him. It had taken her a long time to know and appreciate him and his dedication to the Message. In understanding him, she felt she had learned many things that helped her to unfold understanding in others. "If I can only extend this deeper understanding through the medium of TV and radio, I feel we could bring the world into balance," she told Emelia.

Lao and Guy drove back across country, and on June 1, 1968, they reached Fulton, New York, where they met the Lombardis at a comfortable motel, and joined Dr. Lavender at his commodious home for the board meeting the next day. Emelia thought Lao seemed fresh and rejuvenated by events in California. "You look wonderful," she wrote her soon afterwards. "Traveling and lecturing must agree with you because you look better every time we see you."

Lao asked the Lombardis to consider who they might suggest for the board if anything happened to Dr. Lavender. She considered asking Waynesboro newspaper editor and publisher Louis Spilman or Pikeville, Kentucky, banker John First to join the board.

Lao knew that Guy Chipman wanted to be elected to the board. She was increasingly impressed with his commitment to her and to the work. "He says and has always said that all he wants to do is help in any way he can in spreading The Message," she wrote John and Emelia. "He has paid all the traveling expenses for this trip and of course I could not have made it without him.

"It is a tough job and I know that if I had not made these trips these past three years, it would have been difficult to keep going. I had to build all over again after Doctor's long illness and then attract new people continuously for many of the first students have died or discontinued their support after taking the course and buying the books. I shall always be grateful to Guy for making the lecture trips possible and with all of his faults I know he is sincere in his desire to help give God's Message. He does take a lot of understanding but basically his great desire is to give and to serve selflessly."

Lao was single-minded in committing her every effort to promoting the University and its teachings. "I know without a single doubt that the Message is the only thing that will save the world now. I see it in every department of life. The misery and plain unhappiness is evident everywhere. As long as I live I shall try to awaken man to Love for this is his greatest need," she told the board. After discussion, it was decided that the University should expand its distribution of tapes of Lao's lectures, as there appeared to be a definite demand.

It had been five years since Walter had refolded, a term the Russells always used to refer to death. Lao felt the University had made great progress in these years by gaining worldwide acceptance of the Message. She regretted that the University could not yet afford to issue the books in paperback, but she knew that to do so efficiently would require her to print and sell a much greater volume than she was selling at the time.

Lao and Guy visited Niagara Falls after the board meeting and soon were back at Swannanoa. Again road construction at the Swannanoa entrance had blocked access to the palace and diverted traffic to the secondary route 610. This would soon become the only entrance to the palace, and required additional signage to ensure that it was readily indicated to the increasing thousands of tourists who passed through the Rockfish Gap entrance to the Blue Ridge Parkway and Skyline Drive only a mile away.

In midsummer, Lao and Guy Chipman went to Florida on another lecture tour that occurred during the same time as the Republican Convention in

118. Bowan and Geri Jones.

Miami. They visited Arthur and Adele Jones, whose health was rapidly declining. Their son and daughter-in-law, Bowan and Geri Jones, were keeping the elderly couple under watchful care.

After successful lectures in Atlanta, Georgia, and Huntsville, Alabama, Lao returned to Swannanoa on August 17, 1968, and at once began working with Guy Chipman in preparation for the initial Youth for Character rally that was scheduled to be held at the palace on September 8. Inspired by her book *Love*, the Youth for Character movement had evolved from her conviction that "Youth with its energy, idealism, and dissatisfaction with the status quo will work constructively toward their goals for a lasting peace and prosperity once they understand the cause of mankind's present dilemma." The movement was intended to encourage arts and crafts centers, pride in learning trade skills, and giving tangible service to others.

Reverend Paul H. Pike, pastor of Pleasant Valley Church of the Brethren at Weyers Cave and director of youth counseling programs for sixty regional churches, brought several hundred young people to the meeting and served as master of ceremonies. Anita Kelly, a Pennsylvania state representative who had appeared with Lao at the recent conference in Atlanta, told the group that they could serve as an example for youth all over the world. Maybelle Saville, composer of the Garden Club of Virginia's official song, played the organ and accompanied vocalists Evelyn Jones and Susan Reynolds. All of them were longtime friends of Lao. There was free time for all participants to see the palace and gardens and enjoy a box supper together.

In the afternoon, Lao spoke on "Character, How and from Where?" After supper her topic was "Character, Why and for What?" She described the oneness that humans must feel for one another to exist in a completely happy society. She likened the human race to a tree, saying that the trunk represented the world, the limbs the countries, and the leaves the people. She stated that people must learn to remain as a unit like the tree. To do this, one must love one another and give completely of himself to others. She said that true happiness only follows unselfishness and joy for others. She cautioned her audience to use God's gift of free will to spread love and not hate. "'Love ye one another' is the Law of God, not just a cute saying," she said.

Lao told the young people she never saw Walter Russell take anything without giving something in return, and that he firmly believed that genius is

119. First group meeting of the Youth for Character Clubs.

self-earned and mediocrity is self-inflicted. She expressed optimism for the future because of the high quality of today's youth, and stressed that character consisted of loyalty, kindness, service, and true love.

Well over 600 young people attended the rally. Their comments reflected their enthusiasm. One concluded, "I truthfully didn't think that I would enjoy it, but it has been a wonderful experience." Another marveled, "The lady has so much to say!" Newspapers gave the event extensive coverage. Lao particularly enjoyed an article about the rally published in *The Roanoke Times*. At that time, her book *Love* was recommended reading in a class in human development at Marshall University in West Virginia. Within weeks, Youth for Character Clubs had been established in Waynesboro and Harrisonburg, the latter under the sponsorship of Samuel Spicher. Members of each group were encouraged by Lao and entertained at Swannanoa with a special reception and personal tour of rooms not generally open to the public. Lao told them that as leaders of tomorrow they could usher in a new age of character by living and practicing the high mental, physical, and spiritual qualities that lead to service to others.

She tried to build on her "Youth for Character" idea by corresponding with like-minded youth counselors across America, but demands on her time and her increasing tiredness prevented her from making a special cross-country tour to focus on organizing youth chapters.

The Russells' early supporters were passing from the scene. Her old friend and longtime supporter, former University director Arthur Jones, died in Florida in September 1968. After Arthur's death, Adele Jones moved to Fort Lauderdale to live with their son, Bowan. Arthur had played a major role in sustaining their work at Swannanoa during the first decade. He loved Walter and Lao deeply, and donated the summer cottage adjoining Swannanoa to the University. Florrie wrote that she "did not think Arthur ever realized how much you did while Walter was alive, but as you have become so well known and in such great demand these last few years, it became clear to him that it was you who counted as a person and not simply because you were the wife of Dr. Walter Russell."

Emelia wrote Lao that Val Thompson, now eighty-nine and widowed, had sold her house in New Jersey and moved permanently to Florida. She and Emelia had become close friends, and she gave Emelia several file cabinets filled with the Thompsons' long correspondence with Walter Russell.

Marie Dunn had become a close friend to Lao. The talented composer had repeated the *Home Study Course* several times and did her utmost to promote the work, writing Lao, "I shall begin again with the first unit and study and meditate with you and Dr. Russell and God as long as I am permitted to live in His beautiful universe. I think I have found the Golden Thread woven by you and Dr. Russell through this inspiring study course and your immortal books. It is the admonition to 'Love Ye One Another,' give of yourself and serve your neighbor, and be ever aware of that precious tie that binds mankind and God together. These things will always be my guiding light."

In October Lao addressed an English department forum at nearby Blue Ridge Community College, prompting the professor, Wilson L. Seay, to call her remarks "a glimpse into a Utopia where man ceases to fortify his ego with the greed and material gain that has brought so much destruction into this world of ours." Her address was publicized over area radio stations for a week or more in advance, and she spoke in the college's largest auditorium to a standing room only crowd. The following Sunday the college's dean brought a group of faculty members and their families to Swannanoa and purchased a number of books. The dean stressed to her, "Not only do all youth need the Love you have to give, but we need it, also."

Lao spoke on "The Importance of Love in the Family" to the Fort Defiance chapter of Future Homemakers of America on the night they honored their fathers. Mrs. Nancy Waybright introduced her, telling the audience that Lao had a message as valuable as silver or gold for the fathers and their daughters. The speech led to invitations from other youth groups in the region.

Groups of disabled veterans, often forty at a time, visited Swannanoa from the Salem Veterans Hospital two hours away, always leaving inspired and more confident after meeting with her.

A University of Virginia student came to Swannanoa and was amazed to learn that May 19, 1971, would be the centennial of Walter's birth. He had recently been given a Jehovah's Witness tract that stated that on May 19, 1971, the planets and sun of our solar system would form the configuration of the Christian cross with earth at the angle of intersection. This purportedly was to signal an end that would be a beginning. The student's own research in the University's astronomy department had borne out the celestial configuration.

Throughout the Southeast, Dr. R. C. Bolen, her longtime chiropractor friend, regularly introduced many patients and acquaintances to the Russell course and books. In Harrisonburg, Virginia, Sam Spicher, one of Lao's favorite friends and students, achieved success in his growing waterless-cookware sales business through his generous custom of giving Lao's book *Love* to every customer. He extended this practice throughout his entire organization, and discovered that it virtually eliminated his company's problem with bad debts. Soon his entire sales force emulated his practice with remarkable success. Lao considered this a classic example of the giving-regiving principle in action. She was happy to meet with Spicher's salesmen, and she always stressed the importance of putting love into cooking. "Even a simple item like tea must be made with love," she told them, adding, "Food cooked without love fills but half man's hunger. It fills your stomach, but not your soul."

The mother of a young military school cadet wrote to thank Lao for encouraging her son to remain in the tough disciplinary atmosphere of his Virginia boarding school. After meeting Lao at Swannanoa, the young teenager had written his mother, "I have just returned from one of the most beautiful Thanksgivings of my life. Jesus Christ set the circumstance for me to meet the wife of one of the most important and interesting philosophers and scientists in the history of mankind, Mrs. Lao Russell. I felt love between God and us. It was beautiful! She brought me to realize so many new and fresh ideas and ideals—I am back at school ready to fulfill my joy in everything Christ places before me."

Lao told Emelia that every letter she received "seems to need a very special answer. Everyone seems to be in great trouble in some way or another. All want special direction." It no longer satisfied people simply to be referred to the *Home Study Course* or books. They all seemed to demand a personal relationship with Lao herself, and maintaining this individual correspondence was a daunting task. Despite this, Lao wrote her sister Florrie that she felt extraordinarily well and was enjoying her busy life. Unfortunately, Florrie was slowing down and suffering more acutely with angina.

Time constraints prevented Lao from sending out her usual 20,000 Christmas messages, but Lloyd Hawkins printed 2,000 special Christmas cards for her to send to special students and friends. At New Year's 1969, Emelia wrote to recall their many lovely holidays together on the mountain, "especially the quiet ones when we were snowed in." She hoped Lao would not be so busy during the coming year, but prayed it would bring about the fulfillment of all her dreams and desires.

Soon afterwards, as Lao contemplated leaving for Florida, she learned that her old friend Val Thompson was very ill there. Lao hoped to visit her again, but the rush of business forced her to cancel her trip. It was the first year she had not been south since Walter had refolded.

In March 1969, the famous actor Eddie Albert and his wife, Margo, wrote her from Pacific Palisades, recalling their past acquaintance and telling her, "We have found great satisfaction in living by your principles and certainly hope that we may continue to grow in that direction."

The actress Joan Crawford sent her a Christmas greeting and wished her good health and happiness for the New Year. Miss Crawford praised Lao's book *Love* and hoped to come to Swannanoa, but she never made the trip. She and Lao corresponded for five or six years.

Gloria Swanson wrote Lao, "I wish all my thoughts of you had been written messages. Unfortunately, this world is spinning too fast. Love, Gloria S." Lao maintained contact with movie stars who had read her books. Messages from well-known students like these famous film actors always brought her cheer.

A broadened advertising program was attracting many new students to the work. On March 16, *God Will Work with You but Not for You* was displayed in a full-page advertisement in the religious book section of *The New York Times*, and, a week later, *Love* was similarly promoted in the same forum.

It amused Lao that the *National Observer*, a popular newspaper that hardly seemed discriminatory in the articles it published, declined to advertise her book *Love*, because it treated a subject the editor did not feel acceptable for advertising.

Her tapes and records were selling well across the country through students and groups who she had addressed on her lecture tours. A British Columbian student praised the recording of her lecture "A Living Philosophy for Today," calling it "a wonderful speech in which you simplify living as you do in all of your books." A bookstore in Santa Monica, California, was successfully marketing the book *Love*, and intended to advertise it at their own expense in two national magazines. A New Age bookseller in Perris, California, took the liberty of including *Atomic Suicide?* in its widely circulated book list, calling Walter Russell one of this century's great geniuses and terming *Atomic Suicide?* "one of the books I would want along with me if I had to face fifty years alone in the 'wilderness.'"

Students came to Lao with the simple problems of day-to-day life. An Oklahoma factory worker wrote,

> If I do too much work I get into big trouble. I was confined to one machine when I enjoyed the whole department. I have been a foreman but even that was not enough for I would get orders handed down from the bosses that were of no good. That is when I quit my godly nature. A voice kept saying not to, but I did any way.
>
> Dear Lao, does this comply to what you teach? Give and it shall be

> given? Will your study course help me if I will no longer strive for perfection? There was a voice I heard but from my story does it sound like it was God's voice?
>
> I am at the crossroads of my soul searching.

Lao urged him to read *God Will Work with You but Not for You* and consider taking the *Home Study Course* as a means of bringing his effort and aspiration into balance.

Dr. Lavender died in Fulton, New York, in March 1969. He had served on the University's board for twelve years and been its vice-president since 1967. Lao was ill with pneumonia and unable to travel to the funeral, but she immediately contacted Howard's son and daughter-in-law, writing, "Your blessed father was one of our most cherished friends, and nothing will ever erase my deep love for him, for he was such a vital part of both our lives. Loving Howard as we did and knowing what little things can mean when one is incapacitated, I have consistently and frequently written and telephoned him to not only give him my love, but to give him every scrap of good news about our work, which has been so close to his heart these many years. I cannot reproach myself with not being present for the funeral, for knowing your father so well, I know that he would have understood why I was not present." Lao had been too ill to leave her room.

One of the last things she and Dr. Lavender had discussed was the dedication of Walter's bust of Mark Twain in the Sacramento Union building in California, which they both considered a great accomplishment because of the public recognition it brought to Walter's work.

Jim Goodwin, her old friend in Salem who had helped Walter and Lao from the time of their arrival in Virginia in 1948, died a few weeks later in the spring of 1969. It seemed to Lao that all her longtime stalwarts from the early years were leaving her. Emelia tried to console her: "One of the saddest things as the years creep up is the inevitable loss of old friends." They both took pity on Adele Jones, ill in Florida and feeling absolutely lost without her husband, Arthur, despite the love and care of Bowan and Geri Jones, her son and daughter-in-law.

Lao thought long and hard before she filled Arthur Jones and Howard Lavender's vacancies on the board. She feared that Louis Spilman was too involved with the Methodist Church and promoting Waynesboro and the Shenandoah Valley in general to focus necessary attention on the University and Swannanoa.

She conferred with the Lombardis, and they agreed on choosing Aubrey Perry, Sr., owner of Perry Buick Company in Norfolk, Virginia, to replace Arthur Jones. Lao had worked closely with Perry since he first came to Swannanoa in 1953 and enrolled in the course. He had been a serious Russell student ever since, as well as an active leader in Tidewater Virginia civic affairs and a state and national leader in the Alcoholics Anonymous organization, through which he had introduced the Russell books to tens of thousands of individuals. Lao knew him to be a devoted friend and a great advocate of their teachings. He had generously helped her procure her new Buick at a fraction of its cost. Lloyd Hawkins, her professional photographer friend from Jackson, Mississippi, was named to succeed Dr. Lavender. The board committed resources to expanding the network of International Age of Character Clubs, and applauded the exceptional success of two such groups that had been recently established in Delaware and California.

Guy Chipman was upset at not being selected for the board vacancy and was irritated to learn that the Lombardis had opposed his election. He began spending more time away from Swannanoa in connection with his own business activities, and made certain he was not present when the board meeting met there. Guy and Lao cancelled their proposed respite at the beach.

The Russells' work was reaching many like-minded groups. Beta Sigma Phi International Sorority named Lao to honorary membership for her services to mankind. The leaders of Zarathustra Unlimited in Clinton, Iowa, called Lao "a sincere leader in the ever-increasing movement towards greater Awareness and Unification (spiritual, emotional, physical, mental, etc.) of Mankind." Duncan S. T. Faurie, a Philadelphia scientist, wrote to tell Lao that he was working with ecologist Ian McHarg on a course called *Man and His Environment*, which used nature to demonstrate the theories and ideas expressed by the Russells in *Atomic Suicide?*

On May 27, 1969, a Trappist monk from the Abbey of Gethsemani in Kentucky wrote that he had just finished reading *God Will Work with You but Not for You* and told Lao, "I have never read anything so dynamic, moving, and inspiring in all my life. Lao, you are a true Mystic. I have read the works of many of the mystics, but never have I read anything so powerful and moving, so heavenly, yet so practical and down-to-earth. If this book were in the hands of all men, we would truly be on the way to an era of peace on earth." This began a long correspondence and introduced Lao to a Catholic group that gladly endorsed the University's teachings. Soon she received greetings from members of the Motherhouse of the Sisters of Loretto at Nerinx, Kentucky, who had learned of the University from the Trappists. Since these contemplates had devoted their life to solitude and deep meditative study at the motherhouse, earning just enough to support their barest needs, Lao sent them copies of the *Home Study Course* as a gift in return for their giving service to humanity.

Swannanoa was named a Virginia historic landmark and placed on the National Register of Historic Places. At the same time, Lao mourned the fact that road-building crews were destroying hundreds of beautiful trees near the palace entrance in connection with construction of the Rockfish Gap interchange of the new Interstate 64 Highway. In August 1969, Hurricane Camille swept through Central and Western Virginia, causing unparalleled death and destruction in the Rockfish Valley below Swannanoa. It was a terrifying time for everyone in the area, but Lao and the staff were safe on the mountain.

The remainder of the year had its good fortune and its disappointments. At the time of the hurricane, Lao had been confined to bed for several days with a summer fever. Her sister Florrie suggested the cause might be mosquito bites and prescribed by mail a homeopathic remedy that effected a cure. Florrie's own health problems prevented her from coming to Virginia in 1969.

In December, Lao concluded arrangements with the St. James Press in London to handle her and Walter's books on the British market. Sam and Martha Spicher drove her to Palm Beach, Florida, where she spent three weeks of rest and recuperation as the guest of Pat duPont and her husband, James Stephanis. As always, Pat was a kind and extravagent hostess. She arranged for Lao to meet many influential people in the context of private luncheons and small receptions, opportunities that allowed Lao to extend her work without the pressure of a demanding lecture schedule.

On her return to Virginia, Lao suffered from a long spell of sickness that lasted throughout the winter. It was clear that her health was not as strong as it had been. She described her illness that winter as long and almost fatal. "At least I know that I cannot over-do and expect to keep going as of yore!" She was unable to leave the mountain for lectures and was very disappointed, because she had planned a trip to California early that spring and had arranged a personal visit with Eddie Albert and his wife, Margo.

Guy Chipman occasionally visited Lao at Swannanoa, but there was a coolness between them now. Florrie wrote her sister regularly, reassuring her, "You will soon be feeling on top of the world again," It was early April in 1970 before Lao seemed to be on the road to recovery.

Her mail proved good medicine. A typical student letter in February 1970 told her, "Your readings have freed me from myself, given me joy, strength and an unshakable faith in God, theretofore not experienced. It is such a big and beautiful new knowledge, ever deepening and I am still awed by it. To start every day with God, to be constantly with him, to be grateful to him and so simply love him and to know with him all is well makes all the difference. It is just too big and powerful for words."

A couple leaving for Vietnam a few months later wrote to ask if they could learn the lessons of the course in several months instead of a year. "I wouldn't be cheating myself since my entire life force depends on learning such schooling," one of them told Lao, who cheerfully accommodated them.

In May, *The Spirit*, the yearbook of Virginia's Blue Ridge Community College, contained the following tribute to Lao Russell, written by its Editor-in-Chief Richard L. Thompson: "To have known you has been a great delight in my life. You have been an inspiration to me in this book and in my entire life. God Bless you always." A special section of this yearbook contains fifty-three photographs taken of the students in the gardens and palace at Swannanoa. These included a full-page color photograph of Lao. "Thanks must go to Lao Russell," the editor wrote. "No greater proof is needed than my experience at Swannanoa to prove to the doubting world that all knowledge exists in the Mind universe of Light—which is God—that all Mind is One Mind, that men do not have separate minds, and that all knowledge can be obtained from the Universal Source of All-Knowledge by becoming One with that Source." Lao entertained the staff at the palace after the volume won national honors.

By then Lao was experiencing good effects from a biochemical system of natural medicine using cell salts. She was still working on restoring her body to a balanced condition and was eating very little meat. In fact, her appetite had greatly decreased. Lao was learning and putting into action all she could about organic foods, using as her guide the experience and research of the Rodale organization of Emmaus, Pennsylvania. She believed that their publications coincided in a great measure with natural law.

120. 1970 board meeting at Swannanoa: Lloyd Hawkins, Jim Stephanis, Lao Russell, Guy Chipman, Patricia duPont Stephanis, Aubrey Perry.

The board of directors met at Swannanoa on June 10, 1970, and spent much time discussing plans for celebrating the 100th anniversary of Walter's birth the following May 19.

Pat and Jim Stephanis arrived from Florida for the board meeting. Pat was still upset about her husband's deep involvement with politics, but they were in good spirits, and things went well while they were at Swannanoa. Aubrey Perry came from Norfolk, Virginia, and Lloyd and Rowena Hawkins from Jackson, Mississippi.

The Hawkinses wanted Lao to appear in a daily minute television spot all over the country. They suggested that these programs be sponsored by students in the various regions. Lao felt that she could not spare the time to make ten different spots. "Each day the details of the mail, running Swannanoa, and seeing people ties me up, and then I feel too tired to tackle something else." A few weeks after the board meeting, she went to Virginia Beach for a brief vacation.

At last her sister Florrie came to see her, arriving in New York on July 8. Lao had expected that Guy Chipman would meet Florrie there, but instead Sam and Martha Spicher drove to New York and brought Florrie to Virginia.

She remained at Swannanoa until mid-September. Then Guy Chipman drove Florrie and Lao to New York, where Lao spent over a week in Manhattan after her sister sailed for home on September 17. Pat Riccardi hosted a large reception to introduce Lao to an important group of diplomats, show-business executives, and newspaper, magazine, television, and radio journalists. "They literally hung on every word I said and now are trying to fit in visits with me during what was already a booked-up October," she ruefully wrote her young friend Richard Dulaney, grandson of Alvin T. Dulaney, Sr. Lao took the opportunity to visit Gloria Swanson and many of her other New York friends. Guy returned to New York to drive Lao home to Virginia. Soon after returning to Swannanoa, she suffered a painful fall in the palace, from which she quickly recovered.

Jim Dulaney had been operated on for lung cancer and was having extensive radiation treatments. Lao knew that the failure of the ski run he had built on Afton Mountain near the former Swannanoa entrance had been very hard on him, but she hoped he would survive.

Lao enjoyed a quiet Christmas at the palace, sending out her New Year's message and "writing letters like crazy. Now I have hundreds more coming in and only me to answer them," she wrote Emelia. The widely-distributed greeting pictured Lao at the palace and contained the following text: "Let us, together, light the candles of love that man may become aware of his oneness and true purpose on earth. Remember, always, that no man is an enemy in God, his Creator. Only the sense of man divides him in his purpose in life. In Mind we are eternally One and shall be forevermore. Let us, in this New Year of 1971, see the birth of an era on earth where man has discovered that 'something beyond' and lives knowingly with God experiencing the ecstasy of all-knowledge, all-power and all-presence."

CHAPTER TWENTY

A Balance of Equals (1928-88)

Women, as well as many men, praised Lao for emphasizing woman's role in history. They agreed with her that throughout time woman had been "the stone that the builders neglected." From the story of Jacob's daughter in Genesis, slightly lifted from obscurity in Thomas Mann's *Joseph and His Brethren*, to the legend of paradise being lost through Eve, Lao felt strongly that women's essential equality with men had been ignored. Many philosophers and historians felt that this lack of respect for woman as man's equal was the fundamental reason for civilization's development of a belief in a duality, the concept of good versus evil that had long been the cause of endless suffering. To Lao, this was an irrefutable fact.

In the years before she had met Walter Russell, Lao's recognition of the integral role women played in the New Thought and Christian Science movements had been strengthened by her association with Eleanor Mel and the Boston Home of Truth. Mary Baker Eddy had reached legendary status as the founder of Christian Science. Emma Curtis Hopkins, who left Christian Science to become the greatest New Thought teacher of her generation, dramatically influencing the Unity, Religious Science, Divine Science, and the Home of Truth movements, had successfully advanced women to leadership roles. In Hopkins's first graduation ceremony in 1889, twenty of the twenty-two graduates of her college were women.

Hopkins had encouraged such women as Eleanor Mel to take leadership roles in all arenas of spiritual and temporal activity. To these women, as to Lao, it was critical that the playing field be leveled so as to give women an equal opportunity with men. At times, Lao referred to Joachim of Fiore's concept of the Trinity, which charted the advance of civilization through three historical eras. God the Father represented the patriarchal ideal of the earliest era, and Jesus Christ exemplified an era of individual freedom, but the third era of ultimate illumination focused on the Truth or Mother principle, represented by women.

As the years went by, more and more Russell students recognized that Lao was a pioneer and a force to be reckoned with in the struggle for women's rights. They compared her favorably not only with Mary Baker Eddy, but also with the California Four-Square Gospel evangelist Aimee Semple MacPherson and such relatively obscure cynosures of the sex as Alexandra David-Neel, who had earlier become the sole ordained female Lama priest. Some students thought it would be Lao herself who would restore mankind's direct communication with God that was lost in the Garden of Eden.

Lao knew that she and Walter had been fortunate to be living in what Woodrow Wilson had called "the age of men and women working together as equals." She understood that the thesis of their *One-World Purpose* was to herald a new era in cooperation between the sexes. From her earliest days, she had been consumed by the need to bring balance into the relationship of man with woman.

Years before meeting Walter, Lao had read Benjamin Kidd's *The Science of Power* and Dorothy M. Richardson's four-volume, fictionalized work, *The Pilgrimage*. She was familiar with Florida Scott-Maxwell's *Women—And Sometimes Men*. She owned a copy of Lady Julian's *Revelations of Divine Love*. All of these books reinforced the actual life experiences of equality between the sexes that Lao had experienced early in life in her relationship with such men as Walter Powell, and ultimately in her marriage to Walter Russell.

Lao was intrigued to realize that in French the opening verses of "The Gospel According To St. John" showed "Word" and "Light" in the feminine case. She thought this was one more wonderful instance demonstrating the correctness of viewing God as both Father and Mother. She was always thrilled at seeing women at the top of their profession, realizing that all walks of life needed more women to balance the ways and thoughts of men and bring the sexes into a state of working together as one mind.

During her years at Swannanoa, Lao knew that she lacked sufficient time to devote herself solely to the campaign for Man-Woman Equality. She felt that progress was accelerating on this front throughout the western world, and that it was only a matter of time before women in the third-world countries awakened to their rightful destiny. She often stated, "Truly there never will be peace on earth until the spirituality expressed in the female principle is understood and put into practice in all of man's human relations."

Lao sought to clarify that balance must be achieved in the spiritual and mental realms, and that emphasis on physical mating alone was woefully inadequate. "Truly men and women contain within their Beings both the male and female principle, but how many know this as fact?" she asked one student, adding, "Man is always seeking his mate, as is woman also, but the human race so far has stressed physical mating alone, whereas only when we find our spiritual and mental mate can we know a perfect physical mating."

Mary R. Beard's *Women As Force in History* inspired Lao and strengthened her longstanding conclusion that women had started civilization and must now must take the initiative in cleaning up the mess man had made of the world through thousands of years of warfare. The Russells' book *The World Crisis* included inserts with quotes from Mrs. Beard's book.

She carefully read new works on the status of women and stressed that "young people especially need the security of knowing that God is Love." She disagreed with many of the tactics used by the Women's Liberation Movement. "While I agree with the complete equality of man and woman in action, I have never felt that any violent mass demonstration was the way to bring acceptance of an idea. Woman's greatest power lies in her spiritual contribution to life, and the great need is for women to comprehend that the home is the center and basic source for world peace." This was somewhat in conflict with her lifelong admiration of powerful women.

Lao had always felt that there was a special message for women in her living philosophy, and when she wrote *God Will Work with You but Not for You* in 1955, she hoped it would strike a chord in the hearts of women all over the world because it emphasized that the survival of the human race was directly dependent on the balance that women alone could bring to human affairs.

She truly felt that this balance between women and men should permeate business, politics, science, philosophy, and all fields of endeavor. When the president of Nova Scotia's Mount St. Vincent University lectured on the subject "Women Executives and the Future," Lao was quick to encourage him to follow through with the subject. Her students in the provincial government had forwarded the speech to her from Halifax, and she corresponded with the speaker about the Russells' long efforts to promote male-female equality in business and society. As usual, she used uncomplicated examples: "I am finding that many truly intelligent men are realizing the need for the balance of the male-female principal in all departments of life. I gave someone a simple example of the need of balance even in lighting a fire. One could not get a fire with one log alone, but two logs created an explosion."

Irene Fickes of Altoona, Pennsylvania, the top woman on the staff of District 50, United Mine Workers of America, an all-encompassing auxiliary union to the mine workers that embraced many industries, had visited the palace with her colleagues the September after the May 1949 dedication. They had accepted the Russells' invitation to return to the mountain for the first two weeks of October for a special series of lectures Walter was giving, noting that they considered it a priceless privilege and "if the way opens for us, [we shall] stay for four weeks."

After her stay, Mrs. Fickes credited Walter Russell with teaching her the difference between greatness and humility. She promised with all earnestness to "try to dispose of the 'I,' the Ego, and apply that lesson to my life, keeping constantly in the mind, that I, of myself, do nothing."

Lao, she said, had equally impressed her and given her much to ponder. "I have always more or less resented the fact that women (to my way of thinking) are destined to play the minor roles in life. Perhaps it is due to the fact there is prejudice in the business world today, particularly in this town. A woman can do the same job as a man, but never earn the same salary or position. You taught me that is not important, that a woman's role is inspiration for man, that she is actually the one who has the vision, which is why she was created the Mother. History (man's history) reveals so few women as spiritual leaders, and I could not understand it, but now I know. Women were the true leaders and were so great that they could forget Self. It is a lesson I much needed."

It was a lesson Lao had been espousing for decades, since she first had read such books as *Salome: My First Two Thousand Years,* and had come into her own as a successful business woman in England in what seemed a lifetime ago.

She read with interest of the early work of Guru Maharaja Ji, whose Divine Organization for Women seemed to be spontaneously growing across America, seeking to reestablish God's balance by educating men and women as to a true identity not limited or confined to traditional social, economic, or political roles defined by sex. She hoped this group would provide a practical way to spread the message of sexual balance and equality the Russells had espoused for years.

To Lao, the concept of man-woman equality was far more than a matter of semantics. She was frequently chastised for referring to God as "He." She stressed that she was merely following the practice of the centuries. In reality, she knew that God was not a personal being, but instead the inviolate Law of Love!

In 1982, when the battle for the Equal Rights Amendment to the United States constitution had polarized opinions across the country, she was chastised by a Rockville, Maryland, correspondent for her use of non-inclusive language. "It would be so nice if you could remove sexism from your talks," the writer told her. "This in and of itself would be such an excellent example to others since I can see you are well-intentioned. I am sure the mother/father God would be so grateful if you would. These are not trivial matters, and I hope the enclosed newspaper article will give you a small inkling of what is happening in the world. You needn't mention ERA [the Equal Rights Amendment] at all."

Lao's response was comprehensive: "I have dynamically illustrated the equality of man and woman in my books, as we did in the *Home Study Course*. I have found throughout my life that in giving and explaining a principle with love, one can make a point much more acceptable than with an aggressive attitude."

She stressed her optimism: "I truly believe that the time is very close when there will be a full acceptance of the man-woman balance or equality principle. I believe that the members of the ERA movement and all people desirous of bringing balance to our world would do well to study our new cosmogony.

"I have found in my life that in giving truth it is better to state things in simple terms that people can understand than to criticize the way others express their viewpoint. There is an old saying that one can be damned for a few words. That is why I urge you to read our books and know the sum-total of my thinking on the male-female principle. I am fully aware of things that are happening in the world, and I live but to awaken Love (God) into the hearts and souls of all people, regardless of race, color, creed, or sex." Lao ended her letter with a sentence that surely, if unintentionally, further aggravated her reader: "Love is the single answer to all of the problems which now beset mankind."

CHAPTER TWENTY-ONE

How God Works (1970-71)

In February 1970, television personality Art Linkletter telephoned Lao and asked to see her when she came to California later in the year. He was greatly distressed. Two weeks after his daughter had committed suicide, his son-in-law had done the same because of depression over a business failure. Joan Crawford wrote Lao with a similar request for a meeting. She and Lao had corresponded for eighteen months, hoping to find a mutually agreeable time to meet, and they planned to do so that year in California.

Due to her heavy schedule at Swannanoa, and the demanding work in connection with reprinting three of Dr. Russell's books, Lao found herself unable to fulfill any of the many invitations and requests for lectures she received that year from all over the country. Emelia helped proofread and otherwise prepare the books for publication from her home in New Jersey. She welcomed the opportunity to keep busy. John Lombardi was busier than ever. "If it's not work, then it is a council or a planning board meeting here in Far Hills. Doesn't leave too much time for socializing," Emelia said.

Lao's own plans to go west in the spring of 1970 may have been thwarted by palace business, but she sent "three wonderful young men" as her ambassadors. On July 12, 1970, Lao wrote letters to introduce her "friends on the west coast" to Richard Dulaney, his brother Charles, and their friend Taylor King, who she described as "beloved students and friends who were inspired to go to California to meet and speak with you to help in any way possible awaken the light in their fellow man."

The three young students had taken a van-load of Russell books with them to sell along the way. Lao was very proud of their commitment to the work, noting, "They are 100 percent for me and 'The Message.' It is wonderful and strange how God works."

She was particularly close to Richard Dulaney, who she described in a letter as "one of those rare souls whose deep desire is to give to life instead of to take from life and who knows his true purpose on earth through knowing his relationship to God and to his fellow man." For over a year Richard had maintained a regular correspondence with Lao and often placed large orders for the Russell books, which he liberally distributed among his colleagues and teachers at Yale.

Richard, whose grandfather had been instrumental in leasing the palace to the Russells in 1948, and whose uncle Jim Dulaney was the managing owner now, was a graduate of Episcopal High School in Alexandria, Virginia. Richard had responded half-heartedly to the religious training he had received at school, but found that the Russells' Message left a deep impact on him. He completed the *Home Study Course* on May 19, 1970, the year before he graduated from Yale University.

Lao was extremely proud of the Dulaney brothers' dedication to the Message. "Surely God borned you both as messengers for this age," she had written Richard, "for the world's greatest need is the enlightenment contained in our *Home Study Course* and our books."

At Yale, Richard had entered an intensive major in American Studies, and wrote his senior honors' essay on the American development of Rosicrucianism, a subject he had selected only after his faculty advisor, Sydney E. Ahlstrom, convinced him that he was too close to his preferred subject, the University of Science and Philosophy, to be objective. Richard's discussions with Dr. Ahlstrom, chairman of the American Studies Program, convinced the professor that the University at Swannanoa and its teachings belonged "to a great and honorable tradition in the western world. It honors many of the greatest religious and moral thinkers of all time, and it is definitely committed to the principles of peace and love." The distinguished religious historian felt that the Russell teachings "lead as directly and legitimately to conscientious objection to war and violence as those of the historic peace churches such as the Friends and Mennonites."

Dr. Ahlstrom included much accurate information on the Russells in his monumental reference work, *A Religious History of the American People*, which was published by Yale University Press in London and New Haven in 1971, and came to Lao's attention through a Delaware student in June 1976.

In a section on cosmic consciousness and the science of spiritual man, Dr. Ahlstrom cited Richard Maurice Bucke and the latter's 1901 experience of a new plane of existence resulting from an illumination of cosmic life and order and a sense of immortality. Recognizing Bucke's effort "to absorb scientific materialism in a highly generalized form of mysticism," Ahlstrom credited the Russells with giving institutional form to the ancient impulse Bucke represented.

Recounting the Russells' illuminations (Walter's in 1921 and Lao's in 1946), the author described the work of their University, noting it had been founded in 1957 with the motto "World Peace through World Balance." Ahlstrom traced the harmonial traditions of the Russells' central doctrine through Emerson and Whitman, but he took note of the distinctiveness of their belief in the "coequality of man and woman, caused by a balance of elemental forces."

In one of the most scholarly descriptions of the Russell teachings, the Yale professor summarized his section on their work as follows: "The Russells' outlook is also marked by a fairly strident apocalypticism, which, along with their stand of women's rights, even won them a hearing in the student protest movements of the 1960s. They designated 1960 as 'the crucial year' for reversing man's way of life 'to serving man instead of preying upon him,' and they regarded 1963 as the 'point of no return' in this race with time. The white race they considered 'on the eve of its downfall' and in need of drastic transformation, despite its persistent belief in itself as the 'world master.'"

Ahlstrom took note of the *Home Study Course*, and the fact that "there are no organized 'churches' to unite the hundreds of thousands who thank the Russells for having given them religious peace in a troubled world."

Other scholars took note of the University's work. In 1971, Dr. Carl L. Moore, a professor of business and economics at Lehigh University, wrote a book titled *Profitable Applications of the Break-Even System*, which he presented to Lao with deep gratitude and best personal regards. In the acknowledgments he wrote, "Special recognition is given to Lao Russell and the late Walter Russell of the University of Science and Philosophy for general guidance that led to the publication of this book." Professor Moore had previously read and studied the complete curriculum of the University of Science and Philosophy. At the time he wrote his book, he realized the importance of the Russell Law of Rhythmic Balanced Interchange in the business world.

Arthur Carl Piepkorn, graduate professor of Systematic Theology at Concordia Seminary in Missouri, prepared a theological profile of the University for his multi-volume work, *The Religious Bodies of the United States and Canada*, but the last three volumes covering metaphysical bodies were never published.

Ingo Swann, an internationally known psychic, whose secret work for government intelligence agencies was often cited as invaluable by officials whose favorable statements technically violated official security rules, visited Lao in 1970 to discuss matters of mutual interest. Their mutual friend Coral Gaynes introduced them. Both Lao and Dr. Swann were interested in the decades-long research into cosmic art undertaken by Dr. Raymond Piper, whose widow, Lila, had given his manuscripts to Swann to prepare for publication. After so many disappointments at the lack of acceptance afforded occult and spiritual art by the public in general and the art establishment, Swann hoped that Piper's work, and possibly a proposed new journal that Swann himself proposed to edit, would bring spiritual research itself into better tolerance. He was impressed with the Russells' books and the University's purpose and frequently discussed them among the various elite intellectual circles in which he moved. Lao seems to have enjoyed meeting the man whose creative work in worldwide research centers, alleged involvement in psi warfare, and obvious creative genius earned him the sobriquet of "parapsychology's most tested guinea pig."

Lao knew that the University needed a national radio or television program broadcast from Swannanoa itself. A television producer in Washington tried to arrange this in his broadcast area and encouraged Ralph Nader to come to Swannanoa, but there is no record that the great consumer advocate came to speak with Lao. Popular but controversial Alabama Governor George Wallace had written her a surprisingly supportive letter.

Lao urged her friend Earl Nightingale to undertake publication of some of their works. She stressed the need for broader circulation of *Atomic Suicide?* "Had the deep message of this book been heeded from 1957, when we first released it, much of the agony that we are witnessing in the world today could have been avoided. Unfortunately, it takes a tragedy like the California earthquake to make people think. The undermining that has happened throughout the whole world through the use of atomic fission cannot be measured at this time. Only unfolding events will prove how right Dr. Russell was when he stated that atomic fission should not be used for war or industry."

Bishop M. S. Medley, of the Omniune Church in Texarkana, Texas, suggested that Lao should be able to draw dedicated workers from both young and old folks. "Their greatest need is to be needed. You could give them a chance at new self-respect," he told her. He urged her to adopt a better marketing program: "Your university needs publicity. Too few persons are aware of its existence, much less the marvelously valuable lessons it has to teach. It is obvious that your teachings are not so well known as many foolish and faddish ideas are. What is needed here is a new approach. Your best advertisement is your philosophy itself. The problem of publicity would be solved by getting basic facts about U.S.P. and its teachings into the hands of a great number of people." He urged that she publish an inexpensive paperback book that would carry her most important message in short, easy-to-read form.

"The Unitarian-Universalist Association is having good success with this method," he told her. "They are selling a paperback, *Challenge of a Liberal Faith*, both by mail and through other dealers." He believed that much greater interest in the *Home Study Course* could be generated if a degree title came with the diploma. "I truly believe that an education in basic Truths, such as you offer, is at least equivalent to, if not better than, the type of 'higher education' offered by standard colleges," he told her.

Lao explained why she had no desire to pursue the accreditation process that would be necessary if the University were to seek to bestow academic degrees. "The greatest teachers the world has ever known have not had degrees. What a man knows must always eventually be expressed, and he will make his mark in the world. I founded this worldwide University and studying under me now are many doctors with degrees from Sc.D.s to Ph.D.s. Edison is a great example of a man who contributed much to the world and yet had not one degree after his name. There are many such men," said Lao.

Dale Torkelson and David Brandy of the Melchizedek Order in Albuquerque, New Mexico, wrote her that *The Secret of Light* and other Russell works that they had been studying since 1965 had been a tremendous help in the Order's research work. "We are hoping that sometime in the near future we can demonstrate mind-over-matter before scientists," they said.

The Churches' Fellowship for Psychical and Spiritual Studies in London, England, discussed their books at its council meeting and advised its members about the course. The Order of Natural Christians in Perthshire, Scotland, was actively promoting the University and its course and books.

In Detroit, Michigan, the Lewis Hypnosis Center featured the Russells in its *Concept Transition* newsletter. Lao corresponded with the newsletter editor about Stewart White's reportage of his wife Betty's incredible experiences and activities. Betty's paranormal divulgence of the continuity of personality after death of the physical body had been extensively explored in White's books, *Across the Unknown*, *The Betty Book*, *The Job of Living*, *The Stars Are Still There*, and *The Unobstructed Universe*, and Lao found much of this information congruent with the Russell work.

Jeffrey R. J. Bond of Southwell, England, wrote her, "I have become more impressed with *Atomic Suicide?* as I have continued reading it. Something of this kind of writing and explanation, put in a suitable way, is needed in all the schools of the world so that children grow to appreciate the universal principles at work everywhere and that everything, whether studied as physics or as spirituality, is an expression of the same principle derived from God. *Atomic Suicide?* is unique in more ways than one, yet I have been greatly interested to see how the great insights of other philosophical systems have been confirmed therein." Sir George Trevelyan wrote that he planned to recommend *Atomic Suicide?* to his friends.

Lao read with interest of the work of New York's Philosophical Research Center. "All such work is greatly needed to awaken the world to its great need of inner direction," she wrote its director, Doris Herzog. "Greater knowledge of many things not yet known on earth is necessary to make man realize that all things which he seeks outside of himself are already within himself."

Lao was concerned that polluted air and water had become a major problem all over the country. She and Walter had tried hard to awaken people to this danger for many years. *Atomic Suicide?* had been written not only to accomplish this, but also to give a solution. Lao considered the volume "truly the parent book on pollution and radioactivity, and many thinking people are reading it with deep concern and interest today."

She emphasized that her immediate concern was for the planet itself. She drew hope from the fact that a number of senators and congressmeen had found the arguments the Russells made in *Atomic Suicide?* inspiring and persuasive.

Lao took heart from the fact that many college-age young people were reading *Atomic Suicide?* and comprehending the new science. Their enthusiasm seemed boundless, and Lao felt that in these young people there was great hope for the world. She promoted *Atomic Suicide?*, since it contained the scientific knowledge of *The Secret of Light* and was profusely illustrated with more than eighty drawings by Dr. Russell, who had considered it a more comprehensive study of their new science than *The Secret of Light*, despite the fact that most deep students felt that the two books together gave a fuller picture of the Russell science than either did separately.

Elizabeth Hogan, co-author with Richard Curtis of a book called *Perils of the Peaceful Atom*, corresponded with Lao and suggested that they seek a loose coalition of groups opposing nuclear plants to bring worldwide attention to the unprecedented hazards related to America's civilian nuclear power plant program. They both agreed that, although they were armed with increasing amounts of scientific data, they were no match financially for the promotional efforts of the Atomic Energy Commission and nuclear industry. Mrs. Hogan had written to several hundred responsible social service and religious organizations, emphasizing the points made in Lao's book and her own, and stressing that failure to act against nuclear plants could be disastrous to the planet.

Dr. W. Ballantine Henley, a man of outstanding ability and the new president of the United Church of Religious Science, read *Atomic Suicide?* and corresponded with Lao about other Russell books.

Lao still received inquiries on Walter's early book *The Russell Genero-Radiative Concept*. She had hesitated to reprint this book, because Walter himself had felt the new scientific knowledge and his Charts of the Elements had been more clearly explained in the *Home Study Course* and their book *Atomic Suicide?*

She believed that nothing in the Message was more critically important than for humanity to understand its own potential and the danger of radiation to the very survival of the Earth. "Mankind has never yet generally understood that man's greatest asset is man himself," she wrote, "but actually he is left with no choice at this stage but to work together for the survival of the planet itself. There is enough atomic waste in the world to destroy our whole civilization. My late husband said there was not any metal or material of any kind that could permanently contain atomic fission, and that was why he always stated atomic fission should not be used for war or industry. It was to warn the world of what would happen if they continued to use it for war and industry that we wrote our book, *Atomic Suicide?*"

She heard from Winifred Babcock, author of *The Palestinian Mystery Play* and co-publisher of the writings of Preston Harold. Lao appreciated this work. She found Preston Harold's book *The Shining Stranger* of more than passing interest, but had little time to read for pleasure and often apologized for not having the time to read the manuscripts people sent her. "I greatly regret being unable to write you constantly about your work," she replied, "but if you spent just one day at Swannanoa, you would realize the reason for my seeming uncommunicative way of life. My working day is anything from eighteen to twenty hours a day, and surprising as it may seem to you, I have not had an opportunity in all of the twenty-five years since I met Dr. Russell to read all of his countless writings.

"Frankly, if I read all of the poetry and manuscripts for books that are sent to me by students, I would never get any of my own work done at all. Perhaps someday I shall have more time for such things, but in the foreseeable future, it seems impossible."

On February 14, 1971, Lao left Swannanoa for Kingsport, Tennessee, to meet with her printer. That day, she sent Emelia and John Lombardi one of her several priceless copies of Walter's long out-of-print masterpiece *The Universal One*. She urged them to come to the May 19 centennial celebration of Walter's birth. She expected a large turnout for that event and hoped that they would stay through Emelia's birthday on May 22. She told Emelia she planned to make a change in the board of directors and ask Jim and Pat duPont Stephanis to step aside. "We need practical help now, not ten years from now when I may not be here," she noted. They would be replaced by J. Mitchell Ellis of Glasgow, Kentucky, who had done much to help her for twenty years, and Dr. Raymond John, who had been married at Swannanoa and wanted to help spread the Message. Lao was planning for Walter's centennial to be quite a festive occasion. A singer from the New York Opera Company would be at Swannanoa to entertain the guests on the centennial event. Lao believed that the occasion would mark the beginning of a great new era for the University.

Emelia was thrilled to receive *The Universal One*. She told Lao that she had once only had the opportunity to glance at a copy and had always longed for the opportunity to read it. She and John were studying it slowly and finding it very deep.

From Kingsport, Lao went to Florida for a long rest, lecturing at Key West and several other places. Lao took great interest in the April 21, 1971, issue of *Look* magazine. She wrote, "The five articles of the *Five Who Care* series concerning Earth Day clearly outline the world's great needs, and our teachings cover every need mentioned in these five articles—and more. Dr. Marga-ret Mead, one of the five, was quoted as saying, 'We need a religious system with science at its very core.' That is exactly what our teachings give!"

Because of the cold weather and late spring in Virginia that year, Lao delayed returning to Swannanoa until April 28. She had barely twenty days to rest at Swannanoa before the centennial of Walter's birth. When she returned from Florida, she told Emelia, "My body was awfully tired, and it has taken much time to build it up a bit. I still have some problems but am grateful to be alive!"

As Lao had hoped, the May 19, 1971, celebration of what would have been Walter's hundredth birthday proved to be a gathering of students from all over the country. A number of Canadian students also came to the two-week celebration.

121. Centennial celebration of Walter Russell's birth, Swannanoa, May 19, 1971. (Front row, left to right: Mrs. Albert Doss, Dr. Doss, Guy Chipman, Lao Russell, Patricia Hall, Evelyn Jones, Angela Carr (with Emelia Lombardi immediately behind her), Rowena Hawkins.

The two volumes of *The Message of the Divine Iliad* were off the press and were at Swannanoa by May 19. *The Secret of Light* took longer, because it had to be entirely reset due to changes and corrections on nearly every page that Walter had marked some years before he refolded. Lao was disappointed that *The Secret of Light* would not be available for the centennial gathering, but Kingsport Press told her they could not deliver it until early July.

Dr. Clifford Chaffee and his wife and family came to the May 19 celebration from California. They had hoped to stay at the summer cottage, but three young students from California and Oregon had offered to come and stay the entire week and help with whatever was needed at the palace or in the gardens. Lao had promised the cottage to them and found other accommodations for the Chaffees.

She was thrilled when James Mitchell Ellis brought three generations of his family to Swannanoa, including his infant grandson. "Never forget that a baby only 'looks' like a baby, for his Mind is part of the great eternal Mind which is ageless, and little James Robert could have been in a million bodies before coming to you in this body," she told the baby's parents. Mitchell Ellis served on the University's board for a decade.

She invited the Lombardis to stay at the palace. John was not able to come, but Emelia came and charmed all who she met with her usual bright and beautiful personality. Many of those present told Lao, "I fell in love with Emelia." The Lombardis had sent a substantial donation, and after Emelia returned to New Jersey, Lao wrote her and John, "You know how deeply I appreciate the gift, but I also want you to know that if you never did one little or big thing ever again for the work, I would and shall ever be, eternally grateful for all the big and little things you have done for so long."

It was a warm yet formal gathering in the participants' spiritual home on God's mountaintop. Lao gave an intimate talk about Dr. Russell and played some of his recorded lectures. Richard Dulaney spoke to the group, emphasizing the impact the Russells' work was having on college students and young people in general. Students played musical instruments and sang, and those who felt inspired described how the Russells had influenced their lives.

122. Yale honors graduate Richard A. Dulaney speaks at Walter Russell centennial.

Twenty-two years before, the Russells had opened the doors and dedicated Swannanoa as a world cultural center. Lao believed that in many respects their purpose had been fulfilled.

A meeting of the board of directors was held at Swannanoa in connection with the Walter Russell centennial celebration. Many copies of the new printing of *The Message of the Divine Iliad* volumes were sold.

Interest had revived in the Temple of Light. Although the general purpose and intent of constructing the Temple of Light was encouraged, the University was not in a position to proceed directly with the project.

A film on the University, which could be loaned to various educational and religious groups at a nominal cost, was authorized. Lao reported that *The World Crisis*, *Atomic Suicide?*, and *God Will Work with You but Not for You* were presently required reading in many college courses, including one at the University of Virginia, and also that the teachings were spreading into such major industries as the Western Electric Company.

Lao reported that she had received several requests for translating *God Will Work with You but Not for You* into German, French, Portuguese, and Spanish. The board determined that the best interests of the University would be served by permitting such translations, and Lao was authorized to enter into the necessary contracts as the need arose.

The possibility of a Portuguese translation of *God Will Work with You but Not for You* was the most definite. On May 1, 1971, Paul Lojnikov, a spiritual-minded businessman of Rio de Janeiro, wrote of his pleasure in reading that book, and his belief that it should be translated and distributed throughout Brazil. He was likewise certain the *Home Study Course* would prove popular if translated into Portuguese.

Brazil had a population of eighty million people, seventy-six million of whom Paul felt were practicing "low" spiritualism. "Your book and courses will be very helpful in this country," he told Lao. She wrote Paul on May 26 to tell him that the board had voted in favor of allowing him to have *God Will Work with You but Not for You* tranlated into Portuguese for sale in Brazil. She told him that all the money the University received from the sale of its publications and books was reinvested in disseminating the Russell teachings, and asked that a fair royalty be sent to the University on copies of her book translated and sold in Brazil.

Lao had read with interest the altruistic objectives of Paul's organization, Ordem Revelacionista Evangelica, and told him, "My sole purpose on earth is to extend to my fellow man—regardless of race, nationality or creed.... Because our teachings are very basic, they do not appeal so much to the emotions in man as to his Mind-intellect, so therefore, it has taken more time for them to be integrated into universal acceptance. However, there are so many signs that our time has come."

She added, "The world is in desperate need of basic knowledge of man, himself, and of his true purpose on earth. The whole world of man is at the very crossroads of life when he will completely destroy himself and his planet unless he is awakened in awareness of who he is, what he is, and the very purpose of the Play of Creation." She invited Paul to come for a visit to Virginia and discuss the possibility of translating, not only *God Will Work with You but Not for You*, but also all of the Russell writings into Portuguese for distribution in Brazil.

Paul Lojnikov soon replied that he had commissioned a skilled linguist, Dr. Viegas, to translate *God Will Work with You but Not for You* into Portuguese, telling Lao, "I am very glad because I don't believe there is a better man in Brazil to do this job. Herewith I enclose several pages translated by him from your brochure." He hoped to visit Swannanoa in the fall with his colleague Matero (Nelson Moreita de Queiroz). Paul told Lao that Dr. Viegas had translated the works of Mary Baker Eddy into Portuguese.

Lao wrote Paul, "Each letter that comes from you tells me more of the depth of your desire to bring God-awareness to our fellow man, and with the fire of your dedication—and with the additional help of your dedicated associates, we cannot fail!"

Lao was disappointed that Jim and Pat duPont Stephanis had not come to the May 19 meeting and seemed to have a waning interest in the work. On June 1, she wrote to tell them that she had replaced them as directors:

> The time is here when I must have more help—a great deal more help—and knowing you cannot be here at a moment's notice, we have now elected two directors who have been dedicated students and helpers for a long time—one since 1955—and the other one lives close and comes frequently. Both of these students have done extensive work through distributing the *Home Study Course* and books and are qualified to help here—or anywhere—and live but to help with our work in any way they can.
>
> We decided to elect the two new directors on May 19 when students came from all over the country for Doctor's 100th anniversary. I knew it would be a special day, but was amazed when so many students arrived. Many of them stayed for a whole week.
>
> As you know, directors are only elected for a one-year term so we feel those who are able to help more actively now should be elected. Pat mentioned last June that it was difficult for you to come in June and that she did not think you could come at all in 1971. It is essential now for us to have Directors who can come at a moment's notice, if necessary, and we realize this is difficult for Jim.

She told them, "I treasure all the years we have shared and all of Pat's personal help in the past. Now, we must all look upon this experience as a good experience. Everyone has learned a great deal from it, the greatest thing being that only by working together with loving cooperation can everyone fulfill their main purpose of being here, which is to express Love in Action."

Pat duPont Stephanis replied immediately. Her own personal and business problems prevented her from objecting to their being removed from the board. She wrote, "I don't know how you stand it, Lao. You have so much love and truth and goodness and help to give to the world, and people will not listen. What great strength you must have to hold up against all the ignorance and stupidity of the human race!

"I dearly, dearly love you and I am so grateful for all you have given me. Your teachings are the only true ones that exist in the world, and you are the greatest, most intelligent, and most divine woman in the world."

During the winter of 1971, Lao encouraged Richard Dulaney with his efforts at establishing an organic farming project on some of the Swannanoa acreage behind the palace grounds. Anti-war sentiment had split the nation largely along generational lines as the conflict in Vietnam continued to rage. Lao was advised by her tax attorney that it would be most unwise for her to write the Virginia Director of Selective Service of her plan to employ conscientious objectors at the University in connection with the farming project. She had recently received a letter from the Internal Revenue Service asking pertinent questions regarding the University's non-profit status. Rumors were rife that the militarists in the federal government were exhausting all avenues to put pressure on citizens and groups supporting the peace movement, and Lao feared reprisal if the University appeared to be a haven for so-called "peace-niks."

In the meantime, Richard was gathering a fine group of young people for the project. Lao agreed that the excess acreage at Swannanoa would be an ideal site for organic farming, but she referred Richard to her student and friend John Saxman, a thirty-five-year-old West Virginian who was planning to undertake biological and organic farming on his hundred-acre farm there. Lao was excited at the prospect. She knew the danger atmospheric radiation and dangerous chemical fertilizers posed to the world's food supply. She had recently received a large order for copies of *Atomic Suicide?* from the Valley Farm Organic Foods Conservation Project in York, Pennsylvania, and also from the Los-Angeles-based Help Unlimited organization.

Plans for the farming project on Swannanoa mountain were postponed indefinitely when Richard Dulaney entered the College of William and Mary School of Law in September 1974. The previous month, Lao wrote Richard of her happiness that all was unfolding the way he desired.

Throughout the Vietnam War era, students of draft age wrote Lao for written confirmation that they were attending the University of Science and Philosophy, hoping to thus qualify for a student deferment from active military duty, but she was forced to advise them that Swannanoa did not fall under the category of a theological organization or a divinity school, despite the fact that she had many ministers of all denominations studying with her. Letters she had written in more peaceful times for students who were conscientious objectors had proven helpful to them in officially obtaining that status. She agonized over the Vietnam War and lent support to those who were working for world peace. Leaders in the Peacemakers Mission from New Jersey visited her again, remembering their visits to Swannanoa during Walter's lifetime, when America was relatively uninvolved in war, and they could sit on the porch of the summer cottage sipping tea with the Russells with more optimism that an era of international peace might indeed be on the near horizon.

Lao encouraged students who were entering second marriages: "You mentioned that your husband is forty-five and I presume that you are in your late thirties or early forties. I have known so many women of this age who have made wonderful second marriages. If one can look at the ending of one experience as something that had to take place in order that a greater cycle could come into being, one often finds another door opens into another experience in marriage."

She was pleased when the head football coach at the Virginia Military Institute ordered copies of *The Man Who Tapped the Secrets of the Universe* for members of the team and coaching staff. Faculty members at the University of Alaska also ordered their books.

She encouraged her friends and students to introduce the teachings to others. "Surely to awaken the Light of God's Love in the hearts of our fellow man is the greatest service one can ever give to him," she wrote. Nonetheless, she cautioned a Michigan student regarding students teaching their own classes from the *Home Study Course*: "Dr. Russell and I always advised our students that discussion groups only should be formed since the knowledge in this course is new and scientific, and Dr. Russell did not feel that students would be ready after one year's study to teach the new science of the Russell Cosmogony. It was for this reason that we always urged every student to have his or her own copy of the lessons so that he or she could study alone and then get together for discussion."

All the while, Lao was inundated with letters from students with problems of all levels of severity. Regarding cremation, Walter and Lao both felt strongly on the subject and personally did not like cremation, believing that when a body returns more slowly to the elements from which it was created, there is a more balanced regiving to the earth, which gives us our life and sustenance. Lao strongly recommended use of aloe for healing.

She told a mental health nurse that she knew that working with patients who were spiritually unaware could be very draining, "but when one learns to look beyond the physical man, realizing that every soul is born to unfold in understanding of Mind-Consciousness, one will find seeming previous barriers disappear. Think of this, also: Jealousy, hate, fear, and greed spring from a sense of inner insecurity. That is why the more that one unfolds in God-awareness, the more secure and positive one becomes in one's actions. These negative emotions disappear with Mind-Consciousness."

Lao received repeated inquiries as to whether or not there were regular classes scheduled at the University. Her normal reply was that there were no special activities scheduled owing to the tremendous demand on her time for personal interviews and the necessity of speaking to visiting groups daily at Swannanoa. During the past six years, she had lectured all over the country during the winter months, and spent the summer months talking with groups at Swannanoa, as well as holding special meetings and personal appointments. The curriculum consisting of the *Home Study Course* and the books seemed to fill a greater need for the students by allowing them to study at their own pace in their own homes.

Lao reassured such inquirers: "When one is ready for further spiritual unfolding, God never fails to open a new door for growth. There is always the right time for desires to come to fruition, and never has there been a time that man has needed basic knowledge as today."

Regarding a student's question as to how to achieve balance in daily responsibilities, Lao replied, "Naturally, this depends upon the size of your family and the depth of your desire in serving your community. It would be most unbalanced to give more time to community affairs than to your own family obligations. Actually, it is a case of doing those things that are most needed. There is only one 'yardstick' for giving service, and that is the 'yardstick' of Love. Love means Balance, so therefore, when giving love to your family, household chores and the community, one is guided to the length of service where the need is greatest at that particular time."

A student from Pittsburgh told her, "After reading your reference to might vs. right in one of the later lessons, it reminded me of how I admired and read the words Napoleon said during his exile on Elba: 'I have come to the conclusion that nothing taken by force can ever have permanence.'"

Lao continued to receive occasional letters from Ghana and South Africa. The Sermon on the Mount was popular among African students and they appreciated her concept that it was identical to the "inviolate Law of Rhythmic Balanced Interchange," which she felt to be truly "Love in Action."

She was not so involved with her international work as to ignore those who were personally close to her. She was particularly concerned with young Rodger Hostettler, who had taken ill and been hospitalized while she was in Florida. She greatly valued this young man who had been working on the staff and studying the philosophy. She was very disappointed to find him discouraged and depressed. He was a talented musician. "You also know I want you to have great joy out of your music. That is why I have encouraged you to use the organ," she told him.

She was also very congenial with her neighbors, particularly with the cultured and cosmopolitan Virginia Dillon and her mother, Lottie Hinton, whose beautiful Rossmont Farms estate was less than a mile from Swannanoa. She was unfailingly thoughtful when Virginia was forced to leave her mother alone from time to time. Although she knew the Hintons had servants, Lao kept in touch daily with the elderly Lottie Hinton during these periods.

Water service to the palace once again grew intermittent. For three weeks there was no water pressure except in the basement. James F. Dulaney, Sr., had died of cancer in 1970, and Lao was uncertain as to whom she should turn. John Lombardi told Lao that she had a legal right to water as a necessary part of the rental. John advised, "I feel that if you talked with Dulaney's brother you could get most anything from him. You have a very persuasive way. You are very diplomatic and have a way of making people want to do things for you. I will bet you could get him in the palm of your hand."

She appealed to the owners for help, reiterating the importance of the work she was doing at Swannanoa in a particularly detailed letter to Alvin T. Dulaney, Jr., that included a veiled warning that revealed the depth of Lao's frustration with the poor palace maintenance and her determination to persevere.

Lao emphasized that the Russells' motive in establishing the shrine of beauty at Swannanoa had never been one of self-aggrandizement. Both she and Walter had previously known great success in the material world, she reminded Mr. Dulaney.

"When we came to Swannanoa in September 1948, I was startled to be in the place of my vision of January 1946, wherein God made known to me the science of man and what I was to do to give the new knowledge to the world. It is for this reason that for twenty-five years I have worked ceaselessly from sixteen to twenty hours per day."

In pleading for help she stressed, "My long-range concern is for all the valuable works of art at Swannanoa to remain safe and intact to inspire future generations of their innate and powerful potential. Everything at Swannanoa, including all of the copyrights on our writings, belongs to the University of Science and Philosophy. These things belong to posterity and my personal concern is for their safe custody in dedicated hands."

"I know in God's time we shall have national publicity," she told Mr. Dulaney. "There are always important people coming who want me to give lectures, and this fall I hope to be able to get away for T.V. appearances in Washington, D.C."

The owners took corrective measures, but the water system on the mountain continued to be unreliable.

She did not fail to remind Mr. Dulaney that his son was deeply committed to the work at Swannanoa, adding, "Because of Richard's dedication and understanding of God's Message, I feel that it will be his destiny to continue with our work."

CHAPTER TWENTY-TWO

Messengers of Love (1971-75)

Jerome Canty, whose works would be proclaimed by John David Mann in *Solstice* magazine as among the "most challenging and adventurous books" in macrobiotic literature, authored *The Eternal Massage*, *The Sounding of the Sacred Conch*, and the privately issued *Spiral, Lord of Creation*, all of which cited the Russells' work extensively and were credited with introducing the Russells' thinking to a venturesome circle of macrobiotic students. During the 1970s *The Eternal Massage* in particular enjoyed an extensive readership.

In 1971, Jerome Canty published a column in the widely circulated magazine *East West Journal*. As usual, he extolled the Russells and their work, and as a result, many readers of the popular periodical wrote the University for books and ultimately enrolled in the *Home Study Course*. Lao was always delighted to learn that a new student had sought out the University on Jerome Canty's recommendation. She knew he had studied and participated in many spiritual groups, and she considered him "an outstanding student of the Science of Man and the Science of the Cosmos upon which all our teachings are based." Lao called him one of the "great messengers of love," and was not surprised when inquirers from as far away as Sweden told her they had come to the University through Canty's recommendation.

Several years later, students in New Mexico urged her to come to Albuquerque and Santa Fe, where Canty was conducting a series of lectures on harmony and the wave principle in March. Her heavy schedule at Swannanoa made it impossible for her to attend, but she paid high compliments to Canty as "a dedicated and great worker for God's Message," adding, "I know that he will be wonderfully successful for his one desire is to awaken his fellow man to the cause of his problems and give him the solution that only comes from the practice of God's ways and processes."

The scope of the Russells' radical scientific vision, embracing as it does what John David Mann termed a "remarkably practical understanding of the yin/yang principle" and its application "to physical entities, human relationships, and the social order," had indeed been echoed by George Ohsawa and Michio Kushi in their macrobiotic science. "For example," Mann explained in his definitive comparison of the two, "Russell contended that matter is not held together by an attracting force generated from the center of mass, but by compression generating from the outside toward the center. This view, one of the Russell statements that flies most abruptly in the face of accepted scientific tenets, is echoed precisely in Kushi's cosmology, where conventional 'gravity' is discarded in favor of centripetal 'Heaven's force.'"

Lao was delighted at the widespread publicity the University seemed to be getting from many sources. Richard Dulaney sent her a copy of *The Psychic Observer* containing Evelyn McKeever's recent review of *The Secret of Light*. Lao had not previously seen the review, but she considered it excellent in its treatment of the voidance principle, and sent copies to many of her students and friends.

She was pleased to read an article on the balanced "giving-regiving" law of nature in the April 1970 issue of *Psychic* magazine that demonstrated Bruce Barton's familiarity with the Russell principles. The great advertising genius and author of many popular books understood it well, Lao remarked. *The National Exchange*, Vol. 1, No. 3, included Kathy Redmond's review of Glenn Clark's *The Man Who Tapped the Secrets of the Universe*, and was of great interest to Lao.

Lao was frequently interviewed for important magazine articles. Irene Preston of *Southern Living* magazine visited her in the 1970s. The same year a favorable article by Pat Matheny appeared in *The Roanoke Times*.

An Oregon film producer wrote Angela Carr at the palace, "If Lao ever writes of the Cosmic Romance, I certainly would want to know of it. As for making a full-length movie of their lives, that would be the movie! It would be an undertaking that would be expensive no doubt, but the important thing in my opinion would be that Lao insure its accuracy and truthfulness and make certain that the actors involved would know what it was all about."

Merta Mary Parkinson of Kansas City included excerpts from the Russells in her new book, *Sing a New Song!*, which dealt with the importance and necessity of all humans understanding and applying the dynamic energies of forgiveness. Lao was pleased that Parkinson had included them with such other widely known intellects as Charles Fillmore, Winifred Babcock, and Diane Pike.

Lao had been hard at work on her new book on reincarnation. In September 1971, she sent Emelia a copy of the working manuscript, and Emelia became deeply involved in helping Lao edit the book. It took as its starting point the words "In the beginning God," because, Lao stressed, "these words are truth, everlasting truth, scientifically stated." She began another book she would never publish, *Out of the Silence*, which would extend her explanation of the continuity of life as God had impressed on her in the words "Thou shalt know space but never emptiness, for behold I am space, and I fill all of it."

In November 1971, Walter's great-granddaughter came to visit her at Swannanoa. Lao introduced her as "the last one from his immediate family who 'inherited' the spiritual quality of my beloved." Years later, other relatives of Walter came to the palace and demonstrated a similar spiritual awareness.

In April 1972, Emelia and the Hawkinses joined Lao for the board meeting. Dr. Raymond John, who had served for a year, was not reelected. *The Secret of Light* was selling well, and the University was reprinting the third edition of the *Home Study Course*. The Christ of the Blue Ridge statue in the palace gardens had been severely damaged by the weather, and the board authorized major reconstruction in order to rebuild it.

On May 9, the Honorable James G. Martin IV, presiding judge of the Juvenile and Domestic Relations Court in Norfolk, Virginia, brought a delegation from the Norfolk Institute to discuss applying the Russell principles to Virginia's prison system. Lao often referred to the 1970-71 Annual Report of the Norfolk, Virginia, Juvenile and Domestic Relations Court, which described how Judge Martin had used the University's curriculum to improve the lives of the young people in his charge through a training center called the Norfolk Institute. The report confirmed how his court, "in endeavor to discover the key to the solution of juvenile crime and delinquency, has established formal liaison with Swannanoa, taking advantage of its propinquity, to see whether the key lies within the lore of that institution. The fundamental concept of the Norfolk Institute is that juvenile crime and delinquency are rooted in a delinquent society; that the eradication thereof must contemplate revolutionary reformation and stabilization of society itself. Founded by the Mayor's Youth Commission of the City of Norfolk, pursuant to authorization by the City Council on May 19, 1970, it is envisaged as an institution for local research and development of the problems and panaceas appurtenant to juvenile crime and delinquency." Judge Martin asserted that, through its liaison with Swannanoa, his court had set the pattern for the juvenile court to come of age in a nation in cultural decline.

Lao and the judge discussed at length their negative opinion of the current television industry. Lao ruefully expressed relief that television had not opened up as a means of furthering the University's work. She told Judge Martin that she had intuitively canceled her acceptance of an invitation to judge the Miss Universe contest in Wilmington, Delaware, and the final competition in Puerto Rico. She felt that such a role would not effectively project the true mission of the University.

Judge Martin, who helped Lao fund additional staff for the University through his personal generosity, also arranged for her to talk with his long-standing friend and Virginia Military Institute classmate Frank McCarthy, who had produced the recent film *Patton* and who Judge Martin described as an anomaly in the film industry. Lao dared to hope that McCarthy was one who God had prepared to lead mankind out of the wilderness of the senses to the peace and fulfillment of mind-knowing and direction.

On July 1, 1972, a national politician sent the University its first order for *Why You Cannot Die!* Despite advance publicity, the book would not be published for six more months.

123. Lao Russell with Angela Carr and Johnny Miles.

With Pat Hall busy downstairs greeting visitors, Lao did her own packing for her upcoming lecture tour, and signed several boxes of books before leaving for Georgia with Sam and Martha Spicher. Lao's faithful Scottie Wendy was ill, and she feared leaving her. In fact, Wendy died soon after her return. Pat, Angela Carr, and Johnny Miles remained at Swannanoa.

In July, Lao gave three lectures to more than 2,000 doctors of chiropractic at the Life University Dynamic Essentials meetings at the Marriott hotel in Atlanta, Georgia, by invitation of the University's founder, Dr. Sid E. Williams. This led to a tremendous extension of interest in the University of Science and Philosophy over the next year.

During this trip, she spent several days at the Monastery of the Holy Spirit located at Conyers, Georgia, thirty-five miles east of Atlanta. She was no stranger to this community of members of the Cistercian Order of the Strict Observance (Trappists), who followed the Rule of Saint Benedict. In early 1969 Father Peter Assard, the Abbey's retreat master, had read a copy of Lao's book *Love* and had shared it with Father Anthony, master of liturgical rites at the Abbey, and Brother Louis Galletti, who wrote her at once to express his delight in her book, and to advise her that at his request the Abbey community had granted her Letters of Association, by virtue of which she and her work would perpetually be remembered in the prayers and masses at the Abbey. She had sent Brother Galletti her other books and seems to have strengthened her relationship with the community through regular correspondence.

124. Author's reception in Albany, Georgia.

She often reflected on her 1972 visit to this tranquil retreat. She was warmly received by the monastic community, and enjoyed long discussions with the Abbot and other leaders. She relished the fact that she was the only woman at the Abbey at the time, but more significantly, she often related details of her conversations while there. The Abbot asked her if she believed in the virgin birth of Christ. Her reply was clear. She told him that she believed that God never violated any of his natural laws. To her surprise the Abbot seemed satisfied with her answer.

Clearly it was not only the famous to whom she related. When she lectured in Albany, Georgia, she gave an autographed copy of her book *Love* to one of the maids who cleaned her room. This lady shared the book with her entire church school. The members wrote Lao that *Love* should be in the home of every family with children, and should be mandatory reading for every young couple contemplating marriage.

Dr. Earl St. Dennis wrote to tell her of the impact she had on one of his patients when she addressed the Chiropractic Society Meeting in Albany. "One young lady, only twenty-two years of age, who was faced with extensive psychiatric treatment, stated to me after reading your book *Love*, 'This did me more good from the standpoint of understanding than anything else I have ever read on the subject of sex, love, and life.' You will be pleased to hear that with this new concept of thought, in addition to her physical treatment, this patient is now taking on a new interest in life which includes broadening her goals for the future. Her way back to a normal life has been made just that much easier because of the contribution your excellent book has helped play in her life."

Why You Cannot Die! was finally released in December 1972. Unity churches and Association for Research and Enlightenment groups from coast to coast promoted it. The New York Public Library had experienced a demand for the book even before it was advertised in *The New York Times*. A senior consultant at the DuPont Company purchased ninety copies. Lao hoped the book would prove the catalyst of God's Message. She wrote her students that the silent voice within her had whispered, "When man knows that the Light of God is the sole Source of Life, he will individually and collectively give to life instead of taking from it." She told her friends that this was what Jesus knew would some day happen when he spoke the words "on earth as it is in heaven."

Peter Parker had designed the dust jacket for *Why You Cannot Die!* as a blend of the modern today and the traditional past "to symbolize that the 'I' of today is the sum of all the 'I's of the past."

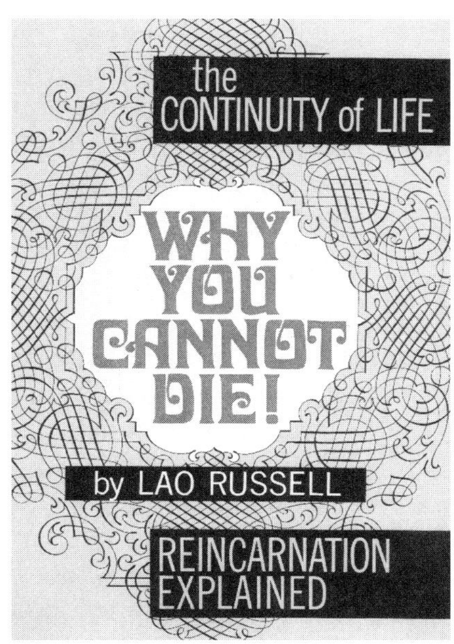

125. Why You Cannot Die!

He explained his inspiration further in a letter she often quoted: "A richly beautiful piece of continental calligraphy was chosen to frame the title. It is one continuous line. Place your finger on any part of the design and follow the line to its end. You cannot. It has no beginning or end.

"There is yet another reason, a romantically symbolic reason, why calligraphy is appropriate to a book such as this one. As drawn by the monks, scribes and artists of ancient times, the remarkable beauty of manuscripts of calligraphy was so highly prized that even conquering barbarians considered such manuscripts valuable booty. Thus did the beauty of immortal art preserve and guard the sciences and the accumulated wisdom of the ages.

"The history of this form of art which men call calligraphy is such as to make it uniquely appropriate to the purpose of this book—appropriate that it inspire the reader to come forth once again to preserve and guard the truly cosmic knowledge and ageless wisdom contained within the pages of your book."

Lao strongly defended her reincarnation teaching to Biblical literalists who doubted its validity. She wrote Cheryl Hopper of Tampa, Florida, in early 1973, "Regarding your question, actually the Bible has many references to reincarnation, but people put their own interpretation into what they read according to their spiritual unfolding. For instance, in looking up Hebrews 9: 27, which you mention, at the bottom of the page in our Scofield Reference Edition of the Holy Bible, my eyes lit on this sentence: 'The soul and spirit live, independently of the death of the body, which is described as a "tabernacle" (tent), in which the "I" dwells, and which may be put off' (2 Corinthians 5: 1-8; 1 Corinthians 15: 42-44; 2 Peter 1: 13-15).

"There are other sentences in this interpretation at the bottom of the page, and all speak loudly of reincarnation. A number of our minister students from orthodox denominations are now reading my new book on reincarnation, *Why You Cannot Die!* One minister of a First Christian Church (Disciples of Christ) wrote the following about it: 'There was not one word in it that was not truth. If I had the money, I'd buy enough copies to give to everyone I know and put one in every library in the world.'"

Lao advised students that when one lived a long life, one's self desired a longer rest period in the light of God before unfolding in another body. She stressed that God works with us constantly, and that in reincarnation it was "a Soul's deep desire that unfolds a new cycle in a new body."

At Christmas 1972, Lao sent out more than 30,000 printed messages and hundreds of handwritten letters. She also inscribed thousands of copies of her new book.

Winter was difficult on the mountain, and Lao felt badly in need of a vacation. She wrote Emelia, "My heart is pounding away all day and all night, and I am aware the altitude does not help! Perhaps a miracle will happen and I can get away in a week or so. Guy has not written or called.

"Perhaps this is the way God wants it! When I think of all that has happened, I cry inside, but then I know if all were right, things would be smooth and beautiful. Pat is not as well as she should be too, and that makes leaving difficult, also. If I could only be strong as in the past, but my poor old body is wearing low."

On New Year's Eve 1972, Neva Dawkins's review of *Why You Cannot Die!* appeared in the Huntsville, Alabama, *Times*. Neva had studied at Swannanoa during Walter's summer courses in the early 1950s, and later gave Lao a virtual transcript of his lectures from that time. Her brief review succinctly summarized the Russell Message in a single paragraph: "The Russells are internationally known for a distinctive body of philosophy relating to the science of man. The universal laws of rhythmic balanced interchange basic to the Russell Cosmogony are restated in this volume, particularly as they apply to the continuity of life or the reincarnation principle, which is shown to parallel all the myriad examples of repetitious life cycles evident in the world about us. Man is idea. Idea cannot die. Man's body manifests ideas by eternally changing and eternally repeating. Eternal changing, eternally repeated, can have no end. Bodies, therefore, cannot die, for eternal change, eternally repeated, is an ageless continuity which, like the mind of God itself never began and can never end." The review stimulated sales of Lao's last book throughout the Southeast.

Lao learned from J. Paul Getty's secretary that the capitalist and philanthropist had read *Why You Cannot Die!* with interest. Henry C. Mulberger, the Raytheon scientist and longtime Russell student, considered the book "the most complete and comprehensive work on science and metaphysics" he had ever read. A number of readers wrote that *Why You Cannot Die!* was the capstone of all the Russell writings.

A December windstorm had severely damaged all but the superstructure of the base of the Christ statue. In January 1973, a seeming miraculous week of unseasonably warm weather allowed Sam Spicher and his helper, Benjamin Baer, the opportunity to replace and repair the supporting masonry and restore the lofty pedestal to its original proportion. Little more than a month later Sam and Martha Spicher again drove Lao to Florida.

On February 24, Lao arrived safely in Palm Beach for much-needed time away from her extremely heavy schedule at Swannanoa. She stayed with her old friend Hildegarde, now Mrs. Carl Meibes. Hildegarde immediately took Lao to her homeopathic doctor. "He took a cardiograph of my heart. My blood pressure is high, and that is one cause of the fast heartbeat. I shall not know the results of the tests he took until next week. He is testing a list of things from my blood. He is a Mexican and treats only with homeopathic medicine."

Hildegarde was a fantastic cook, but she put Lao on a five-day fast on fruit and vegetable juice alone. "She says her own blood pressure went down on this so I pray this will happen to me! I wish that I could tell you I feel fine but perhaps I shall be able to in a few weeks," Lao wrote Emelia.

Lao told her friend she spent an extremely happy day reading *Siddartha* by Thomas Mann, a book that Hildegarde had recommended. "I enjoyed it more than anything I have read in a long time and I thought of you constantly as I read. How clear it explains the thoughts of mankind today. Man has so far to go to even bring a semblance of Balance on earth. One hears one unhappy story after another."

Lao's own books were favorably reviewed in the March 1973 issue of *Murmuring*, published monthly by the Center for Truth in Portland, Oregon. Its editor, Charles Detloff, quoted the Russells often. Walter and his work were described in an article titled "Silent Partner" in the February 1973 issue of *Guideposts*. This prompted Sergeant E. L. Allen, who was featured on the cover and in the first article in the December 1972 *Guideposts*, to write Lao, telling her that he was successfully using her book *Love* to bridge the gap between prison authority and the sixty-five hard-core killers among the inmates for whom he was responsible. He was the head correctional officer at one of the largest prisons in the country, and several years before had heard Lao speak on love at a Unity Church. He told her the experience had changed his whole life. A top official in the Beverly Hills, California, police department wrote that he was using the Russell teachings in his master training plan for the academy he ran for all new officers.

Lao was in communication with United States Senator Mike Gravel of

Alaska, who referred to *Atomic Suicide?* in a statement included in the Congressional Record. She told Richard Dulaney that she and Senator Gravel had discussed the Frankenstein monster America was creating by its growing use of atomic fission and had agreed that the nation was sitting on top of a powder keg. They both feared that some error of judgment or careless act could destroy the whole world.

Professor Enoch Palm, a mathematician on the faculty of the University of Oslo, Norway, obtained Lao's public support in opposing the building of two nuclear reactors in Norway. She was appalled by the human lack of care for the environment. "To save the planet has been my greatest concern for many years," she wrote Bud and Carmen Mushier of the Today Church in Dallas, Texas. Lao also spoke regularly with Dr. Ernest Sternglass of Pittsburgh, who was leading the fight to convince the Atomic Energy Commission to halt the proliferation of atomic reactors in America. Larry Bopart had introduced Dr. Sternglass to *Atomic Suicide?* years before. Dr. Sternglass had single-handedly taken on the scientific establishment throughout the western world. He told Lao, "I have never had any doubt that we have grossly underestimated the dangers of radiation."

The problem of nuclear waste was also a constant worry to Lao. Twenty-one of the fifty American atomic reactor plants had been closed temporarily for investigation and repair for leakage. The weekly news magazines featured prominent articles on the difficulties in storing such waste, and Lao heard firsthand from a French colleague of similar concerns shared by Jacques-Yves Cousteau. She often warned students that Walter had repeatedly said there was not an element in the world that could contain atomic fission or atomic waste indefinitely, and that sooner or later it would seep through any type of container that was used.

A leading mechanical engineer wrote to Lao with the following endorsement: "*Atomic Suicide?* is a cosmic classic, which should be compulsory reading for all scientists as well as all others who are capable of grasping the tremendous import of every truth expressed therein. It has certainly confirmed a number of my beliefs and informed me of many other facets of nuclear fission of which I had never even thought."

By March, Lao was staying with her friend Alice Touchberry on Worth Avenue in Palm Beach. Miss Touchberry was a Florida registered nurse, whose patented interlavage unit had helped Lao regain her strength. She brought the talented healer and her invention to the attention of Dr. Timothy A. Binder, her colleague and friend in Boulder, Colorado, who had distributed hundreds of copies of the Russell books through his eminent Chiropractic and Naturopathic practice. He ordered *The Man Who Tapped the Secrets of the Universe* by the hundreds and also recommended *My Experiences Preceding 5,000 Burials*, the classic book by Hamid Bey, the great Coptic mystic. Dr. Binder's own book, *Position Technic*, in which he outlined his unique innovative healing practices, was widely circulated, and he also sought to perpetuate the interlavage technique after Miss Touchberry's death.

Florrie wrote to Lao from England, "Knowing how busy you must have been with the dispatching of your books and the Christmas Message I knew you would be exhausted. When I didn't hear from you, I thought you would be winging your way to Florida for a rest in the sunshine so I wasn't surprised when your letter came saying you were there. I do hope by now you are feeling more rested and much better. I should have replied before. I was sorry to hear you have had the upset with Guy [Chipman] and that it has lasted so long." Guy Chipman soon returned to see Lao, but by now she had set aside any thought of pursuing a romantic attachment with this longtime friend.

In Florida, as at Swannanoa, Lao thirsted for quiet in which to work. "Both Doctor and I did our greatest work when we had each other," she wrote Emelia. "I did my last book because I had known love with Doctor. I thought of him strongly with every word I wrote." Yet she was lonely and told Emelia that they both needed oneness in matehood here on earth. "It is the need for matehood that brings the deepest sense of depression. I believe the cause of my physical ills lies in this need. I say this because of the ecstasy I always knew with Doctor and the great things we accomplished together that neither of us accomplished when we were alone!"

She encouraged the recently divorced Emelia to get out with people her own age. "You are young and beautiful with an intellect that should be shared. You are a little powerhouse of love and spiritual awareness, and the world around you needs your light, and you need the balancing love of another light." She wrote Emelia that a minister had tried to kindle a romantic interest in her, "but he is not my type—at all!"

By April 14, 1973, Lao was back at Swannanoa and addressed a large church group from Washington. Soon Judge Martin arranged another meeting at Swannanoa, at which Lao addressed eighteen influential court officers and other judicial personnel from Norfolk and Richmond. They all expressed a desire to use the Russell teachings to stem the growing tide of crime and violence in Virginia. "This is going to take time, of course, but it will be the beginning of nationwide exposure to our work in regard to the number one problem of the country," Lao wrote.

Paul Lojnikov sent Lao copies of the Portuguese translation of *God Will Work with You but Not for You*, which had been published in Brazil on April 20. He described his success in promoting her work there, and emphasized the need for her to attract film or television attention in all parts of the world, adding, "I understand that you don't like publicity and propaganda, but it is essential in order for your precious work to be spread more and more."

In late summer she left Swannanoa for two weeks on the Carolina coast. Some students, who had met Guy Chipman on his previous travels as driver and escort on her lecture tours, inquired as to the progress of his proposed book about Lao, *A Universe to Share*, but she advised them that he had never completed it. That summer, the nationwide shortage of gasoline greatly affected tourism in Virginia, but Swannanoa welcomed many groups and a number of special visitors. Book sales were greater than ever, and the demands on Lao's time were unrelenting. Sam and Martha Spicher drove her to Far Hills, New Jersey, for several weeks of rest at Emelia Lombardi's quiet and commodious retreat.

Peter and Midge Soderberg had moved to Charlottesville, where he was now associate dean of the School of Education at the University of Virginia. His wife had first come to Swannanoa with a Silva Mind Control group from Pittsburgh in November 1972, and soon proved herself to be a tremendous ambassador for the Russells' work. She told Lao that her life had never been the same since the day she first came to Swannanoa.

In November Lao ordered an additional 10,000 copies of *God Will Work with You but Not for You* and *Love*, and 2,000 copies of the new edition of *The Universal One*. It had taken courage for Lao to reprint *The Universal One*. Walter had expressed his feeling that the 1926 book had been succeeded by his later *Cosmogony* and *The Secret of Light*. In the new edition, Lao explained in a special notation, "In the interim between the writing of *The Universal One* from 1921-1926, to 1947, when *The Secret of Light* was released—and also our book, entitled *Atomic Suicide?* published in 1957—Dr. Russell's thoughts and awareness matured in expression and he clarified and rectified errors he felt that he had committed in his earlier writings."

Curtis Wallace told her he had been present when a scientist gladly paid at an auction $6,000 for a copy of the 1926 edition of *The Universal One*, of which the reprint was an exact copy.

Again in 1973, she was too busy to issue a general Christmas message. In late October, Skyline-Swannanoa, Inc., had proposed a new lease for the palace. Essentially, it reflected the practice the parties had been following over the years. The gross admission receipts would be divided between the parties. The University would bear all repair, utility, maintenance, liability insurance, and personnel expenses. The lease was unassignable and had a one-year extension provision.

John Lombardi reviewed it and asked for an automatic year-to-year renewal unless prior notice was given by either party of an intention not to renew. He also asked that the University be given a right of first refusal that would allow it to purchase the premises in the event the owner received an acceptable bona fide offer to buy it.

These provisions were not acceptable to Skyline-Swannanoa, Inc. The owners hinted to Lao that the International Playboy Club had expressed an interest in the property. She felt as if she had no alternative but to sign the lease as presented. It was to take effect January 1, 1974.

In the meantime, on November 11, she left for Florida with Guy Chipman to look for possible winter headquarters for the University. A month later she was back at Swannanoa and reported to Emelia that their search had been fruitless.

By April 1974, she had received delivery of a thirty-minute documentary filmed at Swannanoa that included a talk by her and testimonies by several students of all ages. Albert Ashe, the previous owner of *Pathe News*, had produced it for her after coming to Swannanoa and hearing her speak extemporaneously to a group of visitors. Her book *Love* had greatly impressed him. He told her that if it could be distributed around the world by the millions, it alone could save the world.

In May 1974, Lao left Swannanoa for several days' vacation at the beach, but returned to the palace before the board of directors met there in June. Emelia could not attend the meeting, but the Hawkinses and Mr. Perry were present. Lao was pleased to report that the reprinted edition of *The Universal One* had been well received, and that both the fourth edition of *God Will Work with You but Not for You* and the third edition of *Love* were selling briskly. She described the success study groups in Delaware and Puerto Rico had experienced in attracting new interest in their work.

Lao also told them that she had written lyrics to a new song, "Stand Up for God," with music by Marie Dunn and Bill Pape. It was to be published later in the year. They had been inspired by Walter's Four Freedoms sculpture and hoped that the triumphant anthem would be popular during the national bicentennial. The Four Freedoms sculpture figures, which had been located at the former entrance to Swannanoa, had recently been placed in the nooks of the fountain at the base of the gardens.

Emelia was concerned about Lao's declining energy and urged her to watch her diet more carefully and increase her intake of vitamins and brewer's yeast. Lao often expressed the wish that she were twenty years younger and more able to keep up with the demands of her work. She began to watch her diet and thereafter used brewer's yeast as a regular dietary supplement. She often quoted *Vansant's Discourses*, a European vegetarian diet source. She found the vegetarian diet preferable, because she knew the truth of the maxim "You are what you eat." Even more important, she said, was the inescapable fact that "You become what you think."

It amused Emelia that people were always so observant when they were with Lao. Long afterwards, they could describe what she wore, what she looked like, and what she ate. Lao pressed her students to follow a diet that kept their cholesterol at a safe level. Lao corresponded with H. H. Matz of

Mesa, Arizona, regarding his hydroponic unit for sprouting grains, seeds, and herbs. She told him that these unprocessed foods had enabled her to keep Walter in good health for so many years. She was feeling much better herself and remembered how the diet she had prepared for Walter had rejuvenated him and given him many additional years of life. "He was on a very poor diet when I met him," she told friends.

Lao was still in contact with Forrest Griffith, who had mixed medicinal herbs for Walter in the early years of their marriage. She often met with her friend A. P. Thomson, an orchardist from Front Royal, Virginia, and other members of the Virginia Association of Biological Farmers.

Pressed to describe her diet, she wrote a student in Hollywood, "I have been a vegetarian on and off all of my life, but now there are times when I feel the need for a little meat. I do enjoy and feel that all good vegetables and fruits are good for one, and when eating salads—or meat—I always like onions and garlic."

Students of Dr. Ann Wigmore, whose dietary work with the Hippocrates Health Institute had brought her national attention, often came to Swannanoa. Dr. Wigmore was one of Lao's personal friends, and had frequently been her guest at the palace over the years. Lao greatly admired the work Dr. Wigmore was doing to bring greater health to millions of people.

Lao cautioned those who had difficulty in curtailing the habit of smoking tobacco: "The reason you have not been able to control your smoking habit or any other destructive habit is because you only read words concerning the destructive effects of smoking. When you truly know the cause you will stop at once. We only live that which we know!"

Lao knew that many members of Alcoholics Anonymous had been among her students, and that many heavy smokers had stopped smoking and drinking when studying the *Home Study Course*. She felt that excesses of any kind indicate a deeper need than either alcohol or nicotine, and knew that the deeper need is for man to know who he is and what he is and the desire to know and fulfill his true purpose on earth, which is to discover his divinity and live it. She often related how Aubrey Perry had told her that he was an alcoholic on his first visit to Swannanoa in the early 1950s, adding, "He, today, tells the story that when he was leaving, I put my hand on his shoulder and said, 'You know, Mr. Perry, you need never take another drink!' He never did, and since that moment and has done great work for the Alcoholics Anonymous movement on a national basis." This was by no means the only alcoholic she had directly helped, but he always told her that through him she had forcefully, if indirectly, helped thousands of alcoholics. Mr. Perry resigned in 1977, after eight years on the board, because of a need to reduce his extensive commitments.

In 1974, University of Virginia Professors James S. Payne, Cecil D. Mercer, and Michael H. Epstein published a book titled *Education and Rehabilitation Techniques*. It was dedicated to "Clare W. Graves for theory, Jeffrey D. Chaffin for application, and Lao Russell for inspiration." In the preface is the statement, "We are indebted to Lao Russell, President of the University of Science and Philosophy, Swannanoa, Waynesboro, Virginia, for her inspiration. Her graciousness consistently generated renewed life within the authors." On page twenty-six, the authors wrote, "The life and work of Walter Russell as reported by Glenn Clark (1946) provide many illustrations of the type of thinking which is derived from meditation and is inherent in an eight-lever existence." In Dr. James S. Payne's class at the University of Virginia, Clark's book *The Man Who Tapped the Secrets of the Universe* was required reading.

In late August, Lao left Swannanoa to deliver a series of lectures in North Carolina. The next month she received a group of longtime students from the Aquarian Age Yoga Center in Virginia Beach, Virginia, and helped them arrange an October yoga retreat near Swannanoa. In mid-November she left for Florida for rest and interviews, and did not return until shortly before Christmas. She stayed with William and Sue Goza in Madeira Beach, Florida.

A minister from the Mind-Life Fellowship surprised her with criticism of her celebrating Christmas because of the alleged pagan origin of the holiday. She replied that she endorsed Christmas because it was a time when people express love. "I might also add that this world is still pagan for as long as one man is killed, it will be pagan!" she emphasized.

As the holiday came, Lao recalled the large Christmas gatherings that she and Walter had hosted for students at Swannanoa in the past. "I trust that one Christmas in the future we can again have another lovely gathering for students and friends," she wrote Emelia.

CHAPTER TWENTY-THREE

Giving Every Moment (1975-76)

On February 2, 1975, the *Staunton News Leader* ran an extensive, complimentary, but superficial feature story titled "Lao Russell, Mistress of Swannanoa Palace." It described her making tea "the English way with tea leaves and poured through a strainer into fine china cups, sweetening the tea with honey and adding milk." She did not consider white sugar or coffee healthy and neither was used at Swannanoa Palace. Occasionally she enjoyed a cup of a grain-based coffee substitute, but she much preferred tea. She told the reporter, "Once in a while I enjoy a glass of champagne, but only one glass."

Thousands of miles away in Hawaii, Phillip Yee was still spreading the University's scientific and philosophical teachings and obtaining far more substantial publicity. His articles, "Balance in All" and "Ozone or Aerosol" were given prominent coverage in the *Honolulu Advertiser* during March 1975 and publicized the Russells' long-espoused fear that the buildup of fluorocarbons may be causing destruction of the upper atmosphere, which blocks out much of the potentially cancer-causing ultraviolet radiation from the sun.

Citing the Russells, Yee wrote, "The sun is the seed of our solar system's creation, and contains the whole record of earth's creation. The various layers of our atmosphere are the spherical system of curvature that constitute the Creator's lenses that project the sun's rays to refold and unfold our earth's cycles of creation. This it does through the rhythmic balanced interchange processes of gravity and radiation; compression and expansion; condensation and evaporation; growth and decay; life and death.

"The Creator's spherical and radial systems of curvature control the shape and form of every particle of growth which unfolds into any species of body into its proper pattern. An understanding of the Russell Cosmogony will give one insight to the Creator's processes and emphasize how vitally important it is that man should emulate nature and maintain a proper balance in all of his activities."

On March 15, the *Honolulu Star Bulletin* published Yee's commentary on the same subjects. His key point was as follows: "Nuclear power and fossil fuel employ energy of the radioactive or 'death' half of Nature's energy cycle. Its unbalanced use will continue to endanger our environment. The Russell Cosmogony explains Nature's manner of multiplying both generoactivity and radioactivity. Assimilation of this new knowledge can uplift man to the higher status needed for a new civilization."

Phillip Yee sent clippings of these articles to Lao, who had already heard of their publication through a sudden increase in inquiries from Hawaii. Lao told Phillip, "There are times when I think of all of the years that I have given every second of my life to try to awaken mankind to his true purpose on earth that I feel like Lao-tze did when he left the world of man because he could take man's unawareness no longer. Then a message comes such as yours this morning, and once more I go on giving every moment."

Lao seldom released information on her date of birth or early life. She told a young college student from North Carolina, who was preparing a history project on Walter Russell, that except for the dates of her marriage (July 29, 1948), the dedication of Swannanoa (May 2, 1948), the dedication of the Christ of the Blue Ridge (July 29, 1950), and Dr. Russell's refolding (May 19, 1963), she seldom made note of the date or hour of special occasions. Her date of birth did not appear in print until after her death.

Nevertheless, as an English-born, naturalized American, Lao was proud to have been selected for inclusion in the Bicentennial Edition of *Who's Who in America*. She was requested to state in a few sentences the source of her personal success in life and wrote the following, which was included with her sparse biographical data: "Love is the key to all success and eternal happiness, for Love is Cause and is expressed in the inviolate law of Rhythmic Balanced Interchange. This law, in individual and collective action, will ultimately lead to man's fulfillment, which is to live the Brotherhood of Man and know Heaven on Earth. Knowing the Source of all things and of my Oneness with the Creator and my fellow man—and with all things else—is the secret of my personal success."

She had been included in the first edition of *Who's Who of American Women* in 1956, and twenty-two years later would be ranked in *Who's Who in the World*. Dr. Russell had been included in the *International Who's Who* and *Who's Who in America* for over sixty years before his death and thereafter in *Who Was Who in America*. He also merited a biographical article the *Encyclopedia Britannica* before it was greatly abridged for mass-marketing purposes.

In March 1975, Lao spoke to an enthusiastic audience of students and faculty at the University of Virginia, arranged by Dr. Jim Payne, who praised the rapport she had developed so instantly with what was generally a critical and difficult audience.

The next month she was keynote speaker at the first seminar of the newly established Creative Living Institute at Madison College in Harrisonburg, Virginia. She was introduced as "a radiant soul with a living philosophy to share. Both Lao and her late husband, Dr. Walter Russell, have tapped the secrets of the Universe, and she continues to dedicate her life to sharing them. This is a rare appearance for Lao and cannot be missed." Rosalind Knight, director of the Creative Living Institute, wrote her afterwards: "You were fabulous and people appreciated you very much! The spiritual aura of the group built up throughout the day and ended on a great high—thanks to your contribution." Rosalind knew how busy Lao was and that she turned down many invitations. She appreciated Lao's kind words about the future of the Creative Living Institute. It gave Rosalind inspiration as she worked as a channel to unfold spiritual creativity to her students. Pat Hall, Angela Carr, and Sam Spicher accompanied Lao to the seminar.

126. Sam Spicher, Evelyn Jones, and Sam Spicher, Jr.

The winter had exhausted Lao, and she longed for sun and rest to restore her strength. "I have been very sick again as the result of too much tension through too heavy a load!" she wrote Emelia, fearing "I guess this is the last year I can do so much whatever happens." In mid-May, Lao at last escaped for several weeks of "quiet time" before her heavy summer season began.

Students often wrote Lao to inquire about so-called "light bodies," and she always replied that they needed "a full explanation of what bodies are and what the Light within man truly is," adding, "It was to answer such questions that I wrote my book, entitled, *Why You Cannot Die!* You are confused on this subject because you do not understand the scientific principle of life itself, nor do you understand how 'everything is of everything else that is.'"

She was asked whether it was a good idea to pursue extra-sensory perception and other psychic phenomena. These subjects intrigued many of her students, but Lao believed such matters were better off left alone.

Lao frequently stated that although she did not believe in the mystical significance of natural phenomena, she could not help being curious about the recurring rainbow in the sky just above the palace. In 1974, either she or her friends or members of her staff saw a rainbow over Swannanoa seven times, always on a fair day, most recently on Christmas Day, when the phenomenon appeared to come straight down from the heavens to hover over the palace. She was intrigued but not entirely persuaded when a longtime resident from the Afton area near Swannanoa told her that an unusual light had seemed to bathe the mountain on the very morning in November 1904 when Lao was born far away in Ivinghoe, England.

Lao definitely rejected extreme forms of spiritualism. Paul Lonjinov asked her if it were possible for dead people to talk to the living. She replied, "It is not possible in the way that people do on this planet, Earth, but it is possible for you or anyone to tune in to the soul record in the Mind of a soul either in this world or in the one Light-Mind of God."

She reassured Paul that no disincarnated soul could hurt an individual who was living God's ways and processes as expressed in his inviolate Law of Love (Rhythmic Balanced Interchange). She was distressed that some of his friends in Brazil were asking him to sponsor a demonstration of black magic. "It is well to leave such things alone," she told him, "and no one knowing God's ways and processes would desire such phenomena."

She was asked if she believed the devil existed. "This is too big a subject to go into in less than a full book," she replied. "Suffice it to say, man's senses often produce experiences which demonstrate devilish thoughts and actions!"

Interest in witchcraft was reviving in many quarters. Lao termed it "something beyond my awareness, for I know nothing of witchcraft and have always thought of this as something not to be considered as Truth. The one way to protect one's self and family against such people," she added, "is not to have any relationship with them whatsoever. The whole experience is definitely not in accord with God's inviolate Law of Love (Rhythmic Balanced Interchange)."

Donald Lawrence, a film and television producer, came to ask her help in producing a series of specials focusing on man's efforts to gain control of his inner mind power. The series would deal with many forms that the attempt to control mind power had taken, including witchcraft, voodoo, and more modern metaphysical beliefs. The series would approach the subject from an informative as well as an historical viewpoint, and Mr. Lawrence argued that it would be very salable as well as educational. Lao encouraged him to study the *Home Study Course*, believing that it would spare him the effort of exploring false claims, and enable him directly to educate and guide his viewers to realizing their own potential through personal study of the new science on their own.

She was bombarded with questions in every mail. One reader posited the following queries: "You say sin and evil do not exist, but I see it every day. You mention sinful thoughts and evil ways that drive love away. This is a big stumbling block for me. What about the rise in black magic, witchcraft and Satan worship? Pornography and abortion are rising, and I can hardly believe what I read in the daily newspaper. It seems as though the world is going mad. Some people go from cult to cult searching for the truth, and have the Messiah complex. Please explain what this complex is. Just recently I was at our Planetarium, and they have just discovered Quasars and neutron stars, but do not know what they are. Can you tell me?" Patiently she referred the inquirer to the *Home Study Course* and the Russell books, where through careful study, she assured him, he would be led to the answers to all of his questions.

Lao was very defensive when writers questioned why she seemed to deviate from the precise language Jesus Christ had used. By now she was at ease in replying that this was a creating universe and not a created universe. She felt that God had sent the world new knowledge to equip people to handle the problems of today. "Jesus Christ came on earth to teach man the same lesson we are now endeavoring to teach in man's language of today. If Jesus had tried to teach man what Love and Light truly are, he would undoubtedly have been crucified in three days, not three years."

A Silva Mind Control graduate mentioned the difference between the fundamentalist Christian, who takes all of Christ's words in the Bible literally to prove his chosen religion, and the metaphysician, who explains how Christ's words proved that he understood and manifested the immutable laws of the universe. He asked Lao, "Since Satan, Hell, and eternal punishment are man's own inventions, what was Christ's meaning when He repeatedly spoke of all these horrors? Throughout the gospels, Christ refers to Satan, the devil, and the judgment of Hell. Why? Are these particular statements misquotes? Is my reasoning unsound?"

Lao's reply was succinct: "It is always well to remember that not anything was written that was purportedly said by Jesus until some two hundred years after his death. Also, always remember that Jesus was God's Messenger of Love. I would like you to read in the *Encyclopedia Britannica* what was written under the heading of the Bible. There were many changes made, including additions and deletions. I do not personally believe that Christ Jesus ever talked of Satan, the devil, or the judgment of Hell for he knew that man was on earth to unfold in God-awareness. That is why every experience one has is a good experience, for from every experience one learns something. Jesus may have used the words 'sin' and 'punishment' in his day instead of cause and effect for the people of his day were not as ready for Truth as many are today."

At times, her writings on Christ Consciousness confused readers. To Lao the term implied ultimate awareness of the "God-Light" within. "Jesus had this complete awareness, and some far day all mankind will unfold in complete Christ Consciousness, as did Jesus," she believed.

Lao said she was always happy to meet a scientist who professed to be a Christian, "for truly Jesus proved how great a scientist he was when he told mankind that God was Light and God was Love."

Lao always reminded those who took the Biblical Jesus too literally, "When Jesus was on earth, he said, 'I have yet many things to say unto you, but ye cannot bear them now.' Man is now not so new, and many are ready to accept the how and why of Creation itself."

The board met at Swannanoa on June 11, 1975. Lao gave a confidential report about scientists who had come to Swannanoa to tell her of their progress in the transmutation of metals, according to the principles outlined in the Russell books on science, thereby uniting the modern scientific approach with recognition of God's natural law. Many students had written to ask the names of scientists or physicists who had given form to the Russell scientific principles. Most of those who had put the cosmogony in practice asked her to respect their privacy, but frequently some gave her permission to use their names. Dr. Oscar L. Morphis of Fort Worth, Texas, was one such individual, and he welcomed the opportunity to discuss his special work with cells with interested parties. Walter Baumgartner of Magdalena, New Mexico, used the Russell theories in his work. He had visited Swannanoa and examined many of Walter Russell's laboratory notes.

Lao outlined her contacts with prison officials throughout the country, many of whom reported marked rehabilitation of hardcore inmates after they had been introduced to the University's teachings.

127. Lao with Pat Hall.

Pat Hall, who had long been Lao's mainstay on the palace staff, was suffering from serious foot problems and feared she could not long remain on staff. When she was compelled to retire after more than twelve years of service, Lao praised her as the best hostess she had ever had at Swannanoa.

In August, Lao received a visit from an orthodox Muslim prince, who bought five of the Russell books and wrote her a week later, "I have been up every night since, reading them until 3:00 and 4:00 in the morning."

Although Lao took delight in addressing civic clubs in Waynesboro, Staunton, and the surrounding area, she seldom participated in large conferences any more. An exception to this rule occurred on October 7, 1975, when she spoke to a large audience before the Divine Science Federation International during a three-day retreat at Airlie House in Warrenton, Virginia, on the subject of healing through prayer.

Cozy Baker, a popular southern writer, had read Lao's books and was knowledgeable about the work at Swannanoa. She included a chapter on Lao in her 1975 book, *Cozy Getaway*, which Lao considered somewhat inaccurate but basically inspiring. Four years later, Miss Baker based two chapters in her *Holiday Frame of Mind* on Swannanoa, but Lao felt she had failed to emphasize the University's Message. Nonetheless, the exuberant Ms. Baker was eager to see Lao adapt the *Home Study Course* for children, a project that was unfortunately never undertaken.

Lao spent a quiet Christmas holiday. Guy Chipman joined her for several days at Swannanoa. By New Year's, Lao had not been able to find a satisfactory replacement for Pat Hall, whose retirement had left a noticeable void in the palace staff. Florrie consoled Lao, writing her, "I do hope you can soon get permanent help. I know how wearing temporary help can be. I know how you must miss Pat Hall. It was obvious to me she put her whole soul into her work. Such people are very rare today." Within two months Lao was able to write her friends that she had "good help now, including two excellent young men, a mature woman secretary, a willing and lovely young girl, and other good occasional help." Nonetheless, she would always miss the gracious presence of the lovely and capable Pat Hall.

In January 1976, a major television network spent five hours at Swannanoa filming and interviewing Lao. This was the *P.M. Magazine* interview that she long used in connection with palace tours.

Lao often enjoyed reviewing Walter's early correspondence and work. It pleased her greatly when a student sent her an early and profusely illustrated brochure depicting the Hotel des Artistes, one of the famous buildings that Walter had designed in New York, telling her, "I thought you would enjoy seeing the swimming pool and the other pictures, not to mention its historical value." This led Lao to a rereading of Christopher Morley's *Parnassus on Wheels*, which she and Walter had enjoyed together. Lao treasured the following quotation from Christopher Morley: "If we discovered that we had only five minutes left to say all we wanted to say, every telephone booth would be occupied by people calling other people to stammer that they loved them. Why wait until the last five minutes?"

Students from as far away as Sweden enrolled in the course and bought Russell books after reading information on the octave wave principle and the book *Atomic Suicide?* in a publication called *The New Age Science Journal*.

A new International Age of Character Club had been formed in Nigeria. Lao was delighted with the report of its inaugural meeting and distributed the minutes among the University's students. It proved helpful to others in both countries as they worked to expand the movement.

She received many course enrollments from the Philippines. The Science of Mind Center in Manila promoted the *Home Study Course* along with its own seminar, which over 6,000 students had completed within the first three years.

A woman chiropractor in Paris, France, enrolled in the course after many years of studying macrobiotics with students of George Ohsawa and reviewing the Tao. She wrote Lao that she had found in the *Home Study Course* "the linking chain which is the real illumination," and thanked her for giving cosmic knowledge to humanity, offering to begin a study group in Paris if she could obtain a French translation of the course.

Baroness Hella von dem Bussche wrote her from Munich, Germany, urging her to pursue a program of translating the course and books into German. The Baroness's daughter had visited Lao at Swannanoa. Lao had always felt that there would be a great thirst for the Russell teachings in Germany. In later years, Dagmar Neubronner would translate into German *The Man Who Tapped the Secrets of the Universe*, *The Secret of Light*, and other Russell works.

She received reports from a student in Israel who was making good progress in his project of placing Lao's *Code of Ethics* in every youth hostel in his country, after which he intended to do the same thing in South Africa and possibly Europe.

Her longtime Arizona student Minette Crow went to Portugal with her husband and discussed the Russells' work at length with the scholar and genius Don Luis de Castro e Almeida at the Castle de Milfontes.

An English businessman in Washington wrote Lao that he had told the Lord Bishop of Liverpool in England that he had never known and loved two more truly Christian people than Walter and Lao.

Dr. Peter Stevens, who had met Lao through Paul in Brazil, was actively promoting the new paperback edition of *God Will Work with You but Not for You* throughout Australia, New Zealand, and Asia. Harold Oliver also promoted the Russell books in Australia, and met a number of Lao's students in Sydney at a 1973 Psychical Research meeting. He had visited Lao at Swannanoa in 1972 and hoped to return soon.

Her Bombay student H. S. Ureskar had long urged her to take the lead in creating a United Religions organization similar to the United Nations. He told her that a logical first step to accomplishing this would be for Swannanoa to sponsor a Parliament of World Religions similar to the one that had brought the great Vivekananda to America in 1893. He also reiterated his longstanding invitation to her to visit India, "the land of Lord Krishna whose song celestial, the *Bhavagad Gita*, has inspired and influenced you considerably." He told her that like Napoleon, Lao had had to turn back from Egypt on her way to India, but he told her he was certain she could achieve what Napoleon could not, "because you are coming not to destroy but to build a bridge of friendship and a highway of understanding between the two great nations." She responded that she longed to visit him in India, but her health and schedule would not allow her to make the journey.

Students and visitors sought her advice on virtually every aspect of the human condition, and she seemed always ready to dispense her thoughtful and pertinent wisdom, despite the pressure of her busy schedule.

She took pleasure in making detailed suggestions as to how loving parents could use the Russell principles in preparing their preschool children to interact in school and face the outside world. As parents took the *Home Study Course*, Lao advised them, "Know that your child will be absorbing your thoughts and way of life constantly and this will give him a tremendous fulcrum of knowing as he spreads his own wings in the great world. Constantly tell him how God does everything with him and that this invisible power is something that he can know even though he cannot see it—only the expression of it in the beauty and balance which can be seen in every manifestation of Nature. Show him the beautiful butterflies—how their wings are equal and centered from their fulcrum—as he is centered from God's fulcrum. Teach him the male-female principle that is illustrated even in the lock and key. Always illustrate the beauty of the male-female principle of balance. As your child matures into adulthood, he will think of the beauty and balance of all of life and live his life reverently. There are countless illustrations one can give to a child of how God does everything with him."

Parents often wrote her that they had problems with young children who were not being challenged in the public education system. The mother of a seven-year-old wrote that her daughter was a bright and unusual child, yet she was beaten down, repressed, and bored. She formerly drew a lot, pictures with many suns, flowers, trees, and animals, all of which had smiling faces, even the clouds. Now her clouds had scribble marks all over them. Lao suggested the parents use the lessons in her book *Love*, and when they did, they achieved good results. They urged her to author a home study course especially for children.

Lao was acutely aware of humanity's need for mind motivation, particularly the great need to create a desire to work in employees. She wrote an industrialist, "It is the lack of putting love into what workers do that is the cause of such poor workmanship today, and unless we create a desire to work in man, the economy, itself, will fall flat on its face. Industry has the greatest opportunity to be the savior of the world for without the interchange of products, there would be no economy." She advised another student that what he feared, a dual personality in himself, was in fact a habit of "voiding the happy, positive you with negative, frustrated feelings."

She encouraged students who were lonely: "Although I cannot write you at length at this time, I would like you to know at this time of your great loneliness that my love is strongly extended to you.

"I would also like to urge you that whenever you are feeling especially lonely to rest your thoughts on the fact that God centers your whole being. When you can become fully aware of the God-Light, all sense of 'aloneness' will fade away. One's sole purpose on earth is to become aware of this Oneness with God, and that is why every experience in your life is truly purposeful and ultimately leads you to the fulfillment of your divine purpose."

A letter to a particularly depressed inquirer reveals Lao's encouraging approach:

> I wish I could talk to you for a little while for I know how your deep hurts have created a great sense of frustration and fear. Dear one, know first that in spite of everything that you are an extension of God. Do not let your frustrations and fears lead to self-hate. See every experience as teaching you something—that 'something' is true values.
>
> Instead of seeking companionship in emotions, seek it in aloneness with God for awhile. At first you will feel lonely but after a while you will feel the ecstasy of Oneness with the God-presence.
>
> Think of that old English saying, "The nearer the dawn, the darker the night—and in going wrong all things come right." Wonderful things will unfold for you. First, you must clear the slate in your own thinking. Think of your experiences as stepping-stones. Every Soul in this life—or past lives—has been through every difficult (and bad) experience imaginable. It is never too late to start anew. Every moment can be a new beginning.

Tension in the world seemed to Lao to have risen to epidemic proportion. Many correspondents and visitors asked her for her views on suicide after they had lost a friend or loved one in this way. She knew how to reassure a person after they had experienced the greatest of losses. "Losing a parent is always a traumatic experience whether there has been a close relationship or not, but this, too, is part of a soul's unfolding into the Light of God and teaches one much of self-reliance," she wrote. "A divorce, also, is a very traumatic experience because one does not marry in the first place without deep feeling for the mate. However, this experience teaches one that unless there is a balanced spiritual and mental unfolding of both, the 'partnership' becomes unbalanced and there is born a desire for a change."

She often explained the loss of loved ones to their grieving relatives: "actually, there is no such thing as death since everything is of everything else that is. Regarding death of the body, when one—as we say—dies, the elements of the body return to the earth and to the heavens from whence they came, and the soul returns to the Source. It was to clarify these statements that I wrote my book, *Why You Cannot Die!*"

She told another, "It matters now that we understand our eternal oneness in each other. The great void is heartbreaking, sometimes for several years. However, in the silence of God's Love there gradually comes a healing and someday I know that you will be able to relive moments you have shared without the great grief you know today."

Those who prematurely lost a loved one often wondered why good people seemed to die young. Lao explained that each life brings man the opportunity to advance one step further in unfolding his soul. The good person dying young had doubtless accomplished what he had come to Earth to do either for himself or for another.

Disabled or handicapped individuals who could not accept their physical limitations often asked her for help. In 1975, Lao clearly outlined her feelings about such a situation: "The frustration you experience with your physical condition would disappear with awareness of the God-Light that centers you. One's body is an inanimate thing. The life within one's body is the God-Light that centers it. You will have a further explanation of this in *God Will Work with You but Not for You*.

"I can give you no better illustration of the foregoing statement than the illustration of the awareness which Gil Sonastine so gloriously demonstrated in his life. Gil had polio as a young man and for more than forty years he could only speak and hear. His body was completely paralyzed and he could not see, and yet he started a great movement for shut-ins, wrote inspirational articles, and was completely self-supporting, paying a secretary to help him with written work and a nurse who saw to his physical needs. When Dr. Russell and I went to see him on our honeymoon, his voice was full of joy, and during a conversation with him, he said he would 'rather have his body and know God as he did than have a perfect body and not know God.'"

To a nursing professional, who felt unfulfilled in her work and found hospitals depressing, Lao stressed the fact that more than anyone else on earth, people who are sick need love. She told the nurse that she should find inordinate satisfaction in giving the kind of love her patients needed to allay their frustration and tension.

Her advice to teenagers was always unique. "I thoroughly understand your problem, for yours is the problem of many young people of both sexes," she wrote one young girl who felt inadequate on a date. "Do not be discouraged because you have not met the special boy at this time.

"When I was your age I had many boys who wanted me to be their one girl, but if I went out with them once and was bored with their conversation,

I would not go out again with that particular one. This did not mean that they were not wonderful young men—for someone else.

"As far as being a tomboy, I was that, too, and that was why I had so much fun with boys of my own age."

The *Love* book prompted many questions from young people who were caught in the middle of the sexual revolution sweeping the western world. A fourteen-year-old boy asked whether he should insist on having sex with his girlfriend when he felt certain he loved her, and, more specifically, how could someone know whether or not he actually loved a person. Lao replied by answering his last question first: "When you truly love a person, you know deep within your heart and soul and you will put that person's feelings before your own. You say that you have a girlfriend who has a dream of being a virgin until she becomes married and that you respect her feelings but feel that it is alright to have sex before marriage. My first answer answers this question." She added, "At such a tender age of fourteen, there are many reasons why sex can bring all kinds of complications and obligations that one so young could not comfortably handle. Also, remember that bodies do not love each other, they only sense each other, and so often when the senses are satisfied, there is a terrible emptiness that people feel unless they have love with sex."

On July 13, 1976, Lao wrote to a student in Edmonds, Washington, "Your answer to the one who asked you about oral sexuality was a good one! The great tragedy regarding any or all sex practices has been born from the fact that man has been taught that sex was sinful. My answer to all of the confusion and untruths about sex being sinful is that sex is God's Holy Law of Creation. To say that sex is sin is like saying the Creator, Himself, is sinful for without sex there would be no form.

"If sex had been understood for what it truly is—God's Holy Law of Creation—mankind would reverence any kind of sexual action and there would be no stigma of sin."

A student from Illinois asked Lao to comment on homosexuality. He had read the sections on sex in the second volume of the *Divine Iliad* with great interest and inquired, "If there is anything else in your's or your husband's writings that deals with this, please let me know, or if you could, please share a few words of truth with me or another book from which I could better understand this problem. I do not consider myself a homosexual but a Son of God. However many times I have had problems in dealing with these urges within me. It seems as if I cannot control them. I am a young man of twenty and have been trying to walk by the Spirit for the last five years. I feel I am beginning to level out spiritually but cannot seem to deal with this problem."

She replied at once, "I feel sure that as time passes you will be able to better control the physical aspect of your desires. As you study our writings, I feel sure you will realize that 'wholeness' and 'balance' are derived when the male-female principles are equal.

"Perhaps your greatest help at this time would come from a concentration on creativity for when one is engaged in any creative endeavor, one's thoughts are not centered on physical sex, and the inner satisfaction that comes to a creative person brings with it the accomplishment great ecstasy and fulfillment. I tell you this because I know this to be true from personal experience."

Although she made clear in many writings that she did not consider an active homosexual lifestyle as balanced or healthy as a heterosexual one, she was often sympathetic in her advice to men who asked if their lack of sexual attraction to women was abnormal. Often, she noted, this could be a matter of delayed sexual development. "I do understand your quandary, but I want you to know that there is nothing abnormal about the way you feel about girls or sex. I remember Walter Russell telling me that he matured very late in a desire for sex," she wrote an Australian student. Walter clearly thought of age in relative terms, for he had married for the first time at the age of twenty-three.

"Also," she added, "when you think of your life from the standpoint of reincarnation, it might well be that it is not in the pattern of your desire in this life to marry and have children!"

In 1987, when a twenty-four-year-old artist and writer from Northern Virginia suggested that Lao had spoken negatively about homosexuality in Chapter IV of her book *Love*, she was quick to explain her feelings on the subject: "Since I am aware of the strong power and force of the male-female principle in all unfolding Creation, I have a deep desire for this balanced male-female principle to be known and expressed in all life. However, I have no condemnation regarding homosexuality, for to me every experience is good and valuable, and in every experience we learn some valuable lessons in the school of Life."

Lao feared that many young people were confusing mere concentration with meditation, and expressed particular concern for the growing number of teenagers who seemed unable to cope with life. She expressed alarm that the suicide rate among youth was growing. On the other hand, she treasured letters she received from those who had found life's meaning through her teachings.

She constantly warned students that instead of trying to meditate, they should simply be quiet within themselves "and gradually you will realize that your Inner Voice is directing you."

Lao described her practice of often writing late into the night, adding that frequently she woke up and immediately started writing in a notebook kept beside her bed. Many times she hurriedly wrote down her thoughts in the dark without turning on a light. "When in a deep sleep," she explained, "one becomes unaware of the body and tunes in to the universal mind. This mind awareness is real knowledge. Through the process of decentration one expands into the mind universe."

She was frequently questioned as to the advisability of hypnosis. She knew that Paramhansa Yogananda had advised his students never to allow themselves to be hypnotized, but that his successors now suggested the practice was suitable if done for medical purposes. Lao believed decentration was far preferable, because it enabled the individual to remain in control of his own mind as he tuned himself into the "Universal Mind."

Despite her frequent disappointments, Lao epitomized the eternal optimist. She often told Emelia, "My heart is singing because I know God is with me, and somewhere along the line we shall come out on top!" Lao greeted every new year with joyous expectation. She wrote Peter Parker, "I believe 1973 will be the year! Of course I have always said this about every year. I remember saying it to the Joneses when they were here on New Year's, and they said, 'Lao, you always say that' with the connotation that so far it had never come true! If I had not thought that way these many years, I could not have worked on from sixteen to twenty hours a day seeking to manifest it." Emelia always seemed to give Lao added encouragement. Lao wrote to her longtime friend, "You cheer my heart so! I cannot tell you how much it means to me. There are times—and today is one of them—when I wonder how things will end. And then your brilliant light shines on me and I feel all will be right. It just takes time." Lao truly believed that ten days after Walter Russell's death, God had told her, "This time you will not fail." She likewise believed in her deepest heart that humanity itself must not fail because the earth itself was in jeopardy.

Years before, Lao had told a young girl of eleven who aspired to a theatrical career about her own background in theatre. Now the young girl was a woman and a successful actress. Her mother wrote Lao, "Your words to her were never forgotten. You told her, 'You won't always dream. You will make your dreams come true!' And you were right."

CHAPTER TWENTY-FOUR

Dramatic Impact (1976-79)

On March 20, 1976, Sam Biser, editor of *The Healthview Newsletter*, wrote her from Belmar, New Jersey: "I have some ideas on how you could logarithmically accelerate the spread of your work. I'd like to discuss them with you in a visit sometime in the next several months." That meeting would have a dramatic impact on both their lives.

The board met at Swannanoa on May 2, and later the same day the directors traveled to nearby Fredericksburg, Virginia, where at Mary Washington College they presented a bronze casting of Walter's last sculpture, the bust of George Washington, as a gift to the Commonwealth of Virginia in commemoration of the 1976 national bicentennial. Lao stressed that the bust was Walter's final message of love to the American people, and dedicated it with sincere hope that it would serve as an inspiration for generations to come. She heralded "the qualities of love, humility, courage, loyalty, and great compassion which came from the soul of George Washington and gave birth to our great nation."

She told the large audience in Fredericksburg, "If humanity can be inspired to give of themselves, they will discover that it is in giving that one can know the 'heaven on earth' which all so deeply desire, and that it is in the living of God's inviolate Law of Love—Rhythmic Balanced Interchange—that all shall know true peace and prosperity. This was the great law that God gave to Walter Russell to give to mankind through the demonstration of his own magnificent life, and if mankind everywhere can be reinspired to express these qualities, then the whole world can unite in a lasting peace."

The bust was to be permanently displayed in the museum of the Masonic Temple in Fredericksburg, where George Washington had been initiated into Freemasonry.

Much to Lao's delight, Guy Chipman was present to help with the ceremony. She wrote her sister Florrie that Guy always enjoyed such ceremonial events and had made an excellent impression on the public. The Alleluias, a musical group from Delaware, provided inspiring music on the occasion. Lao noted that their "glorious voices [had] resounded in concert through the

128. Lao dedicating Walter's bust of George Washington at Fredericksburg, Virginia.

marble hall at Swannanoa the previous day."

Some months later, Florrie wrote Lao a long letter in which she shared her sister's recurring cynicism about Guy Chipman. "All your remarks about Guy and his work—and it is always something different—reminds me of old Huckesby and his pet word for describing someone like that. Do you remember? 'Lacking stickability.' How we used to laugh about it! It is not a word that is in the dictionary, but it does describe such people. Guy has all the charm of the Irish and because of it one cannot help but like him, but it doesn't pay to rely on him completely."

John Lombardi had left the board by 1976 after his divorce from Emelia. She and Lao felt that it would be wise to select another attorney to replace him as a director, but it was more than a decade before this was accomplished. Judge Martin was willing to offer her advice but felt he could not ethically serve on the board, even in an advisory capacity. J. B. Yount, Jr., her Waynesboro attorney and close friend since 1949, had died in 1974, and his son thereafter provided her with legal counsel.

It did not surprise Florrie to hear that people thought Lao looked younger than she had twenty years before. "At that time you were beginning to get very worried about Walter's health and trying to prevent him from overdoing things. Your condition today shows how you have adjusted to life without him, and although you have other worries, it is not the same as when one is worried about the health of a loved one."

By December 1976, Lao had formed a highly favorable impression of Sam Biser and his brother Loren, calling them both "very special souls who I fully believe have come to earth to fulfill a special mission that can ultimately unite our disunited world through their understanding of man's greatest need, which truly is the Law of Love—Rhythmic Balanced Interchange in action!"

129. Samuel Biser.

Sam Biser's *Healthview Newsletter*, sold in

organic and health food stores up and down the east coast, was touted as a forum for varying expert viewpoints on nutrition, health, and the frontiers of medicine. Biser's frequent references to Lao Russell and Swannanoa led a number of these merchants to contact her for permission to stock the Russell books as well. A 1977 issue contained a review of Lao's book *Love*, which Sam Biser highly recommended to all readers. "The answers and knowledge contained in this book can improve your well-being in ways that even the best foods could never do," he stated, adding, "This book contains a living philosophy which is really a comprehensive and logical way of life."

The next month Biser wrote, "I was amazed and pleased at how many readers ordered the book *Love* by Lao Russell, which I mentioned in our last issue. Shortly after the announcement appeared in the *Newsletter*, hundreds upon hundreds of orders poured in from all over the country. This confirmed my feeling that our readers are far above average in their spiritual awareness and that they are ready for the new and basic knowledge contained in Lao Russell's books."

Biser added that ordering the book "will be one of the best things you ever did for your health because there is no vitamin, food, or exercise that can produce the joy and well-being that true love will give you." He also extolled the virtues of Lao's first book, *God Will Work with You but Not for You*, which, he said, "answers in clear, understandable language many of the questions that man has been asking himself for centuries." He continued, "Two of the subjects covered in the book include 'The Basic Cause of All Disease' and 'What Is Mind-Healing and When Can It Help.' The two discussions alone would make the book required reading for *Healthview* readers."

Biser related that he had been introduced to Lao Russell's writings through *God Will Work with You but Not for You*. "I said to myself, 'This is it! This is what I have been looking for all my life. It is like coming home.' And my brother Loren said the same thing."

In 1976, Lao often referred to Laara Lindo of Qualicum Beach, British Columbia, as "a wonderful student who happens to be a teacher and also has given our whole set of books to libraries in her area. She has been a student for many years, and it will be such people who will bring the much-needed balance to our very sick world." Lao wrote Laara that on January 23, 1976, God told her that all doors would open for the University's work.

Lao was strict in observing the giving-regiving principle and seldom gave her books away, but she usually found a reason when she thought an exception to the rule was in order. When a student wrote that an office fire had destroyed his copy of the *Home Study Course*, she expressed her sympathy and sent him a duplicate course at once "in repayment," she noted, "for the thoughtful and loving gift of red roses you sent to me after your visit."

A Norfolk newspaper article in March 1977 quoted Swannanoa owners Wendell Wood and James F. Dulaney, Jr., as hoping to convert the estate into a luxury resort within the next five to ten years. Admitting that they did not have the funds to do so at present, they stated, "Once the change is made, people will come to dine in the gardens, swim, ride, dance, play tennis, and see the palace." When told of this when she was interviewed for the same article, Lao put on a brave front and said she was not concerned about the luxury resort plans. "I don't think of myself personally," she told the reporter. "I am concerned about mankind, and I think we will be a far more understanding world when we know man's principles. I know what God has told me. I will go on with my work, come what may."

The day after the article appeared, Lao wrote, "I was feeling discouraged about events on our mountaintop. I awoke early in the morning as God imprinted the following words on my consciousness which I want to share with you, 'Heed well, my daughter, what I am about to give to thee. You must remain on my mountaintop in Virginia!'"

Elsie Benney was widowed now and still in correspondence with both Lao and Florrie, and both sisters thought that Elsie should come to live with Florrie once Anna, Elsie's daughter, was married.

Macalester Park Publishing Company wrote to inquire about the University's authority to publish and distribute copies of *The Man Who Tapped the Secrets of the Universe* by Glenn Clark. Clark was dead, and there was new management at the press. Lao wrote that Clark had agreed that Macalester Park would continue to print the paperback editions, and the Russells could print hardcover editions free of any royalty payment. She sent the publishing company a copy of Clark's letter authorizing the arrangement.

Lao was in New York on business the first week of April 1978, but in May and June she was ill again. She cancelled the board meeting, advising the directors she would call a new meeting as soon as she felt able. It took place in October. There were technicalities to handle. Although Guy Chipman and Winston S. Purvis had been elected to replace Jim and Pat duPont Stephanis in 1976, that election was flawed for lack of a quorum. In the meantime it was deemed preferable to elect instead Marie Dunn and Sam Biser in their place. Marie served until 1984, when William Cranwell was elected in her stead. Sam Biser served until 1988, when he resigned to pursue his own business interests.

Purvis, who was vice president of the Fidelity Bank of Lynchburg, Virginia, and had supported the work of the University for many years, often speaking to groups on its behalf, was properly elected to the board in 1978 and served for the next eight years. Gary Scrogham, a longtime student from nearby Crimora, Virginia, who faithfully contributed time and effort to the maintenance and upkeep of the palace and grounds, served on the board from 1981 to 1984, when he was succeeded by Waynesboro attorney J. B. Yount III, namesake and grandson of the man who had sold the Swannanoa land to Major Dooley in 1908. Yount's father, Lao's longtime friend and local attorney, had met the Russells at the palace dedication in 1949, which he attended with his wife and children.

Aubrey H. Perry, Sr., her longtime student and friend from Norfolk, resigned from the board in 1978 after nine years as a director, reassuring Lao that that he would always love her and the work, adding, "Please count me as one of your dear friends and call on me any time if I can be of help."

130. St. Barbe Baker with Lao.

St. Barbe Baker visited Lao again in 1978. *The News Virginian* related, "The founder of The Men of the Trees, a Society of Earth Healers who are working to create a universal tree sense, is visiting America as a guest of the University of Science and Philosophy, Swannanoa, Waynesboro, Virginia. He brings his latest lecture: 'Trees, Water, Food, and Man.' Baker, the author of over twenty books, had recently completed a marathon horseback ride of 1,200 miles from northland to southland through the length of New Zealand, giving talks to 90,000 school children and university students. He had won honorary life fellowship of the Institute of Arts and Sciences for his book, *Green Glory—Forests of the World*, and had launched the Sahara Reclamation Program as the long-term answer to freedom from hunger. His planting plan for New Zealand in 1931 had resulted in the largest man-made forest in the world. He had earned for himself the reputation of being the greatest living authority in the English-speaking world on the supreme value of silviculture from the standpoint alike of scenic beauty, economic importance, dominant climatic influence and human health."

On his final journey to Swannanoa he and Lao discussed in particular God's message to Lao that dramatic changes in world weather conditions would ultimately draw international attention to the University's teachings.

Lao regularly corresponded with old friends who she had met decades before at the Boston Home of Truth. She referred to her "lovely nostalgic memories" of those experiences in Boston during the 1940s.

When Pat and Bob Beazley, who she had met in California, asked her views on the wisdom of relocating their health store to Waynesboro, Virginia, from the west coast, she gave them cautious encouragement, was delighted when they moved east and opened their store several miles from Swannanoa, and embraced them as treasured friends.

Another new venture in the area that pleased Lao deeply was Kay Allison's establishment of the Quest Bookshop in Charlottesville in 1978. Lao was one of her first customers, and the two women established a close friendship that led to many conversations, both at the palace and in the wholesome, stimulating atmosphere of what was to become central Virginia's largest and most popular metaphysical bookstore. Kay Allison recounted her delight at seeing Lao's effervescent interaction with people of all different backgrounds who came to Swannanoa from all over the world.

Volunteers, who came to enjoy a week or more "working" vacation at Swannanoa, often wrote her of the "spirit of Love and Hospitality" they found pervading the mountaintop. "Cooperation was the watch word," wrote one such laborer, "and I enjoyed every minute!"

When the board met in October 1978, Emelia was not present. She had decided to resign from active participation in the University's affairs. Samuel Spicher was elected to fill her vacancy and served until 1985, when he was succeeded by Richard Dulaney. Sam Biser, the new corresponding and recording secretary, noted that Mitchell Ellis, Marie Dunn, and the Hawkinses were all present. The office had been moved downstairs into the old kitchen in the English basement, greatly facilitating the packing and delivery of books and supplies and the preparation of mass mailings. The old office, directly across from the upstairs drawing room, had been redecorated and furnished as a sitting room for Lao to use in receiving special students and visitors.

On Sunday, October 15, 1978, a time of the harvest moon, Michael P. Hudak of Abbott Pharmaceuticals in Akron, Ohio, visited Lao for the first time with a friend, Mr. Pat Egan. They met at length with Lao upstairs in her private quarters. Michael recounted the experience in a Christmas letter to her later that year: "It is impossible to express in words the profoundness of the spiritual experience I had with you, Mrs. Russell. You quite literally read my thoughts when you offered to take me up those heavenly stairs to share the privacy and intimacy of your thoughts and the beauty of your living quarters. It is burned into my mind forever. A long, searching journey was fulfilled on the mountaintop that day.

"I have read Dr. Russell's *Message of the Divine Iliad* and I am currently receiving absolute clarity from *The Secret of Light*. At the time of my visit, I also purchased thirty copies of *The Man Who Tapped the Secrets of the Uni-*

verse. I made a commitment to you that I was going to give that little book to those souls whom I 'felt' were ready for seeds of spiritual light. I have given out all thirty copies in about six weeks; already much activity has been created by those efforts." He sent a check to purchase additional copies to give as Christmas gifts and pledged to continue the work of spreading "the urgent message man must awaken to soon."

Lao's beloved eldest sister, Florrie May French, died in Rushington, Sussex, on January 3, 1979, at almost eighty-four years of age. This was Lao's last close family tie with her youth. Lao was delighted, however, when her handsome and intelligent nephew, Peter Harold Summerfield, successful in the leadership of the English scouting movement, came to Swannanoa for a visit with his charming wife, Betty, in 1980. Florrie bequeathed Lao her diamond and sapphire ring, antique gold watch and chain, and a "coral hand" brooch, as well as all her photographs and half of the proceeds of her real estate and savings. She left the residue of her estate to be divided among her niece and nephew, Olive Margaret Morley and Peter Summerfield, as well as Harry French's son, John William Ernest French, and his wife, Alice Winifred French, to whom she also referred in her will as her nephew and niece.

The board met at Swannanoa on the anniversary of Walter's birth, May 19, 1979. The most dramatic news they shared was the enormously increased interest in *Atomic Suicide?* since equipment failure and human error had caused the worst nuclear accident in United States history two months before at the Three Mile Island nuclear plant in Harrisburg, Pennsylvania. Sam Biser had been successful in attracting renewed attention to this pertinent Russell volume through articles and advertisements in his *Healthview Newsletter*. The board was growing more receptive to using direct-mail marketing techniques to market the books. Biser had brought the University many orders when he used his extensive mailing list to promote *Love* and *God Will Work with You but Not for You*. He was also working on a video movie on the University to be titled *The Spirit of Swannanoa*. Samuel Spicher, ever generous and supportive, had donated two new signs for the entrance to Swannanoa. He and his family did volunteer work at the palace on a regular basis, and by the 1980s, his son Sammy was likewise an integral part of Lao's ongoing support system.

A new Russell study group had been formed in Sarasota, Florida, and its leaders inquired as to whether the University had issued any special supplements for group leaders. Lao replied that study groups had always been formed by students thoroughly familiar with the *Home Study Course* itself and that in such cases additional materials were unnecessary.

She stressed to those forming study groups that it was the usual practice for each member to have his or her own copies of the books and course. She knew that the group members achieved better results when they studied alone and then met to discuss what they had read. In this way, interest generally spread into the members' families and working lives. "We receive glowing accounts of transformed lives through these group meetings where each student finds a listening ear to his reactions and to the desires fulfilled through living the principles outlined in our teachings," Lao wrote.

Larry Tiegs, a certified personologist from Nampa, Idaho, began working with Lao in 1973, telling her that he and his wife and partner Patti were "great followers of your teachings." Lao was impressed with their work, adding, "Your brochures show good imagination and are well-done." He and his wife later conducted well-attended discussion groups on the Russell teachings in Burlingame, California, with Lao's long-distance help and blessing. Larry proved a valuable adjunct to the University for the rest of Lao's life.

She often received inquiries from students desiring to form International Age of Character Clubs in their home cities. In her instructions for forming these local chapters, she stressed that the sole purpose "is to give the people of every race, nationality, and creed, and in every walk of life, an opportunity to share the greatest joy on earth—interchange with loving understanding." This could be accomplished, she said, by lifting humanity one individual at a time to a higher mental and spiritual level of understanding as manifested by the teachings of the University of Science and Philosophy.

Lao was always reluctant to advise such students that she no longer had the time to direct the local groups personally. She explored proposals by communications firms who desired to put the *Home Study Course* on cassettes for worldwide marketing.

Howard Hall's study class still drew many excellent students in Newark, Delaware, home of the University of Delaware. The class included staff members from the prestigious St. Andrew's School in nearby Middletown. "Each member of his group enrolls in the year's *Home Study Course*," Lao reported. "Howard starts each group with Unit One, and others join the group at any time. If they join when the group is studying later units of the Course, they study previous units on their own until they catch up with the unit the class is currently studying."

In later years, three of the most successful Age of Character Clubs were founded in Virginia by Glenn P. Kellam in the Chesapeake-Virginia Beach area, by Leona Kondas in Staunton, and by Georgia Papadopoulos in Arlington.

Kellam, a minister and family counselor, had ordered *The Divine Iliad* in September 1981. He came to Swannanoa for the first time thirteen months later and came to know Lao well over the next six years. She felt that his classes truly highlighted the Russell principles.

Lao much preferred that students receive the home study lessons by the month rather than all at once. "The psychology of receiving lessons monthly is a stimulating one and it keeps you on your toes," she said.

The top musical arranger for Walt Disney Productions had completed the *Home Study Course*. He wrote Lao, "It has helped untap my creative resources in my work of composing and orchestrating music, and it has helped me when I read books in other fields. After reading your and Dr. Russell's writings, there isn't anything else I want to read!"

In a letter of September 27, 1977, to Phillip Smith, Port of Spain, Trinidad, Lao described how she and Walter had come to write the course: "The first two units of our *Home Study Course* were written by me for I knew that we needed a course to explain the principles God had given to both of us. When Doctor read these first units, he realized the worth of a full year's course of study, and we wrote the first two editions of the course together. However, when we started to write the final and last edition—the third edition—together, Doctor became so ill that he could not work on this from the sixth unit onward."

Lao advised those who desired accredited study, "I greatly regret that I have no idea of a university or college at this time that gives degrees in parapsychology. I feel sure that at some future time they will, but it is still a far-out subject to date. However, I would not be too concerned about degrees, for if one can prove one's self in any field, one can know great fulfillment without degrees. Some of our greatest historical characters have but little formal education. In the end it is what a man knows that stands him in good stead rather than what he remembers and repeats."

She reassured a Beverly Hills physician, Dr. Paul Cantalupo, that the University had "many Sc.D.s, M.D.s, Ph.D.s, etc., studying with us who say that our Home-Study curriculum contains the key for which they have always sought to the whole answer as to the how and why of Creation itself!" Students who apologized for lacking formal education, "this time around," were usually told, "I can tell from your letter that you have the most important thing of all—inner awareness."

The Russells appealed to an impressive array of people. Psychologists and psychiatric counselors, who utilized the teachings of Dr. Carl G. Jung, wrote Lao that Jung's principles were very congruent with those of Walter and Lao Russell. Dr. Ernest Holmes had sent many of his advanced students to the University of Science and Philosophy throughout the years, and many Divine Science ministers had followed the Science of Mind author in taking the *Home Study Course*. This accounted for the continuing interest in the Russell books and course among Divine Science church members.

Ted De Renzi, who conducted one of America's highly successful Montessori schools in Collingdale, Pennsylvania, corresponded frequently with Lao on educational techniques, and assimilated many of her teachings into his curriculum. They shared articles on psychic phenomena, discussed such magazines as *World of Psi*, and believed that students could progress from the most ordinary existence into the higher creative state. He sent Lao books on Maria Montessori, and specifically called attention to the great educator's cosmic curriculum in Standing's book *Maria Montessori—Her Life and Work*. Lao told him she was familiar with Montessori's work and considered her "one of the greatest and most enlightened of Souls." She had always felt that it would be advantageous to children to incorporate the Montessori and Russell principles in a basic curriculum.

José Silva, who visited Lao at the palace and referred his Mind Control students to her by the dozens, had often told her that he felt the Russells' course was seriously underpriced. Lao thanked him for selling thousands of their books in his Silva Mind Control Centers around the world.

Marcelino Alcala, an attorney in San Juan, Puerto Rico, offered to translate *God Will Work with You but Not for You* into Spanish. He had been an official Spanish-English translator for the United States Army, owned a bookstore handling materials on psychic phenomena, and was a successful Silva Mind Control instructor. Lao offered him the same terms she had offered Paul Lojnikov, who had financed the Portuguese translation of the book in Brazil. Publication would be at the translator's expense, and ten percent of the gross receipts would be returned to the University. By 1974, Alcala had established successful Russell study groups in San Juan and Arecibo, Puerto Rico. In July of that year he visited Lao at Swannanoa with his family and a group of interested professionals, including Dr. Castro, a well-known psychiatrist from San Juan. Later Alcala extended his work in Silva Mind Control techniques to other Caribbean countries. By the early 1980s, students from Columbia in South America had enrolled in the *Home Study Course* at his suggestion. Lao was devoted to Alcala and his family.

Jeanette Mendez from Old San Juan, Puerto Rico, one of Alcala's friends and former students, wrote Lao in March 1976, while studying at the Harvard graduate school of education. She had read *Love*, and her dream was to have a school that would teach people to live up to Jesus' commandments to love God and your neighbor. She ordered a large supply of the Russell books for herself and others and enrolled in the *Home Study Course* that June. After corresponding with Lao for several months, Jeanette Mendez expressed an immense desire to speak personally with her. She visited Swannanoa on several occasions and was a very strong supporter of the Message in Puerto Rico.

In 1978, she offered to translate Lao's book *Love* into Spanish. Some years later she used passages from the Russells' human relations book regarding profit sharing while presenting ideas for the platform of a major candidate for governor in Puerto Rico.

Albert Roy Davis and Walter C. Rawls, Jr., wrote Lao, "We have spent thousands of dollars in the presentation of our two books, *Magnetism and Its Effects on the Living System*, released in 1974, and *The Magnetic Effect*, released in 1975, published by Exposition Press, Inc., New York." A colleague in the medical field had noted the similarity between their magnetic theory of cancer research and the principles of Walter and Lao.

Lao regretted that neither she nor Walter had ever met Edgar Cayce, the world-famous Virginia Beach clairvoyant, whose philosophy Lao believed to be consistent with the Russell principles. She considered Cayce "a very fine soul who helped many people during his lifetime." It stimulated her when students of Edgar Cayce's Association for Research and Enlightenment and students of Unity enrolled in the *Home Study Course*. "Both teachings bring a special unfolding awareness as a preparation for the Science of Man and the Cosmos contained and explained in our writings and teachings," she advised them.

She often regretted the fact that there was no adequate facility at Swannanoa for large groups to use in holding their own retreats. On a number of occasions, groups from the Cayce center in Virginia Beach and various Unity congregations implored her to allow them to use the mountaintop for several days, but this was impossible since the palace and gardens were open to the public the year round, and she had not yet acquired the commodious Lesser house that became her guest facility.

Per-Axel Aterrbom, a Swedish scholar who was translating the Edgar Cayce books into the Scandinavian languages, wrote Lao that he hoped to have the opportunity to do the same for the Russell works.

Lao acquiesced when Mormon friends asked her consent to perform a proxy baptism for Walter in the Latter-day Saints temple in Los Angeles according to Mormon practice. Members of the Reorganized Church of Jesus Christ of Latter-day Saints in St. Louis told her that they believed her concept of Rhythmic Balanced Interchange was the same thing as what the Church called the "Celestial Law," part of a revelation given to Joseph Smith in 1834 at Fishing River, Missouri, by Jesus Christ himself. Lao agreed that Joseph Smith's revelation accurately reflected the Russells' Law of Rhythmic Balanced Interchange, even though it was couched in a different language.

Students of Astara praised Lao's book *Love*. The head of the group had written Lao's friend Billy Prior Bates, "I'll put it next to Ralph Waldo Emerson's books and will continue to go to it often for inspiration and love and wisdom." Astara, founded in 1951, sought to elevate the consciousness and health of humankind by initiating people from all faiths into esoteric teachings and mystic philosophy from its headquarters in Upland, California.

Lao received a group of visitors from Mt. St. Mary's Seminary in Emmetsburg, Maryland, and was pleasantly surprised at the favorable comments this Roman Catholic audience accorded her. A Sister of Mercy found her idea of gradual illumination "something I like and can relate to. That's what I've always thought life was all about."

The president of the new Atlantis University in Los Angeles wrote of his plans to locate a campus in Bimini. It was to include the school building and a pyramid, the former for teaching the laws of balance as they are found in nature, and the latter for helping people achieve cosmic consciousness. "I believe that Walter Russell's books might well be adapted to our curriculum, if such is agreeable to you. Please let me hear from you," he wrote. Lao responded enthusiastically.

Valmore T. Jones of the Founding Church of Scientology in Washington, D.C., wrote her, "Your goals and ideals are the same as mine and those of other Scientologists. We agree with you that man is capable of much more than he often believes." She sent Lao books by L. Ron Hubbard and visited her at Swannanoa. Commander Yvonne Jentzsch, president of the Church of Scientology Celebrity Centre in Los Angeles wrote, "I enjoy your writings, and I will enclose something that you may enjoy, written by L. Ron Hubbard." They met and immediately sensed a spiritual kinship.

Charles Burlage, a prominent Norfolk, Virginia, attorney, wrote to Lao, "The aspect of your philosophy that particularly intrigued me is that you seem to say that somewhere in the labyrinth of the human body there is contained in effect a 'receiving set' which either through chemical interaction or some other force is somehow occasionally able to 'tune in' on the universal wisdom which permeates the atmosphere. This would explain flashes of brilliance that occur to some of us occasionally."

Mrs. Pat Nixon, America's First Lady, had given Secretary of State Henry Kissinger a copy of Lao's book *God Will Work with You but Not for You*. One of Dr. Kissinger's friends told Lao that the great statesman, strategist, and diplomat had read the book and written to her from Beirut, asking, "Why was I not acquainted with this book before? It is most amazing. It contains answers to all the world's problems. I want to go to Waynesboro some day." The friend, Mrs. Van Houten, told Lao that she had closely followed Dr. Kissinger's public statements and activities during the Mid-East Crisis at the time and was certain he had been using principles outlined in Lao's book.

Across America increasing numbers of the Baha'i faith found the Russells' thesis that science and religion were one and the same remarkably consistent with Baha'i principles. Years ago, a Baha'i student had informed her that Bahá'u'lláh had made the statement that one would come who would give a scientific explanation of the light, which is God.

The famous Egyptian Coptic Hamid Bey, whose temple in Los Angeles,

California, was well known to Lao, offered a series of lectures on *Atomic Suicide?* there and bought many copies of the book when conducting his classes on the nature of radioactivity. He also taught from and recommended Lao's book on reincarnation, *Why You Cannot Die!*

When Jo and Vonn Hoffman, Coptic students who were close to Lao, sent her the sad news that Hamid Bey had transcended from life on Friday, July 16, 1976, she greatly regretted the fact that the great spiritual leader with whom she had shared so much by correspondence had not been able to come to Swannanoa the previous September as he had hoped to do. Besides enjoying his letters, Lao had felt even closer to Hamid Bey because of their strong mutual friendship with Dr. Tim Binder. Lao wrote the Hoffmans of her sorrow at losing Hamid Bey, adding, "I shall always treasure his beautiful letters to me and know that someday we shall meet and work together for the good of all of God's great Creations." Several months later, the Hoffmans attended the Coptic Convention and wrote Lao, "The consciousness was high, the lecturers excellent, but I missed you because I knew there was a slight chance that you would come. The Coptic teachings are very similar to yours."

Many students had told Lao that they had heard Gloria Swanson expound on Lao's virtues, and admit that she had first learned of the danger of pollution through nuclear reactors through Lao. The two women had remained friends for nearly twenty years, and the great film actress had always supported the University's work. "When we have people in the public eye speaking so favorably about our work, I know that we could gather tremendous national momentum," Lao told Larry Tiegs.

It was nevertheless true that in many instances people in positions of authority ignored the Russells' warnings. Her loyal student Larry Bopart constantly bought copies of *Atomic Suicide?* to give to influential friends. He presented a copy to Governor Nelson Rockefeller of New York, but after months passed, and it elicited no response, Lao wrote Emelia, "Guess it fell on deaf ears as usual."

Lao recalled that some years before she had sent a collection of their books to Henry Ford II, who had acknowledged them in a personal letter and told her he had placed them in the company's library for employee reference. "What he should have done," Lao commented, "was to put the principles we expounded in *The Scientific Answer To Human Relations* to work in his business practices, and the Ford Motor Company may not be in the trouble it is today!"

Students asked her to recommend a church denomination to them. Her reply was plain: "I always hesitate to introduce anyone to organizations for, frankly, I am not familiar with many other people's teaching since all of our teachings have come directly from God. To me, God's greatest Church is in Nature, and when I take a walk in the forest or by the seashore, I know the ecstasy of my Oneness with God and all things else."

CHAPTER TWENTY-FIVE

Introducing a Man Like Gandhi (1979-82)

131. Governor Melford Okilo takes the oath of office in Nigeria.

Melford Okilo, a Russell student since 1965, paid his third visit to Swannanoa in October 1979. He had devoted much of his time since the 1960s to building genuine democracy in the vast nation of Nigeria. Since first meeting him, Lao considered him a beautiful soul with a very special mission in life.

He told her he had been elected the first civilian governor of Nigeria's important Rivers State, a sprawling region whose capital is Port Harcourt. He served in this capacity from October 1979 to December 1983. As governor of Rivers State, he told Lao he would develop a form of government with policies that would reflect and incorporate a new philosophy based on the principles of love. He introduced a form of government that became popularly known as government by decentralization. Federal in structure and democratic in character, it eliminated over-centralization of power in few hands and exemplified love in action in a practical, uniquely effective way.

At the time Governor Okilo took office, Rivers State was notorious for its disunity, abject poverty, fear, threats of inter-tribal conflicts, and lack of modern amenities. He faced the enormous challenge of creating unity among diverse peoples, with complex interests, in an effort to resolve them into a harmonious working entity for the good of all parts of the state.

This remarkable governmental strategy brought enormous benefits to the Rivers people, whose standard of living rose sharply during the years of the Okilo administration. Although he was far too humble to claim credit for these achievements, it was undeniable that improvements in their day-to-day existence and opportunities would have been unthinkable without the enlightened policies that stimulated economic growth and social awareness in the citizenry, by appealing to the most benevolent qualities of their individual and collective spirit. A recitation of some of these results charts more specifically what "Love in Action" came to mean to the people of Rivers State.

132. Governor Okilo addresses his fellow citizens.

Hand-pulled canoes in riverine areas of the state gave way to powered outboard engine boats that people could afford to buy for the first time. Quality food, shelter, clothing, and drinking water became the standard rather than the exception. The Kolo Gas Turbine Station, the largest rural electrification project in Nigeria, was implemented to introduce electricity to hundreds of remote and isolated towns and villages. Health and transportation services were extended throughout the state.

His political party had been elected in 1979 by a slight majority, but in the fair and democratically conducted elections of 1983, he was not only reelected, but the "unity in diversity" movement he exemplified and headed won sixty-one of sixty-two vigorously contested parliamentary seats. He valued this unique mandate not as the obvious personal compliment he had been paid by the voters, but because it clearly indicated that his heterogeneous people were recognizing the strength and progress their newfound unity was producing.

It was the first large-scale effort to implement the Russell philosophy throughout the political and educational system of a large geographical entity. It proved an effective answer to the economic and social problems of a large population. "I saw the system as Love in Action," Governor Okilo recalled in his subsequent memoir. While in office, he truly applied the principles of the Russell philosophy. Looking for a way to best serve his people, he decentralized government power and distributed government money to his people for their own welfare, allowing local government to flourish at the various community levels.

This love in action brought peace, prosperity, and unity to the Rivers State people. As a result, Rivers State became one of the most influential states in Nigeria and West Africa.

To Lao's delight, Governor Okilo emphasized the Russells' Message in his development of an enlightened public education system in Rivers State. He redirected the mission of the public schools from the traditional curriculum based on memorization and information by rote to the new science of man, which aimed to bring to the forefront the student's spiritual, loving, and Godly qualities. "This system brings out the genius in man by emphasizing such qualities as honesty, humility, kindness, intelligence, wisdom, courage, truthfulness, consideration and sympathy for others, and sharing the joys and sorrows of others," he wrote.

New schools were built in the smallest villages. In August 1980 Governor Okilo founded the first University of Science and Technology in Nigeria. He imported the Russells' books in large quantities and distributed them from University to local school level throughout the Rivers State. "I bought these books," he explained, "because I found them to be some of the best books in the world which bring out the genius qualities in man, and [because they] first married Science, religion, and philosophy into one."

Not only did Governor Okilo's administration bring the economic status of the average Rivers State citizen to the highest level in the region's history, it also was enormously successful in valuable, unexpected ways not usually associated with the political system. Besides tapping and developing human and material resources in every community, by providing full employment and promoting community consciousness and the art of self-government throughout the state, it created an atmosphere conducive to breeding statesmen and future leaders. As one chronicle attests, "It gave every citizen a sense of belonging. It was Love in action, as it gave power, peace, stability, wealth, happiness and unity to the masses." One political scientist called it "a form of participatory democracy from the village level." An enthusiastic student of the new form of government declared, "If the ideal of government by the people, for the people is something attainable, then it is this form of government by decentralization that we must look into."

Lao was deeply impressed by the letters and visitors she received from Nigerians studying the *Home Study Course* and Russell books. Largely influenced by Melford Okilo, many important citizens of Africa's most populous country soon came to appreciate the potential that the Message of universal love held for the future development of their nation. Each day's mail brought course enrollments and book orders from eager young Nigerians, and it was a rare month when influential professional or military leaders failed to visit Swannanoa to meet Lao personally. Their character and wholesomeness, buttressed by their determination to keep their own culture intact while establishing a distinct national identity in the modern world, deeply moved Lao. She found that many of the qualities she so admired in Governor Okilo seemed to typify his countrymen. Their spirituality overwhelmed her, and she admired their resolve to preserve their own traditional medicines and cures. She and Emelia Lombardi often discussed the fact that Nigeria might someday prove the springboard from which other African countries would achieve their democratic destiny and succeed in bringing enlightened brotherhood to the continent and thence the world.

Lao had passed her seventy-fifth birthday, but young men admired her for her beauty and vivacity and turned to her for advice on their most intimate sexual problems. A thirty-year-old Quaker humanist, who had absorbed himself in eastern religious teachings for much of his adulthood, came to Lao when he began to question his guru's view of total abstinence from sexual involvement. He had earned a doctor of philosophy degree but felt that his "higher learning" poorly prepared him to decide if his continuing sexual desires were natural or sinful. She assured him there was nothing unnatural in selfless physical love for another.

Lao never forgot the horrible experience when she was twelve years old, and her mother died suddenly one night at the age of fifty-two. Her father had died the following year, and she always claimed that after his death "it was not until I met Dr. Russell that I could truly share my deep thoughts with anyone as I did with both of my parents."

She always identified with those who had known a similarly agonizing loss. Losing Walter Russell had been equally terrible, she told people, even though it was not unexpected, for they had been each other's whole life. Lao's ever-present smile charmed her visitors. She always claimed that her smile came from the knowledge that Walter was always beside her. Lao remembered that it had been at least five years after Walter's death before she could smile with absolute peace of mind. By then, although she still knew moments of great sadness, "I can relive moments that we shared and know again the joy that those moments brought to me."

She constantly reassured those in grief that love would always bring together those who desired to be together. "Desire," she stressed, "is the single force of Love and the depth of one's desire is motivated by Love."

Lao loved to recount the experience of summer 1978, when visitors had taken three Polaroid photographs of her standing on the main marble staircase at Swannanoa. She took great comfort from this incident and believed it could give others the peace of knowing that their departed loved ones were with them always. The three pictures were difficult to describe, she recalled,

> for I have never seen anything like them before or since. A man was taking a picture of his wife standing beside me on the double marble staircase. She had a white dress on and is prematurely white-haired.
>
> The gentleman had taken two or three pictures, which he informed us were not coming out and was crushing them and putting them in his pocket. I said, "Do let me see the one you have just taken," and when I looked at it, my heart jumped for joy for there superimposed on his wife's body and head was my Beloved's body! In place of her white hair was a dark beret and covering her white dress was a bright colored coat such as Dr. Russell liked to wear.
>
> The two previous pictures he had crushed showed light rays—one stronger than the other coming into focus on the woman's body. I have known Oneness with my Beloved from the time of his refolding, but this was the only time that I have ever had a picture or seen a presence. One needs only one such experience to know the everlasting comfort of our eternal Oneness with those we truly love.

She encouraged students who had difficulty in understanding the course to take heart. "This is not a year's course of study but a lifetime study. I often receive letters from students who have had the course for more than twenty years and who tell me that each year as they restudy it, the entire course becomes much clearer to them."

Lao believed sincerely that lack of character was often manifested in poor work. "Every nut, bolt, and screw in every type of workmanship should be done with precision. Today most of our workmanship is not done with perfection because man has put materialism before himself."

Thirteen years earlier, in her book *Love*, she had endeavored to instigate a worldwide network of Age of Character Clubs, but for the most part, the movement had fallen on deaf ears. She urged an Arizona student to encourage his colleagues in the fire department to read *Love*.

She was often reminded of Paul Stixrud's anguish over the death of his son and the latter's family in a plane accident. His correspondence with Lao was included in Lao's *Vital Message* in 1986. He had written Lao, "Now that I am filled with this terrible void, nothing will comfort me." She replied in a letter that he felt had saved his life. "Love will forever bring together those who desire to be together," she advised him.

She enjoyed hearing visitors play their personal compositions for her at the palace on her piano or Hammond organ and encouraged them to sing their songs for her. Music was important to Lao. When Allan Stocker wrote that his main and deep desire was to express his soul through music, she told him that the very concept warmed her heart. She knew that one of Walter's unrealized desires was to compose symphonies, but he had felt constrained instead to concentrate on the written word in order to fill what they knew were man's more critical needs. She applauded Allan for his *New Age Songbook* and thanked him for generously making copies of the Russell books available to others.

Brantz Mayer, professor of parapsychology at Northern Virginia's Lord Fairfax Community College, invited Lao to give a lecture to his classes on February 7, 1979, and brought his fascinated students on a field trip to Swannanoa two days later.

Her book *Why You Cannot Die!* was reviewed favorably in comparison to a highly successful treatise on the subject by Manly P. Hall, published earlier by the Philosophical Research Society in Los Angeles. The reviewer favored the simplicity and logic of Lao's treatment. Lao was not personally acquainted with Hall but had heard Walter praise him as a beautiful soul who had given much to enlighten mankind. When she read Hall's book on reincarnation, she was happy to find it congruent with her own in every important respect.

Students inundated her with writings they considered similar to the Russell works. Some of these were obscure books only recently translated into English. Some she gave a cursory glance. Others impressed her deeply. She particularly enjoyed a book called *Paneurhythmy* by Peter Deunov, a Bulgarian mystic and spiritual teacher who developed a sequence of carefully formed, distinctively spiritual communal dances. This esoteric Christian, an academic as well as an accomplished violinist, was saintly and charismatic. He had died in 1944, but Lao appreciated the techniques he developed for creating unity, harmony, and inner love. She enjoyed hearing his music played and watching his dances performed by students at Swannanoa. She considered his work more personal and significant than the similar *Eurythmy*, which the Austrian genius Rudolf Steiner and his wife, Marie, had developed before the First World War.

In August 1979, Charles Duncan, United States Secretary of Energy, acknowledged that Earl Starcher, Jr., a Russell student, had sent Walter's books to the department, urging them to evaluate his diagram on solar energy. The request was ultimately lost in the bureaucracy, although Lao corresponded briefly with Frederick H. Morse, director of the Office of Solar Applications. Starcher was deeply intrigued by Walter's octave multiplication by white light and conducted his own experiments to expand on the theory.

In late February 1980, Lao was back in California where she visited friends and lectured to small groups of students until early May.

Lao believed that no medicine was superior to a healthy diet. She endorsed the efforts of her longtime friend and student Jerome Canty, who had helped so many ill and injured people recover their health through a nutritional diet. In June 1981, she assured an inquirer, "I am quite familiar with Mr. George Ohsawa through our valued student, Jerome Canty, and know of the great value of Zen macrobiotics." Canty's popular macrobiotic summer camp was thriving and continued to be an important source of *Home Study Course* enrollees. Lao considered him "an inspired and valued student of all of our teachings," and knew that he realized "the great value of the basic knowledge contained throughout our whole home-study curriculum."

Although she advised students that *The Healthview Newsletter* was an incomparable source of information on natural methods of healing, and considered Sam and Loren Biser two very special young men dedicated to promoting good health, she read with more skepticism the account in *Healthview Newsletter* of a woman who had lost her finger in an accident and was growing another one through the use of a patent bone tea. Nonetheless, she praised Sam Biser for what she perceived to be his integrity and dedication.

Silva Mind Control students had always been drawn to the Russell teachings, and many of the major Silva centers regularly gave copies of *The Man Who Tapped the Secrets of the Universe* to each student as a graduation gift. Lao felt that this illustrated the universal love and advanced thinking of the organization. She introduced Silva instructors to Melford Okilo's work in Nigeria.

Students of the *Home Study Course* promoted the University on radio and television. A broadcaster in Hawaii read excerpts from the book *Love* over local radio for two hours, between three and five in the morning, for weeks at a time and received many telephone orders for the book. After a few weeks, he followed the same practice with *God Will Work with You but Not for You* and the *Home Study Course* with like results. Another student, Gordon Banta, frequently mentioned the Russells on his syndicated radio and television programs across the southeastern United States.

Lao found some resistance to her work. People intimately associated with popular daytime television host Phil Donahue gave him a copy of *Love*, but he advised them he had no interest in inviting her to appear on his program. "Frankly," she wrote a friend, "I was most happy that he did not invite me to go on his show. I only do that which God inspires and directs me to do personally, and my instructions from God are crystal clear."

A noted English physicist, who had read both *The Secret of Light* and *Atomic Suicide?*, told her he could not understand why orthodox scientists had rejected their theories. "The explanations are water clear to me, and I have seen electrographs of an atom of oxygen made by modern British physicists that show the spiraled shape anticipated in 1926 by your Beloved," he wrote, noting *The Loom of Creation* by Dr. Dennis Milner and Dennis Stuart, a book he recommended that Lao include in her list of suggested readings "as providing positive experimental proof of your teachings."

A like-minded scientist, Jorgé Resines, told her in April 1980, "The science taught in both your mentioned books is so far reaching that I have designed machines to effect the transmutation of matter with simple equipment and a regenerating chamber to stop and reverse the process of aging."

Lao could still enthrall a prospective student. As one wrote, "My mind is at one with your message, and I feel a spiritual union. A mere phone call has opened my world to the truth."

She sought earnestly to lift the spirits of students suffering from depression, urging them to realize that "every action in life is purposeful for every action is unfolding within you the pattern of your life." She reminded them that thoughts are things and that one's experiences were directly affected by one's own thinking. "Try to think of the purpose of every single experience that you have from the time you get up in the morning until the time you go to bed at night. Truly, happiness is self-bestowed and misery is self-inflicted."

Lao frequently asserted that the only way to have a happy and fruitful life is to do all things with love. She told a depressed student from the California coast that he was fortunate to be living by the sea, and should walk along the ocean near San Diego and realize the beauty and rhythm of nature as the waves brought music to his ears.

Her books *God Will Work with You but Not for You* and *Love* had helped many married couples through the physical and mental strain of long, career-induced separation. She had files full of letters attesting to this.

Lao had frequently reminisced over past times with her late sister Florrie, but her correspondence with Emelia Lombardi seemed to evoke the fondest memories. Each year around the date of Walter's birthday, they regularly recalled their many times together before and after he had refolded on his ninety-second birthday. "Thank you for being such a precious part of those years," she told her New Jersey friend, "and may the happiness you gave us be regiven to you in whatever way you desire." Emelia recalled that it had been thirty years since she and her brother, Peter, had spent their first day at the palace with Walter and Lao.

In July Lao lost yet another of her precious Scottish Terriers. Jimmy Love died at Swannanoa, much to her sorrow. Mitchell Ellis and Emelia both wrote her touching messages of sympathy.

Lao frequently received marketing proposals from businesses and others, who promised to work with her to achieve broader circulation of the Russell teachings. Without exception she declined to allow such individuals or organizations to imprint their own names on University literature. To allow one such promoter to do so would open the door to others, she knew, and she and Walter strictly refused to yoke the University officially with any other organization. While this kept the University's curriculum and method of operation free of outside thought or influence, it may at times have stymied its growth, given the large number of influential and highly educated business, educational, and professional people who were among her deepest students and yearned to implement the Russell principles in their respective fields of endeavor.

Lao never joined in what she called "the tearing down process" when others sought to expose fraudulent people and movements because she knew that only basic knowledge of God and man could effect a positive change in civilization.

Frank Kearns sent the Russells' book *The World Crisis* to United States President Jimmy Carter as he campaigned for reelection in 1980. Kearns had enjoyed and absorbed more from this book than any other, and it had helped him pull his life together. He called the University "a school with no walls, world-wide in student body," and attributed to it sole responsibility for the ninety-five percent positive change he had made in his lifestyle over a few short years.

A chiropractor encouraged Lao to expand the *Home Study Course* into a three- or four-year curriculum to keep it from being so concentrated. He also recommended that an effort be undertaken to publish a special edition of the course for children by rewriting it in very simple language on the level of a ten-year-old. They both agreed that the course would be ideal for young children, who as a rule lacked the closed minds of most adults. Lao knew that many children were seeking a new way for themselves. She had written *Love* to appeal to a younger audience and was not surprised when children interested their parents in the Message, but her optimism seemed to wane at times. "There is ever growing interest for our teachings in universities," she wrote, "but this is a slow process, and time is of the essence for man is now in his midnight hour."

Lao wistfully recalled how she had worked to begin the Age of Character Clubs movement in 1966. It was planned for every age group, but leaders failed to come forth and put it into operation. The same had been true with the Man-Woman Equalization League she had espoused a decade earlier in *God Will Work with You but Not for You*. She felt that the Russells' 1960 book, *The One-World Purpose*, as well as their 1951 treatise, *A Scientific Answer To Human Relations*, had been largely ignored by the general public. Now with the whole world in chaos, she said, it would not really matter who was elected president unless the great mass of people changed their own human relations practices, but more and more she found comfort in God's assurances to her that she would not fail. It encouraged her when the governor of Maine sent for a copy of *Atomic Suicide?* in late 1980. On November 10, she wrote in her bedside notebook, "Life is the unfolding of a flower, and the full blossom is the fulfillment of every petal's unfolding. Love is the law of creation."

Dr. Henry Kordus, a physicist who had received his doctorate in agricultural science from the University of Warsaw, termed *The Universal One* "the most magnificent, majestic book I [have] read in my life." He compared it favorably with Einstein's work, praised its logical and scientific simplicity, and wrote Lao that it demonstrated the universe in endless dimensions. By now Alexis Carrel's *Man the Unknown* was out of print. Lao considered reprinting it in a limited edition but was not certain the copyright laws would allow it.

Lao regularly received high praise from students who asked her to respect their anonymity. "A great man who has attained a very important position in this country told me recently that from the time he met me and studied our books and teachings miracles seemed to happen to him," she wrote, adding that "Life itself is a miracle, for man makes his own heaven and hell on earth and right now we are witnessing man-created hell on earth." Students sought to help expand the Message. One gave her a professionally recorded tape of the first four lessons of the *Home Study Course*, suggesting she might reproduce it for sale. She thought that this medium would have particular value in helping reach the blind.

A reader suggested there was little unique in the general structure of the Russell philosophy, except its exemplification in the life of Walter Russell and in Lao's own overwhelming spirit.

Lao seldom left the mountain but made herself available to visitors whenever she could. At times she would sit in the garden working on her Christmas message and stop to talk with those who passed by.

Lao enjoyed it when aspiring artists brought their works for her to see. She was quick to recognize artistic genius and offer encouragement, although recognizing the fact that the world seemed to have set mediocrity as its standard.

Friends told her she seemed impervious to the effects of age. An article in the Staunton, Virginia, *News Leader* featured her current photograph and prompted many compliments from those who thought she was as beautiful as ever.

Lao had not changed her philosophy since she met Walter. She repeated time and again that the only solution to the world's devastation was to put love into action. A book distributor in Texas begged for the opportunity to publish and disseminate the University's books and materials after her death. Over 6,000 copies of *Atomic Suicide?* were now in circulation in Nigeria.

She encouraged young people to plan their weddings in the palace garden. She understood why they felt it was a perfect setting for exchanging lifetime vows. Two psychics wrote her that Walter's image had appeared before them. Their description of him stroking the beard on his chin as he commented seemed accurate in the extreme and moved her deeply.

To her consternation a crank tourist had written to the United States Postmaster General, the Virginia Travel Service, the producers of the television program *P.M. Magazine*, and other state and national officials, alleging that all of the statements he heard during his palace tour were false and misleading. The complaint put her to undue trouble, but she was firm in her response, offering the complainant and all his hearers joint and individual invitations to come to Swannanoa, and hear firsthand her explanation of the truth and validity of every statement made on the tour and every sentence in the "Romance of Swannanoa" promotional brochure she herself had written. She noted that for all the thousands of complimentary letters she had received over her thirty-two years at Swannanoa, this was the first formal complaint.

It pleased her when students who were members of the Mormon Church told her that her book *Love* was fundamentally in line with the church's own *Articles of Faith*. During her western trip in 1982, she visited Salt Lake City, stayed at the Hotel Utah, and lectured to several small groups of interested students, almost all of whom were active members of the Mormon Church.

A Latin-American student wrote to tell her that it had taken him initial courage to look within instead of without, as she had encouraged him to do, but assured her it had been well worthwhile. Gail E. Otto advised Lao that her successful completion of the *Home Study Course* had earned her academic credit at California's University of Redlands.

Governor Okilo visited Lao again in late August 1981 and kept in regular touch with her from Nigeria. They had developed an abiding friendship. She considered him a modern Gandhi.

October was always Lao's busiest month at Swannanoa. She declined the opportunity to participate in a broad-spectrum New Age program, because she was determined not to imply that she endorsed teachings other than their own. "This does not mean that I do not value any teachings that others are inspired to give for I know that everyone is drawn to that which they feel will benefit them," she explained.

She offered the simplest demonstrations of their principles. "One can put one's hand on a hot stove, and all of the prayers in the world would not take that hand off the stove until one desires to lift it off one's self," she said. "That is God working with you!"

She enjoyed answering questions from perceptive students. One inquired why vibration frequencies multiplied in the direction of density according to *The Divine Iliad*, although the outer Mind was said to be characterized by low speed in *The Universal One*. "Think of a spinning top," she replied. "The faster it spins, the more still it appears, and when it is in its highest vibration of motion, there appears to be no motion at all. A book could be written on this question alone."

In her mind, Lao was composing another book to be called *Out of the Silence*, but her work at Swannanoa was too demanding to afford her the atmosphere and time she needed to make progress on this book.

In an increasingly violent society, Lao urged her students to face pressure with equanimity. She knew that in times of trauma it was hard to control one's emotions, and that one could best help himself by focusing a strong awareness of the power that lies within. "When I face unpleasant occurrences here, I hold strongly to the thought that the God-Light centers everyone and that includes those causing the immediate agony. Everyone today is subject to violent attacks because the whole world is under universal tension. Fear creates hate and greed, and hate and greed create violence. The deep-rooted cause of fear is frustration, and mankind is frustrated because it does not know God."

Walter and Lao had always maintained that fear does not and cannot exist in Nature. When a student countered by saying he had often seen wild animals displaying fear toward one another, she replied, "It is not fear they display. It is fright. Man has created an expression of fear toward each other because of an unnatural way of life. When God's ways and processes are thoroughly understood and lived, we shall not have fear in the world, but cooperative service to each other."

To those who sought an answer to their problems, she offered a simple solution: "The unfortunate thing about all life in the world today is that we have too little quality of thought because man has concentrated on materialism, which has given him the emptiness that comes from bitterness and greed because he has attained the quantity of material wealth not through Rhythmic Balanced Interchange, but through exploitation and unbalanced dealings."

For her birthday in 1981, Governor Okilo sent Lao beautiful ivory gifts from Nigeria. She was seventy-seven and wrote to Richard Dulaney, "I am as busy as ever and know 1982 will be a momentous year."

She no longer sent out thousands of Christmas messages, but there were hundreds of old friends and faithful students who she could not ignore as the holidays came. High on the list of these individuals was Emelia, to whom she sent a Christmas letter in 1981 filled with nostalgia for their past times together. Emelia seldom came to Virginia these days, but Lao made it clear that she had a standing invitation.

CHAPTER TWENTY-SIX

Turning Point (1982-86)

On January 31, 1982, Lao received a letter from Gary Starbuck of Carmel, California, which she treasured and often quoted. It read in part: "I cannot adequately express my gratitude for your having again made *The Universal One* available to the world. It marks a profound turning point in the development of human culture. The science of the future, of the conscious fusion of mind, matter, and spirit is now born. This is the seed of the new age planted and nourished in the heart of consciousness. It cannot fail to burgeon into the blossom and fruit of a civilization founded on the symphonic unison of all that is."

He told her that the book embodied the quintessence of all art, science, philosophy, and religion and signified the dawn of a new Light and a new Creation. "To designate Walter Russell as the greatest scientist we have yet known would be an extreme understatement," he added. Starbuck had hesitated to purchase the book when he saw the republication price of $200, but on reading it, he determined it was priceless. He encouraged Lao to quote his comments anywhere and anytime, and she gladly did so.

Fortuitously, Starbuck's letter came the day before a rather sad letter from Emelia. Lao's longtime friend obviously felt that time was in danger of passing the Russell Message by. She wrote, "Our hopes and dreams that the Russell philosophy would be absorbed by millions of people in our lifetime and change the course of this barbarous age don't seem to be materializing at this point. Maybe we all have to suffer some more. And maybe, as you predicted, we need to feel the consequences of these unusual weather con-ditions to make people stop and go within.

"At least there is one concession: The people are standing up together to block the atomic energy buildup or erase it altogether. Maybe if they succeed in this, it will give them the impetus to right other wrongs." Emelia told Lao she still felt the need to shout the Russells' teachings to the entire world, but when she tried to do it among her circle of acquaintances, she found that they were simply not ready. "They want their fun, their money, and they want to live it up now," she mused. To Emelia, the Russells' teachings meant more than anything else in the world. She felt better when Lao shared Gary Starbuck's letter with her.

Lao was beginning to depend more and more on Sam Biser, editor of *Healthview Newsletter*, whose business she supported financially, and whose attention she clearly appreciated. As she grew older, she felt the need of a male presence at the palace, and Sam Biser spent much time with her. She clearly referred to this young friend in her letter to Emelia: "I do have a glorious love in my life. Someday I will tell you more about it. I am growing stronger every day and at the right time I shall proclaim my love and live in a home we shall call 'Tranquility.'" She hoped that Emelia would find a new love.

Somewhere in Time, a romantic film with Christopher Reeve, Jane Seymour, Theresa Wright, and Christopher Plummer, was Lao's favorite film. She enjoyed screening it for special friends and had the theme music played frequently over the garden loudspeakers. "I often play this as I go to sleep at night," she wrote a student. "The music is romantic and soothing."

Among other gifts, she sent Emelia recordings of the music from *Somewhere in Time* and the *Love Songs of Elvis Presley*, a personality who Lao felt had been a deeply spiritual, greatly misunderstood individual. "Someday," she wrote Emelia, "we might write a book on the real Elvis!" To her own amazement Emelia found that she likewise enjoyed Presley's music, as different as it was from the classical fare she generally preferred.

Lao had thought for some time that an increasing number of unhappy and broken marriages were caused by universal tension, rather than a breakdown in the personal relationship between the parties. She urged people trying to save their marriages to avoid creating tension by projecting a warm and happy atmosphere. Nonetheless, she advised many heartbroken correspondents that the hurt of breaking up with someone they love was often a necessary experience. "It may be some years ahead before you will see why this break had to come," she often advised.

She reacted warmly to those who gave of themselves to others: "The only thing that life can give to us is that which we first give to life. This is the hardest lesson that man has to learn, and it is the one principle that will bring happiness and security to individuals, as well as to the whole world."

The winter of 1982 was treacherous at Swannanoa. Ice covered the mountaintop for weeks on end.

The Honorable Takeshi Araki, mayor of the City of Hiroshima, Japan, read *Atomic Suicide?* in 1982 and corresponded with Lao on their mutual interest in the abolition of nuclear war, and the need to bring unity and cooperation through every avenue of human endeavor. He was interested to know that Walter Russell had charted the two elements, Uridium and Urium (which were renamed Plutonium and Neptunium in 1934), and was impressed that Walter had always stressed that these two elements should never be used for war or industry. In 1984 the mayor sent Lao a Peace Declaration adopted by the city council in Hiroshima, which she distributed to everyone on the University's growing mailing list. Lao felt a deep kinship with the people of this great city, which in 1945 had known the tragedy of the first war use of an atomic bomb. She told Susan Christie, her friend at Denver's Rose Medical Center, "I wish everyone the world over could read the mayor's letter and Peace Declaration."

Lao had little patience for students who complained that their workload was so heavy that they could not continue studying the *Home Study Course*. "Throughout the years businessmen and others living and working full time under great stress have written us of the tremendous comfort and inspiration just one paragraph of our writings has brought to them."

A student wrote that he was overwhelmed by laziness when he tried to pursue the *Home Study Course*. "I am aware of the need for self-improvement," he told her, but seemed unable to progress past the first few lessons. Lao reassured him in a letter she later used often for other students who felt they were facing a similar mental block. "Anything that is new takes longer to absorb, but as you absorb new knowledge, you become aware of an inner ecstasy and all things in life become more meaningful and colorful." She urged the student to focus on the good points in his character instead of his negative aspects, cautioning him that people attract to themselves what they think. "If you believe and think you are lazy, you will lack not only desire for action but you will keep away from yourself people who will aid in creating a desire in you for action." She urged her students to continue expressing love for their fellow man. "People often do not seem to respond," she said, "but no one ever forgets a kind word or action."

Lao had broken her wrist in late winter and spent several months unable to write her usual personal responses to special letters. Emelia was suffering severe arthritic problems in her joints. She was seriously considering selling her Far Hills estate and moving someplace where it would be simpler for her to live, but Emelia had grown to love her villa. She had always felt that her nine-acre enclave in New Jersey might provide an ultimate refuge for Lao and the University in the event circumstances, or the Dulaneys, forced a move from Swannanoa. "I do love this place of quiet, lovely country with rabbits and deer and birds all over the place. It's a haven from the outside world around me."

Lao advised a student of *A Course in Miracles* that she had not read the three volumes, but had been told by friends that Helen Schucman, who channeled the course, had read the Russell books and studied their work. Lao frequently avoided rendering an opinion on other popular courses by suggesting that she was not familiar with their content. She seldom criticized what she considered to be less-important alternative teachings, although she always suggested that the Russell *Home Study Course* could take the student a step beyond on the quest for enlightenment. A longtime student confirmed that *A Course in Miracles* had been a stepping stone that helped prepare him to understand the Russells' course.

Her book *Love* seemed to be popular with audiences of all ages. She was extremely happy when an official of the National Health Federation in Utah ordered copies for the members of his board of directors. Likewise, it thrilled her when an educator who was close to retirement wrote her, "You wrote this book for teenagers, but it belongs to everyone!"

In May, Lao reported to the board that Governor Okilo had sent a personal donation of $250,000, and instructed that it be used for the purchase of the two houses and lots closest to the palace entrance, as well as a lot of two acres at the rear entrance of Swannanoa for the protection of the premises. This was a major addition to the University's presence on the mountain. The larger of the two houses became a three-story guesthouse.

Lao worried that after her death the teachings might be altered. She reminded the board that when the Russell work had begun at Swannanoa in 1948, and when the University had been chartered in 1957 to succeed the old Walter Russell Foundation, the basic principle had been adopted that the Russell teachings not be changed by addition or deletion. She noted that this policy had been adopted because so many spiritually inclined movements were changed when the originators were no longer in active control.

She received frequent requests from authors desiring to quote from the Russells' books. William B. Conner used references in his book *Harmonic Mathematics*, published by the Tesla book company. The Russells' work was referenced in a book titled *Suppressed & Incredible Inventions* by John Freeman. Lao received inquiries through this source from as far away as Saudi Arabia. She had not been aware that their work had been mentioned by Freeman and was interested to see the book.

Lao was attracting more and more attention in South Africa. The School of Truth, a recognized ecclesiastical and educational group with the same standing as churches in South Africa, had been founded in 1937 under the direction of Nicol C. Campbell. Some of the members compared the Russell teachings to the publications of the School of Truth, particularly *The Path*, a guide for true students published by the organization. "Somehow your teachings are much deeper," a sixteen-year-old member of the South African organization wrote her, "but it is all based on truth."

Emelia's health had prevented her from coming to Virginia, and she wrote in October that she would have to postpone her trip until the spring of 1983. She had greatly anticipated visiting her friend and staying at the new guesthouse.

Lao's old friend Richard St. Barbe Baker died June 9, 1982, while visiting his native Saskatchewan. He was ninety-two, active to the end, and his biographer recalled that he had "brought excitement and adventure to a life spent in the cause of conservation and exemplified a philosophy of life and the eternal dependence of man upon trees." He had helped Lao and the University in many ways.

In December 1982 she announced that the University intended to reprint Walter Russell's three early children's books, *The Sea Children*, written in 1898, and *The Bending of the Twig* and *The Age of Innocence*, both written in the first decade of the twentieth century. Walter's close friend President Theodore Roosevelt had stayed up all night to read these books. Peter Parker, Emelia's brother and the artist who had so often helped Lao in the past, cautioned her not to economize in reproducing Walter's illustrations for these children's books, reminding Lao, "Walter Russell's soul and thinking talk to us from these pictures with their delicate tonal values. To alter them would risk loss of subtle meaning." Unfortunately, the books were not reprinted.

Harry French's son, John, and his wife sent Lao a loving Christmas message from their retirement home in West Sussex, Rustington, England. "It is quite a long time since you and I went putting on the green at Hart Hill in 1923. I was about thirteen then. There is a lot to remember."

133. Margaret Ruhe holds a copy of Lao Russell's book Love *for her to autograph.*

Lao's Canadian secretary, Margaret Ruhe, impressed visitors with the fact that her voice patterns had grown so similar to those of Lao. One noticed that the rhythm, the phrases, and the slight accent were very suggestive of Lao.

In a cover story in the March 3, 1983, issue of *The Declaration*, a newspaper published by students at the University of Virginia, reporter John Martin focused on what he termed "The History and Mystery behind Swannanoa."

After a vivid account of his "startling first impressions," he described how he and his roommate had discovered the palace somewhat by accident after a day of hiking in the Blue Ridge Mountains. Describing their drive up the road to the palace as dusk began to settle like "taking a climb in a small Cessna," he described their awe at suddenly seeing the palace "glaring from the light of the spots focused on it." Amazed at the spectacle, they hastily retreated, but the next weekend their curiosity led them to make a legitimate visit. Martin had called the day before in hopes of meeting Lao personally, but they were greeted instead by Margaret Ruhe, who advised them, "Mrs. Russell is very busy, and constantly on the phone. She's talking to one of her students in Australia right now, but she may be able to see you later, perhaps in half an hour."

The two University students, who had dressed in the typical preppy style for their visit, were amazed at the array of sculptures, busts, paintings, medallions, certificates, and books in the dimly lit room. Naturally, their eyes were drawn to the white marble staircase and "enormous Tiffany stained-glass window at its landing, sunlight streaming through. Its colors scattered across the steps." Margaret showed them the videotape of Lao's interview on *P.M. Magazine*, which she said would give them "a good idea of what this place is about."

Later, as they were looking into some of the Russells' books on display in the library, Lao appeared on the marble steps, descending slowly. "She was smiling radiantly, wearing a blue-green gown that set off her silvery hair and blue eyes. After greeting us very warmly, she sat down in front of the fireplace, and told us stories of the past, her feelings that day, her visions of tomorrow," Martin recounted.

"The greatest thing that has disunited man," Lao told them softly, "is not knowing who he is. It's all very simple, you know. Like a tree. The branches are the countries. The leaves are the people. But all get their sustenance from the one root. Man has made life so complex."

She gave them advice on romantic pursuits, cautioning, "You attract to yourself what you think. That's why it's important to think right. You must not compromise. Every time you compromise, you make a detour. You waste precious time." She advised them, "I live solely to try and bring an awareness to man of really how great he is."

Lao escorted the two college students to the second floor of the palace. Martin described her sitting room, decorated in pink, aqua, and lavender, with its "spectacular view of the Sculpture Gardens behind the palace centering around the Christ statute inspired by Lao's vision." They admired the panoramic view of the Rockfish Valley, which other windows afforded. "Far below," Martin wrote, "buildings looked like mere spots, as if seen from a plane."

Their upstairs tour included all the highlights special students had come to know well from their visits to the palace. Lao showed them the intricate watercolor paintings of old harbor scenes with incredibly detailed sailing ships, works of art that she had executed as a very young girl. They saw Walter's precise drawings from the Spanish-American War. "One depicted some drowning sailors struggling on their capsizing ship. Another was a court martial scene. Every one of the over twenty people in that picture had a distinctly different face. From ten feet away, the drawings looked just like black-and-white photographs," Martin wrote.

Returning to the main floor with her fascinated visitors, Lao showed them Walter's early scientific paintings, which Martin described as looking "a lot like modern posters of outer space done in psychedelic, fluorescent colors. One appeared to be the rings of Saturn. These futuristic paintings were actually done over sixty years ago, long before such colors or concepts became popular." She pointed out details of Walter's Mark Twain Memorial Sculpture and his award-winning painting *The Might of Ages*. By the end of the visit she had clearly charmed her guests. This is apparent from the last paragraphs of Martin's story in which he urged his readers to visit the palace: "As we were leaving, Mrs. Russell showed us to the door. 'Come back and see me. Bring some of your friends,' she said, smiling as brightly as when we had met her a couple of hours ago. She closed the heavy doors quietly behind us.

"'You know, she's gotta be one of the most charismatic people I've met,' I told Joe. 'Yeah, almost ageless, in a way.'"

Lao felt that the best path to meditation was to fill one's soul with desire for ecstasy. Many people misunderstood meditation, she felt, because they have been taught to concentrate either on some part of the body or some object. That often led to motion rather than stillness.

Lao explained that scientific demonstrations of the mechanics of Walter Russell's scientific principles were generally the copyright of the inventors and producers. The technology was valid, she assured her readers, and had been frequently demonstrated.

Lao's great friend Gloria Swanson, the quintessential glamour girl who reigned in Hollywood's Golden Age, died on April 4, 1983, at a New York hospital at the age of eighty-four. She had been hospitalized for several weeks following a slight heart attack. Miss Swanson and Lao had kept in touch over the years and had last communicated with each other just before Christmas 1982. The great actress believed she had found truth in the teachings of the Russells and that they helped her become a better person. "I thought she would live to be a hundred. She took such good care of herself," Lao said. "Loneliness must have killed her. When she didn't have a man in her life, she was so lonely," she added. Subsequently, Lao was given to understand that the medicines given to Miss Swanson in the hospital had been a fatal shock to a system that had been spared chemicals and toxic substances for years.

In 1983, the Cold War was in full sway, and it appeared that a nuclear holocaust would be the certain fate of mankind. Lao received a deep and thoughtful letter from a Los Angeles student named Marv Hudis, who asked the simple question, "What can I do now to help prevent world war?" Lao's reply developed into a message that she came to share with many deep thinkers. She told him that his letter had touched a deep chord in her heart and soul. Not a day passed that Lao did not hear the same plea of what could be done to prevent a world war. She truly believed that "man is so close to his annihilation, and that only the miracle of awakening him to the Source of his power and purpose can bring the necessary balance to stop man from destroying himself and the entire planet." She told Marv Hudis that there truly is a single answer to the prevention of world holocaust, "and that single answer is for mankind to be awakened to the cause of our problems by putting into practice God's inviolate Law of Love, which is Rhythmic Balanced Interchange. Lao said that God had told her during her three-day and -night illumination, three months before Walter Russell and she met, that the greatest problem in the world had been created by the unbalance in the male-female principle, both in human relations and in science itself. Lao recalled that "in that period God made known to me that half the sun was blue and the other half of the sun was red, as were all the planets of our solar system. That is why Nature has always balanced itself even though that balancing may take a million years or more!" Mankind, she stressed, had but one lifetime to balance his human relations. She truly believed that because of lack of balance in the world, humanity had unfolded a mile technologically, but only an inch spiritually.

She believed that only a natural-law catastrophe would awaken man to the solution to the problem. In 1972, when she had just completed her book *Why You Cannot Die!*, she sensed intuitively that it would be the weather conditions that would make man listen to the Russells' Message. She knew that when she and Walter had written *Atomic Suicide?* in 1957, it was a voice crying in the wilderness, yet twenty-six years later, the book was being sent for and used by scientists and thinking people all over the world. In 1982, Nigeria alone had ordered 6,000 copies of the book.

Lao applauded Soviet dissident Andrei Sakharov, who echoed her own opinion regarding nuclear proliferation in a devastating open letter to American physicist Sidney Drell in mid-1983. The Russells were a hundred percent against the use of atomic fission for war or industry, because it represented the extreme degree of the death principle. She looked for "the miracle of an awakening of world leaders in all countries to the fact that all mankind needs is to cooperate in order to save the world. "This may sound like an impossible happening," she wrote Hudis, "but God has told me five times, since my beloved refolded, that, 'this time I shall not fail,' and that, 'all men shall come unto me.'"

Lao said that the answer to Hudis's question was absolutely simple. "The greatest help today is for each and every soul to unfold within himself the awareness of the God-light which centers all men equally. Great accumulative power could accrue from groups of people becoming aware of the God-power that centers them when they put the principles into practice." She circulated an article on "radioactive waste" by ABC television producer Stanhope Gould and NBC legal consultant and San Francisco attorney Brian McTigue. She quoted a letter from a physician, Dr. William Chagares, whose life demonstrated the power that came to him upon putting into practice the principles of the Russells' teachings.

Lao realized that what she had written would sound to some as "too simple a solution for the prevention of war." She knew that the very simplicity of God's creation and his laws had led to man's confusion. Mankind insisted on making all of life complex, because he followed sensed-thinking instead of mind-knowing. He had resorted to drugs, alcohol, and perverted sex, instead of knowing the ecstasy of love through the balance of mental and spiritual interchange, which alone brought the fulfillment of an individual's desire for true love and matehood. Man had abused sex and failed to realize that sex was God's holy law of creation. She considered it a tragedy that man was so full of fear, hate, greed, and violence that he failed to recognize his own true worth. She recognized that the modern educational system, built on empirical knowledge and not on natural law, had failed to give mankind the knowledge of his inner power nor allowed him to unfold his awareness as to the how and why of creation. "The hardest lesson man ever has to learn is that the only thing one can ever have to hold forever is that which one first gives."

She told her students *The Man Who Tapped the Secrets of the Universe*, *Love*, and *God Will Work with You but Not for You* were three books that could give them new vistas of thought, ever greater awareness of man's true purpose on earth, and the fulfillment of their deepest desire.

"Always remember that Love (God) is the strongest force in the world. You are an extension of that tremendous power and there is no power that can destroy the power of Love (God)."

Her longtime student Minnette Crow of Prescott, Arizona, recommended several anti-nuclear films that were sponsored by Common Cause and Prescott College. One was titled *If You Love This Planet*, and another *In the Nuclear Shadow—What Can the Children Tell Us?*

Lao and Emelia shared information on a regular basis as to the increasing practice of radioactive wastes being dumped into the oceans.

In a September 1984 letter to Ms. Ruth Drury, a deep student of the Russell works who had learned of them while attending the World Harmony Peace Conference in New Zealand, Lao compared education by "knowing" with more traditional higher education: "We must cultivate imagination and inspiration rather than memory. The accepted concept of higher education is a more intense, empirical, physical knowledge, whereas higher knowledge is, in reality, the recognition of the cosmic Light which opens the door to awareness of man as a cosmic, spiritual entity. We have hundreds of conventionally educated engineers, doctors, lawyers, industrialists, and others in all walks of life, who leap suddenly ahead when they awaken their cosmic, divine basis. There is a profound reason for this. Each man who thus transforms himself is beginning to find that the well of cosmic knowledge is within himself not outside of himself." Ms. Drury, a businesswoman who used the Golden Rule as the basis of her work, edited *The Living Word* newsletter and promoted Lao's philosophy.

Lao liked to quote a businessman from Trinidad who wrote her that by applying the principles taught by the Russells, "I find that I am over 100 percent more efficient, and this is apparent in my business to the extent that the profits of the company of which I am managing director were the best in its entire existence of over forty years!"

She tried hard to clear up students' confusion regarding the difference between good and evil. "The hardest thing for most people to understand," she said, "is why the innocent have to suffer with the guilty. The explanation of this phenomenon is because all people are truly one."

"The cause of the present world crisis could be put in one phrase—taking instead of giving—which always leads to experiences we describe as evil," she explained.

134. John Denver with Lao at Swannanoa.

John Denver came to see Lao the week of June 20, 1983, and they enjoyed a wonderful visit. He landed his helicopter on the front lawn of the palace, which caused much excitement for everyone there. Dr. Tim Binder, his personal physician and Lao's great friend from Colorado, accompanied him. John Denver was greatly inspired by what he found at Swannanoa, and Lao considered him a very beautiful, spiritual soul whose world vision made him a kindred spirit.

Lao was most impressed when she read his speech three years later at the Choices for the Future Symposium: "With consciousness about who we are and what we are, with the awareness of the problems we are faced with, with a commitment not only to ourselves but to each other, we can make it work." She thrilled to the words he proclaimed to his colleagues at Windstar in Aspen: "We can end hunger. We can rid the world of nuclear weapons and the rhetoric war. We can begin to live the reality of the family of humankind on this planet. It's a possibility!"

Franca Dal Toso-Bourne of Taringa, Queensland, wrote Lao of her efforts to alert every member of the Australian parliament to the dangers of radioactive waste. She was one of the strongest leaders of the anti-nuclear movement there and had kept in close contact with Lao.

Lao described in detail the difference between extra-sensory perception (ESP) and mind-knowing, or ISP (inner-sensory perception), which she defined as the light of God. She said that ESP was not always true spiritual awareness, because it could be governed by one's own personal sense-desires and imaginings, whereas inner-sensory perception came from giving form to one's knowing in the stillness of the God-light. She likened ESP to empirical information and ISP to basic knowledge of God.

The autumn 1983 issue of *Nexus: The Connection* featured an informative article about Lao by Grace J. Mazza. It contained the usual description of the palace, gardens, and artwork, but, more than most such articles, it included some of Lao's conversation with the reporter. These reveal the soft but certain logic with which she approached cosmic subjects. "As tea was served and we continued to chat," Miss Mazza wrote, "Ms. Russell summed up in one statement the one truth that can change everyone's life and make it richer and fuller. 'If you understand the laws that govern you, and you work in harmony with them, nothing is impossible. If we are to elevate man beyond hate and war, we must act individually and with respect. This effort will benefit us collectively. Love has only one constant. It must be given and received. It can never be kept. Its constant movement is its survival. The more you give it the more it becomes. Its intensity can permeate all living matter.'"

Lao sympathized with traditional artists. She discussed trends in modern art with her friend Dr. George Speck, telling him that she had told one traditional art student from California, "I know how you feel at the seeming unappreciation of your work, for the same thing happened to Walter Russell when modern art became popular. In truth, however, it proved the

135. Lao with Dr. George Speck.

beginning of the greatest point in Walter's life."

Lao believed that Mother Nature was the best doctor in the world. She strongly recommended cod liver oil as a medical remedy, and recommended that students take out their frustrations through physical work. One of her students loved to escape from the rigors of his high-pressure work in big city advertising to spend four or five days at Swannanoa weeding the gardens.

As always, there were problems with people using the Russells' names under false pretenses. Lao was quick to counter any such unauthorized abuses. Plagiarists continued to offend her by publishing extracts from the Russell works as their own. Lao always protested such illegal action, but generally concluded that court proceedings would do little more than give the pirate greater publicity. Students in Canada advised her that Paul Twitchell (also known as Eckankar) had taken long extracts from Walter Russell's book *The Secret of Light* and had plagiarized it in *The Tiger's Fang*, as if it were a message channeled directly to Twitchell from God. He had come to Swannanoa in 1949 and purchased a copy of Walter's book. The office staff had recorded the purchase on his card in the University files. Lao had been told that Paul Twitchell had also been accused of plagiarizing Joel Goldsmith's writings in the same way he had Walter's. Soon afterwards, the plagiarist was killed in a car accident in Washington, D.C. "I never hear the name of Paul Twitchell or Eckankar," she said, "without feeling a sense of pity and sorrow for one who was doing spiritual work and yet was so unaware of God's inviolate law of balance."

Lao's prison mission was expanding. She received letters from many chaplains and prisoners saying that *God Will Work with You but Not for You* was one of the most inspiring books they had ever had in their prison libraries.

Lao did not know whether or not Walter had known Paramhansa Yogananda, but she was certain her husband knew of the great teacher's spiritual classic *Autobiography of a Yogi*. In answer to an inquiry, she wrote, "If Paramhansa Yogananda had been in New York, he undoubtedly had heard of Walter Russell, if he did not know him personally, for at the time you mentioned Walter Russell was a prominent figure in New York as you know from *The Man Who Tapped the Secrets of the Universe*."

In November 1983, Lao wrote Emelia that she had scarcely been off the mountain for the previous three years. "The last time I drove the car I felt that it was running away from me down the mountain, so I knew that it was time for me to stop driving for awhile," she reported.

Nevertheless, she had quietly developed friendships with some of the well-established old Waynesboro families. She enjoyed warm philosophical conversations with Ruth and Bernard Keiser and relished the opportunity to get to know their vivacious and intelligent children. When their daughter

Sandy Keiser married Clayton Edwards in August 1983, Lao prepared a special reading for them to use in their wedding at Hickory Hill, their commanding home just west of Waynesboro.

Lao's medical care was being directed by Dr. Paul Eck of The Eck Institute of Applied Nutrition and Bioenergetics, Ltd., Analytical Research Labs in Phoenix, Arizona, who she had met through Sam Biser. Dr. Eck had been a nutritional scientist for well over thirty years and had produced exceptional results for his patients, even including those who were severely mentally handicapped. Described by his colleagues as a pioneer in hair mineral testing, Dr. Eck incorporated the stress theory of disease, metabolic typing, natural healing theory, and modern biology in interpreting the test and prescribing palliatives. Lao followed his advice carefully and was extremely pleased with the results. "I have been on his program steadily for some time now," Lao was swift to tell all who asked, "and I consider him tops!" She wrote Dr. Eck, "I bless you every day for all your help to get me well and strong."

Lao hoped to get a Christmas message out for 1983. She wrote half of it in October, but she had so many special interviews that it was impossible to complete it in time for printing and mailing before Christmas. She wrote her friend Howard Hall, whose Conquadco, Inc., was dedicated to "Advancement of Man, Managers of Natural Resources, Industry and Commerce," describing her work day at that time: "I was downstairs talking to special people on Saturdays and Sundays for five, six, seven and eight hours at a stretch, as well as having special appointments during the week."

In November 1983, Governor Okilo visited Lao. She was excited to learn firsthand of the progress he was making in bringing universal education and long-needed government reforms to Nigeria's Rivers State. They had an exceptionally productive visit, and Lao was more confident than ever that the Message was being effectively disseminated in his great African nation by this far-thinking and selfless humanitarian.

Melford Okilo stressed that the Russells had confirmed for him that the Law of Love was God's only law, and that it was applicable to all men and all creation. "Like every other law, it has it own sanctions. Its obedience brings its own rewards and blessings, while its disobedience brings its own punishment and suffering," he explained. "The Law controls the rise and fall of men, nations, governments, and civilizations, including everything that men and nations do to each other. It is the law by which Nature takes its Course without conflict and confusion. It regulates the ebb and flow of the tides, the orderly succession of day and night, the seasons of the year, the orderly movement of the sun, moon, stars, and all other heavenly bodies in their respective orbits. It is the same law by which all created things are produced and are allowed to develop themselves in such an orderly manner that none can injure the other except for the purpose for which they were created. It keeps our planet and the Universe in an eternal state of balance." He sought to exemplify in his life this unalterable universal law.

Governor Okilo urged Lao to travel to Nigeria to see for herself the impact the Russell teachings were having on the country. She had wanted to go but felt the trip would be too strenuous. Months later his cousin visited her and took several hundred copies of her books back to Nigeria by air. Others told Lao that the rest of Africa looked to Nigeria for direction, and she began to feel that she might "have a part in the influencing of God's ways and processes in the Africa of tomorrow."

Within weeks after Governor Okilo's return to Nigeria on December 31, 1983, the world was stunned to learn that a military government had seized control of the country. Lao desperately sought news as to Governor Okilo's welfare. She intuitively felt that he would be safe, but it was months before she learned that he had been imprisoned on his removal from office at the time of the coup. She contacted American and Nigerian officials in Washington and London, and used the limited means at her disposal to promote his well-being.

When the military took power, they again centralized money and power in the state and federal government, bringing many hardships to the people Governor Okilo had done so much to liberate. But even after the military coup had effectively ended his remarkably successful experiment in participatory democracy, it was obvious to every unbiased observer that his visionary government by decentralization had produced many long-lasting, beneficial effects. The economic impact of the program was apparent. "The government gave power and money to all the governed for their physical, economic, moral and social development through their own [local] organs of government, and the people responded by regiving of service to each other for mutual cooperation," he explained, adding that the program benefited every citizen "from the humblest to the highest." His determined efforts had brought peace, unity, stability, and prosperity to the diverse people of his jurisdiction.

After seeing the nuclear holocaust film *The Day After*, a student telephoned to tell Lao that she should have been portrayed giving the solution to the nightmare depicted in that film, instead of commentators who had no solution to abate the fear in millions of hearts. He ordered seventy-five copies of *Atomic Suicide?*, which he sent to prominent American and world leaders, including the governors of all fifty states. Within weeks he had received more than thirty substantive replies, he advised Lao, noting that many of the recipients were demonstrating "more than a passing interest."

Abbey Cowen in Johannesburg had undertaken the mission of spreading Lao's *Code of Ethics* throughout South Africa. A student had come to Swannanoa from Switzerland after reading the *Code of Ethics* and bought copies of all the Russell books to take back to Switzerland, saying they were the greatest teachings she had ever known, and telling Lao that her *Code of Ethics* "should be used all over the world by everyone."

Lao sensed an increasing uneasiness in those who corresponded with her. She wrote long and reassuring letters to these individuals, often concluding, "In these days of worldwide tension, to become aware of the stillness of God is one's greatest achievement, as well as one's greatest security. Living Love is truly a challenge, but it is the single answer to personal and world peace and happiness."

Sam Biser was helping Lao more and more with staff decisions and organizational work at the palace. He encouraged her to maintain a careful, balanced diet, as well as to do regular exercises. When her nephew, Peter Summerfield, and his wife, Betty, paid her a visit in 1983, they found her in excellent health and were delighted to see the dedication with which she pursued her health routine. It was obvious to them that Sam Biser was a major source of encouragement to her.

Lao was greatly interested in another book, *Frozen Flame*, which told the story of the dangerous usage of liquefied frozen gas all over the world. She added this book to her list of supplementary readings.

On April 29, 1984, she spent a productive and mutually stimulating day at Swannanoa with Etel DeLoach, an internationally known psychic healer, who was brought to see Lao by her friend Mary Frances Arpante, the director of the Positive Healing Center in Arlington, Virginia.

Witter Brynner's translation of Lao Tzu's *The Way of Life* remained her favorite, and she recommended that special students try to obtain the out-of-print edition from a used-book dealer. She had replaced it on her book list with a lovely edition of the timeless classic, translated by Gia-Fu Feng and Jane English and beautifully illustrated. "I am sure you would enjoy this if you cannot find the translation mentioned in the Course," she advised her new enrollees.

In April 1984, a student with an active prison ministry in Ohio purchased the *Home Study Course* as a gift for a particularly interested inmate who posed pointed questions to Lao in a letter: "I perfectly understand that God is in all of us, but Who is the God Head? How did we get separated in the first place? I realize that we are NOT separated, but we think we are. How did we forget? Who remained in control when the others forgot?? How was it that all (the God-Head) did not forget? Are we as enlightened beings considered as the God-head?? Is there such thing as Godhead? Who is in control and why, and for how long, and why?"

Lao's response was definite: "To answer your questions regarding the God-Head, we do not use the language of the God-Head but rather, we refer to one's God-Self. As this term expresses, the God-Self is truly the God-Light, which could be called the Soul that centers all living things whether it be man, animal, bird, fish or tree."

Lao was not a graphologist, but she knew from experience that she possessed an uncanny ability to tell much about a person through letters they had written her. In May 1984, she wrote a particularly sensitive inquirer, Jeff Arthur of Tampa, Florida: "The power in your handwriting [when I read your letter this morning] truly touched my heart, and I know how greatly you will appreciate the book about my husband. I say this from judging the way you write and your handwriting."

William B. Connor sent Lao a copy of his *Concordphone* book, which had received a disappointing reception. Lao understood the reason. "Truly there are all too few awakened souls in the whole world, and to try to extend the knowledge you have in color and music is like a voice crying in the wilderness," she wrote him. "I believe that it would help you extend the knowledge you have in your lectures and writings if you use a language which might be considered suitable for a child of ten, for truly the world's understanding and comprehension is that of a child."

Lao kept in regular contact with her "treasured friend" Michael Hudak of Akron, Ohio, who referred many of his friends and acquaintances to the University. Through him she met Mark Worrell of Cuyahoga Falls, Ohio, who visited her and was eager in promoting the University's teaching among those who he taught and counseled. Michael had sent Mark a copy of *The Universal One* as a birthday gift in September 1980. Over the next decade Michael Hudak sent many gifts of the Russell books to friends and loved ones, including his brother on the latter's wedding day and his friend who owned and published the Warren, Ohio, *Tribune*. Michael was a leading figure in a worldwide peace organization called Legacy, through which he gave many copies of *Atomic Suicide?* and *The Secret of Light* to such luminaries as Dr. Helen Caldicott and Dr. Benjamin Spock.

To students under unusual stress and tension, Lao wrote, "The best advice I can give you is to know that every single thought and every single action has an equal reaction." She often added the following experience: "I told this to a woman who had twelve beds to make every day, as well as all of her other work. She told me that she hated making beds. After doing her work for several weeks with the thought that the God-Light centered every cell of her body and, therefore, God did everything with her, she wrote me and said that she not only made all of the beds and did all of her other work with joy, but never felt tired anymore with all of her work!"

Lao wrote a student from Portales, New Mexico, "It is wonderful that you are working in a hospital which has the reputation of caring for the people who use it, for most people who become ill have known the frustration of unfulfilled love."

When a student suggested that Jesus had said, "Whoever marries a divorced woman commits adultery," Lao replied, "I doubt very much that this statement was made by Jesus, and I agree with you that there are quite a few statements attributed to Jesus that were really made by the church fathers of the day. I remember a woman coming to see me several years ago who had had a divorce and doubted whether she should ever marry again because she had been married in church. Her husband had remarried, and she was very lonely. She was so relieved when I told her my feelings on this matter. Then she remarried, and for the first time in her life knew true love. This was because she had learned as an individual that only when one knows his or her Oneness in God can one learn to know and live true love."

"The single purpose of any one is to know one's divinity and live it!" she generally concluded.

136. Bridget Killen and Kevin Mitchell.

In Pittsburgh, Bridget Killen, a beautiful and spiritually mature young student with an operatic voice and deep insight into the Russell work, had organized a Character Club to discuss the Russell philosophy. This delighted Lao, who was very fond of Bridget and wrote her often. "It is wonderful to hear indirectly from your precious friends that you have started and are getting strongly underway with your Character Club chapter. When the members of a Character Club put into practice the principles given throughout all of our writings, a great change can take place within their characters and way of life. When Love is put into practice in all things one does, it brings an inner joy to one's heart and happiness is attracted to the person."

Soon afterwards, Bridget came to Swannanoa to devote her full energies to escorting visitors through the palace. Lao felt that Bridget radiated light. She was on staff until after Lao's death, and subsequently married a fellow student at Swannanoa, Kevin Mitchell, a talented craftsman. They settled in the area near Charlottesville, Virginia, and reared their family, reflecting the highest principles in their lives.

After surviving three bouts with death within a year and each time experiencing the near-death phenomenom, Dr. P. M. H. Atwater was starting over, recreating her life, when she came to visit Lao Russell on a foggy September day in 1984, Lao recognized her at once, although they had never met before.

She told Dr. Atwater, "You have important work to do. You'll be speaking to thousands of people." Lao spoke to her about love and how to direct that love to her audience in such a way that each person not only heard but felt what was being said. Ms. Atwater often returned to see Lao over the next four years, and followed her advice during decades of clinical verification of the near-death phenomenom, research that was verified in her books and in such prestigious professional periodicals as *Lancet Medical Journal*. "It was love that brought me to Lao, love that she sent me away with, and love that has guided me ever onward," Dr. Atwater wrote.

Lao enjoyed hearing from Tesla scientists, and often recounted how she had persuaded Walter not to follow the great inventor's advice on limiting access to the Russell knowledge: "I was also glad to know of your appreciation of Nikola Tesla," she wrote one such student in 1984. "My husband was very close to him in the last years of his life. Tesla told my husband that he should lock all of his new scientific knowledge up in the Smithsonian Institute for he said not only was the world not ready for it, but they would crucify him for trying to give it. However, when I met my Beloved after my own Illumination, I told him that the world desperately needed the new scientific knowledge NOW and from the moment we met, we worked together giving our combined Messages from God to the world. I am grateful to say that many scientists and other deep thinkers are not only listening, but acting upon our teachings and my deepest desire is that great action will take place in time!"

Cicely Allan, director of the White Lodge, an English center for esoteric studies in color research and spiritual therapies, wrote Lao, "Your work as outlined in *Atomic Suicide?* is a natural complement to the Cosmic Science/Earth Science aspects of our work, and it would be my pleasure to incorporate the knowledge drawn from your material in our own work. I should therefore like to have permission from you to do this so that all may continue in a straightforward manner. Since it is your wish that not only your work but the knowledge enclosed within it shall reach as many people as possible, I am hopeful that such cooperation will be forthcoming. We look forward to a closer association." This was typical of the broad range of like-minded organizations that recommended the University teachings with Lao's blessing. All she desired was assurance that the integrity of the Russell work not be compromised or diluted in the exchange of information.

Sam Biser's frequent references to the University and its publications in

The Healthview Newsletter brought Lao into contact with many forward-thinking men and women. Her letter of September 6, 1984, to a scientist named Paul Scardina reflects the range of this increasing volume of correspondence: "Thank you for your valued letter which you were inspired to write upon reading the article on the transmutation of free hydrogen. Walter Russell has pictured the orderliness, the symmetry, and the balance that all Nature expresses. He explains how Nature polarizes and depolarizes in its every expression, just as man does in his every action and in every second of his life in his breathings, although he is not aware of it. The fulcrum from which all power springs is knowledge. When man has the omniscience which is unfolding in cosmic man, he will no longer misuse, break, or disobey God's Law because of being unaware of it. He will command it because he will know the law. The 'life and death' cycles of man and of the elements of matter do not vary. They are the same, for man's body is a compound of these elements."

Lao spoke frequently with Emelia by telephone. Her friend was increasingly handicapped by arthritis but deeply appreciated word from Lao, writing her, "Your calls always give me a great emotional boost, and I treasure them dearly. You seem to have a direct line to my heart and emotions. It is incredible how you can tune in, and it has always been that way."

Students coming to Swannanoa were more and more interested in the archival material supporting their work. Lao made transcripts of many of the newspaper clippings covering Walter's work in the 1920s and 1930s available for researchers.

She also continued to give wide distribution to the letter Dr. Francis Trevelyan Miller had written Walter when *The Secret of Light* had been published. She enjoyed recounting that Dr. Miller had said that the free verse poetry of Walter Russell's *Book of Early Whisperings* "out-Whitmanned Walt Whitman for beauty."

137. Dr. Grace Faus.

When a student wrote Lao about walking with her husband in the Muir Woods of California, Lao replied, "I shared the joy of your walk with your husband. It brought memories of my walks around the mountain with my Beloved. We used to take a daily walk with our little Scottie, and it was on these walks that we would talk about the writings you are now studying in our *Home Study Course*."

In September, Dr. Grace Faus, the legendary Divine Science minister so well-known for her many years as minister of the First Divine Science

Church at 2600 16th Street in Washington, D.C., held another of her successful seminars from her active retirement home in Baily, Colorado. Dr. Faus and her husband had attended the first summer class at Swannanoa in 1949. Gracious and understanding, she had always championed the important work Lao was doing from Swannanoa. A number of Dr. Faus's seminar participants wrote the University for more information about the Russells and their work. One such student, Meredith Bauman of Denver, described Dr. Faus's seminar as "absolutely marvelous and inspiring. She is such a beautiful soul. How lucky she was to have had the opportunity to study with Walter Russell and you."

The popularity of her "You Are Important" stickers pleased Lao. "I would like to see these signs in every home, office, store, church and prison—in fact, everywhere people live, work, or visit. Man's frustration has arisen from his own sense of inadequacy. When all men at last know that they are an extension of God and of each other, we can look forward to the greatest period of peace, happiness, and prosperity that the world has ever known," she wrote Mary Davey of San Juan Capistrano, California, who had ordered a supply of the stickers.

In a general letter to students dated October 6, 1984, Lao advised, "Knowledge is the only power which any man has to make himself superior to himself each succeeding day of his life. We shall forever have conflict and wars until men know their oneness in each other. To know oneness is to know the unlimited power of Love."

In 1984, Michael Hudak requested that many of the Russells' books be sent to Tom DeFrange, the author/songwriter of the nuclear disarmament-themed play *Alice in Blunderland*, which they would sponsor across America and as far away as the Soviet Union. Hudak delighted in recounting for Lao how he began sharing the Russell books with Tom DeFrange and soon afterwards took a family vacation with the DeFranges, during which Tom read the Russell books constantly. "He awoke every day at dawn and meditated on your teachings at the waterfront. He then retreated to a silent place and wrote a new song every day for fifteen days."

On October 6, 1984, Lao sent out signed, six-page, individual letters of reference to several important students, who she described as deep and able teachers of the University's curriculum. They were Dr. Timothy Binder, Neal Chaves, Thomas A. Concert, and Dennis L. Ricketts, each of whom offered to conduct lectures and seminars on the Russells' teachings in universities, schools, business and social organizations, and churches.

John David Mann later described how Binder, "a naturopathic doctor whose client list includes John Denver and other well-connected environmental advocates, has studied and championed the Russell teachings along with macrobiotics, the climate crisis/soil mineralization thesis of John Hamaker, and other vital fields of perspective." Binder emerged in the late 1980s as a leading standard-bearer in what *Solstice* magazine termed "the massive project of reintroducing the Russells' revision of science to the world. While his own interests naturally lean toward matters of human health and diet, Dr. Binder has thrown the University's focus and resources full-force into documenting and publicizing the possible ozone-radiation link." Binder crusaded for years to bring nuclear sanity to a world in which the proliferation of atomic power plants had led to such disasters as those at Chernobyl and Three Mile Island. He also buttressed Lao's belief that the ozone crisis would finally compel the scientific world and the general public to recognize the validity of the warnings the Russells had given the world in the 1950s through their open letter to scientists and their book *Atomic Suicide?*

A student sent Lao a photograph of the gravestone he had erected as his future memorial. The epitaph read, "Life is Light in Motion. Death is Light at rest. Rest=Motion." She replied, "It is wonderful to see such a marker, for this will someday be recognized as meaning that no one can truly die. You are indeed a special soul!"

In June 1984, she was visited by Claes Nobel, grandnephew of the famous Alfred Nobel of Sweden. Claes had bought seven of the Russell books at the Bodhi Tree Bookstore in Los Angeles, and after reading them had telephoned Lao to say that he had never read such truth and knowledge in all of the thousands of books he had read. He had felt an immediate and deep commitment to extending the Message throughout the world.

There was a growing demand for the books and *Home Study Course* among Unity students across the country. It had been nearly thirty years since Lao had spoken before her first Unity audience at Unity Headquarters in Lee's Summit, Missouri.

She referred students in Southern California to a spiritual leader named JacQueline at the Los Angeles Triune Light Center on Wilshire Boulevard, who regularly led study groups on the *Home Study Course* and was always willing to give helpful advice to others who wished to organize and teach such classes.

Emelia was unable to come to Virginia for Lao's birthday, but several weeks later enjoyed a long visit to Swannanoa that extended through mid-December. The two old friends always struck the perfect balance between sharing memories and exploring new horizons. "I enjoyed being with you very, very much! It was like old times. You made my visit so lovely," Emelia wrote on her return to New Jersey. She had met the new staff for the first time. "I was happy to meet Margaret, Dolores, and David. Now I know the whole 'family.' I'm so glad they're all there with you."

Betsy Fleet, a well-known Virginia writer, was preparing an article for the

Virginia State Library's scholarly and well-illustrated quarterly, *Virginia Cavalcade*, but both Sam Biser and Lao were too busy to devote the time necessary for interviews with her, and Lao had a "strong intuitive feeling that the delay has a very definite purpose!"

Sam Biser left Swannanoa on an urgent and extended business trip, and Lao was deluged with urgent mail and work in connection with the reprinting of *The World Crisis* and the *Home Study Course*. Lao knew that 1984 had been a difficult year for countless people. As she reviewed *The World Crisis*, she wrote Betsy how she "wished this book could reach the leaders of the world and every businessman. So many of the topics and violent things of today are described in that book which we wrote in 1958. The subtitle is *A Blueprint for Peace and Prosperity*."

Students constantly asked if Walter had built any machinery to test his theories. "It seems to me that extremely energy efficient devices for electrical generation could be built based on Dr. Russell's theories of light and derived energy configurations" was a typical student view. "I was particularly delighted by Dr. Russell's knowledge of the ring system of Jupiter. That was only discovered in the past two years or so," a student wrote Lao in late 1983.

In September 1984, Lao had a challenging weekend with scientists and teachers in a seminar at the palace.

In November Lao heard from Johnnie Lee Macfadden, fourth wife of the great physical culturist Bernarr Macfadden. Lao had met him in the early 1930s and was delighted to become acquainted with Johnnie Lee, who had married Macfadden in 1948. Johnnie Lee Macfadden, a well-known health expert who authored a dramatic bestselling memoir titled *Barefoot in Eden*, always enthusiastically recommended the Russell writings to her many friends, including a number of individuals who were prominent in the New York theatrical world. Jerry Adler came to know and corresponded with Lao as a result of this introduction. Mrs. Macfadden often visited Lao at Swannanoa.

A tourist visiting from Fredericksburg noticed that the plaque on Lao's bust in the Swannanoa music room described her as a humanist. "I always thought humanists do not believe in God. Please explain your belief as a humanist," the tourist wrote a few days later. Lao was quick to respond and firm in her conviction: "I presume you saw the sign under my bust, which my late beloved husband made in 1959. Dr. Russell certainly did not know how the word 'humanist' would be used and interpreted in the 1980s, for both of us used this word as one would use the word 'humanitarian.' I was more than shocked to look up 'humanist' in a present-day dictionary. Both my late husband and I have lived only to awaken God-awareness in our fellow man. To us God is all there is! The world will never know peace on earth until the world awakens to the Cause (God) of all things. It was to give emphasis to God's Love that we sculptured and erected our statue of Jesus in the gardens with the message, 'Love Ye One Another,' on the pedestal."

She was quick to relate her religious background. "Regarding my denomination, I was born in England, was christened when I was three weeks old, and was confirmed by the Bishop of St. Albans in the Church of England when I was eighteen years of age. My grandmother's family, the Lester family, sent the first missionaries out of England, and I have never forgotten my heritage." Walter Russell, she added, "was brought up in a Baptist Church and was the church organist when he was only nine years old. He loved the spiritual quality of organ music and played it all of his life."

Robert Wooler, administrator of the Centre for Universal Harmony and Service in Devon, England, advised Lao that he was preparing his thesis on Walter Russell, who he believed to have been a forerunner of the new group of world servers, adding, "We believe that God has never left himself without a witness and that through the ages the path of Ageless Wisdom has been charted and developed by one pioneering thinker after another." She sent him detailed information on the University and told him, "Our work has encircled the world strongly with students in practically every country and of every race, nationality, and creed." She recounted the history of the University's precursor, the Twilight Club, through the various eras of its existence, since Herbert Spencer had founded it in the 1870s.

Lao wrote Ginger Evans, a physiotherapist of note who had visited her at the palace, "I wish every physiotherapist could become acquainted with our teachings, for so much could be given to our fellow man when man understands how the Light of God centers every cell of one's body, and there could be great healing power through the hands of doctors for their patients."

Despite the political situation in Nigeria, she received many inquiries from that country. Because of difficulties in the exchange of currency between the two countries, the only way money could be remitted to the United States was through banks in such other countries as England and Switzerland. This made it difficult for Nigerian students to purchase the University's books and enroll in the *Home Study Course*. William Cranwell, who had befriended Lao and the University so often in recent years, established a large scholarship fund especially for Nigerian students, making it possible for the Message to continue its growth in that country, even during the political imprisonment of Lao's beloved friend and colleague Governor Okilo.

Lao wrote that she had searched her soul for the greatest message of love and peace that she could give her friends and students for Christmas 1984, hoping that it "would also bring comfort and happiness to you through every day of the New Year. My Soul echoed the four greatest words ever spoken, 'Love Ye One Another.' What greater celebration could the whole world have for the birthday of God's Son of Light and Love, than the dedication of service of all men to all men through the most dynamic, activating force on earth or in heaven? Love Ye One Another! Know that my love is extended to you at Christmas and each day of the New Year—and forever. Devotedly, Lao Russell."

Lao received numerous requests to include books written by students on the supplementary reading list she sent to those enrolled in the course. The authors often asked her to sell their books at Swannanoa. Typically she felt obliged to reply as she did to a Missouri college professor in early 1985: "I regret that we cannot distribute your book, but you have no idea how many booklets and books are sent to us for such distribution, and it is impossible for us to do so due to lack of space on our book tables for books other than those directly used in our teachings."

Lao was past eighty now, but she still demonstrated a great affinity for children. This was obvious whenever she encountered them in the weekend groups she met at Swannanoa. She felt that children had a special understanding of truth. One example she loved to relate concerned the letter a nine-year-old girl had written her soon after Lao published her book *Love*. The little girl's mother had died, and she was blaming herself, thinking she had not done enough for her mother to save her life. People in the foster home where she was being cared for gave her Lao's *Love* book to read. When she read it, the little girl realized that she had done the best she knew how to do and immediately lost her guilt complex. She wrote Lao that the book had saved her life.

Lao was asked her opinion of tithing, the custom practiced in many churches of giving a tenth of one's earnings to the church's work. "I am sure that you have answered that question yourself long before this, but the reason I did not answer your letter upon receipt was because it is not our practice to ask students to tithe," Lao wrote. "We have always preferred to earn the right to spread God's Message through the sale of our books and *Home Study Course*. All money that comes in from our work is used solely for our work. Sometimes students do send donations, and, naturally, it is heartwarming when they do because they have said they could never repay in money what the teachings have done for them in improving their whole lives. As you well know, we have never asked people to tithe or send donations, for we know that whatever one gives to life, one is re-given although this is not necessarily a material giving or regiving."

Lao was eager to produce and distribute cassettes of their books. A cassette-tape edition of *Atomic Suicide?* was in the planning stages. John Denver had promised to join her in recording the introduction. She wrote her friend Billy Bates that the actor Eddie Albert had agreed to record a cassette tape of "The Eleventh Hour," the first chapter in Lao's book *God Will Work with You but Not for You*.

Lao was working on a special summer message that she hoped would be published in early 1986.

She was quick to make known to all that she and the University abhorred racial discrimination. This was not only fundamental to her beliefs, but was recorded in the University's legal documents and made known to its students.

In November 1985, her longtime student Minette W. Crow of Prescott, Arizona, wrote to congratulate Lao on a *Washington Post* article about her, titled "Relentless Optimism." "While happy to see the article, I think they did not do you or Dr. Russell justice concerning your astounding accomplishments," Mrs. Crow wrote, "yet I know what editors can do toward cutting an informative story. Bless you for holding your torch high for all of us while living on Swannanoa!"

The same month the owners of Swannanoa advised Lao that Skyline-Swannanoa, Inc., would not be willing to renew her lease for the palace when it expired on May 31, 1986, but would enter a new lease with her at an increased rental of $4,000 per month. This caused her great concern.

In 1985, Claes Nobel visited her at Swannanoa three times, accompanied on each occasion by important opinion makers. They were all impressed by her work, and she felt that each of them had come into the orb for the special purpose of aiding the spread of God's Message for today during the most crucial period in mankind's unfolding. Christopher Hills featured Lao's work in the Winter 1985 edition of his *Enlightener Newsletter*, published in Anaheim, California, and widely distributed among New Age students in the western United States. Its editor, Christopher P. Humphries, recalled Lao's words to him when they had met on September 7, 1984: "Anything we can do to make men aware of the grave danger of the continued use of atomic fission is of great importance."

In 1985, Lao's Christmas correspondence was extremely heavy. She wrote Billy Bates that on some days she received literally hundreds of letters. It was a burden to reply at times but a joy to know she was remembered.

CHAPTER TWENTY-SEVEN

A Vital Message (1986)

Thousands of copies of Lao's *Vital Message* were mailed out to her worldwide student body in March 1986. It received a mixed reception. The appearance and quality of the booklet were exceptional, yet there was a commercial aspect to it that had not been found in her previous books or publications. In addition, at the insistence of Sam Biser, who had edited and produced the *Vital Message*, the booklet contained a discreet but obvious solicitation of donations to support the University, a practice Walter and Lao had hitherto always eschewed.

It distressed Lao when recipients of the *Vital Message* or her latest catalog objected to what they felt was an over-commercialization in presentation. "I greatly regret your reaction," she wrote one such correspondent. "Try to remember how difficult it is to try to awaken the average person in today's world. This was prepared to do just that!"

Emelia encouraged her. "I, too, feel, as you say in your *Vital Message*, 'This time we shall not fail.' It is a tremendous undertaking, and I wish I could help in some way, but as yet I am still incapacitated, although improving daily." Though besieged with tremendous medical expenses at the time, Emelia again sent Lao a handsome donation for the University.

138. Lao Russell's Vital Message.

Nonetheless, the *Vital Message*, filled with beautiful photographs, many in color, contained much biographical information about both Walter and Lao that had not appeared elsewhere in as succinct a form. It was a magnificent publicity piece, but yielded disappointing results as a tool for increasing course enrollments or book sales.

Publication had been delayed because of the time Lao had spent overseeing the computerization of the University's office, a project funded through the generosity of William Cranwell, which required transferring some 60,000 current addresses on the University's mailing list to computer files. Lao felt that there was an additional reason for the delay in sending out her *Vital Message*. It always seemed, she felt, that her letters and messages reached students at precisely the right time in their lives. She wrote her students, "I know that you will receive it at the right time—God's time—just as my brief Christmas letter reached our students and friends, as so many stated, when their need for my Love was so great."

139. William C. Cranwell, Dr. Timothy Binder, Emelia Lombardi, Richard A. Dulaney, J. B. Yount III.

Bill Cranwell spent many hours with Lao on numerous occasions. A football star at Virginia Tech during his college years, he had been featured in *Sports Illustrated* magazine, and later rose to prominence in the business world as an entrepreneur with wide-ranging interests. By the time he met Lao he had served on the board of his alma mater by appointment of the governor of Virginia, and his reputation as a hard-driving businessman was tempered by his dynamic, nonsectarian spiritual qualities. His brother and sister felt that the affectionate regard he held for Lao was in part an outreach on his part to a kindred soul who reminded him in many ways of his recently deceased mother. Lao and Bill shared long discussions on the nature of life and the universe and enjoyed mutual respect for each other, always tempered by enjoyment of each other's sense of good humor.

Lao's uniqueness of character and unpredictability delighted Bill. He remembered sitting with her in the second-floor tower room one afternoon when a deafening noise heralded the arrival of a large group of leather-clad motorcyclists on their Harley-Davidsons. Fearful that these unexpected tourists might alarm her tour guides downstairs, Lao excused herself to greet the cyclists personally. Bill wondered if perhaps Lao were about to face a group she would be hard put to handle, and after a few minutes he followed her downstairs, only to find Lao happily welcoming the smiling cyclists, each of whom seemed thrilled and responsive as she gave them a personal tour of Swannanoa and a heady dose of Russell philosophy.

Not the least of Bill Cranwell's effective efforts at extending the Russells' Message was his establishment of a scholarship fund, which he later named in honor of Emelia Lombardi, for the purpose of providing free Russell books to inquiring prisoners. This perpetual endowment brought the University many letters from inmates and prison officials describing remarkable transformations in the lives of those who had received the books.

Constantly besieged with questions from younger readers who seemed perplexed at how to develop a satisfactory marriage, Lao stressed the fact that the sexual side of the marital relationship was secondary. She wrote a Missouri couple, "The most important thing for two people who are contemplating marriage to know is that only when there is a Oneness of mental and spiritual understanding does the physical side of life remain beautiful."

She found it increasingly difficult to answer individually the daily flood of letters she received and often replied in general terms. "These days it is impossible for me to answer all personal questions," she would write, "but as you know, as you read, reread, and restudy all of our writings, you will find you are able to answer all of your inner questions. That is why we wrote our whole curriculum, knowing that when a student is ready, he can answer his own questions with this knowledge."

When asked if Walter Russell had known or worked with Baird T. Spalding, author of the multi-volume *Life and Teaching of the Masters of the Far East*, who had died in 1953 at the age of ninety-six, Lao replied, "Dr. Russell never mentioned to me having known him." Spalding's basic account had been written in the 1890s and first published in 1924, but he issued successive volumes in the 1930s, and others were compiled from his writings and published after his death.

Students asked her opinion of Alice Bailey, whose voluminous works, kept in print by the Lucis Trust in New York, were receiving renewed interest. Lao considered Bailey to have been a good Theosophist. "However," she stressed, "our teachings are scientific, and when Alice Bailey was writing, the world was not then ready for a scientific explanation as it is today."

Lao heard from modern Theosophists, some active as near as Richmond, Virginia, and always afforded them a warm welcome when they came to Swannanoa. "With your background in Theosophy, I know you will be more than fascinated with the whole demonstration here at Swannanoa," she wrote one of them. "I have always thought of Theosophists as the New Age people of yesterday! I had, not long ago, a lovely visit with two Theosophists from

Switzerland. They were very much impressed and left with a sense of something such as they had never experienced before! They recognized that our teachings have gone one step further by giving the scientific explanation of what the Theosophists are teaching today!"

Writers often asked to reproduce Walter Russell's illustrations and diagrams in their own scientific treatises. She advised one such author, Dean Wickersham, "We do not like to have a great number of Dr. Russell's scientific drawings used indiscriminately. If you desire to use one or two, be sure to send a detailed request for the ones you wish and provide us an appropriate acknowledgement in the book." She assured inquiring students that she knew of scientists and engineers who were constructing energy-producing devices using the Russell principles. "We certainly do have students who have done and are doing these things, but I am not at liberty to give their names and addresses. I am sure you will understand why," she explained.

A Texas scientist wrote her asking for copies of Walter's detailed laboratory procedures for conducting the experiments described in *The Russell Cosmogony*. Lao advised him, "Naturally, we do not have available for readers details for conducting experiments using our principles in science. As our advanced students read and study these scientific principles, they are experimenting in their laboratories with great success."

In April 1986, Lao spent an enjoyable day discussing the University's goals and books with a group of professors from Washington and Lee University and the Virginia Military Institute, both located in nearby Lexington.

A twenty-three-year-old Englishman, to whom Lao referred to as "one of the greatest art critics of our day," had enthusiastically taken the *Home Study Course* and came to Virginia to meet her. He had entered the United States at sixteen to study music at Tanglewood in Massachusetts. There he learned of Swannanoa from two young Russell students who became well-known opera singers in Chicago.

It pleased Lao that the course seemed as relevant as when it had first been written, and that students found its message truly timeless. "When you read the final unit of lessons," she wrote a California student, "you will realize that herein is a blueprint for building a whole new civilization!"

She recognized that the course appealed to all ages. A new student of eighty-seven wrote to tell her of the many hours of comfort and joy it had given him. A Florida student, who had studied both earlier editions of the *Home Study Course*, learned twenty years later that a third edition had been published in the 1960s and promptly enrolled again.

She gave an eighty-eight-year-old student who was fearful of dying the impetus to keep going. The student had read all of the Russell books, and at last Lao persuaded her to enroll in the *Home Study Course*. This so revived her spirits, Lao noted, that she called Swannanoa to report that on her eighty-ninth birthday she had taken her driving test and had her driver's license renewed for the first time in twenty years.

Lao's first husband, Lionel Stebbing, died of heart failure at Crawley, West Sussex, England, on May 23, 1986, less than a month before his eighty-first birthday. Notices of his death focused entirely on the many publications he had written or edited in connection with the Rudolf Steiner Institute and made no mention of his marriage to Daisy Cook (Lao) or their lucrative business partnership of fifty years before.

Lionel was survived by his second wife, Margarita, and their two sons, Nowell and Peter, as well as two grandchildren, Clare Zoe and Benjamin. After providing in his will for Margarita and establishing libraries for his grandchildren, he left personal items and a small legacy to each of his sons and established a trust to receive the balance of his estate. Its purpose was to keep his books in print for a period of fifty years after his death, after which time all remaining corpus would revert to the Anthroposophical Society of Great Britain. In addition to his work with the Steiner organization, Lionel still maintained his own mail-order business, with Ellen Crabb running his office as she had at Dean's Street in London during the 1930s. His mail-order business focused now on business advice instead of health and beauty.

At the time of his death, he lived with Margarita at 18 Elizabeth Crescent, East Grimstead, Sussex, near Emerson College, where teachers were trained to educate children in Waldorf schools throughout the world, using the pedagogical principles of Rudolf Steiner, the founder of Anthroposophy.

The well-known director of a highly successful Phillipi, West Virginia, counseling center was one of many who wrote to tell Lao of the lasting impact a visit to Swannanoa had made on her life. "You don't know me," the director wrote, "but you gave me a very vital message one summer day two years ago when my husband and I stopped by Swannanoa on a whim and took the tour. You came into the room when the guide was called to the telephone and made a statement that was directed to us, if to no other person in the room. You said that too often people give up in a new business just as things are about to happen. We had recently started a Counseling Center and were both involved in learning Primal Integration Therapy. I was discouraged with the business and thinking about going back into public employment. Each time that I felt discouragement I remembered that day and retrenched." The director of the Physical Therapy Institute in Poway, California, wrote Lao that *The Universal One* was being used by the Institute for educational purposes. "We act as a clearinghouse for the most advanced and dynamic educational media available," he wrote her.

Lao consistently urged her eager students not to be concerned if they lacked formal education. "Walter Russell left school at nine and one-half years of age," she wrote a discouraged student from Arizona, "and when you read what he accomplished when working knowingly with God, you will realize that when you truly understand your Oneness with the Creator, you become a co-creator yourself. If you read the history of our greatest creators, you will find that many of them did not shine in school because they were listening to their Inner Selves, which is the Light of God."

She took care in explaining the need for stillness and decentration to a talented musician who was taking the course. "As a musician you surely realize that the need for stillness in the Light is necessary truly to tune into the God-Light and all that lives. All idea springs from the stillness of the Light of God. You can practice decentration, which means to stop thinking, at any time. This is what we all do when we sleep, so during the night is the best time to decentrate. If one deeply desires an answer to a question or a problem, one should deeply desire the answer to that question or problem before going to sleep at night. If the desire is deep enough, the answer will come upon your awakening."

"Regarding what type of music to listen to," she added, "this, too, depends on the personal desire of a soul, for what would appeal to one person may not touch another. You should play the music that touches your soul!" Lao gently guided new students into decentration.

When she received questions as to meditation techniques from beginners in the *Home Study Course*, she could always tell if the student was actually concentrating instead of decentrating. One such student bombarded her with questions: "What do I do with this attention once I have reached zero thought and complete stillness? Should I look into the darkness in front of me in a relaxed way, but looking for light? Should I concentrate this attention into the darkness before me looking for light? Should I not look and not concentrate into the darkness and just relax totally? In that case should attention remain in the area above the eyes? What do I do with this attention? If any light is seen, what do I do then—concentrate into it, or disregard? Please take the time to answer these questions for me. For the whole benefit of the course can only be realized through proper meditation and I want to start out on the right foot."

Lao's reply to him was prompt and specific:

> Thank you for your lovely letter. I know that with your attitude, desire and understanding you will ultimately gain great knowledge and wisdom from our teachings. Your many questions regarding the proper method of meditation indicate to me that you have not yet learned to entirely "let go."
>
> When you meditate do not be concerned with the "attention." What you are actually doing is concentrating rather than decentrating. The whole

> purpose of meditation is to decentrate, which means to expand thought into the Mind universe of stillness! Do not be concerned with any sound that you may hear. This also indicates to me that you are not reaching that Zero-Stillness. There is absolutely no sound within the Zero-Stillness for sound is motion, and the goal of meditation is to "Be still and know," as it states in the Bible.
>
> I have always taught my students to work meditatively throughout the day. When you keep a busy life in doing service for your fellow man, you gradually earn the ability properly to decentrate. God provides us with this special technique of meditation for daily renewing.

Lao avoided reading publications that emphasized hunting. "It hurts me to kill a fly, and when I read how they kill deer and birds, I feel sick. I know that many people kill animals to maintain balance in nature, but still it distresses me," she wrote Michael Rutkaus, who had sent her a beautiful wildlife periodical, which he was involved in producing.

The gardens at Swannanoa were still a major tourist attraction. Angela Carr augmented her full-time efforts in the University office by working a virtual second shift in tenderly caring for the magnificent terraces. Although the various blossoms yielded their beauty from springtime to autumn, Lao advised those who inquired that the best time to see the flowers at Swannanoa was in August and September. The gardens were at an altitude of 2,400 feet above sea level, and the start of the growing season on the mountain was a month behind that of the valley below.

Professional singers and classical musicians often inquired as to the possibility of offering benefit concerts at Swannanoa in the evenings. Lao had welcomed such activities from time to time in the past, but the pressure of being open to the public seven days a week, and of spending most of her evenings maintaining her worldwide correspondence, now prevented her from holding such pleasant diversions.

Lao's friend Bill Cranwell, to whom she was devoted for the selfless manner in which he responded to the teachings, wrote to tell her of the sudden death of a close friend and business associate. She sought to comfort him: "Your dear friend returned to the light of God with your loyal and great love comforting him! What a precious soul you are! The love and loyalty of a friend is our greatest gift on earth."

In late April 1986 the Chernobyl nuclear power plant disaster occurred in the Ukraine. Flawed reactor design, poorly trained personnel, and inadequate safety precautions combined to cause a steam explosion and fire that released five percent of the radioactive reactor core into the atmosphere and downward. The accident caused many radiation-related fatalities; contaminated

140. Lao Russell and Michael Hudak.

large areas of Belarus, Ukraine, and Russia; exposed seventy-five million people to dangerously high radiation levels; and led to enormous concern throughout the world.

The University's students had long formed a determined network of nuclear control proponents and agreed with Lao that the explosion at Chernobyl could have been avoided if the warnings in *Atomic Suicide?* had been heeded. Reenergized by their horror at the consequences of the Chernobyl incident, Dr. Tim Binder and Michael Hudak stood in the forefront of University supporters who launched new efforts to curtail nuclear proliferation, and worked with like-minded groups to build an effective anti-nuclear global coalition. Hudak, who had brought his three daughters and his wife's parents to visit Lao at Swannanoa the month before, had joined the University's board of directors the previous year and would succeed to the presidency on Lao's death in 1988.

The University's prison outreach was effective and growing. Lao received the following letter written on Mother's Day 1986: "I first learned of your late husband Walter when another prisoner (whom I didn't even know) was reading *The Man Who Tapped the Secrets of the Universe*. I begged him to allow me to read it and to copy from it. I stayed up most of the night writing page after page of your husband's philosophy, and then I wrote to you. Before I received your own books I would study those excerpts (and I still read and study them). This is just a short note to let you know that you hold a special spot in my heart. I have adopted you as my spiritual mother. I have read your book *God Will Work with You but Not for You* for the third time, and I will continue to do so for I find it so inspiring. I know now that I am the master of my own fate, the creator of my own destiny."

Lao encouraged her students to care for their physical bodies. She recommended deep muscle therapy and reflexology. Remembering her early years as a physical culture advocate and recognizing the results of her lifelong penchant for physical activity, she welcomed the growing popular awareness of advanced techniques of healing through diet and exercise. "I can just picture your beautiful body now as it expresses your eighteen-year-old thinking and acting," she wrote a young dancer.

She met with James F. "Fil" Dulaney, Jr., in an effort to reach a compromise on the proposed 100 percent increase in rent he had imposed. She urged him to agree on "a rental amount that would be fair and reasonable to both parties," reminding him of the extent to which she and Walter had restored and maintained the palace and gardens since November 1948. They spoke at length about the matter but to no avail. The rent was raised to $48,000 a year. Nonetheless, Lao professed a special fondness for young Fil Dulaney, writing him affectionately, "I have never forgotten your eyes when you were a little boy and I gave you a huge Hershey chocolate bar one Christmas. It endeared you to me at that time, and I have never forgotten that 'something special' in you since!" It hurt Lao to feel that the University's outreach would be adversely affected by the burden of the additional overhead, but she had little alternative but to pay the additional rent. She was eighty-two years old, and to have vacated the palace and relocated her God-directed work to a site other than her sacred mountain would surely have killed her. In addition, she remained confident that she would never be forced to leave Swannanoa, and that the University's work would continue to flourish.

Howard R. Davis III of Atlanta had dedicated a week at Swannanoa in 1976, helping to maintain the palace, and remembered that even then the great Tiffany window was dirty and needed care. At the time, he was told that it could only be touched by a stained-glass master. He wrote Lao to advise her that he had spent many years in the interim building and restoring stained glass and offered to return to Swannanoa to help maintain the priceless window. "I am sure that I could help you do what needs to be done to keep that window in good shape," he told a grateful Lao. "Cleaning is relatively easy, but the window should also be examined for broken solder joints, weak bracing, et cetera." Soon Lao was able to report that the Tiffany window had been well cleaned and was being admired more than ever. "Like everything at Swannanoa," she reported, "the basic work of structure [of the window] was perfect."

A student of science, as well as a humanitarian, Howard Davis had endeared himself to Lao by his efforts to encourage the global rescue organization Amnesty International to intercede on behalf of Governor Okilo during his political imprisonment in Nigeria. Later, Lao and Howard discussed the discrepancy in Walter Russell's chart of the elements, which was shown as ten octaves in *The Universal One* and nine octaves in his later writings. Lao correctly asserted that if one compared the science of *The Universal One* with that contained in their later work, one found fundamental consistency. Nonetheless, she advised Howard, "when Dr. Russell and I first met and worked together on the *Home Study Course*, I reminded him that one can never go beyond nine in mathematical calculations, and he then redrew his chart of the elements accordingly."

James E. Yehl of Boulder, Colorado, founder of a publicly owned optical manufacturing firm and a student of the metaphysics of light, vision, and illusion, advised Lao that the advent of the scanning tunneling microscope now allowed science to verify what philosophers and metaphysicians had known since the beginning. "About a month ago," he wrote, "I saw an amazing photo of an atom magnified 100 million times. To my amazement it was a blueprint of the description of the wave described by Walter Russell on page 180 of *The Universal One*. I do not know why it should amaze me as I have studied *The Secret of Light*, *Atomic Suicide?*, and the rest of the books you have published. Walter discusses studying the variegation of matter via the spectroscope and the spectrophotometer. On page 182 of *The Universal One* he mentioned the complexity of the wave and that in the second volume it will be charted in all of its complexities while considering the structure of the atom. I would like to see some of the work he did on the spectroscope. There is very little information like this available elsewhere."

This led to a lengthy exchange of ideas with Lao, who advised Mr. Yehl that Walter Russell had pictured the orderliness, symmetry, and balance, which all nature expresses, and explained how nature polarizes and depolarizes in its every expression, just as man does in his breathing without being aware of it in every action and every second of his life. She told him she anticipated preparing another book on Dr. Russell's new cosmogony that would include new information that would help him proceed with his advanced study of the wave. In the meantime, she urged him to study and restudy their published works, assuring him, "You should be able to answer all of your inner questions by studying and restudying these books."

141. Lao Russell with Sri Swami Satchidananda of Yogaville.

In early 1986, Sri Swami Satchidananda, the guru who years earlier had opened the Woodstock rock festival by calling music "the celestial sound that controls the whole universe," visited Lao with a number of his colleagues. His primary purpose was to discuss with her the Lotus Shrine and Yogaville community he was constructing on 600 acres along the James River in nearby Buckingham County, Virginia. His philosophy of Integral Yoga echoed the Russells' belief that "truth is one, paths are many," and he and Lao shared several hours of conversation and deep thought. Later that year he invited Lao to participate in the dedication of the Lotus Shrine, an international occasion attended by political figures and religious leaders of many faiths. Two Bengal tigers, a juggler, and a baby elephant added to the festivities. Lao sent warm personal greetings but decided against attending such a strenuous event.

She often reflected on other great religious teachers with whom she had shared the basic philosophy and science that she and Walter espoused. Among them was Dr. Ernest Holmes, founder of the Religious Science movement and author of *Science of Mind*, who would often tell his advanced students and church members that he had taught them all that he could, and now they were ready for the Russells' teachings.

This had also happened in the last years of the Reverend Starr Daily's life. "He, also," Lao wrote, "was truly a wonderful and spiritually unfolded man who had an Illumination in prison and was released because of his record in prison and because of his tremendous character and desire to serve God. He sent many beautiful souls to us whom he knew needed our teachings to renew their lives."

It pleased and amused her that visitors still commented on her physical attractiveness. In June 1986 she received what she described as "a love letter" from a visitor of several days before. She sent Emelia a copy of the missive, which read in part as follows:

> Yesterday I fell in love with a woman—a very special woman who gave me, in just the short time we had, a brilliance of light which will last a lifetime. This woman also gave me the inspiration to strive for a serenity that I did not feel I could own. I have been fortunate in my life to know and love many beautiful women. The woman I fell in love with yesterday was far more beautiful than all the women I have ever known together because her beauty transcended the physical and was of the spirit. Her presence mesmerized me with an overpowering, yet serene, aura. Her words and gestures were a gala celebration of life. And her eyes, more than anything else, sparkled and glimmered with a myriad of lights that radiated all the beauty within her. I have known and loved many beautiful people and of those there are those that are "special." This woman was among the most "special" of the "special," and I feel honored to have known her just briefly. I write to tell you this because the name of this enchanting and gloriously beautiful woman is Lao Russell.
>
> Thank you for the loving guidance you gave me when we visited last week. I was the handsome man with the red beard, straw hat, gold framed glasses, who represents the Foundation for Perfect Children. I also loved

> you on the tape that *P.M. Magazine* did, especially when you said that women should "make love" to men sometime. The pure, joyous sacredness of your view of men and women together encourages me that I may be able to find a woman like yourself!
>
> I couldn't help but be spiritually, emotionally, and sexually attracted to you. Yes, I'm thirty-five. Yes, you're still beautiful. Yes, I'm aware how old people think you are. Yes, you are eternal youthfulness! Love and Kisses.

She and Emelia enjoyed the irony and straightforwardness of the letter. Lao told her that it seemed typical of the way many younger men spoke to her. Emelia replied that she was not surprised: "Men have always been very much attracted to you as long as I have known you, and time has not touched you as it has the rest of us. You exude that special sensuality. My memory of the first day we met you and Dr. Russell is as vivid as if it were yesterday. You were a beautiful vision all in white. Your visitor sees you now as that same vital, vivacious, beautiful self. More power to you, Lao! You surely are an inspiration."

In fact, time was taking its toll on Lao's health. "I am having a tough time with what is called retracing," she confided to Emelia. "Dr. Paul Eck says the painful rash I have had sounds like the small pox shot I had coming out. It has been a tough year all through and all round. I feel there are some great things about to happen, and that keeps me going."

On July 27, 1986, she telephoned Emelia with extraordinary news. Most important of all, Melford Okilo had been released from prison and wholly vindicated by the highest court in Nigeria. After the military coup of 1983, he and the other democratically elected government officials had been arrested and detained. Many of them were tried and convicted on spurious charges. Melford Okilo was the notable exception. At last, the nation's supreme court had acquitted him of all charges, leaving his record without blemish and officially acknowledging his indisputable integrity. Lao was jubilant at the news.

By coincidence, the famous actress and author Shirley MacLaine had stopped at Swannanoa to visit Lao for two hours on the same day. The two women both understood the cosmos and found that they took an instant liking to each other. Claes Nobel had given the great actress Lao's books *Why You Cannot Die!* and *Love*. She told Lao that the former was the book that impressed her so much. Lao wrote Emelia, "She said she will soon be ordering all of our books for close study. She recognizes how truly advanced and practical our teachings are and that they are beyond anything she studied previously."

Dr. Tim Binder introduced Lao to the actor Dennis Weaver, with whom he shared an active interest in the Self-Realization Fellowship in California. In 1983, the noted actor, humanitarian, and past president of the Screen Actors Guild, had founded Love Is Feeding Everyone (L.I.F.E.), an organization that helped feed 150,000 hungry people a week in Los Angeles County and grew to have global impact as a role model for similar organizations. In 1986, this work had earned Mr. Weaver the Presidential End Hunger Award. Dennis Weaver told Lao that her *God Will Work with You but Not for You* was high among his favorite books because it was so comprehensive.

A student from Ohio asked Lao to suggest the best sequence in which a student might read their works, and her reply was definitive: "The best textbook for all of our teachings is *God Will Work with You but Not for You*. However, for new readers and students I recommend that our books be read in the following order: (1) the brief biography of my late beloved husband's life by Glenn Clark, *The Man Who Tapped the Secrets of the Universe*; (2) my book entitled *Love*; (3) *God Will Work with You but Not for You*; (4) *Why You Cannot Die!*; (5) *The Secret of Light*; (6&7) Volumes I and II of *The Message of the Divine Iliad*; (8) *The World Crisis*; (9) *Atomic Suicide?*; (10) *The Electrifying Power of Man-Woman Balance*, formerly *The One-World Purpose*; and (11) *Scientific Answer to Human Relations* and *Scientific Explanation of Sex*."

Since two of the principal supplementary books on the University's recommended list, *Dawn of Conscience* and *Man, The Unknown*, were out of print, she again explored the possibility of republishing them at Swannanoa, but for copyright reasons was unable to do so and instead was forced to refer interested students to rare book dealers. "These books are beautiful and important, and we trust that someday they will become available again," she advised.

On September 1, 1986, the nearby Charlottesville newspaper *The Daily Progress* ran a long, somewhat inaccurate article titled "Cosmic Consciousness: Restored Palace Is Shrine To Philosophy of Light, Love." It was uncomplimentary in many respects, teasing readers with descriptions of "drought-brown cedars [that] line the scarred road leading to the Shrine of Beauty" and "the late afternoon autumn sun filtering through a Tiffany window at the staircase landing, casting a sulfurous glow on the dark portraits that line the walls." The writer noted that "none of the carvings or the bizarre paintings of the rings of Saturn attract the same attention as the petite, elderly woman with the girlishly golden curls, who is attired in a formal gold lamé evening dress and matching gold slippers. Like a metaphysical Miss Havisham, Lao Russell, the widow of Walter Russell, waits for the dream that she and her husband shared to reach fruition. She maintains Swannanoa—and the University of Science and Philosophy that it houses—as a shrine to her husband and their quasi-scientific quest for human perfection. Drawing on Zen Buddhism, Christianity and sub-particle physics, the Russells' teachings aim at stripping away the self and putting the individual in direct touch with creative workings of the universe."

The writer described Lao's Sunday afternoon discussion with the people touring the palace. That day she was relaxing in her chair in the great hall, sipping tea and dispensing autographs and words of kindness. "She [spoke] effusively about the visitors who have traveled from all parts of the world to see her." She described the recent visits she had received from Shirley MacLaine and John Denver, fascinating the young people in the audience with a vivid description of Denver landing his helicopter on the front lawn. She described the importance of Walter Russell's work to averting world disaster, and told of her 1946 first meeting with him in Boston and their subsequent marriage and coming to Swannanoa.

The article was punctuated with quotes from skeptical scientists who claimed to know nothing of Walter Russell's work. These included a so-called "specialist in the history of science at the American Institute of Physics in New York" and a professor of physics at the University of Virginia, who confessed, "I'm afraid that I am unfamiliar with Dr. Russell and his particular theory."

Nonetheless, the writer included favorable comments from Professor Wayne Shebilske, a professor of psychology at Texas A&M University and a Russell student for the past ten years. "I can't comment on Russell's scientific theories," he said, "but I do know that since I've been a student, I have come to grips with the importance of my own incarnation. Their teachings have helped explain to me why God would need me." Dr. Shebilske argued that the Russells' teachings complement any of the world's formal religions by adding a new rational dimension to faith. "When people look for answers, they turn to religion or psychology and don't get what they're looking for," he concluded in a telephone interview from College Station, Texas, "but the Russells have taken the Bible and put it in a modern framework. That's what makes their teachings viable."

Cathy Edwards, a student of the Russells for eight months who was volunteering in the University office, described her interest to the reporter as follows: "Religion has always meant fear to me, but that has changed since I have been a student of Mrs. Russell. With her you find out the meaning of life and your purpose. It's all so simple; it all feels right."

The article concluded on a positive note: "Students like Wayne Shebilske and Ms. Edwards confirm Lao Russell's purpose in life. They make the criticism and the doubts bearable. And they fill the long Sunday afternoons with pleasant memories and optimism. 'I think the time is close when people will become aware that they have to take action,' Mrs. Russell said as she tugged at one of her dangling gold earrings, 'and that is when they'll find us.'"

A pacifist, who had been imprisoned at Fort Leavenworth for several years because of his refusal to perform his military service, wrote Lao a stirring letter concerning the extent to which her teachings had helped him: "I will be released from this school of life next month. I have learned a lot about myself and look upon these past four years as the lessons of life I needed to experience in order to understand the simplest of universal principles—the unity of man with man and with God! I only harvested the seeds of hatred, selfishness, and greed, which I had been sowing for years. In many ways I am happy I got this opportunity to pause and to see where I was really heading [and] to learn of you and your husband Walter. I am grateful that I have this opportunity to begin anew."

He visited Lao at Swannanoa and told her that he had enrolled in Kansas State University and would major in agriculture, hoping to be a pioneer in the organic food movement by getting organic farmers recognized by the government and society. "It is my firm belief this is the right path for me and I know, as you do, this is the solution to this country's health problems and farm economic situation," he told her, emphasizing the Russells' often stated maxim that by working with nature, rather than against her, many problems could be solved. The young man told her that he had learned through the *Home Study Course* to seek no sympathy or revenge. Citizen Soldier, Inc., a New York organization, had supported him and helped him obtain his release. The details of his saga strongly suggested that he had been unfairly imprisoned.

Lao loved to show visitors to Swannanoa the Latin proverb that the Dooleys had carved into the library mantel when they built the palace. Its English translation was "Everyone is divine when he knows that he is divine." Lao felt that it was more than coincidental that she and Walter found this message awaiting them in the home to which God had led them.

She was pleased to see that health, educational, and motivational groups across the country and in Canada were adding her curriculum to their programs. Students of an electromagnetic phenomena class in San Diego enrolled in the course, and told Lao they were constantly finding proof of the Russells' new scientific principles. Nevertheless she was concerned over growing inflation and economic depression. "The people who will survive the depressions," she advised, "are the people who give loving service."

She consoled those who had lost loved ones in the growing spread of cancer, a disaster that she and Walter had foretold in *Atomic Suicide?* She recalled that Eddie Albert had told her he was restudying the *Home Study Course* and had found "the teaching he needed to keep going" in her book *God Will Work with You but Not for You* after losing his beloved wife of forty years to cancer. Decades before, Margo Albert had introduced her husband to Lao's work.

Lao was somewhat impatient when a student called her attention to seeming paradoxical statements on nature in the course after reading only a few of its units. The student had questioned how natural disasters could possibly occur in a truly balanced Universe. Lao urged her to continue and restudy the course, advising her, "Not until you understand God's inviolate

Law of Rhythmic Balanced Interchange will you understand the complete answer to your questions."

She continued her explanation in a brief précis of the Message that was seldom better expressed elsewhere in any of the Russell writings: "Tornados and any unbalanced condition of Nature must be balanced even if it takes a million years or more to restore that balance. However, balance is always restored in Nature and in life. That is why it is so important to understand God's Laws which govern us and to live them even though it takes a million lives to understand them. Through understanding His inviolate Law of Rhythmic Balanced Interchange in all givings and regivings, you can better understand the concept of sex-divided pairs of opposites in all our human relations as well as in the planet itself! We and Nature continually violate the inviolate Law of Balance. Man violates this Law of Balance physically and mentally and constantly pays by agony of Mind and lack of opportunity in form. In Nature we have catastrophic violence in storms, and there are also physical delays in Nature like misshapen plants and flowers, but Nature has no choice but to balance itself. God gave mankind the free will choice of decision in balancing His inviolate Law of Rhythmic Balanced Interchange. However, sooner or later in his present life or lives to come, God's Law must be lived before one becomes truly One in the Eternal Light of God, our Creator."

Lao was interested in health publications. Although the University itself did not publish such works, she advised a student whose book on arthritis reflected the Russell teachings to contact her close friend and student Palo Abney, Jr., who had just started his own publishing business in Orlando, Florida. Lao considered Mr. Abney "a successful businessman who has put our principles into practice and has devoted much of his time to the furtherance of God's Message."

Ever mindful of her own diet, Lao corresponded extensively with vegetarians and vegans. To Craig Rabinowitz, who wrote from Hawaii for her views on eating meat, she replied, "Always keep in mind that 'everything is of everything else that is'! I too share your feelings about eating meat or meat products; however, I go one step further in my feelings and understanding of the consumption and eating of grass, berries, and fruit by animals and the cutting of vegetables and fruits for man's consumption. We have to remember that all life exists through an interchange of one form of life for sustenance of another form of life. For instance, our bodies are put into the earth and they feed the soil which brings forth the grass for the consumption of animals and thus life continues for every other form of life. Some bodies need the protein and minerals that is found in meat as others need the calcium found in milk products. Everyone's metabolism is different. Different bodies need different diets. One reason we have not gone into detail about diets is because it is truly a matter of finding whatever the individual needs through mineral testing or such. I was on a complete vegetarian diet, but being unable to obtain organically grown food, I found I needed, occasionally, to eat fish or chicken." She added that she had read the writings of Rudolf Steiner and the Yoga sutras of Pantanjali and thought they were excellent and instructive.

Friends continued to send donations for the long-planned Temple of Light. Lao stressed that if the colossal Christ were ever erected on Afton Mountain, it would be "the greatest fulfillment I could ever experience because it was the vision of Christ and God's Message to me that gave me the courage and strength to come to Swannanoa and restore the ruined palace and gardens." She wished in vain that the project could be undertaken and kept all donations made specifically for that purpose in a separate Temple of Light trust account.

At Christmas 1986, the message she sent to students and friends around the world concerned the occurrence that had brought her the most happiness during the year: "My dear friend and student, Melford Okilo from Nigeria, has now been released and is now devoting all of his time to the dissemination of our teachings in his country!"

CHAPTER TWENTY-EIGHT

When Nature Has a Plan (1987-88)

Lao's friend Ben Novick, a prominent securities consultant in California who was well-connected with many major American businessmen, introduced her to the famous capitalist Armand Hammer, with whom she exchanged letters in early 1987. Mr. Novick had read *The Man Who Tapped the Secrets of the Universe* in its entirety over the telephone to Dr. Hammer, who told Lao he was eager to speak with her in person. Dr. Hammer's longstanding economic contacts with the Soviet government dated back to the 1930s. Both he and Lao believed there was a desperate need for world leaders to heed the warnings in *Atomic Suicide?* and avert the ultimate nuclear disaster, which each of them felt might well be the final outcome of the Cold War arms race. Lao found Dr. Hammer "a deeply concerned man who truly works for world peace and balance." It pleased her greatly to make his acquaintance and learn of their shared commitments.

Ben Novick had known Albert Einstein intimately and confirmed the reports Lao had often heard that, in his last years, the great Einstein had expressed regret that he had not followed through with his study of Walter Russell's new science. Einstein had been one of the first recipients of *The Universal One* on its private publication in 1926. Mr. Novick told Lao that Einstein had told him personally that even then he intuitively knew that Walter Russell possessed new scientific knowledge so desperately needed by the world.

As always, Lao enjoyed encouraging young women to enter professions from which custom had largely excluded them in the past. She told a female law student of the success the principal domestic relations lawyer in Tidewater Virginia had experienced in his practice by giving copies of Lao's book *Love* to couples contemplating divorce. She told the story frequently, mentioning the attorney by name. "He has had tremendous success in bringing couples back together through the use of my book! He comes to Swannanoa frequently to buy the book by the case. He told me that when couples come to him wanting a divorce, he first gives them my book to read. In most instances these couples return to him arm-in-arm, totally reconciled! I said to him, 'You must be losing a lot of business!' and he replied, 'Oh, no, Mrs. Russell, since using your *Love* book, my business has gone up and up and up!"

There were inexplicable instances of healings experienced by people who visited the palace and by their loved ones. In early 1987 Lao wrote a number of her friends: "I just had a wonderful call from a young lady who visited Swannanoa five years ago. She said her visit here was 'magical.' When she returned home to her parents, she insisted that they also visit Swannanoa. Her mother at that time was suffering with stomach cancer. I had the opportunity to meet them. Just three days after their visit, the mother was scheduled for surgery. When the doctors opened her up, all they could find was a slightly inflamed stomach lining. Today, five years after her incident with cancer, she is healthy and well!"

This was not unlike the experience of her late friend and local attorney, J. B. Yount, Jr., years before, when his doctors at the University of Virginia had diagnosed terminal bladder cancer, only to discover relatively minor benign conditions when they performed surgery the day after Lao had gone to Charlottesville and spent the entire afternoon encouraging her longtime counselor, assuring him, "Tomorrow God's hand will guide the surgeon's hands."

The Russells' warnings of impending natural and nuclear disasters echoed earlier prophecies, Lao learned. She had recently reviewed the writings of Nostradamus, who, she realized, had accurately predicted most of the major events of the past 400 years. She obtained a documentary video titled *Nostradamus, The Man Who Saw Tomorrow*, narrated by Orson Welles. "The prediction for today and the next few years should inspire everyone into action," she wrote Gary Schlagenhauf of Walnut Creek, California. "It was one of the most powerful warnings of destruction I have ever seen." She was more and more convinced that "only a concentrated effort to improve man's human relations worldwide will save us from the threatened Armageddon."

Lao's English friend Cicely Allan, principal of the White Lodge Soul Therapy Association, had relocated her organization to Sedona, Arizona, and was now an important distributor of the Russell books, all of which she had read while she was still in England. She saw to it that her students were well acquainted with the Russell cosmogony. "The genius of your work," she wrote Lao, "is that you are able to express in understandable terms scientific principles so that minds without such training can absorb them. It is only by this understanding that the mass of the people can be reached." *Atomic Suicide?* had been her introduction to the teachings and remained the book she most often consulted.

Cicely invited Lao to visit her in Sedona, describing it as "a glorious place to be, having the most extraordinary energies I have as yet experienced, like a 'breather area' of cleansing for planet and human alike, so much so that many cannot remain for long, a phenomenon familiar to us since it happened often at White Lodge, England." She told Lao that such an atmosphere could be very uncomfortable to certain people and things, "even stopping watches for instance!" Lao understood precisely what her friend was describing. She often reflected on the spiritual intensity sensitive people experienced on her own Swannanoa mountain.

Russell students in Atlanta held a three-day conference at the Church of Daily Living in May 1987 in conjunction with the World Peace Foundation. They invited her to speak on the subject "Peace—Weapons of Peace," but she declined. By now she seldom left the mountain, due to the exhausting pace she maintained in keeping up her worldwide correspondence and conferring with groups of students and special visitors at the palace.

Gary Schlagenhauf was eager to implement the University's principles in his agricultural business. Lao told him not to be too concerned if he felt that he lacked the technical know-how to accomplish this. She referred him to her friend and student Edward Heft of Alpha, Ohio, who had successfully devoted his life to agricultural research using the Russell science. Mr. Heft and John Cejla offered a seminar in Ohio based on their understanding of the Science of Man and the Science of the Cosmos teachings as presented throughout the Russell curriculum. They accepted Lao's invitation to meet with other like-minded advanced thinkers at Swannanoa on the first weekend in April.

They were joined by William Howdon, a well-known economist who provided the keynote address, as well as Jerry Henderson and sales expert Randy Carlson, both of whom outlined means by which the Russell teachings could be extended to a broader audience. Two attorneys and a major Virginia capitalist who were members of the University's board of directors participated in the two-day proceedings. Informal brainstorming sessions occupied all of Saturday, and on Sunday afternoon Lao formally introduced each of the special guests as they addressed the large gathering of students and visitors that filled the palace's great hall.

John Andreadis, the brilliant co-founder of New York's Eternal Values Corporation, was present with several of his colleagues and offered stimulating remarks. Heralded by popular New Age writer Ruth Montgomery in her bestseller *Aliens Among Us*, Andreadis was a spellbinding writer and speaker. He and his colleagues had distributed hundreds of copies of *The Secret of Light*, proclaiming that the book included the most succinct and explicit explanation of creation in print. In addition he had co-produced a number of documentary videos, which his organization circulated at no charge for the use of public television stations in major metropolitan areas. Two of these videos directly depicted the Russells and their work, one a panel discussion on the genius of Walter Russell and Nikola Tesla, and the other an interview on Walter and Lao and their University with their learned Egyptian-American physician friend, Dr. Albert Hugh T. Doss.

142. John Andreadis.

Dr. Doss, the most important link between the University and its many important Rosicrucian students, was an Egyptian who later moved to America to practice medicine. Although Lao was aware of the Rosicrucians, she had not read many of their writings, but it pleased her that many advanced Rosicrucians had eagerly enrolled in and successfully completed the Swannanoa *Home Study Course*. She was extremely proud of a highly complimentary letter she had received from Dr. Doss, who had originally come to the United States to attend a Rosicrucian meeting. Lao was in Missouri on a lecture tour when Dr. Doss had first visited Swannanoa, and he left this letter for her and then traveled from Virginia to Missouri to hear her speak. He had previously donated sets of the Russell books to the great Rosicrucian library in San Jose, California, and saw to it that this important repository of spiritual and scientific books received a copy of the new edition of *The Universal One* as soon as it was republished. Later, when he and his wife visited his homeland, he presented a copy of *The Universal One* to Egyptian President Anwar Sadat, just prior to the latter's assassination. Dr. Doss often told Lao that he considered the *Home Study Course* the greatest course ever given to the world. He strove to see the complete Russell curriculum taught in America's schools and universities, and also presented a complete set of the Russell books to the United Nations library in New York.

143. Dr. Albert H. T. Doss.

Dr. and Mrs. Doss had invited Lao to accompany them on a journey to Egypt that included a sixteen-day cruise on the Nile and the opportunity to meet President and Mrs. Sadat. Her duties at Swannanoa precluded her from joining them, as much as she wanted to visit Egypt again. Lao often reminisced about her experiences in Egypt in the 1930s. Dr. Doss was particularly interested to learn of the impact his native country had left on the awakening philosopher. Lao longed to return to Cairo. "Perhaps when world affairs become more settled," she told him, "I can spend more happy days there." He took additional copies of her books as gifts to his medical colleagues in Cairo and to other Egyptian leaders and opinion-makers. He proved a constant source of encouragement to Lao and shared her feelings that the time of fulfillment might well be near for the University. They grew excited to learn that scientists and physicians in several states were building special apparati designed to demonstrate the Russells' scientific principles, and were impressed when the work was favorably recommended by the Union of Concerned Scientists.

Lao tried to help those with addictions by demonstrating that the cause of most human weaknesses lay in a deep sense of insecurity or inadequacy created by severe frustration. "When one at last becomes aware of the God-Light which centers him, he naturally feels secure and has an awareness also of the unlimited power of his God-Self. When one attains this, one's desire for any such addiction is voided!" She often recalled the many friends and students whose addictions had vanished once they studied the Message.

One of Lao's most valued colleagues, Dr. Wayne Shebilske, the psychologist who had been so supportive of the work at Swannanoa while he was a faculty member at the nearby University of Virginia, wrote a stunning account of her personal impact on his life and gave her permission to use it to encourage other potential students of the University of Science and Philosophy. Lao considered it to be one of the most heartwarming and impressive letters she ever received. It read in part as follows:

> Until I met you personally, Swannanoa scared me. I had been taught to fear the potential evil of any spiritual ideas that did not come from the conservative Christian religion in which I was raised. I was afraid of being stalked by an authoritarian cult that would control my thoughts, separate me from friends and family, and reduce me to a zombie that would sit and sway all day.
>
> Uncertainties in my career accentuated these fears. I had recently obtained tenure in the Department of Psychology at the University of Virginia. This promotion was like having in my hand the brass ring for which I had been reaching as long as I could remember. The question was, "What would I do with it now that I had it?" I thank God that you propelled me inward in search of an answer.
>
> Your books and *Home Study Course* helped me to know myself better and to live in an active partnership with God. As a result, I did not relinquish control but gained far greater control of myself. Similarly, I did not lose touch with friends and family but grew much closer because knowing and loving myself more was a giant step toward knowing and loving others

> more. Finally, I did not become immobilized and unproductive but energized and prosperous. I wrote a successful textbook, served two years as the Study Director for the Committee on Vision at the National Academy of Sciences, participated for a summer in an international workshop in Germany, and accepted a full professorship at Texas A&M University where I have recently been elected to head a committee that is striving to establish a multidisciplinary center to foster the integration of the University's research resources and the application of those resources to today's pressing problems.
>
> Most importantly, my work and my life in general are a joy. Can you imagine, for example, the joy I felt when I worked together with my father, who was a house painter, to paint my house shortly before he died? That is the kind of joy that I now experience working with God. My father and I knew no limits to our joy or energy as he shared with me all he knew about painting. Similarly, God and I know no limits to joy and energy when we work together. Lao, I pray that this letter will help others find God in themselves.

Lao was confident that if Soviet Premier Gorbachev could read *Atomic Suicide?* he would take the initiative to reduce the nuclear arms race. It thrilled her when John Denver and his physician, Dr. Tim Binder, took copies of the book to Russia and distributed it among important government officials. Soon after their return, a top scientist with the American Academy for the Advancement of Sciences, Dr. Harold Chestnut, took copies of the same book to a meeting of his fellow scientists in Russia.

She told her newer students, "More and more deep-thinking people are recognizing the importance of this book because it gives the cause and solution for man's dilemma regarding the destructive elements of radioactivity and pollution. Its deep purpose is to unfold not only vital New Age scientific concepts but to enlighten man to the urgent need of unity of purpose for the very survival of man and of the planet that sustains him."

Her own first book, *God Will Work with You but Not for You*, remained one of the University's key tools in extending its work. Walter Russell had considered it to be the greatest textbook of their teachings. Lao never released the names of the ladies who had told her the story, but she took enormous pride from their assurance that the great transformation of Malcolm X's character before his assassination was due in no small part to the powerful message of her book.

She often related the story as follows: "Two special women came to see me from Chicago, and they said that Malcolm X had introduced them to our work. He then explained that his study of *God Will Work with You but Not for You* made him realize his oneness with white people and with all races, and with this new understanding he said he could no longer be a leader who advocated violence. He became a leader of Love! He refused to call his movement the Black Muslims, but renamed it and allowed white membership!

"This clear demonstration of Malcolm X's dramatic change of character from one of great violence to Love and loving service illustrates the great need for this book to reach into every country so that all races heed its vital message of man's oneness with God and with his fellow man. We could at long last have a world united with peoples of all nations and races knowing—and living—their oneness with all others!"

Although the story of Malcolm X and Lao's book was never broadly publicized, because of the reluctance of the visitors who told it to Lao to be identified, she was well aware that Malcolm X had experienced an enormous change in his outlook in his latter days. She knew that the forceful leader had realized that he had been mistaken in his race-conscious philosophy and had understood that following the path to the "Brotherhood of Man" was the only way to peaceful living. Rumors abounded that this change in his heart was the real reason for his murder by former colleagues who could not accept his enlightenment.

Lao actively corresponded with groups of all kinds who promoted women's rights. In England, the movement to allow women to be ordained as Anglican priests caught her attention. One reason for the church's refusal to allow this was that a woman priest could not celebrate Communion because she might be menstruating. "How absurd these men are!" an English colleague wrote her.

Three leaders of the Holistic Health Counseling Center, Kiribat-Yam, Israel, directed by Pinchas Kuziner, enrolled in the *Home Study Course* after reading her books. These scholars, who were teaching the impact of the music of the spheres in the development of higher consciousness, found the Russell information on octaves of great help. Lao granted them permission to translate limited information and cite it in the essays their group was publishing. They appreciated the compatibility of the Russell principles with similar approaches found in the Kabbalah, the works of Khrisna, and the writings of Gurdjieff. To Lao this was additional confirmation of the universality of the Russell work.

The arts editor of the *World & I* magazine had read *The Man Who Tapped the Secrets of the Universe*. Lao arranged for materials and a proposed article to be prepared by a University student, John Thomas LaValley of Tarrytown, New York, and sent to the periodical for possible publication.

During 1987 Lao enjoyed visits and long conversations with Dr. Sumer Sahin, who was general secretary and chief executive of TUBITAK, the scientific and technical research council of Turkey. A prominent scientist and engineer, he also served as vice chairman of the United Nations Intergovernmental Committee on Science and Technology for Development, and his duties in New York prevented his coming more often to Swannanoa. He pleased her greatly when he wrote, "Our discussions on science and philosophy are always most interesting and stimulating of thought. Wouldn't it be marvelous if the world could be receptive to ways to live in harmony and mutual support? Perhaps, one day, our ideas and the way we live will be shining examples to the generations to come."

Lao reminisced with Dr. Sahin on how *The Scientific Answer To Human Relations* had come to be written. "There were very serious labor problems worldwide, and they weighed heavily on my Consciousness for I could foresee the culminating agony of man's dissensions. One night I slept soundly until about three o'clock after retiring about midnight. From 3:00 A.M. until 8:30 A.M. I wrote rapidly, and when my beloved read the many sheets of manuscript after breakfast, he said, 'Darling, this message will change the relations of the whole industrial world.' It seems but yesterday that I heard his voice expressing this verdict. I also remember my reply to him. 'Darling, if it does so in a hundred years, man will have come a long way, but some day he will be forced to listen or he will have no world in which to live.' Even then with all the conspicuous evidence facing him mankind was blind, even as many are today, to the cause of his calamities." Lao told Dr. Sahin she had always stressed that knowledge alone and not money would bring balance to an unbalanced world.

A New York student put Lao in contact with Basil Bova, who had recently been named president of the Pathe Film Company. She recalled for Mr. Bova how Walter had skated a full programme for *Pathe News* in 1922, at the age of forty-nine, at Lake Placid, New York, with the then national women's champion, Beatrice Loughlin. Lao had been told that this film had been used in a recent documentary on the history of figure skating. Walter had won three first prizes for figure skating twenty years later, competing against people who were all under thirty.

She recounted that years before an original owner of *Pathe News* had visited Swannanoa. He was a man then in his nineties who had just read Lao's book *Love* and told her that if he were a younger man, he would see that it was distributed by the millions. She explored with Mr. Bova suggestions she had received from many well-known figures in the film industry that a documentary should be made about her and Walter. Eddie Albert had recently reiterated his desire to do the introduction to such a film. Cary Grant and Gloria Swanson had both suggested such a project in previous years.

In mid-August 1987, a large group of visitors from Japan, Russia, and Poland arrived simultaneously at Swannanoa and stayed to discuss the University's teachings with Lao. The group included a woman physician from

Moscow and the current Polish ski champion. Lao always told her staff that one never knew who would be the next person to walk through the magnificent front doors of the palace. The Japanese visitors had just attended a spiritual training program in New Market, Virginia. Their visit with Lao was so productive that their leader, Mr. Takahama, persuaded them all to change their flight arrangements so they could return to Swannanoa for further discussions over the weekend. On their return to Japan, Mr. Takahama wrote Lao that he had hired one of the top Russell students in Japan, a former leading atomic laser researcher there, to translate *Atomic Suicide?* into Japanese. "They were all entranced with what they found here on our mountaintop," she wrote Mr. Bova.

144. William B. "Butch" Carter.

William B. "Butch" Carter, a nutritionist from Norlina, North Carolina, joined a large group at Swannanoa over the astrologically significant last weekend in August. He wrote to thank her for her "gracious reception and hospitality," and noted, "I cannot think of a place where I would rather have been for the harmonic conversion from the Piscean to the Aquarian Age than at Swannanoa." He returned often with others to do volunteer maintenance and garden work for Lao at the palace. These professionals found such activity both refreshing and enlightening.

A senior officer in the Nigerian Navy, who was attending the United States War College, wrote her that his reading of the Russell books in his homeland had made visiting her one of his top priorities on coming to America. When they met at Swannanoa, he told her that henceforth his primary desire would be to work for true peace instead of studying war.

Charles Lutes, one of the most popular speakers on the teachings of Maharishi Mahesh Yogi, brought a large group of his students to see Lao at Swannanoa that summer. Every one of them was so impressed that they bought at a minimum the University's three core books. Mr. Lutes bought a copy of *The Universal One* for the famous guru. Lao was pleased that so many students of eastern religions found the scientific principles of the Russell curriculum both a valid and significant addition to what they believed. They continued to send busloads of their members to Swannanoa.

In 1987 Lao spoke to a large Baptist church group, and after her talk, they invited her to Danville, Virginia, to give a sermon in their church. Lao recalled that she even mentioned "reincarnation" to them but they seemed to love her entire talk. A large assembly of Lutherans came to the palace soon afterwards.

"The reaction of these varied groups to our teachings illustrates how our work knits together the Western and Eastern philosophies," she wrote. "This truly indicates how both the West and the East are still looking for that 'something beyond' which they are now finding in our *Home Study Course* and books!" Lao was in her thirty-ninth year at Swannanoa, and the Message emanating from the mountain seemed ever more popular.

Television personality Joyce DeWitt, a star of the popular situation comedy series *Three's Company*, telephoned her to express her eagerness to study the Russell works. Lao sent her *The Man Who Tapped the Secrets of the Universe* and *Love* through a California student, and Miss DeWitt called to order *God Will Work with You but Not for You* even before she had opened the other two books. She told Lao she intended to give copies of the books to many of her friends. "She sounds like a wonderful person," Lao wrote Emelia.

Dr. Marcel Vogel, a deep student of the Russells for many years, came to Swannanoa. He had great respect, admiration, and appreciation for Walter Russell's new cosmogony and had studied and used it in his own teachings for many years. He was but one of many individuals seeking greater knowledge of the healing powers of crystals, who found that the *Home Study Course* and other Russell books clearly revealed for them the true nature of crystals.

Dr. James Payne, former special education professor at the University of Virginia, who had made *The Man Who Tapped the Secrets of the Universe* required reading in his courses for many years, wrote that he had been appointed dean at Mississippi State University. He still recommended the Russells' books to his students, he assured Lao.

Tony Cordero, who had come to the palace years before, was reportedly advising others that Lao's health was failing and that she had designated him as her successor to continue the University's work after her death. She corrected this misimpression, adding that while Mr. Codero had been neither her close student or friend, she hoped he was living "the inviolate laws of God which alone can bring happiness and success to anyone's life."

Lao confided a combination of past frustration and growing hope to her economist friend William Howdon in the fall of 1987: "In all the years I have been carrying this Message and disseminating it, I can count on one hand the number of special souls who really understand it and have done something about it. Since Walter Russell refolded, this university has actually been a 'one-man' university. I have worked long hours every day whether it be attending to the daily details of running the university, maintaining my important correspondence, or meeting with our many visitors and students, not to mention the continued writing of my books. I have seen too many movements collapse within just a few short years through lack of real work and action. But through all this, I have stuck to it. I wrote my books, *Love* and *Why You Cannot Die!* They have encircled the world and are most successful. Now I seem to have gained the momentum in giving this Message, and important people of position are contacting me daily."

Lao had little patience with much of the younger generation's New Age rhetoric. Many people thought the New Age would prove the tidal wave that swept the Russell work into the consciousness of the general public. "Unfortunately so much of the so called 'New Age' language is so repetitive that it has lost the power of its original message. It is not practical enough to inspire people to action. I have always said that many of the metaphysical movements have done as much harm to the world as the orthodox religions have in the past in that they give people a pseudo sense of security. These people will have to experience the same 'hard knocks' as everybody else before they will have a real awakening," she told William Howdon.

It astounded Lao to see the American government support the $4.4 billion super-collider project, which physicists claimed would prove definitively what matter is and how it is created. She felt that the world could easily obtain this knowledge for a few dollars by reading and studying Walter's book *The Secret of Light*.

Lao noted that only in 1986 had the top scientists at NASA discovered through space probes that the planet Uranus was spinning on its side. "They have spent millions in discovering this, and yet they still do not know why Uranus is doing this. Walter Russell gave a full explanation of this phenomenon in 1926 in his book, *The Universal One*, and he was giving that book away when it was first printed! Likewise, he gave a full explanation of the rings of Saturn, and the scientists are only just beginning to verify this also!"

She wrote Sanford Edward at Harvard University, "Some far distant day my husband's new Cosmogony will receive the attention it deserves." Lao had never authorized a student discount on orders of this book, but when a Harvard graduate student ordered it, she made an exception, relying on his assurance that he would do his best to introduce it to the "mainstream academia where they desperately need it!" W. I. Wilson, a Chicago physician, told her that *The Universal One* had moved him to tears. "This is the book I have been waiting and looking for throughout my whole life as a physician, a metaphysician, and scientist."

The week before Thanksgiving, Mr. Gueye, the First Counsel from the Embassy of Senegal, West Africa, came from Washington, D.C., to meet Lao. He had learned of the University the week before from an oil businessman in Austria.

The same week, Dr. Ken Lipke, president of Gibraltar Steel Company in Buffalo, New York, flew to Charlottesville in his private jet, accompanied by Shirley Calkins Smith, an evolutionary tutor from Lily Dale, New York, who had introduced him to the Russells' works. They drove to Swannanoa and enjoyed an exciting meeting with Lao, who recognized that Dr. Lipke was in touch with leading business executives all over the world, and felt very strongly that he might be the person who she had long awaited to spread God's Message and secure the long-range mission of the University. She likewise found Shirley Calkins Smith an engaging and delightful person, and in coming months they agreed that Shirley would come to Swannanoa in May 1988 to join the staff as Lao's principal assistant.

145. Dr. Ken Lipke, president of Gibraltar Steel.

Dr. Lipke was Chairman of the Board of the Freedoms Foundation at Valley Forge, held the Silver Helmet Americanism Award, had served on the USO World Board of Governors, and had been a featured speaker for more than 500 national civic and governmental organizations. He had found *The Man Who Tapped the Secrets of the Universe* inspiring and wrote Lao that he had been mesmerized on meeting her. After she died, he became a creative, energizing member of the board of directors of the University of Science and Philosophy and was instrumental in helping it meet many challenges, until his own sudden death several years later.

These events cheered Lao enormously, and she spent much of December communicating her excitement and encouragement to friends and students around the world. She celebrated Christmas with Sam Biser, Angela Carr, Margaret Ruhe, and a local couple who often brought their young children to see her on holidays. Lao appeared in good health, but it would be her last Christmas at Swannanoa.

Emelia wrote that in the world of American business she saw little reason for encouragement, "so hearing of your progress at Swannanoa is like a breath of fresh air!"

For years Lao had drawn inspiration from Angela Morgan's poem "When Nature Wants a Man," which ranked with John Burroughs's "Waiting" as her favorite verse. Since her youth, Lao had admired Morgan's first book, *The Hour Has Struck*, and she found in the subsequently published and later anthologized "When Nature Wants a Man" a perfect description of the need for influential world leaders and dedicated, cosmically inspired motivators to step forward and take the lead in transforming mankind. She quoted from Morgan's three-page poem in her correspondence as long as she lived. She used it as a challenge to those whom she thought could bring the urgent message of Rhythmic Balanced Interchange to all humanity, and Dr. Lipke was no exception.

Lao especially loved the opening section of Morgan's dramatic, cadenced verse: "When Nature wants to drill a man / And thrill a man, / And skill a man, / When Nature wants to mould a man / To play the noblest part; / When she yearns with all her heart / To create so great and bold a man / That all the world shall praise, / Watch her method, watch her ways!" Likewise she frequently quoted these subsequent lines from the poem: "When Nature wants to take a man / And shake a man / And wake a man; / When Nature wants to make a man / To do the future's will; / When she tries with all her skill / And she yearns with all her soul / To create him large and whole… / When the force that is divine / Leaps to challenge every failure… / Then doth Nature show her plan / When the world has found—a man!"

Just after the New Year, Eddie Albert telephoned her again. He told her it was his intention to devote 1988 to doing anything he could to help Lao spread her work. He recounted that throughout the entire morning of New Year's Day, he was thinking how deeply he desired to retire from the entertainment business and do something of much greater value for the world. He told Lao that he believed her work was the single answer. She viewed this as a highly important harbinger of greater success for the University.

She believed that change was in the air for the long-troubled world. She was convinced of Soviet Premier Gorbachev's sincerity and believed that he was eager to do his part to make the world safer and less threatening. She only hoped he would be recognized and appreciated by America's leaders so that he would feel encouraged to press onward with his plans for peace. She truly believed that Gorbachev had a very special destiny to fulfill, and she envisioned him sitting with other world leaders around the big oak dining table at Swannanoa.

Lao was greatly concerned with the deterioration of the earth's ozone layer, which she and Walter had predicted in 1954, when the world's major governments began making immense capital outlays for developing nuclear power sources. By now she was receiving reports that the ozone layer had grown so thin in Antarctica that researchers there were regularly suffering severe radiation burns. Lao knew that this severe thinning of the ozone layer, to the extent that it was no longer protecting life below, was an ominous warning to the world at large. She often discussed this fearful situation with Dr. Tim Binder, who kept her apprised of details of what they both believed would result in world calamity if corrective measures were not undertaken.

Another California student, connected with the National Aeronautics and Space Administration and involved in studies of the ozone layer, wrote Lao that tests being conducted by the government revealed these conditions to be much worse than the experts had anticipated.

Rabbi S. Y. Cohen, the Chief Rabbi of Haifa, Israel, visited Lao at Swannanoa after a Russell student from New York had sent him *Atomic Suicide?* and *The Book of Early Whisperings*. He had specifically requested extra time on his schedule so that he could meet Lao on his next official trip to America. "He had so many deep questions, all of which were unanswerable within his own spiritual training and background," Lao wrote Emelia on January 4. "He was in great awe during his entire visit and had a wonderful appreciation for the demonstration of what Walter Russell and I had done together. As he was leaving, one of my staff overheard him say to his escort that his visit here with me had been his greatest spiritual experience."

"Such wonderful things are happening," Lao told her longtime friend. "Dr. Lipke called me Christmas Day and New Year's Day!" She was preparing a special letter and group of documents to send to the spiritually minded New York steel industrialist whose visit had so encouraged her the preceding fall.

Jess Stern, whose numerous popular books by now included the bestselling *Edgar Cayce, The Sleeping Prophet*, visited Swannanoa in 1987, twenty-seven years after he had first met Walter and Lao. She told Emelia that the prolific author was "incredulous to see how I looked. He said I looked better now than I did twenty-seven years ago! Then a few minutes later he exclaimed, 'If anyone can prove that there is no such thing as age, it is Lao Russell!'" Compliments like these gave Lao confidence that God was keeping her alive until her destiny of giving God's Message to mankind could be fulfilled.

Emelia had been shocked to learn that the Dulaney group had raised the rent on the palace and grounds to $48,000 a year. She felt that the owners had placed Lao in an indefensible situation and were trying to pressure her to surrender the premises after forty years. "At this point they probably wouldn't let you buy Swannanoa, even if you were able to," Emelia ruefully wrote her friend. Emelia hoped that Dr. Lipke could persuade the owners to transfer the palace to the University.

"It is amazing that there are people who have forty million dollars to pay for a Van Gogh painting, and yet we can't seem to find one individual to buy Swannanoa for humanity," Emelia wrote Lao. "Be that as it may, and even though it seems like an impossible dream, I strongly feel, as you do, that it will come to pass that Swannanoa will be the permanent foundation for the Message." Neither Emelia nor the palace's owners realized the extent to which Lao and the University had slowly accumulated capital over the decades, waiting for the day when the palace might be offered to them for purchase. Extending the Message throughout the world was the more important mission, both friends knew, but the security of owning the palace as the University's permanent home remained their dream.

Lao wrote a special New Year's message to her many friends, concluding, "There is so much more I wish I could share with you. I feel that in this New Year everyone needs a special message of Love and Hope. I know such a deep desire to hold the whole world to my heart—every man, woman and child and all the animals, birds and fish of the sea."

Enrollments in the *Home Study Course* had grown, and book sales were encouraging. A therapist in West Germany appealed to Lao to provide translations of the books, assuring her that the Russell teachings could easily be translated into every major foreign language by computer. Lao suspected this would not be as simple a task as he suggested, given the complicated nature of some of their works, but she agreed that her mail indicated there was a growing demand for such translations.

"It is an interesting fact that without advertising our work has encircled the globe," she replied, "and many deep students come from far countries to visit with me at the headquarters of the University of Science and Philosophy on our mountaintop at Swannanoa."

The brilliant young macrobioticist John David Mann, who edited and published his popular magazine *Solstice* in nearby Charlottesville, visited Lao with his colleague Steve Gagne and described the University in several excellent articles, beginning in February. He also introduced her to Super Blue Green Algae, which he felt certain could prove indispensable in helping restore her health.

The same month Lao awakened numerous times one night with the strong realization that God was urgently calling her to action, and warning her that the planet itself was already in a dying stage due to the overuse and abuse of atomic fission, pesticides, and chemicals.

Lao had just become acquainted with the efforts of industrialist Paul C. Fisher, president of the Fisher Space Pen Company in Nevada and inventor of the pen the astronauts used in outer space. His book *The Plan* outlined his efforts to promote a revolutionary constitutional amendment to "abolish all income, payroll, sales, inheritance and gifts taxes and put $700 billion extra into the pockets of those who must work for a living."

146. Paul Fisher, inventor of the space pen.

Fisher proposed to balance the federal budget by "taxing hoarded wealth on a graduated basis, as suggested by Thomas Jefferson." He advocated a tax on assets, including those of foundations, corporations, churches, unions, and even governments. This would produce a thirty-trillion-dollar tax base. "A fair tax averaging three percent a year will more than balance the federal budget," he insisted.

Paul Fisher telephoned Lao on February 16 and ordered seventeen copies of *Why You Cannot Die!* as gifts for family members and close associates. Lao's philosophy had touched the well-known inventor and capitalist greatly, he told her, adding that it was not until he had read her books that he realized that his businesses had been successful because he had in fact been putting God's laws into practice in his every transaction without fully realizing it. Lao likewise felt that the Russell teachings were reflected throughout Fisher's important thesis set forth in *The Plan*.

He called her again in March, ordering copies of all of the Russell books. Lao told him his actions proved to her that he was "truly in character and spiritual awareness what I felt from the first chapter of your book." She told him that he obviously recognized in their mutual writings the truth and knowledge they had both been trying to give to the world.

Eddie Albert called Lao again in April, expressing delight that she had met Paul Fisher, who he intended to call himself. Mr. Albert had an appointment in Washington, D.C., the following month, after which he planned to visit Lao at Swannanoa.

Lao would not live to see Eddie Albert at Swannanoa, but she was delighted when Paul Fisher flew into Charlottesville by private jet on April 12 and drove to Swannanoa to visit her. After what she described as a marvelous visit, he left early the next morning, leaving her a loving note: "Dear Lao, I woke a little early, well rested and happy. So, I shall be on my way soon. Thank you for your hospitality and for helping to inspire me to do a better job. Please thank Sam, Margaret and Bridget for their kindness and consideration. They, too, have helped me. I shall call you and plan to see you again soon. Love, Paul."

Lao regularly heard from Melford Okilo, who was living in Port Harcourt, Nigeria, and devoting himself to building his country's educational system. He was a greatly honored statesman there, and his own book, *Love Creates Balance*, would be published by the University the following year. Lao felt that no one else had a deeper knowledge of the University's teachings and writings and credited this brilliant and gentle man with introducing the Message to all of West Africa. He actively promoted the *Home Study Course*, and supported the strong International Age of Character Clubs that had over the years been founded in various parts of Nigeria. He also encouraged new students to organize such clubs in their own areas of the country. Over a hundred letters a month came to Swannanoa from Nigerian students. Other prominent leaders of the country, including Captain Dele Osunmakinde of the Nigerian Navy, supported Lao and Melford Okilo in bringing the Russells' teachings of world peace and brotherhood to their fellow citizens.

The University was receiving new *Home Study Course* enrollments from across America. A student of esoteric philosophy wrote Lao from California that the first lesson had "answered questions I have had for years."

Another West Coast student called her to suggest that the University undertake a renewed effort to promote the Man-Woman Equalization League, which Lao had introduced thirty years ago and still believed held the key to bringing peace and progress to the world. Lao recognized that the world had not been ready for the idea then but told her caller, "Now the world is ready and desperately needs the multiplied power that comes from Man-Woman Balance."

It seemed strange to Lao that the obvious need for balancing the male-female energy had not been recognized from the beginning of time. She wrote, "There are all too few men or women who comprehend the wholeness of true matehood. Creation is but a multiplication of the male-female principle!" She recalled, that in her 1946 illumination, God had made known to her that man would never know peace on earth until he was awakened to this balancing factor of Creation, which was applicable to scientific principles as well as all living things.

In early April 1988 Lao wrote Dr. Donald C. Profenno in Waterville, Maine, outlining exciting events that were occurring among the University students. She described her meeting with Kenoll Wilson of Brussells, Belgium, a WANG computer executive responsible for the company's governmental computer work for all of Africa, much of Europe, and many parts of Australia. He was currently organizing development programs for forty African institutions to train government employees and others in efficient use of computers, and told Lao that one of his main goals was simultaneously to implement principles from the *Home Study Course* in his overall curriculum.

Lao was alarmed to learn that many European governments had allowed five times the acceptable radiation level in their dairy and vegetable products. Mr. Wilson told her that virtually all of Europe's produce had been severely affected by the Chernobyl nuclear accident in Russia. Australia had remained strict in enforcing regulations prohibiting the use of radioactive food and had banned many food imports from Europe. Lao was confident that the relatively wide distribution of *Atomic Suicide?* in Australia and New Zealand had provided the governments of these South Pacific countries an early warning to the dangers of such contamination. Lao was in regular discussion about these alarming conditions with Michael Hudak, Dr. Tim Binder, Bill Cranwell, and other members of her board of directors.

Dennis Weaver encouraged Lao with frequent telephone calls. He knew implicitly that true leadership must come from parts of society other than politics. It thrilled them both to learn that at last copies of *Atomic Suicide?*,

Why You Cannot Die!, and *The Man Who Tapped the Secrets of the Universe* had been personally delivered to General Secretary Mikhail Gorbachev in the Soviet Union by a leading Virginia educator, who had spoken on ozone depletion in a speech, "The Hole in the Sky," at a Soviet-American conference for young people that April. John Denver, Tim Binder, and Harold Chestnut had all brought these books to the attention of Mr. Gorbachev's top aides in the past and asked that he be given them, but the young Virginian assured Lao that she had personally given her copies to the Soviet leader himself.

Visitors energized Lao, and she never seemed too tired to receive them. Two weeks before she refolded into the next life, she wrote a Massachusetts lady who had come to Swannanoa for the first time in April and had written to thank Lao for their conversation and the hospitality she had received at the palace. "It is always like the touch of God's hand to be told that a visit to Swannanoa brought greater Light to a Soul," Lao wrote, "and we never fail to experience an ever greater desire to give more of the new Cosmic knowledge God has bestowed upon us."

In late April, Laara Lindo, now a widow living in North Vancouver, British Columbia, wrote that she was coming to Swannanoa in early May. Lao replied immediately, "I cannot tell you what it meant to me to have your letter this morning and to know that we shall soon meet face-to-face on God's beautiful mountaintop." Over the thirty-two years of their friendship, they had often planned to meet, both in Canada and Virginia, but this was the first occasion it proved possible. Lao invited her to stay at the guesthouse and welcomed her offer to be "put to work" during her visit. "There is nothing greater than to share in every possible way with all the goings on here at Swannanoa. It makes one's visit a most memorable one," she wrote her Canadian friend.

Lao spent Sunday afternoon, May 1, in the great hall of the palace, speaking individually and collectively with a large group of visitors. One of them was a professional photographer, and the informal portraits he took that afternoon reflected her vibrant energy and spirit.

Nonetheless, her strenuous pace was taking its toll on her heart. Although she was forced to rest more often, her closest friends and staff members at the palace

147. Lao with an unidentified student the Sunday before she died.

did not realize that she was seriously ill. Her demeanor remained bright and cheerful, and she seemed energetic until the end. In later weeks her secretary Margaret Ruhe recalled indications that should have alerted them that all was not well: "In retrospect, she hinted that she did not have the strength to do all she wanted to do. We always thought God would give her a greater renewal. Deep down I feel that she did accomplish her life's mission of giving God's Message. There was not too much more that she could do to help further awaken mankind. She and Dr. Russell supplied the entire University's curriculum, and all the tools for awakening mankind are within their teachings. It would not have been fair if Mrs. Russell had to go on with the work while not having the strength of body she desired. She used to say, 'When your body gets old and creaky, why not trade it in and get a new one?'"

Margaret Ruhe had been at Swannanoa for some ten years, having left college in Canada to come to help Lao after reading their books. She recalled, "When I came to Swannanoa, I immediately felt 'at home.' I stayed almost a week and in that time I met Mrs. Russell for approximately ten minutes. In that brief time Mrs. Russell touched me so deeply. I knew that I was not alone! I knew that I was not alone in my thinking! What a relief it was for me. Actually, I realized that I had felt so much alone because there are still so few who really know God."

On Wednesday afternoon, May 4, Lao relaxed with four visitors, including Laara Lindo, who had arrived from British Columbia, and Mary Louise De Marchi, a deeply interested new student from near Niagara Falls, New York. Two women from North Carolina were also present. Laara recalled the afternoon as a "very natural visit as though very longtime friends had met again and found the time between visits to be as no time." Part of their colloquy was preserved by tape recording. Laara had brought Lao a beautiful bouquet of pink carnations, which Lao told them had been her mother's favorite flower. They enjoyed a lively exchange, a delightful conversation among five brilliant women, who obviously were in tune with *The Message of the Divine Iliad*.

148. Laara Lindo.

It was warm and happy talk, serious enough but punctuated with friendly banter and occasional humor. All of them participated fully in the hours-long discussion over tea with honey.

Mary Louise was smart, inquisitive, and a good businesswoman herself. Laara was happy to be at Swannanoa at last, and to have the opportunity to discuss in person the many things about which she and Lao had corresponded and spoken by telephone over three decades. Naturally both of the visitors were interested in Lao's opinions, little suspecting that she would refold from her mortal life in little more than twenty-four hours.

Lao recounted many of the difficulties Walter had experienced before he met her, noting that it was always thus with illuminates. She reminded them that the wise men and not theologians had discovered Jesus. She told them she had learned never to talk about the subtleties of their science with those who she suspected could not understand it, for many people were quick to condemn anything they had difficulty in comprehending. She knew that Laara and Mary Louise realized the importance of the Russell teachings and recognized that relatively few people shared their realization.

They discussed astrology and numerology. Lao told them to remember always that when you understand God's processes and live God's ways, you control your stars and your numbers. She cautioned that the physical universe is an illusion. The only reality is the God Light, which is the Mind.

They spoke briefly about national and world politics and racial intolerance. Lao stressed how impressed she had been with many of the African and African-American people she had met. "They are so fantastic," she said. She related many of her experiences with her Nigerian friend, Governor Melford Okilo, who in her eyes was a second Gandhi.

They discussed the tensions that existed in Nigeria due to the division in its population between Christians and Muslims. Lao stressed that every religion is fundamentally the same. She had studied the life of Mohammed and seen a biographical film on him, but she saw clearly that many present-day Muslims were no more true to Mohammed's teachings than present-day Christians adhered to the precepts of Jesus.

In his time, she told them, Jesus had brought the greatest message to the world. "If He had said what He knew about the Light of God, they would have crucified Him in three days instead of three years," she stressed. "His message has never been left alone. It is fundamentally a message of 'I love you and love each other,' but people fail to love each other. They let some little prejudice come up and put them right off the loving. If we had had real Christianity, we would never have had wars or enmities like we have had, nothing but one war after another. Every twenty years we build up to go and kill each other."

They talked about the growing interest in witchcraft. A policeman visiting the palace the previous Sunday had told Lao that witchcraft seemed to have become one of the worst entrapments of present-day young people. Lao found this virtually unbelievable and recalled the years she had spent in trying to interest her students in forming character clubs to guide the young. It was such a simple way to expand worthwhile knowledge to the next generation.

Lao believed that lack of character was the world's most fundamental problem. It intrigued her that the University's character club movement was more vibrant and alive in Nigeria than in any other country. She told her friends that the thousands of letters she had received from Nigeria revealed feelings, understanding, self-awareness, and desire for God consciousness that were stronger than that of any other group she had encountered.

"Today people emphasize physical, sensed things, ignoring the spiritual, and the spiritual is the strongest force on Earth," she said. "How many people know God? That is the tragedy. The teachers and professors in this country say that they have become nothing but babysitters. They are not allowed to teach what character really is, and that is the whole problem with the world. It's become characterless."

They discussed Lao's hopes for the future, her excitement at Eddie Albert's impending visit, and the keen interest that Dennis Weaver and John Denver were showing in the teachings. They spoke of the growing emphasis on sex instead of love and on the rampant increase in both heterosexual and homosexual promiscuity. All of this worked against the concept of balance, Lao stressed. She knew that in any relationship it was the little acts of kindness and not the animal sex that counted. "It's heaven when it is mental and spiritual first," she told them. "That is why I'm urging the youth today not to marry until they find their mental and spiritual mate."

People felt sorry for her when she and Walter first married, she remembered, pitying the young bride of such an old man. Their pity was misplaced. "I was the luckiest woman in the world with Walter Russell. He was the youngest man I'd ever known," she told her friends that afternoon.

"When Walter Russell and I came together, I was completely happy and integrated within myself and had this tremendous oneness with God, and, frankly, I was almost afraid to marry, and Walter Russell, of course, was the same way when I met him. What we had together was 100 percent balanced.

"When we wrote those books and courses together, I would be in the office, and he would be in the studio. We would discuss what we were going to do, you know, and time after time we found we had written the same thing word for word. I couldn't believe it. I didn't think anybody on this earth could ever think like I thought. That is why *The Man Who Tapped the Secrets of the Universe* had such an impact on me. It was the first time in my life that I read the words of someone who thought like I did."

Lao described the impact that her "You Are Important" motto had had on a variety of people in need of positive support. They also discussed at length Lao's *Code of Ethics*. Lao told them Walter had referred to it as "the Ten Commandments of today."

She discussed the burden of running the University alone, recounting that she had raised the funding herself and never taken one penny of royalty on anything she and Walter had written.

Lao asserted that the coming period in history would be woman's time. "Women are the ones who are going to give birth to a new era. I have a lot of faith in women, because when a woman starts doing something, really doing it, she puts her heart and soul into it and does it. Isn't that right? Now don't think I'm against men. I'm 100 percent for men, but not as leaders acting alone. They need women with them. We have never had a peace table. We have only had bargaining tables. Women have unfolded farther spiritually than men. You can see this in your churches, your movements, everything. In anything to do with spiritual things you will find ninety-five percent women and five percent men."

She bewailed the fact that many men were reluctant to enter what they considered menial jobs like construction. Without carpenters, plumbers, and bricklayers, we would have no homes. These jobs should be revered. She felt the same way about waitresses. They should be respected and not demeaned.

She was proud of the tenure of her loyal staff, Angela with twenty-five years of service and Margaret Ruhe with ten.

She listened to the Oprah Winfrey show, she said, because well-connected Russell students were trying to arrange for the television personality to interview Lao. "She's a brilliant woman, and I can't wait for her to read my *Love* book."

They spoke of the view of the Rockfish Valley from the guesthouse windows. She told them it was the same view of the valley that she had seen when God brought her there during her illumination three months before she met Walter Russell. They talked of animals, particularly the Scottish Terriers Lao had loved, and the condition of the palace itself when the Russells arrived in 1948.

They asked her about ghosts, astral projection, mediums, spirit guides, and the power of crystals. She suggested such concepts had little value because when one truly understood the universe, they knew it consisted only of God's imaginings and our imaginings. Death was a rest period. "Mind is all there is. The brain is nothing but a computer registering the senses. Everything of the senses is transitory, but everything of the mind is eternal. When you truly understand the ways and processes of God, you understand all of these things in a correct perspective."

It was a glorious afternoon of sharing, and the four women who talked with Lao would long remember every aspect of the occasion, from the warmth and smiles to the wisdom and truth.

That very day, May 4, 1988, a huge flare had erupted from the sun. An Associated Press story published two days later described the resulting geomagnetic storm "sweeping over the Earth," and quoted a spokesman for the Space Environmental Services Center in Boulder, Colorado, who said, "It took about a day for the effects to reach Earth. The storm may interfere with

149. *Lao Russell, May 1988.*

satellite, radio and telephone communications."

Her students wondered if this phenomenon had fatally affected Lao Russell. She died at 6:00 P.M., Thursday, May 5, in her upstairs suite at Swannanoa Palace. Margaret Ruhe was with her when she collapsed, and Angela Carr was nearby.

The funeral service was held at 3:00 P.M. on Mother's Day, the following Sunday afternoon, in the great marble hall of Swannanoa. Music permeated the occasion, including the great hymns "Abide with Me," "The Lord's Prayer," and "Peace, Perfect Peace," beautifully sung by Reverend Robert J. Richards, a Lutheran pastor from Waynesboro. Several hundred people were present, including press and curiosity seekers among dozens of old friends and students, many who had come from as far away as Michigan and California to pay their respects. Floral tributes included one from the British consulate. Shirley Calkins Smith, who had arrived in preparation for beginning work at the palace the next day, instead attended her prospective employer's funeral.

Michael Hudak, the board member from Akron, Ohio, who succeeded Lao as president of the University, delivered the memorial address. After recounting many events of Lao's life and warm experiences he himself had shared with her, he quoted from Walter's words describing "the crowning achievement of her life" as "the founding of a world university, with its student body in practically every country on the globe, in which to spread our teachings to those increasing numbers of people who have become ready and eager for higher knowledge of their relation to God." Michael Hudak repeated Walter's conclusion that only an extraordinary person could have accomplished such a miracle.

Her fellow directors spoke from scripture, read her *Code of Ethics*, and bore her casket to the hearse, which transported it to the nearby grave next to Walter's in the forest clearing behind the summer cottage. Gary Scrogham and Samuel Spicher served as honorary escorts.

There, as several hundred gathered on the lovely mountain, a prayer was said, followed by an excerpt from Edna St. Vincent Millay's sonnet on the death of Elinor Wylie, and slowly the mourners made their way back to the palace.

CHAPTER TWENTY-NINE

In Retrospect (1998)

Ten years later, in an upper-scale suburb of London, a remarkable man of eighty-six occupied his days caring with humor and compassion for his invalid wife of nearly sixty years.

His steps were halting and deliberate, and his day-to-day burdens weighed down heavily on him, but his eyes were bright and his memory keen.

He spoke with a distinct hint of the accent found in England's industrial midlands at the time of World War I, but his grammar was impeccable, and there was a cosmopolitan quality to his voice that bespoke the decades he had spent as a professional construction engineer in Toronto. He was a fascinating raconteur. There was melody in his diction, and he possessed descriptive powers.

He spoke of his dreary boyhood in Luton, where his father was the city's wealthiest wholesale grocer. He recalled his youthful insecurities as an asthmatic lad, torn between estranged parents, awkward in society. He described his good fortune in surviving the London blitz, the months he spent in a London hospital during World War II, and his postwar adventures in the New World.

In many ways he was little different from thousands of ambitious and intelligent young Englishmen who took advantage of their opportunities and found their fortunes across the ocean in various parts of the English-speaking world.

On one particular subject, however, John French had a unique story to tell. He had known Daisy Grace Cook as a country girl from Ivinghoe during her early years in Luton, and he remembered Mrs. Lionel Stebbing, the successful and glamorous prototype of English beauty during the 1930s. He had known Lao Russell, philosopher and visionary, who with her husband, Walter, on several occasions in the 1950s, had welcomed him and his wife to Swannanoa, the Russells' Italian Renaissance marble palace in the Blue Ridge Mountains of Virginia.

Daisy Grace Cook, Mrs. Lionel Stebbing, and Lao Russell were, of course, one and the same person, successive stages in the life of the most remarkable person he had ever met.

He smiled to remember her, the beautiful woman filled with natural genius, insatiable curiosity, the ability to stimulate and captivate any audience, and, above all, unceasing and unbounded love.

He reflected on the amazing journey she had made, from working as a teenager in his father's bustling office to her decades as an author and illuminate a world away on her American mountaintop. At once he seized upon the consistent quality he felt best characterized this exceptional woman throughout her lifetime.

"She was the kindest person I ever knew."

150. Lao Russell, May 1988.

APPENDIX 1
SOURCES, NOTES, AND ACTIVITIES

The principal source from which this book was drawn is the extensive collection of the University of Science and Philosophy Archives (USPA), which includes personal records of both Walter and Lao Russell covering most of their respective lives. In addition to official documents, books and other publications, business records, and photographs, the USPA includes voluminous correspondence files on the Russells' associates, friends, and students. These provided a wealth of information from which Lao Russell's life story was drawn.

Although in many instances privacy rights precluded the identification of an individual, the reader may be confident that unless specifically identified in the text or the following notes, the source of every statement in the book is found in the USPA. Its hundreds of thousands of documents, letters, and photographs are destined to be made available to qualified scholars and Russell students in the future by the board of directors of the University of Science and Philosophy, which holds the materials in trust under the last will and testament of Lao Russell.

Footnotes have not been used in the text for several reasons. First of all, much of the information has been drawn from personal correspondence, many of which may not legally or should not ethically be attributed. Secondly, because so many of the sources are not public documents, it was clear that use of footnotes would seriously detract from the readability of what was in any case a long and complicated story.

Most individuals mentioned in the text are listed alphabetically in Appendix 2 with a brief biographical citation where available. Publications and unpublished manuscripts cited in the text are listed by author in the bibliography.

The University of Science and Philosophy left Swannanoa Palace in 1997, after its offer to purchase the palace and gardens was declined by the owner. The organization still owns and maintains a number of properties on the mountain immediately adjacent to its former home. Friends and students of Walter and Lao Russell often visit their graves behind the summer cottage and enjoy the matchless view of Rockfish Valley from Russell Way, the road just below the palace. From the lofty vantage point, despite the progress of almost sixty years, the panorama is little changed from the day Lao Russell visited the mountain for the first time in 1948 and recognized the valley as the view she had experienced in her illumination of two years before.

The University still extends the Russell's message through its web sites and activities, and publishes the works of Walter and Lao Russell, including their books and the *Home Study Course*. The published works of Dr. Walter Russell and Lao Russell and other publications of the University of Science and Philosophy may be obtained from University of Science and Philosophy, Post Office Drawer 520, Waynesboro, Virginia 22980, and via the following: Facsimile Number: 330-650-0315; Telephone Number: 1-800-882-LOVE (5683), Websites: www.philosophy.org, www.twilightclub.org.

APPENDIX 2
LINE BIOGRAPHIES OF CERTAIN INDIVIDUALS IN THE TEXT

[R=Russell; WR=Walter Russell; LR=Lao Russell (Daisy Cook Stebbing); Swan=Swannanoa; USP=University of Science and Philosophy]

Abney, Palo, R friend and student in Orlando, Florida.
Ahlstrom, Sydney E. (1919-84), Yale University professor; examined USP in his 1971 *A Religious History of the American People*; winner of the 1973 National Book Award.
Albert, Eddie (1906-), entered films in 1938 after radio and stage, enjoyed long and successful screen and television career.
Albert, Margo (1917-85), actress; wife of Eddie Albert; played Maria in film *Lost Horizon*.
Alcala, Marcelino, Puerto Rican attorney; taught R philosophy, Silva Mind Control system in Caribbean and South America.
Alexander, E. S., English banker friend of LR.
Allan, Cicely, director, "White Lodge" center for esoteric studies in England and America.
Allison, Kay, confidante of LR; founder in 1978 of Charlottesville, Virginia, comprehensive Quest Book Shop, e-mail: Questka@mindspring.com.
Andreadis, John, co-founder of New York's Eternal Values; featured in Ruth Montgomery's *Aliens Among Us*; promoted R works in public service videos.
Araki, Takeshi, mayor, Hiroshima, Japan; corresponded with LR regarding *Atomic Suicide?*
Arpante, Mary Frances, directed Positive Healing Center, Arlington, Virginia.
Aterrbom, Per-Axel, translator of Edgar Cayce books into Scandinavian languages.
Atwater, Dr. P. M. H., near-death researcher and visionary author; web site: www.cinemind.com /atwater, e-mail: atwater@cinemind.com.
Aull, Warner, early R supporter from Hollywood, California.
Babson, Roger (1875-1967), American statistician, forecaster, and author.
Bailey, Alice (1880-1949), theosophist; New Age movement predecessor.
Baker, Richard St. Barbe (1889-1982), environmentalist who founded international conservation movement, The Men of the Trees.
Baliles, Gerald L. (1940-), Virginia governor, met LR/WR as Fishburne Military School cadet.
Bamberger, Joseph Jay, film producer, first in England, then California.
Bankhead, Tallulah (1903-68), American stage and film star; radio personality; father was Speaker of U.S. House of Representatives and grandfather a U.S. Senator.
Barton, Bruce (1886-1967), advertising genius and inspirational author.
Bates, Billy Prior, California attorney; promoted USP; friend of LR.
Beazley, Bob and Pat, friends of LR, who patronized their health food store near Swan.
Bedford, Rev. Eugenia, minister, Chapel in the Pines, Idyllwild, Calif.
Bellamy, Ralph, editor, *Cleveland Plain Dealer*; his father wrote *Looking Backward*.
Bellwood, Arthur B., entrepreneur and promoter of new inventions.
Bennett, R. Wheeler, conductor of Boston Youth Symphony.
Benney, Elsie and Bennie, staffed Sun Haven for LR.
Berlin, Edward P., Jr., Managing Editor, *Waynesboro News Virginian*.
Bertheau, Don, minister, Long Beach, California, Science of Mind Church.
Bey, Hamid (d. 1976), Coptic mystic and author.
Biddle, Charles W. (1895-1971), international banker of the Philadelphia Biddles; befriended LR.
Binder, Dr. Timothy A., LR friend and colleague; chiropractic and naturopathic physician; author; promoted new energy and nuclear disarmament; USP officer.

Biser, Samuel, editor, *Healthview Newsletter*; friend of LR; USP officer.
Blake, Sarah Weld, spiritual teacher.
Bolen, R. C. (1909-93), South Carolina chiropractor; R supporter.
Bopart, Larry, USP student; introducted Dr. Ernest Sternglass to *Atomic Suicide?*
Borsook, Dr. Henry, California Insitute of Technology; developed Meals-for-Millions after World War II.
Boulware, Lyle (1901-85), American architect who employed LR (1945).
Brandy, David, Melchizedek Order, Albuquerque, New Mexico.
Brick and Boyers, two women who were business partners from Des Moines, Iowa; attended and filmed summer classes at Swan; established USP study groups.
Brunton, Paul (1898-1981), British philosopher, mystic, traveler, and author.
Bucke, Richard Maurice (1837-1902), physician; wrote *Cosmic Consciousness.*
Buist, Olah (Mrs. David Buist), Michigan supporter of WR/LR.
Burkhart, Dr. Roy, pastor, Community Church, Columbus, Ohio.
Burlage, Charles, Norfolk, Va., attorney.
Burmeister (Leibe), Hildegarde (1894-1984), R friend in New York, later at Swan and in Florida.
Burns, William Heydon (1912-87), mayor of Miami, governor of Florida (1965-67).
Buttons, Patricia, singer and actress; LR friend from Hollywood years; testified for her in naturalization proceedings; later married Robert Levoff; visited Swan.
Burroughs, John (1837-1921), American poet and naturalist.
Byington, Spring (1893-1971), American stage, screen, and television actress.
Canty, Jerome, macrobiotic author and practitioner; supporter of USP; friend of LR.
Carlson, Randy, sales expert and supporter of USP.
Carpenter, Rev. Clifford, pastor, Unity Temple, Glendale, California.
Carr, Angela, name given by LR to Phyliss McConnell, Iowa educator who became the longest-tenured (thirty years) USP staff member at Swan.
Carroll, Sydney W. (1871-1958), English film and theatre critic, author, and journalist.
Carter, William B. "Butch," nutritionist; LR volunteer; USP supporter; Norlina, North Carolina.
Cassin, Pat and Marie, English friends of LR; Marie worked at USP.
Cayce, Edgar (1877-1945), American seer, psychic, and clairvoyant.
Cayce, Hugh Lynn, Edgar Cayce's son; led Association for Research and Enlightenment, Virginia Beach, Virginia.
Chaffee, Dr. Clifford, Religious Science minister in California.
Chestnut, Dr. Harold (1918-2001), electrical engineer famous for his work on stability, reliability, and power systems automation, his work on the Apollo space missions, and his post-retirement efforts to apply engineering principles to political realities.
Chipman, Jesse Guy, motivational expert who accompanied LR on her national tours.
Cipelletti, Dr. Giusepe, Milanese physician; friend of LR in 1930s.
Clark, Dr. Gene Emmett, minister, Beverly Hills Church of Religious Science; religious commentator on radio in western U.S.
Clark, Glenn (1882-1956), founded Camps Farthest Out; prolific spiritual author; books include WR biography, *The Man Who Tapped the Secrets of the Universe.*
Clinton, Clifford, California businessman who headed international Meals-for-Millions program.
Cook, Alfred William (1850-1918), LR's father.
Cook, Emily Anne (1897-1962), LR's sister; wife of Harold Summerfield.
Cook, Florence Lizzie Hills (1864-1917), LR's mother.
Cook, Florrie May (1895-1979), LR's eldest sister and guardian; known later as Florrie French.
Cook, George (1828-1909), LR's paternal grandfather, Ivinghoe, England.
Cook, Dr. James T., surgeon in St. Louis, Mo.; LR's cousin.
Cook, Sarah Lester (1826-1907), LR's paternal grandmother.
Corelli, Marie (1855-1924), English author.

Cowen, Abbey, promoted LR's *Code of Ethics* in South Africa.
Crandall, Jack, sought R relocation to Colorado Springs.
Crane, Ruth, licensed minister, clairvoyant, and Cayce student.
Cranwell, William, benefactor and board member, USP; friend of LR.
Crickmore, M. R. and Joan, of Ellerton Abbey; friends of LR in England and Jamaica.
Cripps, Lady Isobel (1891-1979), British public figure; friend of WR/LR.
Cripps, Sir Stafford (1889-1952), British statesman.
Cummings, Constance (b. 1910), English star of stage and screen.
Daily, Rev. Starr, inspirational author; reformed prison inmate; colleague of Glenn Clark.
Daniel, Dr. Robert P., president, Virginia State College.
Daniels, Bebe (1901-71), American movie star; wife of Ben Lyon.
Darden, Dr. Colgate, Jr. (1887-1981), governor of Virginia (1942-46); later president of the University of Virginia; dedication speaker at Swan, May 2, 1949.
David-Neel, Alexandra (1868-1969), sole ordained female Lama priest at one time.
Davis, Howard R., III, USP supporter; LR friend; Atlanta, Georgia.
Davis, Neil C., Success Training organization, Toronto, Canada.
Davis, Richard Harding (1864-1916), American writer and journalist.
De Kock, Gertrude, R supporter in South Africa.
De Marchi, Mary Louise, friend of LR; spiritual leader; Niagara Falls, New York.
deZevallas, Mary, author who aspired to write WR biography.
DeLoach, Etel, director, Aescupapian Institute, Lilburn, Georgia; psychic healer.
Denver, John (1943-97), American singer, composer, environmentalist, and humanitarian.
Detloff, Charles, editor of Portland, Oregon, journal *Murmurings*.
Deunov, Peter (also known as Beeinsa Douno) (1864-1944), Bulgarian spiritual teacher whose music and communal dance movements (Paneurhythmy) appealed to LR.
Devi, Gayatri (1906-95), first Indian woman ordained to teach Vedanta in America; led Vendanta Centre in Boston; friend of LR.
DeWitt, Joyce (b. 1949), American television actress.
Dickson, Dorothy (1893-1995), American film and stage star, noted for musical roles.
Dillon, Virginia, LR's neighbor at Rossmont estate near Swan.
Dilworth, William, Maj. and Mrs. Dooley's butler at Swan.
DiRenzo, Ted, directed Montessori school, Collingdale, Pennsylvania.
Dooley, Maj. James (1841-1922) and Sallie May (1846-1925), built Swan.
Doss, Dr. Albert Hugh T., Egyptian-born medical doctor; American Roscicrucian leader; supporter of USP.
Drummond, Grace L., provided scientific equipment to WR.
Drury, Ruth, Palmyra, N.Y.; editor of *The Living Word*; Golden Rule businesswoman.
Dulaney, A. T., Sr., stockholder in Skyline-Swannanoa, Inc., when WR/LR came to Swan.
Dulaney, A. T., Jr., held ownership interest in Swan.
Dulaney, James F., Sr., son of A. T. Dulaney, Sr., stockholder in Skyline-Swannanoa, Inc.
Dulaney, James F., Jr., stockholder in Skyline-Swannanoa, Inc.
Dulaney, Richard A., attorney; son of A. T. Dulaney, Jr.; USP board member; friend of LR/WR.
Duncan, Winifred, Alabama theosophist; USP supporter.
Dunn, Marie, USP board member; musician and composer; co-composed music for LR's lyrics.
Dunn, Ruby, nutritionist; USP supporter; Tulsa, Oklahoma.
Dunnington, Dr. L. L., author, minister, and USP supporter; Mercer Island, Georgia.
DuPont, Patricia (Mrs. Alfred I.), later Mrs. James Stephanis; USP benefactor and board member.
Earley, Charles, physician and phrenologist; WR friend; USP supporter.
Eaton, Cyrus (1883-1979), American industrialist, financier, and philantropist.
Eck, Dr. Paul, LR's personal physician in later years.
Eckankar. *See* Paul Twitchell.

Eddy, Mary Baker (1820-1910), founder of the Christian Science movement.
Edwards, Margaret Davies, director, Montreal Truth Centre.
Edwards, William and Virginia, neighbors of LR at Swan; Mrs. Edwards authored *Conspiracy of 30*.
Ellis, J. Mitchell, Kentucky pharmacist; USP board member.
Elson, Dr. Edward Lee Roy (1906-93), Presbyterian minister; U.S. Senate chaplain; Pres. Dwight Eisenhower's personal minister.
Evans, Ginger, physiotherapist; USP student.
Faurie, Duncan S. T., scientist, Philadelphia, Pennsylvania.
Faus, Rev. Grace L., Science of Mind minister, Washington, D.C.; R friend and student.
Fee, Thomas E., president, Preferred Accident Insurance Company, Boston.
Fickes, Irene, official, District 50, United Mine Workers of America.
Fillmore, Charles Sherlock (1854-1948), co-founder, Unity School of Christianity, with his wife, Myrtle Fillmore (1845-1931).
First, John, Pikesville, Kentucky, banker.
Fisher, Paul C., president, Fisher Pen Company; inventor of the space pen; author, economist, and industrialist; USP board chairman.
Flanaghan, Rev. and Mrs. Ross, New Jersey students of WR/LR.
Fourton, Bessie (Elizabeth Shields), friend of WR for decades; promoted R work.
Ford, Henry, II (1917-87), president, Ford Motor Company.
Fortescue, Priscilla, friend of LR in Massachusetts.
Fosdick, Dr. Harry Emerson (1878-1979), minister, Riverside Church, New York.
Frank, Dr. Martha, director, Mothers' and Children's Educational Foundation, Child Guidance Center, Pacific Palisade, California.
French, Eva Rosaline, wife of William Henry "Harry" French.
French, John William Ernest, engineer in England and Canada; son of William Henry French.
French, Muriel, secretary, Harvard Musical Association; past chairman, Boston Youth Symphony.
French, William Henry "Harry" (d. 1952), Luton businessman; employer of LR and sister Florrie.
Gabrilowitsch, Clara Clemens, singer; daughter of Mark Twain and wife of Ossip Gabrilowitsch.
Gabrilowitsch, Ossip (1878-1936), Russian-born American pianist and conductor; Mark Twain's son-in-law; friend of WR.
Gallean, Dr. W. J., Scientologist, Riverside, California.
Garnett, Maj. John B. (1879-1976), professor, Fishburne Military School, Waynesboro, Virginia.
Garroway, Dave (1913-82), television personality, host of *Today* show.
Gerhard, Rev. Henry, Laguna Beach Science of Mind church.
Getty, J. Paul (1892-1976), American oil industrialist and philanthropist.
Gianokos, George and Aristea, owners, Southern Restaurant, Waynesboro, Virginia.
Gibilaro, Salvatore, Bridgeport, Conn., WR student.
Gibran, Kahlil (1883-1931), philosopher, poet, and painter whose thoughts appealed to LR.
Gibson, George and Dorothy, R friends, Columbus, Ohio.
Glass, Harvey, worked on Rs' science projects at Swan.
Gohmsted, Arthur, chemical engineer in Ohio; WR student.
Goldberg, Arthur (1908-90) U.S. Supreme Court justice; American statesman.
Goldsmith, Joel (1892-1964), practical mysticist; founder of "The Infinite Way."
Goldwater, Barry (1909-98), U.S. senator; unsuccessful presidential candidate in 1964.
Goodwin, Allen Orizon, founder, The Creative Institute; sponsored R study groups.
Goodwin, James R., Jr. (d. 1969), R friend and insurance broker from Salem, Virginia.
Gorsuch, Dr. Thomas L., physician and heart specialist, Waynesboro, Virginia.
Graves, John S., president, Skyline-Swannanoa, Inc. (early 1950s).
Grewal, Dr. Sadhu, recommended to LR as successor to WR.
Griffith, Forrest, head of Westward Health Products, California; USP supporter.
Grimmond, Gwen and Sid, USP supporters, Vancouver, British Columbia.

Gueye, Mr., First Counsellor, Embassy of Senegal, West Africa.
Gurdjieff, George Ivanovitch (1866-1949), Russian mystic; founded school to advance human potential.
Hall, Derward (1910-2001), U.S. congressman from Missouri (1961-72).
Hall, Howard, Conquadco, Inc.; led USP classes in New Castle, Delaware.
Hall, Manly P. (1901-90), founded Philosophical Research Society; author.
Hall, Pat (d. 2000), friend of LR and hostess for twelve years at Swan.
Hammer, Armand (1898-1990), U.S. oil industrialist and philanthropist; longtime advocate of broadening U.S.-Soviet trade ties.
Haney, Lucille, co-owner, Haney's Pharmacy, and premiere hostess, Waynesboro, Virginia.
Hanna, Mark (1837-1904), U.S. political leader; senator in post-1890 era; his descendant gave his banquet table to LR/WR at Swan.
Hardy, Ray Morton, Detroit businessman inspired by LR's business skill.
Haslet, Dame Caroline, English student of USP.
Hawke, George, Waynesboro, Virginia, historian.
Hawkins, Lloyd and Rowena, Jackson, Mississippi; operated a photography studio; longtime USP benefactors and board members.
Hawly, Vicar Treffry, baptized LR in Ivinghoe, England, 1904.
Hbalary, Professor, Indiana University; simplified Einstein's gravity formula, reflecting prior WR work.
Heft, Edward, Alpha, Ohio, LR friend and student.
Henderson, Jerry, USP researcher and supporter.
Henley, Dr. W. Ballantine, president, United Church of Religious Science.
Hennessy, Frances Margaret (1798-1848), LR's great-grandmother; wife of Lt. Parker.
Herzog, Doris, director, New York's Philosophical Research Center.
Hills, Alice Anne (1854-1917?), LR's maternal aunt.
Hills, Ellen Eliza Parker (1825-77), LR's maternal grandmother.
Hills, Richard Thomas Hennessy (1866-1917), LR's maternal uncle.
Hills, Thomas (1824-92), LR's maternal grandfather.
Hills, William (1783-1881), LR's maternal great-grandfather, curator of the Chichester Museum.
Hinton, Lottie, Swan neighbor of LR at nearby Rossmont estate.
Hoffman, Jo and Vonn, Coptic students; friends of LR.
Hogan, Elizabeth, co-author of *Perils of the Peaceful Atom*.
Holman, Edward L., president, Carson Long Military Institute, New Bloomfield, Pennsylvania.
Holmes, Dr. Ernest (1887-1960), founder of the Religious Science movement; author of *Science of Mind*.
Hone, Harry, friend of LR/WR; author; had near-death experience.
Hopkins, Dr. Clarabelle (1913-2004), Waynesboro, Virginia, chiropractor; treated LR.
Hopkins, Emma Curtis (1853-1925), the "teacher of teachers"; termed founder of New Thought movement.
Hopper, Lillian, First Church of Religious Science, Oakland, California.
Hostettler, Rodger D., LR student and friend during the 1960s.
Hovey, Charles F., capitalist and member of the Board of Boston Symphony.
Howard, Dr. Christopher, London physician; friend of LR from 1930s.
Howard, Sydney (1885-1946), English film actor known for his unique comedic style.
Howdon, William, economist who spoke at Swan seminar.
Howes, Ron, early leader of Scientology.
Hubbard, Elbert (1856-1915), American writer; died in sinking of *Lusitania*.
Hubbard, L. Ron. (1911-86), founder of Scientology.
Hubbard, W. W., Washington, D.C., economist; edited *The American Motorist*.
Hudak, Michael P., Ohio student of USP; pharmaceutical company executive; board member of

USP, succeeded LR as its president.
Hughes, H. B., LR's solicitor in her separation and divorce from Lionel Stebbing.
Hughes, Thomas, LR's real estate agent in England.
Hulbert, Jack (1892-1978), English actor, dramatic author, manager, and director.
Hunter, Dr. John H., dean of Virginia State College, Petersburg, Virginia.
Hutton, Barbara (1912-79), American heiress to Woolworth fortune.
Hyde, William and Christine, R supporters in Detroit, Michigan, during 1940s.
Jackson, Jill, author of hymn "Let There Be Peace on Earth (And Let It Begin with Me)."
JacQuiline, prominent in Los Angeles' Triune Light Center on Wilshire Boulevard.
Jaquin, Noel (1894-1974), English psychic known for work in establishing scientific basis for palmistry.
Jentzsch, Yvonne, president, Church of Scientology Celebrity Centre, Los Angeles.
Johnson, Stanhope (1882-1973), Virginia architect.
Johnston, Dr. Everett and Martha, acquired scientific equipment for WR laboratory.
Jones, Adele, wife of Arthur Jones; friend, benefactor, and colleague of WR/LR.
Jones, Arthur (d. 1969), May Department Stores executive; USP director; benefactor of WR/LR.
Jones, Dr. Bowan (d. 2004), naturopathic physician and therapeutic massage therapist; son of Arthur Jones; Fort Lauderdale, Florida; wife Geri.
Jones, Evelyn, friend of WR/LR.
Jones, George Arnsby, London editor; founder of Unified Word Communion.
Jones, Stanley, New York economist and stock market analyst.
Jones, Valmore T., member, Founding Church of Scientology, Washington, D.C.
Jones, Wendy, pianist; Arthur Jones's daughter; helped WR/LR at Swan.
Jordan, Clark L., WR's New York attorney; negotiated 1948 lease on Swan for LR/WR.
Kai, Fung, wife of Dr. Shag Okubo; research scientist with WR at Swan.
Katz, Mr. and Mrs. Jay, R students; he was a chemist; founded USP scholarship fund.
Kearns, Frank, USP promoter who sent *The World Crisis* to Pres. Jimmy Carter.
Kennedy, Ann, R student; retired bookkeeper who helped with USP accounting at Swan.
Keogh, Eugene James (1907-89), U.S. congressman from New York (1937-66).
Keyser, C. C., scientist who assisted WR in developing science projects at Swan.
Killen, Bridget, USP student; organized a Character Club; staff member at Swan.
King, William Lyon Mackenzie (1874-1950), prime minister of Canada.
Kiser, Sherman, New York businessman; supporter of WR in New York years.
Knight, Rosalind, director, Creative Living Institute in Virginia.
Kolb, Hans, Austrian businessman in New York; champion swimmer; friend of LR.
Kopf, Dr. Carl Heath (1902-58), minister on radio in Boston and D.C.; author.
Kordus, Dr. Henry, physicist and R supporter.
Korn, Joey and Jill, promoters of LR/WR in his work on dowsing, Kabbalah, e-mail: Joey@dowsers.com.
Kuziner, Pinchas, director, Holistic Health Counseling Center, Israel.
Lahde, Clarence W., lecturer and photographer.
Landon, Dr. Brown, studied teleois of the Great Pyramids as evidence of future.
Lane, David, Natural Living Foundation, Denver, Colorado.
Laning, Capt., chaired Radar Committee for U.S. Army and Navy.
Lao Tzu (ca. 600 B.C.E.), Chinese philosopher and father of Taoism.
Lavender, Dr. H. Walter (d. 1969), Fulton, N.Y., chiropractor; early USP board member.
Law, Robert E., president, Colorado Chamber of Commerce, during late 1940s.
Lawrence, Donald, film and television producer.
Lawrence, Frank (1891-1966), Virginia banker; founder, Virginia Athletic Hall of Fame.
Levy, B. E., director and past president of Coty International.
Lewis, Fulton, Jr. (1903-66), radio news commentator.

Lewis, Samuel L., Pakistan educator.
Lindo, Laara, Canadian poetess, educator, and author; USP director and officer; friend of LR.
Linky, Raymond and Kay, R friends, Colorado Springs, Colorado.
Lipke, Dr. Ken (1929-92), president, Gibralter Steel Company; USP board member.
Lipton, Sir Thomas (1850-1931), Scottish entrepreneur in tea business.
Livingston, C. D., Scottish promoter of R works.
Lloyd, Guy, founded pioneer Character Clubs among R students in Delaware.
Lojnikov, Paul, Rio de Janerio businessman who financed translation of *The Man Who Tapped the Secrets of the Universe* and *God Will Work with You but Not for You* into Portuguese; headed organization, Ordem Revelacionista Evangelica.
Lombardi, Emelia Lee (1918-97), edited many USP publications; longtime director, officer, and benefactor of USP; friend of WR/LR after 1949.
Lombardi, John, attorney; husband of Emelia Lombardi; USP counsel and board member.
Lorraine, Guy, La Crescenta, California, Science of Mind Church.
Lorraine, Lilith, founder of Avalon and editor of *Flame*.
Loughlin, Beatrice, U.S. national women's skating champion.
Lutes, Charlie, advocate of teachings of Maharishi Mahesh Yogi.
Lyon, Ben (1901-79), matinee idol; co-starred with wife, Bebe Daniels.
Macfadden, Bernarr (1868-1955), American physical culturist; publisher.
Macfadden, Johnnie Lee (1904-92), fourth wife of Bernarr Macfadden; author of *Barefoot in Eden*.
Machaty, Gustav (1911-63), Czech film director of 1933 classic film *Ecstasy*.
MacLauren, C., Australian doctor who wrote *Mere Mortals* and *Post Mortem*.
MacPherson, Aimee Semple (1890-1944), American evangelist; founder of the Foursquare Gospel Church.
Maday, Henry (1910-96), Detroit, Michigan, business leader; sponsored WR 1947 lecture tour.
Maguire, Russell, oilman and munitions manufacturer; owner of *American Mercury* magazine (1962-70).
Maharishi Mahesh Yogi, founder of Transcendental Meditation and the Spiritual Regeneration Movement.
Manch, Dr. Martin G., headed Institute of Musical Art, Staunton, Virginia.
Mandus, Brother (1907-88), founder of World Healing Crusade, Blackpool, England.
Mann, John David, American macrobioticist; former editor and publisher of *Solstice* magazine; friend of LR; e-mail: johndmann@earthlink.net.
Manser, Rodney, USP promoter in South Africa.
Martin, Hon. James G. IV, judge, Juvenile and Domestic Relations Court, Norfolk, Virginia.
Matero (Nelson Moreita de Queiroz), colleague of Paul Lojnikov.
Matz, H. H., Mesa, Ariz., hydroponic gardening expert.
Mayer, Brantz, professor of parapsychology, Northern Virginia's Lord Fairfax Community College.
McCain, Virgil, president, Athens College, Athens, Alabama.
McCarthy, Frank, producer, U.S. film industry.
McConnell, Phyllis, thirty-year USP staff member; LR renamed her Angela Carr.
McElroy, Neil (1907-72), U.S. Secretary of Defense (1957-59).
McVeigh, Norman R., president, Mick-or-Mack grocery chain.
Mead, Dr. Margaret (1901-78), American anthropologist and writer.
Medley, Bishop M. S., Omniune Church, Texarkana, Texas.
Meibes, Mrs. Carl, formerly Hildegarde Burmeister; LR friend in New York and Florida.
Mel, Eleanor (d. 1964), successor of Emma Curtis Hopkins; directed Boston Home of Truth Center.
Meneken, H. L. (1880-1956), American newspaperman, reviewer, and writer.
Michelson, Albert E. (1852-1931), American physicist who won the 1907 Nobel prize for measuring the speed of light using an optical interferometer.

Militz, Annie Rix (1856-1924), founder of Home of Truth (New Thought) movement.
Miller, Dr. Francis Trevelyan (1877-1959), American historian.
Millikan, Robert (1868-1953), American physicist who determined an electron's charge by using oil drop experiments in 1909.
Milner, Dr. Dennis, author with Edward Stuart of *The Loom of Creation*.
Mitchell, Kevin, USP staff member; husband of Bridget Killen.
Montessori, Maria (1870-1952), innovative Italian educator.
Moore, Dr. Carl L., professor of business and economics, Lehigh University.
Moore, Myrtle, natural healer who offered services to USP staff.
Morgan, K. Z., director, Oak Ridge Atomic Laboratory.
Morley, Christopher (1890-1957), American author whose books LR favored.
Morphis, Dr. Oscar L., scientist; interested in USP.
Morris, Harry C., supported USP scientific experiments; briefly headed USP staff.
Morris, John R., president of Skyline-Swannanoa, Inc., in 1948.
Moshier, Bud and Carmen, Today Church, Dallas, Texas.
Mulberger, H. C., Raytheon Company scientist; worked with WR/LR on science.
Murphy, Dr. Joseph, founder, The Truth Forum.
Murrow, Edward R. (1908-65), American broadcaster who set the standard for television journalism.
Mycroft, Walter Charles (1891-1968), directed production at Elstree Studios; British film industry pioneer.
Newhouse, Rev. Flower A. (1909-94); with her husband, Lawrence, founded Questhaven Retreat, Escondido, California, in 1940, and the Christward Ministry.
Nichols, Henry, Boston Naturalization and Immigration officer.
Nightingale, Earl (1922-89), advertising genius; innovater in multi-media self-improvement education.
Nimmo, Dr. Raymond L., Forth Worth, Texas, chiropractor.
Nizer, Louis J. (1902-94), American attorney; author of *My Life in Court*.
Nobel, Claes, grandnephew of Alfred Nobel, Swedish inventor of dynamite.
Novick, Ben, securities consultant.
Okilo, Hon. Melford, Nigerian statesman, humanitarian, businessman; USP officer.
Okilo, Otio, son of Melford Okilo; Fishburne Military School alumnus; Nigerian educator.
Okubo, Dr. Shag, University of Hawaii physicist who worked at Swan laboratory.
Oliver, Harold, promoted USP in Australia.
Ohsawa, George, Japanese practitioner who refined macrobiotics and popularized it through his writings.
Osunmakinde, Capt. Dele, Nigerian Naval officer; humanitarian.
Oursler, Fulton (1893-1953), American author on spiritual subjects.
Paderewski, Ignance Jan (1860-1941), Polish pianist, composer, and statesman.
Page, Dr. Robert M., U.S. government expert on radar.
Palm, Enok, mathematician on the faculty of the University of Oslo, Norway.
Palmer, Dr. B. J., (1881-1961), succeeded his father, chiropractic founder Dr. D. D. Palmer, as president of first chiropractic college, 1906.
Palmer, C. E., scientist; headed USP staff during absence of WR/LR.
Pantanjali (ca. 200-300 A.D.), Indian philosopher to whom authorship of the Yoga Sutras is attributed.
Pape, Bill, musician, composer.
Parker, Lt. Henry Lucas (1793-1842), LR's great-grandfather; officer, Royal Marines.
Parker, Peter (1913-92), commercial artist; brother of Emelia Lombardi.
Parkinson, Merta Mary, author; included R concepts in her book *Sing a New Song!*
Parks, Gordon (1912-), African-American photographer and writer.

Paxton, Sir Joseph (1803-1865), English architect; designed London's Chrystal Palace.
Payne, Dr. James S., professor, University of Virginia; dedicated book to LR.
Peale, Dr. Norman Vincent (1898-1993), famous American clergyman; author of *The Power of Positive Thinking*.
Perry, Aubrey, Norfolk, Va., automobile dealer; member of USP board.
Phillips, Mr. and Mrs. George E., Boston friends of LR, ca. 1938.
Phillips, William C., American ambassador to Belgium, brother of George E. Phillips.
Piepkorn, Arthur Carl (1907-73), American historian and theologian.
Pinto, Manuel, professor at the Phillips Academy, Andover, Massachusetts.
Pizarro, Alex, publisher in South Africa.
Plough, Rev. Willard I., pastor, Church of the Christian Brotherhood, Rivanna, Ohio.
Poling, Dr. Daniel A. (1884-1968), American clergyman; editor of *The Christian Herald*; delivered eulogy at WR's funeral.
Pollard, Dr., Chief Director, Oak Ridge Laboratory, Oak Ridge, Tenn., who resigned to become an Episcopalian priest.
Poole, Maj. Tudor, originated London's worldwide Big Ben Silent Minute for World Peace observance.
Purvis, Winston, Lynchburg, Virginia, banker; member of USP board.
Quillian, Dr. William F., president, Randolph Macon's Women's College.
Randolph, Mrs. Thomas Jefferson, IV, Waynesboro, Virginia, portraitist and artist.
Redmond, Kathy, reviewer for *The National Exchange*.
Reid, Georgia Eliza, Boston advertising executive.
Resines, Jorge, scientist, author, expert on free energy devices.
Reventlow, Lance (1936-72), sports car enthusiast; produced the Scarab sports car.
Reynolds, Catherine, personal secretary to actress Gloria Swanson.
Rice, Grantland, professional photographer; worked on R scientific experiments.
Richards, Robert J., Lutheran pastor who sang at LR's funeral service.
Ricketts, Dennis L., conducted USP seminars.
Roberts, J. Gordon, Omaha, Nebraska, commercial dairyman.
Rockwell, B. A., director of research, Pennsylvania Farm Bureau.
Roosevelt, Elliott (1910-90), son of U.S. Pres. Franklin Delano Roosevelt.
Roosevelt, John Aspinwall (1916-81), son of U.S. Pres. Franklin Delano Roosevelt.
Rose, Murray (1939-), Australian Olympic swimming champion; American sports businessman.
Ruhe, Margaret, Canadian staff member at USP; LR's private secretary.
Rubert, Euell, USP supporter; Midwestern commercial builder; wife Joyce.
Russell, Helen (d. 1953), WR's first wife; they married in 1893, divorced in 1948, had two daughters, Helen (wife of Edward Tracy and mother of Joan) and Louise, who died in 1947.
Sadony, Joseph (1877-1960), prophetic Michigan author of *Gates of the Mind*.
Sahin, Dr. Sumer, General Secretary and Executive Chief of Tubitak, the scientific and technical research council of Turkey.
Saltonstall, Mrs. Richard, supporter of the Boston Youth Concerts.
Sandow, Eugene (1867-1925), pioneer body builder, "iron man," and physical culturist.
Sarfraz, Mohammad, editor of *The Pakistan Times*.
Sargeant, Maj., U.S. Air Force scientist who worked with WR on gravity reactor project.
Satchidananda, Sri Swami (1915-2002), founder, Integral Yoga community, Yogaville, Virginia.
Schlagenhauf, Gary, USP student from Walnut Creek, California.
Schmiedigen, August F., New York architect; prominent in 1939 World's Fair.
Schucman, Dr. Helen (1909-81), psychology professor who "scribed" *A Course in Miracles*.
Schuller, Dr. Robert (1926-), television evangelist; founded Crystal Cathedral, Garden Grove, California.
Seay, Wilson L., professor, Blue Ridge Community College, Weyers Cave, Virginia.

Shapley, Harlow (1885-1972), American astronomer; discovered dimensions of our galaxy and the location of its center in 1918.
Shaw, Elmer W., conducted USP classes in Lacey, Washington.
Shebilske, Wayne, professor of psychology, Texas A&M University.
Sheldon, Rev. Charles M. (1857-1946), author of *In His Steps* and other Christian books.
Shenoy, Dr. B. R., Indian scholar of the *Bhagavad-Gita*.
Sheridan, William H. "Billy," New York City automobile dealer in the 1930s.
Silberg, Dr., Raytheon Company corporate scientist.
Silva, Jose (1911-99), started the Silva Mind Control movement.
Smathers, George A. (1913-), U.S. senator from Florida (1951-68).
Smith, Dr. Enid S., sociology professor, Pfeiffer College, Misenheimer, North Carolina.
Smith, Gerald L. K. (1898-1976), radical right-wing American evangelist.
Smith, Joseph (1805-44), founded Church of Jesus Christ of Latter Day Saints (Mormon).
Smith, Margaret Chase (1897-1995), U.S. senator from Maine (1949-72).
Smith, Shirley Caulkins, evolutionary tutor, Lily Dale, New York.
Snow, Chauncey, attorney in Beverly Hills, California.
Snyder, Frederic, rated as one of the ten leading platform speakers in the U.S.
Soderberg, Peter, Associate Dean, School of Education, University of Virginia.
Sonastine, Gil, R friend who overcame disability and was an inspiration to many.
Spalding, Baird Thomas (1857-1953), author of *Life and Teaching of the Masters of the Far East*.
Spann, Owen, television personality in San Francisco, California.
Speck, Dr. George, artist and pioneer art therapist, New York City.
Spencer, Herbert (1820-1903), British philosopher and sociologist; provided inspiration for founders of the Twilight Club.
Spicher, Sam and Martha, USP supporters in business in Harrisonburg, Virginia.; he served on USP board.
Spilman, Louis, founder, owner, and editor of the *Waynesboro News Virginian*.
Starbuck, Gary, scientist who praised *The Universal One*.
Stauffer, Marjorie, cousin of U.S. Pres. Dwight D. Eisenhower.
Stearn, Jess (1914-90), biographer of Edgar Cayce; prolific writer on the occult.
Stebbing, Charles William, father of Lionel Stebbing.
Stebbing, Daisy Ellen Claypoole, mother of Lionel Stebbing.
Stebbing, Lionel Charles (1905-81), LR's first husband; fitness expert, author, and Anthroposophy expert.
Steiner, Marie (1867-1948), wife of Anthroposophy founder Rudolf Steiner.
Steiner, Rudolf Steiner (1861-1925), Austrian-born founder of Anthroposophy.
Stephanis, James, husband of Patricia DuPont; USP board member.
Sternglass, Dr. Ernest, Pittsburgh scientist active in anti-nuclear proliferation.
Steven, Rev. Robert L., pastor, San Diego Christ Church, Christian.
Stevens, Dr. Peter, promoted USP books throughout Australia, New Zealand, and Asia.
Stevens, Virgila Tiffany, journalist, *Washington Times-Herald*.
Stoddard, Marie, Hollywood drama coach during the 1940s.
Stone, Robert B., president, Associated Plan Service, Inc.
Stone, Vida Reed (1893-1990), author and supporter of LR/WR.
Story, Charles H., active in U.S. nuclear control efforts.
Stuart, Edward, author with Dr. Dennis Milner of *The Loom of Creation*.
Suhiro, Rev., pastor, Los Angeles Holiness Church.
Summerfield, Harold (1894-1971). LR's brother-in-law; husband of Emily Rose Cook.
Summerfield, Peter, LR's nephew; British Navy veteran; Scouting official; wife Betty.
Sutherland, Dr. William G. (1873-1954), father of osteopathy in the cranial field.
Swanson, Gloria (1897-1983), American film star and Academy Award winner.

Swedenborg, Emanuel (1688-1772), scientist, philosopher, and spiritual explorer.
Symington, Stuart (1901-88), U.S. senator from Missouri (1953-76).
Taft, Edward A., officer of the Boston Symphony and Youth Concert Association.
Tesla, Nikola (1856-1943), inventor, scientist, and pioneer in transmission of high-voltage electricity.
Thomas, Lowell (1892-1981), U.S. broadcast journalist and explorer.
Thompson, Arthur Van Renssalear and Valborg, early WR and USP supporters.
Thompson, Richard L., Editor-in-Chief, 1970 Blue Ridge Community College (in Weyers Cave, Virginia) yearbook, *The Spirit*.
Thomson, A. P., orchardist, Front Royal, Virginia.
Tiegs, Larry, certified personologist, Nampa, Idaho; active promoter of USP.
Tillich, Paul (1886-1965), American theologian and philosopher.
Torkelson, Dale, Melchizedek Order, Albuquerque, New Mexico
Touchberry, Alice, medical nurse who invented an Interlavage unit useful in healing.
Tourma, Michael George, Commissioner General of Tourism in Lebanon; influential Middle East opinion-maker active in international tourism.
Trevelyan, Sir George M. (1876-1962), noted English historian.
Twitchell, Paul (1908-71), founder of the modern Eckankar movement.
Ureskar, H. S., promoted USP in Bombay, India.
Van Meter, Rose, Summit, N.J., spiritualist who integrated R principles into the curriculum she used for studying the Kabbalah.
Vanneman, Donald K. and Hilda, R supporters from Chamblee, Georgia.
Vannerson, Dorothy, USP staff member in the early 1950s.
Vannerson, Dr. J. F., naturopathic and chiropractic physician who treated WR/LR.
Viegas, Dr., Brazillian linguist who translated *God Will Work with You but Not for You* into Portuguese.
Vivekananda, Swami (1863-1902), Hindu mystic; exponent of Vedanta philosophy.
Voyer, Claire, illegally used R names to establish center to receive space people.
Wagner, Robert F., Jr. (1910-91), New York politician; mayor of New York City.
Walsh, John, nephew of U.S. Sen. David I. Walsh (1872-1947) of Massachusetts.
Watson, Thomas J. (1874-1956), American industrialist and philanthropist; founder of IBM.
Watts, Dodo (1910-90), actress who played many leads in British movies in the 1930s.
Way, A. Warren, Philadelphia scientist interested in USP.
Weald, Kitty, secretary to LR during her years in business in New York (1933-35).
Weaver, Dennis (1925-), American television actor and humanitarian; wife Gerry.
Webster, Edwin S., officer of the Boston Symphony and Youth Concert Association.
Weisserts, Mr. and Mrs., Vienna, Austria; Hans Kolb's mother and stepfather.
Wheeler, C. L., editor, *Mind* magazine, San Francisco, California.
White, Antonia, translated Dr. Alexis Carrel's *Reflections on Life* from French to English.
White, Stewart Edward (1873-1946) and Betty (d. 1939), studied paranormal divulgence of the continuity of personality after death of the physical body.
Wickersham, Dean, author who asked to use Russell drawings in his own work.
Wigglesworth, Richard B. (1891-1960), U.S. congressman from Massachusetts (1927-58).
Wigmore, Dr. Ann (1910-94), Living Foods Lifestyle founder; author and educator on sprout diet.
Willey, Victor, Religious Science minister; R supporter.
Williams, Edna K., African-American osteopath in Philadelphia.
Wilson, Andrew C., Scottish scientist who worked with WR on transmutation of free hydrogen.
Wilson, Kenoll C., promoted R teachings in Australia.
Wise, Jennings C., American historian and author, associated with Virginia Military Institute.
Wolfe, Thomas (1900-38), American novelist; author of *Look Homeward, Angel*.
Wooler, Robert, administrator, Centre for Universal Harmony and Service, Devon, England.

Wright, James C., U.S. congressman from Texas (1955-89); Speaker, House of Representatives.
Wylie, Elinor (1885-1928), American poet.
Yeang, Dr. C. H., USP supporter in Malaya.
Yee, Phillip K. H., manager of Honolulu, Hawaii, municipal water system; USP supporter.
Yehl, James E., founder of an optical manufacturing firm, Boulder, Colorado.
Yogananda, Paramhansa (1893-1952), author of *Autobiography of a Yogi*; founder of the Self-Realization Fellowship.
Young, Gilmour, marketing expert and USP organizer on U.S. West Coast.
Younkin, Dr. Audra, homeopathic physician and Egyptologist; founder, Esoteric School of Cosmic Sciences in Indiana.
Yount, J. B., Jr. (1897-1974), LR's local attorney and friend, Waynesboro, Virginia.

APPENDIX 3
BIBLIOGRAPHY

BOOKS

Allen, James. *As a Man Thinketh*. New York.
Baker, Cozy. *A Cozy Getaway*. Washington, 1976.
Beck, L. Adams. *The House of Fulfillment: A Spiritual Romance of the Himalayas*. Los Angeles, 1927.
Bey, Hamid. *My Experiences Preceding 5,000 Burials*. Coptic Fellowship of America, 1938.
Bigmore, Peter G. *The Bedfordshire and Huntingdonshire Landscape*. London, 1979.
Binder, Dr. Timothy A. *In the Wave Lies the Secret of Creation: Scientific Paintings and Charts of Walter Russell with Commentaries and an Outline of the Russell Cosmogony*. Swannanoa, 1995.
———. *Position Technic: The Science of Centering*. Hamilton, Montana, 1977.
Burroughs, John. "Waiting." In *Collected Works*, Riverby edition. Vol. XI.
Campbell, Florence. *Your Days Are Numbered*. New York, 1931.
Canty, Jerome [Jeronimo]. *Holoscene II: The Book of Spiral Logic*. 1975.
——— [Jerry]. *Eternal Massage*. Oroville, California, 1977.
———, and Richard France. *Healing Naturally, The Commonsense Macrobiotic Approach to Cancer and Other Diseases*. Boulder, Colorado, 1982.
Carrel, Alexis. *Man the Unknown*.
———. *Reflections on Life*. Translated by Antonia White. New York, 1953.
Clark, Glenn. *A Man's Reach*. Harper Bros., 1949.
———. *How to Find Health through Prayer*. Harper Bros., 1940.
———. *I Will Lift up Mine Eyes*. Harper Bros., 1937.
———. *The Man Who Tapped the Secrets of the Universe*. Macalaster Press, 1946.
———. *The Soul's Sincere Desire*.
———. *What Would Jesus Do?* Malacaster Press, 1950.
Clark, Miles. *Glenn Clark: His Life and Writings*. Abingdon Press, 1972.
———. *The Man Who Tapped the Secrets of Creative Power*. Malacaster Press, 1962.
Corelli, Marie. *The Life Everlasting, A Romance of Reality*. Los Angeles, 1911.
Cowles, Virginia. *The Rothschilds, A Family of Fortune*. New York, 1973.
Druett, Walter W. *The Stanmores and Harrow Weald through the Ages*, London, 1938.

Eddy, Mary Baker. *The First Church of Christ Scientist and Miscellany*. Boston, 1913.
Edwards, Virginia Davis. *Conspiracy of 30: Misuse of Music from Aristotle To Onassis*. Waynesboro, Virginia: Conspiracy Press, 1994.
Gheon, Henri. *Secrets of the Saints*. New York, 1944.
Gofman, John W. *The Case against Nuclear Power Plants*. Emmaus, Pennsylvania: Rodale Press, 1971.
Harding, Glenn. *Saga of Glenn Clark*.
Henry, Robert. *A Century Between: The Story of the Descendants of Nathan Rothschild*. New York, 1937.
Hollander, Bernard. *Scientific Phrenology*.
Hone, Harry. *The Light at the End of the Tunnel*. Williamsburg, Virginia: American Biographical Center (P.O. Box 473, Williamsburg, VA 23187), 1996. (Harry Hone, P.O. Box 395, North, VA 23128, 804-725-2234, e-mail: harry@villagepop.com.)
———. *The Day I Met Walter Russell*. North, Virginia, 1996. (See preceding citation.)
Kopf, Carl Heath. *Personal Crisis*. New York, 1945.
———. *Windows on Life*. New York, 1941.
Korn, Joseph W. *Dowsing: A Path To Enlightenment*. Augusta, Georgia, 1997. (E-mail: Joey@dowsers.com.)
Lao Tzu. *Tao Te Ching* (numerous editions). (A new translation by Yashuhiko Genku Kimura was published by the University of Science and Philosophy in 2000.)
Levi. *The Aquarian Gospel of Jesus the Christ*. 1907.
Marks, Richard and Rita. *Ivinghoe As It Was*. Wing, England, 1990.
Macfadden, Johnnie Lee. *Barefoot in Eden*. Prentice-Hall, 1962.
Maclaurin, Charles. *Mere Mortals: Medico-Historical Essays*. New York, 1925.
———. *Post Mortem: Essays, Historical and Medical*. New York, 1922.
Mee, Arthur. *Sussex: The Garden by the Sea*. London, 1938.
Merrill, A. Marion, and Grace E. W. Sprague. Angela Morgan in *Contemporary Verse*. Boston, 1936.
Okilo, Melford. *Art of Government and the Okilo Administration*. Riverside Communications, 1992.
———. *The Law of Life*. Swannanoa, 1989.
———. *Love Creates Balance*. Swannanoa, 1989.
O'Leary, Elizabeth L. *From Morning To Night: Domestic Service in Maymont House and the Gilded Age South*. London and Charlottesville, 2003.
Piepkorn, Arthur C. *Profiles in Belief*. Vol. V (n.p.). Harper, 1978.
Russell, Lao. *A Christmas Message*. Swannanoa, 1963.
———. *God Will Work with You but Not for You*. Swannanoa, 1955.
———. *Love: A Scientific and Living Philosophy of Love and Sex*. Swannanoa, 1966.
———. *My Love I Extend To You: A Christmas Message and Announcement of Events*. Swannanoa, 1966.
———. *Why You Cannot Die!* Swannanoa, 1972.
Russell, Lao and Walter. *Scientific Answer To Human Relations*. Swannanoa, 1951.
———. *The Electrifying Power of Man-Woman Balance: World Peace through World Balance*. Swannanoa, 1960.
Russell, Walter. *A New Concept of the Universe*, with an epilogue by Lao Russell. Swannanoa, 1953.
———. *Scientific Explanation of Sex*. Reprint (from *The Message of the Divine Iliad*, Vol. II). Swannanoa, 1949.
———. *The Book of Early Whisperings*. Swannanoa, 1949.
———. *The Message of the Divine Iliad*. Vol. I, New York, 1948.
———. *The Message of the Divine Iliad*. Vol. II, Swannanoa, 1949.
———. *The Secret of Light*. New York, 1947.
———. *The Universal One*. New York, 1926, and Swannanoa, 1974.
———. *Think: The First Principle of Business Success, Excerpts from the IBM Lecture Series*.

University of Science and Philosophy, 2000.
———. *The Book of Early Whisperings*. Swannanoa, 1949.
———. *The Russell Genero-Radiative Concept* or *The Cyclic Theory of Continuous Motion*. New York, 1930.
Russell, Walter and Lao. *A Vision Fulfilled!* Swannanoa, 1989.
———. *Atomic Suicide?* Swannanoa, 1957.
———. *The World Crisis: Its Explanation and Solution*. Swannanoa, 1958.
Stebbing, Lionel. *A Guide To Occult Books and Sacred Writings of the Ages*. Horsham, England, 1967.
Stocking, Charles Francis. *Thou Israel*. Chicago, 1922.
Stone, Vida Reed. *Behold My Song*, with an introduction by Walter Russell. 1947.
———. *Come Now into Your Freedom*. Montrose Press, 1946.
———. *The Cosmic Age Is Dawning*. Hollywood, 1952.
Twitchell, Paul. *The Tiger's Fang*, 1969.
Viereck, George S., and Paul Eldridge. *Salome, The Wandering Jewess: My First Two Thousand Years of Love*. Duckworth, London, 1930.
Warren, Patricia. *Elstree: The British Hollywood*. London, 1983.
Watson, Thomas J., and Peter Petre. *Father and Son & Co., My Life at IBM and Beyond*. New York, 1990.
White, Stewart Edward. *The Betty Book: Excursions into the World of Other Consciousness Made by Betty between 1919 and 1936*. New York, 1937.
Wilson, Lawrence D., M.D. *Nutritional Balancing and Hair Mineral Analysis*. Prescott Arizona, 1998.
Winbolt, S. E. *The Chilterns and the Thames Valley (from Iffley to Staines)*. London, 1932.
Windsor, William. *Phrenology, The Science of Character*. Big Rapids, Michigan, 1921.
Wise, Jennings C. *The Philisophic History of Civilization*. New York, 1955.
Zevgolis, Lula. *Grace and Truth: The Story of Grace L. Faus, Ordained Minister in the Nation's Capital*. DeVorss & Company, 1985.

PERIODICALS

Del Mar, Rita. "Faith and Genius: Walter Russell: Teacher and Disciple of a New Age Philosophy." *Astrology* (December 1981).
Korn, Joey. "Quest for the Blue Books: The Russell Connection To Dowsing." *Mid-Atlantic Geomancy* 9 (Spring Equinox 1998).
Mazza, Grace J. "Lao Russell." *Nexus: The Connection* (Autumn 1983).
Mann, John David. "The Macrobiotic Genius of Walter Russell." *Solstice—Perspectives on Health & the Environment* (May/June 1989). (E-mail: johndmann@earthlink.net.)
Sakharov to Drell, *Time*, 4 July 1983.
"Swannanoa's Walter Russell: The Most Versatile Man in America." *Albemarle* (August-September 1990): p. 42.

NEWSPAPER ARTICLES (chronologically)

Daily Mail (London), 13 July 1933.
"Where are the Rich?" *New York World-Telegram*, 23 October 1942. (Article on Mr. and Mrs. Arthur VanRensselear Thompson.)
"Walter Russell to Open Lectures Sunday, May 11." (Detroit, Michigan) N.p., n.d. (1947).
Stone, Woodrow W. "Russells Turning Swannanoa Estate into Art Lover's Paradise." *Waynesboro News Virginian*, 2 December 1948.
Stevens, Virgila Tiffany. "Swannanoa." *Washington Times-Herald*, 25 October 1953.
Stephenson, Roy T. "Actress Gloria Swanson Visiting at Nearby Swannanoa Residence." *Staunton (Virginia) News Leader*, 24 October 1958.

Rabon, Florence. "Hale and Hardy at 90 Is Artist Walter Russell. He Recalls Keys During Spanish Hostilities." *Miami Herald*, 26 February 1961: sec. B-1.

Coker, JoAnn. "Her Work: World's Thinking." *Charlotte Observer*, 22 April 1964: sec. 1B.

"Mrs. Russell Guest Speaker Here Today." *Lynchburg (Virginia) News*, 29 November 1964: sec. C-8.

"Noted Author to Speak on 'Love' at Local Church." (California) N.p., n.d. (May 1965?).

"Lao Russell to Lecture at Religious Science Church." (La Crescenta, California), N.p., n.d. (May 1965?).

"Philosopher Author to Give Two Lectures." *Pomona (California) Progress-Bulletin*, 26 April 1965: p. 7.

"Mrs. Russell Will Address SD Ruritans." *Waynesboro News Virginian*, 14 February 1966.

Spilman, Louis. "Are We Truly Aware of Swannanoa and the Philosophy It Radiates?" *Waynesboro News Virginian*, 12 April 1966.

"Lao Russell Lectures on Love." *Miami News-Record*, 31 January 1967: sec. 2B.

"Lao Russell Speaking on Love." *Key West Citizen*, 8 February 1967: p. 2.

"Lao Russell Speaks Here." *Palm Beach Times*, 4 March 1967: p. 7.

"Lao Russell." *Abilene (Texas) Reporter-News*, 1 April 1967.

"Mrs. Russell Speaks on 'World Crisis.'" *Menlo Park (California) Recorder*, 17 May 1967.

"Lao Russell to Speak at Area Unity Center." *Birmingham Eccentric*, 24 August 1967: sec. 7-C.

"Youth for Character at Swannanoa Sunday." *Waynesboro News Virginian*, 6 September 1968: p. 7.

"Youth for Character Rally at Swannanoa." *Waynesboro News Virginian*, 8 September 1968.

Evans, Paul. "Love of Mankind, Selflessness Said Necessary in World Today." *Waynesboro News Virginian*, 9 September 1968.

"Swannanoa: Attraction for Tourists and Mecca for Students of Philosophy." *Roanoke (Virginia) Times* (1968).

"Youth for Character Club Organized Here." *Waynesboro News Virginian*, 30 September 1968.

"Mrs. Russell Plans Seminar at Blue Ridge Community College, November 14, 1968." *Waynesboro News Virginian*, 8 November 1968.

"Character Group Ends First Project." *Waynesboro News Virginian*, 7 December 1968.

Review of *God Will Work with You but Not for You*, by Lao Russell. *New York Times*, 16 March 1969: p. 39.

Carroll, John. "Mrs. Russell Hosts CQ Staff at Mountain Top Palace." *C.Q.*, Fishburne Military School, Waynesboro, Virginia (November 1970).

Dixon, Mike. "Lao Russell: Mistress of Swannanoa Palace," *Staunton (Virginia) News Leader*, 2 February 1975.

"Sculptor's wife dedicates bust of Washington," *Fredericksburg (Virginia) Free Lance-Star*, 3 May 1976: p. 3.

"A Swannanoa Playland?" *Norfolk Virginian-Pilot*, 3 March 1977, sec. D4.

Jones, Brad. "Russells Came To Swannanoa Mansion 30 Years Ago Today." *Waynesboro News Virginian*, 2 November 1978: p. 1.

Hooper, Doug. "You Are What You Think." *Alameda (California) Times Star*, 5 January 1984.

Bowman, Curtis L., Sr. "Millionare Dooley Built Swannanoa." *Waynesboro News Virginian*, 1 August 1987.

Bowman, Curtis L., Sr. "Swannanoa a Mountaintop Marvel." *Waynesboro News Virginian*, 3 March 1988.

Harter, Dale. "Enlightened Philosophy Taught from Afton Mountain 'Shrine of Beaut.,'" *Harrisonburg (Virginia) Breeze*, 14 April 1988: pp. 16-17.

"Service Set Sunday for Mrs. Russell." *Waynesboro News Virginian*, 6 May 1988.

"Magnetic Storm Sweeps Earth." *Richmond Times-Dispatch*, 7 May 1988.

Shatz, Ellen. "Swannanoa: Palace in the Blue Ridge Shows off Its Treasures." *Staunton (Virginia) News Leader*, 15 June 1988: sec. C-1.

Sides, W. Hampton. "The Wizards of Odd." *Washington City Paper*, 7-13 October 1988: pp. 14-16.

Nuckoles, Christina. "Draft Woman Reaches Settlement with Swannanoa." *Staunton (Virginia) News Leader*, 16 June 1992: sec. B-1.

"Biser Drops His Claim to Be Lao Russell's Heir." *Charlottesville (Virginia) Observer*, 28 June-1 July 1992.

Berry, Sharon. "'The Science of Man' Is Taught at Swannanoa." *Waynesboro News Virginian*, 24 September 1992.

Austin, Natalie. "Area Structures Prominent in New Architecture Book." *Staunton (Virginia) News Leader*, 24 November 1992: sec. A-3.

Farrell, Dena Hogan. "The 21st Century Science of Dr. Walter Russell." *Dimensions* (July 1993): p. 6.

"Notables Will Attend Swannanoa Homecoming." *Waynesboro News Virginian*, 10 September 1993.

"Whither Swannanoa?" *C-ville (Charlottesville, Virginia) Weekly*, 4-17 May 1994: pp. 8-10.

Fox, Jonathan. "Space Mountain; What They're Really Teaching at Swannanoa." *C-ville (Charlottesville, Virginia) Weekly*, 12-18 November 1996.

Shulman, Terry. "Built as a Summer Home, Swannanoa Still Beckons." *Staunton (Virginia) News Leader*, 18 May 1997: sec. A3.

Carter, Sam. "Swannanoa to Return To Brilliance; Internet New Home of University of Science and Philosophy." *Staunton (Virginia) News Leader*, 2 October 1998.

"East of Eden." *C-ville (Charlottesville, Virginia) Weekly*, 10-16 August 1999.

Provence, Lisa. "The Great Divide: Swannanoa and the University of Science and Philosophy Face off on Afton Mountain." *C-ville (Charlottesville, Virginia) Weekly*, 10-16 August 1999: pp. 15-20.

UNPUBLISHED MANUSCRIPTS

Atwater, P. M. H., L.H.D. "My First Meeting with Lao Russell." (P. M. H. Atwater, L.H.D., P.O. Box 7691, Charlottesville, VA 22906-7691, 434-974-7945, web site: www.cinemind.com /atwater, e-mail: atwater@cinemind.com.)

Dawkins, Neva. *The Legacy of Walter Russell, A Modern Leonardo Da Vinci: His Formula for Success in Business, Science, the Arts, and Human Relations; Walter Russell's Own Teachings as Recorded by Neva Dawkins*. 1985.

Grimmond, Gwen. *Address on the Life and Teachings of Doctor Walter and Lao Russell*. N.d.

INDEX